Studies in Art, Heritage, Law and the Market

Volume 3

The book series *Studies in Art, Heritage, Law and the Market* provides an international and interdisciplinary forum for volumes that

- investigate legal, economic, and policy developments related to arts, heritage, and intellectual property;
- critically assess how and for whom art and heritage values come about;
- promote novel forms of user engagement, participatory presentations, and digitalization of arts and heritage;
- examine the processes that transform cultural objects and practices into arts and heritage; and
- highlight new approaches in preservation and conservation science.

The series addresses a need for research and practice in the fields of art, culture, conservation, and heritage including a focus on legal and economic aspects. It deals with complex issues such as questions of authenticity and provenance; forgery and falsification; the illicit trade, restitution, and return of cultural objects; the changing roles of museums; the roles of experts and expertise; and the ethics of the art market.

More information about this series at https://link.springer.com/bookseries/16197

Vanessa Tünsmeyer

Repatriation of Sacred Indigenous Cultural Heritage and the Law

Lessons from the United States and Canada

Springer

Vanessa Tünsmeyer
Department of International and European Law
Maastricht University
Maastricht, The Netherlands

ISSN 2524-7425 ISSN 2524-7433 (electronic)
Studies in Art, Heritage, Law and the Market
ISBN 978-3-030-89046-9 ISBN 978-3-030-89047-6 (eBook)
https://doi.org/10.1007/978-3-030-89047-6

This Springer imprint is published by the registered company Springer Nature Switzerland AG.
The registered company address is: Gewerbestrasse 11, 6330 Cham, Switzerland

The PhD version of this work was published at Maastricht University under the ISBN 978-94-6380-952-8.

To Melanie, Michaela and Peter Tünsmeyer—with all my love and gratitude for your unwavering support. Who would have thought that all of our museum visits would result in this?

Preface

Recent discussions on the return of colonial heritage located in European museums have reminded me frequently of discussions, narratives, articles and books I read on the subject of repatriation in the context of Indigenous Peoples.[1] While not everything is the same, neither in lived experiences nor legally, there are enough similarities to make it worthwhile to take a deeper look at the repatriation of heritage to Indigenous Peoples in legal systems outside of Europe. I hope that by looking at this topic through the lens of human rights the discussion will be of use not only to us in Europe, but also to those of you who have been engaging with this topic in their own countries and institutions for some time already.

As diverse as the legal systems and geographical locations that we find ourselves in are, so are the backgrounds that shape us and the way in which we approach each other. It is quite clear to me that the question of dispossession of heritage is only a small piece of the past and present experience of Indigenous Peoples. The journey towards decolonization—and I often fear that we are still on the road struggling to achieve it—does not end with a ceremony in which heritage is handed over and apologies are made.[2] However, cultural heritage can be a good entry point for many of us to consider our (colonial) past. When we visit museums, we can ask ourselves how did this object come to be here? What do I feel about it being here? Do I know some of what the object has witnessed? Each piece of heritage becomes a microcosmos that showcases many of the difficulties, pain, suffering, and the continuing tension that surrounds our shared past. It is also a lens through which we can approach legal questions: Who do we call the 'owner' of the heritage in question? Why? Which cultural tradition are we applying when we begin to talk about the ownership of heritage in the law, whether it is religious heritage or not? Why do we accept that the legal rules continue to have the effect of cementing past wrongs?

[1]Please note that this preface adopts the capitalization of the terms Indigenous Peoples and Indigenous (except for when used in citations) for reasons explained in Chap. 1.

[2]The latter still seems to be a problem for numerous institutions and countries by the way.

Suffice to say, there is more to each object and more questions to be asked and answered than I could possibly hope to answer in this volume.

Yet, by presenting my research and analysis of the legal experiences in repatriation that exist already, contrasted with the advances we have made so far in Indigenous rights on the international (legal) level, I can highlight some of the possibilities that exist. I believe that the law (if we can speak of it as an entity) can be used to enable us to meet each other with respect rather than as an excuse or obstacle to repatriation, and possibly reconciliation. Ultimately, my wish is of course that my work will be of help to Indigenous Peoples and other actors who are engaged in this process.

Lastly, I also hope that the ongoing conversations on repatriation can be an opportunity to take a step back, evaluate our shared history and look honestly, humbly and respectfully at past wrongs and how they continue to shape the present. I know that delving into the issue of repatriation was such a moment for me. It is a road of learning, which does not have a clear ending in sight. To confront one's own history, and even scientific discipline, and to see the continuing influence of colonial experiences and mindsets is sobering. For this reason, I would like to thank you, my reader, for picking up this book, and for deciding to walk a bit of this path with me. I hope we can continue to learn together. I am always open to reflection, critical comments, questions and suggestions.

Maastricht, The Netherlands Vanessa Tünsmeyer

Acknowledgements

The book you hold in your hands is the result of my PhD research and would not have been possible without the support of many individuals, both in the professional and personal sphere. I would like to express my gratitude to a number of colleagues who provided helpful thoughts and suggestions throughout the writing of this volume. First and foremost, my thanks go to Prof. Hildegard Schneider and Prof. Fons Coomans, for their guidance and advice throughout this journey. My thanks also go to the members of the Assessment Committee who volunteered their time to read my manuscript and pose critical questions at my defense: Prof. Dr. Cees Flinterman, Prof. Dr. Yvonne Donders, Prof. Dr. Robert Paterson and Prof. dr. Bruno de Witte. I would like to express my appreciation to Professor Robert Paterson for agreeing to host me at Peter Allard Hall Law School (even though I came the autumn after he had just officially retired).

I am similarly indebted to colleagues from the Maastricht Centre for Human Rights (MCfHR) for feedback and questions they posed during our Lunch Talk Sessions and great friendships throughout my time there. Many thanks also to the members of the Steering Committee at the Maastricht Centre for Arts and Culture, Conservation and Heritage (MACCH) for the inspiration you bring and the warm welcome you gave me. Thank you also for your kind acceptance of the manuscript in this series.

I would also like to thank the many colleagues and friends I made along the way, whom I met during conferences, in faculties, libraries, on research visits and online, who supported me, challenged me and helped shape this book in one way or another. You are too numerous to name here: thank you for your support, the sharing of your expertise, knowledge and lived experiences.

Lastly, my thanks go to my family and my friends. I am incredibly fortunate to have you in my life—Ich kann mich glücklich schätzen, euch in meinem Leben zu wissen.

Contents

List of Select Abbreviations

ADRM	American Declaration of Rights and Duties of Man
AIRFA	American Indian Religious Freedom Act
ARPA	Archaeological Resources Protection Act
BIA	Bureau of Indian Affairs
CERD	Committee on the Elimination of Racial Discrimination
CESCR	Committee on Economic, Social and Cultural Rights
CMH	Canadian Museum of History
CPEIA	Cultural Property Export and Import Act
FNSCORA	First Nation Sacred Ceremonial Objects Repatriation Act
HRCee	Human Rights Committee
ICCPR	International Covenant on Civil and Political Rights
ICESCR	International Covenant on Economic, Social and Cultural Rights
NAGPRA	Native American Graves Protection and Repatriation Act
RAM	Royal Alberta Museum
RBCM	Royal British Columbia Museum
RFRA	Religious Freedom Restoration Act
SCC	Supreme Court of Canada
SCOTUS	Supreme Court of the United States
UN	United Nations
UNESCO	United Nations Educational, Scientific and Cultural Organization

Chapter 1
Introduction

1.1 Current Claims for Indigenous Cultural Heritage in Museum Collections

> 1. Indigenous peoples have the right to manifest, practise, develop and teach their spiritual and religious traditions, customs and ceremonies; [. . .] the right to the use and control of their ceremonial objects; and the right to the repatriation of their human remains.
> 2. *States shall seek to enable the access and/or repatriation of ceremonial objects* and human remains in their possession *through fair, transparent and effective mechanisms* developed in conjunction with indigenous peoples concerned.—Article 12 of the United Nations Declaration on the Rights of Indigenous Peoples (adopted in 2007, emphasis added)

> I believe, in line with the Commission's first recommendation, that by taking possession of cultural goods against their will, the original population of the colonial territories has been wronged.[1]—Ingrid van Engelshoven, Dutch Minister of Education, Culture and Science, 2021

Many (Indigenous) objects that are currently located in museums have a tumultuous, even violent history. Invasions, armed conflicts and other forms of violent clashes between different cultures have been the setting for the collection and exportation of cultural objects out of their original and into a new cultural context. This has happened on a massive scale during different historical periods, notably during

[1] I. van Engelshoven, Beleidsvisie Collecties uit een koloniale context (29.01.2021) [Letter of government, Appendix], p. 4. Retrieved from: https://www.rijksoverheid.nl/ministeries/ministerie-van-onderwijs-cultuur-en-wetenschap/documenten/kamerstukken/2021/01/29/beleidsvisie-collecties-uit-een-koloniale-context. Unofficial translation, original quotation: "Ik ben van oordeel, in lijn met de eerste aanbeveling van de Commissie, dat door het tegen hun wil in bezit nemen van cultuurgoederen, de oorspronkelijke bevolking van de koloniale gebieden onrecht is aangedaan." [last accessed 30.07.2021].

V. Tünsmeyer, *Repatriation of Sacred Indigenous Cultural Heritage and the Law*, Studies in Art, Heritage, Law and the Market 3,
https://doi.org/10.1007/978-3-030-89047-6_1

European colonialism, beginning in the fifteenth century.[2] Members of the civil and military services of European colonial powers, such as the Netherlands, Great Britain or Germany, took objects for private or governmental collections or sold or donated cultural heritage to other collectors. This history of cultural dispossession also occurred under settler colonialism in countries such as the United States or Canada. Objects may have been taken violently, under duress, in accordance with colonial legislation but in unequal power relationships, or they may have been part of a sale or gifts between parties.[3] All of these modes of acquisition have to be evaluated against the colonial (legal) background that created significant power inequalities between the parties. Current museum collections remain as evidence of such practices, for example in the British Museum or Dutch colonial collections of Indonesian and Benin objects.[4] These are subject to international claims for their return, issued by governments, museums or individuals of former European colonies.

Within former settler colonies, the claims for the return of Indigenous heritage (referred to as repatriation, see Sect. 1.4.1) by Indigenous communities cover cultural heritage located abroad and located in museums that are situated within the same country as the community. Both private and public collections encompass cultural heritage of mixed origins: some may have been legally owned (gifted or purchased) at a certain point in the past, others may have been taken against the will of the owner or maker. These objects can thus be legally owned by a museum today, but may originally have been taken from their owner or creator by illegal or unethical means. Due to the nature of the art market (longevity of the object and trade in the object) we, as a society, are thus continuously confronted with the question: how did an object arrive in a collection? Should a certain piece of cultural heritage be returned? And, if yes, to whom?

Recent decades have witnessed a growing trend of a critical examination of colonial collections and a confrontation with these questions in the wider museum community and public debate that has finally entered the wider European debate. Calls for returns of colonial-era heritage occurred first in connection with the decolonization wave in Africa,[5] then in the context of settler colonialism, notably

[2]Other historical examples are Hitler's specific targeting of art collections all over Europe or Napoleon's collection of art for the glorification of France. Looting of cultural objects during conflict has a long history, we can even read of Caesar's looting campaigns in the poet Virgil who rhymed "*Mighty Cæsar, thund'ring from afar, Seeks on Euphrates Banks the Spoils of War*" Virgil (1792), line 809–810. For a long time, looting was considered a right of the warring parties, the *ius praedere.* W. Kowlaski views 1815 and the end of the Napoleonic wars as a fundamental date which marked the emergence of a generally accepted ban on looting, Kowalski (2005), p. 87. See also Lubina (2009), pp. 54–55.

[3]For another typology see van Beurden (2017), p. 41.

[4]van Beurden (2014). For a general overview of different colonial takings and return proceedings, see van Beurden (2017).

[5]As exemplified by the famous speech of the Senegalese Director-General of UNESCO Amadou-Mahtar Mbow 7.06.1978.

in the United States, with the adoption of a law facilitating the return of human remains and sacred objects in 1990.[6] Finally, the discussion on returning colonial (including Indigenous) heritage recently regained momentum in Europe. In 2017, newspapers all across the globe reported on Emmanuel Macron's pledge to return colonial heritage to African countries.[7] "France", it has been observed, "has electrified an old debate by pushing to repatriate art works".[8]

Current examples of international requests range from requests to return works of art looted from Royal Palaces of Abomey in Benin to requests by Rapa Nui elders for the return of important statues.[9] Macron has called for the necessary legal changes to be made to French heritage legislation to enable the return of colonial heritage. A report by the French art historian Bénédicte Savoy and the Senegalese economist Felwine Sarr, commissioned by Macron, called for developing new "relational ethics" between France and Africa through the restitution of African cultural heritage that is hoped to have a much larger greater impact on the relationship between the two continents.[10]

In Germany, the discussion has arisen anew both in the context of establishing the Humboldt Forum and the call by Hermann Parzinger for rules on the restitution of colonial objects.[11] In April of 2021 the German government announced an update on their part of the Benin dialogues, including a timeline for publishing details on Benin bronzes in public collections online and a confirmation of their intention to return the bronzes in 2022.[12]

In the Netherlands, several initiatives are underway.[13] Most well-known has been the recently issued by an advisory body to the Dutch government on a future framework policy for colonial collections.[14] The minister has stated her intention to largely follow the advice and to act upon the recommendations of the commission[15] and, as indicated in the quote at the beginning of this chapter, will proceed with the admission and understanding that the original population was wronged by the taking of heritage during colonialism. At the time of editing this volume it is still too early to evaluate the outcome of this process. The Rijksmuseum started with provenance research into parts of its collection, as well as engaging in talks with

[6]The Native American Graves Protection and Repatriation Act (NAGPRA), Pub. L. 101-601, 25 U.S.C. 3001 et seq., 104 Stat. 3048 was enacted 16.11.1990.

[7]Harris (2017).

[8]Thomas (2018).

[9]Thomas (2018).

[10]Sarr and Savoy (2018).

[11]Hickley (2018); Braun (2019). See also interview (in German) Parzinger and Polenz (2016). [Last accessed 29.05.2016].

[12]Federal Foreign Office of Germany (30.04.2021) Press release: Statement on the handling of the Benin Bronzes in German museums and institutions.

[13]Hickley (2019).

[14]Gonçalves-Ho Kang You et al. (2021).

[15]I. van Engelshoven, Beleidsvisie Collecties uit een koloniale context (29.01.2021) [Letter of government, Appendix].

former colonies. The National Museum of World Cultures[16] has published principles on how to deal with claims for the return of colonial objects. These principles reflect some of the changes in the museum community, including the desire to place "communities on an equal footing as national collections" and to engage in a dialogue with both source communities and source nations.[17]

In sum, both the taking of cultural objects as well as the debate over their return has a long tradition. There has been a progression towards actual returns in some areas, but a slow one. This is also illustrated by the selected quotations on page one. While colonial Indigenous collections have been the subject of debate in some settler colonial systems for several decades now, the discussion in Europe, which had already been initiated by notable African scholars and politicians after the independence movement of African states was met with resistance by different actors, including European politicians and museum professionals, at the time.[18] Only since 2017 has it gained renewed momentum and more widespread support amongst European museums and politicians. Moreover, not all of these initiatives have been inclusive, in the sense that Indigenous communities were involved or consulted where their heritage is being discussed. In fact, it often appears to be an intergovernmental affair. This has many reasons, legal, historical, and political. For one, the current structure of international law still reserves the majority of legal power in international dealings for states. Moreover, Indigenous objects taken during colonialism are at the intersection of several processes, namely the quest for the realization of Indigenous rights by the communities in question, decolonization of museum collections, and the realization that to impose conditions for return discussions on the governments of former colonies unilaterally would be akin to imposing neo-colonial structures.[19] Of course, such observations are not new, and it is to be hoped that they will not be "forgotten" in a way that happened to the earlier debate in Europe which took place between the 1960s and 1980s.[20]

However, from an Indigenous rights perspective this also bears the potential for conflict. Ultimately, this approach means that decisions on international returns are at the discretion of the respective state governments. Some governments support their Indigenous populations in their efforts for international repatriations, if not of cultural heritage then at least for the return of human remains.[21] Talks can be inclusive, featuring all interested parties coming together to negotiate (governments,

---

[16]The Dutch National Museum of World Cultures is in fact an amalgam of the Museum Volkenkunde, the Tropenmuseum and the Afrika Museum.

[17]Nationaal Museum van Wereldculturen, Return of Cultural Objects: Principles and Process National Museum van Wereldculturen (7 March 2019), p. 2.

[18]Savoy (2021).

[19]Gonçalves-Ho Kang You et al. (2021), Recommendation nr.3.

[20]See Savoy (2021), on p. 193 who describes an open letter written by a German politician member of the green party in July 1985 as one of the final moments of the first of the restitution debate in Europe.

[21]For example, the Australian government has been actively negotiating for the repatriation of ancestral remains of the country's Indigenous population on the international level. Feikert (2009).

communities, museum representatives and representatives of the Diaspora, for example). It also means that where the government of a former colonized power is unwilling to involve an Indigenous community from their territory—even if the latter may have expressed their desire to be involved—their involvement is unlikely. This is a result of both the historical evolution of international law and its current legal structure. However, all governments do have obligations towards their Indigenous populations under international human rights law, as will be discussed in Chap. 2. This is crucial as it means that, in the absence of any direct involvement of Indigenous populations in international return negotiations (which would be preferable from an Indigenous rights perspective) there are still rights that such communities hold vis-à-vis the respective state government of their territory and which come to play in intranational returns. Or to put it simply, any international return of Indigenous heritage holds the potential for an intranational repatriation. In how far such rights can be claimed against an unwilling government in practice is of course a different matter.

So far, no clear, internationally undisputed answer has been found to the question whether or not, and how, items taken during colonialism should be returned, be it to the state or to descendants of those from whom they were originally taken. There is no obligation to return colonial-era heritage under international law. On the international level, the Human Rights Council has called for the establishment of an international repatriation mechanism,[22] which so far does not exist (setting aside the Intergovernmental Committee acting under the auspices of UNESCO, for reasons that will be discussed in Chap. 3). The Expert Mechanism on the Rights of Indigenous Peoples in its report on repatriation recommends that stakeholders take a human-rights based approach to repatriation.[23] This contribution follows this call and seeks to concretize how such a human rights-based approach would look like exactly. Different legal mechanisms of regulating returns have sprung up and, in the context of international returns, the standards so far are comparatively loose and broad, as can be seen in the principles issued by the National Museum of World Cultures in the Netherlands, the policy vision adopted by the Dutch government, or the bottom-up proposal that has recently been published by a number of academics and heritage actors in Belgium.[24] However, for returns *within* individual countries legal repatriation mechanisms have already been adopted or are being considered at this moment, both in the form of hard and soft law. In fact, the context of the takings, the cultures and the identity of the actors are so diverse that a one-size-fits-all solution does not seem likely or even advisable. How then, should repatriation be regulated legally within a specific context?

---

[22] Human Rights Council, Resolution 42/19 on Human Rights and Indigenous Peoples, U.N. Doc. A/HRC/42/L.24 [26.09.2019], para 18.

[23] Human Rights Council, Report of the Expert Mechanism on the Rights of Indigenous Peoples, Repatriation of ceremonial objects, human remains and intangible cultural heritage under the United Nations Declaration on the Rights of Indigenous Peoples, U.N. Doc. A/HRC/45/35 [21.07.2020].

[24] Boele et al. (2021).

This study focusses on the claims for the repatriation of Indigenous heritage by Indigenous claimants for three main reasons: first, during colonialism, Indigenous Peoples were the group who, across the globe, lost a significant part of their cultural objects. Different peoples have been trying to reclaim this heritage, both as distinct communities as well as through state organs since the start of the decolonization process. Second, given the rise of Indigenous rights on the international level and the disadvantaged position of Indigenous Peoples across the globe, the relationship between Indigenous rights and the repatriation of cultural heritage deserves further attention, especially in light of the renewed wave of (calls for) repatriation. Third, there have been successful negotiations on repatriation and laws mandating the repatriation of Indigenous colonial heritage. There is thus a comparative wealth of materials to draw lessons from.

1.2 Research Questions and Methodology

1.2.1 Normative, Comparative Legal Research

The question of how repatriation should be regulated legally is of a normative nature. It requires us to make a value judgement about one regulatory choice over another. This implies both the existence of different regulatory options and a standard by which to measure them. To answer this, we thus first have to establish whether there are different ways of regulating repatriation in the form of different repatriation models. To explore whether different repatriation legislation in effect uses different methods for regulating this matter, the author will use comparative legal research to analyse a sample of legal repatriation frameworks that already exist. The author has chosen the United States and Canada for the reasons motivated in Sect. 1.3.3 below.

Second, there must be a standard against which to measure these frameworks or models. To establish such standards, the author will make use of international law for a number of reasons: By having ratified relevant international treaties, states have incurred legal obligations. The research thus works on the understanding that international law (a) qualifies as law (not purely international relations) that (b) gives rise to obligations either towards other states or individuals or communities under international law, (c) irrespective of whether a treaty has been implemented in domestic law or not, and regardless of whether (d) a legal system is monist or dualist. While rights arising out of human rights treaties might not be enforceable at the national level depending on state (in)action, this does not negate the existence of the legal right or the state obligation on the international legal level. As a result, assessing national repatriation schemes in light of these international standards is warranted regardless of how Canadian or US domestic law structures its relationship to international law. The focus on national regulatory frameworks on repatriation therefore does not imply that there is no role for international law in the examination. In fact, there are two fields of public international law that directly relate to the repatriation of Indigenous cultural heritage: international cultural heritage law and international human rights law.

International cultural heritage law evolved as a field to enhance the protection of cultural heritage in light of different dangers. It first arose in light of the dangers of war to cultural heritage, evolved to encompass natural dangers and the risks of an increased art trade and globalization. It imposes duties upon states in connection with different categories of cultural heritage. International human rights law in turn enshrines a large catalogue of rights that are held by every human being by the simple virtue of their existence. It imposes obligations upon states to respect every individual in its territory, irrespective of their citizenship. There are a number of rights that connect to sacred Indigenous cultural heritage, notably cultural rights, the freedom of religion, minority rights, and Indigenous rights. Both impose obligations that a state must respect within its territory, with respect to either cultural heritage or Indigenous Peoples.

Since the main treaties of human rights law are almost universally recognized, different countries that seek to learn from existing repatriations can also use this standard to measure their respective drafting legislation. Since the aim of this research is to identify how best to regulate repatriation legally, both national and international law must be incorporated into the examination. These observations raise the first, main research question:

How Should the Repatriation of Sacred Indigenous Cultural Heritage Be Regulated Legally in Light of International Cultural Heritage and Human Rights Law Standards?

This research question raises three sub-questions, namely: How is the repatriation of sacred cultural heritage regulated in the selected examples? What international standards apply to repatriation? Which method of repatriation is the most in line with these standards?

Neither international cultural heritage law nor international human rights law explicitly regulate repatriation. However, they affect repatriation incidentally, as repatriating sacred cultural heritage connects to questions of heritage protection, rights held by Indigenous individuals, communities or the general public to cultural heritage and the exercise of religious practices. Moreover, since these objects are mostly held by museums, standards that bind museum behaviour, even soft law, can also affect how repatriation is handled. In short, repatriation does not occur in a vacuum. It is connected to diverse legal and policy areas. For example, if repatriation legislation intends to ensure the revitalization of religious practices, other factors that undermine religious practices affect in how far Indigenous communities can engage in such revitalization practices. Alternatively, if repatriation seeks to remedy the effects of a long tradition of trading in Indigenous art works, how can this be successful if no measures are taken to protect against their contemporary trade?

This requires an examination of national repatriation legislation and an evaluation of national cultural heritage legislation, the legal-historical conditions under which the objects were taken, museum (self-) regulation, and laws governing Indigenous religious freedoms. Repatriation frameworks are embedded in this wider framework, and the choice for one over another framework was taken against this backdrop. To portray an accurate picture of repatriation, both in the national legal context and in light of international standards, goes beyond an examination of the repatriation law to examine linked policy areas. The national examination will thus consider these areas not only to consider whether they affect the repatriation framework but also to evaluate these areas in light of the standards derived in part I. This is done in the understanding that broader questions of cultural heritage law and policy are connected to and affect the repatriation experience of Indigenous communities and are, simultaneously, subject to relevant human rights standards. This leads to the second main research question that this research will answer, namely:

What—If Anything—Can We Derive from the Findings of the Country Analysis in Light of the International Standards for the Cultural Heritage Law and Policy of the Selected Countries?

This research thus seeks to establish how to best regulate repatriation within its given legal context, considering both the specific repatriation legislation by itself and the legal context in which it operates. This context includes national heritage law and policy and international legal standards, in particular in human rights law. The recent decades have seen a strengthening of Indigenous and cultural rights, and these standards have not (yet) been fully taken into account by those engaged in repatriation and heritage management. This study aims to remedy this gap and to further the repatriation discussion by incorporating the developments of human rights law more explicitly in repatriation laws. It thus also builds upon an existing debate that began with the question whether to repatriate or not, which is summarized below.

1.2.2 To Repatriate or Not to Repatriate: And If Yes to Whom? The Repatriation Dilemma and the Existing Debate

Many factors appear to influence whether an object is repatriated, i.e. the context of the original taking, the current location of the object, its role in its current environment, the original nature (and value) of the objects for their maker or original community, the nature (and value) for the current possessor and owner, the ethnic (social and/or institutional) background of the claimant and current possessor, the media attention the claim for return has triggered and, last but not least, the legal framework in place at the time of the taking and at the time of the request for return.[25] This multitude of factors, which ultimately decides whether or not an object which is (re-)claimed will be retained or returned, gives a first impression of the

[25] Compare Prott in Prott (2009), p. xxii. She observes that "the nature of the taking of the cultural property is never the sole concern in the dispute and often only a minor issue compared, for example with cultural arguments."

complexity which lies at the heart of the return of colonial-era cultural objects to Indigenous Peoples.

To gain a better understanding of this complexity, the next section summarizes common arguments brought forward in the debate, focussing on the return of Indigenous cultural heritage taken during colonialism.

1.2.2.1 Actors in the Repatriation Debate[26]

To start the discussion on repatriation, the decision to repatriate objects of questionable origins is not self-evident to all actors in the debate. In Europe, the discussion on returning colonial-era heritage has only recently picked up speed and is slowly starting to mirror some of the discussions on repatriating Indigenous heritage in North America in or since the 1990s.

Depending on the actors involved, perspectives can differ significantly. Some scientists and archaeologists may advise against the repatriation of objects on conservationist grounds, for fear that the object, once returned, may be destroyed and/or not available for future scientific research.[27] Others may argue in favour of repatriation to establish new partnerships with Indigenous Peoples and out of ethical motivations. Some museums might fear the precedent which the return of one object can set (this is the well-known 'we will have nothing left in our collections' argument).[28] Other museums might be much more open towards repatriation, viewing it as a possibility to create the foundation for a lasting relationship with neighbouring communities and to learn more about their cultures.[29] At times, it may be the museum community of the formerly colonized country that pleads for their return.[30] In fact, repatriation claims have raised difficult questions for museums, both specific to their Indigenous collections as well as challenging their role as an educative and scientific institution.[31] For example, if a museum is to preserve, for

[26] As the focus of this analysis rests on repatriation, not international returns, the position of the Diaspora, which should be taken in account in international returns, is not considered separately. In repatriations by contrast, attention as to be paid to the Indigenous Peoples living outside of their communities, i.e. in urban areas.

[27] Such scientific considerations were *inter alia* highlighted by the Museums and Galleries Commission (2009), pp. 131–132. Krzystof Pomian, by contrast, has argued in favour of conservation but highlights that repatriation and conservation can be combined (presumably if conditions are made to which the Indigenous community has to agree to), Rivière et al. (2007), p. 50.

[28] Critically, Prott (2009), p. 43.

[29] As Argued by Bernice Murphy, Chair of the ICOMOS Ethics Committee in Rivière et al. (2007).

[30] Abungu (2009), p. 121.

[31] Compare Welsh (1992), p. 847. He enumerates a number of what he calls fundamental contradictions that have guided museums: "First, they attempt to preserve collections in perpetuity and yet desire to make them accessible to everyone. Second, they strive for new understanding, yet speak in the simplest terms to their audiences. Third, they encourage scientific inquiry, but rarely do it. Fourth, they attempt to foster cross-cultural respect, yet are thrown into turmoil when faced

whom does it do so? If a museum is to educate, whom should it educate, and which story or stories should it tell?

One group which has frequently voiced claims for the return of (their) cultural objects are Indigenous Peoples, both internationally and nationally. Repatriation claims can involve contradicting claims by different groups. At times, due to the nature of the object, an Indigenous community might require it back for its collective spiritual wellbeing or may not wish to receive it back for precisely the same reason and would prefer it to stay in the collection of the museum. It might also be that a community desires the return of all objects held in a museum, irrespective of their nature (sacred and everyday objects). Claims of an international dimension concern objects which were taken by European colonial powers in the past and now remain abroad. These were, for example, exported to be displayed by the colonial power in its own territory. Universally known examples of this are in the British Museum and the State Museums of Bavaria in Munich.[32] Claims of a national dimension concern those objects which are now located within the state where the specific Indigenous community resides but which they no longer own (referred to as intra-national throughout this book).

This change of ownership may have a variety of causes. The items could have been taken against the will of the Indigenous community but in accordance with the law at the time. They could have been sold under duress or sold by the caretaker of the object, yet without the consent of the community, or they could have been stolen.[33] Past takings may also have been motivated by a number of different reasons. Depending on the number of objects taken and their importance, to remove the object could suppress resistance, disrupt the transmission of cultural knowledge, which in turn rendered younger generations more open to being influenced by the colonial culture and could highlight (similar to how looted objects have been used in the past) the importance of the colonial power.[34]

Current requests for return, in contrast, can be linked to such diverse concerns as treaty negotiations, claims for self-determination, the increase of political power within the state, attempts to revitalize the community or attempts to further the reconciliation between Indigenous Peoples and the state.[35] The refusal to return objects in turn can be motivated by a fear that it would set a precedent, which could in turn mean the loss of a significant part of its collection or alternatively the loss of a more valuable collection. Alternatively, to return where there is no legal obligation

with representatives of another culture calling for the return of an object for use with a religious purpose."

[32] I.e. Samoan artefacts in the Staatliche Museum für Völkerkunde, see this exhibition as reported by the Bavarian Ministry for Culture: http://www.km.bayern.de/kunst-und-kultur/meldung/2474/bayern-und-samoa-eine-ausstellung-zeigt-ein-spannendes-stueck-kolonialgeschichte.html [last accessed 30.07.2021].

[33] The loss of sacred objects of other religions is often as or even more convoluted. Compare O'Keefe (2009), pp. 226–229. Section 'How Sacred Objects are Lost and Repatriated'.

[34] Bengs (1996), p. 511.

[35] Glass (2004), p. 116.

to do so has an apologetic note to it, and not every institution or country is open to admitting that past actions were at least unethical or immoral, if not unlawful, and would in all likelihood qualify as illegal if judged by contemporary standards. Yet, even if an institution acknowledges past wrongs and is not afraid to set a precedent, to return an object might violate its trust-holder position,[36] considering that public collections are held for the general public of the region and country in which the museum is located or even for humanity in general (as museums, which identify themselves as universal, claim[37]).

Representatives of the art market, in turn, are likely to be focussed on the economic aspects of a repatriation dispute, where the demand for ethnographic material is high and the return to Indigenous communities could make it less likely that these objects enter the art market again.[38] Next to Indigenous communities, governments of previous colonies may also reclaim the cultural heritage of Indigenous Peoples from former colonial powers as part of their national cultural heritage. These government representatives could either favour repatriation to Indigenous communities as a step in a wider reconciliation project or be opposed to repatriation fearing that it may increase ethnical tensions in their territory, that past violations are brought back into public consciousness, that the cultural heritage is national cultural heritage, or that it may increase claims for the self-determination of the Indigenous community within the state. Having considered the different interest groups involved, it is not surprising that a variety of arguments have been made in favour and against repatriation. These arguments are summarized briefly below.

1.2.2.2 Arguments on Whether to Repatriate or Not

The arguments on repatriation can roughly be divided into four themes: the place of an object within an Indigenous culture, the value of the object to the non-Indigenous community (educative, scientific or financial), the history of the object, and Indigenous rights (including the value of the object for the community).[39] First, proponents of repatriation cite the cultural value of an object to the community which

[36] Excerpts from 'Restitution and Repatriation: Guidelines for Good Practice' 2000 issued by Museums and Galleries Commission (2009), see Sects. 2.1 and 2.2.1.

[37] Declaration on the Importance and Value of Universal Museums 10.12.2002, "we should acknowledge that museums serve not just the citizens of one nation, but the people of every nation."

[38] Of course other arguments are advanced in favour of the free trade of cultural objects, *inter alia* that, by means of the market, objects will move towards the person or institution which has sufficient funds to care for them and ensure their safety, that the art market because of its global nature will in fact increase the accessibility of the objects in question or that it aids in educating the public. For a brief yet rightfully critical summary see Gerstenblith (2001), p. 206.

[39] Sarah Harding distinguishes three approaches to justify the repatriation of Native American Cultural Property [compensation for past destruction, relationship between importance of an object and ownership and impossibility to own cultural property] in Harding (1997). For an insightful discussion of the value of cultural heritage more generally see Harding (1999), p.

produced it as an important reason for repatriation.[40] Repatriation then gains an important role in the preservation or revitalization of the source community.[41] This argument is therefore highly relevant for sacred objects. The link of this argument to the cultural diversity concept is clear. Proponents of cultural diversity will highlight the need to revitalize a culture. Sceptics will oppose it for its emphasis on cultural revivalism and a fear of increased ethnic or religious tensions.[42] Fears of revivalism aside, the revitalization argument operates on the assumption that the object is first and foremost important to the group which produced it. If the group decides that the proper method of handling an object in line with its cultural tradition is a ritual use, which will lead to its destruction, then this must be accepted under this approach. The idea that a group is hindered in exercising its religious freedom if it is not allowed access to vital religious objects is another argument in favour of repatriation.[43]

The centrality of reclaimed objects within the source community disregards arguments made by cultural internationalists, including the renowned art law expert John Merryman, who viewed heritage mostly in global terms, as the heritage of mankind, best cared for by market nations.[44] Coombe describes this approach as originating in the law of war.[45] To condemn the destruction of cultural property in times of war requires a strong justification, this restriction is justified by elevating heritage from objects of national importance to objects of international concern. She criticizes Merryman, arguing that one of his most central assumptions was ill-founded, namely his argument that rich 'market' states are those most suited to preserving and finding pleasure in the objects.[46] Nafziger and Paterson similarly criticize the internationalist approach, and the debate in itself. They argue that the concept seeks to legitimate a type of international art trade which benefits the private individual rather than the wider public. This being said, they find this and similar confrontational concepts to be "yielding to more cooperative approaches for accommodating the many diverse interests in the cultural heritage of humankind."[47]

As indicated above, the debate on the value of repatriation is linked to a central concept in the area of cultural heritage, the concept of a cultural heritage which is of

[40] Welsh (1992), pp. 847–848.

[41] Welsh (1992), pp. 847–848.

[42] Singh (2009), pp. 128–129. K. Singh, influenced by the history of violent clashes between the Hindu and Muslim communities in India, has observed: "We are not, we are never returning things to the past – that moment is gone- we are assisting contemporary revivalism. And coming from India where we have a history of current Hindus avenging themselves on current day Muslims for 800 years of Islamic rule, current day low castes waiting to get into a position to avenge themselves against 5000 years of oppression by the upper cases, I have to say that even the well-intentioned acts of respecting other cultures which then lead to revivalism terrify me."

[43] Welsh (1992), p. 846.

[44] Merryman (1986).

[45] Coombe (2004), pp. 541–542.

[46] Coombe (2004), pp. 541–542.

[47] Nafziger and Paterson (2014), p. 16.

value to humankind. The conceptual foundation of this term lies in the destruction of heritage in times of war.[48] This loss of heritage eventually caused states to attempt to regulate cultural heritage on the international level. The first international treaty which accorded cultural heritage 'universal importance' was the Convention for the Protection of Cultural Property in the Event of Armed Conflict with Regulations for the Execution of the Convention 1954, commonly known as the 1954 Hague Convention.[49] This universal importance was then picked up again in later UNESCO instruments, such as the 1972 World Heritage Convention. Its most central tenet is that a specific category of heritage (be it tangible or intangible heritage) is of such fundamental importance to all of humanity that it must be preserved for present and future generations.[50] The present owners of the heritage in question are thereby placed in the position of a trustee who has the (ethical) obligation to care for the object and to preserve it for the future beneficiaries.[51] It has to be observed, however, that this conceptualization of heritage does not *per se* support or contradict repatriation, as long as repatriation does not equal the loss of an object which is deemed to be of such importance or rather *value* that it is classified as part of the common heritage of humankind. Fechner has described the concept as being weak in the sense that it has been used to support both repatriation claims as well as to support ownership and management by the international community as a whole.[52]

These different positions agree on the importance of the object to different entities (the individual, the community, the nation-state, or humankind) but differ in whose affiliation with the object is ranked highest. The ranking hinges on what value of the object is prioritized, for example its financial, aesthetic, spiritual, or its evidentiary value for a specific culture or history.[53] The value of a reclaimed object is thus a recurring theme in the repatriation debate, even apart from the common heritage of humankind debate. Financially, there is a significant market for cultural objects and Indigenous objects form part of this market. To return the objects not only results in the financial loss of the object itself, but for museums it is also a potential loss in the future revenue from visitors.[54] But it is not only the financial loss which opponents of repatriation fear. Where the main goal is preservation, museums have argued in the past that they are in a better position to preserve the object than a small, community-based museum would be, since they have more funds to do so.[55]

[48] Forrest (2007), p. 128.

[49] Forrest (2007), p. 129.

[50] 1972 World Heritage Convention, recital 6 and Art.6. Forrest (2007), p. 129.

[51] This idea also appears in Museums and Galleries Commission (2009), p. 131. "Global significance of cultural and natural heritage, which belongs to us all".

[52] Fechner (1998), pp. 387–388.

[53] This also links to the construction and maintaining of specific identities, be they national or communal.

[54] Kenney (2011), p. 517.

[55] Museums and Galleries Commission (2009), p. 132.

The objects also hold a scientific value. Future research methods, which are not yet available, might yield new knowledge and the return of objects to communities prevents this.[56] On the other hand, partnerships between Indigenous communities and museums have the possibility to accommodate new avenues of collaborative research and other activities.[57] The consultation of Indigenous experts, i.e. on production methods, could provide new insights and rectify existing misconceptions.[58] The inclusion of Indigenous representatives both in the creation of exhibits and among museum staff would also ensure that the public is educated in a way that acknowledges diverse cultural expressions.[59] Moreover, it could ensure that the educative value an object holds is not lost with its repatriation but potentially even enhanced. The role of an object in educating the wider public (by a museum) is often advanced as an argument against repatriation.[60] Moreover, museum displays allow urban Indigenous populations to have access to their cultural heritage.[61] These arguments against repatriation hold true only if the items are actually displayed. Where museums do not display the item, be it for curative reasons or avoiding negative publicity, this does then not hold true.

The third group of arguments advanced can be linked to the historic and cultural context of the time in which the item was taken. One argument in favour of repatriation views it as an integral part of a wider societal confrontation of historical wrongdoings and as a form of redress.[62] This acknowledges the unethical method in which the object was likely taken from Indigenous communities in the past. In a sense, the possession of the object by the museum is tainted by the original, unethical, acquisition. Given the power asymmetries in which the original taking occurred, combined with the fact that many museums continue to hold colonial heritage of Indigenous groups who dispose significantly less resources, the refusal to repatriate can be seen as reinforcing colonial power inequalities.[63] To repatriate cultural heritage can help a society that is embarking on a wider reconciliation journey to address some of its difficult past.

Repatriation can also be used as a form of reparation for harm suffered in the past. Reparation describes substantive remedies[64] that are granted to a victim who has suffered a violation of his or her rights. Restitution is to restore the victim to his/her position before the violation occurred (if this is possible) and it is the primary form of

[56] Welsh (1992), pp. 846–848. Museums and Galleries Commission (2009), p. 131.

[57] Museums and Galleries Commission (2009), p. 132.

[58] Welsh (1992), p. 844.

[59] Welsh (1992), p. 844, 846.

[60] Welsh (1992), p. 848. Museums and Galleries Commission (2009), p. 131.

[61] A comparable argument can be made against returning everything that classifies as colonial heritage, to ensure access for example for members of the Diaspora.

[62] Museums and Galleries Commission (2009), p. 132. "Acknowledgement of past wrongful taking and/ or misunderstandings of complex customary ownership concepts, and attempt to redress;"

[63] Bell (2009), p. 20.

[64] There are also procedural remedies, access to justice via a court proceeding, for example.

substantive reparation.[65] Indigenous Peoples have suffered violations of their human rights in the past and this continues. This includes harm suffered during colonialism, such as the confiscation of their land and their cultural heritage. Both need to be present for the community to survive, both physically and culturally. For Indigenous Peoples, restitution is therefore a crucial form of reparation for harm suffered.

While international law identifies restitution as one of the primary means of reparation for gross violations of human rights,[66] reparation for wrongdoings committed during colonialism remains the subject of intense international political and legal debate.[67] In terms of cultural heritage, many Indigenous Peoples continue to suffer from the continued absence of cultural heritage. The harm suffered can be both spiritual and cultural in the wider sense. For example, the loss of cultural heritage has gone hand in hand with language prohibitions and other policy measures. To return cultural heritage can help in the revitalization of cultural traditions, even supporting the reclaiming of cultural identity. However, it is important to acknowledge that to return Indigenous cultural heritage (i.e. to repatriate)[68] simply cannot return the community to the situation that it experienced prior to the confiscation of the property (and colonialism). It is one of many methods that (may) have to be taken to address the continuing effects of colonialism. This also connects it intimately to efforts of reconciliation. In the efforts of decolonization, both internationally and nationally, this means finding a new balance between different communities, peoples and states, also legally.

The OED defines reconciliation as "[t] he action of restoring estranged people or parties to friendship; the result of this; the fact of being reconciled"[69] or "the action or an act of bringing a thing or things to agreement, concord, or harmony; the fact of being made consistent or compatible".[70] To achieve agreement or harmony can require the return of cultural heritage in order to remedy its unequal distribution. On the other side of the spectrum of the debate on the historic-cultural context of the object, is the importance of the object for the rest of society. For example, British museums have, *inter alia*, highlighted the history of the piece within the museum and the UK in general.[71] This can then add an additional difficulty to repatriation

---

[65] Desmet (2008), p. 98.

[66] UN GA Resolution 60/147, Basic Principles and Guidelines on the Right to a Remedy and Reparation for Victims of Gross Violations of International Human Rights Law and Serious Violations of International Humanitarian Law (16.12.2005), also termed the Van Boven/Bassiouni Principles.

[67] This also occurred in connection with adopting the van Boven/ Bassiouni Principles, see Desmet (2008), p. 74.

[68] See terminological clarification in Sect. 1.4 below.

[69] OED, entry reconciliation available at: http://www.oed.com/view/Entry/159781?redirectedFrom=reconciliation#eid [last accessed 30.07.2021].

[70] OED, entry reconciliation available at: http://www.oed.com/view/Entry/159781?redirectedFrom=reconciliation#eid [last accessed 30.07.2021].

[71] Museums and Galleries Commission (2009), p. 132. "Extended history of the material's presence in the museum makes it now part of the scientific or cultural heritage of the United Kingdom".

attempts. As culture fluctuates and develops (see above) one object can become important to several communities.

The fourth group of arguments are motivated by human rights concerns, in particular the advancement of Indigenous rights in international and regional human rights law. One of the crucial arguments is that Indigenous Peoples have a right to control and interpret their heritage.[72] This also connects to the right to revitalize their traditions and the return of colonial heritage, which will also be addressed in the international law section. This is especially the case where sensitive objects may only be handled by a limited group of people or one gender only. Western conservation standards may risk the desecration of the object and the disclosure of sensitive information.[73] Moreover, the absence of religious cultural heritage from the community impairs the right to practise their religion.

The arguments in favour of repatriation are manifold and the reason for a holding institution or state to adopt a repatriation framework can thus vary significantly. As has become apparent in the brief summary of the discussion above, the question of whether or not an item should be repatriated cannot be answered with a clear yes or no. It is also not just a purely legal question. It involves a multitude of interests, not all of which are reconcilable. This is also expressed by the title of this section, the 'repatriation dilemma'. The Oxford English Dictionary describes a dilemma as "A form of argument involving an adversary in the choice of two (or, *loosely*, more) alternatives, either of which is (or *appears*) equally unfavourable to him."[74] For example, when faced with demands for the return of an object, a museum must consider that to retain the object will preserve the object but reinforce the power inequalities which existed at the time of the original taking and the return of the object might be morally advisable but it could violate the museums' responsibility vis-à-vis the local citizenship or even under its duties under national law.[75] Alternatively, a cultural institution may very much desire that an object be returned and the creation of a new partnership with an Indigenous community but be hindered due to existing national law.

The legal obstacles which may (partially) create this dilemma need not necessarily remain or even have been adopted with the conscious decision to create this interaction. The question for legal research is then not so much whether there should

---

[72]This understanding is also reflected in Art.31 UNDRIP, "indigenous peoples have the right to maintain, control, protect and develop their cultural heritage, traditional knowledge and traditional cultural expressions".

[73]Kenney (2011), discusses a 'right to cultural privacy' that would take this into account, comparable to the privacy of medical information.

[74]The Oxford English Dictionary Online, available at www.oed.com, entry "dilemma" [[last accessed 30.07.2021], emphasis on appears added.

[75]This conflict becomes apparent when one reads the Guidelines prepared by Museums and Galleries Commission (2009). This being said, when reading the Guidelines, it becomes very clear that they stem from a country whose collections are very much influenced by its colonizing past. This can be seen *inter alia* in the concern that, by returning an object, a precedent is created and by the emphasis of the guidelines on the object having become part of British culture over time.

be repatriation or not—this is a debate that involves ethical, moral, societal, cultural, and many other components and which will have to be answered in their respective context. Instead, this work proceeds on the assumption that repatriation is desirable in a variety of different circumstances and that we need to find ways to enable it legally. In this sense, the research is based on the general academic debate on the value of repatriation that already exists. Authors such as Sarah Harding, John Moustakas and Rosemary Coombe considered the question from manifold angles, *inter alia* in light of reconciliation and its link to identity in the nineties.[76] More recent explorations have also been undertaken in a collection of essays under the title 'The Ethics of Cultural Appropriation'.[77] Instead, here the focus is not on whether cultural heritage should be repatriated but how repatriation should be regulated. Given the diversity of actors, interests, cultural heritage, and the legal-historical context of the cultural heritage (and human remains) that are reclaimed, how to regulate the return of cultural heritage in the law cannot be answered uniformly. The diversity of claimants, objects and the historical context of dislocation explored above mandates a narrowing of focus.

1.3 Research Focus

1.3.1 Focus on Sacred Cultural Heritage in Public Collections

As highlighted above, repatriation claims can cover a wide variety of forms of heritage. Cultural heritage can be tangible or intangible, moveable or immovable and can comprise everything from songs to baskets and fishing hooks.[78] The calls for the repatriation of Indigenous cultural heritage (both by communities and governments) cover a wide variety of cultural heritage, including everyday items, such as arrowheads and baskets, important pieces of Indigenous cultural objects such as wampum belts, sacred cultural heritage and associated funerary items, which were dug up together with human remains. They also cover Indigenous human remains, which have been conserved and displayed in museums and were—for a long time—not treated as human remains but as cultural heritage.

In this volume, the research will focus on repatriation claims by Indigenous communities for the return of their moveable, tangible, sacred cultural heritage. The focus on Indigenous religious objects is motivated by the need to narrow down the scope of the research to make it feasible and the importance of the selected group of objects to the culture in question. The absence of spiritual objects affects not only

---

[76] Harding (1997), pp. 740–743; Moustakas (1989); Coombe (2004).

[77] Young and Brunk (2009).

[78] For the specific definition of cultural heritage employed in this volume, please consult Sect. 1.4 below.

the cultural rights of Indigenous Peoples more generally but also their freedom of religion. The focus on religious objects is also motivated by the fact that, judging on the basis of current practices, states and museums seem more open to consider claims for the return of objects whose retention is more difficult to defend to the public, due to the spiritual nature of the object.[79] In this respect, there is a common element in the repatriation of sacred objects and ancestral remains. This research will therefore explore how to regulate the repatriation of sacred cultural heritage to Indigenous Peoples legally. Indigenous Peoples also experience difficulties in connection to their immoveable (religious) cultural heritage, notably in the access, protection, and use of sacred sites. An in-depth analysis of the latter, however, is beyond the scope of this research. As a result, the national legal examination will only touch upon this incidentally as part of considering the freedom of religion under national law. As was explained in Sect. 1.2.1, the freedom of religion is considered as part of the legal context in which the repatriation of sacred cultural heritage takes place.

Moreover, this research will focus on the repatriation of sacred Indigenous cultural heritage from public collections for two reasons: the regulatory capabilities of a government in designing a model that affects public collections, held on behalf of its populations, are far greater than for private collections. Concerns of government expropriation of privately held property, for example, do not arise (to the same degree). Moreover, the decision to repatriate or not, taken by the body that administers the collection on behalf of the government for the citizens of a territory, can also be attributed to the government. This is crucial in evaluating the human rights compliance of repatriation mechanisms. 'Public' in the sense employed here does not refer to whether items are on display. Instead, 'public' refers to whether there is a governmental or rather state dimension in the legal nature of the collections, its holding institutions, or its financing structure. There are different ways in which collections can be classified as public: they could for instance be owned by a governmental agency, or cultural heritage could be held and displayed by a state museum (for and on behalf of the people in the respective territory).

1.3.2 Intra-national Versus International Repatriations and Returns

Sacred Indigenous cultural heritage that has been moved outside the community can either still be located within the same nation state as the claimant community or it can be located abroad, for example in English museum collections. We can therefore differentiate between repatriation claims that occur within a national legal system and those that cross territorial boundaries and legal systems. In the cases of intra-national repatriation, communities bring claims against a holding institution within

[79] At least the existing repatriations, both under NAGPRA and international returns of ancestral remains, would suggest this.

the same country. These can be regulated through national legal frameworks, as has been done in the United States with the well-known Native American Graves Protection and Repatriation Act (NAGPRA). This is not the case for international repatriation claims which involve different national legal frameworks that may be applicable to the claimed cultural heritage.

Repatriation claims on the *inter*national level largely remain in the realm of international politics. There is no widely applicable treaty which obliges states to return cultural objects to Indigenous communities. Moreover, in terms of returns of colonial-era heritage internationally, we also frequently witness a state-heavy model, in which discussions on the returns of heritage taken during colonialism is discussed amongst states, possibly with the involvement of museums. There are a number of reasons for this, both legally and politically.

Apart from the structure of international law which places power on state governments, this approach of state-state negotations connects to historical power imbalances between the respective countries and territories. Connected to this is the express desire not to instate neo-colonial structures in which return returns are driven, and at worst dictated, by the West. The drafters of the recently published Dutch report on the return of cultural heritage taken during colonialism to the governments of former colonies expressly warned the Dutch government against taking such an approach.[80] International repatriations of Indigenous objects to the source community are the outcome of international negotiations between states and varying degrees of communal and institutional involvement.[81] If we want to learn how to best regulate repatriation legally and base this recommendation on existing practice, it is therefore advisable to examine it on the national level and evaluate returns that are effectuated within one country.

However, as was observed in Sect. 1.1. above, if international returns exclude communities who expressly want to be involved (for whatever reason), there is still the potential of intranational returns to communities by a government of a former colony under national law (albeit not necessarily in practice if the community was previously excluded because of said government). The lessons learned may in effect be applicable not only to future intra-national but also to international repatriations and indeed also for international returns to governments of former colonial powers. The extent to which such lessons can be transferred to the international context, will be considered further in Chap. 10.

[80] Gonçalves-Ho Kang You et al. (2021).

[81] For one example in which multiple parties are involved see the return of Toi Moko from overseas to New Zealand with governmental support, see information provided by Te Papa Tongerewa (Museum of New Zealand) at: https://www.tepapa.govt.nz/about/repatriation/repatriation-maori-and-moriori-remains [last accessed 30.07.2021].

1.3.3 Focus on the United States and Canada

As the number of Indigenous people worldwide is extensive and the scope of the research project is limited, a choice had to be made as to the countries to be examined. The author selected the United States and Canada for a number of reasons, both individual to the country as well as to allow for a better comparison between different repatriation frameworks.

For this research, the United States is a very obvious and necessary choice. The first law mandating intra-national repatriations were introduced in the United States. The Native American Graves Protection and Repatriation Act stimulated a heated debate in the early 1990s when it was adopted. It led to numerous returns of Indigenous cultural objects and also sought to facilitate the return of Indigenous ancestral remains which were located in US museums as an inheritance of state-sponsored grave-robbing. The discussion will focus on the federal level, given the federal law nature of NAGPRA and the semi-sovereign status which Native American peoples hold under US constitutional law.

It was only when the Native American Graves Protection and Repatriation Act (short NAGPRA) entered into force in the United States in the early 1990s that museums all of the country systematically started to search for the origins of their Indigenous collections.[82] Not only had Native American material been collected in the process of colonizing the country, but American anthropologists and other scientists intentionally sought to collect cultural material to safeguard evidence of what was then considered to be a culture on the verge of extinction.[83] This gathering of knowledge, however well-intentioned, frequently occurred in an unequal power relationship between the representative of the 'Western' culture and the Native American culture, with all the damage that such inequalities entail: dispossession under threat or exercise of violence, theft or the conscious search of deceased Native Americans by the military.[84] Furthermore, the display of the material was, for a long time, in degrading conditions, possibly motivated by the need (consciously or subconsciously) to justify the general behaviour towards dealing with Native Americans.

NAGPRA (Native American Graves Protection and Repatriation Act) set up federal repatriation legislation, aiming at the return of objects to their 'culturally affiliated' community.[85] To answer the two research questions for the American legal context, NAGPRA and connected legal areas such as federal Indian law, heritage legislation and policy, and museum law and policy will be considered in Chap. 4. While the NAGPRA was only concerned with the repatriation of cultural objects to native communities within the US, it triggered a review process within the communities of several First Nations in Canada on how to better protect and reclaim

[82] Harding (1997).

[83] Kenney (2011), p. 510.

[84] Kenney (2011), p. 510.

[85] Nafziger (2009), pp. 118–119. He views NAGPRA as a piece of human rights law.

their cultural heritage.[86] Moreover, it led to a growing awareness of the need to consider Aboriginal rights in general and Indigenous cultural resources in Canada in particular.

The choice for Canada is motivated by a number of reasons: First, in order to consider the relationship between law(-making) and repatriation, it must be recognized that there are very different ways in which the law can engage with repatriation. In the United States, a federal law mandates repatriation under certain conditions. In Alberta, a province in Canada, the provincial legislature adopted a law facilitating the return of very specific objects to allow for the return of cultural objects which had been negotiated between a museum and Indigenous claimants. This was necessary due to the public nature of the museum and the corresponding deaccessioning prohibitions laid down in provincial law which previously had hindered successful repatriation, despite a successful negotiation between the two actors. In the province of British Columbia, by contrast, the absence of historical treaties which settled rights between the crown and an Indigenous nation elsewhere in Canada, in combination with case law of the Supreme Court, has led to a modern-day, comprehensive treaty-making process that started in the 1990s. These modern-day treaties address a variety of Indigenous rights, including different cultural rights and can be used to negotiate the repatriation of Indigenous religious objects. Moreover, legislation that articulates the goal to implement the United Nations Declaration on the Rights of Indigenous Peoples into Canadian law has been adopted both at the federal level as well as in the province of British Columbia.[87] This makes examining the compliance of the relevant Canadian law on repatriation with human rights standards articulated in the Declaration all the more timely and important.

Examining these three examples in the two countries shows how law and repatriation can interact in different ways. To be able to distil models and their comparative advantages and disadvantages to learn from these experiences, another point is crucial. The countries compared must have enough in common to make deductions which can reasonably be attributed to the differences in the specific legal forms examined rather than the differences in their legal systems, differences of historical contexts etc.

Both countries are members of (most of) the relevant international legal bodies and instruments, as well as the relevant regional body, the Organization of American States (OAS).[88] As a result, both relevant UN instruments and OAS instruments will be considered in the search of relevant international legal standards. Domestically, both countries examined are countries in which Indigenous Peoples are recognized groups of the society but in the numerical minority. Both share the common law

[86]Bell and McCuaig (2008), pp. 358–359.

[87]United Nations Declaration on the Rights of Indigenous Peoples Act (S.C. 2021, c. 14).

[88]The United States has not ratified one of the core human rights treaties, the ICESCR. However, this is less problematic as one might presume in the present context, as Art.27 ICCPR firmly enshrines minority and Indigenous rights within the international bill of rights. The ICCPR has been ratified by the United States. For more see the discussion on Art.27 ICCPR and Art.15(1) (a) ICESCR in Chap. 2, section 6.2.3.

legal system, which allows for a better comparison of the legal choices made. Moreover, in both systems, Indigenous Peoples hold a distinct constitutional law status (even if the status is a different one). Also, both were former colonies of the British Empire, resulting in certain similarities in the historical evolution of the relationship between the Indigenous population and the incoming settler governments. In both countries, laws have been used to force the assimilation of Indigenous Peoples into mainstream culture. Lastly, both countries are federal systems: Canada[89] is a federal, parliamentary democracy under a constitutional monarchy, while the United States is a federal presidential republic.[90] This makes it possible to consider how the co-existence of the federal and provincial or state level can have an effect on the repatriation of Indigenous religious objects. Of course, there are also differences in the countries. Indigenous Peoples are manifold and varied, as are their cultures and historical experiences. Moreover, there are differences between groups in terms of the peace treaties which were concluded in the process of colonization, many of which extinguished Indigenous rights and therefore remain relevant when contemplating current legal affairs.

In order to be able to compare the repatriation frameworks of the two countries, the repatriation framework will be examined in a number of key areas, in particular: scope (definition of Indigenous Peoples and sacred objects), whether they mandate a particular outcome, procedure or combination thereof, who takes the final decision on a repatriation request, whether there is a dispute resolution mechanism, and in how far costs associated with repatriation are considered. This will allow for a better comparison of the models and the application of the standards derived in Chaps. 2 and 3 in the final part of the research. However, there are a number of limitations that are inherent in the adopted approach that cannot be mitigated by the adopted methodology. The limitations are addressed in Sect. 1.3.4 below.

1.3.4 Limitations or Potential Dangers of the Adopted Approach

1.3.4.1 In Solely Choosing English Terminology for Repatriation Efforts, the Original Problem May Be Misconceived/Misrepresented in the Eyes of the Indigenous Population

A central concern in any analytical endeavour is the language to be used; the language of the material analysed, and the language chosen for writing the analysis, which then becomes the framework for defining and thereby limiting the problem to

---

[89] See *Constitution Act, 1867*, R.S.C. 1985, Appendix II, No. 5, s. 9 (authority vested in the Crown). *See also Marleau and Montpetit (2000), section on parliamentary institutions.*

[90] *Constitution of the United States*, Art.I s.1-3 read in conjunction with Art. II s.1.

be solved. In choosing the English language to phrase a particular question, there is an inherent danger that the solutions become limited to those conceivable within English/Western (legal) thought. This may, although not intended, disadvantage Indigenous Peoples from the outset, since they rely on a world view so very different, that the solution ultimately found may not answer the original, Indigenous problem. If an adequate solution to the problems surrounding repatriation claims is to be found, these differences must be acknowledged.[91]

One example is provided by the Canadian context. One difficulty in dealing with repatriation claims of cultural property is the difference in understanding the term by First Nations and Western (Canadian) legal scholars. First Nations have a wide understanding of what they view as cultural property, for many things are needed to restore and maintain their way of life.[92] The sheer diversity of Indigenous languages in the areas analysed and the financial and temporal implications of any endeavour to learn them sufficiently to bridge the gap between the different cultural systems makes it impossible for this study. The choice for English, regardless of this danger, is quite simply motivated by the fact that it is the language of the law being analysed. I address this gap slightly by the inclusion of Indigenous authors, but the fundamental role of the English language for the construction of applicable law remains with all of the disadvantages this has for the Indigenous claimant who acts within this system.

1.3.4.2 The Cultural Diversity Debate

This second point is less a weakness of the adopted approach and more a general danger one has to be aware of when researching in the area of cultural rights or cultural heritage. The contemporary emphasis on cultural diversity and the ensuing emphasis on preserving and/or strengthening cultures which diverge from the dominant culture, be they Indigenous Peoples or minority cultures in general, can lead a legal system to the edge of what is compatible with its own value and belief system.[93] Ultimately, cultural diversity means, if not accepting, then 'accommodating' other customs and beliefs which can run counter to one's own customs and beliefs.[94]

Moreover, preservation efforts are frequently set against a historic background of (forced) assimilation. In this context, Welsh cautions "[p]reserving one's own culture and preserving another's culture are two very different things. Preserving one's own culture is an expression of human rights, while working to preserve someone else's culture without their input or participation is, at best, paternalism."[95]

---

[91] Compare Asch (2009), pp. 403–404.

[92] Bell et al. (2008), pp. 39–42.

[93] Welsh (1992), p. 850.

[94] Welsh (1992), p. 850.

[95] Welsh (1992), p. 839.

This certainly holds true for repatriation and returns (be they regional, national or international) and thus has to be taken into account when debating repatriation schemes at the national level. One could argue that this statement also holds true for the attempt to research this issue and depending on one's disciplinary background it may similarly encompass the attempt to analyse and solve a problem 'from the outside'. In this context it is worth drawing attention to the two goals of this research: first, to synthesize repatriation legislation with Indigenous rights which position Indigenous Peoples at the centre as the main actor with whom governments and other actors *have* to consult and cooperate. Second to draw lessons from systems in which museums and Indigenous populations share a territory and have interacted for a considerable period of time, to help those actors and policy-makers who are only now starting to engage with these issues and may not have much if any familiarity with some of the problems and potential wins of repatriation.

1.3.4.3 Changing Values

Values are not stagnant. Beliefs and acceptable modes of behaviour can change, sometimes over a long period of time, or suddenly, and these changes can find their way into the law. Not only does this mean that the analysis of the respective countries in later chapters is partially transient but it also means that, when debating whether or not to return items which have been displaced for a considerable period, past actions are viewed through the lens of contemporary ethical and moral standards.[96] The past is transformed into a distinct entity which can be judged, with the temporal distance creating a certain feeling of safety. This is not necessarily to be avoided, simply because an 'injustice' has its origins in the past does not mean that it should continue into the present.[97] It is here that the discussion on repatriation becomes more complex ethically, since the continuing presence of an object in the museum or public collection means that it may have gained an additional function for the community in which it is displayed. One object can have multiple pasts, as it can speak for the previously oppressed and victimized and it can speak to the descendants of past colonial powers as well as ethnic groups which may not have had a tie originally but have developed one after prolonged exposure to the object. The question that arises for this research is in how far the law negotiates these complexities of meaning underlying a heritage object in the repatriation framework.

[96] Barkan (2009), p. 84.

[97] Barkan (2009), p. 84.

1.3.4.4 Enforcing or Working on the Basis of Stereotypical Understandings of What 'Indigenous' Means

Aaron Glass has highlighted that the emphasis on sacred objects employs a "stereotype of Native people as intrinsically spiritual and the argument that the objects are needed to maintain culture provides strong rhetorical value for such terms."[98] He cautions that if the central distinction in the classification of requests for return is the differentiation between sacred and non-sacred objects, it thereby reduces the relationship of reclaimable objects to the sacred dimension to the exclusion of all others.[99] These remarks could similarly be applied to the present undertaking. One may ask why the result of a balancing exercise between the 'property' interests of current owners, scientific concerns of preservation, the cultural rights of the broader public and the Indigenous minority, often set against a backdrop of colonial wrongs and efforts of reconciliation apparently leads a number of actors to primarily focus on sacred objects. This is of course not per se a legal question, and certainly deserves further attention. For the purposes of the present discussion and her choice to focus on sacred objects as the material scope the author would like to highlight the following: The discussion of the return of sacred objects at present is not done to reduce Indigenous Peoples to their religious dimensions but rather a necessary contextualization of a category of repatriation efforts in the wider context of a legal system. In the present volume it is undertaken because a number of existing Indigenous rights standards that connect to the exercise of religion enjoy a relatively strong protection under binding international human rights treaties. This is done with the understanding that there are, of course, rights and elements to Indigenous (legal) existence other than sacredness.

1.3.4.5 Approaching a Non-Legal Problem from a Legal Perspective

As has become obvious from the previous sections, repatriation is very much a multidisciplinary research subject. It comprises elements of historical research, anthropology, heritage and museum studies, law, politics and sociology. As it is simply impossible to encompass all of these dimensions adequately within a single study, two choices remain: to choose one and try to go into as much depth as possible within the existing limits, or to choose multiple disciplines but keep the discussion either broad and superficial or narrow and limited to one particular case study. The adopted singular disciplinary that analyses the legal dynamics that structure, underlie and connect to repatriation focus brings its own problems. One might criticize that I am characterizing repatriation as something which it is not, namely a legal phenomenon. To this, I would answer that this volume is not trying to represent repatriation as singularly legal, but only as a phenomenon or process that has legal aspects.

98 Glass (2004), pp. 119–120.

99 Glass (2004), p. 122.

1.4 Terminology and the Focus of the Research: Indigenous Peoples, Cultural Heritage and Other Relevant Terms Defined

Having clarified the scope of the research, the question it addresses and the methodology it uses, the last point that requires consideration before proceeding to the analysis of the selected legal areas is the terminology used. My focus on such contested terms as culture, religion, heritage, and indigeneity warrants a brief terminological exploration to prevent misconceptions. I limit myself to defining seven terms that are integral to the discussion,[100] as I consider these to be either highly amorphous or controversial, or both. I would like to highlight that I am not trying to replicate the entirety of the discussion on each of these terms or concepts; nor do I wish to reduce them to the statements I make for the sake of future debate. I am simply providing a working definition and my reasoning for adopting it so that I can proceed on a common basis of understanding.

1.4.1 Repatriation: Restitution—Recovery—Return

Different terms describe the action of returning an object, be it to a state, an institution, an individual, or a community. So far, academics and practitioners have used repatriation, restitution, recovery, or return. Different meanings have been attached to these terms,[101] and a clear, uniform approach to these terms is missing.[102] All of these terms have in common that they "address the undoing of some past deed through use of the common prefix 're'."[103]

Repatriation is not a purely legal term,[104] yet this does not speak against its use. As was elaborated upon above, the repatriation of Indigenous material has several dimensions, legal and non-legal. Recovery, by contrast, denotes the "gaining or

[100] Kenney (2011), p. 507. As Kenney emphasizes, terms in this field can be 'loaded' and the focus of much controversy. Nevertheless, common definitions are needed as a basis if we are to debate about the strength and weaknesses of the respective legislative systems. Therefore, an attempt has been made to identify the most suitable, least 'loaded' term so to speak, and this choice has always been motivated. Yet, it has to be acknowledged that the choice for one over another definition is a value choice and, as such, ultimately subjective.

[101] Welsh (1992), p. 846. He, for example, is clearly influenced by the US experience and the NAGPRA legislation when he writes "I use the term 'repatriation' to label a variety of actions to return museum collections to cultures of origin."

[102] Compare, for example, Kowalski's understanding of the terms with Prott or the understanding Barkan has of restitution: Kowalski (2005); Prott (2009), pp. xxi–xxiv; Barkan (2009), p. 80. Another approach is given in Gerstenblith (2001), p. Gerstenblith views restitution as a broad term denoting the return of objects, of which there are different categories.

[103] Glass (2004), p. 118.

[104] O'Keefe (2009), p. 225.

regaining" of a lost or taken object.[105] Prott rightly criticizes that 'recovery' does emphasize the position of the previous owner in a way that the usage of this term already implies previous ownership.[106] This does not sufficiently capture the different dimensions that returning an item to Indigenous communities, including the long period of absence, the potential fact that the community may not have been recognized as an owner under the applicable law governing the original removal etc.

Restitution is a legal term, which has different meanings depending on whether it is employed in a common or civil law system.[107] Moreover, it has two connotations which are not in line with the discussion of inner-state returns to Indigenous Peoples. First, it refers to returning objects to their owner, which, under the applicable law, often is not the case for returns to Indigenous Peoples. Second, it refers to returning objects which were taken by a foreign nation during armed conflicts,[108] which does not match the colonial classification of Indigenous nations as non-sovereign entities under international law (however critical one may be of this fact). The term 'return', by contrast, is more neutral, as Prott observed, but it is also used in many other circumstances. Repatriation, as a legal term, is specific to humanitarian law, as well as cultural heritage law.

Whitby-Last contrasts restitution and repatriation as follows: "Restitution is the return of an object to its owner, based on an analysis of property rights. ... Repatriation, in contrast, is premised upon the culturally specific value of the object. ... [B]ecause of the difficulties that attend actions of restitution, many claims by Indigenous Peoples are claims for repatriation, phrased in terms of moral obligation, rather than claims of restitution based on an assertion of property rights."[109] It is interesting that Whitby-Last classifies repatriation in relation to the position of the object for the claimant community. The research focus adopted here has a similar direction, but it is the result of a broader category of objects which can be reclaimed, which is then narrowed to a sub-group that has a particular value within the community, namely sacred objects.

For the purposes of this study, the action of returning an object that was taken in a colonial context[110] to a descendant Indigenous community will be discussed as repatriation. The term 'repatriation' has already been used to refer to the return of objects to Indigenous Peoples.[111] Moreover, it is acknowledged to go beyond the dimensions of inter-state actions and to include those returns which take place

---

[105]The Oxford English Dictionary Online, available at www.oed.com, entry "recovery" [last accessed 30.07.2021].

[106]Prott (2009), p. xxi.

[107]Prott (2009), p. xxi.

[108]Prott (2009).

[109]Whitby-Last (2010), p. 36.

[110]In or against a colonial context is to be understood to include both early European colonialism, settler colonialism and including internal colonialism and forced assimilation up until the 1960s.

[111]This is especially the case for the discussion on the United States which is of course rooted in the choice made in the NAGPRA for the term 'repatriation'. See in this context Glass (2004), p. 119.

between an institution and a community and to also include those returns which occur in the same country, rather than between different states.[112] International returns, in the way as they are currently being discussed between state governments (for example the Netherlands and Indonesia) will be referred to as returns. In these cases, Indigenous communities are not necessarily involved in the negotiations and may not be final recipient of the heritage in question.

1.4.2 Culture

Culture is a concept which is notoriously difficult to define.[113] First, it is ever changing and refuses to be fixed in time.[114] As a consequence, any attempt to define it will have to take this fluidity into account.[115] Second, it has different facets, the importance of which will vary depending on the context in which the term culture is employed. Two of these facets are societal and the individual.[116] Thus, in the author's opinion, a *'Wechselwirkung'*, an interdependency, exists between culture and society. While societies shape and develop a culture,[117] a culture which has developed can shape the direction in which society moves, which in turn will also influence the future evolution of the society's culture. Not only can the culture shape and be shaped by the society, but it also has an influence on the micro-level, contributing to how an individual constructs its identity.[118]

Moreover, it has to be acknowledged that diverging definitions of the term culture exist, depending on how and by whom the term is used, also in connection to the term heritage. For that reason, a clear choice must be made in the beginning to avoid any confusion as to the basis of the discussion. In light of this, a choice was made to follow the definition of culture as given in the preamble of the UNESCO Universal Declaration on Cultural Diversity which states "culture should be regarded as the *set of distinctive* spiritual, material, intellectual and emotional *features* of society or a social group, and that it encompasses, in addition to art and literature, lifestyles, ways of living together, value systems, traditions and beliefs".[119] The reasons for

---

[112] Prott (2009), p. xxiii. Also, Welsh (1992), p. 846.

[113] See Metcalfe (1996), p. 172. "[C]ulture, however, is a troublesomely broad term".

[114] Donders (2008), pp. 3–4.

[115] This understanding of culture as fluid also appears in the preamble of the Convention on the Protection and Promotion of Cultural Expressions 2005 which states: "Taking into account that culture takes diverse forms across time and space and that this diversity is embodied in the uniqueness and plurality of the identities and cultural expressions of the peoples and societies making up humanity".

[116] Donders (2008), pp. 3–4.

[117] Compare Donders (2008), pp. 3–4.

[118] Donders (2008), pp. 3–4. This is not to say that a culture will *determine* the individual's identity, as many other factors may contribute to this.

[119] UNESCO Universal Declaration on Cultural Diversity, 2.11.2001, [emphasis added].

this choice are threefold. First, its inclusion in an international legal instrument, even though it is non-binding, evidences a certain measure of support for it within the sphere of international law. Second, the notion of 'distinctive features' gives it both a flexibility which will encompass future changes and a boundary, albeit a wide one. Third, the focus on the different elements that the term culture can encompass connects it well to the concept of cultural heritage, which is also important for this study.

1.4.3 Cultural Heritage/Cultural Property

> Objects of cultural property have two distinct, conflicting aspects which are inseparable. The first is a physical aspect. Cultural objects are physical items; therefore, they may be legally owned according to traditional western notions of property. However, a cultural object is also imbued with a certain significance by the culture that created it.... This second aspect of art is critical because it relates to the function of the art itself. The physical object alone may be worthless, but the value attached to it by an individual or group makes it priceless. Therein lies the root of the conflict.[120]

Similar to the concept of culture, cultural heritage has several dimensions. First, the material dimension, which refers to the substance of tangible objects, is very static, unless damaged or destroyed by an outside force, which is different from the fluid nature of the cultural concept. Second, a theoretical, almost ideological, dimension which is subject to change.[121] This is a consequence of the close link between culture and heritage. Some argue that "heritage is selected and cultures are constructed".[122] Indeed, at times, the link between an ancient civilization and the state which claims its artefacts is purely geographical and, even then, the borders of the respective territories will rarely align completely. Over time, the association of a given culture with a specific heritage might change. Similarly, the interpretation of cultural heritage is subject to change, depending on who interprets it and when. Because of this, a clear understanding of what is subsumed under the term 'cultural heritage' has to be set. In the area of art and cultural heritage law, both the concept of cultural heritage and cultural property are used. As a result, not only will cultural heritage be defined and used as a concept in this study, but the difference between the concepts will be explored briefly and the reasons for the choice made will be given.

As Prott and O'Keefe have pointed out, *'cultural property'*, while clearly an accepted legal term, carries with it all the connotations which property holds in national property law.[123] This not only includes its economic emphasis but also the *prima facie* understanding that the owner of an object may dispose of it however he wishes, which can include the destruction of the object or rendering it inaccessible to

---

[120] Bengs (1996), p. 505.

[121] Forrest (2010), p. 2.

[122] Niezen (2010), p. 3.

[123] Prott and O'Keefe (1992), p. 310.

whomever he or she does not want to see it.[124] This emphasis is partially reflected in international instruments such as the Unidroit Convention of 1995 or the UNESCO Convention of 1970, which ultimately seek to prevent illegal export and/or excavation and attempt to return these stolen objects, all of which emphasize the ownership dimension of the objects in question.[125]

'Cultural heritage', in contrast, speaks more to the linkage between generations across time. It is often discussed in connection with an emphasis on maintaining heritage or preserving it for future generations. This need was emphasized, for example, in 2001 in Art. 7 of the UNESCO Universal Declaration on Cultural Diversity which provides:

> Creation draws on the roots of cultural tradition, but flourishes in contact with other cultures. For this reason, heritage in all its forms must be preserved, enhanced and handed on to future generations as a record of human experience and aspirations, so as to foster creativity in all its diversity and to inspire genuine dialogue among cultures.

Cultural heritage appeared on the international legal level as a binding concept in Art.1 of the UNESCO Convention Concerning the Protection and Preservation of the World Cultural and Natural Heritage 1972.[126] Art.1 defines it as immovable objects, including monuments, groups of buildings and sites. The convention draws a clear distinction between 'cultural' and 'natural' heritage. Art.2 encompasses certain natural elements free from human intervention.[127] Despite the distinction between 'cultural' and 'natural', the convention clearly made a choice against using the concept 'cultural property', which is mentioned in the preamble but not in the body of the instrument.[128] The 1972 convention emphasizes the need to conserve the objects it seeks to protect,[129] which was taken up in the 2001 Declaration. This focus might explain the drafter's choice for the term cultural heritage rather than cultural property, considering that heritage implies a certain continuity and almost an intrinsic value which should be transmitted to future generations.[130] Yet, the

---

[124]Prott and O'Keefe (1992), p. 310. Nafziger and Paterson similarly highlight the ownership dimension of 'cultural property'. "Strictly speaking, however, the term 'property' connotes ownership and imputes rights to owners and possessors of objects and intangibles under national property law, whereas 'heritage' does not imply such ownership and concomitant rights", see Nafziger and Paterson (2014), p. 1.

[125]This argument does not hold true for the 1954 Hague Convention, which mainly seeks to protect structure and objects of value from destruction.

[126]In the 1954 Hague Convention it is subsumed under the notion of cultural property, see article 1 (a).

[127]Art. 2 "physical and biological formations", "geological and physiographical formations" as well as "natural sites" to classify as natural heritage if they fulfil certain conditions.

[128]Prott and O'Keefe (1992), p. 318.

[129]See Art.7, Art.26 Convention Concerning the Protection and Preservation of the World Cultural and Natural Heritage 1972.

[130]Prott and O'Keefe (1992), p. 307. At 309 "The fundamental policy behind cultural heritage law is protection of the heritage for the enjoyment of present and later generations". Compare also, Forrest (2010), p. 2.

interpretation of the 1972 convention was narrow and it had a Western European focus, as can be seen in its clear emphasis on immovable objects. One of the major advantages of the cultural heritage notion, in contrast to the concept of cultural property, is that it can easily encompass both the tangible, movable and immovable objects, and the intangible, such as folklore, language, song, or oral histories and traditions.[131] It is this broader understanding of the concept which will be followed in the next chapters.[132]

1.4.4 Minority

So far, a widely accepted definition of the term 'minority' and which groups fall under it does not exist.[133] In the early 1990s Lerner suggested that terminological problems with the term "minorities" had resulted in a turn towards using the term "group".[134] While the notion of group rights (being the more accurate term when describing the difference between individual and group rights) has indeed been used on the international level, it would be wrong to assume that international usage of the term 'group' implies a definite turn away from the notion of minority in international law. This is *inter alia* ensured by the fact that one of the main international human rights instruments and part and parcel of the International Bill of Rights explicitly mentions minorities, namely Art. 27 ICCPR.

Within the UN apparatus, different definitions have been suggested to clarify which entity can be classified as a minority. For the purposes of this study, it suffices to distil the common elements of these definitions. Francesco Capotorti put forward a definition which categorizes minorities as: "A group numerically inferior to the rest of the population of a State, in a non-dominant position, whose members—being nationals of the State—possess ethnic, religious or linguistic characteristics differing from those of the rest of the population and show, if only implicitly, a sense of solidarity, directed towards preserving their culture, traditions, religion or language."[135] Both he and Jules Deschênes enumerate a sense of solidarity as a

[131] Kenney (2011), p. 507. Kenney rightly describes it as a 'broad category' and views 'cultural artefacts' as a sub-category.

[132] Compare Harding (1999), p. 303. Cultural heritage is defined as "an individual or group creation of either a tangible or intangible good which, by virtue of the creation process, customary use, historical event, or simply geographic proximity, becomes an important expression of human or cultural life".

[133] Martinez, A., UN. Special Rapporteur on Treaties, Agreements and Other Constructive Arrangements between States and Indigenous Populations, Study on treaties, agreements and other constructive arrangements between States and Indigenous populations [1999] U.N. Doc. E/CN.4/Sub.2/1999/20, para 70. UN Office of the High Commissioner for Human Rights (2010), p. 2.

[134] Lerner (1991), pp. 28–29.

[135] Francesco Capotorti, U.N. Doc. E/CN.4/Sub.2/384/Rev.1 (1977), para. 568 as referenced in UN Office of the High Commissioner for Human Rights (2010), p. 2.

characteristic of a minority but qualify it differently. To Capotorti, solidarity has to be purpose-bound, that is to say to be "directed towards preserving their culture, traditions, religion or language." Jules Deschênes, by contrast, seems to understand his proposed solidarity characteristic more as solidarity among the members of the respective minority, without necessarily being purpose-driven.[136] Meijknecht also highlighted another definition of Asbjörn Eide, who proposed a more inclusive definition, in that minorities can also be made up of residents of a state (not nationals).[137]

In its General Comment No. 23, the Human Rights Committee, in connection to Art. 27, observed that a minority was a group within a state, whose members "share in common a culture, a religion and/or language" and whose members were residents of that state.[138] Moreover, the Committee emphasized that the existence of a minority depended on the fulfilment of objective criteria and was independent of any state action.[139] Having considered the different elements proposed, next the working definition adopted in this study will be addressed. For present purposes, minorities are:

1. Groups within a state
2. Which are non-dominant
3. Whose members are residents or nationals of a state
4. Whose members share a culture, ethnicity, religion, and/ or language

By dispensing with the numerically smaller characteristic, it is recognized that it may very well be that a numerically smaller group sits in government institutions, governing bigger groups. This seems to be in line with the aim of the minority rights provision in international law, which constitutes an attempt to ensure the cultural rights of individuals, recognizing that some of them might only be exercised in community with others and that such groups might require additional protection when they are situated in an unequal power relationship vis-à-vis the state and the main governing institutions. Similarly, the solidarity element has been dispensed with. The author can identify no valid justification for introducing such an additional obstacle to the identification of a minority if the focus is merely on ensuring that members of a minority may enjoy their cultural rights, similar to members of the majority. It would be different if the notion was merit-based, i.e. only a minority which seeks to preserve its culture is 'worthy' of extra protection, which undoubtedly is a dangerous notion, in violation of the notions of human dignity and equality. The fact that a common culture, ethnicity, religion and/ or language is identifiable

---

[136] Deschênes, J., United Nations Sub-Commission on the Prevention of Discrimination and Protection of Minorities Proposal Concerning a Definition of the Term 'Minority' U.N. Doc. E/CN.4/Sub.2/1985/31 & Corr. 1, para 181.

[137] Meijknecht (2001), p. 83.

[138] HRCee (26.04.1994), General Comment No. 23 (50) on Art. 27, U.N. Doc. CCPR/C/21/Rev.1/Add.5, para 5.1 and 5.2.

[139] Ibid, para 5.2.

from the outside and that this differentiates the minority from the majority should be sufficient to classify it as such.

1.4.5 *Indigenous Peoples*

1.4.5.1 Etymological Approach

Etymologically speaking, 'indigenous' derives from the latin *'indigenae'*, which means 'born in a country', 'native'.[140] It therefore has a specific geographical connotation and also, when contrasted with those who 'arrive' (*'advenae'*), a temporal connotation, namely being somewhere prior to the undefined other.[141] However, while this is a preliminary definition which is useful in distinguishing minorities from Indigenous Peoples, it is not sufficient as a legal definition. In international law, Indigenous Peoples is usually spelled with a lower case "i", whereas the practise of capitalization is common in countries like Australia and Canada.[142] This volume discusses both international law, as well as Canadian and U.S. law, and even discusses the national context in light of international standards. For this reason, to ensure a respectful use of the term, capitalization of the term is used throughout (even when international law is considered within the national context), except for in Chaps. 2 and 3 and Sects. 1.4.5.2 and 1.4.5.3 in this chapter, where the discussion is predominantly focussed on international law. In the remainder of this chapter, and Chaps. 4 to 10, the terms Indigenous Peoples and Indigenous are spelled with capital letters to clearly differentiate between the term Indigenous in its etymological meaning and Indigenous Peoples as sovereign entities. The only time when lower case is used in these chapters is to keep true to a citation.

1.4.5.2 Analysis of the Existing Definitions and the Definition Adopted in This Study

How 'indigenous peoples' should be defined under international law is a difficult question. While it is possible to trace the development of the concept of Indigenous people in the past, a precise definition has not been adopted by the UN apparatus.[143] One of the reasons for this is the fact that, as has been argued elsewhere, regardless of

---

[140] The Oxford English Dictionary Online, available at www.oed.com, entry "indigenous" [last accessed 9.12.2019].

[141] Asmuss (2011), p. 35.

[142] See also https://www.stylemanual.gov.au/format-writing-and-structure/inclusive-language/aboriginal-and-torres-strait-islander-peoples [last accessed 30.07.2021].

[143] On the evolution of the term "indigenous" and its appropriation by Indigenous groups see Niezen (2009), pp. 26–27.

how a definition is phrased, certain Indigenous groups will be excluded due to the sheer diversity of Indigenous Peoples.[144]

According to Niezen, the evolution of the term 'indigenous peoples' occurred in distinct phases. Up until the 1920s, Indigenous people did not exist as a distinct entity in international law. In the 1920s this was evidenced by Art. 22 of the Covenant of the League of Nations which speaks of "Indigenous population" rather than people. They were viewed as being under the "tutelage" of more "advanced nations".[145] A first conceptualization started in Latin America in the 1930s to 1950s with the concept of "*pueblos indígenas*" in the Spanish literature and the emergence of the term Indigenous Peoples in the English language elsewhere.[146] The real breakthrough occurred in the third phase in the 1970s to 1980s with the legal construction of the term.[147] Convention No. 169 on Indigenous and Tribal Peoples in Independent Countries (1989) has to be highlighted as one of the earliest references to "indigenous peoples" in an international legal instrument. Its predecessor, the much-criticized Convention No.107, still referred to "indigenous populations" and adopted a paternalistic approach.[148] Convention No. 169 partially followed Convention No. 107 by defining Indigenous People in the personal scope of application of the convention as:

> peoples in independent countries who are regarded as indigenous on account of their *descent from the populations* which *inhabited* the country, or a geographical region to which the country belongs, *at the time of conquest or colonisation* or the establishment of present state boundaries and who, irrespective of their legal status, *retain* some or all of their *own social, economic, cultural and political institutions* (Art.1(1)(b) ILO Convention No. 169).[149]

Moreover, it added the very important criterion of "self-identification" by means of Art. 1(2), thereby enabling Indigenous Peoples to adapt their group membership to different social and legal climates in a very flexible manner.[150] Even more

---

[144] Kenney (2011).

[145] Covenant of the League of Nations, 28 April 1919. Commenting on this *perceived* dependency of Indigenous People, Niezen (2009), pp. 25–26.

[146] Conceptualization of the phases Niezen (2010), pp. 115–123.

[147] Niezen (2010), pp. 115–123. According to Niezen, the fourth phase is a gradual acceptance of the term in everyday language, but for present purposes this phase can be ignored as the focus rests on the legal definition.

[148] Criticism i.e. by Donders (2002), pp. 208–210. Art.1(1)(b) limits the personal scope of the convention to "members of tribal or semi-tribal populations" "which are regarded as *indigenous* on account of their descent from the *populations* which *inhabited the country*, or a geographical region to which the country belongs, at the *time of conquest or colonisation* and which, irrespective of their legal status, *live more in conformity with the social, economic and cultural institutions of that time* than with the institutions of the nation to which they belong." (emphasis added).

[149] In the eyes of the UN Permanent Forum on Indigenous People, this cannot be described as a definition, rather it has to be seen as "statement of coverage", see UNPFII, Background paper prepared by the Secretariat of UNPFII on the concept of Indigenous People [2004] UN Doc PFII/2004/WS.1/3 para. 4.

[150] On Art.1(2) see Background paper prepared by the Secretariat of UNPFII on the concept of Indigenous People, PFII/2004/WS.1/3 para. 5; Battiste and Henderson (2000), pp. 62–64.

importantly, they can do so while still being able to raise a claim as "peoples". This combination of flexible group membership with the self-determination aspect is unparalleled for an entity other than a nation-state.[151] The element of self-identification is all the more important given the fact that Indigenous Peoples have refused to acknowledge both the necessity as well as the desirability of a definition. Self-identification has two important elements: an individual as well as communal one. First, to be regarded as Indigenous, an individual should identify him- or herself as Indigenous. Second, the respective community has the right to identify its members.[152]

The two most well-known descriptions of the concept of Indigenous Peoples were written by Special Rapporteur Jose R. Martinéz Cobo and Erica-Irene Daes, then Chairperson of the UN Human Rights Subcommission on Discrimination and Minorities.[153] Being asked to find common criteria, Erica-Irene Daes identified "historical continuity, distinctive cultural characteristics, traditional lands, non-dominance, self-identification and group consciousness."[154] The Cobo report highlighted that Indigenous Peoples preferred states not to adopt a common, international definition of the term 'indigenous peoples'. States seem to have agreed, as the United Nations Declaration on the Rights of Indigenous Peoples does not include any such definition. In the words of the Permanent Forum of Indigenous Issues, "the prevailing view today is that no formal universal definition of the term is necessary. For practical purposes the understanding of the term commonly accepted is the one provided in the Martinez Cobo study".[155]

> Indigenous communities, peoples and nations are those which, having a historical continuity with pre-invasion and pre-colonial societies that developed on their territories, consider themselves distinct from other sectors of the societies now prevailing in those territories, or parts of them. They form at present non-dominant sectors of society and are determined to preserve, develop and transmit to future generations their ancestral territories, and their ethnic identity, as the basis of their continued existence as peoples, in accordance with their own cultural patterns, social institutions and legal systems.[156]—*J. R. Martinéz Cobo*

For the purposes of the application of international law, the thesis follows UNPFII and adopts the concept of Indigenous People as advanced by Cobo as the working definition.

---

[151] Niezen (2009), p. 30.

[152] Desmet (2011), pp. 75–77.

[153] Highlighting Cobo and the ILO treaty definition, Donders (2002), pp. 204–205. Battiste and Henderson (2000).

[154] As summarized in Daes, E., Standard-setting Activities: Evolution of standards concerning the rights of Indigenous Peoples [1996] U.N. Doc. E/CN.4/Sub.2/AC.4/1996/2, para 5.

[155] Background paper prepared by the Secretariat of UNPFII on the concept of Indigenous People, PFII/2004/WS.1/3 para. 8.

[156] Martínez Cobo, J. Special Rapporteur, Study of the Problem of Discrimination Against Indigenous Populations Final report (last Part) [30.09.1983] U.N. Doc. E./CN.4//Sub.2/1983/21/Add.8, Chapter XXII para 379. Paragraph 380 elaborates on the element of historical continuity.

Asmuss criticizes this pragmatic approach of the Secretariat. In her view, to improve the protection of Indigenous Peoples requires a uniform definition at the international level.[157] I disagree. For the reasons that Asmuss outlines[158] and that have been highlighted already (the sheer diversity of Indigenous cultures, disagreement of focus between state and Indigenous population, migration patterns of Indigenous Peoples), a rigid definition of Indigenous People does not seem possible. It would seem that, to improve the protection of Indigenous People at the international level *per se*, a flexible definition, which can then be defined further at the national level in implementing or supplementing legislation, or through case law, would achieve the necessary agreement in principle and not alienate States further. While binding agreements can be entered into at the international level, the majority of the enforcement and implementation of international law still occurs at the regional and especially the national level.

In terms of statistics, according to Statistics Canada and as result of the 2016 Census of Population, "In 2016, there were 1,673,785 Aboriginal people in Canada, accounting for 4.9% of the total population. This was up from 3.8% in 2006 and 2.8% in 1996. Since 2006, the Aboriginal population has grown by 42.5%—more than four times the growth rate of the non-Aboriginal population over the same period."[159] Aboriginal peoples in this context comprises the First Nations of Canada, the Inuit and the Métis populations.[160] According to the United States Census Bureau in 2019,[161] the American Population amounted to a total of 328,239,523 with "American Indian and Alaska Native alone" representing an estimated 1.3% of the population and "Native Hawaiian and Other Pacific Islanders alone" representing 0.2% of the population.[162] Collectively, this would amount to an estimated 4,923,593 individuals and does not take into account the 2.8% category of "Two or more races" listed.[163]

1.4.5.3 Indigenous Peoples as Minorities?

Indigenous peoples have been firm in their resistance to being classified as minorities under international law, despite being considered as rightholders of the right to enjoy their minority culture under Art.27 ICCPR. Thornberry contrasts various definitions

---

[157] Asmuss (2011), p. 36.

[158] Asmuss (2011), pp. 40–41.

[159] Canadian census data of 2016, available at: http://www.statcan.gc.ca/daily-quotidien/171025/dq171025a-eng.htm [last accessed 30.07.2021].

[160] Ibid.

[161] The definite results of the 2020 Census were not yet available at the time of final edits.

[162] https://www.census.gov/quickfacts/fact/table/US/RHI525216#viewtop [last accessed 18.08.2021].

[163] https://www.census.gov/quickfacts/fact/table/US/RHI525216#viewtop [last accessed 18.08.2021].

of Indigenous Peoples with the different attempts to definite minorities and observes "In the light of all the above, elements in the indigenous descriptors (not commonly found in descriptions of 'minority') relate to: precedent habitation; historical continuity; attachment to land; the communal sense and the community right (including those societies which do not have a strong conception of individual rights); a cultural gap between the dominant groups in a State and the indigenous, and the colonial context. To these may be added the specific of self-identification as indigenous peoples."[164] On the lack of needing a coherent definition, Thornberry observes: "The principles which animate the need for definitions in municipal law and at the level of the community do not necessarily carry over into international law. The level of abstraction required for international legal principles, the dynamic nature of the system, the need to be receptive to inputs from the variety of national practice and the openness of tis prescriptions, make parts of the human rights system in particular unsuitable for the imposition of definitions as a kind of deus ex machina."[165]

This is essential in light of the resistance of Indigenous Peoples to being qualified as a minority.[166] In the drafting process of the article, a number of states insisted on the phrase "In those states in which . . . minorities exist", hoping that this would limit the reach of the provision. Examples of such problematic points of view are evident in numerous cases, and the argument is often made that no minorities exist within its territorial borders, as all citizens are awarded equal rights without discrimination.[167] Yet, it has to be emphasized that, whether or not a group qualifies as a minority is a matter of fact and not of law, as emphasized by the PCIJ already in 1928.[168] It is to be answered through the use of objective criteria.[169] This restricts a state's margin of discretion, obliging it to create a set list of criteria to be used in any given situation which can be objectively justified. This has made it less likely that a state will recognize a minority or grant it rights depending on the current political climate.

It is more problematic that international law is lacking a commonly accepted definition of both minorities and Indigenous Peoples.[170] The fact that Indigenous Peoples qualify as a minority for the purposes of Art.27 ICCPR has been highlighted by different UN actors. In its guiding document "Minority Rights – International Standards and Guidance for Implementation", the OHCHR acknowledged conceptual difficulties in defining Indigenous Peoples as minorities and acknowledging

[164]Thornberry (2002), p. 55.

[165]Thornberry (2002), p. 57.

[166]Vrdoljak (2014), p. 163.

[167]One such example was France. The HRCee observed in this respect "The mere fact that equal rights are granted to all individuals and are equal before the law does not preclude the existence in fact of minorities". See Human Rights Committee, Concluding Remarks France [8.04.1997] UN Doc CCPR/ C/79/Add.80.

[168]Vrdoljak (2014), p. 161. PCIJ *Rights of Minorities in Upper Silesia Minority Schools 1928* Series A, No 15,29.

[169]HRCee, General Comment No. 23, para 5.2.

[170]UN Office of the High Commissioner for Human Rights (2010), pp. 2–3.

them as possessing minority rights.[171] This distinction remains important, as highlighted *inter alia* by Thornberry, as neither historical origin nor rights under international law are identical, but there are ‘overlaps’ such as Art.27 ICCPR.[172] One of the dangers for Indigenous Peoples in being subsumed under ‘minorities’ is that it misrepresents the pre-settler relationship with their territory and any ensuing treaties which were effectively concluded between different nations.[173] Moreover, being subsumed under the minority heading entails being affected on the international legal-political level by the effects of ethnical violence and conflicts which are fought on minority grounds.[174] It is telling that the OHCHR Guiding Document, apart from the short discussion on definitional difficulties, focusses on non-Indigenous minorities.[175] However, Indigenous individuals have successfully submitted individual complaints under the individual complaints mechanism of the ICCPR. Well-known cases in international law involving Indigenous Peoples are, for example, Sandra Lovelace v Canada, Lubicon Lake Band v Canada and Apirana. For these reasons, this chapter thus follows the current international legal opinion and considers Indigenous Peoples as entities distinct from minorities but enjoying some of the same rights, as well as others that are particular to their Indigenous status.

1.4.6 Sacred Ceremonial/Secret Objects

As was explained above, sacred (ceremonial/secret) objects (as opposed to items of everyday, non-religious use) will be the subject of this study and are considered a sub-category of Indigenous cultural heritage. Before going further into how best to define sacred objects, it is first necessary to justify why the term sacred objects was chosen. Welsh has argued that, instead of ‘sacred’, we should refer to ‘potent’ objects. In his view, potent is the more neutral term, as sacredness is a term not limited to the religious field. It has different dimensions, including emotional and moral. To invoke the sacredness of an object, according to Welsh, is to claim the “the moral and philosophical ‘high ground’”.[176] While it is undoubtedly true that the term sacred has various connotations, it is the link between these objects and religion which is the reason to consider them separately. The objects in question are not easily replaceable, as they are specific items which cannot be mass-produced or they lose the meaning which is intrinsic to them when they are copied outside of their

[171] UN Office of the High Commissioner for Human Rights (2010), pp. 3–4.

[172] Thornberry (2002), p. 34.

[173] Even if Indigenous Peoples were never accepted as sovereign nations under international law, which is not surprising given that it was made by the power colonizing Indigenous territories.

[174] Thornberry (2002), p. 35.

[175] UN Office of the High Commissioner for Human Rights (2010), p. 4.

[176] Welsh (1992), p. 858.

original context.[177] To refer to them as potent will not change this but rather hide an integral element.

To define these objects and to make repatriation exercises dependent on whether objects fall within this category or not raises difficult questions. Someone will have to make the decision which modes of behaviour can be considered Indigenous religious practices and which cannot be classified as such.[178] Even more important is the question who judges whether an object can be considered sacred, and this question will have to be considered on the domestic level, in the chapters that follow.[179]

Having considered these preliminary concerns, the term 'sacred objects' will be defined for further use in the following chapters. Given that sacredness will depend on the community in question and that the element is used merely to distinguish claims for the repatriation of sacred material from claims for the repatriation of non-sacred materials, as identified by the claimant, the definition adopted will be a broad one by necessity. Simply stated, a sacred ceremonial or secret object is an object that fulfils a spiritual function or has a spiritual identity according to the beliefs practised by an Indigenous community. It should be noted here that there is no formal element imposed on 'beliefs practised by Indigenous communities'. Sacredness can be known to many or few, what matters is whether it can be classified as spiritual in accordance with rules internal to the belief system. The practise element is necessary to remove the question of sacredness from something purely internal to something which can become observable and claimable in the application of a legal rule. I will use the terms sacred object, Indigenous religious object, ceremonial object, and secret object interchangeably to refer to this definition.

---

[177] Similarly, Kenney (2011), p. 515.

[178] Compare Graber and Lai (2011), p. 10. They make a similar argument in respect to judging the authenticity of an object.

[179] As an example of how (religious) importance depends on who is asked, consider the Guidelines which were issued by the Museums and Galleries Commission UK which sought to aid museums in judging the 'cultural and religious importance' of the requested objects:

1) Where a request relates to religious or sacred objects and communally owned cultural patrimony, attempt to assess the continuing links between the original community in which the material was made, used and valued, and the contemporary community on whose behalf the request is made. [..]
2) Attempt to ascertain whether the:

   a. Material is **central** to maintaining the identity and cohesiveness of the community and/ or the revival or survival of traditional practices;
   b. Return of these items will contribute to the confidence and self-esteem of the community;
   c. Material plays a key role in the continuing practice of traditional religion;
   d. Material is of outstanding symbolic significance in the history of the community; i.e. whether it is a cultural icon.

Source: Museums and Galleries Commission (2009), pp. 136–137.

Lastly, my choice of the term 'object' is also a choice against using the term 'art' in this context. While cultural heritage or sacred objects can be viewed as 'art' by certain stakeholders, the term has strong connotations[180] connected to the art market, including the idea that objects can be traded, possessed and disposed of by individuals and is inherently biased against a world view that rejects commodification of the sacred. The use of the term 'object' is an attempt to adopt a more neutral approach, considering the sacredness of the contested object is (part of) what makes it attractive to the art market and to the scientific community and important to Indigenous Peoples.

1.4.7 Sovereignty

Sovereignty, as a legal concept, has been and remains heavily debated. It has been described as "the supreme authority within a territory" and "the ultimate power within a territory".[181] Sovereignty can be classified as having an internal (power to regulate internal affairs) and an external dimension (power to regulate external affairs). This is complemented by differentiating between domestic and international sovereignty, which consider the concept of sovereignty from different perspectives. Domestic sovereignty is shaped by domestic law that regulates the internal and external affairs of a state. International sovereignty refers to the rights and duties of a state in relation to its territory and people under the international legal order.[182]

Indigenous Peoples were sovereigns before colonization, that is they were domestic sovereigns with internal and external sovereignty in accordance with their own legal traditions. They were not, however, accorded the status of sovereign in the international legal order. This is not surprising, given that international law at the time was dominated by colonizing powers who had a vested interest in not recognizing Indigenous Peoples as equal partners. As part of the continuing decolonization effort in law,[183] this research therefore identifies Indigenous Peoples as sovereign entities who had power over a defined territory and people in accordance with their own legal traditions at the time of colonization.

As a result, in the following chapters, sovereignty is used in three different ways: first, Canada and the United States are sovereign states as recognized under international law (international sovereignty). They are also domestic sovereigns under their own legal tradition. Second, Indigenous Peoples are sometimes referred to as

[180] Compare Glass (2004), p. 116. Glass, for example, argues that "the marking of many objects as 'art' adds a certain kind of cultural value, often to the exclusion of others".

[181] Besson (2011). Besson gives these examples of very different aspects of sovereignty based on Customs Régime between Germany and Austria (Protocol of March 19th, 1931), Advisory opinion, PCIJ Series A/B No 41, ICGJ 287 (PCIJ 1931), Individual Opinion of Judge Anzilotti, p. 57.

[182] Besson (2011), pp. 69–73.

[183] For one example of this see Watson (2015), who critically assesses the colonisation of Australia from the perspective of Aboriginal law.

sovereign, for example Native Americans in Chap. 4. This is to recognize that they were domestic sovereigns at the time of colonization under Aboriginal law, albeit not recognized or treated as such under international law. Their domestic sovereign status at the time of the conquest or settlement of a territory was rejected unilaterally by the colonizing powers, but it continues to exist under Aboriginal law. This continues to be ignored by a multitude of actors for very obvious reasons (the risk they may pose for territorial integrity is one example). The legal analysis still follows existing international legal standards of treating Indigenous Peoples as an undefined entity under international law that resides between the state and individual, in order to reflect the state of the law accurately. Third, the domestic laws of the selected countries have their own way of navigating the difficulties of dealing with the quasi-sovereign status of Indigenous Peoples prior to the establishment of the settler government. This has also resulted in separate terminology, including the status of Native-Americans as "domestic dependent nations", which evokes the image of a quasi-sovereign nation. The relevant national legal terminology is used to be accurate, but it is used with this legal struggle between different sovereign entities in mind. The continued struggles in different domestic legal areas and bodies will become more apparent in the respective national analysis.

Overall, it must be acknowledged that much of the difficulties described in the national country chapters occur because of the continuing need to undertake a decolonization of (inter-) national law. This has not or has only partially happened. Uncertainties over land, governing and membership structures, rights protection and co-governance are not surprising if we examine the historic evolution of the legal status of Indigenous Peoples (nationally and internationally). The use of the term sovereign in connection with Indigenous Peoples is thus also a reminder of the legal root of contemporary difficulties.

1.5 Structure

This research is structured in four parts to answer the two central research questions. The first question asks how the repatriation of Indigenous sacred cultural heritage should be regulated legally in light of international cultural heritage and human rights law standards? This question is split into three sub-questions, namely: How is the repatriation of sacred cultural heritage regulated in the selected examples? What international standards apply to repatriation? Which method of repatriation is the most in line with these standards? As was explained above, the research also asks a second question, namely what—if anything—can we derive from the findings of the country analysis in light of the international standards for the cultural heritage law and policy of the selected countries? This goes beyond the specific repatriation law to consider related legal areas that affect the claims of Indigenous Peoples to their Indigenous cultural heritage.

Part I analyses relevant international law, with a view to distilling standards that can be applied to measure national repatriation and heritage law and policy to answer one sub-question. Chapter 2 considers international human rights law, in particular cultural rights and Indigenous rights in international instruments. This is supplemented by a consideration of the Inter-American system, since both countries under examination are members of the OAS. Chapter 3 builds on this by evaluating international cultural heritage law to see whether it imposes any standards in addition to those distilled in Chap. 2. Since much of the binding instruments in the field do not consider Indigenous Peoples or their heritage, many instruments will only be summarized briefly, before turning to the more recent treaties.

The next step towards answering the first main research question is the analysis of national repatriation legislation in the United States and Canada. This will yield answers to the sub-question how the repatriation of sacred cultural heritage is regulated. Part II analyses American law and policy on the repatriation of Indigenous cultural heritage, in particular, and Indigenous cultural heritage and Indigenous religious practices in general. The mapping of American law, in this part, and Canadian law in part III, will then provide the material from which one or more model(s) can be developed to regulate repatriation. Part II starts by exploring the historic foundations of federal Indian law, the field which includes NAGPRA, and the constitutional framework that has facilitated—or even required—the adoption of a nation-wide law that mandates repatriation. This is complemented by an examination of the legal protection of Indigenous religious freedom, given the particular focus of NAGPRA on the protection of graves and the return of remains, associated funerary objects and sacred objects.[184] Finally, museum law and policy will be examined to discover how museums have approached their statutory duty to repatriate under NAGPRA in light of their other fiduciary and ethical obligations. This part will conclude by applying the standards set in part I to accumulate the data necessary to answer which method of regulating repatriation is most in line with these standards.

Part III analyses Canadian law and policy on the repatriation of Indigenous cultural heritage, in particular, and on Indigenous cultural heritage and Indigenous religious practices in general. Chapter 6 considers the relevant national legislation. In particular, it examines the evolving legal relationship between the different governments (federal and provincial) and Indigenous field, Aboriginal rights, religious freedom and the federal regulation of cultural heritage and museum management, in so far as these relate to Indigenous sacred heritage. Because of the constitutional split of competences, cultural heritage and repatriation legislation differs on the provincial level. As justified in Sect. 1.3.3 above, Chap. 7 will examine how repatriation is regulated in the provinces of Alberta and British Columbia. On this basis, Chap. 8 will evaluate existing repatriation efforts and apply the standards derived in part I to evaluate their compliance with human rights.

Part IV brings all of the strands together to develop repatriation models, their advantages and disadvantages and their compliance with human rights standards in

---

[184]NAGPRA also covers important cultural patrimony, but this is a very restrictive category and most of the repatriation occurs under the other headings.

Chap. 9. Chapter 10 will summarize how the research findings answer both central research questions, outlining the main ways to regulate repatriation to align with international human rights and cultural heritage law standards and summarize the main lessons for future repatriations. Parts II and III evaluate the repatriation legislation in the context of connected laws that also affect the position of Indigenous Peoples vis-à-vis their cultural heritage. On this basis, Chap. 10 will also consider whether the research findings suggest any lessons for Canadian or American cultural heritage law and policy, in answer to the second research question. Finally, the transferability of these lessons to the international context will be considered, in light of the renewed attention in Europe on international returns to the governments of former colonies, to give an outlook on the potential of returns versus repatriation in so far as they relate to colonial objects that remain in European collections.

References

Abungu G (2009) The declaration: a contested issue. In: Prott L (ed) Witnesses to history - a compendium of documents and writings on the return of cultural property. UNESCO Publishers, Paris, pp 121–122

Asch M (2009) Concluding thoughts and fundamental questions. In: Bell CE, Paterson RK (eds) Protection of First Nations cultural heritage. UBC Press, Vancouver, pp 394–411

Asmuss K (2011) Ansprüche indigener Völker auf Rückführung rechtswidrig ausgeführten Kulturgutes: Eine Untersuchung für Ansprüche aus Art. 5 UNIDROIT-Konvention 1995 und aus allgemeinem Völkerrecht. Veröffentlichungen aus dem Institut für Internationale Angelegenheiten der Universität Hamburg, Vol 36, 1st edn. Nomos, Baden-Baden

Barkan E (2009) Making amends: a new international morality? In: Prott L (ed) Witnesses to history - a compendium of documents and writings on the return of cultural objects. UNESCO Publishing, Paris, pp 78–94

Battiste M, Henderson JY (2000) Protecting indigenous knowledge and heritage: a global challenge. Purich, Saskatoon

Bell CE (2009) Restructuring the relationship: domestic repatriation and Canadian law reform. In: Bell CE, Paterson RK (eds) Protection of first nations cultural heritage: laws, policy, and reform. UBC Press, Vancouver, pp 15–77

Bell CE, McCuaig H (2008) Protection and repatriation of Ktunaxa/ Kinbasket cultural resources: perspectives of community members. In: Bell CE, Napoleon V (eds) First Nations cultural heritage and law: case studies, voices, and perspectives. UBC Press, Vancouver, pp 312–364

Bell CE, Raven H, McCuaig H (2008) Recovering from colonization: perspectives of community members on protection and repatriation of Kwakwaka'wakw cultural heritage. In: Bell CE, Napoleon V (eds) First nations cultural heritage and law: case studies, voices and perspectives. UBC Press, Vancouver, BC, pp 33–91

Bengs B (1996) Dead on arrival? A comparison of the unidroit convention on stolen or illegally exported cultural objects and U.S. property law. Transntl Law Contemp Probl 6:503–535

Besson S (2011) Sovereignty. Max Planck Encyclopedia of public international law. Oxford University Press

Boele V, Busselen L, de Clippele M-S, De Palmenaer E, Francken R, van Beurden S, Van de Ven A, Zian Y (2021) Ethical Principles for the Management and Restitution of Colonial Collections in Belgium. https://restitutionbelgium.be/en/report. Accessed 4 June 2021

Braun S (2019) Looted colonial art: Is there the political will to return pilfered artifacts? Deutsche Welle 5:01

Coombe RJ (2004) The properties of culture and the politics of possessing identity: native claims in the cultural appropriation controversy. In: Gerstenblith P (ed) Art, cultural heritage, and the law. Carolina Academic Press, Durham, North Carolina, pp 541–547
Desmet E (2008) The UN basic principles and guidelines on the right to a remedy and reparation: a landmark or windowdressing? An analysis with special attention to the situation of indigenous peoples. South Afr J Human Rights 24(1):71–103
Desmet E (2011) Indigenous rights entwined with nature conservation. Intersentia International Specialized Book Services, Cambridge; Portland
Donders Y (2002) Towards a right to cultural identity? Intersentia, Antwerpen, New York
Donders Y (2008) The history of the UNESCO convention on the protection and promotion of the diversity of cultural expressions. In: Schneider H, van den Bossche P (eds) Protection of cultural diversity from a European and international perspective. vol Maastricht Series in Human Rights. Intersentia, Antwerp, pp 1–29
Fechner F (1998) The fundamental aims of cultural property law. Int J Cult Prop 7(2):376–394
Feikert C (2009) Repatriation of Historic Human Remains: Australia. Library of Congress, Law. https://www.loc.gov/law/help/repatriation-human-remains/australia.php
Forrest C (2007) Cultural heritage as the common heritage of humankind: a critical re-evaluation. Comp Int Law J Southern Afr 40:124–151
Forrest C (2010) International law and the protection of cultural heritage. Routledge, Abingdon
Gerstenblith P (2001) The public interest in the restitution of cultural objects. Connecticut J Int Law 16(2):197–246
Glass A (2004) Return to sender. J Mater Cult 9(2):115–139. https://doi.org/10.1177/1359183504044368
Gonçalves-Ho Kang You L, Balai L, Bloksma B, Gosselink M, Lidchi H, Smeulders V, Tarekat Dipowijoyo H, Visser J, Bersee S, Keizer E (2021) Colonial collections and a recognition of injustice. Raad voor Cultuur, The Hague
Graber CB, Lai JC (2011) Indigenous cultural heritage and fair trade: voluntary certification standards in the light of WIPO and WTO law and policymaking. SSRN Electronic Journal. https://doi.org/10.2139/ssrn.1792382
Harding S (1997) Justifying repatriation of Native American cultural property. Indiana Law J 72 (3):723–774
Harding S (1999) Value, obligation and cultural heritage. Arizona State Law J 31:291–354
Harris G (2017) What restitution experts have to say about President Macron's pledge to return African artefacts. The Art Newspaper, 29.11
Hickley C (2018) Berlin Museums chief calls for rules on restitution of colonial artefacts. The Art Newspaper, 16.02
Hickley C (2019) Dutch museums take initiative to repatriate colonial-era artefacts. The Art Newspaper, 14.03
Kenney CC (2011) Reframing Indigenous cultural artifacts disputes: an intellectual property-based approach. Cardozo Arts Entertain Law J 28(3):502–552
Kowalski W (2005) Types of claims for recovery of lost cultural property. Museum Int 57 (4):85–102
Lerner N (1991) Group rights and discrimination in international law, vol 15. Martinus Nijhoff, The Hague
Lubina K (2009) Contested cultural property - the return of Nazi spoliated art and human remains from public collections. Maastricht University, Maastricht
Marleau R, Montpetit C (2000) House of commons procedure and practice. Canada, Parliament, House of Commons
Meijknecht A (2001) Towards international personality: the position of minorities and indigenous peoples in international law. Intersentia, Antwerp
Merryman J (1986) Two ways of thinking about cultural property. Am J Int Law 80(4):831–853
Metcalfe E (1996) Illiberal citizenship? A critique of will Kymlicka's liberal theory of minority rights. Queen's Law J 22(1):167–207

Moustakas J (1989) Group rights in cultural property: justifying strict inalienability. Cornell Law Rev 74(6):1179–1227

Museums and Galleries Commission UK (2009) Restitution and repatriation: guidelines for good practice 2000. In: Prott L (ed) Witnesses to history - a compendium of documents and writings on the return of cultural objects. UNESCO Publishers, Paris, pp 130–149

Nafziger J (2009) The protection and repatriation of indigenous cultural heritage in the United States. In: Bell CE, Paterson RK (eds) Protection of first nations cultural heritage: laws, policy, and reform. UBC Press, Vancouver, pp 110–152

Nafziger J, Paterson RK (2014) Cultural heritage law. Handbook on the law of cultural heritage and international trade. Edward Elgar Publishing, UK

Nationaal Museum van Wereldculturen (7 March 2019) Return of Cultural Objects: Principles and Process. available via: https://www.volkenkunde.nl/sites/default/files/2019-05/Claims%20for%20Return%20of%20Cultural%20Objects%20NMVW%20Principles%20and%20Process.pdf

Niezen R (2009) The rediscovered self: Indigenous identity and cultural justice. vol 56. McGill-Queen's University Press, Montréal [Que.]

Niezen R (2010) Public justice and the anthropology of law. Cambridge University Press, Cambridge

O'Keefe P (2009) Repatriation of sacred objects. In: Prott L (ed) Witnesses to history - documents and writings on the return of cultural objects. UNESCO, Paris, pp 225–238

Parzinger H, Polenz R (2016) Wir müssen den Mut zu schwierigen Themen haben. https://www.preussischer-kulturbesitz.de/newsroom/dossiers-und-nachrichten/dossiers/dossier-sammlungswelten/wir-muessen-den-mut-zu-schwierigen-themen-haben.html

Prott L, O'Keefe P (1992) Cultural heritage or cultural property. Int J Cult Prop 1(2):307–320

Prott LV (ed) (2009) Witnesses to history - documents and writings on the return of cultural objects. UNESCO Publishing, Paris, France

Rivière F, Pomian K, MacGregor N, Murphy B, Loyrette H, West R, Valdés JA, Piotrovsky M, Cummins A, Godonou A (2007) UNESCO forum on memory and universality, UNESCO headquarters Paris, 5 February 2007. In: Prott L (ed) Witnesses to history. UNESCO, Paris, pp 45–77

Sarr F, Savoy B (2018) The resitution of African cultural heritage. Toward a New Relational Ethics. vol N 2018-26

Savoy B (2021) Afrikas Kampf um Seine Kunst. C.H. Beck, Ulm

Singh K (2009) Universal museums: the view from below. In: Prott L (ed) Witnesses to history - a compendium of documents and writings on the return of cultural property. UNESCO Publishers, Paris, pp 123–129

Thomas N (2018) Should colonial art be returned home? Financial Times, 6.12

Thornberry P (2002) Indigenous peoples and human rights. Manchester University Press, Manchester

UN Office of the High Commissioner for Human Rights (2010) Minority Rights: International Standards and Guidance for Implementation. New York and Geneva

van Beurden J (2014) How to Break the Deadlock in the debate about colonial acquisition? In: Vadi V, Schneider H (eds) Art, cultural heritage and the market. pp 165–182

van Beurden J (2017) Treasures in trusted hands - negotiating the future of colonial cultural objects. Interdisciplinary studies in culture, history and heritage. Sidestone Press, Leiden

Virgil (1792) The Works of Virgil - Volume II (trans: Dryden). J. Rivington and Sons

Vrdoljak AF (2014) Human rights and cultural heritage in international law. In: Lenzerini F, Vrdoljak AF (eds) International law for common goods. Hart, Oxford, pp 139–173

Watson I (2015) Aboriginal peoples, colonialism and international law. Raw law. Routledge, Abingdon

Welsh PH (1992) Repatriation and cultural preservation: potent objects, potent pasts. Univ Mich J Law Reform 25(3&4):837–866

Whitby-Last K (2010) Legal impediments to the repatriation of cultural objects to indigenous peoples. In: Turnbull P, Pickering M (eds) The long way home - the meanings and values of repatriation. Berghahn Books, New York, pp 35–47

Young JO, Brunk CG (eds) (2009) The ethics of cultural appropriation. Wiley-Blackwell, Chichester

Part I
Sacred Indigenous Cultural Heritage in International Law

Chapter 2
Repatriation of Sacred Indigenous Cultural Heritage Under International Human Rights Law

2.1 Introduction

Indigenous peoples have been at the mercy of international law for a long time while at the same time rejecting this treatment with persistent and impressive resistance. Despite Indigenous activism on the international level dating back to the early nineteenth century,[1] international law as a legal framework justified colonialism. For well into the twentieth century, Indigenous Peoples were not recognized as subjects but rather as objects of a global assimilation project that was deemed inevitable. A paternalistic approach geared towards the assimilation of Indigenous Peoples into national communities dominated.[2] This stance is embodied in the ILO Convention No. 107 and has been heavily criticized in academic literature and by Indigenous organizations both for its assimilationist approach and for the ILO's failure to consult Indigenous Peoples in the drafting process.[3]

The approach towards Indigenous Peoples on the international level slowly started to change in the late 1960s and early 1970s,[4] and Indigenous activism bore fruit. International bodies started to consider Indigenous Peoples' rights explicitly, notably in connection with minority rights and Art.27 ICCPR. In 1982, within what was then the Sub-Commission on Prevention of Discrimination and Protection of Minorities, a Working Group on Indigenous Populations (WGIP) was created.[5] Two

[1] Lenzerini and Scott (2012), p. 69. For example, there were several Maori visits to London, including Moehanga of Ngāpuhi who visited London in 1806 and met with King George III.

[2] Lenzerini and Scott (2012), p. 70.

[3] Donders (2002), pp. 209–210.

[4] Lenzerini and Scott (2012), p. 70 See also Antkowiak (2013), pp. 122–123.

[5] UN DESA website, information on Indigenous Peoples > UNDRIP [last accessed 05.07.2021]. https://www.un.org/development/desa/indigenouspeoples/declaration-on-the-rights-of-indigenous-peoples.html.

V. Tünsmeyer, *Repatriation of Sacred Indigenous Cultural Heritage and the Law*, Studies in Art, Heritage, Law and the Market 3,
https://doi.org/10.1007/978-3-030-89047-6_2

years later in 1985, the WGIP began what would turn out to be a 20-year long drafting process to draft a declaration on the rights of Indigenous Peoples. In line with these developments within the UN, a Committee of Experts (created by the ILO) deemed the Convention No 107 'obsolete' in 1986.[6] This changing perspective on the role of Indigenous Peoples within society led to a revision of the Convention in 1988 and 1989. This resulted in the adoption of ILO Convention No 169. It was ratified by 24 countries, albeit neither by Canada nor by the United States.[7] During the last 30 years,[8] and with the changes explored as well as the proclamation of the first International Decade of the World's Indigenous Peoples (1995–2004), indigenous rights have been recognized on the international level. Much of the advances in Indigenous rights are undoubtedly due to the actions of the Indigenous Peoples themselves.[9]

This shift towards recognizing Indigenous Peoples as subjects of international law has culminated in the adoption of the United Nations Declaration on the Rights of Indigenous Peoples. The UNDRIP was adopted in the General Assembly with a vote of 143 countries in favour, 11 abstaining, 4 countries vetoing its adoption (Australia, Canada, New Zealand and the United States).[10] However, all four countries later issued a statement in principle to show their support for the convention and retracted their earlier veto. It contains a number of cultural rights that focus on recognizing and preserving the Indigenous right to their cultural identity. Examples are the right to protect, preserve and manage their cultural heritage, the right to the revitalization of Indigenous cultural practices, and the right to the use and control of their ceremonial objects.

Relatively recently, the Human Rights Council adopted resolution 42/19, in which it "[e] ncourages the development of a process to facilitate the international repatriation of indigenous peoples' sacred items and human remains through the continued engagement of the United Nations Educational, Scientific and Cultural Organization, the World Intellectual Property Organization, the Expert Mechanism, the Special Rapporteur on the rights of indigenous peoples, the Permanent Forum on Indigenous Issues, States, indigenous peoples and all other relevant parties in accordance with their mandates".[11] At the time of editing, no such mechanism exists, but the Expert Mechanism did adopt a report on repatriation and considered potential mechanisms and best practices.[12]

---

[6] ILO (2013), p. 4.

[7] Overview via www.ilo.org[last accessed 18.08.2021].

[8] Human Rights Council, Report of the Special Rapporteur on the situation of human rights and fundamental freedoms of Indigenous Peoples, S. James Anaya, U.N. Doc. A/HRC/9/9 [11.08.2008], p. 6 (para 18).

[9] Lenzerini and Scott (2012), p. 70.

[10] Voting Record for A/RES/61/295, via https://digitallibrary.un.org/?ln=en [last accessed 18.08.2021].

[11] Human Rights Council, Resolution 42/19 on Human Rights and Indigenous Peoples, U.N. Doc. A/HRC/42/L.24 [26.09.2019], para 18.

[12] For more see Sect. 2.4.2.2.5 below.

This chapter will answer whether international human rights law sets any standards for the repatriation or the protection of Indigenous rights to their sacred cultural heritage that states have to respect under national law. Next to the specific rights in the UNDRIP that were highlighted above, a number of articles included in the core human rights documents remain crucial to any analysis of state obligations under international Indigenous rights standards. These span across the different human rights categories contained in the international bill of rights, encompassing civil, political, economic, social, and cultural rights. The most important rights are the right to self-determination (which is of a mixed nature, containing both political, collective as well as cultural aspects), the right to non-discrimination, the freedom of religion and the prohibition of discrimination (both forming parts of the civil rights catalogue), the right to property and the rights included in the categories of cultural rights as well as minority rights. However, repatriation not only touches upon the rights of Indigenous individuals who reclaim the object, but also upon the wider population's cultural rights, if the object is housed in a museum. Similarly, depending on the identity of the owner, the right to property may come into play. As in the case of any conflict between conflicting human rights, this requires a balancing exercise. For this reason, first the rights which favour repatriation (Sects. 2.2 to 2.4) will be considered before considering rights that may conflict with Indigenous interests and how to balance them against each other (Sect. 2.5). Based on this, a human rights 'toolbox' will be proposed comprising both principles and limitation tests. The principles will guide the evaluation of national repatriation and heritage legislation. The tests help to evaluate whether state measures that limit human rights amount to a violation. To reach these results the author will interpret international provisions as explained in the following two sections.

2.1.1 *Method of Interpretation ICCPR/ICESCR*

The rights that connect to repatriation claims belong to different covenants, as well as different categories of rights. The question as to their interpretation is complicated further by the fact that the ICCPR and the ICESCR approach the creation of rights differently. Traditionally, it has been argued that the ICCPR mostly creates negative obligations (duty to refrain from infringing human rights) whereas the ICESCR rights are more positive in nature.[13] These positive obligations are, however, subject to the limitation in Art.2 (1) ICESCR which obliges states:

> to take steps, individually and through international assistance and co-operation, especially economic and technical, to the maximum of its available resources, with a view to achieving progressively the full realization of the rights recognized in the present Covenant by all appropriate means, including particularly the adoption of legislative measures.

[13] Tomuschat (2010), pp. 27–29.

Thus, as the Committee on Economic, Social and Cultural Rights [CESCR] clarified, States are obliged to ensure the "minimum essential levels of each of the rights" and have an "obligation of conduct" in trying to realize the content of the rights in question to the maximum of their abilities.[14] Under this view, the interpretation of the ICESCR requires the identification of those obligations, which can be viewed as essential, positive obligations, and those which states have to fulfil progressively, depending *inter alia* on their financial resources. In this respect, it has to be observed that, not only is it theoretically difficult to establish a 'core content' for a given right, but to do so can be problematic in a political reality where states are already far from enthused about the concept of cultural rights. It might lead them to do no more than what is absolutely necessary, claiming to fulfil their obligations and ignoring the warnings issued by the CESCR in its General Comment No. 3.[15]

Still, rights enshrined in the two covenants are interconnected and do not exist in isolation.[16] Rights contribute to the interpretation of other interconnected rights.[17] In spite of the differences between the ICCPR and the ICESCR highlighted in the past, it is possible to employ a uniform methodology for these different instruments, namely the respect/protect/fulfil approach. The threefold typology developed[18] by the CESCR applies to all categories of rights.[19] States have negative duties to refrain from violating a right themselves (duty to respect a right), as well as a duty to protect an individual from violations by others (duty to protect). The last dimension suggested by the CESCR then includes the broadest positive obligation, namely the obligation to ensure that individuals enjoy the substance of a right (duty to fulfil).[20] This has also been emphasized by a number of important human rights scholars in the Maastricht Guidelines on Violations of Economic, Social and Cultural Rights. They emphasize that the tripartite typology (protect, respect, fulfil) applies to all human rights and that "the failure to perform any one of these three obligations constitutes a violation of such rights."[21] Measures of the fulfil dimension may be "legislative, budgetary, administrative, judicial" or take any other possible

[14] CESCR, General Comment No. 3, The Nature of States Parties' Obligations (Art. 2, Para. 1, of the Covenant) [1990] U.N. Doc. E/1991/23, paras 9–10 and 2.

[15] Similarly Donders (2002), pp. 90–91.

[16] Thornberry (2008), p. 2.

[17] Thornberry (2008), p. 2.

[18] Initially, in the context of a study on the right to food in 1989, see footnote 1 in CESCR, General Comment No.12 (1999).

[19] CESCR, General Comment No.12: The right to Adequate Food [1999] U.N. Doc. E/C.12/1999/5, para 15 ["The right to adequate food, like any other human right, imposes three types or levels of obligations on States parties:"]. See also Nowak (2005), p. 36.

[20] CESCR, General Comment No.12, para 15.

[21] Maastricht Guidelines on Violations of Economic, Social and Cultural Rights, (Maastricht, 22–26.01.1997) Sec. II.6, available at: http://www1.umn.edu/humanrts/instree/Maastrichtguidelines_.html [last accessed 18.08.2021].

form.[22] It has to be realized that States also possess a certain margin of discretion within which they can act.[23] While the content of each dimension differs depending on the (category of the) right in question, obligations exist under each dimension. With respect to the ICESCR, this means that a state has to be able to show "measurable progress" with regard to the fulfil dimension, i.e. evidence that it is taking active steps towards improving the protection of the right in question.

2.1.2 Status and Interpretation of the UNDRIP

Next to the treaty provision, the UNDRIP is an important instrument for Indigenous rights standards. Strictly speaking, the UNDRIP is a soft law instrument and not legally binding by itself.[24] However, this approach would not reflect the current reality of international law, notably treaty body jurisprudence and the proliferation of Indigenous rights standards in both state practice and (inter)national legal opinion. This begs the question as to the precise legal force of the rights selected to measure state practice.

There appears to be scholarly agreement on the fact that a number of UNDRIP rights in effect reflect existing customary law.[25] Concerning the UNDRIP rights that do not correspond to customary international law, there are three ways to approach their interpretation. First, one could argue that the provisions that are not already binding as part of customary law or existing treaties are binding if they are necessary to realize the principles enshrined in the UN Charter.[26] The problem with this approach is the difficulty in its application as an analytical benchmark to measure the binding force of the declaration's normative content. Which provisions would be strictly necessary and what would the realization of the Charter look like exactly in a specific case? Even if the application of the UN Charter is followed, we are still confronted with the question how the comparatively broad principles and purposes listed in Art.1 and Art.2 of the UN Charter (i.e. "encouraging respect for human rights and for fundamental freedoms for all without distinction as to race, sex, language, or religion" Art.1(3) UN Charter) can be specific enough to decide which UNDRIP rights are classifiable as a form of 'proper realization'. Next, one may follow the ILA Committee on the Rights of Indigenous Peoples which highlighted the interconnected nature of Indigenous rights and recognized a number

---

[22]Ibid.

[23]Ibid.

[24]ILA, The Hague Conference Report – Committee on the Rights of Indigenous Peoples (2010), p. 2.

[25]Human Rights Council, Report of the Special Rapporteur on the situation of human rights and fundamental freedoms of Indigenous Peoples, S. James Anaya, U.N. Doc. A/HRC/9/9 [11.08.2008], para 41. ILA, The Hague Conference Report – Committee on the Rights of Indigenous Peoples (2010), pp. 51–52.

[26]Proposed on the basis of UNDRIP, preamble recital one by Lenzerini and Scott (2012), p. 71.

of broader Indigenous rights that reflect customary international law.[27] Those parts that are not customary international law are characterized as principles that drive the evolution of international law forward.[28] The research conducted by the ILA on the congruence between the UNDRIP and customary international law is important in establishing the strength of the relevant Indigenous rights. However, the legal status of those cultural rights that cannot be claimed to be customary law remains uncertain.

James Anaya, as Special Rapporteur on the situation of human rights and fundamental freedoms of Indigenous People, instead approached the UNDRIP as applying existing international state obligations and human rights to the context of the life of Indigenous Peoples. He argued that the UNDRIP:

> elaborates upon these fundamental rights [of universal application] in the specific cultural, historical, social and economic circumstances of indigenous peoples. These include the basic norms of equality and non-discrimination, as well as other generally applicable human rights in areas such as culture, health or property, which are recognized in other international instruments and are universally applicable.[29]

Anaya's conceptualization of the UNDRIP has certain consequences for the interpretation of the selected human rights. As a "contextualized elaboration of general human rights principles and rights as they relate to the specific historical, cultural and social circumstances of indigenous peoples",[30] the UNDRIP is thus transformed into material to be taken into account in the interpretation of the rights created under the ICCPR and the ICESCR. This understanding of the UNDRIP is reinforced by the observation made by CERD that the UNDRIP "could be used as a guide to interpret the State party's obligations under the Convention on the Elimination of all Forms of Racial Discrimination as far as it relates to indigenous peoples (see CERD/C/US/CO/60)."[31] The CESCR has also used the UNDRIP to interpret Art.15 for Indigenous Peoples.[32]

To opt for this contextualized reading of the UNDRIP means that the specific UNDRIP provisions can be viewed as interpretations of existing, binding treaty provisions and have significant authoritative force. This does not mean that all UNDRIP rights are immediate, absolute obligations. Some undoubtedly are. Others may provide guidance as to the measures states should take to respect their obligation 'to fulfil' dimension of the respect, protect, fulfil typology. This approach then

---

[27] ILA, The Hague Conference Report – Committee on the Rights of Indigenous Peoples (2010), p. 43.

[28] Ibid, p. 51.

[29] Human Rights Council, Report of the Special Rapporteur on the situation of human rights and fundamental freedoms of Indigenous Peoples, S. James Anaya, U.N. Doc. A/HRC/9/9 [11.08.2008], para 40.

[30] Ibid, para 86.

[31] Annual Report of the United Nations High Commissioner for Human Rights - The rights of Indigenous Peoples, U.N. Doc A/HRC/10/51 [14.01.2009], at 6.

[32] CESCR, General Comment No.21, Right of everyone to take part in cultural life (Art.15(1) (a) ICESCR) [2009] U.N. Doc. E/C.12/GC/21, para 16(e).

respects the soft-law nature of the instrument as well as its broad support in the General Assembly (which was support expressed for a *soft-law* instrument). In this sense, I agree with Anaya's observation that "the Declaration provides a framework of action towards the full protection and implementation of these rights".[33] It should be remembered that the binding instruments, as well as the Declaration, concern the obligations of states and not private individuals. The state retains its central role[34] as the guarantor of rights, even if these rights have more of a collective rather than individual nature. Even the repatriation provisions do not concern the status of Indigenous cultural property held by private, non-state entities under domestic law.[35] There are a number of reasons to follow this understanding of the UNDRIP. First, there is vast international and state support of the UNDRIP. These provisions therefore constitute widely accepted legal sources that can be used to measure state behaviour. Second, it follows the approach taken by international treaty bodies who are the authoritative force in the interpretation of the respective treaties. Third, the UNDRIP was developed in collaboration with Indigenous Peoples. This approach therefore respects the position of Indigenous Peoples as entities under international law in their own right. For all of these reasons, this volume follows the guidance of the UNDRIP in the interpretation of the relevant treaty articles in order to derive principles that can help to evaluate Canadian and US repatriation and cultural heritage law. In parallel, the limitation clauses included in the treaties themselves will be decisive in establishing whether a specific state action that limits Indigenous cultural rights is in violation of its obligations under the respective treaty article. They represent the current standard by which state limitations can be measured authoritatively and to which states have agreed upon by the ratification of the treaties.

2.1.3 Indigenous Rights and Connected UN Bodies

The dominant platform for the discussion of Indigenous rights is the UN Permanent Forum on Indigenous Issues (UNPFII), which is an advisory body to ECOSOC. Next to UNPFII, the bodies which focus on human rights also touch upon indigenous or cultural rights. Another important entity that considers Indigenous rights is the Expert Mechanism on the Rights of Indigenous Peoples (hereafter Expert Mechanism) as a subsidiary body of the council.[36] Its main task is to provide

[33] Human Rights Council, Report of the Special Rapporteur on the situation of human rights and fundamental freedoms of Indigenous Peoples, S. James Anaya, U.N. Doc. A/HRC/9/9 [11.08.2008], para 43.

[34] Ibid, p. 14.

[35] Paterson (2014), p. 313.

[36] By means of HRC Resolution 6/36 [14.12.2007].

"thematic advice" to the Human Rights Council.[37] The now extinguished[38] Sub-Commission on the Promotion and Protection of Human Rights (formerly Sub-Commission on Prevention of Discrimination and Protection of Minorities) which operated under the Commission on Human Rights is also worth mentioning. This is complemented by special procedures including the Special Rapporteurs and the work of treaty bodies. The following special procedures and treaty bodies are the most relevant for research on Indigenous Peoples and culture/cultural heritage:

- Treaty monitoring bodies
  - The Human Rights Committee (CCPR)
  - the Committee on Economic, Social and Cultural Rights (CESCR)
  - the Committee on the Elimination of Racial Discrimination (CERD)
- Special Procedures (incorporated through HRC)
  - Special Rapporteur in the field of cultural rights
  - Special Rapporteur on the rights of Indigenous Peoples
  - Special Rapporteur on minority issues
  - Special Rapporteur on contemporary forms of racism, racial discrimination, xenophobia and related intolerance
  - Special Rapporteur on freedom of religion or belief

The Indigenous rights bodies—the UNPFII, the Special Rapporteur and the Expert Mechanism—contribute to the operationalization of the UN Declaration of the Rights of Indigenous Peoples (UNDRIP).[39] The various UN bodies were entrusted with this task through Art.42 UNDRIP,[40] which requires them to "promote respect for and full application of the provisions of this Declaration and follow up the effectiveness of this Declaration". A first step in this direction was made when the forum adopted the UNDRIP as its legal framework.[41]

Many Indigenous rights concerns have been contemplated by UN bodies and individual cases have been considered by treaty bodies. Unfortunately, the issue of the tangible cultural heritage of Indigenous Peoples and its connection to cultural rights has not yet been examined by the treaty bodies. Most discussed by the monitoring bodies are "land, poverty, education and health, participation and consultation, the question of access to justice, census data and self-identification as well

[37] Human Rights Council, Report of the Special Rapporteur on the situation of human rights and fundamental freedoms of Indigenous Peoples, S. James Anaya, U.N. Doc. A/HRC/9/9 [11.08.2008], p. 20.

[38] Operated from 1947–2006.

[39] Human Rights Council, Report of the Special Rapporteur on the situation of human rights and fundamental freedoms of Indigenous Peoples, S. James Anaya, U.N. Doc. A/HRC/9/9 [11.08.2008], p. 19.

[40] Ibid.

[41] Ibid, pp. 19–20.

as civil status registration."[42] However, the Expert mechanism considered the repatriation of ceremonial heritage and human remains to Indigenous communities in light of human rights law in 2020.[43] This advice will be considered below in Sect. 2.4.

2.2 Civil and Political Rights

2.2.1 Right to Self-Determination: Common Art.1

2.2.1.1 Article 1

> 1. All peoples have the right of self-determination. By virtue of that right they freely determine their political status and freely pursue their economic, social and cultural development...
>
> 3. The States Parties to the present Covenant [..] shall promote the realization of the right of self-determination, and shall respect that right, in conformity with the provisions of the Charter of the United Nations.

2.2.1.2 Evolution of the Right to Self-Determination in Relation to Indigenous Peoples

The link between self-determination and minority cultures has a long history in international law.[44] In the early twentieth century, a notable example of the interaction of self-determination and minority cultures in international law arose in the case of the Åland Islanders. When they desired to secede from Finland and unite with Sweden, the International Commission of Jurists was tasked with considering the question.[45] It found that a "common object" existed between self-determination in the sense of the right to form a state and minority protection in order "to assure to some national Group the maintenance and free development of its social, ethnical or religious characteristics".[46] It furthermore argued that, should this common object (of maintaining and protecting the minority culture) be denied, the exercise of

---

[42] Report of the United Nations High Commissioner for Human Rights - The rights of Indigenous Peoples, U.N. Doc A/HRC/10/51 [14.01.2009], p. 3.

[43] Expert Mechanism on the Rights of Indigenous Peoples, Repatriation of ceremonial objects and human remains under the UN Declaration on the Rights of Indigenous Peoples: report, U.N. Doc. A/HRC/45/35 [21.07.2020].

[44] See Fink (2000) who links the consideration of minorities back to the Treaty of Westphalia.

[45] Cassese (1995), pp. 27–31.

[46] Report of International Commission of Jurists as cited by Vrdoljak (2008b), p. 45.

self-determination by a group within a state could not be ruled out.[47] It clearly linked minority rights, culture and the principle of self-determination. With the adoption of the UN Charter, self-determination was situated at the core of modern international law.[48] Nevertheless, there was still much resistance to the recognition of the concept as a legal principle. Only later did the right to self-determination become a standard in international law. Ellen Desmet observes that the right "is among the most controversial rights in international human rights law" and attributes this predominantly to the lack of conceptual clarity and continuing misunderstandings as to its implications.[49] In fact, it appears that "the sole undisputed point is that peoples living under colonial rule or comparable alien subjugation" can make use of the right to self-determination.[50]

In relation to Indigenous groups, we can trace an evolution from the UDHR, which was remarkable in its lack of provisions on the rights of collectives, to early regional treaties to the application of common Art.1 ICCPR/ICESCR beyond a colonial context. With the 1970 UN Declaration on Friendly Relations, the internal dimension of self-determination was finally recognized in relation to ethnic groups.[51] The Banjul Charter in 1981 signalled another shift, albeit on a regional level, which was followed up by ILO Convention No.169, recognizing peoples' cultural rights in a number of provisions.[52]

2.2.1.3 Substance of the Right and Application to Indigenous Peoples

Common Art.1 ICCPR/ICESCR replicates UNGA Res. 1514 (XV), transforming self-determination into a "legally-binding, human right" and the self-determination discourse from a colonial-context oriented debate into one of contemporary global relevance.[53] Self-determination in the sense used in the treaties has several dimensions: political, economic, cultural, and social. It also includes the freedom of each people to develop in these areas without being influenced or coerced. The ICJ furthermore affirmed that the right has customary law status.[54] At the time when the right was drafted, the term 'peoples' referred to national cultures, the peoples of a nation and not Indigenous Peoples.[55] Nowadays, it is clear that the right applies to Indigenous Peoples. However, it is unclear how far this application reaches. The

[47] Vrdoljak (2008b), p. 45.

[48] Arts. 1(2) and 55 UN Charter.

[49] Desmet (2011), pp. 204–205.

[50] Nowak (2005), p. 22.

[51] Åhrén (2008), p. 101.

[52] Åhrén (2008), pp. 102–103.

[53] Vrdoljak (2008b), pp. 52–53.

[54] *Case Concerning East Timor (Portugal v. Australia),* International Court of Justice (ICJ), 30 June 1995.

[55] Lenzerini and Scott (2012), p. 72.

discussions on the right to self-determination of Indigenous Peoples during the drafting phase of the UNDRIP did not solve the question in how far a right to self-determination can be claimed by such groups.

At first glance, it might be argued that a group cannot be a 'people' and a 'minority' at the same time, at least not in the way the two terms are used in international law. States resist(ed) according Indigenous groups the status of peoples to avoid fragmentation of their territory. Vrdoljak observes that it is the legacy of both decolonization and the Cold War that self-determination is a process, which requires states to employ political, civil, social, and cultural rights in order to guarantee both the effective participation of its inhabitants as well as the respective identities of its groups.[56] If grave violations of these rights persist, according to Vrdoljak, this could become a matter of international concern, rendering self-determination as secession "the ultimate mechanism for protecting group identity and the cultural rights of its members."[57]

Scheinin maintains that the work undertaken by the Human Rights Committee (HRCee) so far evidences that, where groups identify themselves as Indigenous, they can be classified as minorities and that some of these groups also classify as 'peoples' in the sense of Art.1.[58] The author agrees with Scheinin and others that Indigenous Peoples can be classified both as 'peoples' as defined in the UNDRIP and as minorities under the main treaties of international human rights law. This fits with the HRCee approach, which has applied both Art.27 and Art.1 to IndigenousPpeoples. This was visible for example in Apriana Mahuika et al. v New Zealand, when the Committee considered Art.1 as an aid in the interpretation of other rights, notably Art.27 on minority rights.[59] This relates to the internal aspect of self-determination only, not to an external right of secession. In this context, in its concluding observations on Canada in 1999, the Committee also emphasized that the state should abandon its "practice of extinguishing inherent aboriginal rights", which it considered incompatible with the right of self-determination as enshrined in Art.1 of the convention.[60] Due to the fact that the Optional Protocol only allows individual claims and that Art.1 can only be exercised collectively, the HRC has however only had a limited possibility to consider Art.1 so far (this approach was visible in Lubikon Lake Band, for example).[61]

It is frequently emphasized that the Art.1 right to self-determination is a collective right. One such instance was *Lubicon Lake Band (Bernard Ominayak) v. Canada*, where the HRCee stated that, due to the collective nature of the right, the

[56] Vrdoljak (2008b), p. 78.

[57] Vrdoljak (2008b), p. 78.

[58] Scheinin (2005), p. 4.

[59] Desmet (2011), p. 205.

[60] Also, Scheinin (2005), p.11. UN Doc CCPR/C/79/Add.105 (1999), Concluding Observations on Canada, para 8.

[61] Scheinin (2005), pp. 12–13.

complainant could not bring a claim as an individual under Optional Protocol 1.[62] Vrdoljak observes that, although the right to self-determination is *per se* less contested in relation to Indigenous Peoples than minorities, its exact content in this respect is still very much debated, as could be seen both in the drafting process of the ILO 169 as well as during the drafting process of the UNDRIP.[63] In relation to Indigenous groups, it has certainly been shown that the usage of the term 'peoples' can be very problematic to governments who fear to "inadvertently be recognizing a right to secession" by referring to Indigenous populations within their territory as peoples.[64]

The best conceptualization of self-determination might be the distinction between an internal and external dimension[65]—at least with respect to Indigenous Peoples. These two elements are visible in a number of Indigenous rights instruments, such as the UNDRIP. UNDRIP recognizes the right to self-determination while protecting territorial integrity (Art.46(1)) "with the result that the reference to self-determination is generally interpreted to limit indigenous peoples to the exercise of autonomy within existing states."[66] The internal dimension provides Indigenous Peoples with a certain degree of autonomy to develop their own institutions. This autonomy is not without limits and *inter alia* depends on how their participation at all levels of decision making of the respective state is ensured.[67] Both rights, autonomy and participation are procedural rather than substantive. Together with the notion of FPIC, which is a partial specification of the participation dimension, they frame the way in which Indigenous substantive rights can and should be realized.

2.2.1.4 Application to the Repatriation Debate

If there is such an intense debate about whether Indigenous groups constitute 'peoples' in the sense of Art.1 ICCPR/ICESCR, the question arises in how far this right is helpful for the discussion at hand. The answer is twofold: on the one hand "[i] nternational law has inextricably linked the right of self-determination to the control of land and resources, and the return of cultural objects since the early nineteenth century."[68] Chamberlain and Vroldjak highlight that export controls are an

---

[62] Vrdoljak (2008b), p. 61. HRCee, *Lubicon Lake Band v. Canada*, Communication No. 167/1984 (26 March 1990), U.N. Doc. Supp. No. 40 (A/45/40) at 1 (1990) sec. 6.1.

[63] Vrdoljak (2008b), p. 72.

[64] Swepston (2005), p. 59.

[65] As defined for example in CERD, General Recommendation XXI (1996), para 4.

[66] Shelton (2013), p. 940.

[67] At the same time, struggles also arise when the state or its organs (including the judiciary) encroach on the internal dimension of self-determination, see for instance HRCee, Views adopted by the Committee under article 5 (4) of the Optional Protocol, concerning communication No. 2668/2015 (Tiina Sanila-Aikio), U.N. Doc.
CCPR/C/124/D/2668/2015 [20.03.2019].

[68] Vrdoljak (2008a), p. 244.

important dimension of the right to self-determination which "includes the right of a peoples to determine how their cultural heritage is preserved."[69]

For Indigenous Peoples, by contrast, the right to self-determination is linked to the possession of a distinct cultural identity, separate from that of the majority. An internal right to self-determination implies the cultural self-determination of these groups. In order to maintain their culture, which includes traditional religious practices as an integral part, Indigenous groups need to be able to reclaim their religious artefacts. This stance is mirrored in claims of Indigenous Peoples, who, according to Vrdoljak, "emphasize the importance the importance of the collective nature of self-determination and. . . cultural development, in reversing 'the impact of racism on the expression of indigenous identity'."[70] This way, Indigenous communities can link their claims to a cornerstone of international law (thereby increasing the legal legitimacy of such claims). However, despite the importance of cultural heritage to identity, it seems too far-reaching to interpret self-determination as comprising a right of a people to reclaim their cultural property.[71] To derive such a right of repatriation from common Art.1 is not in accordance with an interpretation of the provision as required by Art.31 VCLT.

Leaving purely legal concerns aside, to link the right to self-determination with repatriation claims might not only strengthen but it can also weaken repatriation claims. This is due to the fact that, as was already observed above, states are very reluctant to recognize Indigenous groups as 'peoples' for fear that the external dimension of the right to self-determination might be claimed successfully. Consequently, to link a claim to the repatriation of objects to self-determination in its internal dimension might be supported less or even rejected in order to avoid setting a precedent. In this (admittedly pragmatic) sense, it might be asked whether self-determination truly "is the ultimate safeguard protection of identity of particular groups and the cultural rights of their members".[72] This might be true if the conceptual capabilities of this provision were to be realized in political reality. Until then, the poltical struggles surrounding territory and sovereignty might even negatively impact the dialogue on cultural rights and heritage between Indigenous Peoples and the states they live in.

2.2.1.5 Indigenous Self-Determination Since the Adoption of the UNDRIP

Art.3 UNDRIP affirms the applicability of the right to self-determination to indigenous peoples. It mirrors Art.1(1) ICCPR/ICESCR. It likewise includes the different dimensions of the right to self-determination, including the cultural dimension. It is

[69] Chamberlain and Vrdoljak (2014), p. 568.

[70] Vrdoljak (2008b), p. 76.

[71] Kuprecht (2014), p. 82.

[72] Vrdoljak (2008b), p. 46.

further elaborated on by Art.4, which specifies the political dimension of Art.3 but is mitigated by Art.46(1), which safeguards the territorial integrity of the state in which Indigenous Peoples are situated.[73] In this sense, UNDRIP confirms the reading of Art.1 ICCPR that provides Indigenous Peoples with an 'internal' right self-determination. Reading Art.1(1) ICCPR in the light of Art.3 UNDRIP, it may be observed that Indigenous Peoples have the right to choose and maintain their cultural traditions[74]—as long as they do not violate international rights norms (Art.46 (2) UNDRIP). Stamatopolou suggested that a significant part of what is sought to be realized can actually be achieved through cultural rights: "The implementation of minority and indigenous peoples' cultural rights, far from being a soft agenda can also achieve, if taken seriously, transfer of resources to them from the dominant society and thus mend age-long injustice and discriminatory practices."[75] In this sense the right to self-determination and cultural rights complement each other. This holds true especially for the case of the return of Indigenous religious objects.

2.2.2 *Right to Non-Discrimination and Substantive Equality*

Another more general human right is the right to non-discrimination. Neither the ICESCR nor the ICCPR provide for the right to non-discrimination in the form of a specific isolated right; rather it frames the entire catalogue of rights in both instruments. It appears in Art.2(1) ICCPR as well as Art.2(2) ICESCR and acts as an umbrella which covers all other, more specific rights.[76] It requires states to ensure that all human rights can be enjoyed by the different members residing in its territory, irrespective of their differences. Prohibited grounds of discrimination are listed and part of this framing provision. Non-discrimination is undoubtedly a pillar upon which all other human rights rest, as is the concept of human dignity. Yet, it is only in combining the right to non-discrimination with the specific rights catalogue that the right becomes truly effective.

Patrick Thornberry has emphasized that many contemporary forms of discrimination are rooted in cultural differences. It is crucial to remember that freedom from discrimination requires both formal and substantive equality.[77] Substantive equality implies the recognition that to achieve true equality for different groups will require that they are treated differently. There are four different types of measures which can be necessary to guarantee the equality of an Indigenous People or minority group:

---

[73] Tsosie (2012), p. 225.

[74] In agreement Graber (2012), pp. 6–7.

[75] Stamatopoulou (2008), p. 7.

[76] Nowak (2005), p. 34.

[77] CESCR, General Comment No.20 Non-discrimination in economic, social and cultural rights (art. 2, para. 2, of the International Covenant on Economic, Social and Cultural Rights) [2009] U.N. Doc. E/C.12/GC/20, para 8 for Art.2(2) ICESCR.

first, temporary measures necessary to eliminate existing substantive discrimination (which should be "reasonable, objective and proportional means to redress the de facto discrimination");[78] second, permanent measures necessary to avoid substantive discrimination (which should also be "reasonable, objective and proportional means to redress the de facto discrimination");[79]; and third, temporary measures which need to be taken by the state to guarantee existing Indigenous or minority rights under Art.27 ICCPR. If these measures aim "at correcting conditions which prevent or impair the enjoyment of" Art.27 rights "they may constitute a legitimate differentiation under the Covenant, provided that they are based on reasonable and objective criteria".[80] The choice of words "correcting conditions" by the HRCee highlights that such measures derogating from Art.2(1) and Art.26 ICCPR are of a temporary nature until the conditions have been rectified. The fourth and final measure are permanent positive measures which need to be taken by the state to guarantee existing Indigenous or minority rights under Art.27 ICCPR.[81] These must respect both art.2(1) and Art.26 ICCPR.[82]

Freedom from discrimination also affects the relationships between individuals, as the state is under a duty to protect individuals from violations committed by other individuals.[83] Freedom from discrimination thus not only grants minority groups leeway to express their cultural differences but it also limits it by requiring that individuals do not infringe upon other individual's human rights.[84] One way in which this has happened in the case of Indigenous Peoples is the question of group membership, especially as regards discrimination against Indigenous women in Canada.[85]

---

[78] CESCR, General Comment No 20, para 9. Compare HRCee, Human Rights Committee, General Comment No.18 Non-Discrimination [1989] U.N. Doc. HRI/GEN/1/Rev.9 (Vol. I), para 10 allowing for affirmative action.

[79] CESCR, General Comment No 20, para 9.

[80] HRCee, General Comment No.23, para 6.2.

[81] The Human Rights Committee has also observed "that not every differentiation of treatment will constitute discrimination, if the criteria for such differentiation are reasonable and objective and if the aim is to achieve a purpose which is legitimate under the Covenant." HRCee, General Comment No.18, para 13.

[82] HRCee, General Comment No.23, para 6.2. The reference to Art.2(1) here should not to be misunderstood as requiring formal equality. As highlighted in this section, the Committee itself has emphasized that the provision encompasses substantive equality.

[83] Nowak (2005), p. 39.

[84] Compare Thornberry (2008), p. 14.

[85] HRCee, *Sandra Lovelace v. Canada,* Communication No. R.6/24, U.N. Doc. Supp. No. 40 (A/36/40) at 166 (1981).

2.2.2.1 Discrimination Against Indigenous Peoples as Racial Discrimination

In so far as specific categories of discrimination are concerned, racial discrimination has also been the subject of a separate convention, the International Convention on the Elimination of Racial Discrimination. The corresponding treaty body (CERD) has assisted in clarifying the content of freedom from racial discrimination and, by analogy, also freedom from discrimination more generally. CERD has covered discrimination against Indigenous Peoples as a result of its mandate[86] and issued a number of helpful statements or observations. More generally, the Committee has emphasized that non-discrimination does not equate to identical treatment. Rather "differential treatment will constitute discrimination if the criteria for such differentiation, judged in the light of the objectives and purposes of the Convention, are not applied pursuant to a legitimate aim, and are not proportional to the achievement of this aim."[87]

CERD has issued an instrument specifically directed at the situation of Indigenous Peoples such as its General Recommendation No. 23 on the Rights of Indigenous Peoples. The Committee called upon States to:

> "(a) Recognize and respect indigenous distinct culture, history, language and way of life as an enrichment of the State's cultural identity and to promote its preservation;
>
> (b) Ensure that members of indigenous peoples are free and equal in dignity and rights and free from any discrimination, in particular that based on indigenous origin or identity;
>
> (c) Provide indigenous peoples with conditions allowing for a sustainable economic and social development compatible with their cultural characteristics;
>
> (d) Ensure that members of indigenous peoples have equal rights in respect of effective participation in public life and that no decisions directly relating to their rights and interests are taken without their informed consent;
>
> (e) Ensure that indigenous communities can exercise their rights to practise and revitalize their cultural traditions and customs and to preserve and to practise their languages."[88]

For present purposes, subparagraphs (a) and (e) are of particular importance. Subparagraph (a) is broader, covering culture, history, language, as well as way of life, but it also requires less positive action on the side of the state. State actions are those which are necessary to ensure the recognition and respect of cultural rights and

---

[86] CERD General Recommendation No.23 U.N. Doc. A/52/18, annex V at 122 (1997), paras 1–2.

[87] Thornberry (2008), pp. 13–14. Also CESCR, General Comment No. 20 para 13.

[88] CERD General Recommendation No.23 [1997] U.N. Doc. A/52/18, annex V at 122, para 4.

may also qualify as measures to ensure the preservation of the state's more general cultural identity if the presence of Indigenous culture has been accepted as a part thereof. Paragraph (e), by contrast, exclusively focusses on the position of indigenous peoples and even requires the state to ensure that Indigenous communities are able to 'revitalize their cultural traditions and customs'. This connects to the repatriation of Indigenous objects and suggests that procedural thresholds, which requires a continued cultural practice in which the object would have been used, may run counter to the state's obligations under CERD. Art.5(e)(vi) ICERD obliges states to guarantee equal rights to participation in cultural activities. States may have to take separate legislative and policy measures to ensure that Indigenous Peoples substantively enjoy this right, including in ensuring access to their cultural heritage.

As far as the practice of states under this instrument is concerned, it is telling that special rapporteur James Anaya observed in 2008 that "[m]ost of the specific country situations that have been dealt with or are currently being monitored by CERD under its early warning/urgent action procedure are related to Indigenous communities and peoples."[89] The balance shifts, depending on the current political climate. For example, due to the conflicts in the Middle East and the resulting refugee crisis, but the situation of Indigenous Peoples remains a central point of concern. To illustrate this point, between the years 2010 and August 2016, the Committee issued 4 decisions,[90] 3 statements[91] and 64 letters. These documents *almost exclusively* concerned alleged violations of the rights of Indigenous Peoples (66 out of 71), albeit several of the letters were addressed to a particular country and concerned the same situation which had not yet been addressed adequately. This also holds true for the countries under consideration. The letters addressed to both the United States and Canada in recent years were exclusively concerned with possible violations of the rights of Indigenous Peoples.[92]

---

[89] Human Rights Council, Report of the Special Rapporteur on the situation of human rights and fundamental freedoms of Indigenous Peoples, S. James Anaya, U.N. Doc. A/HRC/9/9 [11.08.2008], p. 8.

[90] CERD, Decision 1/85 Iraq [2014]; CERD, Decision Côte d'Ivoire [2011] U.N. Doc. CERD/C/CIV/DEC/2; CERD, Decision Kyrghystan [2010] U.N. Doc. CERD/C/KGZ/DEC/1; CERD, Decision Nigeria [2010] U.N. Doc. CERD/C/NGA/DEC/1.

[91] CERD, Statement on Recent Migrant Crisis [2015], CERD, Statement on Libyan Arab Jamahiriya [2011], CERD, Statement on Syrian Arab Republic [2011] all three of which concerned the Middle East conflict and its consequences.

[92] Those available for Canada between 2008 and 2019 and the United States between 2006 and 2019 via https://www.ohchr.org/EN/HRBodies/CERD/Pages/EarlyWarningProcedure.aspx [last accessed 18.08.2021].

2.2.3 *Freedom of Religion*

2.2.3.1 Article 18 ICCPR

1. Everyone shall have the right to freedom of thought, conscience and religion. This right shall include freedom to have or to adopt a religion or belief of his choice, and freedom, either individually or in community with others and in public or private, to manifest his religion or belief in worship, observance, practice and teaching.
2. No one shall be subject to coercion which would impair his freedom to have or to adopt a religion or belief of his choice.
3. Freedom to manifest one's religion or beliefs may be subject only to such limitations as are prescribed by law and are necessary to protect public safety, order, health, or morals or the fundamental rights and freedoms of others.
4. The States Parties to the present Covenant undertake to have respect for the liberty of parents and, when applicable, legal guardians to ensure the religious and moral education of their children in conformity with their own convictions.

In considering the content of the freedom of religion/belief as present in international law, three main sources have to be consulted: Art.18 UDHR, Art.18 ICCPR and the UN Declaration on the Elimination of All Forms of Intolerance and of Discrimination Based on Religion or Belief.[93] While the Declaration is a soft law instrument,[94] it has been used consistently by the different UN Special Rapporteurs on Freedom of Religion.[95]

In relation to the freedom of religion, it has to be observed that different approaches to interpreting the terms 'thought', 'beliefs' and 'religion' exist.[96] If read separately, a comparatively narrow reading of 'religion' would mean "some entity or force, which if not divine, is at least spiritual".[97] The HRCee clarified the matter in General Comment 22, observing that Art.18 "protects theistic, non-theistic and atheistic beliefs, as well as the right not to profess any religion or belief."[98] Alternative Indigenous religions are thus protected, as is their religiously motivated connection to the land and nature. Conceptually, it could be argued that the freedom

[93] UN Special Rapporteur on Freedom of Religion or Belief, Framework for Communications – International Standards on freedom of religion or belief, available at: http://www.ohchr.org/EN/Issues/FreedomReligion/Pages/Standards.aspx [last accessed 18.08.2021].

[94] Ahdar and Leigh (2005), p. 106. They observe that "recommendations from two Special Rapporteurs that a Convention of this kind be adopted have so far come to nothing".

[95] Wiener (2015).

[96] de Jong (2000), p. 21.

[97] de Jong (2000), p. 21.

[98] HRCee, Human Rights Committee, General Comment No. 22 Freedom of Religion (Art.18) [1993] U.N. Doc. CCPR/C/21/Rev.1/Add.4, para 2.

of religion can roughly be classified into four aspects: the freedom to adopt/change or renounce one's religion, the freedom from coercion, the freedom to manifest one's religion in worship or in practice, and the freedom to teach one's religion to one's children. The difficulty for Indigenous communities rests in the fact that the freedom of religion has been classically interpreted as an individual not a group right,[99] even though it does protect the collective manifestation of religion.[100] Where group elements of religion, such as a sacred site or communally owned sacred objects are concerned, their protection goes beyond the classic approach of treating religious freedom as an individual right that does not demand much positive obligations from states. However, Art.18(1) ICCPR read in conjunction with Art.27 ICCPR, protects the communal dimension of Indigenous freedom to manifest their religion in addition to the protection offered by Art.18. ICCPR[101] This reading is reinforced by Art.12 UNDRIP. The linkages between the freedom of religion and cultural heritage are explored below and linked to the repatriation/Indigenous practices debate where a substantive connection can be established.

2.2.3.2 Content of the Right and Application to Indigenous Heritage

The first aspect comprises the basic right to adopt, change or renounce one's religion.[102] For the present debate this means that Indigenous populations have a right to adopt their traditional beliefs. A state must thus recognize Indigenous beliefs in the same way it does other religions. No discrimination may result from adhering to an Indigenous belief, directly or indirectly, *de lege* or *de facto*.[103] For instance, the definition of who is recognized by the state as Indigenous on the national level, and any ensuing benefits, may not depend on the individual adhering to any particular belief. In addition, the state needs to ensure that Indigenous individuals seeking to adopt a different belief are not prevented from doing so by the group due to traditional customs.[104]

As a second aspect, the freedom from coercion prohibits any kind of coercive action aimed at influencing individuals to adopt a certain religion (be it directly through threats of penal sanctions or indirectly by restricting access to certain services such as health care or education to members of a certain religious

[99] Xanthaki (2018), p. 290.

[100] Nowak (2005), p. 419.

[101] Nowak (2005), p. 658.

[102] Art.18 UDHR, Art.18(1) ICCPR, Art.1(1) Declaration on the Elimination of All Forms of Intolerance and of Discrimination Based on Religion or Belief, UN GA, UN Doc A/RES/36/55 (25.11.1981), hereafter 1981 GA Declaration. Human Rights Committee General Comment No. 22 paras 3, 5.

[103] This also applies if the Indigenous religion is different from any official state religion. See HRC General Comment No. 22, para 9.

[104] This is a consequence of the state's duty to protect an individual's freedom of religion against incursions/violations by other parties.

group).[105] In the ordinary use of the word, 'coerce' denotes "to constrain or restrain (a voluntary or moral agent) by the application of superior force, or by authority resting on force".[106] General Comment 22 echoes this: "including the use of threat of physical force or penal sanctions to compel believers or non-believers to adhere to their religious beliefs and congregations, to recant their religion or belief or to convert" or "[p]olicies or practices having the same intention or effect".[107] Relating this to repatriation, it is clear that practices which resulted in the 'relocation' of Indigenous cultural objects would be prohibited under contemporary human rights law. Examples of past practices include governmental agents or missionaries coercing the local Indigenous group to dispense with their religious items using threats of imprisonment and using residential schools. Yet, no such prohibition existed at the time. However, it could be argued that this value, if shared by a society, influences modern-day repatriation debates. Thus, even in the absence of legal ownership claims by Indigenous communities, a shared understanding of the importance of religious tolerance can colour a social retrospective and be introduced into the repatriation debate as a moral concern.

The emphasis of the first two aspects thus rests on the term 'freedom' and 'everyone' in the sense of every individual him-or herself. As Special Rapporteur on the Freedom of Religion Heiner Bielefeldt observed, the result of the strictly individual choice in favour or against a specific belief means that:

> the State cannot 'guarantee' the long-term development or identity of a particular religious minority. Instead, what the State can and should do is create favourable conditions for persons belonging to religious minorities to ensure that they can take their faith-related affairs in their own hands in order to preserve and further develop their religious community life and identity.[108]

In the view of the author, such favourable conditions necessitate private access to and use of religious material as far as these objects are an integral part of rites/ ceremonies or customs. Creating favourable conditions can thus require the protection of access by communities to sites and resources, as this may be necessary for the individual to manifest his or her religion. This is under the condition that this is compatible with the applicable restrictions laid down in the relevant treaty provisions.

As a third aspect of the overall right, religious freedom includes the right to manifest one's religion (be it in private or public, as an individual or in community

[105] Art.18 UDHR, Art.18(2) ICCPR, Art.1(2) 1981 Declaration of General Assembly, Human Rights Committee General Comment No. 22, para 5.

[106] OED entry 'coerce', http://www.oed.com/view/Entry/35716?redirectedFrom=coerce#eid [last accessed 18.08.2021].

[107] HRC General Comment No. 22, para 5.

[108] Report of the Special Rapporteur on freedom of religion or belief [24.12.2012] U.N. Doc. A/HRC/22/51, para 24.

with others).[109] It covers ritual and ceremonial acts as well as customs.[110] Article 6 (a) 1981 UN Declaration clarifies that this includes the right to "establish and maintain places for these purposes". Conversely, states are under the obligation to "exert the utmost efforts, in accordance with their national legislation and in conformity with international human rights and humanitarian law, to ensure that religious places, sites, shrines and symbols are fully respected and protected and to take additional measures in cases where they are vulnerable to desecration or destruction."[111] It is this third aspect of the freedom of religion which most clearly contains a fulfil dimension and one where the state has certain minimum steps it needs to take. The main problem for Indigenous Peoples in relation to places of worship lies in the fact that they are sites rather than buildings.[112] In addition, these are frequently not owned or managed by Indigenous groups. Such sites, for example, can be part of nature reserves or even military areas, meaning that these grounds are in governmental hands. If an Indigenous site is on public land, the state needs to protect it against desecration and ensure Indigenous access to it. Yet, the Indigenous right to access such sites is not absolute; access may be subject to governmental restrictions. These must meet the general requirements for restrictions under the Art.18 (3) ICCPR, discussed below and be in line with Art.27 ICCPR.

The right to manifest is also relevant for the repatriation claims of Indigenous groups in so far as the material subjected to a claim could be subsumed under the categories of "religious symbols". Art.18(1) ICCPR protects their use as part of the right to manifest one's belief.[113] If Art.6(c) UN Declaration is accepted as a clarification of Art.18(1) ICCPR, the right to manifest then also includes the freedom "to make, acquire and use to an adequate extent the *necessary articles* and materials related to the rites or customs of a religion or belief".[114] A minimum obligation to ensure an Indigenous communities' right to manifest their religion would certainly be to implement export prohibitions on religious artefacts in their national legal framework to prevent export without FPIC of the relevant community. In addition, if objects are located in public institutions, or institutions which receive public funding, the state needs to ensure that guidelines are in place which prevent the desecration of the object or its destruction without community consent.

A selection of two examples can show some of the problems of non-Indigenous ownership of sacred objects, ultimately leading to desecration. First, those instances where religious objects are sold into private hands are highly problematic. While the new owner has a financial interest in maintaining the object (preventing destruction), Indigenous communities may have certain practices which have to be observed in

---

[109] HRCee, General Comment No. 22, Para 4.

[110] Ibid.

[111] Art.6(a), (c) 1981 GA Declaration, Human Rights Council Resolution 6/37 para 9(e).

[112] de Jong (2000), pp. 388–389.

[113] HRCee, General Comment, para 4.

[114] Art.6(c) 1981 GA Declaration, Human Rights Council Resolution 6/37 para 9(e). Emphasis added.

caring for an object and may even only be undertaken by a specific individual of the community. Therefore, private ownership may endanger the sacred integrity of an object both by the standard of care employed as well as through the mere fact that it is handled by the new owner rather than the caretaker. Another case is the question of adequate audience: who might view the object? Displaying the object to the general public may be prohibited by Indigenous customs, leading to cases where objects are hidden in museum storage rooms, neither displayed nor repatriated. In a research project undertaken by Catherine Bell and Val Napoleon, Indigenous communities in the Canadian province Alberta were consulted on the proper manner of caring for the medicine bundles of their communities still located in museums: Francis First Charger observed "[t]he way you treat those sacred items is the same way you would treat your children."[115] Frank Weasel Head agreed, arguing that "[i]n our way, the old people would say they have become orphans. And those bundles in museums are all orphans waiting for somebody to adopt them and bring them back and get painted for them so they can be put back into use".[116]

Another, fourth aspect of the freedom of religion is the right to teach one's religion and the right of parents to "ensure the religious and moral education of their children".[117] At first glance, there is no link between repatriation claims and the right of Indigenous groups to teach their religion. However, such a link exists where religious teachings depend upon the availability of certain sacred objects necessary for ceremonies, such as traditional clothing. Where the rituals can neither be exercised nor practised without the regalia in question, the absence of such objects hinders this aspect of the freedom of religion as well.

2.2.3.3 Possible Limitations

There are two possible ways in which a right may be limited in accordance with the ICCPR. First, under the general limitation clause under Art.4 ICCPR. The freedom of religion is one of the rights which is protected from derogations in times of public emergency under Art.4(2) ICCPR. Second, as part of a limitation clause included in the specific article. The right to manifest one's religion is a form of individual freedom that is embedded in a wider structure of numerous individuals having similar rights. As a result, this dimension of the right is "necessarily subject to certain limitations to preserve social order and the rights of other citizens."[118] It thus requires the state to take steps but, at the same time, it is not an absolute right for the individual to manifest his or her religion.) This is also reflected in the limitations expressed in 18(3). The ICCPR thus only allows limitations on the right to manifest one's religion not on the other elements of the right, including exercising one's

[115] Bell et al. (2008), p. 206.

[116] Bell et al. (2008), p. 206.

[117] Art. 5, 6 (d)(e) 1981 Declaration GA, Art.13(3) ICESCR, Art.18(4) ICCPR.

[118] Ahdar and Leigh (2005), p. 100.

religion in private.[119] This is in marked contrast to the standard developed in the UDHR in which Art.29(2) provides acceptable limitations for all declaration rights.[120] Under Art.18(3), any limitation on the freedom to manifest one's religion or belief must be prescribed by law and be motivated by one of the five following concerns: a necessity to protect public safety, order, health, morals, or the fundamental rights and freedoms of others. Moreover, as the Commission on Human Rights Resolution 2005/40 evidences, these exceptions are only permitted if they do not invalidate the right.[121]

2.2.3.3.1 Prescribed by Law and Serve a Recognized Purpose

Any restriction of the right to manifest one's religion has to be laid down in legislation "or an equivalent unwritten norm of common law in a manner adequately specified for the enforcement organs."[122] The second step of the test requires the measure to pursue a legitimate purpose. Art.18(3) gives an exhaustive list[123] of objectives justifying restrictive measures: public safety, public order, public health, public morals or the fundamental rights and freedoms of others. Public order is to be construed narrowly as Manfred Nowak points out. As becomes apparent from the different language versions, public order under Art.18(3) is not to be confused with an *ordre public* exception. Instead it only permits measures "to avoid disturbances to public order in the narrow sense."[124] With regard to public morals, it is important to highlight that limitations for this purpose must be based on broad principles rather than a single tradition.[125] The objective cannot be used to discriminate against a minority belief through the backdoor by imposing limitations which are solely based on the majority's religious beliefs. The last objective listed, fundamental rights and freedoms of others, implies a minimum level of rights to be protected which are the ICCPR and ICESCR, and rights which are given stronger protection on the national level, i.e. through constitutional provisions.[126]

---

[119] Private practice that does not touch upon the freedom and privacy of others is protected from limitation by virtue of Art.17 in conjunction with Art.18(1), see Nowak (2005), p. 418.

[120] Evans (2001), p. 216.

[121] UN Commission on Human Rights, Resolution 2005/40 on Elimination of All Forms of Intolerance and of Discrimination Based on Religion or Belief, U.N. Doc E/CN.4/RES/2005/40 (19.04.2005) para 12.

[122] Nowak (2005), p. 425.

[123] HRCee, General Comment No. 22, para 8.

[124] Nowak (2005), p. 428.

[125] Nowak (2005), p. 429.

[126] Nowak (2005), p. 430.

2.2.3.3.2 Be Necessary for Attaining this Purpose

The necessity element in the limitation test requires that no less restrictive measure is available to the state. This also implies a proportionality[127] requirement. This requires the state to undertake an evaluation of the expected impact of the planned measure and compare it to possible alternative measures. This needs to be done with a view to the severity of the measure's impact on the right and the relative need for it to achieve the listed purpose. A necessity test also implies that the restriction is temporary. If it is not temporary, this begs the question if it is indeed the least restrictive available measure and thus necessary.[128]

2.2.3.4 Linking Art.18 ICCPR to Repatriation

If we consider how repatriation may be linked with Art.18 ICCPR, there are different possibilities. First, a state could prohibit repatriations to Indigenous communities from public and private museums. This could be argued on the permissible limitation of "fundamental rights and freedoms of others", or more precisely the right to cultural participation and its related access to cultural heritage in this context.[129] Yet, it is important to recognize that the permissible ground for limiting the right to manifest one's belief speaks of 'fundamental rights' (not merely rights). According to Cornelis de Jong, this formulation "requires from States a careful weighing between the freedom to manifest one's religion or belief and only the more important rights of others."[130] This is not to say that other rights will not be considered but simply that they might not prevail over the right in question. As an example, de Jong argues that the principle of non-discrimination is formulated in 'rather absolute terms' and likely to prevail in a conflict with Art.18. De Jong adds that, where vulnerable groups are concerned, and the rights in question do not function on the basis of equality, the state may be required to give the vulnerable party special consideration.[131] The cultural rights of the majority may be one of the fundamental rights speaking against state action. In this context it is important to recognize the vulnerability of Indigenous groups (due to historic/contemporary marginalization) in order to ensure a substantive equality in the protection of the right to manifest one's religion of Indigenous People. Thus, if a cultural institution voluntarily decides to repatriate an Indigenous cultural object, a state may not hinder the return due to a fear of its destruction or lack of accessibility on the basis of its cultural heritage law if the

[127] HRCee, General Comment No.22, para 8 "limitations ... must be proportionate to the specific need on which they are predicated."

[128] In agreement Nowak (2005), p. 426.

[129] On the relative importance of Indigenous heritage for non-Indigenous individuals see Sects. 2.5.1 and 2.5.2 below.

[130] de Jong (2000), p. 91.

[131] de Jong (2000), p. 93.

item is integral to the ceremony. Even in cases where the item is not integral, the vulnerability of the group, and the multitude of other human rights held by the Indigenous group need to be balanced against those of the general public before hindering the repatriation by i.e. listing the item as national/regional cultural heritage which is subject to special protection.

The second example concerns objects under state control. It would be important to consider in how far Indigenous religious objects that are necessary to manifest their religion are generally available to Indigenous Peoples. If past assimilation policies have resulted in an extreme scarcity of the necessary ceremonial items for Indigenous Peoples to manifest their religion, the question may be asked in how far a denial of access to and use of the object under state control would invalidate their freedom of religion. Limitations on the freedom of religion are only permitted if they do not invalidate the right. While the state institution is thus not obliged to repatriate the object, it may, at the minimum, be required to allow access to and use of the object.

The third scenario is less clear. It deals with cases in which a state does not impede repatriations but refuses to encourage them (be it through legislation or by providing financial resources to facilitate such claims). In general, negative obligations upon states under human rights law are easier to enforce in human rights law than positive obligations. The author would argue that a minimum positive obligation is the prevention of the desecration of Indigenous religious material which is under public control by i.e. providing training for those individuals that handle these objects and to mandate certain care standards in private institutions. Providing funds for repatriation or establishing a legislative framework for repatriation, by contrast, are possible measures within the state's discretion to fulfil Art.18 ICCPR (and Art.27 ICCPR).

2.3 Cultural Rights

Cultural rights have been crucial to the protection of Indigenous Peoples' rights on the international and national level.[132] However, as a category of human rights, their development has not been easy. Cultural rights were neglected in the realm of human rights law and human rights studies for a considerable period of time. As a result, they "remained underdeveloped."[133] This lack of substantive (academic)[134] consideration has been acknowledged and recent years have seen more attention being paid

[132]Lenzerini and Scott (2012), p. 75 observed "To properly illustrate the importance of cultural rights for indigenous peoples, one could assert that culture is the cradle of all their rights, which, therefore, exist and are shaped depending on the cultural distinctiveness of the specific community concerned."

[133]Vrdoljak (2014), p. 140.

[134]McGoldrick (2002), p. 447. He observes that "international human rights lawyers discuss culture and cultural wrongs a lot, but discuss cultural rights a lot less."

to this group of rights, also within the human rights bodies of the UN. UNESCO has been considering culture since its inception. Its focus on cultural heritage has also led it to consider/develop cultural rights, at least in the realm of soft law, by means of the 1976 Recommendation on participation by the people at large. The shift within the UN in the perception of cultural rights as being a 'luxury commodity' to being understood as an essential element of human dignity occurred comparatively late. One example of the long delay in the normative support for cultural rights is the fact that General Comment on Art.15 ICESCR was only adopted in 2005.[135]

With the creation of the office of UN Special Rapporteur in the Field of Cultural Rights by means of Resolution 10/23 and her reports on the matter, as well as substantive resolutions on cultural rights adopted by the Human Rights Council, notably on 'cultural rights and the protection of cultural heritage',[136] the development of these rights received important institutional backing. Civil society initiatives have also highlighted the importance of cultural examples, for example through the Fribourg Declaration on Cultural Rights. It proclaims eight cultural rights and notably considers the link between culture, identity and cultural heritage.[137] Even with the scholarly and institutional work that has been done in the field of cultural rights, difficulties remain, as these rights are worded vaguely or contain broad terms. This can render precise interpretative deductions difficult.

Cultural rights thus remain a difficult conceptual category, not least because they are spread out over different hard and soft law instruments. The UDHR includes Art.26 on the right to education and Art.27 on the right to participate in cultural life and in scientific progress. The ICESCR includes the same rights in Art.13 (education) and Art.15 (cultural participation). The ECHR and the American Convention initially both ignored these rights completely.[138] Within the ICCPR, Art.27 protects the cultural rights of minorities but it took time for the right to be given shape by the HRCee. Frequently, other human rights, such as the freedom of speech, are necessary to guarantee cultural rights.[139] As a result, it can be difficult to classify the rights which are part of this category.

Farida Shaheed, then special rapporteur, refrained from defining culture and described the scope of her office in relation to 'rights in the field of culture' preferring to use available 'working definitions', suggesting that she sees cultural rights as rights which relate to culture as defined by other institutions.[140] She

---

135 Stamatopoulou (2007), pp. 48–49.

136 HRC Resolution 33/20 Cultural rights and the protection of cultural heritage [30.09.2016] UN Doc A/HRC/RES/33/20.

137 See Fribourg Declaration, especially Art.3(b): "To know and to have one's own culture respected as well as those cultures that, in their diversity, make up the common heritage of humanity. This implies in particular the right to knowledge about human rights and fundamental freedoms, as these are values essential to this heritage."

138 At least until 1952 with the adoption of the Protocol to the ECHR that included the right to education and 1988 with the adoption of the Protocol of San Salvador.

139 Blake (2014), p. 45.

140 Shaheed (2010), p. 4, para 5.

emphasized that it might be difficult to separate cultural rights from other rights,[141] which is understandable given the centrality of culture in the daily life of both individuals and groups. Stamatopulou has been more precise and classified five rights as cultural rights: the right to education; the right to participate in cultural life; the right to enjoy the benefits of scientific progress and its applications; the right to benefit from the protection of the moral and material interests resulting from any scientific, literary or artistic production of which the person is the author, and the freedom for scientific research and creative activity.[142] For the discussion of cultural rights in the repatriation context, it is not necessary to delve further into classification of cultural rights, as the rights which are important have been widely acknowledged as cultural rights: Art.27 ICCPR and Art.15(1)(a) ICESCR.[143]

Culture is crucial to Indigenous Peoples existing as separate entities and the enjoyment of their other rights. It is thus not surprising, that 17 out of the 46 UNDRIP articles relate to cultural rights.[144] Further cultural rights that will be considered are thus included in the UNDRIP (see Sect. 2.4.2 below). Indigenous claims to cultural heritage (and cultural rights) are frequently collective in nature. Before we can turn to examining the specific cultural rights, we therefore need to briefly consider in how far cultural rights can be considered collectives (see Sect. 2.3.1). Moreover, cultural rights is the category of human rights with the closest connection to international cultural heritage law that was considered in the previous chapter. This link is summarized briefly in Sect. 2.3.2 before turning to discussing Art.27 ICCPR in Sect. 2.3.3.

2.3.1 Cultural Rights as Collective Rights

Having clarified the scope of cultural rights under examination, an additional difficulty remains: cultural rights are not only of an individual but also of a collective nature.[145] Phrases such as "in community with others" can be found in different cultural rights provisions. Collective rights have been the subject of much debate and opinions range from interpreting cultural rights as individual but "exercised in the context of that group"[146] to the view that "it is logically and morally impossible not to recognize the collective elements of cultural rights, when speaking of minorities and indigenous peoples."[147]

---

141 Shaheed (2010), pp. 6–7, para 11.

142 Stamatopoulou (2008), p. 3. A slightly more inclusive list has been advanced by Blake (2014), p. 60.

143 For example, by Art.5 of the Universal Declaration of Cultural Diversity.

144 Stamatopoulou (2008), p. 3.

145 Donders (2002), p. 72.

146 See O'Keefe (2011), p. 7.

147 Stamatopoulou (2008), p. 7.

Another argument in favour of the existence of cultural rights is that the preservation of cultural heritage in international law has been justified by what are essentially collective concerns. In effect, the protection of cultural heritage is often phrased in terms of protection in the form of preservation, for the sake of future generations. Lucas Lixinski argues that, to follow this approach is to adopt a group perspective, as no specific individual is identifiable for those future generations.[148] There is a duplicity in refusing to acknowledge group rights to culture and cultural heritage, on the one hand, yet embedding much of existing cultural heritage in a language which invokes future generations as a justification for the imposition of limitations on Indigenous communities. However, an important distinction between the two remains: the future generations may very well be a group, but it is an unspecified beneficiary. It cannot claim specific rights contrary to existing and identifiable groups under the minority or Indigenous rights regime. By contrast, communities which exist in a given state territory are identifiable beneficiaries of state obligations even if their spokesperson may be difficult to identify. Yet group rights as a separate distinct category still lack "full normative recognition in international law".[149]

One of the reasons for such a resistance rests in the concern that full recognition for a group right not only defends the group vis-à-vis the outside (externally) but could be used internally to subjugate the rights of individuals.[150] To preserve a culture in its traditional sense would then be used to maintain unequal hierarchies to the disadvantage of particular groups such as women or the disabled.[151] The resulting emphasis on the individual over the communal in turn carries another threat with it, namely that of marginalizing the role of the community in creating the necessary framework for the individual to enjoy his or her right.[152] Important questions to consider on the national or local level are thus: who speaks for the community? How are they selected? Is there a way to mitigate tensions between an individual and the community? How is the community involved in the protection of cultural heritage if the focus rests on the individual?

Resistance by some states to the form of collective rights desired by i.e. Indigenous groups and some African States[153] is also rooted in the fear that it would threaten both the 'nation state', as a socio-cultural entity, as well as its territorial integrity.[154] Such concerns were also visible in the drafting history of Art.27 UDHR and state support for certain forms of folklore.[155]

---

[148] Lixinski (2014), p. 211.

[149] Coombe and Turcotte (2012), p. 275.

[150] Thornberry (2008), p. 10.

[151] Shaheed (2012), p. 2.

[152] Lixinski (2014), p. 194.

[153] Blake (2014), p. 53.

[154] Stamatopoulou (2008), p. 8.

[155] Stamatopoulou (2008), p. 8.

As will become apparent in the sections below, internationally recognized actors have come to recognize the collective dimension of the cultural rights presented.[156] Blake argues that this acceptance is not one of rights for the collective but rather the recognition that the individual may have rights from which the group may benefit.[157] However, in the cultural context, individual and group interests are often represented as being in opposition to each other.[158] The violation of individual rights in the name of the collective could occur, were it not for limitations on the recognition of cultural rights, where this would otherwise lead to a violation of human rights. Cultural rights only protect those cultural practices which do not violate international human rights when exercised.

This also obliges states to take steps in advance to prevent such violations where necessary.[159] To identify those practices which would violate human rights if exercised in their traditional sense in turn also raises difficulties. On the one hand, it requires *inter alia* "a legal framework indicating principles on the basis of which cultural rights may be limited and an independent judiciary able to adopt an informed decision on the basis of such a legal framework".[160] On the other hand, such a decision raises difficult questions as to who has the legitimacy to judge cultural practices and whether this may exacerbate cultural tensions and concerns instead of increasing cross-cultural understanding. With regard to repatriation exercises, this limitation could translate into a conditional return. Where a state (institution) is willing to return an item in its possession, the repatriation agreement should make the return conditional upon the Indigenous agreement not to use it in ceremonies which contravene internationally proclaimed human rights standards—if this is at all a concern. A conditional return, however, may very well be contrary to the pursued goals, if the repatriation is embedded in reconciliation efforts, as it will emphasize the power imbalance.

In any event, the possibility of such a clash of rights should not lead to a complete disavowal of the collective dimension. Without the recognition of the collective nature of cultural rights, minorities and Indigenous groups will have a confined, subordinate role[161] to play and their continued existence will be under threat. They lack the backing of cultural policies that a dominant national culture enjoys. This, in turn, would negate the individual cultural rights of its members.[162]

---

[156] Shaheed (2010), p. 6, para 10 for example points out that ""the term 'cultural life' itself strongly suggests the collective", and article 27 of the Universal Declaration of Human Rights expressly refers to the cultural life of "the community", which today must be understood by its plural "communities".

[157] Blake (2014), pp. 53–54.

[158] For example in McGoldrick (2002), p. 448. He speaks of these interests as being counterpoised.

[159] Stamatopoulou (2008), p. 6.

[160] Shaheed (2010), pp. 13–14, para 36.

[161] Nimni (2008), p. 13.

[162] Blake (2014), p. 48.

Having accepted the communal dimension of cultural rights, one is then confronted with the question of whether or not a tradition or custom is essential enough to warrant protection.[163] Not every aspect of cultural life can be protected both for normative as well as practical concerns. However, given the importance of religious beliefs for a community, it can *prima facie* be assumed that they are essential enough to warrant protection and the consideration of cultural rights in this chapter. Of course, this may not always be the true; it will depend on the facts in a specific repatriation case.

2.3.2 *The Link Between Cultural Diversity, Cultural Heritage and Cultural Rights*

Cultural diversity plays a key role both in international cultural heritage law as well as in human rights law. In international cultural heritage law, the main motivation in the protection of cultural diversity is undoubtedly the hope that an appreciation for the diverse forms of cultural expressions and the different cultures in which they originate decreases intolerance.[164] In addition, a diversity of cultures guarantees a multitude of heritage expressions. These various forms of heritage in turn are valued for various reasons, including their emotional, political, spiritual or financial value. To guarantee cultural diversity thus also becomes a means for states to ensure and protect a continuous 'wealth' of heritage. Part of the value (and danger) of heritage for the state rests in its role as a source for the creation of individual and group (cultural) identity. This role of cultural heritage is also fundamental for cultural rights. To protect cultural diversity is to protect different cultural expressions and forms of heritage, to protect heritage and guarantee access to it in turn is to ensure Art.15(1)(a) ICESCR and Art.27 ICCPR (see below). It is therefore not surprising that the CESCR has recognized the link between cultural rights and cultural diversity by expressly linking measures "addressing minorities and indigenous peoples to the promotion of cultural diversity generally."[165] The protection of cultural diversity has thus become one of the concepts which links cultural heritage and human rights. Pineschi has described the strengthening/protective effect between cultural heritage and cultural diversity as 'mutual'.[166] She even goes so far as to state that "it is only

[163] Stamatopoulou (2007), pp. 112–115.

[164] As apparent in the UNESCO Constitution, see discussion Chap. 3, Sect. 3.2.1. See also Vrdoljak (2014), pp. 168–169. "Cultural diversity has been promoted as a common good for a range of reasons including its importance to peace and stability, progress and prosperity, and full realization of human rights and fundamental freedoms and a democratic society."

[165] Vrdoljak (2014), p. 155.

[166] Pineschi (2012), p. 29.

by means of the effective protection of cultural diversity that the preservation of cultural heritage can be achieved in its entirety and in its broadest meaning."[167]

The strength in recognizing the importance of a diversity of cultures, in human rights terms, lies in the implicit recognition of other (minority or Indigenous) cultures and their right to a 'peaceful co-existence' with dominant (state-sponsored/-supported) cultures. The keywords 'cultural diversity' thus not only connects to hopes of tolerance and peace but effectively requires the protection of different cultures. In one of her reports, former Special Rapporteur Farida Shaheed drew attention to the UNESCO declaration on cultural diversity discussed in Chap. 3 and argued that "the defence of cultural diversity is thus an ethical imperative, inseparable from respect for human dignity".[168]

An additional benefit of the protection of cultural diversity lies in the fact that the existence of different cultures within a society can offer all of its members a "wider range of cultural choices".[169] This is not to say that cultural diversity is universally embraced. One of the reasons states may hesitate to implement cultural rights and minority rights within their territory lies in the fear that strengthening minorities and non-dominant cultural groups may increase ethnic or cultural tensions. However, this need not necessarily be the case. Ana Filipa Vrdoljak observed that "[i]t is significant that Africa and Europe, two continents which have been riddled with violent ethnic and religious conflict in recent decades, have adopted multilateral framework conventions focusing on the promotion of cultural diversity and human rights, and heralding a reinterpretation of the protection of cultural heritage."[170]

It is this co-existence of minority cultures with other, more dominant, cultures that explains the link between cultural diversity, cultural rights and the repatriation debate. Equal respect[171] for all cultures requires respect for different cultural manifestations, limited only by the respect for human rights, if one accepts the premise of a universality of human rights or shared values.[172] This is not to be misunderstood as an interpretation of the concept of cultural diversity as mandating the return of cultural Indigenous objects, but it should be acknowledged that a society or state which espouses the value of cultural diversity would, if consistent in its policies/beliefs, support minority or Indigenous rights and instruments such as the UNDRIP and support minority/Indigenous control over its religious objects. To deny such

[167] Pineschi (2012), pp. 29–30.

[168] Shaheed (2010), pp. 10–11, paras 24–25.

[169] Shaheed (2010), p. 11, para 26.

[170] Vrdoljak (2014), p. 170.

[171] Critically McGoldrick (2002), p. 449. He observed "A feature of this revival interest in [the survival of indigenous] 'culture' is that it is taboo to suggest that any one(s) culture is better/ worse than anyone else's. In an international human rights context this is disingenuous, given that many international instruments (for example, on women, race, and children) are clearly aimed at certain 'cultural' practices that they aim to eliminate."

[172] Shaheed has highlighted the importance not to confuse cultural diversity with cultural relativism "which has the effect of raising fears and misunderstandings regarding the recognition and implementation of cultural rights." Shaheed (2010), p. 12, para 32.

control in the name of integrity or the preservation of an object which is of fundamental importance for the cultural integrity of an Indigenous culture is to risk the continuity or presence of another culture in the name of the values of the dominant culture.

2.3.3 *Right of Minority to Enjoy its Own Culture*

2.3.3.1 Art.27 ICCPR

> In those States in which ethnic, religious or linguistic minorities exist, **persons belonging to such minorities** shall not be denied the **right**, in community with the other members of their group**, to enjoy their own culture**, **to profess and practise their own religion**, or to use their own language.

2.3.3.2 Context

Already well before the twentieth century, international law provided for the protection of minorities, albeit only in individual cases. The focus then rested on the protection of religion minorities. Examples are evident in a treaty of 1536 between France and the Ottoman Empire covering French merchants who lived in the Ottoman territory, the 1648 Treaty of Osnabrück and the 1878 Treaty of Berlin in which the religious minorities living in the Ottoman Empire, Bulgaria, Montenegro and Serbia were recognized.[173] This focus on religious minorities continued in the system established by the League of Nations. It enabled religious minorities to bring a complaint if their rights, which had been granted through a treaty system administered by the League, had been violated.[174]

It was only after WWII that minority protection shifted away from the focus on religious minorities and became part of the human rights system. As a result of this shift and the (initial) liberalist[175] focus of the UN human rights discourse on CP rights, much of minority protection was initially focussed on non-discrimination and confined to an individual rights language.[176] In fact, no minority rights were included in the UDHR. In the drafting process of the declaration, the UN Secretariat's draft had included an extensive minority right, covering education, language rights, as well as a right to their own cultural and religious organizations. In the discussions surrounding the draft, a number of countries with considerable

[173] van der Schyff (2004), p. 270.

[174] van der Schyff (2004), p. 271.

[175] Lixinski (2014), p. 194.

[176] Vrdoljak (2014), p. 152.

immigration, notably Australia and Canada, feared that such a right would impede integration.[177]

By contrast, minority rights have been included in Art.27 ICCPR. Art.27 itself relates back to UNGA Resolution 217 C (III) (1948) on the Fate of Minorities.[178] The ethnic conflicts of the late twentieth century underlined the need to consider minority rights beyond the non-discrimination dimension.[179] This realization is reflected in the 1992 UN Minorities Declaration[180] and may have also contributed to the different reception of Indigenous activism on the international level in the 1990s and onwards. The UN Minority Declaration follows the focus of international human rights law and refers to minority rights as individual rights, while situating them in a communal/collective context.[181] This is mirrored in Art.27 ICCPR.

2.3.3.3 Content

Art.27 operates as *lex specialis* to Art.18 for Indigenous Peoples' freedom of religion and supplements Art.15(1)(a) ICESCR with a specific right to Indigenous culture. Art.27, if interpreted strictly on a textual basis, only creates negative obligations for states not to "deny members of minorities the right to enjoy their culture, to profess and practice their religion or to use their own religion." Its vague formulation can be traced to the prevailing views at the time.[182] This entails that much of the content of the minority right to culture questions must be solved by means of interpretation.

It is clear that Art.27 ICCPR grants minorities certain rights, which places it at the heart of the minority rights debate in international law with all the ensuing difficulties. It is only applicable to certain minorities, namely 'ethnic, religious or linguistic' minorities. In addition, it grants minorities a right to their culture, language and religion (in line with the categories of minorities accepted). Traditionally, states have been hesitant to accept minority rights for fear that cultural disintegration (and even desegregation) might ensue. The upheaval and crisis in Yugoslavia during the 1990s was a confirmation for many states of the danger inherent in clearly distinct ethnicities coexisting within one system (on this see section above).[183] However, a limited recognition of minority rights was inevitable in light of the human rights system created, in order to avoid forced the assimilation of minorities which would

---

[177] Charlesworth (2008), para 12.

[178] Vrdoljak (2008b), p. 59.

[179] Vrdoljak (2014), p. 160.

[180] Vrdoljak (2014), p. 160.

[181] In agreement Vrdoljak (2014), p. 162.

[182] Nowak (2005), p. 640. He also describes a comment which perhaps most illustrates the attitudes at the time of discussion in 1961: "The Australian representative even stated that aborigines were too primitive to be able to be considered a minority", referencing A/C.3/SR.1103 para 26.

[183] Vrdoljak (2008b), p. 59.

have negated the principle of non-discrimination.[184] It has also been argued that Art.27 indirectly recognizes a right to cultural identity. The formulation "to enjoy their own culture", according to Janet Blake, "implies the right to self-identification with the group concerned and to the right to consider oneself different from members of other cultural communities."[185] Art.27 ICCPR thus also appears to comprise the Indigenous right to develop and maintain their culture, including in its different cultural expressions meaning tangible and intangible cultural heritage. This raises the question whether such a right to cultural identity only applies to minorities and Indigenous Peoples or to every individual. The existence and scope of such a general right, however, is outside the scope of this research.[186]

The practice of HRCee (as can be seen in General Comment No. 23) has established that the provision includes positive duties, namely to ensure that the right is not denied or violated. This applies "not only against the acts of the State party itself, whether through its legislative, judicial or administrative authorities, but also against the acts of other persons within the State party".[187] The minority right to religion under Art.27 ICCPR therefore imposes multiple obligations on states: first, it imposes a negative obligation on all states to refrain from "conduct aimed at the destruction, damage, alteration or desecration of cultural objects or spaces that are of significant importance for the practice and enactment of a people's culture". Second, it imposes a positive duty to protect the rights of the minority against such interference by third parties. Manfred Nowak has argued that the more severe the interference, the stronger the duties incumbent on the state.[188]

It can thus be argued that Art.27 ICCPR imposes a positive duty to protect cultural objects that are of great importance to a given minority or Indigenous Peoples from destruction/damage by other, third-party actors in order to ensure the cultural survival of the group.[189] Vrdoljak highlights that UN Special Rapporteur Capotori already argued early-on in the history of the provision that Art.27 could be compared to economic and social rights of ICESCR, entailing a state's duty to act pro-actively in the place of its right holders.[190] However, while a state's duty to protect against undue interference seems widely accepted, the extent of a duty to fulfil under Art.27 ICCPR is still debated.[191] One reason for this are the practical difficulties of implementing such a duty in countries with a highly varied ethnic

[184] Vrdoljak (2008b), p. 59.

[185] Blake (2014), p. 52. The importance of self-identification has been highlighted by different international bodies, *inter alia* the Inter American Court in Xákmok Kásek Indigenous Community v Paraguay, Inter-Am. Ct. H.R. (ser. C.) No. 214, para 37 (24.08.2010).

[186] The reader is instead referred to Y. Donders who considered these and many more questions in great detail, see Donders (2002).

[187] HRCee, General Comment No.23, para.6.1.

[188] Nowak (2005), p. 662.

[189] Francioni (2008), p. 8.

[190] Vrdoljak (2008b), p. 62.

[191] Nowak (2005), pp. 664–666.

population.[192] However, it needs to be emphasized that the position of Indigenous Peoples under international law is not identical to the situation of other minorities, which is also reflected in the Committee's jurisprudence.[193] It has more readily highlighted positive obligations to fulfil the rights of Indigenous Peoples than other minorities.

Lastly, it must be observed that, while the Committee emphasized that the right can only be implemented if it is realized within a community, it still conceptualizes Art.27 as an 'individual right'.[194] Manfred Nowak has differentiated between the content of Art.27 which entails communal rights but the enforcement of the rights results in an individual right.[195] General Comment No.23 seems to contradict this interpretation. While the Committee emphasized the rights' dependency on the community culture, language or religion, it classified the rights protected as 'individual rights'.[196]

2.3.3.4 Limiting Art.27 ICCPR

As is the case with other human rights under the ICCPR and the ICESCR, there are two permissible ways for states to limit a right. First, a limitation may fall under the general limitation clauses included in a treaty. Second, a limitation clause can be included in the article itself (i.e. Art.18(3) ICCPR).

Concerning the first scenario, Art.4 ICCPR permits derogations from a number of human rights in public emergencies. This includes Art.27 ICCPR. The purpose of the provision is to protect these rights in situations of emergencies and only in those emergencies that "threaten the life of the nation". Moreover, as the Human Rights Committee has highlighted, there are certain elements of minority rights protection which must be respected even in times of emergency. This includes the protection from discrimination,[197] as well as religious freedom.[198] Given the highly specific and exceptional nature of permissible limitations under Art.4 to emergency situations,[199] the author cannot foresee a scenario where they may apply to Indigenous religious traditions and heritage within the repatriation debate.

The second scenario is somewhat difficult for Art.27 ICCPR to establish, since the article does not contain a clear limitation clause. Rather, the right "shall not be denied". The Human Rights Committee has given some guidance on what this may

[192] Nowak (2005), p. 666.

[193] Nowak (2005), p. 666.

[194] Åhrén (2008), p. 101.

[195] Nowak (2005), p. 657.

[196] HRCee, General Comment No.23, para 6.2.

[197] See also HRCee, General Comment No.18, para 2.

[198] HRCee, General Comment No.29 States of Emergency (Art.4) [2001] UN Doc CCPR/C/21/Rev.1/Add.11, para 13(c).

[199] For a clear and concise discussion of the conditions for and limits to permissible derogation measures, the interested reader is instead referred to Nowak (2005), pp. 93–107.

mean, but the guidance has been limited.[200] It is certain that its limitation cannot be evaluated *in abstracto,* but it has to be evaluated in its context.[201] This is understandable given the vast cultural differences among the minorities and Indigenous Peoples whose cultural practices are protected. However, this also means that only limitations which mirror the cases examined where a breach has been found can be said to be in breach of Art.27 without a doubt. This uncertainty makes it difficult to establish a clear test which can be applied to evaluate state measures taken in Canada and the United States.

For example, where is the line between a limitation and a denial? A denial is a measure whose impact is "so substantial that it does effectively deny" the right of the individual to enjoy his/her culture.[202] If the impact is limited and does not meet this threshold, however, it appears to be permissible. This would suggest that a great many limiting measures are permissible under Art.27. The HRCee has highlighted, however, that, even for limitations adopted by a state that affect or interfere with a right, their permissibility will depend on whether the affected individuals have been consulted.[203] This suggests that measures that deny or whose impact amounts to a denial are prohibited, whereas limitations whose impact is limited are permitted if these are taken after consultation with and participation of the affected minority community in the decision making. Any restriction must also be based on a reasonable and objective justification and be in accordance with other human rights.[204]

The relationship of Art.27 ICCPR to other rights is crucial. Art.27 ICCPR operates as an additional level of protection on top of the existing rights for minority groups and Indigenous Peoples. This leaves the perplexing situation that Art.27 ICCPR is meant to offer additional protection for minorities, but that the limitation clause, as currently interpreted, appears to permit a great number of limitations. On the surface, it appears to permit more limitations than i.e. Art.18(3), which narrows permissible state measures limiting the freedom to manifest considerably. This means that simply implying limitation clauses in Art.27 ICCPR that cover the individual rights it encompasses is not satisfactory (i.e. one similar to Art.18(3) for the minority right to religion).[205] In such a case, the clause would offer no additional protection for Indigenous religious practitioners who practise their religion. However, it is also not satisfactory to simply consider the standards enshrined in other articles, such as Art.18(3) ICCPR as inapplicable,[206] because then there is only a

[200] Notably no specific guidance on permissible limitations was included in General Comment No.23.

[201] HRCee, Kitok v Sweden, 197/1985 para 9.3.

[202] HRCee, Länsman et al. v Finland, 511/1992, para 9.5.

[203] HRCee, Mahuika, 547/1993.

[204] HRCee, Sandra Lovelace v. Canada, Communication No. R.6/24, U.N. Doc. Supp. No. 40 (A/36/40) at 166 (1981), para 16.

[205] In agreement, Nowak (2005), p. 666.

[206] Contrast Nowak (2005), p. 667. Nowak argues that Art.27 acts as *lex specialis* to the general freedom of Art.18 which means that the limitation clauses contained therein are not applicable to minorities. I do not disagree that Art.27 ICCPR acts as *lex specialis* but simply propose using the

very broad formulation "shall not be denied", floating about in a text cloud of uncertainty with limited guidance for either state parties or Indigenous religious practitioners.

Here the following method is used where an Indigenous practice is covered by multiple articles, notably Art.18 ICCPR and Art.27 ICCPR: any limitation has to **at the minimum fulfil** the limitation test under the connected right, i.e. religion, **and in addition** not amount to a denial of the contextualized right under Art.27 ICCPR. This context also includes other limiting measures whose combined impact may result in a denial.[207] In addition, historic treatment that continues to affect an individual's enjoyment of their own culture is also included in the context considered under Art.27 ICCPR.[208] This means that, in order to give some more concrete guidance to practitioners seeking to establish whether the right of Indigenous individuals to practise their religion is concerned, Art.18(3) is used in combination with Art.27 ICCPR. I do not pretend that this makes the article much more concrete than it currently is. However, it does provide a somewhat more structured approach and may thus help the person who has to decide what protection Art.27 ICCPR may offer in a given case.[209]

Lastly, I also want to highlight that this approach does not confuse the two rights with each other. Indigenous individuals have rights both under the general provisions and under Art.27 ICCPR, and the state may have to take measures to fulfil its obligations under both general provisions (i.e. Art.18 ICCPR) and Art.27 ICCPR. Considering the limitation clause of general provisions as subsumed in the clause "shall not be denied" in effect follows the position of the HRCee that the state incurs separate obligations under Art.27 ICCPR.[210]

2.3.3.5 Linking Art.27 to the Repatriation Debate

As was clarified in Chap. 1, Indigenous Peoples qualify as minorities for the purposes of Art.27 ICCPR. In its General Comment No. 23, the HRCee observed that Art.27 imposes specific obligations on the state parties, as the rights it encompasses are necessary for the survival and continued development of a minority, in

limitation clauses of the other overlapping freedoms as guidance to shed light on the minimum level of protection that Art.27 ICCPR entails.

207 HRCee, Länsman v Finland, 671/1995, para 10.7.

208 HRCee, Lubicon Lake Band v. Canada, Communication No. 167/1984 (26 March 1990), U.N. Doc. Supp. No. 40 (A/45/40) at 1 (1990), para 33.

209 This area would benefit from further research and clarification. Moreover, the author is aware that more guidance may come in the future making her approach obsolete.

210 The HRCee emphasized in General Comment 23, para 9 "Accordingly, the Committee observes that these rights must be protected as such and should not be confused with other personal rights conferred on one and all under the Covenant. States parties, therefore, have an obligation to ensure that the exercise of these rights is fully protected."

this case Indigenous communities.[211] In general, the HRCee seems to have adopted a comparatively broad understanding of culture with respect to Indigenous Peoples and Art.27 ICCPR[212] and the cultural practices which can be protected by this right. This author would argue that ceremonies which maintain the spiritual health of a community are essential to its survival as a cultural entity. The right to access and use sacred cultural heritage can thus be argued to be subsumed under Art.27 ICCPR. As a consequence, the repatriation of such objects is a measure to ensure both its survival and religious and cultural development. This is in line with the provision as interpreted by the Human Rights Committee.[213]

The reasoning underlying human rights law efforts to protect Indigenous or minority cultural heritage is similar to the motivation underlying minority rights in general. State heritage policies likely ensure the preservation of cultural heritage that is shared by the majority,[214] and minority heritage requires additional protection. Given the potential costs for preserving heritage, such policies will not necessarily have been consciously directed at undermining or risking minority or Indigenous cultural heritage; they may have simply targeted cultural heritage deemed to be of importance to the greatest number of citizens. It is the function of minority and Indigenous rights to counterbalance such (sub)conscious administrative decisions. In light of the centrality of religious practices to the community, an important element of Art. 27 ICCPR is the community's access to and use of religious objects or sites which are in public ownership or under public control. A denial of such access, unless motivated by the permitted restrictions laid down in the ICCPR, would constitute a violation of Art.27 ICCPR.

So far, the HRCee has not had the opportunity to consider the return of indigenous cultural objects. It has, however, highlighted the importance for Indigenous individuals of participating in their culture in a case that considered limitations on the right of an Indigenous woman to live with her community.[215] More importantly, in *Lubicon Lake*, the HRCee observed that "[h]istorical inequities, to which the State party refers, and certain more recent developments [which] threaten the way of life and culture of the Lubicon Lake Band, and constitute a violation of article 27 so long as they continue".[216] Here a parallel can be drawn to the prevention of religious practices, because of the absence of integral ceremonial regalia which are in public hands due to a historical wrong-doing. The difference rests in the fact the Lubicon Lake case involved a more recent expropriation claim with a historic background,

---

[211] HRCee, General Comment No.23, sec. 9.

[212] Human Rights Council, Report of the Special Rapporteur on the situation of human rights and fundamental freedoms of Indigenous Peoples, S. James Anaya, U.N. Doc. A/HRC/9/9 [11.08.2008], pp. 7–8.

[213] Hadjioannou (2005), p. 206.

[214] Blake (2014), p. 53.

[215] HRCee, Sandra Lovelace v. Canada, Communication No. R.6/24, U.N. Doc. Supp. No. 40 (A/36/40) at 166 (1981*)*, para 17.

[216] HRCee, Lubicon Lake Band v. Canada, Communication No. 167/1984 (26 March 1990), U.N. Doc. Supp. No. 40 (A/45/40) at 1 (1990), para 32.2, 33.

which is not the case for objects which were relocated in the past, and for which prescription or limitation periods barring the claim in national law have long passed. What remains important, however, is the fact that contemporary governmental measures which could possibly qualify as a violation (such as a denial of access to cultural property in public ownership) can serve as an entry point to consider past injustices.

In line with Art.2(3) ICCPR, states have the obligation to provide individuals with an effective remedy which is determined by a competent judicial, administrative or legislative body and to ensure that any remedies that are granted are enforced. The Committee has also highlighted the need to adapt remedies where necessary in the case of "the special vulnerability of certain categories of person".[217] Desmet has argued that, while this was directed explicitly only at children "this observation could be used to plead for remedies that are accessible to indigenous peoples, in the various meanings attributable to the word 'accessible', for instance, in regard to financial resources needed, procedural complexity, and geographical location."[218] Claire Charters, in her analysis of reparations granted to Indigenous Peoples by global institutions, compared the reparations offered by the Committee in the case of individual communications to its concluding observations and found the latter to be more progressive in terms of the reparations offered.[219] Repatriation exercises would thus seem to qualify as a state's measure to ensure Art.27 ICCPR and is a relative dimension, not mandated but also not prohibited. Access to integral religious objects and sites, by contrast, qualifies as necessary measures to protect Art.27 ICCPR and is further guaranteed by Art.18(1) ICCPR and Art.15(1)(a) ICESCR.

2.3.4 *Right to Participate in the Cultural Life*

2.3.4.1 Article 15 ICESCR

1. The States Parties to the present Covenant recognize the right of everyone:
   (a) To take part in cultural life;
   (b) To enjoy the benefits of scientific progress and its applications;
   (c) To benefit from the protection of the moral and material interests resulting from any scientific, literary or artistic production of which he is the author.
2. The steps to be taken by the States Parties to the present Covenant to achieve the full realization of this right shall include those necessary for the conservation, the development and the diffusion of science and culture.

---

[217] HRCee, General Comment 31, Nature of the General Legal Obligation on States Parties to the Covenant [2004] U.N. Doc. CCPR/C/21/Rev.1/Add.13.

[218] Desmet (2011), p. 325.

[219] Charters (2012), p. 177.

3. The States Parties to the present Covenant undertake to respect the freedom indispensable for scientific research and creative activity.
4. The States Parties to the present Covenant recognize the benefits to be derived from the encouragement and development of international contacts and co-operation in the scientific and cultural fields.

2.3.4.2 Context

Having considered the dominant minority right, it is now time to turn to what is arguably the cornerstone of international cultural rights, Art.15 ICESCR. The provision that is central to this research is the right to participate in the cultural life, an arguably "very general and vague assertion".[220] Yet, its fundamental importance can be seen in the fact that numerous binding and non-binding instruments expressly recognize similar rights: Art.27(1) UDHR, Art.5(e)(vi) CERD, Art.13 (c) CEDAW, Art.31 of the Convention on the Rights of the Child, Art.14(1)(a) AP to American Convention, the 1976 Recommendation on Participation by People at Large in Cultural Life and their contribution to it, the 2001 Universal Declaration on Cultural Diversity, a number of UNGA resolutions on Human Rights and Cultural Rights[221] and a series of resolutions of former UN Commission on Human Rights entitled 'Promotion of the Enjoyment of the Cultural Rights of Everyone and Respect for Different Cultural Identities'.[222]

As Pineschi has rightly pointed out, the travaux préparatoires are not very helpful in clarifying the exact scope of the provision[223] and the relationship of Art.15 ICESCR to cultural heritage preservation or repatriation must be distilled from other instruments. UNESCO prepared a preliminary draft version of the Article which featured, *inter alia*, the preservation and development of material cultural heritage as well as States 'guaranteeing the free cultural development of racial and linguisitic minorities'.[224] This was further developed and led to the recognition that an individual may belong to different communities and that the right to participate in the cultural life was in effect a right to participate in *each respective* community in which the individual was a member. However, the proposal to amend the wording of Article 15 accordingly was rejected by state parties.[225] In the final version of the provision, the community element disappeared altogether. Conceptually, the question as to how to interpret the right to take part in cultural life, cultural life being unspecified, remained. Since its inception, the CESCR has been interpreting, clarifying and concretizing the treaty standards, both in its concluding observations on

---

[220] Pineschi (2012), p. 31.

[221] For example, UNGA Resolution 55/91 (4.12.2000) and UNGA Resolution 63/174 (18.12.2009).

[222] For example, UNCHR Resolution 2003/26 (22.04.2003), UNCHR Resolution 2005/20 (14.04.2005). See also UN Human Rights Council Resolutions 6/1, 14/9.

[223] Pineschi (2012), p. 31.

[224] UN Doc E/ CN.4/541 18.04.1951 as reported in Donders (2007), p. 246.

[225] Vrdoljak (2014), p. 153.

state reports as well as its General Comments. Initially, Article 15 received relatively little attention; Yvonne Donders speaks of a 25-year time span.[226] Ana Filipa Vrdoljak observes that the initial post-1945 arguments, which relied on the strength of non-discrimination and the effective realization of human rights more generally to protect minorities, slowly gave way to the realization "that individual human rights alone could not operate as an effective shield against a State hostile to groups on its territory."[227] Gradually, Art.15 ICESCR has come to take the shape UNESCO proposed initially.[228] With their focus on specific treaty provisions, General Comment No.21 and the reports of the special rapporteur on cultural rights are the most helpful for present purposes.[229]

2.3.4.3 Normative Content and Justiciability

Having briefly considered the drafting history of Art.15(1)(a), as well as its institutional background, it is now time to consider first its general content before applying it to the Indigenous repatriation debate.

In light of the vagueness of the provision discussed above, it will not surprise the reader that different interpretations of the right to participate in the cultural life exist.[230] It would be possible to read a right to participate in a very narrow sense, as a right to take advantage of any existing and available cultural opportunities. This would require almost no state action apart from the protection of the individual from private parties interfering with his or her right. Such a limited interpretation would be in line with any position that views state action in the cultural sphere critically. Reasons for this position might even be based on opposite understandings of how a state should be structured. On the one hand, recognition of cultural pluralism entails the recognition of a multitude of cultural interests. The state may then be confronted with such a multitude of competing or even conflicting interests,[231] that to take decisions will become ever more challenging and signify a significant administrative burden. A consequence would be to either not invest in culture or to only invest in those activities or efforts which appeal to the greatest number of individuals. The former would risk a dearth of cultural activities in less affluent sectors; the latter would lead to the formation of what may be termed a dominant, 'mainstream', society. On the other hand, opponents of state intervention in private life might similarly reject state investment in the cultural sector, favouring instead a

[226] Donders (2008), p. 5.

[227] Vrdoljak (2014), p. 154.

[228] Vrdoljak (2014), p. 155.

[229] Before General Comment No.21, a report written by former Committee member Mr. Konaté from Senegal partially fulfilled this function, it resulted from the 1992 Day of General Discussion. See Pineschi (2012), p. 32.

[230] Blake (2014), p. 63.

[231] O'Keefe (2011), para 17.

privately-fuelled cultural sector which could mirror the first of the two outcomes just discussed. The distribution of wealth within a society would thereby be mirrored by an imbalance in the cultural activities offered, as well as their affordability and availability. This is not to say that governmental action will necessarily lead to ideal cultural conditions. Roger O'Keefe correctly summarized: "Perhaps, as Theodor Adorno argued, one is faced with the dilemma that 'culture suffers damage when it is planned and administered', but, when left to itself, 'threatens not only to lose its possibility of effect, but its very existence as well."[232]

General Comment No. 21 clarified a number of uncertainties, including the fact the right can be understood as a collective cultural right.[233] It also highlights that the right is made up of a minimum core combined with a duty of progressive realization. For example, it recognizes that a complete lack of governmental investment in cultural activities will ultimately lead to a denial of the cultural right in question.[234] The comment rejects a selective understanding of culture as high culture, instead adopting the broader ethnological understanding of culture "encompassing all manifestations of human existence".[235] As was observed in the definition of culture in Chap. 1, there are different approaches to defining culture, notably a traditional, narrow understanding and an anthropological understanding.

Prior to the adoption of General Comment 21, it was not necessarily clear which reading of culture was in line with Art.15 ICESCR. The clear advancement of an anthropological interpretation by the committee is a noteworthy advance in the effective protection of cultural rights.[236] The non-exhaustive list adopted by the committee covers oral and written literature, ways of life, religion or belief systems and much more.[237] It is thus safe to say that both specific Indigenous religious traditions can be classified as cultural life under Art.15(1)(a), as can the more general way of life of a respective Indigenous community. Furthermore, the committee clarifies the meaning of participation as a tripartite notion covering "(a) participation in, (b) access to, and (c) contribution to cultural life". In defining participation as including both access and contribution to cultural life, the committee recognizes that a number of basic conditions[238] have to be fulfilled for an individual or a community to exercise their right to participate in the cultural life:

1. *availability* of cultural goods and services,
2. *accessibility* meaning "effective and concrete opportunities for individuals and communities to enjoy culture fully",

---

[232] O'Keefe (2011), para 18.

[233] CESCR, General Comment No 21, para 9 "[T]he Committee recognizes that the term 'everyone' in the first line of article 15 may denote the individual or the collective."

[234] CESCR, General Comment No 21, recognition of need for positive action in para 6.

[235] CESCR, General Comment No 21, para 11.

[236] In agreement Pineschi (2012), pp. 34–35.

[237] CESCR, General Comment No 21, para 13.

[238] CESCR, General Comment No 21, para 16.

3. *acceptability* requires state measures to "be formulated and implemented in such a way as to be acceptable to the individuals and communities involved"
4. *adaptability* translates into the need for state measures to be flexible, relevant and respectful of cultural diversity
5. *appropriateness* requires the realization of other human rights "in a way that is pertinent and suitable to a given cultural modality or context"

These rights are exercised by the individual "alone, or in association with others or as a community". The availability of cultural goods and services also requires the state to take measures to protect cultural heritage resources. The Human Rights Council has emphasized that destruction or damage to cultural property can affect the enjoyment of the right to take part in the cultural life under Art.15 ICESCR.[239] However, it has to be kept in mind that the state obligations under Art.15(1)(a) ICESCR are subject to the state duty to take steps to progressively realize the treaty rights, enshrined under Art.2(1) ICESCR. Heritage conservation and measures protecting cultural goods and services require a state to have some resources that can be spent in this sector. This being said, the CESCR has emphasized that the state is still under a duty to take steps towards the ultimate goal of realizing the right.[240] Moreover, legislative steps may be indispensable in progressing towards this realization.[241] Not all of the measures discussed here are therefore immediate obligations, but they represent some of the steps that a state may have to take to realize the rights enshrined in Art.15(1)(a) ICESCR for Indigenous communities.

Access, as covered by Art.15 is not restricted to physical access and availability of cultural opportunities. It also covers broader access to knowledge and information on different cultures, both one's own and others. Access thus requires education, information and training,[242] which is different depending on the culture in which the individual is embedded. A cultural context can be both chosen or the result of outside influences, such as upbringing, immigration policies of the country of residence, forced relocation due to conflict etc. The possibility of a change in the culture(s) with which an individual identifies depends on education, access to information and other (civil and political) rights.[243] To fully guarantee cultural rights thus requires information and education to be provided on the different cultures. Indigenous individuals should thus have access to education both on their respective Indigenous culture as well as the mainstream culture. Access to not just one but different cultures and their heritage is a consideration which will reappear in Sect. 2.5.2 below. Art.15(1)(a) not only implies a right on the side of the individual to have access to his or heritage as well as the heritage of others, but also the right of other citizens of the respective country to have access to Indigenous heritage. The state accepted the

[239] UNHRC res. 6/1 27.09.2007 8th recital. Similarly, O'Keefe (2013), p. 90.
[240] CESCR, General Comment No 3, para 3.
[241] CESCR, General Comment No 3, para 9.
[242] CESCR, General Comment No 21, para 15(b).
[243] Pineschi (2012), p. 37.

obligation to protect both rights when ratifying the ICESCR. The right of others to have access to Indigenous cultural heritage is however mitigated by positive discrimination measures which take the non-dominant position of Indigenous Peoples into account. This has also been recognized in the reporting guidelines by asking states to create conditions which are favourable for Indigenous Peoples to preserve and develop their culture, traditions and customs.

If Indigenous individuals are denied access to their heritage, it could result in a violation of Art.15(1)(a) ICESCR. Denial of individual, private access by a cultural institution could, for example, be motivated by fear for the physical integrity of the object and the position that museums, academics or other cultural/educational institutions have a 'stronger' right to that heritage than Indigenous Peoples,[244] presumably because of their educational outlook or their broad societal constituency. The former rests on an evaluation of the respective interests of the institution and the Indigenous community. In most cases where such a balance of interests will have to be achieved (i.e. also in the case of presenting Indigenous objects to the public for better societal education), the result is likely to be a compromise of the various interests involved in the attempt to find the least invasive measure, the impact of which should not be disproportionate to the expected benefit. This is a difficult balancing exercise; its outcome is dependent on an underlying value frame which, consciously or not, ranks respective interests according to their (perceived) 'worth'. The latter cannot base itself solely on a simple calculation, such as the number of people who share one interest. This would be a violation of the very basis of the Indigenous and minority rights system. Denial of access may also constitute racial discrimination. As was highlighted in section 2.2.2 on non-discrimination, Art.5(e)(vi) ICERD requires states to guarantee equal rights to participation in cultural activities. Depending on the location and availability of their cultural heritage to Indigenous communities, access prohibitions in relation to Indigenous cultural heritage may constitute *de facto* discrimination depending on the circumstances in the individual case.

As highlighted above, according to the committee, participation includes 'contribution'. The difference between this element and participation in the narrower sense as covered above is not clear. According to the comment, "contribution to cultural life refers to the right of everyone to be involved in creating the spiritual, material, intellectual and emotional expressions of the community."[245] While this sentence highlights the creative aspects of participation, arguably, creating cultural expressions would still classify as participating. Whereas the access element truly takes an aspect into consideration which sets the framework for cultural participation, this distinction cannot be drawn as neatly for an individual's right to contribute to the cultural life of the community. The HRCee has phrased this as a right to be involved in the community's creation of different cultural expressions. The Committee reinforced this understanding by connecting it to "the right to take part in the development of the community to which a person belongs, and in the definition, elaboration and implementation of policies and decisions that have an impact on the

[244] Compare Battiste and Henderson (2000), p. 174.

[245] CESCR, General Comment No 21, para 15(c).

exercise of a person's cultural rights", highlighted in the UDCD and the Fribourg Declaration.[246] Some authors have also emphasized the distinction between the right to participate in a/multiple culture(s) and its prerequisite, the right to a/multiple culture(s) which would be realized under Art.15(2) ICESCR, namely through state efforts to diffuse, develop and conserve a culture.[247] This would juxtapose participation, on the one hand, with access and contribution, on the other.

Lastly, a brief word on the justiciability of the right to cultural participation is warranted. For rights to be effective, they need to be justiciable. Individuals need to be able to "claim and receive compensation if their rights have been violated".[248] Regardless the fact that the ICESCR does not contain an article worded similarly to Art.2(3) ICCPR, the CESCR has emphasized the need for justiciability for the sake of the enjoyment of ESC rights since its early days and General Comment No.3.[249] Criticism of the instrument has focussed primarily on two distinct concerns with regard to the justiciability of ESC rights. The first concerns the fact that obligations under the treaty are weakened by the progressive realization clause. Laura Pineschi argues that the obligation of progressive realization does not mean that no measures have to be taken or that they can be "deferred ad libitum".[250] Groni proposes that no justiciability problems exist if we recognize that the access rights implied in Art.15 are translated into a procedural right to "equal and fair rationing based on objective reasons and qualification, if there are insufficient capacities".[251] Second, some argue that the formulation of the provision is too vague to be justiciable.[252] This argument lost its force with the proliferation of material from international bodies and actors interpreting and clarifying Art. 15(1)(a).

2.3.4.4 Art.15(1)(a) and the Repatriation of Indigenous Religious Heritage

For Indigenous People and their religious practices the deepened understanding of Art.15(1)(a) means, first, Indigenous Peoples have the right to engage in their own cultural practices and to speak Indigenous languages. Second, they have the right to seek and develop Indigenous cultural knowledge and expressions. Third, for the individual and the community to be able to undertake these activities, they must have access to their culture and the cultures surrounding them. Where a way of life requires access to resources, a right to follow a way of life translates into access to resources and, even more important for present purposes, cultural goods. This access

[246] CESCR, General Comment No 21, para 15(c).

[247] McGoldrick (2002), p. 454.

[248] CESCR, General Comment No.21, para 54(a).

[249] Pineschi (2012).

[250] Pineschi (2012), p. 40.

[251] Groni (2008), p. 23.

[252] Pineschi (2012), p. 40.

may be limited, depending on the specific circumstances. This includes "land, water, biodiversity, language or specific institutions, and to benefit from the cultural heritage and the creation of other individuals and communities".[253] The relationship between this element of Art.15(1)(a) and Indigenous cultural objects which are located outside of the community, notably in the storage facilities or display areas of cultural or governmental institutions is clear: non-dominant groups need to access their cultural heritage.[254]

If cultural objects are necessary to live a certain way of life and these objects are owned by a state, the state may be obliged to make these objects accessible to Indigenous Peoples. Whether or not this is an actual obligation will depend on a number of case-specific considerations. First, would a refusal to grant access be in line with the restrictions permissible under the treaty?[255] Consider an item which is so important and singular that a denial of access would prevent a community from following its religious traditions. In this case, denial of access equals an effective denial of an integral part of the communal way of life. A state would be obliged to grant access to the object in its possession under Art.15(1)(a) ICESCR. Second, in how far would granting individuals access to the object threaten its integrity, thereby undermining the right of other individuals to benefit from the respective cultural heritage? Denial of access may also be problematic, not only under cultural rights provisions, but also under the provision of non-discrimination. If we realize that a state may violate this provision if it does not protect the right of an Indigenous community to have access to their heritage, it may also violate the right to non-discrimination. In light of this observation, depending on the justification provided, such a denial of the right to participate in the cultural life could be motivated differently: i.e. the fragility of the object (raising the question whether complete denial of access would in effect be proportionate to the pursued aim, which seems doubtful).

Alternatively, denial of access could be motivated by the argument that museums, academics or other cultural/educational institutions have a 'stronger' right to that heritage than Indigenous Peoples,[256] presumably because of their educational outlook or their broad societal constituency. The former rests on an evaluation of the respective interests of the institution and the Indigenous community. Questions which arise in this context would be whether increasing scientific knowledge is recognized as a legitimate aim in the given legal system (let us presume yes) and whether complete access of one party set off against the complete denial of the other would be proportional to achieve this aim. It seems safe to presume that this is not the case. In most cases with such a balance of interests (i.e. also in the case of presenting Indigenous objects to the public for better societal education), the result is likely to be a compromise of the various interests involved in the attempt to find the least

[253] CESCR, General Comment No 21, para 15(b).

[254] Chamberlain and Vrdoljak (2014), p. 555.

[255] See Sect. 2.3.4.5 on permissible limitations.

[256] Compare Battiste and Henderson (2000), p. 174.

invasive measure, with an impact on the rights which should not be disproportionate to the expected benefit. This is a difficult balancing exercise; its outcome is dependent on an underlying value frame which, consciously or not, ranks respective interests according to their (perceived) 'worth'. The latter cannot base itself solely on a simple calculation, such as the number of people which share one interest. This would be a violation of the very basis of the Indigenous and minority rights system.

Apart from this, if the object is not in state possession, state obligations are limited under Art.15(1)(a) ICESCR. At best, a state could consider a mediating role or provide financial assistance if the private institution (i.e. a museum) would be willing to grant access to or return an object. Conversely, museums and other cultural institutions could be asked not to display religious cultural objects and "other elements of indigenous peoples' heritage ... except in a manner deemed appropriate by the peoples concerned."[257] This would be in line with the protection afforded to Indigenous Peoples under Art.15(1)(a) and in line with the State's duty to protect Indigenous Peoples' rights under Art.27 ICCPR, Art.18(1) ICCPR and Art.15(1)(a). In addition, where a community and a cultural institution have come to an agreement on access restrictions or preservation guidelines, a state should respect such agreements irrespective of the economic or historic 'worth' or the heritage in question. The Committee has emphasized that Indigenous Peoples "have the right to act collectively to ensure respect for their right to maintain, control [and] protect ... their cultural heritage".[258] This would include repatriation negotiations with museums. State measures to support such agreements or to require them for public museums can be seen as measures taken to fulfil Art.27 ICCPR and Art.15 (1)(a) ICESCR.

The broader interpretation of Art.15(1)(a), analysed above, can also be identified in some of the reporting guidelines of the CESCR.[259] With regard to Art.15, the guidelines require states to 'provide information on the institutional infrastructure' or 'indicate' any measures taken. The substantive variety of information covered by the guidelines illustrates the adaptability of the provision with regard to available (financial, technical, temporal) resources, as well as different cultural or societal demands. A state is thus requested to *inter alia*:

- [p]rovide information on the institutional infrastructure to promote popular participation in, and access to, cultural life, especially at the community level, including in rural and deprived urban areas... indicate the measures taken to ensure that access to ... cultural activities is affordable for all segments of the population;[260]

[257] 1993 Daes Draft Guidelines, U.N. Doc.E/CN.4/Sub.2/1995/26, annex, para 23, cited by Chamberlain and Vrdoljak (2014), p. 564.

[258] CESCR, General Comment No 21, para 37.

[259] Included in the regularly updated compilations of reporting standards and guidelines assembled by the Secretary General.

[260] HRI/GEN/2/Rev.6 Compilation of Guidelines on the form and content of reports to be submitted by States Parties to the International Human Rights Treaties [3.06.2009], p.41, para 67 chapeau and 67 (a).

- to *enhance access to the cultural heritage of mankind,* including through new information technologies such as the Internet;[261]
- indicate the measures taken to protect cultural diversity, promote awareness of the cultural heritage of ... indigenous communities, and *create favourable conditions for them to preserve, develop, express and disseminate their identity*, history, *culture,* language, *traditions* and customs.[262]
- [t]o ensure the protection of the *moral* and material *interests of indigenous peoples relating to their cultural heritage* and traditional knowledge;[263]
- [i]ndicate the measures taken for the conservation, development and diffusion of ... culture.[264]

These guidelines not only emphasize the comparatively broader interpretation of Art.15(1)(a) that is favoured by the Committee, but they also help in contextualizing the provision regarding Indigenous Peoples and their cultural heritage. First, access to heritage must be affordable and heritage must be available to all parts of society. Thus, situating the vast majority of Indigenous cultural objects in urban areas, within a country where the respective infrastructure is missing or even where a significant part of the Indigenous population lives in rural or remote areas, could serve as an indicator that their right to participate in the cultural life was violated. Similarly, it highlights the need for a state to grant individuals access to the cultural heritage of others, which GC No. 21 includes but it is not limited to the heritage of mankind. For Indigenous Peoples, this means that not only should their culture be preserved and promoted but that their access to what Thornberry describes as the "outer world" must be ensured "on a non-discriminatory basis."[265] This aspect of Art.15(1)(a) is also reflected in the instruments of ICHL which have taken human rights into account, notably Art.2(a) of the 1976 UNESCO Recommendation, which defines access to culture further as "the concrete opportunities available to everyone, in particular through the creation of the appropriate socio-economic conditions, for freely obtaining information, training, knowledge and understanding, and for enjoying cultural values and cultural property".[266]

The United States has not ratified the ICESCR. However, with regard to indigenous peoples and repatriation Art.27 ICCPR can be argued to operate as lex specialis and contains all that is relevant to develop the necessary standards in this chapter. Art.15(1)(a) ICESCR and its interpretation have aided the elaboration of cultural rights more general, and Indigenous cultural rights in particular. Yet, for the purposes of repatriation of sacred cultural heritage, the protection of the minority right to culture under Art.27 ICCPR encompasses the right of access and use of such heritage as well as the right to develop and maintain minority culture. It is therefore a sufficient legal basis upon which to judge U.S. legislation.

---

261 Ibid., para 67 (b) emphasis added.

262 Ibid., para 68 emphasis added.

263 Ibid., para 71(c) emphasis added.

264 Ibid, para 73.

265 Thornberry (2008), p. 7.

266 In agreement Vrdoljak (2014), p. 156.

This section has laid out the applicability of the provision to Indigenous Peoples and given examples of specific measures which Indigenous Peoples could expect their state to take. The next section will consider which conditions state measures that limit the right have to fulfil under Art.15(1)(a) ICESCR.

2.3.4.5 Limitations Imposed on Art.15 and Limitations Inherent in Considering Cultural Heritage Under Art.15

The rights explored above may be limited by a state, but only to the extent permitted within the treaty and measures may not be designed to destroy the protected rights.[267] Art.4 ICESCR provides a general limitation clause for the rights included in the treaty: they must be "determined by law", "compatible with the nature of these rights", and "solely for the purpose of promoting the general welfare in a democratic society." A measure should also be in line with the proportionality principle. Thus, the aim pursued by the imposed restriction must be legitimate and the measure adopted has to be the least restrictive measure available.[268]

When debating cultural heritage under this article, it has to be kept in mind that such heritage holds different types of value, which may require it to be approached in very different ways. It has monetary, educational as well as social value. The monetary dimension of an object may require its protection and conservation, the educational value may affect its display in Western understanding and use in Indigenous understanding, while its social value is more difficult to define. It relates to our perception of heritage as evidence of past or current ways of life and, as such, is a building block in the construction of our identity. Its use by Indigenous groups (subject to prior repatriation) is a way in which to assert control over the construction of the group's identity vis-à-vis the dominant mainstream culture. The majority, in contrast, values such cultural heritage as evidence of a history it perceives as shared with the Indigenous population; to participate in cultural life for the majority entails to be able to experience evidence of its past and thereby emphasize its present position within society.[269]

However, cultural heritage is not merely a product of cultural life but a prerequisite thereof, as it enables individuals and communities to experience, affirm and create culture.[270] The complexity of interaction between the concept of cultural heritage and Art.15 ICESCR renders any interpretative deductions for the sake of repatriation of Indigenous objects difficult. It asks us in how far the objects that are needed by Indigenous communities to both maintain and affirm their culture are also claimed by the majority in society as part of a historical affirmation of a cultural identity constructed over time. As will also become apparent in the following

[267] Art.5(1) ICESCR.

[268] CESCR, General Comment No.21, para 19.

[269] Harding (1999), pp. 329–331.

[270] Harding (1999), p. 340.

sections, this is the fundamental balancing exercise to be undertaken at the national level, where the value attached to the different positions may vary from country to country.

2.4 Indigenous Rights

Chris Tennant has described the role of Indigenous Peoples in the development of Indigenous rights as being fundamentally characterized by resistance.[271] More specifically by resistance he refers to the two common misconceptions of Indigenous Peoples by the non-Indigenous other: first as the 'ignoble primitive' who, due to said 'primitiveness' is refused the right of self-determination and must assimilate;[272] and second, as the 'noble primitive' who is guardian of traditional knowledge relating to medicine and the environment and thus constitutes an exception in the modern age and requires protection.[273] In reaction to this characterization and the oppression suffered, according to Tennant, Indigenous Peoples have resisted both substantively and procedurally.[274] The former by insisting on their right to self-determination; the latter by claiming greater participation, nationally and internationally. Greater participation of Indigenous Peoples currently takes different forms. An increasing number of Indigenous NGOS have been awarded NGO status with ECOSOC, such as the World Council of Indigenous Peoples, the International Indian Treaty Council, Survival International etc.[275] Moreover, international instruments such as the Operational Guidelines to the WHC, the 2003 ICH (Art.2(3), Art.15), the Operational Guidelines to the 2005 CDCE and Art.41 UNDRIP, all provide for the participation of Indigenous Peoples to various degrees. Substantively, there has been a shift from a paternalistic approach to Indigenous Peoples and their rights to the recognition of Indigenous Peoples as subjects of international law. This shift is reflected in the international legal instruments that proclaim Indigenous rights, from their problematic beginnings in the ILO Convention 107 to the manifold rights contained in UNDRIP.

---

[271] Tennant (1994), p. 4.

[272] Tennant (1994), pp. 7–11.

[273] Tennant (1994), p. 12.

[274] Tennant (1994), pp. 38–39.

[275] Scovazzi and Nafziger (2007), pp. 186–187.

2.4.1 *ILO Treaties*

2.4.1.1 ILO Convention 107 and the Road to Its Replacement

On the international plane, the ILO became "by far the first intergovernmental organization to address indigenous rights", transforming it into the "lead agency" in this area up to the 1970s.[276] It adopted the first convention directly applicable to Indigenous People, Convention No. 107. In the spirit of its time, the generally shared belief was that distinctly Indigenous traditions and customs would soon be extinct.[277] Accordingly, the convention takes a strongly assimilative approach.[278] Special Rapporteur Anaya observed that "although it is somewhat a reflection of the paternalistic and assimilation-oriented assumptions of the time, the protective thrust of the Convention nevertheless contributed to signalling the need for international attention and cooperation with regard to indigenous peoples."[279]

The changing approach within international organizations towards Indigenous Peoples in the 1960s and 1970s[280] undermined Convention No. 107's regulatory thrust towards assimilation and the call for a revision by Indigenous Peoples[281] led to a decision by the ILO to redraft Convention 107 in the mid-1980s.[282] In the words of the ILO "[a]s [is] well known, the main objective of the revision of the Indigenous and Tribal Populations Convention, 1957 (No. 107) through the adoption of Convention No. 169, was to overcome the assimilationist approach embodied in the 1957 Convention."[283]

Convention No. 107 has been replaced by Convention No. 169 (Convention concerning Indigenous and Tribal Peoples in Independent Countries).[284] It is noteworthy that, somewhat at odds with the participatory approach included in the treaty text, the involvement of Indigenous groups in the drafting process was limited.[285] The core provisions of Convention No. 169 focus on the protection of traditions and customs of both Indigenous and tribal people.[286] Both Conventions go far beyond the traditional labour law focus of the ILO, featuring general participation in decision

---

[276] Swepston (2005), p. 54.

[277] Swepston (2005), p. 55.

[278] Donders (2002), p. 209.

[279] Human Rights Council, Report of the Special Rapporteur on the situation of human rights and fundamental freedoms of Indigenous Peoples, S. James Anaya, U.N. Doc. A/HRC/9/9 [11.08.2008], p. 11.

[280] See this chapter, Sect. 2.1.3.

[281] Yupsanis (2010), p. 435.

[282] Human Rights Council, Report of the Special Rapporteur on the situation of human rights and fundamental freedoms of Indigenous Peoples, S. James Anaya, U.N. Doc. A/HRC/9/9, [11.08.2008], p. 11.

[283] International Labour Organization (2008), p. 3.

[284] Except for a number of countries that have not ratified ILO Convention Nr.169.

[285] Yupsanis (2010), p. 444.

[286] ILO Convention No. 169 see i.e. Art.5, Art.7 and Art.8(1).

making as well resource rights and respect of Indigenous customary law.[287] Desmet has described it as the "the most comprehensive binding standard in international human rights law on the rights of indigenous peoples".[288] ILO Convention No. 169 contains economic, social and cultural rights. According to the ILO, the provisions of the Convention No. 169 "as a whole are thus aiming at protecting indigenous peoples and their specific cultural identity."[289]

2.4.1.2 Content of Convention No. 169

The ILO Convention No. 169 focusses on Indigenous and tribal peoples. This distinction only exists within the convention, and generally both groups are captured by the way in which the term 'indigenous peoples' is used within the UN system.[290] The most important part of the Convention, for the present purposes, is Section I on general policy, notably articles 2, 3, 4, 5, 7 and 8. Art.2(1) obliges governments to develop a strategy to take action in collaboration with the relevant Indigenous populations 'and to guarantee respect for their integrity'. This seems to be the precursor to the focus of Indigenous rights on participation that has developed in international law since then. Art.2(2) specifies the action to be taken, including in subparagraph (b) by "promoting the full realisation of the social, economic and cultural rights of these peoples with respect for their social and cultural identity, their customs and traditions and their institutions". This provision, while obliging state parties to adopt a strategy, leaves the specific ways in which cultural rights are to protected open. The wording "full realisation" is in line with the progressive realization duties under the ICESCR. To "guarantee respect for [indigenous cultural] integrity" includes respect for the indigenous right to conduct religious ceremonies with the objects necessary to do so. This seems to be reinforced by the emphasis on religious and spiritual values in Art.5(a) and the need to respect the "integrity of the values, practices and institutions of these peoples" when the Convention is applied (Art.5(b) ILO 169). Since the obligation to take a measure is linked to the need to 'promote' rights, however, and, given the vagueness of the term 'integrity', no Indigenous rights relevant to this study other than participation can be derived from Art.2. Hadjiouannou reads Art. 2 as obliging states to "provide special protections for the cultural identity of indigenous peoples" but does not go on to concretize this.[291]

---

[287] Swepston (2005), p. 57.

[288] Desmet (2011), p. 318.

[289] International Labour Organization (2008), p. 3.

[290] Lenzerini and Scott (2012), pp. 64–65.

[291] Hadjioannou (2005), p. 215.

Apart from its link to Art.2, Art.5 is interesting in the way it considers the cultural dimension that underlies all Indigenous rights.[292] As this section operates in conjunction with the specific provisions of the convention, it is of little practical relevance to repatriation claims, but it is helpful to Indigenous People if it is combined with the provisions in the sections on land or education and communication. If combined with the provisions on administration, it might even confirm that "indigenous peoples themselves need to be closely involved in the decision-making process on measures to protect their cultural identity and cultural values".[293] As far as the scope of application is concerned, the convention has been ratified by a very small number of states. Due to the procedural aspects of the ILO system, the adoption of Convention No. 169 entails that Convention No. 107 is closed for further ratification, meaning that Convention No. 107 is only applicable to those states which ratified No.107 but not No. 169. Neither of the countries selected for this study have ratified either of the two Conventions.

Art.3 and Art. 4 are also worthy of note in the discussion of Indigenous (cultural) human rights. Article 3 reaffirms the applicability of human rights to Indigenous Peoples, linking the ILO Convention to existing human rights treaties. Art.4(1) ILO 169 creates the possibility for states to adopt "special measures" to "safeguard . . . the cultures . . . of the peoples concerned". Repatriation of sacred objects as well as special access and use agreements would qualify as measures that safeguard indigenous cultures because of the importance of religious practices to cultural identity. Art.4(2)[294] addressed the fear that safeguarding a culture could be used by a state to force Indigenous Peoples to maintain a specific cultural form.[295] In its guidance material for Indigenous Peoples, the ILO highlights that special measures "are of particular importance" for a state's duty to respect/protect/fulfil under human rights law.[296] The ILO seems to hold the view that "positive measures may be necessary on a continuing basis, e.g. measures to protect indigenous cultures" and that this would be *prima facie* in line with Art.27 ICCPR if the conditions listed by the HRC in its General Comment No.23 (1994) are fulfilled.[297] Their form is not further specified.

Ahmed, Aylwin and Coombe seem to suggest that safeguarding Indigenous institutions could mean the repatriation of Indigenous objects from private ownership into Indigenous hands, possibly against the will of the property holder, due to the centrality/importance of the object to the community. In their words "[i]f the descendants of the original holders of these properties have neither been assimilated

---

[292] "[I]n applying the provisions of this Convention: (a) the social, cultural, religious and spiritual values and practices of these peoples shall be recognized and protected".

[293] Donders (2002), p. 211.

[294] Art.4(2) ILO 169: Such special measures shall not be contrary to the freely expressed wishes of the peoples concerned.

[295] Similar concerns also arose in the drafting of the UNESCO Convention on intangible cultural heritage, noticeably the fear of fossilization of heritage practices.

[296] International Labour Office (2009) Indigenous and tribal peoples' rights in practice: a guide to ILO Convention No. 169 Geneva, ILO, at 35.

[297] Ibid.

nor extinguished, their human rights to revitalize their traditional social, legal, and spiritual orders should trump the mere private property rights of those who came to acquire them."[298] If this is to be understood as a state being obliged to encourage or foster voluntary repatriation, then it would not be controversial. After all, voluntary repatriations between Indigenous Peoples and private owners will be protected at the national level by contractual freedoms in most cases and, where they might be hindered by state interests in the particular objects, this could even classify as a violation of Art.27 ICCPR. If it is to mean that a state is *required* to oblige a private individual to return an object (as 'trumping' could very well be read) this would be a rather adventurous interpretation of Art.4. This would be a severe interference in the respective individual's rights, not only to property but also to private life and cultural rights. Furthermore, this would classify as governmental expropriation, which is subject to severe restrictions in many legal systems.

Next to articles 4 and 5, the organization has also highlighted the connection of the right to participate in the cultural life in the ICESCR to Art.7 and Art.8.[299] Art.7 (1) gives Indigenous Peoples the right "to decide their own priorities for the process of development as it affects their lives, beliefs, institutions and spiritual well-being . . . **and to exercise control, to the extent possible**, over their own economic, social and **cultural development**."[300] Art.8 requires the state to have "due regard" for Indigenous customs or customary law (Art.8(1)) and highlights that Indigenous Peoples "have the right to retain their own customs and institutions, where these are not incompatible with fundamental rights defined by the national legal system and with internationally recognized human rights" (Art.8(2)). Both of these articles are important from a procedural point of view. The importance of an object, its status within a community and many more aspects which may be elements in a national repatriation law will need to be established according to the procedural rules established in the framework. Articles 7 and 8 suggest that the procedure for determining such factors should be in line with Indigenous customs and customary law as far as this is compatible with international human rights law.

While the convention does not include any specific provisions in relation to repatriation or cultural objects, it is thus useful for the present debate. First the evolution of ILO Convention No. 107 to 169 and the growing number of bodies and institutions on the international level which work in the area of Indigenous rights suggest a shift in international legal theory towards more respect for Indigenous traditions and cultures. Second, the Convention's protection of cultural identity and the need to respect Indigenous customary laws and cultural practices in collaboration with Indigenous Peoples paved the way for the adoption of UNDRIP. Third, the fact that ILO Convention No. 169 is currently only ratified by few countries would suggest that, while there is a shift and a growing recognition of Indigenous rights this

[298] Ahmed et al. (2008), p. 322.

[299] International Labour Organization (2008), pp. 3–4.

[300] It also establishes a participation right for national or regional policies and plans which may affect them directly. Emphasis added by the author.

is limited to the support of what states perceive as soft obligations (like the UNDRIP—which in reality is not purely an instrument of soft law, as explained above). The ratification of a binding convention seems to be a step too far for many states. Special Rapporteur Anaya has evaluated ILO Convention No. 169 very positively, but even this evaluation was linked to the normative effect of the instrument as "a powerful catalyst for the consolidation at the international level of the common normative understanding regarding the rights of indigenous peoples".[301]

2.4.2 *UNDRIP and Substantive Indigenous Rights*

2.4.2.1 UNDRIP: Legislative Context and Status Under International Law

The last two decades have seen a proliferation of Indigenous rights instruments. In addition, the number of international actors whose scope encompasses Indigenous concerns has grown considerably. The previous section examined the two forerunners in the field drafted by the ILO. This section focusses on the main international law instrument on Indigenous rights, the United Nations Declaration on the Rights of Indigenous Peoples [UNDRIP].[302] Its scope is universal; it applies to Indigenous and tribal peoples across the globe.

The adoption of the UNDRIP reflects the shift in international law away from a strictly liberalist approach. This classic approach highlighted individual rights to the exclusion of rights of collectives. Åhrén traces the evolution of international law from the UDHR, which was remarkable in its lack of provisions on the rights of collectives, to early regional treaties, to Common Art.1 ICCPR/ICESCR, which included a reference to self-determination yet was emphatically understood as working on the basis of an assimilation approach not covering Indigenous Peoples.[303] The UNDRIP constituted the next step in the general trend of international law towards the recognition of substantive minority rights. It was made possible by persistent and decades-long of Indigenous activism. The Declaration's preamble establishes it as an instrument which seeks to remedy the effects of historic injustices such as colonization and dispossession.[304] The UNDRIP is thus "packed with

---

[301] Human Rights Council, Report of the Special Rapporteur on the situation of human rights and fundamental freedoms of Indigenous Peoples, S. James Anaya, U.N. Doc. A/HRC/9/9 [11.08.2008], p. 11.

[302] UN GA, United Nations Declaration on the Rights of Indigenous Peoples, U.N. Doc A/RES/61/295 (2.10.2007).

[303] Åhrén (2008), pp. 98–114.

[304] Human Rights Council, Report of the Special Rapporteur on the situation of human rights and fundamental freedoms of Indigenous Peoples, S. James Anaya, U.N. Doc. A/HRC/9/9 [11.08.2008], p. 12 citing recital 6.

provisions that cannot be understood in any other manner than to proclaim cultural rights of indigenous peoples."[305] The drafting process of the UNDRIP, as is frequently reported in the literature, was a long and unique one. The Working Group on Indigenous Populations, established in May 1982, began with the drafting process of the declaration in 1985. In 1993, the Working Group adopted a final version of the Draft and forwarded it to the Sub-Commission which accepted the text without amendment or vote in 1994 and forwarded it to the Commission for adoption.[306] The Commission in turn called for the first meeting to discuss the Draft Declaration in 1995. It was finally adopted in 2007 in the General Assembly with 143 states voting in favour, 11 states abstaining and 4 states voting against (including the countries examined in this study).[307] In the meantime, all four countries have issued statements of support.

The process was a unique one due to the simple fact that the first drafts at the Working Group level were devised in close co-operation with numerous Indigenous representatives.[308] The fact that negotiations also took 25 years has been ascribed to different reasons. Pineschi has observed that the two main reasons were the reluctance of states to recognize an Indigenous right of self-determination, fearing that it would threaten their territorial integrity and concerns about the societal impact of recognizing substantive rights of cultural minorities.[309] The sheer diversity of the actors involved in the multilateral negotiation process also contributed to the duration of the procedure. Yet, this diversity of individuals involved in the negotiation "was central to the emergence, internationally, of a common body of opinion on the rights of indigenous peoples."[310] Originally having a soft-law nature, notable scholars have since argued that some of its provisions have either attained a binding character or are binding because the UNDRIP provision is merely a contextualization of existing treaty obligations. In addition, it also includes aspirational provisions.

A former ILA Committee on the Rights of Indigenous Peoples examined the UNDRIP and observed that a number of elements of the declaration were already part of international customary law and thus are binding.[311] According to the ILA, Indigenous Peoples have five distinct rights rooted in international customary law, even if these may not be exactly congruent with the specific wording adopted in the

[305] Åhrén (2008), p. 114.

[306] Donders (2002), p. 216.

[307] Human Rights Council, Report of the Special Rapporteur on the situation of human rights and fundamental freedoms of Indigenous Peoples, S. James Anaya, U.N. Doc. A/HRC/9/9 [11.08.2008], at 12.

[308] Donders (2002), p. 215.

[309] Pineschi (2012), p. 38.

[310] Human Rights Council, Report of the Special Rapporteur on the situation of human rights and fundamental freedoms of Indigenous Peoples, S. James Anaya, U.N. Doc. A/HRC/9/9, [11.08.2008], at para 34.

[311] ILA, The Hague Conference Report – Committee on the Rights of Indigenous Peoples (2010), p. 43.

UNDRIP. These rights are thus binding on all states regardless of the treaties which they ratified and may even include dependent rights which are a corollary to one of the rights:

- The right to self-determination either in the form of autonomy or self-government.[312] The exact scope is still debated by some, but a right to self-determination which does not threaten the territorial integrity of a state seems to be widely accepted.[313]
- The right to their cultural identity. This is both an obligation for the state to recognize Indigenous identity, a prohibition of ethnocide and a right of indigenous peoples to preserve their cultural identity. To guarantee this a state needs to ensure that "all the prerogatives that are essential to preserve the cultural identity of indigenous peoples *according to their own perspective* must be preserved, including ... the right to profess and manifest their religion in community with the other members of the group, the right to pursue their traditional medicines and burial traditions."[314]
- The right of Indigenous Peoples to their traditional lands and natural resources.[315]
- The right to reparation and redress for the wrongs suffered. According to the Committee where a right of customary law nature was breached the right to reparation is also part of customary international law. There is no obligation on the state to opt for a particular form of reparation but it "must be in any case *adequate* and *effective*, *i.e.* capable to remove – to the maximum extent possible – the effects of the wrong *as they are perceived by the communities concerned*."[316]
- Lastly, states are under an obligation to honour and fully implement "in a manner respecting the spirit and intent of the understanding of the Indigenous negotiators as well as the living nature of the solemn undertakings made by all parties" any agreement with Indigenous Peoples.[317]

As was explained in Sect. 2.1.2, this chapter addresses the declaration as containing provisions that reflect binding provisions contained elsewhere in international law. In particular, the provisions of relevance here (Articles 11, 12 and 31) are understood to contextualize binding treaty provisions. To consider them as part of a customary law right to Indigenous cultural identity would appear to stretch the envelope too far. The frequent violations which occur in relation to Indigenous cultural rights, in particular with regard to sacred sites, their lack of involvement in

[312] ILA, The Hague Conference Report – Committee on the Rights of Indigenous Peoples (2010), p. 16.

[313] See Sect. 2.2.1 above.

[314] ILA, The Hague Conference Report – Committee on the Rights of Indigenous Peoples (2010), p. 51. Emphasis in the original.

[315] Ibid. There are number of facets of this right including the right to restitution or reparation in case of dispossession which can however not simply be transposed to the repatriation of Indigenous cultural objects, the interested reader should consult Ibid, at 16 following.

[316] Ibid, p. 52. Emphasis in the original.

[317] Ibid, pp. 51–52.

the management and protection of cultural heritage in national policies, even at the international level under the World Heritage scheme, suggests that there is not sufficient state practice to support such a view.

2.4.2.2 Specific UNDRIP Provisions

The declaration puts human rights into the context of the circumstances of indigenous peoples in a comprehensive manner.[318] Of the operative articles, 15 articles concern matters of "consultation, participation and partnership".[319] If one adopts a broad understanding of cultural rights as including those human rights "that protect and promote the cultural identity of individuals and their communities", 17 articles concern Indigenous cultural rights.[320] This highlights the centrality of culture in Indigenous rights, at least in their conceptualization through international law. As Vrdoljak observes, Articles 11 to 13 are an application of the rights as catalogued in Art.27 ICCPR to the situation of Indigenous Peoples.[321] Not all of the cultural rights provisions relate to the repatriation debate. Here, the right to self-determination, the right to practise and revitalize cultural traditions, the right to religious traditions, which includes the right of access to and use of ceremonial objects, and the right to cultural heritage are of particular relevance.

2.4.2.2.1 Right to Self-Determination

Arts.3 and 4 UNDRIP provide Indigenous Peoples with the right to self-determination. Furthermore, the ILA Committee on the Right of Indigenous Peoples observed that this right achieved customary law status (see III.2.1). However, self-government or autonomy by Indigenous Peoples only has customary law status when it does not threaten the "territorial integrity or political unity of States".[322] Indigenous self-determination includes the right of Indigenous People to decide in favour (or against) participation in the wider societal structures.[323] This can also be seen in Art.5 UNDRIP. In a two-pronged approach, it affirms the Indigenous right of participation and reinforces the right to pursue economic, social and cultural development, which forms the core of Indigenous self-determination, expressed in Art.3

[318] It features a lengthy preamble of 24 paragraphs and 46 articles.

[319] UNPFII, Indigenous peoples: development with culture and identity in the light of the UNDRIP, A reflection paper of the Inter-Agency Support Group on Indigenous Issues, U.N. Doc. E/C.19/2010/17 [18.02.1010], p. 9.

[320] Ibid.

[321] Vrdoljak (2014), p. 163.

[322] Human Rights Council, Report of the Special Rapporteur on the situation of human rights and fundamental freedoms of Indigenous Peoples, S. James Anaya, U.N. Doc. A/HRC/9/9 [11.08.2008], p. 12.

[323] Ibid, pp. 12–13.

UNDRIP. Another consequence of this right found expression in Art.32(1) UNDRIP. It emphasizes "the right to determine and develop priorities and strategies for the development or use of their lands or territories and other resources."

The Indigenous right to pursue their own cultural development provides the foundation for the right to strengthen and control their own institutions and the right to control their heritage. It does not directly mandate repatriation, but its internal dimension is the basis for those provisions which concern themselves with the repatriation and Indigenous control over their cultural heritage, such as Art.12.[324] Without it, Indigenous cultural rights would rely solely on their status as minorities for the purposes of Art.27 ICCPR or the individual Indigenous right to participate in the cultural life of Art.15 ICESCR. Art.3 UNDRIP, by contrast, allows for the creation of a framework within an Indigenous community that ensures that cultural rights can be realized together with and by Indigenous Peoples themselves.

2.4.2.2.2 Right to Practise and Revitalize Cultural Traditions and Customs

Arts.11 and 12 UNDRIP build upon the broader right to cultural self-determination. They concretize the implications of existing human rights regarding Indigenous (religious) customs and repatriation. Art.11(1) not only protects Indigenous Peoples' right to practise their cultural traditions and customs but also to revitalize them. This is necessary, since past cultural traditions are likely to have been interrupted by assimilation policies and the taking of cultural objects. An Indigenous right to practise their cultural traditions, which does not also allow for revitalization efforts may limit the possibility of many Indigenous individuals enjoying their rights under Art.27 ICCPR. This also means that repatriation legislation, which makes repatriation dependent upon the continued existence of a custom, can in effect violate Indigenous cultural rights. This would not be the case if repatriation was made conditional upon a usage requirement in relation to the object.

Art.11(2) in turn recognizes the need to provide redress for property, including religious or spiritual property, taken without FPIC or in violation of their laws, customs or traditions. The specific form of redress is not addressed further; restitution is acknowledged as one possible option. Instead, there are two formal requirements: states must provide an effective redress mechanism which should be developed together with Indigenous Peoples. Art.11 does not explicitly provide for retroactivity, but instead focusses on contemporary expropriations. This is not surprising, given that the wording adopted was already problematic enough for some states who rejected the proposed collective nature of the cultural rights included in the declaration and disagreed on the inclusion of spiritual property.[325] This reading of the provision is reinforced by the focus of Art.12 and the differences

[324] Lenzerini and Scott (2012), p. 78.

[325] For summary of the drafting process in connection to cultural rights see Xanthaki (2018), pp. 279–283.

in language which between the two (Art.11(2) "states shall provide redress", Art.12 (2) "shall seek to enable access and/or repatriation").

2.4.2.2.3 Right to Spiritual and Religious Traditions

Art.12(1) enshrines the right to manifest, practise, develop and teach their spiritual and religious traditions, customs and ceremonies. This a reformulation of a right that Indigenous Peoples already possess under the ICCPR, namely Art.18(1) for religious and Art.27 ICCPR for non-religious traditions, customs and ceremonies which are not connected to religious beliefs, respectively. This complements the right to maintain, protect, and have access in privacy to their religious and cultural sites. This right is a contextualization of the right to manifest one's religion protected under Art.18(1) ICCPR to the situation of Indigenous Peoples. Due to the high number of relocations of Indigenous Peoples, as well as the dispossession of their lands, this right is undoubtedly of fundamental importance to religious freedom as sites can likely be on public (or even (non-Indigenous) private) lands.

Art.12(1) also encompasses the right to the use and control of ceremonial objects. The right to use ceremonial objects is in fact an element of the right to practise one's religion under Art.18(1) ICCPR.[326] The problems for Indigenous practitioners in exercising this right can occur either because they need materials to create their sacred objects that are protected by law or policy, or because their sacred objects are no longer under their control. Repatriation can only help with the latter and is recognized as one possible measure to do so within Art.12(2). It gives examples of measures states could take to fulfil their obligations to ensure this right, notably: "States shall seek to enable the access and/or repatriation of ceremonial objects and human remains in their possession through fair, transparent and effective mechanisms developed in conjunction with indigenous peoples concerned."

Lastly, Art.12(1) provides Indigenous Peoples with a "right to repatriation" where human remains are concerned. By comparison, the right to ceremonial objects is limited to "use and control". States are merely under the obligation "to seek to enable the access and/or repatriation of ceremonial objects and human remains in their possession". While ancestral remains are covered by an Indigenous right (and consequently state duty) to repatriate, the focus in connection with religious objects lies on the access to the objects in question, leaving the repatriation of such objects open to states as one option. The obligation to return ancestral remains reflects an ethical consensus that has slowly emerged globally.

By contrast, the display of cultural objects of questionable provenance or of ceremonial objects contrary to the customs of the source community remains somewhat less acknowledged. The former ILA Committee on the Rights of Indigenous Peoples has observed that "there is a growing recognition by the international community of the right of indigenous peoples to obtain the return of objects of

[326] See Art.61981 UN Declaration on Religious Intolerance. Similarly: Nowak (2005), p. 420.

special spiritual significance for their cultural identity, especially when these objects are human remains."[327] This observation is based on the return of sacred objects under the UNIDROIT and the examples of the return of human remains. The author agrees that there appears to be a consensus regarding human remains but does not see a similarly strong or uniform consensus, either among states or museums, for ceremonial objects. International returns have predominantly concerned human remains, and the UNIDROIT convention has so far "only" been ratified by 50 states.[328] This is insufficient to evidence a global consensus albeit the reasons for non-ratification are likely to have other reasons as those familiar with the discussion of the instrument will know. This distinction is reflected in UNDRIP and in the Principles and Guidelines for the Protection of the Heritage of Indigenous People developed by Erica-Irene Daes with the input from numerous stakeholders. Guideline 21 reads "Human remains and associated funerary objects and documentation must be returned to their descendants in a culturally appropriate manner", while guideline number 22 provides "Moveable cultural property should be returned wherever possible to its traditional owners, particularly if shown to be of significant cultural, religious or historical value to them."[329] Instead, a central element in the consideration of repatriating religious objects is the revitalization of past cultural traditions element as well the recognition of Indigenous beliefs as alternative religious practices protected by the freedom of religion. In a number of cases, this could be achieved by 'simple' access to an object rather than full repatriation.

2.4.2.2.4 Right to their Cultural Heritage

Art.31(1) UNDRIP provides Indigenous Peoples with a right to "maintain, control, protect and develop their cultural heritage, traditional knowledge and traditional cultural expressions." It also operationalizes the Indigenous right to cultural self-development enshrined in Art.3 UNDRIP, common Art.1 ICESCR/ICCPR, as well as customary international law. In recognizing the central role of cultural heritage in the realization of all cultural practices, it also connects to the more specific rights to practise and revitalize their cultural traditions. The broad understanding of indigenous cultural heritage espoused by Art.31 (1) recognizes the diversity of Indigenous cultural expressions. Along these lines, Rebecca Tsosie warns against the desire to categorize an Indigenous cultural heritage strictly, giving the example of a medicine

[327] ILA, The Sofia Conference Report—Committee on the Rights of Indigenous Peoples (2012), p. 21.

[328] https://www.unidroit.org/status-cp [last accessed 18.08.2021].

[329] Final report of the Special Rapporteur, Mrs. Erica-Irene Daes, U.N. Doc E/CN.4/Sub.2/1995/26 (1995), Annex Guideline 22 continues to discuss the holding of Indigenous cultural objects by non-Indigenous individuals and institutions: "Moveable cultural property should only be retained by universities, museums, private institutions or individuals in accordance with the terms of a recorded agreement with the traditional owners for the sharing of the custody and interpretation of the property."

bundle as tangible cultural heritage which is connected to intangible material, such as a specific ritual or traditional knowledge.[330] Such a separation may lead to inappropriate protection being in place for any of the individual components.

Under the declaration, states are the main duty-holders and Indigenous Peoples are the beneficiaries. Even so, a number of the declaration rights grant Indigenous Peoples responsibilities which need to be exercised for their cultural rights to be fully realized. This holds true for Articles 12(1), 13(1) and 31(1).[331] In addition, to take full advantage of the rights granted under the Declaration, Indigenous Peoples may be required to develop the necessary framework or adapt certain elements. This concerns their institutions, traditions as well as customs.[332] They must adhere to Arts.22 and 34 UNDRIP, that is to say they must prevent discrimination against potentially disadvantaged members, such as women and persons with disabilities, and respect international human rights standards[333] James Anaya has also emphasized that Indigenous Peoples should show "good faith, [and] active participation in a spirit of mutual cooperation, when States consult as they must with indigenous peoples on matters affecting their rights with a view to obtaining their free, prior and informed consent."[334]

2.4.2.2.5 Report of the Expert Mechanism on the Rights of Indigenous Peoples on Repatriation

In the summer of 2020, the Expert Mechanism published a report on the repatriation of ceremonial objects, human remains and intangible cultural heritage under UNDRIP.[335] Unsurprisingly, the report advises using the Declaration as "the main instrument guiding the assessment of indigenous peoples' claims and the development of transparent mechanisms for repatriation at the national and international level".[336] It also underlines the need for state action by characterizing the acquisition, use and retention of cultural items contrary to Indigenous wishes as a violation of their rights to religion and culture.[337] The report does not propose a specific repatriation mechanism, rather it briefly explores best practices across the globe and concludes by urging all relevant stakeholders to comply with Articles 11, 12 and

[330] Tsosie (2012), pp. 227–228.

[331] Human Rights Council, Report of the Special Rapporteur on the situation of human rights and fundamental freedoms of Indigenous Peoples, S. James Anaya, U.N. Doc. A/HRC/9/9 [11.08.2008], p. 22.

[332] Ibid.

[333] Ibid.

[334] Ibid.

[335] Human Rights Council, Report of the Expert Mechanism on the Rights of Indigenous Peoples, Repatriation of ceremonial objects, human remains and intangible cultural heritage under the United Nations Declaration on the Rights of Indigenous Peoples, U.N. Doc. A/HRC/45/35 [21.07.2020].

[336] Ibid, para 7.

[337] Ibid, para 14.

31 of the UNDRIP. This is unsurprising given the focus of each of those provisions elaborated upon above and the driving force of UNDRIP as the main standard-setting instrument for Indigenous rights. Importantly, the report considers states, museums, Indigenous communities and various international actors and highlights the varying obligations of all parties to ensure the development of repatriation mechanisms that respect UNDRIP.

Moreover, the report briefly considers existing treaties in international cultural heritage law in connection with its consideration of international repatriation. Here, comparable to what will be set out in Chap. 3, the problem is that no existing treaty provides for the return of colonial-era heritage to Indigenous communities. The report rightly emphasizes the need to adopt such a framework that is to be based on UNDRIP and respects Indigenous rights, including the right to self-determination, participation and consultation.[338] More specific remarks made in the report on international cultural heritage cooperation will be addressed in Chap. 3, where all relevant instruments are discussed further.

The approach in the Expert Mechanism report is in line with the general consensus of UNDRIP being the standard-setting instrument with regards to international Indigenous rights. It is also mirrored throughout this book as UNDRIP is taken as the main source to interpret binding treaty provisions. In this way, those elements of UNDRIP which have binding force under international law, and which need to be respected can serve as a *minimum standard* for repatriation, with the remainder being recommended standards to follow in addition.

2.4.3 *Indigenous Rights in the Inter-American Human Rights System*

The Inter-American Human Rights System has been at the forefront of developing Indigenous human rights.[339] It comprises both the Inter-American Commission of Human Rights [hereafter IAC], the Inter-American Court of Human Rights [hereafter IACtHR] and a number of individual rapporteurships. The system is part of the Organization of American States [hereafter OAS], of which both Canada and the United States are members. While neither country has ratified the American Convention on Human Rights,[340] every member state of the OAS has ratified the organization's founding charter. As a result, both Canada and the United States have accepted the jurisdiction of the Inter-American Commission to promote the observance and protection of Human Rights.[341] This has been understood to include

---

338 Ibid, paras 85–86.

339 Desmet (2011), p. 213. Notably through the right to property.

340 The United States did sign the treaty in 1977 but has not ratified it, see https://indicators.ohchr.org/ [last accessed 18.08.2021].

341 Art.106, Charter of the Organization of American States.

its competence to consider violations of the American Declaration on the Rights and Duties of Man.[342] Both documents, together with the Commission statute and regulations are binding on all OAS member states.[343] Another document of particular interest in the present case is the American Declaration on the Rights of Indigenous Peoples which will be considered below.

The standards developed within the Inter-American system are important for this research in different ways. First, the principles these bodies have developed, and their understanding of Indigenous rights, have informed and contributed to the development of international Indigenous rights standards, notably UNDRIP. They underline that UNDRIP rights have become widely recognized Indigenous rights standards. Second, the Commission can hear complaints directly against both states, which can bring international attention to violations committed by states. American and Canadian lawyers can also use its work to bolster their advocacy efforts at home.[344] Moreover, while standards developed by the Inter-American Commission cannot directly decide cases before US courts, they do constitute persuasive authority which individual judges can and have taken into account.[345] This section contents itself with the consideration of those Indigenous rights standards that help to establish human rights guidelines which must be respected in a repatriation model. Cases against the United States or Canada are considered in the country chapters, where relevant.

2.4.3.1 Cultural Rights in the Inter-American Human Rights System

The Commission (and the Court) have established a significant body of Indigenous rights case law based on a number of articles that do not expressly consider Indigenous rights, such as the right to property and the right to religion. They take a teleological approach to interpreting the relevant instruments, considering the evolution of the entire Inter-American system since their adoption, which also includes considering relevant international human rights standards.[346] For example, in *Saramaka*, the IACtHR considered the decision of the Human Rights Committee in *Mahuika* to inform its understanding of permissible limitations to Indigenous rights to land under Art.1(1) of the Convention.[347] This approach has also entailed that the Commission has considered the American Convention "an authoritative expression of the fundamental principles set forth in the American Declaration".[348] This means that, while neither country has ratified the Convention, it has played a

[342] Pasqualucci (2006), pp. 282–283.
[343] Bettinger-Lopez (2009), pp. 582–583.
[344] Bettinger-Lopez (2009), pp. 584–585.
[345] Bettinger-Lopez (2009), p. 592.
[346] Pentassuglia (2013), p. 98.
[347] Mazzuoli and Ribeiro (2015), pp. 543–545. Saramaka, at para 129.
[348] Inter-American Commission on Human Rights (2000), para 38.

role in considerations by the Commission involving both Canada[349] and the United States.[350]

Relevant rights are comparable to the international rights considered in this chapter, namely the freedom of religion,[351] the right to property and the right to take part in the cultural life. The right to the benefits of culture in Art.XIII of the Declaration is comparable to Art.15 ICESCR. The American Convention does not feature a minority right position comparable to Art. 27 ICCPR or even a right to culture.[352] In the Additional Protocol of San Salvador, Art.14 enshrines a right to the benefits of culture. Its core resembles Art.XIII of the American Declaration. Art.14 (1)(a) of the Additional Protocol enshrines the right to take part in the cultural and artistic life of the community, also resembling Art.15(1)(a) ICESCR. However, the Commission has also used important cases decided by the UN Human Rights Committee under Art.27 ICCPR to clarify the content of Art.XIII of the American Declaration as it pertains to Indigenous Peoples.[353] It has illustrated that activities that are culturally significant may be protected under Art.XIII. Moreover, it has indicated that a limitation on cultural rights is permissible as long as it is not discriminatory in law or fact.[354]

The Inter-American jurisprudence on Indigenous rights has so far mostly developed in connection with the right to land and resources, based on the right to property as enshrined in Art.21 ACHR and Art.XXIII American Declaration.[355] This core right developed within the Inter-American system for Indigenous People seems to encompass other rights within the jurisprudence, such as the right to culture.[356] The broad protection of the Indigenous right to land and resources is based *inter alia* on the cultural distinctiveness of Indigenous Peoples and their unique connection to their territories.[357] Many dimensions of a right to culture

[349] Inter-American Commission on Human Rights (2000), para 38.

[350] IACHR, Report Nr. 75/02, Mary and Carrie Dann v. United States (27.12.2002), at paras 96–97.

[351] Organization of American States (OAS), American Declaration of the Rights and Duties of Man, 2 May 1948 Art.III. Organization of American States (OAS), American Convention of Human Rights, "Pact of San Jose", Costa Rica, 22 November 1969, Art.12.

[352] Compare Shelton (2013), pp. 968–969. She argues that neither the Declaration nor the Convention actually recognize a right to culture and that the right included in the Additional Protocol is in fact extremely limited. By using the right to property, she argues, both Commission and Court have been able to consider the different elements of Indigenous life without "the need to imply unstated rights."

[353] For example, in IACHR, Report Nr. 61/08 Case 12.435 Grand Chief Michael Mitchell Canada [2008], at paras 74–77.

[354] Ibid, at para 82.

[355] See for example IACHR, Report Nr. 40/04 Case 12.053 Maya Indigenous Communities of the Toledo District Belize [2004], at para 115.

[356] Ibid, para 156. Also, Shelton (2013), p. 968.

[357] For example, in the case of the Mayagna (Sumo) Awas Tingni Community v Nicaragua, Inter Am. Ct. H.R. (ser. C) No 79, at para 149 (31.08.2001). Also, Sawhoyamaxa Indigneous Cmty. v. Paraguay, Inter-Am. Ct. H.R. (ser. C) No 146, at para 118 (29.03.2006). See also Shelton (2013), p. 976.

have been considered. For example, a violation of the right to property was found to have damaged the community's cultural identity in *Xákmok Kásek*.[358] In another case, Judge Cançado-Trinidade even recognized a right to cultural identity based on the right to life "in its wider sense".[359]

The Inter-American jurisprudence has thus played an important part in developing Indigenous rights and the considered rights appear to be in line with the UNDRIP rights that are applicable to repatriation. They reinforce the understanding that Indigenous Peoples require special protection under international law,[360] including the need to protect their cultural distinctiveness. Moreover, the Inter-American jurisprudence highlights that Indigenous Peoples have a distinct relationship with certain forms of property (notably land) that needs special protection. This jurisprudence supports the understanding that the cultural distinctiveness of Indigenous Peoples requires protection that includes cultural and property relationships that are different from non-Indigenous cultures. This supports the argument made in connection with Art.27 ICCPR, namely that the repatriation of cultural heritage is one possible measure to protect the survival of Indigenous communities as distinct cultural entities. In its consideration of the right to religion, the Commission has so far not considered sacred objects, rather it considered traditional burial practices. In the case of the Mayan residents of Chichupac, for example, the Commission found that a clandestine burial of executed Indigenous individuals violated the community's religious freedoms.[361] The Court has likewise condemned disrespect of Indigenous burial practices.[362]

2.4.3.2 The American Declaration on the Rights of Indigenous Peoples

The Inter-American Declaration was adopted almost 10 years later than its international counterpart, the UNDRIP. Both instruments offer a comprehensive approach

---

[358] Xákmok Kásek Indigenous Community v Paraguay, Inter-Am. Ct. H.R. (ser. C) No. 214, at para 174–182 (24.08.2010).

[359] Sawhoyamaxa Indigneous Cmty. v. Paraguay, Inter-Am. Ct. H.R. (ser. C) No 146, at para 28 (29.03.2006) (separate opinion).

[360] Lavrysen (2014), p. 111. States are under a duty to ensure non-discrimination. To guarantee substantive equality in the case of Indigenous Peoples, states are under the obligation to take positive measures.

[361] IACHR, Report 6/14 Case 12.788, Residents of the Village of Chichupac and Neighbouring Communities, Municipality of Rabinal Guatemala [2016], at paras 272–273.

[362] Moiwana Community v. Suriname, Inter-Am. Ct. H.R. (series C) No. 124, at paras 98–100, 103 (15.06.2005) Characterized this a violation of Art.5 ACHR (right to humane treatment). Although not in the case of Chichupac in which the court found no violation of Art.12 ACHR not because there appeared to have been no actions that have violated the religious freedoms of the community, but seemingly because the religious aspects were already considered sufficiently in connection with other rights in the court's reasoning. See IACtHR, Caso Miembros de la Aldea Chichupac y Comunidades Vecinas del Municipio de Rabinal v. Guatemala [30.11.2016] at para 204.

to Indigenous rights, contextualizing existing human rights to the unique situation of Indigenous Peoples. A number of articles are relevant to the repatriation of indigenous religious heritage: Art. VI enshrines the collective rights of Indigenous Peoples, including the collective right to their own cultures and the collective right to profess and practise their spiritual beliefs. This is complemented by these rights being reiterated in separate articles, covering the right to cultural identity,[363] the right to religion[364] and the right to assemble in accordance with their traditions and spiritual beliefs, including on sacred sites.[365] In terms of cultural heritage, the Declaration enshrines both the Indigenous right to their cultural heritage (covering different dimensions, i.e. protect/preserve/maintain/develop)[366] and the right to redress for past taking of property. Here Art.XVI(3) ADRIP makes a distinction similar to Art.12(1) UNDRIP in that there is a right to repatriation (in ADRIP 'recover') ancestral remains versus a right to use and control sacred objects. This does not preclude the repatriation of sacred objects,[367] it is simply not established as a right under either Declaration. This does, however, strengthen the interpretation that the right to use and control a ceremonial object is in fact an authoritative reading of the freedom to manifest one's religion within the Indigenous context. The right to preserve, protect and access sacred sites is covered under the right to spiritual beliefs, as is the right to use and control sacred objects.[368]

Overall, it can be stated that these, and other relevant rights,[369] underline the normative force of Indigenous rights as articulated in UNDRIP. They reinforce the point made above that Indigenous rights are binding obligations upon states. While they may be enshrined in a declaration, their wide acceptance and repeated incorporation in different international and regional instruments reinforces their interpretative authority. As explained in Sect. 2.1.1, the best description seems to be that they are in fact interpretations of human rights included in binding human rights treaties, but they are simply adapted to the unique situation of Indigenous Peoples.

---

[363] American Declaration on the Rights of Indigenous Peoples, Art.XIII and Art.X(1).

[364] American Declaration on the Rights of Indigenous Peoples, Art.XVI.

[365] American Declaration on the Rights of Indigenous Peoples, Art. XX(1)(2).

[366] American Declaration on the Rights of Indigenous Peoples, Art. XIII covers cultural heritage from the perspective of cultural identity. Art. XXVIII protects ownership rights to tangible and intangible cultural heritage, covers its collective and inter-generational nature and the right to control and develop cultural heritage.

[367] See also Art.12(2) UNDRIP asking states to enable access and/ or repatriation of sacred ceremonial objects.

[368] American Declaration on the Rights of Indigenous Peoples, Art. XVI(3).

[369] For example, the Declaration also reflects the contemporary standard on defining Indigenous Peoples, more specifically the decision not to do so. As was highlighted in the introductory chapter and in the discussion of Art.27 ICCPR, rather than defining Indigenous Peoples, the international standard has developed to consider self-identification as a crucial element to establish the right-holders of Indigenous rights. ADRIP follows this approach in Art. I(2) and requires states to "respect the right to such self-identification as indigenous ... in keeping with the practices and institutions of each indigenous people."

Canada and the United States have both shown limited support for this regional variation of UNDRIP. Both countries emphasized their support for UNDRIP and their desire to realize its standards internationally, regionally and nationally. Canada refrained from taking a position on ADRIP, while the United States has "persistently objected to the text of this American Declaration, which is not itself legally binding, does not therefore, create new law, and is not a statement of ... (OAS) member states' obligations under treaty or customary law."[370] The latter limitation was also repeated in its support of the United Nations Declaration, which came several years after the fact. In this sense, one may have been surprised upon reading in the United States comment to the ADRIP of its "longstanding belief that implementation of the ... [UNDRIP] should remain the focus of the OAS and its member states".[371] Whether there will be delayed support of the American Declaration by either country in the future is anybody's guess. However, given the existence of its international counterpart, it seems unlikely. Regardless, it can be said that the human rights guidelines developed in accordance with the other human rights instruments considered in this chapter (which have been accepted and/or ratified by both countries) will also be in line with the standards established in the Inter-American system, given the parallels between their relevant provisions.

2.4.4 *An Indigenous Right (of Access) to Cultural Heritage Under Customary Law?*

James Anaya, as Special Rapporteur, has argued that "an understanding of the rights of Indigenous Peoples on the basis of general human rights norms and a wide array of international instruments" has culminated in a "common understanding of the minimum content of the rights of these peoples as a matter of international law and policy."[372] This raises the question which form such a common understanding with regard to Indigenous cultural heritage should take. There are different ways in which a(n Indigenous) right to cultural heritage may exist, both in terms of its legal nature and its scope. Is it only a dimension of existing human rights, as discussed above? Or can we speak of an emerging customary law or even of a right established by customary law?

---

[370] United States comment to Declaration, AG/RES. 2888 (XLVI-O/16) American Declaration on the Rights of Indigenous Peoples (Adopted at the third plenary session, held on June 15, 2016) footnote 1, at 47.

[371] Ibid.

[372] Human Rights Council, Report of the Special Rapporteur on the situation of human rights and fundamental freedoms of Indigenous Peoples, S. James Anaya, U.N. Doc. A/HRC/9/9 [11.08.2008], at para 30.

There has been a proliferation of instruments on Indigenous rights in recent years. Notable scholars have argued that an Indigenous right to cultural identity exists.[373] It is clear that no right to the repatriation of religious cultural heritage can exist under customary law, as it is not even included as a right under UNDRIP, as was discussed above. In effect, there is neither evidence for *opinio juris* nor sufficient state practice in this respect. This leaves the question in how far a specific Indigenous right to Indigenous heritage exists, independent of and possibly in addition to the broader right to cultural heritage enshrined under Art.27 ICCPR and Art.15(1)(a) ICESCR.

There are two different forms which an Indigenous right to heritage may take in customary international law. First, everyone (including Indigenous Peoples) could hold a right to cultural heritage. Second, Indigenous Peoples could have a group/culture-specific right to their cultural heritage. Indigenous peoples are guaranteed access to their cultural heritage under Art.27 ICCPR, which has almost universal scope, and by virtue of Art.15 ICESCR. Since both the United States and Canada have ratified the ICCPR, it is irrelevant in this research whether or not access to heritage as general human right has reached customary law status.

This leaves the question whether a more extensive customary right to cultural heritage exists under customary law. This would include the right to decide in favour or against the display of cultural objects, managerial rights, access control and it would be comparable to Art.31 UNDRIP. In order to qualify as customary law, there would have to be sufficient evidence of state practice and *opinio iuris*. With regard to *opinio iuris*, several instruments explored in sections 2.2 and 2.3 above recognize the importance of cultural objects to Indigenous identity. In some cases, they also provide for a broader Indigenous right to their cultural heritage, including managerial and access control rights. In addition, decades of activism and lobbying have resulted in Indigenous Peoples across the globe being recognized as a distinct cultural entity in international law with its own (forms of) cultural heritage.

State practice supporting such a right would have to be twofold. First, provisions to ensure Indigenous rights to manage and control their heritage would have to be enshrined in national or local law and be respected by the respective governmental institutions on a global scale. Second, disregarding Indigenous interests in managing their heritage should not be common practice. If such acts occur, they must be isolated and be recognized as violations of an Indigenous right to heritage. Examining state practice reveals that there have been numerous examples of Indigenous Peoples being dispossessed and their right to control their heritage being disrespected. This was documented by Erica Daes in the late 1990s in her study on the Protection of the Heritage of Indigenous Peoples.[374] Since then, other cases in connection with Indigenous heritage sites that suggest that state practice has not yet changed to such an extent as to provide evidence that a corresponding customary law

[373] See Sect. 2.4.2.1.

[374] E/CN.4/Sub.2/1993/28E. Daes, Study on the protection of the cultural and intellectual property of Indigenous Peoples, at para 49, and 53–54.

right has come into existence.[375] However, changes to the World Heritage Guidelines may result in improvement. Repatriations which have occurred do not address a global repatriation pattern. Rather, they are country-specific (such as NAGPRA motivated returns in the United States) or heritage-specific (i.e. most of the repatriations on the international level centre on the return of ancestral remains and even in this case numerous ancestral remains are still located abroad).

The sheer multitude of documents proclaiming that such a right exists could signal an emerging norm in this respect. If more states start to implement the UNDRIP in their territories consistently in the belief that they should do so, there will be more evidence to show sufficient state practice supporting an Indigenous right to their heritage under customary law. However, the widespread distribution of Indigenous Peoples' artifacts, both geographically and considering the many different identities of contemporary owners of such material (public organizations/private individuals/legal persons/non-profit organizations), does decrease the likelihood of a consistent, international and national approach to respecting an Indigenous right to manage and control their heritage.

This being said, alternative viewpoints exist. As was mentioned above, a number of experts in international law and Indigenous rights have argued that Indigenous Peoples possess a right to their cultural identity in customary international law.[376] This includes "all the prerogatives that are essential to preserve the cultural identity of indigenous peoples according to their own perspective must be preserved".[377] The importance of cultural heritage to the cultural identity of communities and individuals in turn has been affirmed by many other actors, such as Faridah Shaheed.[378] Approaching the same connection from the perspective of international cultural heritage law, Blake has argued that cultural heritage is necessary for the constitution of cultural identity. Cultural heritage provisions, she argues "by definition ... are also recognizing this right [to cultural identity]."[379] These arguments reinforce the centrality of heritage to cultural practices. Items which are integral to religious practice (thus essential to preserve Indigenous identity) should thus be preserved in a manner which abides by the wishes of Indigenous Peoples in accordance with existing international human rights norms. Within a nation-state that would indicate the obligation of a state to support Indigenous Peoples in their repatriation requests for sacred material, to enable the return of objects which the state (or one of the institutions funded by it) owns and to pass laws ensuring that third parties who handle Indigenous objects do so in manner that corresponds to Indigenous customs.

However, the author considers that interpeting a far-reaching right to heritage beyond the access dimension into the right to cultural identity that has customary law

[375] Vrdoljak (2018).

[376] ILA, The Hague Conference Report – Committee on the Rights of Indigenous Peoples (2010), p. 6, p. 51.

[377] Ibid, at 51.

[378] Shaheed (2011), p. 4, para 6.

[379] Blake (2014), p. 62.

status would stretch the boundaries of existing state practice too far. Farida Shaheed has highlighted the importance of cultural heritage for the realization of cultural heritage in her study on access to cultural heritage. She did not discuss it in terms of its customary law status but rather as an important element of Art.15 ICESCR. She considered that it was probable that Art.15 ICESCR could be classified as customary law, but she admitted that it was "unclear, in the absence of sufficiently explicit State practice and *opinio iuris*, whether the specific incidents of the right as described below are all customary."[380] Ahmed, Aylwin and Coombe, for example, infer that an access or control or repossession right is included in the right to cultural identity. They maintain that "artifacts necessary to participate in the cultural life of the community can be considered a fundamental human right, as can access to knowledge of a cultural heritage from which a group has been forcibly dispossessed."[381] While they thus create such a right through an interpretation of existing cultural rights, they admit "there is little precedent to guide us."[382] Overall, it therefore seems reasonable not to infer the existence of a customary law right in cultural heritage. At most, we might speak of an emerging norm.

2.5 Human Rights that May Be Limited by a Successful Repatriation

2.5.1 Indigenous Religious Objects as the Heritage of a Wider Community?

It has already been observed in Chap. 1 that cultural heritage can carry multiple meanings to different individuals and groups. For example, over the past 40 years, the notion of a common heritage has been recognized repeatedly in international (cultural heritage) law. This can be seen, *inter alia*, by the widespread ratification of the 1954 Hague Convention, the 1972 World Heritage Convention or the 2003 UNESCO Declaration on Intentional Destruction of Cultural Heritage.[383] This has implications for the conservationist obligations a state has accepted vis-à-vis certain categories of its heritage. However, at the same time the cultural heritage can also have distinct meaning to local communities and Indigenous Peoples. And all of these groups may have different understandings of what it means to use and protect (or conserve) cultural heritage.

A single piece of sacred cultural heritage is unlikely to be so unique and important as to qualify as the common heritage of mankind. However, on the national level, a clash between national heritage interests and Indigenous interests in their cultural

[380] O'Keefe (2011), p. para 3.

[381] Ahmed et al. (2008), p. 333.

[382] Ahmed et al. (2008), p. 333.

[383] Francioni (2008), p. 10.

heritage seems more likely. Repatriation claims (depending on the agreement in place) may result in the complete return of the object to the community and its integration into daily life. Such a return may equal the complete physical preservation of the object for future generations. The Indigenous community could, for example, focus on religious or spiritual preservation at odds with the Western preservationist understanding.

Repatriation can lead to the immediate destruction of the object by i.e. burial or future destruction due to long-term usage. The question then arises in how far the right to participate in the cultural life of the wider national community is affected, and which understanding of preservation of protection is adopted.

2.5.2 Right to Participate in Cultural Life of Majority

2.5.2.1 Content

Cultural heritage protection under (national) cultural heritage centres on the nature of the object, which is deemed so important as to warrant protection. However, heritage preservation can also be approached from a human rights angle. States also have an obligation to protect the cultural rights of those individuals living in their territory who are not Indigenous. The question thus arises whether, and if so in how far, positive discrimination of Indigenous Peoples' cultural rights violates the majority's right to participation in the cultural life.

The different dimensions of the right to 'participate in the cultural life' have already been explored above in connection with the position of Indigenous People. Its most important dimension, upon debating the majority/mainstream society's position on the repatriation debate, related to the accessibility of cultural institutions and objects. This includes the administrative and financial aspects of heritage protection, conservation and potential repatriation budgets. Thus, policy makers need to ensure that budgetary planning is in line with their cultural rights obligations, both to Indigenous Peoples, minorities and other individuals. Moreover, the repatriation of sacred objects from public collections raises another question, namely, how to balance the need for potential secrecy by the community in question versus public access to and knowledge of the object.

This apparent clash between an Indigenous need to maintain the secrecy surrounding certain objects and customs versus a Western understanding of values inherent in the freedom (and spread) of information and knowledge would seem to present a major challenge with regard to finding a compromise between the different points of view.[384] Harding, however, emphasizes that freedom of information and knowledge is embedded in a framework which also protects religious freedom and

[384] Harding (1999), p. 305, pp. 313–314.

reduces inequality.[385] The spread of information and exchange of culture, especially in the UNESCO system, aims at encouraging cross-cultural understanding. Access to heritage and the spread of information at odds with religious Indigenous practices would contradict this. Certain limits on access would thus seem to be compatible both with ICHL and IHRL instruments.

2.5.2.2 Balancing Indigenous and Non-Indigenous Cultural Rights

There is no possibility to answer categorically whether non-Indigenous individuals have a right of access to Indigenous cultural heritage or not. Rather, and this is due to the nature of cultural rights, it depends on the context. To facilitate this rather theoretical discussion, consider the extreme: would a complete denial of access to a particular Indigenous object amount to a violation of the non-Indigenous right to participate in the cultural life? In making the majority claim more concrete, a form of the right is envisaged which could affect repatriation debates. Such a complete denial of access (now and in the future) is the most severe theoretical limitation of a right of access to heritage that is possible. If this can be in accordance with Art.15 ICESCR, all other agreements reached by parties would also be permissible.

In effect, to deny non-Indigenous individuals' access to an Indigenous objects will not constitute a denial of their right to participate in the cultural life. There are multiple cultural opportunities available so that even a complete denial of access to all Indigenous heritage and traditions would not translate into a complete denial of the non-Indigenous individual's right to participate in the cultural life available in his or her territory. Rather, in both cases, what is at stake is a limitation of Art.15(1) (a) ICESCR. As observed above in Sect. 2.3.4.5, such limitations are permissible if they adhere to Art.4 ICESCR ("are determined by law only in so far as this may compatible with the nature of these rights and solely for the purpose of promoting the general welfare in a democratic society"). This also implies a proportionality test ("only in so far"). A measure that bans access to all Indigenous cultural heritage, for example, may not lead to a denial of the majority's right to participate in the cultural life, but it is unlikely to be proportionate to achieve the desired goal and would thus constitute a violation.

Measures that deny access to certain categories of objects first need to be determined by law. A framework should be put in place that regulates access policies. Suffice to say that to require public institutions to adopt an access policy for spiritual/ceremonial objects is actually mandated by international human rights law as part of the protect dimension of both Art.18 and Art.27 ICCPR. An access restriction or denial of access to particular objects by non-Indigenous individuals

[385] Harding (1999), p. 305, pp. 313–314.

would only be compatible with the nature of Art.15 ICESCR and cultural rights if it is aimed at promoting the general welfare in a democratic society.

Even if a goal is permissible, the measure taken must be a proportionate measure. The rights at issue seek to guarantee that all members of a culturally diverse society have the opportunity to realize and take advantage of an important part of daily life—culture. Ensuring the balanced protection of cultural interests, rather than the complete protection of the majority culture to the exclusion of other, non-dominant forms, also contributes to the general welfare in a democratic society, when cultural diversity is considered an important facet of a democratic society in an age of mass migration. Prohibiting any public access to a secret/religious objects would aim to ensure sufficient protection for minority religions and cultures and could satisfy the burden laid down in Art.4 ICESCR. It would not significantly affect the majority right to participate in the cultural life. The reverse may be true for Indigenous Peoples' rights under Art.15(1)(a) and Art.27 ICCPR if access is not prohibited, depending on the objects and religious beliefs being considered.

2.5.3 Right to Freedom of Property

2.5.3.1 Article 17 UDHR

(1) Everyone has the right to own property alone as well as in association with others.
(2) No one shall be arbitrarily deprived of his property.

2.5.3.2 Content

> A most important limit to indigenous peoples' requests for governance over their cultural property is the right to property of others. This right is not only a strong, absolute right of private law, but also the most frequently codified constitutional right and an important universal human rights standard.[386]

The right to own property has been laid down in the UDHR, but it has not been replicated in either the ICCPR or the ICESCR. According to Special Rapporteur Rodriguez, the right itself was not questioned but "there were considerable differences of opinion with regard to the concept of property, its role and functions."[387] Notable differences concerned its possible formulation as a broader right subject to additional specification in national law or a more specific one, as well as possible

[386] Kuprecht and Siehr (2012), p. 262.

[387] UN Commission on Human Rights "The right of everyone to own property alone as well as in association of others, report by Luis Valencia Rodriguez, U.N. Doc. E/CN. 4/ 1994/19, 1993, at para 34.

limitations.[388] Instead, the term 'property' appears as part of the right of non-discrimination in the two instruments, namely in the form of a prohibited ground for discrimination.[389] While it is not part of the ICESCR or the ICCRP, Desmet maintains that "it is commonly accepted that the principles of the Universal Declaration, including the right to property, have attained the status of customary international law."[390]

Some form of the right to private property is recognized in a number of regional instruments[391] and numerous national constitutions.[392] After analysing the existence of the right to property in universal as well as regional instruments and state practice, Golay and Cismas likewise attest that a customary international law right to own property, alone or in association, exists, as does the protection from arbitrary deprivation.[393] In addition, UN special rapporteur Rodriguez observed that many constitutions incorporate the right to own property which is supplemented by administrative or legislative measures in varying forms.[394] To establish a universal human right which is specific enough to be incorporated into national law and claimed before national courts is difficult in light of this variety.[395] Yet, the existence of its basic tenets, according to Rodriguez, seems to be universally accepted and confirmed both in practice as well as legal writing. The standard of compensation to be used is less clear, but this is not a concern at present, given that the primary concern lies in the right to property as a potential obstacle to repatriation requests. It is sufficient here that it appears a widely accepted right that is protected in numerous national frameworks and may thus impede repatriations in a variety of countries.

The right to property thus serves as protection for the individual against expropriation by the state, at least without some form of compensation and sufficient procedural safeguards. This impedes repatriation because many Indigenous cultural objects are in private hands.

---

[388] Ibid, at para 36.

[389] Desmet (2011), p. 214. Property in this context is a status element and includes the lack thereof, see CESCR, General Comment No. 20, at para 25.

[390] Desmet (2011), p. 214.

[391] First Protocol to the European Convention on Human Rights (Article 1), the American Convention on Human Rights (Article 21) and the African Charter on Human and Peoples' Rights (Article 14).

[392] See UN Commission on Human Rights "The right of everyone to own property alone as well as in association of others, report by Luis Valencia Rodriguez (U.N. Doc. E/CN. 4/ 1994/19, 1993) more generally.

[393] Golay and Cismas (2010), p. 10.

[394] UN Commission on Human Rights "The right of everyone to own property alone as well as in association of others, report by Luis Valencia Rodriguez, U.N. Doc. E/CN. 4/ 1994/19, 1993, at para 186.

[395] Ibid, at para 475.

2.5.3.3 Balancing Indigenous Cultural Rights and the Right to Property

The relationship between the right to property and repatriation cases will differ not only from country to country but from case to case, depending on the cultural institution which houses it, its legal status and the level of protection afforded to property by the respective jurisdiction. Balancing the rights in question thus depends on the specific case at hand. However, a number of broader observations can be made. First, individual, private owners of Indigenous ceremonial objects are protected from arbitrary state expropriation. The right to own property may thus be limited, but such restrictions need to adhere to limitations laid down in the national law. In his report, Special Rapporteur Rodriguez observed that the majority of states have enacted legislation which protects individuals from expropriation "except in the public interest, legally proven, on the payment of due compensation in compliance with the law."[396] In spite of national administrative and legislative variations, it seems to be universally accepted that private individuals have a right to property and that the grounds for expropriation are very limited. For state expropriation of private individuals owning Indigenous sacred objects to occur, the expropriation would thus have to be motivated by a strong enough general public interest, the interest of the specific Indigenous community would not suffice in all likelihood. This may be different if the expropriations were embedded in a broader, national restorative justice exercise, combined with appropriate compensation, but this is conjecture. Instead, objects which could be returned are those where the property transfer does not classify as an expropriation by the state of a private individual or institution. This is thus the case for sacred ceremonial objects located in public institutions. In addition, institutions which exist due to public funding might be expected to adhere to more stringent standards of care-taking or farther-reaching access obligations or the state could make its funding dependent on the institution participating in a repatriation framework.

Second, the human right to own property also provides Indigenous communities with the right to own property communally. Thus, if Indigenous customs require a cultural heritage object to be held by a custodian on behalf of the entire community,[397] this is protected not only under Art.15 ICESCR but it is also a dimension of the right to own property.[398] Repatriation requests may not require a specific individual to take ownership of the object. In addition, and this is reinforced by Art.5(d) ICERD, "[a] government's failure to protect Indigenous peoples' collective

---

[396] Ibid, at para 486.

[397] Vrdoljak (2014), p. 159. She has summarized common traits of Indigenous customary law with regard to their heritage as follows: "Whilst customary law necessarily varies from community to community, it usually recognizes the following inherent characteristics of indigenous heritage: it affirms that ownership and custodianship of indigenous heritage is usually collective or communal in character; that such ownership and custodianship over heritage is permanent and inalienable; and, it reinforces the intergenerational nature of custodianship and transmission of their cultures."

[398] For recognition of communal property rights see also regional human rights case-law in the Inter-American human rights system, Sect. 2.4.3.

rights to their heritage may be discriminatory, if this failure is justified by the argument that Indigenous peoples have a lesser right than the state or museums and academic institutions."[399]

Third, international law requires a balancing exercise. The rights of the community to the cultural objects are balanced against the rights of others in a diverse society. As Luis Rodriguez observed on the balance of author's rights versus the right to take part in the cultural life, "it is important to balance the two, to safeguard the one for the realization of the other."[400] Balancing these rights, however, requires careful deliberation. The balance struck will differ on a case-by-case basis. In terms of balancing conflicting rights, there is one last potential conflict that may arise, namely between an Indigenous individual versus the Indigenous community's communal rights.

2.5.4 The Indigenous Individual Versus the Indigenous Community

Various actors have expressed concerns about possible clashes between the rights of Indigenous individuals and community interests. In her position as Special Rapporteur for cultural rights Farida Shaheed asked states to consider how they implemented the cultural rights of women on an equal basis in light of customary restrictions on women's participation in cultural traditions or access restrictions to site.[401] States were asked to "[e]nsure that diverse women's voices within specific communities are heard and that their human rights are not sacrificed in the name of culture".[402]

Lenzerini and Scott, by contrast, stress that Indigenous rights and the remaining human rights framework share a common purpose. Both strive to respect and protect human dignity. They are thus best viewed as "mutually supportive". If rights contradict each other, this should be solved similarly to the other human rights contradictions highlighted above, by realizing that both rights can be limited to a certain, necessary extent to accommodate both interests. Only where this is not possible, it is necessary to consider which right should prevail over the other. By understanding UNDRIP as the specification of existing human rights to the extent necessary to ensure the survival of Indigenous communities it prioritizes Indigenous communal rights over individual Indigenous human rights or non-Indigenous human rights, except where the latter "are of such fundamental importance not to admit any

399 Battiste and Henderson (2000), p. 174.

400 UN Commission on Human Rights "The right of everyone to own property alone as well as in association of others", report by Luis Valencia Rodriguez (U.N. Doc. E/CN. 4/ 1994/19, 1993) at para 478.

401 Shaheed (2012), p. 22, para 79–80.

402 Shaheed (2012), p. 23, para 80.

exception for whatever reason."[403] This also aligns with arguments brought forward by Native American scholar Duane Champagne who argued that, in case of a conflict between individual Indigenous and collective ownership, the latter should prevail over the former. He highlights the need for decisions to be "made by the indigenous community's governing system according to its rules, as long as the decisions are fair and equitable according to the indigenous norms and values of the particular community."[404]

Karolina Kuprecht and Kurt Siehr[405] as well as Christoph Graber highlight the role of Art.34 UNDRIP in such situations, which requires Indigenous Peoples to respect existing human rights standards.[406] Following this line of reasoning, individual human rights would prevail. However, Kuprecht and Siehr are not far from Lenzerini and Scott's approach, as they require a careful evaluation of the respective rights, including their respective "weight",[407] which seems to align with Lenzerini and Scott's emphasis on the survival of the community.

In addition to Art.34 UNDRIP, Art.46(2) UNDRIP makes the exercise of indigenous rights dependent on being in accordance with existing human rights standards.[408] Together, these two provisions create a hierarchy between UNDRIP and the more general human rights provisions. The existing binding human rights standard are the basis upon which the UNDRIP builds, as a concretization of these rights. An Indigenous tradition, which violates any of the binding human rights norms that are put in place, lacks the foundation to be considered a legitimate interpretation of other treaty rights. It's character as a right is contingent upon it being in accordance with existing human rights and fundamental freedoms. This also reflects the standard enshrined in the more recent ICHL instruments, such as Art.5 UDCD.[409]

Lastly, it should be pointed out that there may not only be a conflict between an Indigenous individual right versus the community the person belongs to, but also a conflict between different Indigenous communities. This can occur where it is difficult to establish a cultural connection between a contemporary community and the past community from which the object originated. In this case, both communities may have cultural rights under the Indigenous rights canon, which will have to be balanced against each other. In order to respect the Indigenous right to manage their cultural heritage, as well as the right to cultural self-determination, it would be best

[403] Lenzerini and Scott (2012), pp. 80–81.

[404] Champagne (2012), p. 55.

[405] Graber (2012), p. 15.

[406] Graber (2012), pp. 7–8.

[407] Graber (2012), p. 15.

[408] Art.46(2) UNDRIP. "In the exercise of the rights enunciated in the present Declaration, human rights and fundamental freedoms of all shall be respected. The exercise of the rights set forth in this Declaration shall be subject only to such limitations as are determined by law and in accordance with international human rights obligations..."

[409] Compare in the context of Art.15 ICESCR O'Keefe (2011), para 14.

for the state to ask both communities to come to agreement among themselves before it proceeds with the repatriation.

2.5.5 *Balancing Conflicting Rights*

In the preceding sections, we have seen that actors at the national level will be confronted with the obligation to balance conflicting human rights. This will require careful consideration by adjudicatory bodies. A balance will have to be struck depending on the case and rights in question. This raises the question whether some guidance can be given on the balancing act in general, to guide the relevant bodies.

Other than the permitted limitations within each respective human right, there is no international procedural law that prescribes how the balance should be struck. This is necessary, given that it is generally accepted that there is no hierarchy of human rights enshrined in the treaties. If such a hierarchy exists at all, it rests in the distinction between human rights that allow for no derogation and those rights which permit limitations. In the present case, this means that the national legislator (and judge) is left with a significant amount of discretion in how to balance these interests, as long as the margin of discretion inherent in the respective limitation is not stretched. This means that the concept of general public welfare in Art.4 ICESCR may not be widened beyond what is allowed for Art.15(1)(a) ICESR, the limitation clause under Art.18(3) must be respected and measures that would amount to a denial of the right under Art.27 ICCPR may not be permitted. Further limits may come into play depending on the national legal framework. Guidance on how different rights may clash is difficult to give in the abstract, the balance can only be found in the concrete weighing exercise. The discussion in the country Chaps. 4 to 8 will highlight where different rights are at play that need to be considered.

2.6 Human Rights and Indigenous Cultural Heritage: A Toolbox to Help Align National Cultural Heritage Law with Indigenous Rights

The analysis of applicable human rights law has shown that states have to take a number of measures to respect and protect Indigenous cultural rights. On top of this rests a wide range of possible measures which states can choose from to fulfil the rights in question. The latter is not optional, as steps *have* to be taken, although there is discretion as to how these steps may be taken.

One of the research questions asked *"how should the repatriation of indigenous sacred cultural heritage be regulated legally in light of international cultural heritage and human rights law standards?"* It is now clear that there are binding obligations that arise out of international human rights law. These have to be respected and implemented, and they may affect different elements of repatriation practice.

The lessons learned culminate in 12 standards and obligations that will guide the evaluation of national measures in the chapters to follow. These connect Indigenous (religious) cultural heritage to the necessary state actions that arise under the Indigenous right to religious freedom, the Indigenous right to cultural identity and the Indigenous right to their cultural heritage. As can be seen below, some standards reflect binding obligations (i.e. standard 1) while others reflect concrete measures that can be taken by a state within a discretionary margin but which are not in themselves mandatory (i.e. standard 8). However, all relate to repatriation. To reflect the diverse nature of the evaluating standards, I use the term standards and obligations (standard in short). Each of the standards below is justified by reference to the specific treaty provision(s) it is based on. This illustrates the provisions which were applied to the specific context of Indigenous religious cultural heritage. The analysis also yielded a standard on access to sacred sites (see number 12) which will not be used in the national analysis. The scope of this research on moveable sacred cultural heritage and its legal context prevents me from drawing legitimate conclusions on the state of compliance within the selected countries on this standard. However, it is a standard that resulted from the analysis and should be respected by national governments. It can play an important role for the actual enjoyment of Indigenous religious practices after heritage is repatriated. For this reason, it is still included below.

The standards are complemented by tests which can help actors to evaluate whether specific measures that limit Indigenous rights amount to a violation. We will consider the right to use and the control of sacred objects in Sect. 2.6.2 below. This is the UNDRIP right that connects most closely to the repatriation of sacred Indigenous heritage.

2.6.1 Standards and Obligations

1. *Respect, protect and fulfil indigenous religious beliefs also in designing a repatriation framework so long as these are in accordance with international human rights standards.*
   a. *Legal basis:* This is an obligation that arises out of Art.18(1) ICCPR and has been contextualized in Art.12(1) UNDRIP.
   b. *Example measure(s):*
      i. Do not define sacredness but incorporate definition according to indigenous religious traditions
      ii. Establish custodial rules applicable until repatriation

2. *The repatriation framework and other examined heritage frameworks have to incorporate the consultation of indigenous peoples for measures affecting their cultural rights and FPIC whenever "the preservation of their cultural resources, especially those associated with their way of life and cultural expression, are at risk".*[410]

   a. *Legal basis:* This principle is part of the utmost minimum that a state must do to fulfil Art.27 ICCPR and Art.15(1)(a) ICESCR. It reflects the fact that a state is under a duty to ensure the Indigenous right to participate in decision-making affecting their cultural rights. It is also a minimum obligation at the core of several UNDRIP provisions which operationalize these two treaty rights, most notably Art. 11(1) and Art.34 UNDRIP. A state may take measures interfering with the right to revitalization so long as these do not deny the right (Art.27 ICCPR test), which has to be established within the specific context of the case.
   b. *Example measure(s):*

      i. Consult with Indigenous religious and traditional leaders prior to adopting legislation affecting Indigenous heritage[411]
      ii. consult with Indigenous Peoples to ensure that heritage law and policy that covers Indigenous heritage respects Indigenous traditions as far as possible
      iii. include mandatory consultations and consent with Indigenous Peoples prior to any excavation of Indigenous heritage
      iv. require evidence of FPIC as a precondition for recording, study, display, access and use of Indigenous heritage by non-Indigenous individuals.
      v. Incorporate Indigenous consultation and consent requirements within legislative or regulatory processes that are likely to affect cultural rights. For example, within environmental impact assessments, heritage planning processes and repatriation legislation.
      vi. One may also consider the use of Indigenous representatives, depending on the area and the frequency of contact this may be useful to realize the consultation requirement.[412]

3. *Repatriation of sacred objects guarantees the indigenous right to control the sacred object.* This principle identifies one possible measure within a margin of discretion; there is currently no obligation to repatriate sacred objects under international law.

---

[410] CESCR, General Comment No 21, at para 55(e).

[411] Compare Daes, E, Report of the seminar on the draft principles and guidelines for the protection of the heritage of Indigenous People [28.01-1.03.2000] U.N. Doc: E/CN.4/Sub.2/2000/26, at 15 guideline 23(a).

[412] HRCee Communication No. 205/ 1986 adopted 4.11.1991 CCPR/ C/43/D/205/1986/205/1986.

   a. *Legal basis:* This principle is a means to operationalize Art.12(1) Art.12 (1) UNDRIP and one possible step to fulfil Art.27 ICCPR and Art.18 (1) ICCPR.

4. *States may not interfere with the indigenous right to practise and/or revitalize their cultural traditions and customs, unless this limitation is in accordance with international human rights law.*

   a. *Legal basis:* This principle is part of the utmost minimum that a state must do to fulfil Art.27 ICCPR and Art.15(1)(a) ICESCR. It is also a minimum obligation at the core of several UNDRIP provisions which operationalize these two treaty rights, most notably Art. 11(1) and Art.34 UNDRIP. A state may take measures interfering with the right to revitalization as long as these do not deny the right (Art.27 ICCPR test), which has to be established within the specific context of the case.

5. *Support the indigenous right to practise and/or revitalize their cultural traditions by creating favourable conditions in which to exercise this right.*

   a. *Legal basis:* This principle complements principle number 5 and is one of the many measures in the fulfil dimension of Art.27 ICCPR and Art.15(1) (a) ICESCR, to improve the quality of these rights. It is thus also a way to improve Art.11(1) and Art.34 UNDRIP. Again, state measures that limit revitalization efforts may not vitiate the right. The state is also obliged to fulfil the right to revitalization by creating favourable conditions. There is however a wide margin of discretionary measures that the state can take.
   b. *Example measure(s):*

      i. Provide funds for Indigenous cultural activities
      ii. Strengthen Indigenous languages through support programs

6. *Duty to respect and protect cultural heritage and to mitigate effects of globalization and privatization on culture of marginalized and minority communities, including indigenous peoples.*[413]

   a. *Legal basis:* This is based on Art.15(1)(a) ICECR and Articles 27 ICCPR and Art.18(1) ICCPR, in particular the obligations of the governments to protect these rights against violation by third parties. It is one step to operationalize Art.12(1) UNDRIP, in particular the Indigenous right to use and control their ceremonial objects.
   b. *Example measure(s):*

      i. In light of a flourishing market in 'tribal art', this includes the duty to protect Indigenous cultural rights by legally preventing cultural and sacred objects from leaving the territory without consent of tribe.
      ii. Increase/strengthen export controls

---

[413] CESCR, General Comment No.21, at para 50(a), (b).

7. *Ensure that indigenous sacred objects receive special protection under national heritage law, but that this does not prevent access to heritage by its indigenous community.*[414] *States must actively take steps to eliminate all barriers that prevent indigenous peoples from accessing their heritage.*[415] *Conditions to access are permissible; they have to satisfy the test charted below for limitations on right of access to sacred heritage.*

   a. *Legal basis:* This is based on Articles 27 ICCPR and Art.18(3) ICCPR, in particular the obligations of governments under the protect dimension of the cultural rights. It is one step to operationalize Art.12(1) UNDRIP, in particular the Indigenous right to use and control their ceremonial objects.
   b. *Example measure(s):*

      i. work on the accessibility of heritage to Indigenous Peoples where heritage is centralized and located far from Indigenous communities. Can i.e. include supporting smaller Indigenous museums/cultural centres, or digital access to heritage.

8. *Take measures to prevent conduct aimed at the desecration of cultural heritage.*[416] *This includes encouraging museums not to display human remains and sacred objects unless with FPIC of the affected community.*[417]

   a. *Legal basis:* This is a way to protect Art.15(1)(a) ICESCR, Art.27 ICCPR and Art.18 ICCCPR. There is a sliding scale of possible measures, for example the government could make funding opportunities dependent on an inventory of the collection that is undertaken in consultation with indigenous peoples to identify connected Indigenous sacred objects and remains and agree upon further arrangements. It can also feature an absolute prohibition to display human remains, for example.
   b. *Example measure(s):*

      i. Make funding dependable upon the adoption of guidelines which ensure non-desecration so long as they are in accordance with general human rights standards.

9. *The state has a duty to refrain from undue interference with the indigenous right to their heritage and to protect them from undue interference by third parties. It is also under a positive duty to create conditions progressively in which indigenous peoples can control etc. their heritage according to their own traditions.*

---

[414] Ibid, para 55(d). Indigenous peoples must have access to their heritage.

[415] Ibid. Shaheed (2011), p. 18, para 68.

[416] Pineschi (2012), p. 41.

[417] Compare Daes, E., Principles and Guidelines, guideline 21: "Under no circumstances should human remains or any other sacred elements of an indigenous peoples' heritage be publicly displayed, except in a manner deemed appropriate by the peoples concerned."

a. *Legal basis:* This principle is based on the Indigenous right to their heritage which comprises the right to maintain, control, protect and develop their cultural heritage. Art.31 UNDRIP articulates this right that is a dimension of Art.15(1)(a) ICESCR and Art.27 ICCPR. Any limitations must satisfy the test articulated in Art.4 ICESCR.[418] For states that have not ratified ICESCR, this Indigenous right is also implicit in Art.27 ICCPR, with the result that state measures limiting the right may not deny it. The range of measures to create favourable conditions progressively is wide.
b. *Example measure(s):*
   i. include Indigenous staff in national/regional/local heritage administration to care for Indigenous heritage.
   ii. encourage museums to employ Indigenous staff, support heritage management/museology studies for Indigenous individuals
   iii. accommodate Indigenous heritage laws covering Indigenous lands within the national heritage scheme

10. *The state has a duty to refrain from undue interference with right to cultural identity, which includes a prohibition of enforced assimilation. There are three other duties connected to cultural identity: First, the obligation not to impose definition of indigenous identity from the outside. Second, the positive duty to protect the right-holders from undue interference by third parties, including the duty to ensure that the decision to identify as indigenous does not result in discrimination. Third, the positive duty to take steps to create favourable conditions for indigenous peoples to preserve and develop their cultural identity. This encompasses a wide margin of possible, discretionary measures.*

a. *Legal basis*: This principle operationalizes the right enshrined in Art.33 UNDRIP. It is a contextualization of Art.27 ICCPR, supported by Art.15(1)(a) ICESCR meaning that the state obligations are in effect binding treaty obligation.[419] Any state limitation has to be in line with Art.4(2) ICCPR, Art.5(1) ICCPR and may not amount to a denial of the right within the context of the case (Art.27 ICCPR test).
b. *Example measure(s):*
   i. ensure that state (welfare) programs do not disadvantage or disqualify Indigenous individuals
   ii. prohibit discriminatory practices by third parties against Indigenous Peoples

[418] (1) limitation must be determined by law, and (2) only in so far as this may be compatible with the nature of the right being limited, and (3) purpose of promoting the general welfare in a democratic society (4) proportionate least restrictive measure must be taken when several measures are available.

[419] According to ILA, this is a principle of customary law see ILA, The Hague Conference Report – Committee on the Rights of Indigenous Peoples (2010), p. 6 at 51.

iii. address results of past discriminatory practices that may continue to affect the Indigenous right to preserve and develop their own cultural identity, for example residential schools.

11. *The state has a duty to respect the indigenous right to their own legal traditions*[420] *in accordance with international human rights law.*

a. *Legal basis*: This principle operationalizes the right enshrined in Art.33 UNDRIP. It is a contextualization of Art.27 ICCPR, supported by Art.15(1) (a) ICESCR meaning that the state obligations are in effect binding treaty obligations.[421] Any state limitation has to be in line with Art.4(2) ICCPR, Art.5(1) ICCPR and may not amount to a denial of the right within the context of the case (Art.27 ICCPR test).

b. *Example measures:*

i. courts of first instance for cases on tribal land;
ii. train judges in both national and Indigenous laws

12. *Ensure that legislation and policy measures affecting sacred sites (i.e. environmental or heritage legislation) do not unduly interfere with the right of access to sites. This is important to protect the indigenous right to manifest their religion. There is a wide margin of discretionary measures possible to protect sites*[422] *and protect indigenous religious practices from undue interference by third parties.*

a. *Legal basis:* This principle seeks to ensure that Articles 18(1) and 27 ICCPR are respected as far as sacred sites are concerned. Governmental measures that limit Indigenous access to sacred sites are classified as a restriction upon the freedom of religion and will need to pass both the test under Art.18 (3) ICCPR test and Art.27 ICCPR test.

b. *Example measure(s):*

i. Prevent access to sacred sites during ceremonial practices in collaboration with the Indigenous community
ii. Post public notices to request that the public voluntarily does not access sacred sites under certain conditions

---

[420] Art.34 UNDRIP describes a number of elements of such legal traditions. Indigenous peoples have the right to promote, develop and maintain their institutional structures and their distinctive customs, spirituality, traditions, procedures, practices and, in the cases where they exist, juridical systems or customs, in accordance with international human rights standards.

[421] According to ILA this is a principle of customary law see ibid., p. 6, p. 51.

[422] UN Commission on Human Rights, Resolution 2005/40 para 4(b): "To exert the utmost efforts, in accordance with their national legislation and in conformity with international human rights law, to ensure that religious places, sites, shrines and religious expressions are fully respected and protected and to take additional measures in cases where they are vulnerable to desecration or destruction."

2.6.2 Test to Evaluate Measures Limiting the Indigenous Right to Use Their Sacred Objects

Apart from these principles, there are also tests which arise out of international human rights law. These help us to evaluate whether a state measure that limits an Indigenous cultural right amounts to a violation of this right. Because many of the UNDRIP rights are a contextualization of existing, binding, treaty rights, the limitations have to be evaluated with the help of the limitation clauses that are applicable to the binding treaty rights. Not all countries have ratified the ICESCR, however, all of the cultural rights articulated within UNDRIP can be viewed as a contextualization of Art.27 ICCPR (potentially in combination with other human rights).

Unfortunately, Art.27 ICCPR is an article for which no specific limitation test has been developed. We know from the guidance of the Human Rights Committee that it offers rights protection additional to other rights in the ICCPR. Moreover, a limiting measure has to be evaluated within the specific context of the right, which is understandable, given the cultural diversity of the communities that are protected by Art.27 ICCPR. As a base layer of protection, a limitation may not result in a denial of the right for the specific community. This does, however, make it difficult to give more general guidance on which measures may be permissible or not. Certainly, Art.27 ICCPR gives additional protection. This means that, where a UNDRIP right is a contextualizing of several rights, limiting measures must at the minimum respect the limitations enshrined in other rights and may in addition not lead to a denial of Art.27 ICCPR.

The right to the use and control of sacred objects is articulated in Art.12 (1) UNDRIP. This includes the right to access these objects (Art.12(2) UNDRIP), but there is no right to the repatriation of sacred objects. Instead, it is one measure which a state can take to guarantee the right to the use and control of sacred objects. This right is the contextualization both of Art.27 ICCPR and Art.18(1) ICCPR. Given that the cultural right protected by Art.27 ICCPR is layered on top of the freedom of religion, any state limitation must at the minimum respect the permissible limitations under Art.18(3) ICCPR and they may also not amount to a denial of the right within the specific context of the case.

In the case of the use and control of sacred objects, this means that state measures may not amount to a complete denial of access and use of an Indigenous community to its sacred heritage. We thus consider the use of sacred heritage as a necessary element of the Indigenous right to their religion, the denial of which leads to a denial of the right to practise their religious traditions, which in effect amounts to a denial of the right to enjoy their own culture and manifest their religion. As highlighted below, an important element to evaluate the lawfulness of a measure under the developed framework is whether the measure is necessary and proportionate. If a less restrictive measure is available, the measure will not be proportionate. For example, a state may deny the Indigenous right to control an object in its collection, but still grant access and use it. This would still fulfil the right to manifest Indigenous religious practices. For this reason, in evaluating whether a measure violates Art.12(1) UNDRIP, the minimum level of state protection that is necessary counts, namely access and use of sacred objects. Control of sacred objects and repatriation of sacred objects are important steps a state takes to fulfil Art.18 ICCPR Art.27 ICCPR, but their absence does not imply a human rights violation.

Limitations on the freedom to manifest their religion may thus be permissible for religious communities that represent the majority culture, but the same state limitation can still be prohibited in the case of Indigenous communities. In the absence of clearer guidance from the Human Rights Committee on the content of the Art.27 ICCPR limitations test, the use of a combined test of the two rights is helpful at this point in time. First, the basis of a measure that a state has taken that limits the Indigenous individual in her access and use of Indigenous object is addressed. It is sufficient to show that one of the criteria of the limitation test has not been met, as they are cumulative. We therefore have to ask if the measure is prescribed by law; pursues a legitimate aim; is necessary and proportionate to achieve this aim; and does not vitiate the right of Indigenous practitioners to manifest their religion. If any of these questions are answered in the negative, Art.27 ICCPR is violated. This is illustrated in Fig 2.1 which will be used to illustrate the application of the test for the country analysis that follows in Chaps. 4 to 8.

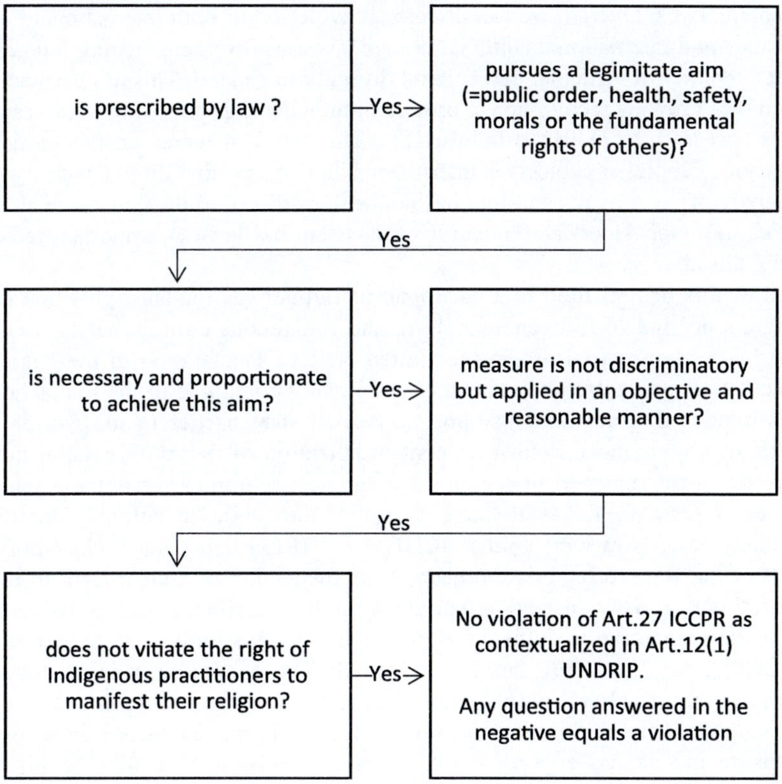

Fig. 2.1 Test to evaluate limitations imposed on the Indigenous right to access and use of their sacred objects

Together, these principles and the test can be used to evaluate both repatriation frameworks, in particular, and Indigenous rights to their religious cultural heritage within the legal framework applicable in the United States and Canada in general.

2.7 Conclusion

The complexity of the repatriation debate was first introduced in Chap. 1, in considering the multitude of legal layers and actors involved. This chapters and Chap. 3 together show that even within international law, repatriation claims are located within a complex web of diverse sources of law. This chapter sought to establish whether international human rights law sets any standards for the repatriation or the protection of Indigenous rights to their sacred cultural heritage that states have to respect under national law. The analysis has shown that international human rights law may not mandate repatriation, but how a state approaches Indigenous sacred cultural heritage connects to a number of Indigenous rights and concurrent state obligations. Overall, we can discern an evolution of both international human rights law and international cultural heritage law towards strengthening Indigenous cultural identity in particular and cultural diversity in general. This has been accompanied by a growing recognition to protect cultural heritage as an important resource that is necessary to realize cultural rights. This trend of increased recognition of Indigenous Peoples as subjects of international law, the proliferation of their rights in a diversity of instruments and fora has not been restricted to the international level. Instead, the Inter-American Human Rights system has been an important factor in driving this change.

All of this has resulted in a catalogue of Indigenous human rights that has a strong connection to Indigenous culture and Indigenous cultural heritage. These rights have been proclaimed in the United Nations Declaration of the Rights of Indigenous Peoples, but they are in effect already contained in the major human rights treaties that are binding upon almost all state parties in the world. This chapter has approached them as a contextualization of the more general human rights that were analyzed in sections 2.2 and 2.3. A number of notable scholars have even gone so far as to infer an Indigenous right to cultural identity in customary law. However, neither ICHL nor IHRL establishes a clear duty on behalf of the state to repatriate objects in its ownership or a clear right to refuse repatriation exercises. Instead, repatriation can be classified as one possible measure a state may take to fulfil the rights of Indigenous individuals under Art.18 (1) ICCPR, Art.27 ICCPR, and Art.15(1) ICESCR. Moreover, it is important to remember that a cultural participation frequently occurs in a communal setting, especially where a religion or belief system and traditional customs are concerned. To ensure the shared enjoyment of the right entails a need to recognize the distinctive value of those resources, including essential Indigenous religious objects which are needed to realize this shared dimension of Art.18 ICCPR, Art.27 ICCPR and Art.15 ICESCR.[423]

Indigenous cultural rights yield important insights into the substantive and procedural content that should be included in a repatriation law in order for it to be fully in line with human rights law. Procedurally, Indigenous Peoples should be consulted before the framework is adopted and consultation has to be included within the framework. Substantively, the framework has to respect the Indigenous right to self-identification and Indigenous religious traditions. The respect for the Indigenous right to manifest their religious practices should also guide the definition of sacred objects within the framework. Essentially, this should be left to knowledgeable Indigenous practitioners. Moreover, to respect the right to manifest their religion, as well as the right to revitalize cultural traditions, the repatriation framework may not require a continuous existence of the respective religious tradition for a repatriation application to succeed.

All of these insights have been distilled into 12 principles that will guide the evaluation of national legislation in the chapters that follow. In addition, a test distilled the admittedly limited guidance on the permissible limitations of Art.27 ICCPR in order to evaluate whether a state measure that interferes with Indigenous access and use of sacred objects amounts to a violation of Art.27 ICCPR. In this respect, it should be reiterated that it is not clear where the dividing line between a denial of Art.27 ICCPR and a limit of Art.27 ICCPR lies precisely, and further research to concretize Art.27 ICCPR is very much needed. Given the broad scope of culture and the diversity of minorities, the difficulty in operationalizing Art.27 ICCPR for the purposes of sacred cultural heritage is not surprising. It does however mean that the application of the test to the different country cases can only be indicative. Whether or not a measure will result in a violation of Art.27 ICCPR will still have to be determined in the application of the repatriation legislation and policy to a specific Indigenous community.

Lastly, this chapter also considered which human rights might have to be balanced against each other in a repatriation. This concerned both the rights of Indigenous individuals, other Indigenous communities that might be affected by a repatriation decision and the cultural rights of the non-Indigenous majority in the preservation and public access of the cultural heritage in question. The picture presented is one of compromise. To the non-legal mind, the language of a right to a given good or activity may appear to be absolute, undeniable in its multiple applications unless violated, sacrosanct. For a certain set of contemporary international rights this is true. In the sphere of cultural rights, self-determination and cultural heritage law, in which repatriation requests operate, however, this is not

[423] International Commission of Jurists (2008), p. 5, para 9. The Commission also cautions "[t]he preservation of these collective goods is of capital importance for the collective practices that inform cultural life and, therefore, their disregard often results in a shared sense of cultural offense."

the case. Instead, compromises[424] must be found which respect state obligations under existing treaty law, Indigenous Peoples rights arising out of an-ever growing body of Indigenous human rights instruments and navigate the difficult landscape of colonial wrongs and contemporary reconciliation efforts. The balancing of contrasting rights and interests is a daily reality of legal practice. To deny this balancing and demand an absolute answer (be it complete repatriation for every object or absolute rejection of every request) is to deny the application of law to repatriation in favor of another solution, for example a political one.

References

Ahdar R, Leigh I (2005) Legal protection of religious freedom. In: Religious freedom in the Liberal state. Oxford University Press, Oxford, pp 98–126

Ahmed MAA, Aylwin N, Coombe R (2008) Indigenous cultural heritage rights in international human rights law. In: Bell C, Patterson R (eds) Protection of first nations' cultural heritage: laws, policy and reform. UBC Press, Vancouver, pp 311–342

Åhrén M (2008) Protecting peoples' cultural rights: a question of properly understanding the notion of states and nations? In: Francioni F, Scheinin M (eds) Cultural human rights. Martinus Nijhoff Publishers, Leiden, pp 91–118

Antkowiak TM (2013) Rights, resources, and rhetoric: indigenous peoples and the Inter-American Court. Univ Pa J Int Law 35(1):113–188

Battiste M, Henderson JY (2000) Protecting indigenous knowledge and heritage: a global challenge. Purich, Saskatoon

Bell CE, Statt G, Mookakin Cultural Society (2008) Repatriation and heritage protection: reflections on the Kainai experience. In: Bell CE, Napoleon V (eds) First nations cultural heritage and law: case studies, voices, and perspectives. UBC Press, Vancouver, pp 203–257

Bettinger-Lopez C (2009) The Inter-American human rights system: a primer. Clear Rev 42 (6):581–595

Blake J (2014) Exploring cultural rights and cultural diversity. Institute of Art & Law, Builth Wells

Cassese A (1995) Self-determination of peoples: a legal reappraisal. Grotius Publ, Cambridge

Chamberlain K, Vrdoljak AF (2014) Controls on the export of cultural objects and human rights. In: Nafziger J, Paterson RK (eds) Handbook on the law of cultural heritage and international trade. Edward Elgar, Cheltenham

Champagne D (2012) Indigenous self-government, cultural heritage and international trade: a sociological perspective. In: Graber CB, Kuprecht K, Lai JC (eds) International trade in indigenous cultural heritage - legal and policy issues. Edward Elgar, Cheltenham, pp 31–58

Charlesworth H (2008) Universal declaration of human rights (1948). Max Planck Encyclopedia of public international law. Oxford Public International Law, Max Planck Institute, Heidelberg

Charters C (2012) Reparations for Indigenous Peoples: Global International Instruments and Institutions. Reparations for Indigenous Peoples: International and Comparative Perspectives. Oxford Online Scholarship

Coombe RJ, Turcotte JF (2012) Indigenous cultural heritage in development and trade: perspectives from the dynamics of cultural heritage law and policy. In: Graber CB, Kuprecht K, Lai JC (eds) International trade in indigenous cultural heritage - legal and policy issues. Edward Elgar, Cheltenham, pp 272–305

[424] Prott made a comparable argument with regard to the right to development and specific (minority) cultures in Prott (1986), p. 15.

de Jong C (2000) The freedom of thought, conscience and religion or belief in the United Nations: (1946–1992). Intersentia [u.a.], Antwerpen [u.a]
Desmet E (2011) Indigenous rights entwined with nature conservation. Intersentia International Specialized Book Services, Cambridge
Donders Y (2002) Towards a right to cultural identity? Intersentia, Antwerpen, New York
Donders Y (2007) The legal framework of the right to take part in cultural life. Human rights in education, science and culture: legal developments and challenges. Ashgate Publishers, Aldershot
Donders Y (2008) Background Paper for the General Day of Discussion - Right to take part in cultural life (article 15(1)(a) of the Covenant). CESCR, E/C.12/40/13
Evans MD (2001) Human rights, religious liberty and the universality debate. In: O'Dair R, Lewis A (eds) Law and religion. Oxford University Press, Oxford, pp 205–226
Fink C (2000) Minority rights as an international question. Contemp Eur Hist 9(3):385–400
Francioni F (2008) Culture, heritage and human rights: an introduction. In: Francioni F, Scheinin M (eds) Cultural human rights. Martinus Nijhoff Publishers, Leiden, pp 1–15
Golay C, Cismas I (2010) Legal opinion: the right to property from a human rights perspective. pp 1–31
Graber CB (2012) Stimulating trade and development of indigenous cultural heritage by means of international law: issues of legitimacy and method. In: Graber CB, Kuprecht K, Lai JC (eds) International trade in indigenous cultural heritage - legal and policy issues. Edward Elgar, Cheltenham, pp 3–30
Groni C (2008) Background Paper for the General Day of Discussion - Right to take part in cultural life (article 15(1)(a) of the Covenant). UN CESCR, E/C.12/40/3
Hadjioannou M (2005) The international human right to culture: reclamation of the cultural identities of indigenous peoples under international law. Chapman Law Rev 9:201–228
Harding S (1999) Value, obligation and cultural heritage. Arizona State Law J 31:291–354
ILO (2013) Understanding the Indigenous and Tribal Peoples Convention, 1989 (No. 169) Handbook for ILO Tripartite Constituents
Inter-American Commission on Human Rights (2000) Report on the Situation of Human Rights of Asylum Seekers Within the Canadian Refugee Determination System
International Commission of Jurists (2008) Background paper for the Day of Gneral Discussion - Right to take part in cultural life (article 15(1)(a) of the Covenant). CESCR, E/C.12/40/7
International Labour Organization I (2008) Comments submitted for the Day of General Discussion - The right to take part in cultural life. CESCR, E/C.12/40/12
Kuprecht K (2014) Indigenous peoples' cultural property claims - repatriation and beyond. Springer
Kuprecht K, Siehr K (2012) International trade in moveable tangible cultural heritage of indigenous peoples: a European perspective. In: Graber CB, Kuprecht K, Lai JC (eds) International trade in indigenous cultural heritage - legal and policy issues. Edward Elgar, Cheltenham, pp 246–271
Lavrysen L (2014) Positive obligations in the Jurisprudence of the Inter-American court of human rights. Int-Am Eur Human Rights J 7:94–115
Lenzerini F, Scott J (2012) International indigenous and human rights law in the context of trade in indigenous cultural heritage. In: Graber CB, Kuprecht K, Lai JC (eds) International trade in indigenous cultural heritage. Edward Elgar, Cheltenham, pp 61–87
Lixinski L (2014) Heritage for whom? Individuals' and communities' roles in international cultural heritage law. In: Lenzerini F, Vrdoljak AF (eds) International law for common goods - normative perspectives on human rights, culture and nature. Hart, Oxford, pp 193–213
Mazzuoli VD, Ribeiro D (2015) Indigenous rights before the Inter-American court of human rights. Indones J Int Comp Law 2:522–553
McGoldrick D (2002) Culture, cultures, and cultural rights. In: Baderin M, McCorquodale R (eds) Economic, social and cultural rights in action. Oxford University Press, Oxford, pp 447–473
Nimni E (2008) Background Paper for the Day of General Discussion - Right to take part in cultural life (article 15(1)(a) of the Covenant). CESCR, E/C.12/40/17

Nowak M (2005) U.N. Covenant on Civil and Political Rights - CCPR Commentary. N.P. Engel, Kehl

O'Keefe R (2011) Cultural Life, Right to Participate in, International Protection. Max Planck Encyclopedia of Public International Law. Oxford Public International Law, Max Planck Institute of International Law, Heidelberg

O'Keefe R (2013) Tangible cultural heritage and international human rights law. In: Prott L, Redmond-Cooper R, Urice S (eds) Realising cultural heritage law - Festschrift for Patrick O'Keefe, IAL Institute of Art and Law, pp 87–95

Pasqualucci JM (2006) The evolution of international Indigneous rights in the inter-American human rights system. Hum Rights Law Rev 6(2):281–322

Paterson RK (2014) Collecting "tribal art"- sacred or secular? Int J Cult Prop 21:305–318

Pentassuglia G (2013) Protecting minority groups through human rights courts - the interpretative role of European and Inter-American Jurisprudence. In: Vrdoljak AF (ed) The cultural dimension of human rights. Oxford University Press, pp 73–116

Pineschi L (2012) Cultural diversity as a human right? General comment no.21 of the committee on economic, social and cultural rights. In: Borelli S, Lenzerini F (eds) Cultural heritage, cultural rights, cultural diversity. Studies in intercultural human rights. Nijhoff Publishers, Brill, pp 29–53

Prott L (1986) Cultural rights as People's rights in international law. Bull Aust Soc Legal Philos 10 (1):4–19

Scheinin M (2005) Indigenous peoples' rights under the international covenant on civil and political rights. In: Castellino J, Walsh N (eds) International law and indigenous peoples. Martinus Nijhoff Publishers, Leiden, pp 3–15

Scovazzi T, Nafziger J (2007) 2005 - Le patrimoine culturel de l'humanité - the cultural heritage of mankind. Martinus Nijhoff Publishers

Shaheed F (2010) Report of the independent expert in the field of cultural rights on the conceptual and legal framework of her mandate. UN General Assembly, A/HRC/14/36

Shaheed F (2011) Report of the independent expert in the field of cultural rights on the right of access to and enjoyment of cultural heritage. UN General Assembly, A/HRC/17/38

Shaheed F (2012) Report of the Special Rapporteur in the field of cultural rights on the enjoyment of cultural rights by women. UN General Assembly, A/67/287

Shelton D (2013) The inter-American human rights law of indigenous peoples. Univ Hawaii Law Rev 35(2):937–982

Stamatopoulou E (2007) Cultural rights in international law: Article 27 of the universal declaration of human rights and beyond. Martinus Nijhoff, Boston

Stamatopoulou E (2008) Background Paper for the Day of General Discussion - Right to take part in cultural life (article 15(1)(a) of the Covenant). CESCR, E/C.12/40/9

Swepston L (2005) Indigenous peoples in international law and organizations. In: Castellino J, Walsh N (eds) International law and indigenous peoples. Martinus Nijhoff Publishers, Leiden, pp 53–66

Tennant C (1994) Indigenous peoples, international institutions, and the international legal literature from 1945-1993. Hum Rights Q 16(1):1–57

Thornberry P (2008) Background Paper for the Day of General Discussion - Right to take part in cultural life (article 15(1)(a) of the Covenant). CESCR, E/C.12/40/15

Tomuschat C (2010) Human rights - between idealism and realism. Oxford University Press

Tsosie R (2012) International trade in indigenous cultural heritage: an argument for indigenous governance of cultural property. In: Graber CB, Kuprecht K, Lai JC (eds) International trade in indigenous cultural heritage - legal and policy issues. Edward Elgar, Cheltenham, pp 221–245

van der Schyff G (2004) The historical development of the right to freedom of religion. South Afr Law J 2:259–272

Vrdoljak AF (2008a) International law, museums and the return of cultural objects. Cambridge University Press, Cambridge

Vrdoljak AF (2008b) Self-determination and cultural rights. In: Francioni F, Scheinin M (eds) Cultural human rights. Martinus Nijhoff Publishers, Leiden, pp 41–78

Vrdoljak AF (2014) Human rights and cultural heritage in international law. In: Lenzerini F, Vrdoljak AF (eds) International law for common goods. Hart, Oxford, pp 139–173

Vrdoljak AF (2018) Indigenous peoples, world heritage, and human rights. Int J Cult Prop 25 (3):245–281. https://doi.org/10.1017/S0940739118000218

Wiener M (2015) Interpretation of the 1981 declaration through the mandate practice of the United Nations special rapporteur on freedom of religion or belief. Changing nature of religious rights under international law. Oxford University Press, Oxford

Xanthaki A (2018) Articles 11(1), 12, 13(1), 15 and 34. In: Hohmann J, Weller M (eds) The UN declaration on the rights of indigenous peoples. Oxford University Press, Oxford, pp 273–298

Yupsanis A (2010) ILO convention NO. 169 concerning indigenous and tribal peoples in independent countries 1989-2009: an overview. Nordic J Int Law 79:433–456

Chapter 3
Repatriation of Sacred Indigenous Heritage Under International Cultural Heritage Law

3.1 Introduction

Chapter 1 highlighted the fact that there is no duty to repatriate sacred cultural heritage in the instruments that set out international cultural heritage law. As the Expert Mechanism on the Rights of Indigenous Peoples [hereafter EMRIP] once observed "(a)lthough some potential avenues for redress or protection might exist in legal terms ... in reality it is extremely difficult for indigenous peoples to receive proper protection and reparation when their cultural heritage... is misappropriated."[1] The analysis of international human rights law has shown that, while there is no obligation to repatriate sacred cultural heritage under binding international law provisions, there are a number of principles that do have to be respected in a repatriation framework. Moreover, the state is under an obligation to enable Indigenous access and use of sacred objects, subject to conditions as explored above. By comparison, international cultural heritage law (hereafter ICHL) largely displays the traditional picture of international law as an arena dominated by states. This is not surprising, since two of its core treaties were adopted in the early 1970s,[2] when Indigenous Peoples were still struggling to achieve recognition of their special status on the international level.

Change has been comparatively slow to come, and instruments of international cultural heritage law do not represent contemporary Indigenous rights standards.

[1] Human Rights Council, Promotion and protection of the rights of Indigenous Peoples with respect to their cultural heritage, Study by the Expert Mechanism on the Rights of Indigenous Peoples, U.N. Doc. A/HRC/30/53 [19.08.2015], para 72.

[2] UN Educational, Scientific and Cultural Organisation (UNESCO), Convention on the Means of Prohibiting and Preventing the Illicit Import, Export and Transfer of Ownership of Cultural Property, 14 November 1970. UN Educational, Scientific and Cultural Organisation (UNESCO), *Convention Concerning the Protection of the World Cultural and Natural Heritage*, 16 November 1972.

V. Tünsmeyer, *Repatriation of Sacred Indigenous Cultural Heritage and the Law*, Studies in Art, Heritage, Law and the Market 3,
https://doi.org/10.1007/978-3-030-89047-6_3

However, as will be seen in the course of the analysis provided in this chapter, protecting cultural heritage as evidence of different cultures has been a cornerstone of cultural heritage law since its early days. This recognizes the importance of protecting a plurality of cultures, including Indigenous cultures. Moreover, the importance of cultural heritage to Indigenous Peoples has increasingly been recognized, not only in soft law instruments, but also in the newer binding treaties in the field. For these reasons, it is important to evaluate whether ICHL instruments impose any duties on the state that would affect repatriation on the national level. In addition, while there is no duty to repatriate sacred cultural heritage that was taken in the past, we can observe an evolving norm in this direction.

To evidence this the evolution of the field as well as the main organizations that have shaped international cultural heritage law will be summarized. This will explain both the absence of repatriation provisions in ICHL treaties as well as the comparatively late arrival of Indigenous rights in the field. Afterwards, attention will be paid to the 1995 UNIDROIT Convention on Stolen or Illegally Exported Cultural Objects. It was the first binding instrument of ICHL that explicitly recognized the importance of sacred cultural heritage for Indigenous Peoples. The more recent UNESCO Conventions, the 2003 UNESCO Convention for the Safeguarding of the Intangible Cultural Heritage and the 2005 UNESCO Convention on the Promotion and Protection of the Diversity of Cultural Expressions, will be explored in Sects. 3.4 and 3.5. Both consider the importance of different forms of cultural heritage for Indigenous Peoples and incorporate some references to human rights standards.

3.2 Evolution of International Cultural Heritage Law

3.2.1 UNESCO: The Leading Organization

UNESCO is an international, intergovernmental organization with 195 Member States and over 50 field offices globally. The United Nations Organization for Education, Science and Culture, is a specialized agency of the UN in accordance with Art.57 UN Charter.[3] The influence of UNESCO on international cultural heritage law rests in its standard-setting instruments which are supported and realized by its wide membership. While the majority of its instruments are soft law instruments and thus non-binding,[4] in the area of international cultural heritage law, UNESCO has contributed the majority of treaty-work and has in effect shaped the way in which international cultural heritage law operates today. As a result, its

[3] Art. X UNESCO Constitution.

[4] Donders (2002), p. 107, observed that "[g]enerally speaking, most of the work of UNESCO does not lie in the field of preparing legally-binding instruments, but in the field of the development of concepts and the attunement of policies."

constituting instrument is incredibly important in establishing the underlying values which international cultural heritage law seeks to realize. Moreover, UNESCO conventions that protect cultural heritage in one form or another are also important for the protection of human rights. Cultural heritage is an important foundation for the enjoyment of the right to take part in cultural life and the right of Indigenous Peoples to their culture.[5]

The UNESCO Constitution identifies ignorance and a lack of mutual understanding as the central cause of war,[6] as it enables the denial of human dignity.[7] Ignorance is to be prevented by the distribution of knowledge, which explains the need for "conservation and protection of the world's inheritance".[8] Mutual understanding was perceived as the only means to ensure long-lasting peace, to which the organization must contribute, in line with Art.1(1). Francesco Francioni has similarly highlighted the relevance of the UNESCO Constitution for cultural heritage.[9] In addition, he underlines the Constitution's importance to international cultural heritage as "cultural property started to be treated as a distinct object of international protection, because of its inherent value as an expression of the different cultural traditions of the world."[10] It was this understanding of the importance of culture, according to Francioni, which lead UNESCO to the adoption of the 1954 Hague Convention which was essential to the development of international cultural heritage law (see section below).[11] It therefore appears as if heritage is valued as a vehicle of culture and knowledge. To preserve and conserve the object in question is to protect knowledge, which combats ignorance and ultimately prevents war. This transforms the protection of heritage into an existential need shared by all states. It is this understanding of conservation and protection as the ultimate purpose of international cultural heritage law that shines through in the 1970 UNESCO convention (examined below) and is the pillar of the 1972 World Heritage Convention. More recently, threats to cultural heritage as part of targeted attacks, looting and the financing of illegal activities has again renewed international attention for cultural heritage and has led to greater cooperation between UNESCO and the UN.[12]

---

[5] Bandarin (2012), p. 307.

[6] Preamble, recital 2: "That ignorance of each other's ways and lives has been a common cause, throughout the history of mankind, of that suspicion and mistrust between the peoples of the world through which their differences have all too often broken into war".

[7] Preamble, recital 3: "That the great and terrible war which has now ended was a war made possible by the denial of the democratic principles of the dignity, equality and mutual respect of men, and by the propagation, in their place, through ignorance and prejudice, of the doctrine of the inequality of men and races".

[8] Art.1(2)(c) UNESCO Constitution. Compare Forrest (2007), p. 129. He has characterized the provision as an expression of universalism.

[9] Francioni (2013), para 1.

[10] Francioni (2013), para 1.

[11] Francioni (2013), para 1.

[12] Scovazzi (2020), p. 740.

Next to the development of standards through treaties and soft law instruments, UNESCO also established an Intergovernmental Committee that acts a mediator in cases where states ask for the return of cultural property. In 1974, UNESCO passed Resolution 3.428, which called attention to the loss of cultural heritage due to colonialism and highlighted the importance of returning such objects, not only as a form of reparation, but also to strengthen international cooperation.[13] This plea was, however, focussed on intergovernmental returns not repatriation in the sense of returning cultural heritage to an Indigenous community. The resolution also asked the Director-General to "defin[e] in general terms the most suitable methods, including exchanges on the basis of long-term loans, and by promoting bilateral arrangements to that end" in order to strengthen restitution efforts.[14]

As a reaction to this and to General Assembly Resolution 3187 on the restitution of art works,[15] an Expert Committee proposed a variety of measures, including a wider ratification of the 1970 UNESCO Convention and the establishment of a Committee, which should facilitate bilateral negotiations and advise the Director General.[16] At the next General Session in 1978, the Intergovernmental Committee for Promoting the Return of Cultural Property to its Countries of Origin or its Restitution in case of Illicit Appropriation was founded.[17] The Committee is made up of twenty Member States, elected by the General Conference.[18] The Statutes provide that any Member State (or Associate Member) may request the return of cultural property "which has a fundamental significance from the point of view of the spiritual values and cultural heritage of the people of a Member State" and which was lost for one of three reasons, including "as a result of colonial occupation".[19] Unfortunately, the Committee has not been as successful in stimulating and settling inter-state return claims as was hoped, which may partially be explained by its intergovernmental nature and the lack of any clear legal mechanism or rules for how return applications. In fact, the mechanism appears to be more diplomatic in

---

[13] UNESCO, 18th General Conference, 18 C/ Resolution 3.428 Contributions of UNESCO to the return of cultural property to countries that have been victims of *de facto* expropriation (1974).

[14] UNESCO, Resolution 3.428 (1974), at para 5.

[15] UN General Assembly, Resolution 3187 [1973] specifically asks states to prohibit the removal of cultural objects still under colonial rule or territorial occupation (at para 3).

[16] Implementation of 18 C/ Resolution 3.428 of the General Conference concerning the Restitution or Return of Cultural Property, General Conference 19th Session, Document Reference: 19 C/109, at para 7.

[17] UNESCO, General Conference 20th Session, Document Reference: Resolution 20 C/ Resolution 4/7.6/5 (1978).

[18] Rules of Procedure of the Intergovernmental Committee for Promoting the Return of Cultural Property to its Countries of Origin or its Restitution in case of Illicit Appropriation, rule 1.1, available via: Statutes and Rules of Procedure | United Nations Educational, Scientific and Cultural Organization (unesco.org) [last consulted 12.07.2021].

[19] Statutes of the Intergovernmental Committee for Promoting the Return of Cultural Property to its Countries of Origin or its Restitution in Case of Illicit Appropriation, Art.3(2). Adopted by 20 C/Resolution 4/7.6/5 of the 20th session of the General Conference of UNESCO, Paris, 24 October–28 November 1978.

nature which may only be suitable for very particular cases, rather than for all possible claims for returns, and certainly ill-suited for repatriations given its state focus.

Instead, it has it has promoted the various conventions, reported on their implementation and generally facilitated the protection of cultural property by States (i.e. by advising States or increasing the effectiveness of the existing instrument).[20] Overall, UNESCO's efforts to engage directly with Indigenous communities appear to be limited by its organizational character and the concerns of sovereign state parties.[21]

3.2.2 The Development of International Cultural Heritage Law

Contemporary international cultural heritage law is a fragmented body of law spread over a number of conventions that deal with very different areas of law. Concern for cultural heritage first arose in the context of war, which caused the destruction of immovable cultural heritage and the looting of moveable cultural heritage.[22] Notable instruments of the law of war which relate to cultural heritage are the American Lieber Code of 1863, which influenced the drafting of the Hague Conventions of 1899 and 1907, and the 1954 Hague Convention for the Protection of Cultural Property in the Event of Armed Conflict.[23] The 1954 Hague Convention defined cultural property in an international treaty for the first time; it was also the first instrument drafted expressly to protect cultural heritage.[24] In the late 1960s, international cultural heritage law slowly started to broaden in scope. This was furthered by a combination of factors. The growing awareness of the dangers of illegal excavation among archaeologists, the growing awareness among officials about the link between illegal traffic of cultural objects and other forms of international crime, the growing awareness among source states of the increasing loss of heritage to market states, the growing environmental awareness globally which also triggered a need to protect natural heritage and, lastly, the growing Indigenous Peoples movement which, *inter alia*, drew attention to non-tangible heritage.[25]

UNESCO reacted to these impulses and, over time, drafted 6 international conventions which, complemented by the 1995 UNIDROIT Convention on Stolen or Illegally Exported Cultural Objects, make up the main body of contemporary

---

[20] Prott (2009b), p. 17.

[21] Kuprecht (2014), p. 148. For an overview of the (evolving) role of non-state actors in international cultural heritage law see the interesting overview presented in Hausler (2020).

[22] Forrest (2010), p. xx.

[23] Bengs (1996), pp. 513–514.

[24] Nafziger and Paterson (2014), p. 4.

[25] Nafziger and Paterson (2014), pp. 5–6.

international cultural heritage law:[26] The 1954 Convention for the Protection of Cultural Property in the Event of Armed Conflict, the 1970 Convention on the Means of Prohibiting and Preventing the Illicit Import, Export and Transfer of Cultural Property, the 1972 Convention for the Protection of the World Cultural and Natural Heritage, the 2001 Convention on the Protection of the Underwater Cultural Heritage, the 2003 Convention for the Safeguarding of Intangible Cultural Heritage and the 2005 Convention on the Protection and Promotion of the Diversity of Cultural Expressions. As the conventions have been drafted as a reaction to the developments explored above, rather than as part of a conscious attempt to draft one coherent body of law, they do not always interact well with each other.[27]

An early example of the possible links between cultural heritage and cultural rights instruments is the 1966 UNESCO Declaration of the Principles of International Cultural Co-operation. It espouses greater cross-cultural understanding in the name of peace.[28] Art.1 of the Declaration provides every people with "the right and the duty to develop its culture", stating that "all cultures form part of the common heritage belonging to all mankind."[29] By transforming the different cultures into part of the common heritage of mankind, one could argue that, rather than a specific object being worthy of preservation and protection for the sake of future generations, the emphasis is instead placed on preserving the specific culture. This could speak in favour of repatriation in much the same way as a cultural revivalist argument, which was explained in the first chapter. This soft-law article is progressive for its time. It would indicate early support for the existence of a collective right to cultural integrity that encompasses other cultural rights, including the right to cultural heritage. It does, however, raise the question who precisely holds the right and the duty to develop a culture and which culture is meant? The preamble lists "governments, authorities, organizations, associations and institutions responsible for cultural activities" as the immediate addressees of the Declaration.[30] This would suggest that the declarations not only seek to encourage states but a wider variety of actors. In this sense, it displays the very first tenets of the participatory model which the youngest UNESCO instruments, the 2003 ICHC and the 2005 CDCE, have transposed into binding law. However, the focus on the culture of each 'people', the duty of 'nations' to develop them 'side by side' (Art.II), cooperate with each other (Art.III), together with the time of adoption would suggest that the focus here was more on national cultures. Moreover, the instrument is not a binding treaty. As a result, the right of every people to develop its culture is not laid down in a manner which would oblige states to respect and protect it.

[26] Forrest (2010), preface lists five and excludes the UNESCO Convention on the Protection and Promotion of the Diversity of Cultural Expressions.

[27] Forrest (2010), p. xxi.

[28] Preamble to UNESCO Declaration of the Principles of Cultural Cooperation, recital 2, 4. See also Donders (2002), p. 111.

[29] UNESCO Declaration of the Principles of Cultural Cooperation, Art.1(2), (3).

[30] Preamble to UNESCO Declaration of the Principles of Cultural Cooperation, recital 7.

Even with this early link between cultural heritage and human rights, and the more recent instruments considering Indigenous rights and human rights more explicitly, the primary goal of international cultural heritage law still remains centred on preserving cultural property. This is motivated by its unique nature; it is not a good that can be mass-produced.[31] This protectionist/ conservationist concern is understandably most visible in the 1954 Hague Convention as well as in the 1972 World Heritage Convention. The former bases this concern on the foreseeable destruction caused to heritage in times of war,[32] while in the latter it is expressly motivated by the importance of the heritage in question.[33] As was highlighted in Chap. 1, where there is an emphasis on conservation, this can translate into a refusal to accept other roles of heritage in so far as they threaten the integrity of the object. Conversely, international cultural heritage law, so far, has not overly concerned itself with the return of cultural objects to Indigenous Peoples. While this also has other reasons, most notably the dominant position of States on the international level,[34] the emphasis on object preservation decreases the likelihood that an international treaty on the repatriation of Indigenous cultural objects will be adopted in the near future. Yet, as will become apparent in the following sections, international cultural heritage law has evolved and has become more and more inclusive and aware of diverse forms of cultural heritage, including the heritage of Indigenous Peoples.[35] This shift towards a greater recognition of Indigenous interests in their cultural heritage first took hold in soft law instruments. The first binding instruments adopted by UNESCO did not consider Indigenous interests.

---

[31] Fechner (1998), p. 382.

[32] See 1954 Hague Convention, preamble, recital 1 "**Recognizing** that cultural property has suffered grave damage during recent armed conflicts and that, by reason of the developments in the technique of warfare, it is in increasing danger of destruction". Emphasis added.

[33] See 1972 WHC Convention, preamble, recital 6,7. The 1972 WHC seeks to protect cultural heritage, because it fears destruction without such protection just as the 1954 Hague Convention seeks to protect heritage from destruction because of its value to humankind (see recital 3). The difference between the two is a question of emphasis not one of fundamental opposition.

[34] With all the consequences this entails for Indigenous Peoples: Lack of international legal personality, lack of self-determination and consequently a lack of participation.

[35] Compare Donders (2020), p. 384.

3.2.3 Lack of Consideration for Indigenous Interests in Their Cultural Heritage in Early UNESCO Treaties

3.2.3.1 1970 Convention on the Means of Prohibiting and Preventing the Illicit Import, Export and Transfer of Ownership of Cultural Property[36]

In order to combat an ever-increasing illicit traffic in cultural heritage, the 1970 UNESCO Convention governs the return of cultural property. It is restricted to the return of cultural property that was illegally exported from its country of origin after the Convention's entry into force.[37] To achieve this, the Convention imposes duties upon a participating member state to implement export legislation, complete with a certificate verifying the compliance of a cultural property with the requirements.[38] The Convention also offers an additional layer of protection to stolen cultural heritage that was part of the inventory of a cultural institution. Specifically, it imposes the duty to prohibit the import of such cultural property.[39]

While the Convention does apply to Indigenous sacred cultural heritage,[40] it does not apply to cultural property that was taken during colonialism and exported out of the country prior to its entry into force. The scope of the Convention is the result of the politically charged atmosphere that dominated its drafting process.[41] This was especially the case where the retroactivity of the convention was concerned. States which had lost much of their heritage before 1970, mostly under colonial rule, wanted their heritage to be returned.[42] The potential negative effect of this on a large number of private owners of cultural objects globally, as well as the feared effect on the respective art markets, would have meant that those states whose acceptance was crucial (such as the United States as one of the major art market states at the time) would not have accepted the Convention.[43] As a result, the Convention does not provide for retroactivity in its articles, and is therefore not retroactive.[44] In effect, its provisions evidence a much deplored problem of international law: compromises between (at times) opposing positions[45] result in unclear

[36] Hereafter referred to as 1970 UNESCO Convention.

[37] Art.3 in conj. with Art.7(b) (ii) 1970 UNESCO Convention.

[38] Art.6 1970 UNESCO Convention.

[39] Art.7(b) (i) 1970 UNESCO Convention.

[40] For present purposes, it seems safe to observe that Indigenous religious objects could be classified on either religious grounds (where the custom in question is still used or revitalized) or secular grounds because of their importance to history or science. They will fall either under Art.1(b) as property relating to history or, more likely under Art.1(f) (objects of ethnological interest).

[41] Prott (2009a), p. 216.

[42] Forrest (2010), p. 41.

[43] Compare Forrest (2010), pp. 166–167.

[44] Similarly Nafziger and Paterson (2014), p. 12.

[45] Forrest (2010), p. 166.

treaty provisions,[46] which may be very difficult to interpret. Similarly, the evaluation of the Convention is difficult. Due to its wide ratification, it could be viewed as successful, but, so far, it has failed in effectively reducing the illicit trade in cultural objects, which was its principal aim.[47]

The Convention does not impose any obligations upon a state that it would have to respect in a repatriation framework. Nor does it advance Indigenous human rights interests. On the contrary, the ultimate power to designate a cultural property is left to the state. While religious cultural property can be protected because of its sacred nature if a state so desires, there is no consideration of the fact that religious practitioners may require the protection of their religious cultural heritage if a state does not categorize it as national cultural property. The 1970 UNESCO Convention protects ICH due to its value to science (as expressed in the preamble and Art.5), its value to national culture (highlighted in Art.4) and its value to humankind (as expressed in the preamble). The fact that the relationship between the Indigenous community and its cultural heritage is not recognized in the Convention is not surprising. It can be explained by the general lack of recognition afforded to Indigenous Peoples in international law at the time. However, national export legislation can (and should) be adjusted to remedy this oversight and incorporate Indigenous rights to their cultural heritage into the national law. Both the United States and Canada have ratified 1970 UNESCO Convention, albeit the former limited its applicability extensively. Their respective export legislation and its (lack of) alignment with the UNDRIP will be discussed as part of analysing the national legal framework.[48]

EMRIP highlights the importance of Art.15 of the 1970 Convention for indigenous peoples in its report on the repatriation of ceremonial objects.[49] Art.15 provides that the convention does not prevent states "from concluding special agreements among themselves or from continuing to implement agreements already concluded regarding the restitution of cultural property removed, whatever the reason, from its territory of origin, before the entry into force of this Convention for the States concerned." It is true that agreements for the return of cultural objects taken during the colonial period to Indigenous objects are permitted under article 15. However, the provision does not contribute much to the repatriation of ceremonial objects as such agreements would be permitted even in the absence of article 15. Quite simply, they fall outside the scope of the 1970 UNESCO Convention and as such, states can decide to conclude such agreements if they so wish. This is a simple outcome of a

[46] Prott (2009a), p. 216.

[47] Forrest (2010), p. 195.

[48] See in particular Chap. 4, Sect. 4.6.1, and Chap. 6, Sect. 6.3.5.

[49] Human Rights Council, Report of the Expert Mechanism on the Rights of Indigenous Peoples, Repatriation of ceremonial objects, human remains and intangible cultural heritage under the United Nations Declaration on the Rights of Indigenous Peoples, U.N. Doc. A/HRC/45/35 [21.07.2020], p. 6.

state's treaty making capacity[50] in conjunction with the fact that any agreement on repatriation of colonial-era heritage to Indigenous Peoples (or to states that would then repatriate it to Indigenous communities in their territory) and restitution of cultural property under the 1970 UNESCO to states after the Convention's entry into force are not the same subject matter.

As such, Art.15 at most provides incentive by highlighting the possibility of concluding such agreements and utilizing the familiarity of states with the instruments. In such a case the long existence of the Convention is used to encourage states to comply with UNDRIP, by concluding an agreement for an international return between states which is then followed by an intra-national repatriation. This seems to be what the EMRIP advised in the case of the Yaqui and Swedish Parties in the dispute surrounding the Maaso Kova.[51]

3.2.3.2 1972 Convention Concerning the Protection of the World Cultural and Natural Heritage[52]

As is the case for the 1970 UNESCO Convention, the 1972 World Heritage Convention's ultimate goal is to ensure the protection (understood as physical preservation) of important cultural heritage. The development of the World Heritage Convention was in effect due to a collision of two spheres, which, in an age of increasing urbanisation, both required protection: cultural heritage and the environment.[53] The former saw both a shift in management methods,[54] as well as a number of instances where important cultural heritage was threatened to such an extent that international efforts were necessary. One such case was the construction of the Aswan High Dam in Egypt and the resulting threat to archaeological monuments due to flooding. Egypt and Sudan's request for assistance caused UNESCO to launch a campaign for financial assistance, which yielded over US$40 million in state contributions.[55] At the same time, the recognition that any impact on the environment nationally could not be separated from shared international environmental spaces also led to joint international efforts in this area.[56] To classify for international protection, natural or cultural heritage site must be of 'outstanding universal value'.[57] Its focus rests on immoveable cultural heritage. Contrary to the 1970 UNESCO Convention, the ultimate designation decision is taken on the

[50] Art. 6 Vienna Convention on the Law of Treaties.

[51] Expert Mechanism on the Rights of Indigenous People, "Technical advisory note on the repatriation request for the Yaqui Maaso Kova" [16.06.2020].

[52] Hereafter referred to as 1972 World Heritage Convention.

[53] Forrest (2010), p. 226.

[54] Forrest (2010), p. 226.

[55] Forrest (2010), pp. 226–227.

[56] Forrest (2010), p. 226.

[57] Arts. 1,2 1972 World Heritage Convention.

international level. This warrants the imposition of a number of obligations upon the state.[58] The convention actually transforms the state into the custodian of designated heritage sites within its territory for the benefit of humankind.[59] This legal transformation of cultural heritage into a shared global common good also entails that, if a cultural heritage is endangered, this triggers action on the international level, including providing resources to assist a state where necessary.[60]

The original convention text does not take the interests of the local (Indigenous) community that lives in the area of the heritage site into account. In effect, the listing of sites as world cultural heritage led to Indigenous rights violations being committed by a number of states in different cases.[61] Over time, however, the system has slowly been moving towards a greater recognition of Indigenous interests in cultural heritage through the Operational Guidelines, which are regularly updated and guide the implementation of the Convention. Their slow evolution mirrors the gradual inclusion of Indigenous Peoples in ICHL instruments and the increasing awareness of the importance of cultural heritage for Indigenous Peoples. For a long time, Indigenous Peoples were not mentioned in the Operational Guidelines. Even local communities, a term which encompasses Indigenous Peoples at the local level, were only included in the Operational Guidelines in 2005.[62] Local communities became participants in the conservation and protection of the heritage site.[63] A further move towards the greater recognition of the importance of cultural heritage for Indigenous Peoples occurred in 2007. On the initiative of New Zealand, then represented by Maori leader Tumu te Heuheu, the World Heritage Committee included communities as a strategic objective of the Convention:[64] the Committee identified the need to

[58] Arts. 4, 5 1972 World Heritage Convention. This identification, protection, conservation and presentation duties, subject to the availability of resources. These duties are fairly strong, even for states with limited resources. Art.4 requires a state to "do all it can to this end, to the utmost of its own resources". This includes the obligation to seek assistance where this is appropriate.

[59] Art.4 1972 World Heritage Convention "transmission to future generations", preamble recital 6 "Considering that parts of the cultural or natural heritage are of outstanding interest and therefore need to be preserved as part of the world heritage of mankind as a whole".

[60] Art.11(4) 1972 World Heritage Convention, see also chapter V (arts 19–26) on conditions and arrangements for international assistance.

[61] Examples of human rights violations are the forceful removal of Indigenous Peoples in the case of the Bwindi Impenetrable National Park, Bwindi Impenetrable National Park or the Thungyai - Huai Kha Khaeng Wildlife Sanctuaries. For a good overview of both the harm suffered by Indigenous Peoples in connection to the world heritage process, and the potential it can have to further Indigenous rights, see Disko and Tugendhat (2014), p. This led to repeated calls for a change of the procedure, as well reparations for past harm done, for example in IUCN World Conservation Congress, Jeju, Korea, 6–15 September 2012, Resolution 5.055, Implementation of the United Nations Declaration on the Rights of Indigenous Peoples in the context of the UNESCO World Heritage Convention.

[62] Bandarin (2012), p. 310.

[63] Bandarin (2012), p. 310.

[64] UNESCO WHC, 31COM 13B, available at: http://whc.unesco.org/en/decisions/5197 [last accessed 18.08.2021].

"enhance the role of communities in the implementation of the World Heritage Convention."[65] To achieve this, communities were identified as partners of state agencies in the protection of World Heritage[66] and states were encouraged to prepare tentative lists with the aid of local communities.[67]

Over time, the Operational Guidelines gradually included not only communities, but Indigenous Peoples explicitly. However, progress has been slow. The first inclusion of Indigenous Peoples in the OGs only occurred in the 2015 version.[68] The operational guidelines are still not fully in line with the United Nations declaration, despite considerable criticism in this regard. In effect, the Special Rapporteur on the Rights of Indigenous Peoples, the Permanent Forum of Indigenous and the EMRIP all called for reforms of the world heritage process.[69] UNPFII especially has been active in trying to ensure effective participation of Indigenous Peoples in world heritage processes.[70] At the same time attempts have been made to revive an older idea of creating a separate, Indigenous, advisory body. A group of experts even proposed specific textual changes in order to facilitate aligning the two instruments with respect to the state duty of free, prior and informed consent.[71] However, even here, progress was slow,[72] and the majority of textual changes for this one right were not made before the 2019 Operational Guidelines.[73] Indigenous peoples remain "partners in the protection and conservation of World Heritage" next to local communities and other stakeholders.[74] More importantly, however, is the recognition that heritage listing can affect Indigenous rights where their traditional lands are concerned. An important step has been made with the UNESCO Policy on Engaging with Indigenous Peoples[75] and the consecutive changes in the Operational Guidelines 2019.[76] For example, before, state parties were only "*encouraged* ... to

[65] UNESCO WHC, 31COM 13B, available at: http://whc.unesco.org/en/decisions/5197 third sentence [last accessed 18.08.2021].

[66] UNESCO WHC, Operational Guidelines 2008, Section I.I, para 40 http://whc.unesco.org/archive/opguide08-en.pdf [last accessed 18.08.2021].

[67] UNESCO WHC, Operational Guidelines 2008, Section II.C, Section III para 123 http://whc.unesco.org/archive/opguide08-en.pdf [last accessed 18.08.2021].

[68] This was accompanied by the first reference to UNDRIP.

[69] Tauli-Corpuz (2014).

[70] Vrdoljak (2018), p. 259.

[71] See for example A Call to Action by the International Expert Workshop on the World Heritage Convention and Indigenous Peoples [Copenhagen, September 2012], available via: https://whc.unesco.org/en/events/906/ [last accessed 18.08.2021].

[72] No mention of free, prior and informed consent up to 2015.

[73] The most current operational guidelines at the time of writing are from 2019.

[74] Operational Guidelines 2015, section I.I para 40 identifies the relevant UNDRIP rights, including Articles 11, 12 and 31 UNDRIP, and applies them to different areas of UNESCO's mandate. See in particular section B.5.

[75] UNESCO Policy on Engaging with Indigenous Peoples, 201 Ex/6 (Paris 2018).

[76] For example the insertion in Operational Guidelines 2019, section III para 123: "Effective and inclusive participation in the nomination process of local communities, indigenous peoples,

demonstrate, *as appropriate* that indigenous free prior and informed of indigenous peoples has been obtained",[77] now they are obligated to demonstrate that FPIC has been obtained. The Guidelines also confirm the right of Indigenous Peoples to the repatriation of their human remains and provides that "[s]tates should seek to enable access and/ or repatriation of ceremonial objects and human remains in states' possession".[78]

Overall, the 1972 World Heritage Convention does not impose any duties on the state that would affect the repatriation of Indigenous religious heritage. In fact, the world heritage process remains decidedly behind the curve in relation to recognizing Indigenous rights on the international level, considering the vast proliferation of Indigenous rights on the international and regional level since the adoption of UNDRIP in 2007. Moreover, the Convention including its Operational Guidelines are not fully congruent with UNDRIP standards. On the positive side, some changes have been made on the international level, and positive examples of collaborative agreements between Indigenous Peoples and regional as well as national government agencies exist on the ground.

3.3 1995 UNIDROIT Convention on Stolen or Illegally Exported Cultural Objects

3.3.1 Drafting History

Both the UNESCO 1970 and the UNIDROIT Convention on Stolen or Illegally Exported Cultural Objects Convention of UNIDROIT Convention on Stolen or Illegally Exported Cultural Objects (hereafter UNIDROIT 1995) seek to combat the illicit traffic of cultural objects, albeit by different means. The 1995 UNIDROIT Convention was drafted upon request by UNESCO and complements the 1970 instrument.[79] In the preamble of the Convention, it becomes apparent that its adoption was motivated by similar concerns as the 1970 UNESCO Convention,

governmental, non-governmental and private organizations and other stakeholders is essential to enable them to have a shared responsibility with the State Party in the maintenance of the property."

[77] Operational Guidelines 2017 section III para 123. Maintained in Operational Guidelines 2019, section III para 123. Emphasis added.

[78] UNESCO Policy on Engaging with Indigenous Peoples, 201 Ex/6 (Paris 2018), para 77(r), at 26.

[79] Affirmed by UNESCO in several instances, i.e. "The UNIDROIT Convention on Stolen or Illegally Exported Cultural Objects (1995), is complementary to the UNESCO 1970 Convention." see 32 C/24, at 1, para 2. This complementarity is also reflected in the fact that the classification of cultural property used in UNESCO 1970 is mirrored in the 1995 UNIDROIT definition of cultural objects, the categories are simply placed in its Annex. There is, however, one important difference between the two definitions: state designation/ inclusion is not necessary in the UNIDROIT Convention, which reflects the fact that it is concerned with the return of stolen objects and primarily seeks to protect private ownership. In agreement, Prott (1997), p. 26.

mainly illicit traffic in cultural objects. Interestingly, the third recital highlights the damage illicit traffic causes not only to states but also to "tribal, indigenous or other communities".[80] This perspective, which goes beyond the nation state, fits well within the overall tenet of the Convention, which seeks to ensure the return of objects to both states and private individuals. While the 1970 Convention focusses on regulating inter-state restitutions, the UNIDROIT instrument seeks to ensure the return of a stolen cultural object[81] to its owner (Art.3(1)) and the return of objects illegally excavated to the state where they were excavated (Art.3(2)).

Institutionally, UNIDROIT is an independent, intergovernmental organization with 63 member states whose purpose is the harmonization of private, especially commercial law.[82] The 1995 Convention therefore constituted the organization's first foray into the area of cultural property law.[83] There are a number of elements in the Convention that lead to a rather critical reception of the text.[84]

3.3.2 Return of Sacred Indigenous Heritage Under the Convention

The Convention is interesting in the present context, because it is the only binding treaty in international law that features a duty to return sacred cultural heritage to Indigenous communities. The provisions of the instrument are self-executing[85] and require no further implementation on the national level if the legal system in question is a monist one.[86] The Convention does not apply retroactively.[87] As a result, sacred objects which were taken during colonial times and left the country before the Convention's entry into force, and which are now located in galleries, museums or in governmental collections abroad, are not covered.[88] However, if a sacred object is

[80] 1995 UNIDROIT Convention, recital 3: "Deeply concerned by the illicit trade in cultural objects and the irreparable damage frequently caused by it, both to these objects themselves and to the cultural heritage of national, tribal, indigenous or other communities, and also to the heritage of all peoples".

[81] Forrest (2010), p. 200. He explains "By 1995 the use of the term 'property' was considered outmoded, and 'heritage' was preferred. This, however, was opposed by some States, and the only way to achieve consensus was to introduce the more neutral term 'object'."

[82] http://www.unidroit.org/about-unidroit/overview [last accessed 18.08.2021].

[83] Prott (2009a), p. 215.

[84] Prott (2009a), p. 216 "The reaction to the text of the Convention was extraordinary. The wildest assertions were made."

[85] Raschèr (2000), p. 70.

[86] As explained later-on in Chaps. 4 and 6, both the United States and Canada can be classified as dualist legal systems and require implementing legislation to effect international treaties ratified by their respective government.

[87] UNIDROIT 1995, Art 10. Also, Prott (2009a), p. 217.

[88] Kuprecht (2014), p. 96.

taken outside an Indigenous community after the entry into force of the convention, exported to another country,[89] and the respective states are parties to the convention, the sacred objects will be restituted, both if they are stolen or illegally exported. If Indigenous cultural objects that are in traditional or ritual use are stolen, the community can reclaim them from the new bona fide owner subject to the rules of the convention.[90] Such objects are afforded special protection and are treated similarly to objects that originate in public collections.[91] Unexcavated materials that have been unlawfully excavated, or lawfully excavated but unlawfully retained, also fall under these rules if the appropriate legislation has been adopted on the national level.[92] As a result, Indigenous burial sites are offered some protection against illegal excavation if the requirements of the convention are fulfilled.

Similar to the protection of Indigenous sacred objects under the chapter on stolen objects, these objects also have to be returned if they have been illegally exported. Again, sacred Indigenous objects are afforded special protection if they were used traditionally or ritually prior to their loss.[93] The chapeau of Art.5(3) restricts the return of illegally exported objects to objects whose absence "significantly impairs" one of the listed interests in the paragraph. However, given that the absence of an object means that it cannot be placed in ritual or traditional use, it seems safe to assume that, as long as there is evidence of this, the threshold of "significantly impaired" is also met. In the case of illegally exported objects, the request for their return will have to be brought by the state in whose territory the community resides.[94]

The Convention also protects sacred Indigenous heritage in museum storage against illegal exportation. Where Indigenous objects have been placed in a museum facility and are not accessible to the community, they would still be protected as long as they are "of significant cultural importance for the requesting State". If a sacred

[89] In effect, the convention applies to object of an 'international character', see Art.1 1995 UNIDROIT Convention. While exported objects are thus definitely covered, it is debated what conditions need to be fulfilled precisely to fulfil this criterion. The explanatory report of the Secretariat on Art.1 of the Draft Convention, which already featured this provision, highlights that the drafters themselves were unclear as to what this terminology should mean: "The chapeau employs the somewhat vague language 'claims of an international character', *any attempt to define more precisely what was an 'international character', having been abandoned in view of the difficulty, if not the impossibility, of reaching agreement on precise criteria*, a problem which is frequently encountered in international private law Conventions." [emphasis added by the author] Draft UNIDROIT Convention on the International Return of Stolen or Illegally Exported Objects and Explanatory Report prepared by UNIDROIT Secretariat [December 1994] Document reference Conf. 8/3, at 23, para 22. Instead, somewhat optimistically, it was to be left to "the case-law in the different jurisdictions to work out a uniform notion" of the term. For further discussion of the term see Prott (1997), p. 22. Also, Groenen (2018), pp. 57–59.

[90] Art.3 1995 Unidroit Convention.

[91] Art.3(8) 1995 Unidroit Convention.

[92] Art.3(2) 1995 Unidroit Convention. For further discussion see Groenen (2018), pp. 410–415.

[93] Art.5(3)(d) 1995 Unidroit Convention and Art.7(2) 1995 Unidroit Convention.

[94] Art.5(1) 1995 Unidroit Convention.

Indigenous object is placed in museum storage (with the consent of the respective Indigenous community), it falls under the first element of Art.5(3)(d), as long as the community has access to it for traditional use.[95]

3.3.3 *An Important Signal of Support for Indigenous Cultural Rights*

The Convention's inclusion of sacred Indigenous heritage was an important milestone in the development of ICHL towards a greater recognition of Indigenous cultural rights. It supports both Art.12(1) UNDRIP and Art.11(1) UNDRIP as the return of these objects is motivated by their current use, be it ritual or traditional.

The special protection of cultural objects in traditional or ritual use[96] is due to the concerted efforts of the Australian and Canadian governments, partially supported by the United States. For example, Art.3(8) was originally not part of the draft Convention. In its explanatory note, the Secretariat acknowledges the criticism which it received for exempting only "public collections" from the definite time limit. The explanatory memorandum observes "[the draft] omitted an extremely important category of objects which are not as a rule accessible to the public, that is to say sacred or secret objects belonging to an indigenous community, a category of the utmost importance for the cultural survival of such communities."[97] The accompanying documents clarify that it was in fact the Australian delegation, supported by their Canadian colleagues, who highlighted the need to include sacred objects whose loss would severely affect the continued existence of their indigenous communities in one of the expert meetings.[98] It is in effect this link which elevates the object to a plane where it is 'worthy' of special protection, of being more protected than the average cultural object owned by a private non-state entity. Prott seems to attribute the lack of inclusion of this proposal into the draft convention to a lack of time to discuss it adequately in the expert meeting.[99] The two States reintroduced a comparable wording at the Diplomatic Conference which was introduced in a reformulated version as a compromise by the United States,[100] familiar

[95] Similarly Prott (1997), p. 58.

[96] Under Arts.3(8), 5(3)(d) and 7(2) 1995 Unidroit Convention.

[97] Draft UNIDROIT Convention on the International Return of Stolen or Illegally Exported Objects and Explanatory Report prepared by UNIDROIT Secretariat [December 1994] Document reference Conf. 8/3, para 53, p. 29 in Acts and Proceedings Compilation made available by UNIDROIT online. In this context, the secretariat also observes that "[a] definition of an indigenous community, based on that of Article 1 of the 1989 ILO Convention No. 169 on Tribal and Indigenous Peoples was proposed in this connection but was not included in the text."

[98] Prott (1997), p. 40.

[99] Prott (1997), p. 40.

[100] Compare, Art.3(6) introduced in the Discussions on the Draft Convention by Australia, Canada and the United States CONF. 8/C.1/W.P. 67 Corr. "In addition, a claim for restitution of a sacred or

with the problem and influential in the drafting process, and the adapted wording found its way into the text by means of Art.3(8).[101]

Similar to Art.3(8), the inclusion of Indigenous cultural heritage in ritual and cultural use under the export provisions[102] was perceived to be essential by Australia, Canada, the United States and UNESCO. It was introduced in a Governmental Expert meeting but, due to the other delegation's unfamiliarity with the subject-matter, it required a substantial amount of debate before it was included.[103]

The fact that the Convention provides special protection to sacred Indigenous heritage is noteworthy for two reasons. First, it is evidence of an awareness of the importance of sacred objects for the continued survival of Indigenous cultures in their territory among government officials in the early 1990s, including in both Canada and the United States.[104] The need for their restitution was justified by the significant damage their absence could cause to the Indigenous communal existence.[105] While neither the United States nor Canada have ratified the Convention, this seems to be motivated by reasons not related to the instrument's protection of sacred Indigenous heritage.[106] Second, it gives evidence that Indigenous interests that are specific to a particular object can be accommodated in binding ICHL treaties. The Convention is still not ratified widely and, while this (may) be attributed to other provisions, the lack of ratification entails that this view cannot be understood to be shared universally. However, there have been a number of new ratifications in recent

---

communally important cultural object belonging to and used by a member or members of an indigenous community in a Contracting State as part of that community's traditional or ritual use [shall not be subject to prescription] [shall be brought within [75] years]."

[101] Prott (1997), p. 40.

[102] By means of Art.5(3)(d) 1995 Unidroit Convention.

[103] Prott (1997), p. 70.

[104] See for example the statements made by Ms Hughes of the Canadian delegation, Diplomatic Conference for the adoption of the Draft UNIDROIT Convention on the International Return of Stolen or Illegally Exported Cultural Objects – Acts and Proceedings, at 162, 256–257, available at: http://www.unidroit.org/english/conventions/1995culturalproperty/1995culturalproperty-acts-e.pdf [last accessed 18.08.2021].

[105] The delegates argued that the objects could not qualify as part of public collections because of access limitations but that they required special protection. See also Groenen (2018), pp. 326–327.

[106] The present lack of ratification of the Convention by Canada also does not seem to equal a general rejection of the Convention. In an answer to a UNESCO questionnaire, the government "indicated its support in principle … and has (in connection with the 1970 UNESCO convention) implemented provisions that are consistent with aspects of the UNIDROIT Convention", see DC8/CS/1 Doc.3 UNIDROIT Secretariat report on the follow-up session in 2012, p. 11 available at: http://www.unidroit.org/english/conventions/1995culturalproperty/1meet-120619/dc8-cs01-03-e.pdf [last accessed 18.08.2021]. The lack of ratification of the UNIDROIT 1995 Convention by the United States may be attributed to other factors, such as the strong lobbying efforts of art dealers in the US against the ratification of the convention notably for its treatment of illegally excavated objects as stolen, see for example Olivier (1996), p. 660 citing Rothman and Fitzpatrick's 'Statement of Position of Concerned Members of the American Cultural Community Regarding the Unidroit Convention on the International Return of Stolen Or Illegally Exported Cultural Objects'.

years.[107] This gives rise to the hope that the protective scope of the instrument may continue to expand in the future.

Overall, the Convention does not impose any duties that affect repatriation legislation on the national level. However, it does impose standards that have to respected that increase the protection of Indigenous cultural heritage that is currently in ritual or traditional use within communities. In addition, states should adopt clear guidelines on unexcavated Indigenous heritage on public lands to ensure that it is protected under the Convention. This need not necessarily entail state ownership for unexcavated Indigenous heritage (which would contradict Art.31 UNDRIP). Instead, prohibiting the excavation of such materials without free, prior and informed of the community, or their retention thereof without permission should be sufficient to trigger the protection afforded under the 1995 UNIDROIT Convention. Similarly, in the same way that sacred cultural objects should be incorporated as a protected category under national export laws, the export of excavated Indigenous heritage without free, prior and informed consent should be prohibited in the respective export legislation. This way, Indigenous sacred heritage, whether in use or unexcavated would be protected under the Convention. For this reason, adoption of the 1995 UNIDROIT Convention is preferable to the patrimonial model. Patrimonial laws seek to ensure inter-state returns of cultural heritage via a law that vests clear ownership of the relevant cultural heritage in the state. To succeed, the ownership right must be absolute.[108] This approach would not protect Indigenous rights in their cultural heritage adequately.

3.4 The 2003 UNESCO Convention for the Safeguarding of the Intangible Cultural Heritage

The 2003 Convention represents a significant step by UNESCO towards aligning international cultural heritage law with international human rights law, including Indigenous rights. This section will briefly explore the drafting history of the instrument before considering the aims of the Convention. Lastly, it will be considered whether it imposes any duties on the state that connect to the repatriation of sacred Indigenous cultural heritage on the national level.

[107] Between 01/2017 and 08/2021, there have been 13 new ratifications or accessions, bringing the total number of state parties to 50 [last accessed 18.08.2021].

[108] Groenen (2018), pp. 408–409.

3.4.1 *Drafting History, Context and Main Aims of the Convention*

Before adopting the ICH convention in 2003, UNESCO had already been considering the protection of intangible cultural heritage for a considerable time. The protection of ICH connects intellectual property law, cultural heritage and human rights law. Within the area of intellectual property law, the protection of ICH had already been considered since 1967 in Stockholm in connection with the revision of the Bern Convention for the Protection of Literary and Artistic Works.[109] In the same time period, UNESCO considered the incorporation of intangible heritage in the World Heritage system at the time of drafting the 1972 WHC, but the idea was dropped.[110] Together with the World Intellectual Property Organization (WIPO), UNESCO adopted the Model Provisions for National Laws on the Protection of Expressions of Folklore Against Illicit Exploitation and other Forms of Prejudicial Action, 1982.[111] Independently from WIPO, UNESCO began to consider 'folklore' in relation to its own more general cultural mandate.[112] This resulted in the adoption of the Recommendation on the Safeguarding of Traditional Culture and Folklore on the 15th of November 1989, which remained the UNESCO instrument for the protection of intangible cultural heritage until the adoption of the ICH in 2003.[113] This evolution of cultural heritage instruments, moving beyond tangible to encompass intangible cultural heritage, could also be seen in soft law instruments. ICOMOS, for example, adopted the Burra Charter which considered not only aesthetic or historic reasons to identify places of cultural significance but also social value.[114] In more recent versions, the Charter has also recognized spiritual value as a reason for cultural significance.[115]

Aside from these normative explorations of intangible cultural heritage, UNESCO also sought to identify and protect existing intangible cultural heritage through programmes such as the Living Human Treasures programme (launched in 1993) and the 'Masterpieces of Oral and Intangible Heritage of Humanity' initiated

---

[109] Srivinas (2008), pp. 530–531.

[110] Blake (2006), p. 3.

[111] Historical Background to the preparation of the preliminary Draft Convention for the Safeguarding of the Intangible Cultural Heritage [Doc. Ref.: CLT-2003/CONF.205/INF.6] available at: http://www.unesco.org/culture/ich/doc/src/04557-EN.pdf. The model provisions are available at: www.wipo.int/wipolex/en/details.jsp?id=6714 [last accessed 18.08.2021].

[112] Blake (2006), p. 2.

[113] Blake (2006), p. 2.

[114] Art.1 The Australia ICOMOS Charter for Places of Cultural Significance ("Burra Charter"), 1979 version: http://australia.icomos.org/publications/charters/ [last consulted 3.09.2019].

[115] Art. 1.2 The Australia ICOMOS Charter for Places of Cultural Significance, first adopted in 1999 (Burra Charter): https://australia.icomos.org/publications/burra-charter-practice-notes/burra-charter-archival-documents/ [last consulted 18.08.2021]. The WHC also shifted towards incorporating the cultural dimensions of landscapes through its Operational Guidelines in 1992.

four years later in 1997.[116] Building on its normative work and the Masterpieces programme, UNESCO adopted a binding instrument on the protection of intangible cultural heritage in 2003. Generally, it can be said that there are distinct similarities between the 1972 Convention and the 2003 ICH Convention. The 1972 WHC was seen as the model to be followed.[117] There were a number of reasons for this approach, including, *inter alia*, the undeniable success of the WHC model, its combination of state duties to protect heritage (especially important for intangible cultural heritage which was frequently not protected at the national level) with international assistance and the creation of a fund.[118] The final approach adopted, including its usage of an international listing mechanism, was highly criticized at the time.[119] For present purposes, however, the focus is on any potential duties that the convention establishes on the national level and which could affect national repatriation provisions.

The final instrument, adopted during the 32nd session of the UNESCO General Assembly on the 17th of October 2003,[120] aims to safeguard oral traditions, languages, social practices, rituals, festive events, folklore, craft skills and traditional knowledge.[121] The duty to safeguard can best be understood as a duty to take measures aimed at protecting intangible cultural heritage,[122] notably through establishing favourable conditions in which it can flourish. The Convention defines safeguarding as having two elements: first, as "measures aimed at ensuring the viability" and second as the "revitalization of" intangible cultural heritage. In its first dimension, safeguarding thus focusses on ensuring that endangered forms of ICH are kept alive, which is based on the implicit valorization of such forms of ICH.

---

[116] Blake (2006), p. 3.

[117] Note that in the First Session of the Intergovernmental Meeting of Experts on the Preliminary Draft Convention for the Safeguarding of Intangible Cultural Heritage, CLT-2002/CONF.203/5 [December 2002] available at: http://unesdoc.unesco.org/images/0012/001290/129000e.pdf [last accessed 18.08.2021]. It was widely agreed upon, as noted in para 7.A. (i) that "In view of the specificity of the intangible cultural heritage, the 1972 Convention should be taken more as a source of inspiration than as a model". However, in light of the structural parallels between the two instruments, this seems to have been more of an ambition than the actual outcome of the drafting process.

[118] Blake (2006), pp. 6–7.

[119] Comments by the United States and Canada, see Second Session of the Intergovernmental Meeting of Experts on the Preliminary Draft Convention for the Safeguarding of the Intangible Cultural Heritage – General Comments received from Member States, Doc Ref Doc.CLT-2003/CONF.205/5, at 25–26 and at 16–18 available via http://www.unesco.org/culture/ich/index.php?meeting_id=00051 [last accessed 18.08.2021].

[120] For a more general overview of the Convention's evolution see UNESCO website: http://www.unesco.org/culture/ich/index.php?lg=en&pg=00310 [last accessed 18.08.2021].

[121] Art.1(a) 2003 ICH Convention. Traditional knowledge in this context is to be understood broadly as "knowledge and practices concerning nature and the universe", see Art.2(2)(d) 2003 ICH Convention.

[122] Art.11 2003 ICH Convention: "Each State Party shall: (a) take the necessary measures to ensure the safeguarding of the intangible cultural heritage present in its territory;"

The convention text and the operational guidelines establish a wide range of possible measures that a state can choose from.[123] It thus seems as if the duty to safeguard ICH on the national level encompasses a margin of discretion, however, a state is under the duty to take some measures towards protecting cultural heritage.[124] Art.13 lists a number of possible measures a state can take, that do not constitute absolute duties, rather a state party shall endeavour to take them.[125] Safeguarding ICH does thus not equal setting a list of cultural heritage in stone, but rather the ambitious aim of fostering a continuous presence of diverse forms of intangible cultural heritage.[126]

Safeguarding also encompasses measures that revitalize intangible cultural heritage, including rituals. In the drafting process, the inclusion of 'revitalization' caused several states considerable concern. It was feared that this could result in the artificial existence of ICH, which would otherwise no longer exist, contrary to the wishes of the community.[127] This is reflected in the report on the first intergovernmental meeting.[128] The glossary provides that, where revitalization refers to practices of a cultural community (such as Indigenous sacred practices), it means "reactivating or reinventing *social practices* and *representations*, which are no longer in use or falling in disuse."[129] For a state, engaging in revitalization through heritage policies means "[t]he encouragement and support of a *local community*, developed with the agreement of that same *community*, in the reactivation of *social practices* and *representations*, which are no longer in use or falling in disuse."[130] The operational guidelines offer no concrete guidance on the exact content of revitalization, which reflects the doubts that already existed at the time of drafting the instrument. A first

---

[123] See Art.2(3), Art.13 2003 ICH Convention, and paras 170–197 of the Operational Directives for the Implementation of the Convention for the Safeguarding of the Intangible Cultural Heritage (as amended June 2018) which centre on aligning the obligation to safeguard ICH with measures of sustainable development in the areas health, education, economic and social development. Chapter IV of the 2003 ICH Convention regulates safeguarding measures at the international level.

[124] At the very minimum, this includes the duty to identify and define the ICH that exists in its territory together with the communities that produce this heritage (Art.11(b) 2003 ICH Convention).

[125] Blake (2006), p. 66.

[126] Art.2(3) 2003 ICH Convention "'Safeguarding' means measures aimed at ensuring the **viability** of the intangible cultural heritage". Emphasis added.

[127] Blake (2006), p. 41.

[128] First Intergovernmental Meeting of Experts on the Preliminary Draft Convention for the Safeguarding of Intangible Cultural Heritage, CLT-2002/CONF.203/5 [December 2002], at 2, para 7.A. (v), "To adopt the notion of "revitalization" so long as it does not underpin a policy of artificial "reactivation" of a given form of the intangible cultural heritage;" available at: http://unesdoc.unesco.org/images/0012/001290/129000e.pdf [last accessed 18.08.2021].

[129] Glossary Intangible Cultural Heritage, prepared by an international meeting of experts at UNESCO 10.06-12.06.2002, available at: http://www.unesco.org/culture/ich/doc/src/00265.pdf [last accessed 18.08.2021].

[130] Glossary Intangible Cultural Heritage, prepared by an international meeting of experts at UNESCO 10.06-12.06.2002, available at: http://www.unesco.org/culture/ich/doc/src/00265.pdf Emphasis in the original [last accessed 18.08.2021].

step towards a textual interpretation of the second dimension of safeguarding provision, namely revitalization, requires the identification of the ordinary meaning of 'revitalize'.

The Convention also seeks to ensure the respect of the intangible cultural heritage of communities, including Indigenous Peoples.[131] Arguably, a duty to respect a variety of cultural rights that are necessary for individual communities to produce these forms of cultural heritage can be read into this provision. It requires state parties to take an inventory of intangible cultural heritage in their state which may be featured in one of the lists established in the Convention: the Representative List or the List of Intangible Cultural Heritage in Need of Urgent Safeguarding.[132] Intangible cultural heritage is protected, not because of its importance to humankind as a whole, but rather as a form of a living expression of individual and group expression that is valued as "a mainspring of cultural diversity".[133] This explains the instrument's considerable emphasis on the communal nature of heritage.[134] It has also led to the express position of ICH within a wider human rights framework, notably the international bill of rights.[135] The 2003 UNESCO convention thus represents an important, albeit small, step in aligning international cultural heritage law more with international human rights law.[136,137]

[131] Art.1(b) ICH 2003.

[132] Nafziger and Paterson (2014), p. 10.

[133] 2003 ICH Convention, preamble recital 2.

[134] 2003 ICH Convention, preamble recital 6: **Recognizing** that communities, in particular Indigenous communities, groups and, in some cases, individuals, play an important role in the production, safeguarding, maintenance and re-creation of the intangible cultural heritage, thus helping to enrich cultural diversity and human creativity.

[135] 2003 ICH Convention, preamble recital 1: **Referring** to existing international human rights instruments, in particular to the Universal Declaration on Human Rights of 1948, the International Covenant on Economic, Social and Cultural Rights of 1966, and the International Covenant on Civil and Political Rights of 1966,

[136] However, while it recognizes non-state actors much more than older UNESCO instruments did, this was not reflected in the drafting process. See criticism by Canada on this particular problem. Second Session of the Intergovernmental Meeting of Experts on the Preliminary Draft Convention for the Safeguarding of the Intangible Cultural Heritage – General Comments received from Member States, Doc Ref Doc.CLT-2003/CONF.205/5, at 17–18 available via http://www.unesco.org/culture/ich/index.php?meeting_id=00051 [last accessed 18.08.2021].

[137] Compare also Hausler (2020), pp. 784–785 who observes "while the Intangible Cultural Heritage Convention marked a significant step forward inhuman rights the participation of non-State actors in cultural heritage governance, it nevertheless did not achieve an equally shared concept of heritage governance between State and non-State actors".

3.4.2 Sacred Indigenous Cultural Heritage Under the Convention

The 2003 Convention pursues the protection of intangible cultural heritage in different ways, some of which directly affect sacred Indigenous cultural heritage and the right of Indigenous People to manifest their religion. First, Art.1(b) provides that the convention aims to "ensure respect for the intangible cultural heritage of the communities, groups and individuals concerned". Indigenous religious practices form part of the cultural heritage that state parties should respect and protect by implementing the Convention. Indigenous sacred rituals can be classified as intangible cultural heritage under Art.2(2)(c) as "social practices, rituals and festive events". While religions in their entirety cannot classify as ICH,[138] individual ceremonial expressions, which form part of such religions, arguably have a ritualistic character and thereby do fall under Art.2(1) ICHC. Oral elements of such practices can likewise be considered as intangible heritage under Art.2(2)(a). The Operational Guidelines indicate a number of measures that a state can take to protect these practices.[139] This can include the adoption of protective measures under intellectual property law or even adopting privacy rights to safeguard sacred intangible heritage.[140]

Second, the convention also covers tangible cultural heritage that is intimately connected with intangible forms of cultural heritage. While this was ignored in the binding UNESCO instruments for a considerable period, the fact remains that the line between tangible and intangible is not that easily drawn. Songs require instruments, and religious traditions require sacred objects.[141] An intangible tradition may require a specific place or an immovable structure. To protect the tradition listed under the ICH will then require protection of the place. The Convention takes account of this by defining intangible heritage both as the "the practices, representations, expressions, knowledge, skills ... that communities, groups and, in some cases, individuals recognize as part of their cultural heritage" as well as "the instruments, objects, artefacts and cultural spaces associated therewith".[142]

The Convention is accompanied by the 'Ethical Principles for Safeguarding Intangible Cultural Heritage' that were adopted by the Intergovermental Committee

[138] They are too broad and manifest themselves in too many different ways for a specific religion to fall under the forms of ICH listed in Art.2(1) ICH.

[139] Respect for the intangible cultural heritage of communities is not a separate state obligation, rather the Convention only cites safeguarding as a clear legal obligation for the state in its territory under Art.11(a).

[140] Operational Directives for the Implementation of the Convention for the Safeguarding of the Intangible Cultural Heritage (as amended June 2018), paragraph 173(b).

[141] In this context Blake (2006), p. 6. She observes "There is no doubt that a 'grey area' exists between the Conventions that will need further elucidation."

[142] Art.2(1) 2003 ICH Convention.

set up to administer the Convention on the international level.[143] These principles were developed not only in light of the 2003 convention, but also international human rights and Indigenous rights standards.[144] They identify good practices and should be complemented by more specific, local or industry codes.[145] The ethical principles are crucial in bringing the convention closer into alignment with the UNDRIP. They require, *inter alia*, collaborative processes with Indigenous Peoples to be based on free, prior and informed consent.[146] Principle number five requires states to ensure "[a]ccess of communities, groups and individuals to the instruments, *objects, artefacts,* cultural and natural spaces and places of memory ...".[147] This brings the 2003 ICH convention in line with Art.12(1) UNDRIP and requires states to ensure that Indigenous religious practitioners have access to sacred cultural objects for the purposes of protecting a particular ritual. Moreover, broader public access may be restricted in order respect customary practices.[148]

Safeguarding under the convention can also entail measures aimed at revitalizing rituals and other practices that qualify as ICH.[149] Measures to aid in revitalizing Indigenous cultural practices could include archival access to evidence of past practices, collaborations with museums to facilitate access and use of sacred heritage that is necessary for particular forms of ICH, or measures aimed at revitalizing endangered Indigenous languages. All of these are thus examples of measures that a state can take to safeguard intangible cultural heritage under Art.11(a) of the Convention. The repatriation of sacred cultural heritage that is associated with rituals that can be classified as an example of ICH under the Convention likewise qualifies as a possible safeguarding measure. This also addresses the research question at the outset of this chapter in relation to this particular legal instrument: the 2003 Convention does not require the repatriation of sacred cultural heritage in particular, but, in the opinion of the author, repatriation or measures that enable Indigenous access to and use of sacred heritage qualify as safeguarding measures under the instrument. While the convention does not require state parties to take any particular measure, it does require it to take *a* measure and to do so collaboratively with Indigenous Peoples where Indigenous intangible cultural heritage is concerned. In this sense, the guidelines identified in the previous chapter to align repatriation laws with Art.12 (1) UNDRIP and Art.31(1) UNDRIP suffice to ensure that a national repatriation law also respects state duties under the 2003 ICH Convention.

---

[143] Intergovernmental Committee for the Safeguarding of the Intangible Cultural Heritage, Ethical Principles for Safeguarding Intangible Cultural Heritage (Windhoek, Namibia, 30 November to 4 December 2015), part of Basic Texts of the 2003 Convention for the Safeguarding of Intangible Cultural Heritage (2018 Edition) available via: https://ich.unesco.org/en/convention [last accessed 18.08.2021].

[144] Ibid, preamble.

[145] Ibid.

[146] Ibid, principle (4).

[147] Ibid, principle (5), emphasis added.

[148] Ibid, principle (5).

[149] Art.2(3) 2003 ICH Convention.

3.5 The 2005 UNESCO Convention on the Promotion and Protection of the Diversity of Cultural Expressions

3.5.1 Context: The 2001 Universal Declaration on Cultural Diversity

Only two years after adopting an instrument on intangible cultural heritage, the 2005 UNESCO Convention on the Promotion and Protection of the Diversity of Cultural Expressions (from hereon: CDCE) followed. The aim of the 2005 Convention is the protection of cultural diversity. Cultural diversity as a concept had already been recognized by the World Commission on Culture and Development in its 1995 Report 'Our Creative Diversity' and was further considered during the 1998 Stockholm Conference on Cultural Policies for Development.[150] In 2001, the concept was expressly protected in the 2001 Universal Declaration on Cultural Diversity, on which the Convention builds.

The **Universal Declaration on Cultural Diversity (UDCD)** was adopted by the UNESCO General Conference in 2001. The declaration draws strongly on one of the central tenets of the UNESCO constitution, the belief that cultural collaboration will contribute to peace[151] and that a wide diffusion of the world's different cultures[152] will combat ignorance, which the constitution identifies as one of the causes of war.[153] The Declaration's preamble reiterates the corresponding Constitution's passages.[154] It also identifies "the preservation and promotion of the fruitful diversity of cultures" as part of UNESCO mandate.[155] The protection of cultural diversity, in turn, is justified by including it under the common heritage of humanity (Art.1 UDCD). But how should cultural diversity be understood, for it to qualify as the common heritage of humanity? And how does Indigenous cultural heritage connect

---

[150] Burri et al. (2009), pp. 361–362.

[151] UNESCO Constitution, Art. I(1).

[152] UNESCO Constitution, preamble, fourth recital.

[153] UNESCO Constitution, preamble, second recital: "That ignorance of each other's ways and lives has been a common cause, throughout the history of mankind, of that suspicion and mistrust between the peoples of the world through which their differences have all too often broken into war". See also Sect. 3.2.1 above.

[154] UNESCO Constitution, preamble fourth recital in 2001 UNESCO Declaration, preamble first recital. UNESCO Constitution, Art.I in 2001 UNESCO Declaration, preamble second recital.

[155] In this context, it is worthy to note that the term the 2001 Declaration employs—fruitful diversity of cultures—is in effect used in the organization's constitution to limit the organization's powers "With a view to preserving the independence, integrity and **fruitful diversity of the cultures** and educational systems **of the States Members** of the Organization, **the Organization is prohibited** from **intervening in matters which are essentially within their domestic jurisdiction** (Art.I (3) UNESCO Constitution emphasis added)." Thus, while the preservation of cultural diversity is not part of UNESCO's mandate explicitly, cultural cooperation is very much in the organization's mandate and the diffusion of culture which the declaration and the convention seek to protect by creating a counterbalance to the WTO.

to cultural diversity? Cultural diversity is not a tangible entity that can be easily described. Rather, it is a concept that describes a state of existence, namely the co-existence of different (*diverse*) forms of cultures. Due to the formative influence of culture on the identity of the individual, the protection of cultural diversity translates into protecting "the uniqueness and plurality of the identities of the groups and societies making up humankind."[156] Moreover, Art.1 UCDC recognizes this plurality as a "source of exchange, innovation and creativity". It is for these reasons that the Declaration seeks to ensure the continuity of cultural diversity for future generations. The continued existence of Indigenous cultures contributes to a continuation of cultural diversity.

As a mirror image of this realization, the increased protection of cultural diversity is closely connected to the realization that globalization threatens non-dominant forms of culture. Indigenous cultures, as well as minority cultures, are especially vulnerable to the influences of globalization. This is reflected in Art.4 UDCD which states that the protection of cultural diversity is a "commitment to human rights . . . in particular the rights of minorities and those of indigenous peoples". Art.7 UDCD requires the preservation of tangible heritage ("heritage in all its form must be preserved") both to inspire the creativity of future generations, as well as a means to further intercultural dialogue, which in turn is believed to increase creativity. Scovazzi highlights the value of the Declaration in filling a gap left by the 1972 WHC and the 2003 ICH, protecting the climate in which artists, architects and other (Indigenous) individuals produce cultural objects.[157]

The Declaration is a soft law and does not create obligations for states in international law. Instead, it informs the interpretation of the Convention as the informal predecessor of the CDCE. This leads to the question whether—in the absence of any explicit repatriation obligations—international cultural heritage law could influence the question of intra-state repatriation of Indigenous sacred objects. Art.4 UDCD and the Declaration's general emphasis on ensuring the continuation of diversity would support measures that strengthen Indigenous cultures, such as the return of sacred objects to ensure the continuity of religious traditions.

Art.7 UDCD could be understood to favour the existence of Indigenous cultural heritage within museums to ensure an intercultural exchange, with the hope of furthering creativity more broadly. If a state enables the repatriation of Indigenous

---

[156] Compare Art.1 UCDC "Culture takes diverse forms across time and space. This diversity is embodied in the uniqueness and plurality of the identities of the groups and societies making up humankind. As a source of exchange, innovation and creativity, cultural diversity is as necessary for humankind as biodiversity is for nature. In this sense, it is the common heritage of humanity and should be recognized and affirmed for the benefit of present and future generations."

[157] Scovazzi and Nafziger (2007), p. 137 "Dans le cas de 'créateurs sans biens culturels', comme l'écrivain ou le musicien, ni la Convention du patrimoine mondial, ni la Convention du patrimoine immatériel ne pourraient s'appliquer. Il faut ici une réglementation plus vaste, visant la culture en tant qu'expression de la société ou du groupe social auxquels ils appartiennent. C'est le domaine de la culture dans son ensemble . . . C'est cette 'culture' qui prend des formes diverses à travers le temps et l'espace et qui pourrait être menacé par la perte de la diversité culturelle."

cultural objects, and the object will not be preserved, this would *prima facie* violate the principle to preserve heritage as expressed in Art.7 UDCD. However, to reject requests for the repatriation of sacred heritage would contradict the instrument's emphasis on Indigenous cultural rights.[158] In addition, Art.7 UDCD cannot have been intended to create an all-encompassing obligation to preserve any kind of heritage, both in light of the sheer scale of available cultural heritage and the logistic and financial constraints a state faces. It would also not fit the Declaration's emphasis on state sovereignty. To summarize, while the Declaration values the protection of Indigenous cultures as a commitment of the state to respect its human rights obligations, and the repatriation of Indigenous objects could be subsumed under this protection, it neither explicitly advocates nor hinders the repatriation of sacred Indigenous objects.

3.5.2 Adoption and Main Aims of the Convention

Not long after the adoption of the Declaration, it was deemed insufficient to protect cultural diversity and UNESCO began to consider adopting a new instrument. This resulted in the adoption of the Convention for the Promotion and Protection of the Diversity of Cultural Expressions. The Convention entered into force mid-March 2007, three months after its 30th ratification (Art.29(1)CDCE). This was less than two years after its adoption by the UNESCO General Assembly in October 2005,[159] making it the fastest ratified UNESCO treaty.[160] 148 states voted in favour of its adoption, 4 abstained (Australia, Honduras, Liberia and Nicaragua) and 2 states voted against the instrument (Israel and the United States).[161] It has been ratified by over 130 states.[162] This quick global acceptance is especially confounding in light of the political sensitivity of cultural matters and the manoeuvring any treaty negotiation entails. UNESCO itself lauds the ratification as a milestone, observing that "hrough this historic agreement, the global community formally recognised the dual nature, both cultural and economic, of contemporary cultural expressions".[163] Others are more critical, Mira Burri suggests that one reason for its wide acceptance rests on the comparative weaknesses of its provisions.[164] It is also important to

[158] Express mention of Art.27 ICCPR in Art.5 UDCD.

[159] UNESCO CDCE Website, Historical Background available at: https://en.unesco.org/creativity/convention/history.

[160] Burri (2013), p. 357.

[161] Donders (2012), p. 165.

[162] In September 2015 the Convention had been ratified by 139 States.

[163] UNESCO Website on the Convention, text section under "about" available at: https://en.unesco.org/creativity/convention [last accessed 18.08.2021].

[164] Burri (2013), p. 360 "[O]ne might venture to suggest that what made the adoption of the UNESCO Convention possible emptied it of some of it stronger and more valuable content...

highlight, as Dominic McGoldrick has done, that the adoption of the CDCE also resulted in a rejection of adopting new, comprehensive cultural rights instruments.[165]

The Convention focusses on protecting and promoting the diversity of cultural expressions[166] and the climate which is conducive to cultural diversity as a whole.[167] All of this occurs under the umbrella of national sovereignty and this is reaffirmed repeatedly throughout the instrument.[168] Similar to the Declaration, the Convention not only seeks to protect cultural diversity, but it also recognizes the potential danger of commerce to culture.[169] In effect, the CDCE is very much a reaction to globalization.[170] It reflects the realization that the strict enforcement of trade rules on a multilateral level can endanger national cultural policies. To safeguard cultural diversity, it recognizes the double nature of objects as vehicles of culture and products of trade. This necessitates both the free circulation of cultural expressions and the protection of cultural objects, cultural services, as well as cultural activities more generally.[171]

The Convention suffers from a number of weaknesses: Different from the UDCD, the CDCE does not cite specific cultural rights.[172] While cultural rights are at least included implicitly in the preamble,[173] intellectual property rights are not included at all.[174] Here, the 2005 UNESCO Convention follows the approach the organization had already taken in the 2003 ICHC.[175] Moreover, the provisions in the CDCE are of a weak nature.[176] The obligations on state parties are softened by the formulation "shall endeavour to" (i.e. in Art.7 CDCE, Art.10(c) and Art.12 CDCE). Lastly, the

---

The Convention's less than bold text is also the result of the starkly different sensibilities and motivation of the parties when drafting an international instrument on cultural matters."

[165] McGoldrick (2002), p. 459.

[166] Art.1(a) CDCE. Different from the declaration, the cultural diversity convention opts for the formulation diversity of cultural expressions rather than cultural diversity.

[167] Art.1(b) CDCE.

[168] Art.1(h), Art.2(2) and Art.5(1) CDCE.

[169] In Declaration, see Art. 8. Compare for UDCD Scovazzi and Nafziger (2007), p. 139.

[170] Burri (2013), p. 358. Also designed as a counterbalance to the WTO see Burri (2013), pp. 366–367.

[171] Scovazzi and Nafziger (2007), pp. 146–150.

[172] Burri (2013), p. 359.

[173] CDCE, preamble 21st recital: "Referring to the provisions of the international instruments adopted by UNESCO relating to cultural diversity and the exercise of cultural rights".

[174] Burri (2013), p. 359.

[175] M. Burri links the division between WTO and UNESCO back to the divide between the EU and the United States on free trade and culture and argues "as the distributive conflict between the United States and the EU continues, the UNESCO and the WTO regimes are highly unlikely to 'converge into a new synthesis, but rather will remain in conflict for a prolonged period.'" Burri (2013), p. 363.

[176] Burri (2013), p. 358.

Convention does not contain a clear solution for a conflict between the CDCE and another international instrument.[177]

3.5.3 *Sacred Indigenous Cultural Heritage Under the Convention*

The CDCE considers the position of Indigenous Peoples in two provisions, Art.2 (3) and Art.7(1)(a). Art.2 lists the general principles intended to guide state parties in the implementation of the Convention.[178] Art.2(3) CDCE requires that measures that protect or promote cultural expressions are taken on the basis of "equal dignity of and respect for all cultures, including the cultures of persons belonging to minorities and indigenous peoples." If we understand equality as substantive equality, respect for the culture of Indigenous Peoples entails the need for a state to take measures that take their specific situation into account.[179] This would be in line with the Convention's overall protection of cultural differences and its incorporation of international human rights standards.[180] Art.7(1)(a) CDCE asks states to "endeavour to create in their territory an environment which encourages individuals and social groups . . . to create, produce, disseminate, distribute and have access to their own cultural expressions, paying due attention to the special circumstances and needs of . . . Indigenous Peoples". This points to the recognition that the environment in which Indigenous Peoples can best express themselves culturally may have specific requirements. Comparable to the Declaration, the repatriation of sacred cultural heritage is not required but it may be classified as a measure which a state can take in order to protect and promote cultural diversity. The Convention does not impose specific obligations that have to be respected in national repatriation legislation. With regard

[177] Burri (2013), p. 359 Art.20 seeks to act as a conflict of laws rule but in effect does not offer a solution to a potential conflict of laws. Paragraph 1 provides that, in case of a conflict between the Convention and other treaties, states shall perform their duties in good faith, without subordinating the 2005 Convention to other instruments. Paragraph 2, by contrast, highlights that the Convention does not "modify the rights and obligations of the Parties under any other treaties". This is the result of a compromise between the United States which wanted the 2005 Convention to be subordinate to other instruments and a number of other States which supported a formulation that would allow States to avoid serious damage to cultural diversity, see Scovazzi and Nafziger (2007), p. 145; McGoldrick (2002), p. 467. He has observed that "[a]rticle 20 was the subject of protracted and difficult debate. Many states considered the provision to be of fundamental importance."

[178] The function of the guiding principles is apparent in the report on the second independent expert meeting which resulted in the first draft of the convention: "[T]he experts emphasized that the advantage of defining principles is to provide States with rules of conduct that are valid in all situations envisaged by the Convention. In light of this, the list of principles should be restricted." Second Meeting of Experts on the Preliminary Draft on the Protection of the Diversity of Cultural Content and Artistic Expressions, UNESCO Doc Ref CLT/CPD/2004/602/6 [14.05.2004], at 5.

[179] Compare Kuprecht (2014), p. 99.

[180] Art.2(1) CDCE.

to national cultural heritage law, the Convention seeks to provide states with the space to promote their own cultural policies and does not require respect for Indigenous cultural rights that goes beyond the incorporation of existing human rights standards.[181]

The question remains whether there is an evolving norm in ICHL instruments that states need to respect the interests of Indigenous Peoples in their sacred heritage. In this respect, the Convention reflects both the growing role of Indigenous People in international cultural heritage and the continuing dominance of state interests in the field. The instrument recognizes the contribution of Indigenous cultures to cultural diversity and takes the special circumstances of Indigenous Peoples into account.[182] While there are provisions which take the position of Indigenous Peoples into account, overall, there is a remarkable lack of consideration of Indigenous cultural rights given the subject-matter of the instrument.[183] This can be explained in light of the drafting context of the Convention.

The instrument was influenced by the need to counteract the WTO. According to Christoph Graber, the references to Indigenous Peoples and their traditional cultural expressions were inserted comparatively late in the drafting process.[184] While the emphasis on state sovereignty can be explained by the desire to counteract the WTO, the instrument does not reflect contemporary Indigenous rights standards, including the Indigenous right to cultural self-determination.[185] While the UNDRIP was not yet adopted in 2005, its drafting and negotiation had already been underway for a considerable time (see Chap. 2). Both the state parties as well as UNESCO as an organization cannot but have been aware of the broader need to respect Indigenous rights. Overall, the instrument thus reaffirms that there is a growing recognition of Indigenous cultural rights in the instruments of ICHL. Yet, this momentum has not reached the stage where there is clear respect for the Indigenous right to their (sacred) cultural heritage and this is reflected in the insufficient incorporation of the latter in both treaties and the soft law instruments that operationalize these treaties.[186]

---

[181] The Operational Guidelines also highlight the need to "foster the full participation and engagement of all members of society contributing to the diversity of cultural expressions, particularly persons belonging to minorities, indigenous peoples and women;" see principle 1.3 on Article 7 'Measures to Promote Cultural Expressions', Operational Guidelines last approved by the Conference of Parties at its fifth session (Paris, 10–12 June 2015).

[182] Compare Kuprecht (2014), p. 99.

[183] The author would not go so far as McGoldrick (2002), p. 471. He has argued that, while there are differences, the CDCE could be classified as a human rights treaty in the sense that it is "strongly premised on the value of cultural diversity as an international public good. It defends human creativity. In those senses it is supportive of individual cultural rights."

[184] Graber (2012), p. 22.

[185] Burri et al. (2009), p. 368.

[186] Anna Meijknecht evaluates the role of the convention for Indigenous Peoples on the whole somewhat more positively. She especially emphasizes its symbolic value: "In the main, however, the added value of the Convention on the Diversity of Cultural Expressions is in its symbolic function: it brings the value of cultural diversity as such to the fore in an international sense", see Meijknecht (2012), p. 226.

3.6 The Return of Indigenous (Sacred) Heritage in International Soft Law Instruments

Earlier it was noted that soft law instruments are ahead of binding ICHL instruments both in the recognition of the connection between cultural heritage (preservation) and cultural rights[187] as well as in recognizing the link between Indigenous rights and cultural heritage.[188] This is apparent both in UNESCO soft law instruments (for example in the 2015 recommendation considered below) as well as in reports adopted by other actors in international law. The importance of sacred cultural heritage for Indigenous Peoples and their contemporary traditions has been considered both by the International Law Association (ILA), and the International Council of Museums (ICOM). The ILA principles are more advanced than the ICOM ethics code in this regard. This is not surprising, given that ICOM is the representative body of museums worldwide, which can be classified as the holding institutions.

3.6.1 2015 UNESCO Recommendation Concerning the Protection and Promotion of Museums and Collections, Their Diversity and Their Role in Society

In its 2015 recommendation on museums and their collections, UNESCO explicitly considered the position of Indigenous Peoples and the presence of their heritage in museum collections. Interestingly, this was done under the heading of the social role of the museum. The position of the museum within greater society was also a particular point of consideration for the Expert Mechanism in their 2015 Report on Indigenous Peoples and their cultural heritage. EMRIP highlighted the museum's role as both a space of education and cultural understanding as well as a contributor to the misappropriation of Indigenous culture.[189]

The Recommendation asks states "to take appropriate measures to encourage and facilitate dialogue and the building of constructive relationships between those museums and indigenous peoples concerning the management of those collections and, *where appropriate, return or restitution in accordance with applicable laws*

[187] Notably in the UNESCO Declaration of the Principles of International Cultural Co-operation 1966.

[188] For example, the 2001 UDCD versus the 2005 UNESCO Convention.

[189] Human Rights Council, Promotion and protection of the rights of Indigenous Peoples with respect to their cultural heritage, Study by the Expert Mechanism on the Rights of Indigenous Peoples, U.N. Doc. A/HRC/30/53 [19.08.2015], paras 67–68.

and policies."[190] While this is an important step forward in terms of recognizing the position of Indigenous Peoples, the provision is relatively soft in terms of wording. Even if the recommendation had been part of treaty it would be a weak obligation at best, especially in light of the fact that many applicable laws and policies may not recognize an Indigenous claims to begin with. After all, this is the reason why many Indigenous Peoples have struggled for so long to success with claims for the return of objects located in museums that are the legal owners of the heritage in many jurisdictions, unless the museum is willing to repatriate and respective government (s) supportive of the claim. On the positive side, Indigenous Peoples are expressly recognized as actors with a claim to their heritage that resides in museum collections and UNDRIP is listed amongst the instruments that directly and indirectly relate to museums and collections.[191]

3.6.2 ILA Principles for Cooperation in the Mutual Protection and Transfer of Cultural Material 2006[192]

The ILA is an international, non-governmental organization established in 1873 in Brussels.[193] Its mandate is "the study, clarification and development of international law, both public and private, and the furtherance of international understanding and respect for international law".[194] The principles do not represent binding law, rather they are a clarification of existing practice as well as a proposal to facilitate matters in international disputes. The principles advance a collaborative approach that aims to establish a process that is available to both international and national claimants.[195] Nafziger and Paterson, respectively the Chair and Rapporteur of the ILA Committee, which adopted the principles in 2006,[196] observe that the principles are to offer guidance for a "broad range of interested parties" in how to deal with repatriation requests with "good stewardship".[197] Their aim is to "facilitate principled collaboration or negotiation between competing claimants in an informal process of first resort."[198]

---

[190] UNESCO General Conference. Recommendation concerning the Protection and Promotion of Museums and Collections, their Diversity and their Role in Society (Paris, 17 November 2015), p. 9, para 18.

[191] Ibid, p. 11, footnote (i).

[192] Principles included in the ILA Resolution No 4/2006 adopted at the 72nd Conference of the International Law Association, held in Toronto, Canada, 4–8 June 2006.

[193] https://www.ila-hq.org/index.php/about-us/aboutus2 [last accessed 27.01.2020]

[194] ILA Constitution, sec. 3.1.

[195] ILA Toronto Conference (2006) Cultural Heritage Law Committee Report, p. 6.

[196] ILA Toronto Conference (2006) Cultural Heritage Law Committee Report, p. 1.

[197] Nafziger and Paterson (2014), pp. 16–17.

[198] Nafziger and Paterson (2014), p. 17.

Three principles relate directly to the discussion on Indigenous sacred objects and their repatriation: **Principle 4** deals with the "cultural material of indigenous peoples and cultural minorities". It requires addressees of repatriation requests by Indigenous Peoples to "respond in good faith" to such requests, regardless of whether they are supported by the government in whose territory the Indigenous community (or cultural minority) resides. Principle 4 bases this obligation on the UN Draft Declaration on the Rights of Indigenous Peoples. Art.13 of the Draft Declaration already included a right to the repatriation of human remains and the use and control of sacred/ ceremonial objects, which was taken over in the final declaration adopted by the UN General Assembly in Art.12 (see Chap. 2). The principles constitute an important affirmation of the connection between international human rights standards and international cultural heritage by notable experts in the field of ICHL. The notes on Principle 4 clarify that the drafters had both inter- and intrastate claims in mind when drafting the provision and they list the different means through which such claims may be settled: legislation, negotiation or litigation.[199]

Principle 5 also reflects the Draft UNDRIP, setting an obligation to repatriate human remains provided that the claimant can demonstrate a sufficient affiliation with the remains. The principle recognizes that remains may at times be subject to competing claims, in which case the remains are repatriated to the party with the closest affiliation. Such disputes also occur in connection with Indigenous cultural objects.

Principle 6 aids Indigenous communities in repatriation claims by requiring state museums and institutions which hold relevant cultural material to make an inventory of it and—even more importantly—to make this register accessible to "interested parties". This provision is essential; having access to information about which material is stored by the holding institution constitutes the foundation of any repatriation dialogue. The Committee Notes show that this principle is a reflection of an emerging trend in the repatriation debate about Indigenous material.[200] It is noteworthy that the US legislation on the repatriation of Indigenous cultural objects (NAGPRA, see Chap. 4), which was first adopted in 1990 includes a comparable provision (25 U.S.C. 3004). Moreover, in the context of restituting Nazi-looted art, the obligation to make records accessible and create them is firmly established, both through the Washington Principles and the Vilnius Declaration.[201]

---

[199] ILA Toronto Conference (2006) Cultural Heritage Law Committee Report, at 4.

[200] Ibid, at 5.

[201] Washington Conference Principles on Nazi-Confiscated Art [3.12.2008], principle II. Vilnius Forum Declaration [5.10.2000], principle 2.

3.6.3 ICOM Code of Ethics

The Code of Ethics was adopted unanimously by the International Council of Museums in 1986.[202] It is discussed here in its most recently revised form available at time of writing, the 2004 Code.[203] The ICOM Code of Ethics remains mostly silent on how museums should deal with requests for the return of items in their collection. Nevertheless, a number of principles relate to Indigenous religious objects, namely provisions 2.5, 2.15, 3.7, 4.3, 4.4 and 6. Principle 2.15 obliges museums to have a policy in place which clearly regulates the deaccessioning of an object in a variety of circumstances, including repatriation. It also highlights that the policy must establish the possibility of a complete transfer of ownership.[204]

The ethics code acknowledges the unique nature of sacred cultural heritage in several instances. Principle 2(5) requires museums to refrain from acquiring human remains or sacred material unless "they can be housed securely and cared for respectfully." Respectful care encompasses not only professional industry standards, but also care in a "manner consistent with . . . the interests and beliefs of members of the community, ethnic or religious groups from which the objects originated, where these are known." Similarly, principle 4(3) provides that such material should be displayed "with great tact and respect for the feelings of human dignity held by all peoples." The code still highlights the museum's position as a custodian of objects which are a source of knowledge, referred to as "primary evidence". However, several provisions indicate the growing awareness among museum professionals of the need for cultural diplomacy and sensitivity towards the needs of (Indigenous) communities. Another example of this is provision 3(7). It does not prohibit professionals from conducting research into human remains and sacred materials. Instead it highlights the need to be aware of the beliefs of the communities from whom the objects originated and to take these into account.[205]

Another part of the code focusses on the collaboration of the museum with communities. Principle 6.1 asks museums to "promote the sharing of knowledge, documentation and collections with . . . museums . . . in the countries and communities of origin". In light of the context of the code, it would seem as if sharing collections is directed at the exchange of collections between museums, but the

---

[202] ICOM Code of Ethics, available at: https://icom.museum/wp-content/uploads/2018/07/ICOM-code-En-web.pdf [last accessed 18.08.2021].

[203] Since the 2019 ICOM meeting in Kyoto a process of review is underway which may lead to changes in the future, this process was not yet completed in July 2021.

[204] Section 2(15) also provides "There will be a strong presumption that a deaccessioned item should first be offered to another museum". In author's understanding, this sentence refers to the removal of an object through means other than repatriation, such as sale and donation. It is not relevant to community directed returns.

[205] Sec.3(7) ICOM Code of Ethics "Research on human remains and materials of sacred significance must be accomplished in a manner consistent with professional standards and take into account the interests and beliefs of the community, ethnic or religious groups from whom the objects originated, where these are known".

exchange of information certainly includes Indigenous communities as the community of origin.[206] 6.2 and 6.3 discuss the possibility to return or the restitution of objects to countries or peoples of origin. The choice of 'peoples' in contrast to communities in i.e.4.4 seems deliberate in order to exclude the requests for the return of Indigenous cultural objects stemming from Indigenous communities from the scope of provisions 6.2 and 6.3. However, this is alleviated by principle 4.4. It addresses requests by communities or groups of origin for the removal of 'their' sensitive material from public display. In these cases, as well as in the case of a request for their repatriation, the code does not indicate whether or not museums are under an ethical or moral obligation to return sacred objects. Instead, it restricts itself to asking museums to handle such requests promptly, placing the main responsibility for such repatriation discussions with the museum.[207]

These provisions represent an awareness of the sensitivity of material that many museums hold in their collections. At the same time, the code's emphasis clearly rests on the museum maintaining its role as an educational and research institution.

3.7 Conclusion to Chapter 3

It is well-established in the literature that there is no binding obligation to return sacred cultural heritage to Indigenous Peoples abroad in international (cultural heritage) law instruments. Instead, this chapter considered whether existing ICHL instruments incorporate provisions which interact with *intra-national* repatriation. Moreover, while there is no obligation to repatriate sacred objects, the strengthening of the Indigenous rights movement raises the question whether there is an evolving norm in international law in this direction.

This chapter examined the nature of UNESCO instruments on the protection of cultural heritage in peace time and their consideration of Indigenous Peoples and their cultural heritage. There is clearly a trend towards a greater recognition of Indigenous Peoples and their unique contribution to cultural heritage. There is, overall, greater respect for their cultural heritage and the importance of that heritage for the individual community.[208] Moreover, the overall trend in the instruments, reports and recommendations examined is a positive one, moving towards greater participation of Indigenous Peoples and recognition of their rights. However, it is also clear that the interests of state parties remain prevalent to a degree that entails that the core documents of ICHL are not yet (fully) in accordance with Indigenous rights standards. If international cultural heritage law is moving towards the recognition of a norm to return sacred Indigenous cultural heritage, this evolution has not advanced sufficiently to influence the outcome of the present research to date. More

[206] Kuprecht (2014), p. 127.

[207] Kuprecht (2014), p. 128.

[208] In agreement, Shaheed (2011), p. 7, paras 19–20.

recent ICHL instruments reinforce UNDRIP by referencing it directly (for example the 2015 UNESCO Recommendation), a trend which is also visible on the national level. However, in terms of repatriation, widespread practice is still lacking.

The examination has shown that binding instruments of ICHL are still too silent on Indigenous rights to their cultural heritage. Earlier ICHL treaties even protect state interests in a way that facilitates disregard for contemporary Indigenous cultural rights,[209] however current practices for example the Operational Guidelines are slowly being used to address such issues. For the 1970 UNESCO Convention, the absence of Indigenous Peoples in the treaty system also means that nothing would stand in the way of an additional instrument(s) in this area, an avenue highlighted by EMRIP in their recent reports. However, in the more recent treaties, there are some provisions that do support Indigenous rights to their sacred cultural heritage, including repatriation requests by Indigenous communities. Things slowly started to shift, also in ICHL, notably with the adoption of the 1995 UNIDROIT convention. While it may not regulate the repatriation of colonial heritage, it does regulate the return of sacred objects that are in use today and were stolen and exported or illegally exported. This also means that if a sufficient number of states ratify the convention, colonial objects that have been repatriated will be better protected from the threat of being taken a second time. This danger still exists, given the existence of a tribal art market. Second, measures that ensure Indigenous access to and use of their sacred heritage qualify as measures a state can take to respect its obligation to protect the connected religious rituals. These rituals can be classified as intangible cultural heritage under the 2003 UNESCO Convention. Consequently, measures that ensure Indigenous access, including repatriation, are classified as measures that a state can take to fulfil its safeguarding obligation under the Convention. The state may not be obliged to take a particular measure, but the Convention quite clearly imposes an obligation to take measures to protect intangible cultural heritage in its territory, including Indigenous sacred traditions. Finally, measures that protect access to sacred heritage, including the repatriation of cultural heritage are also in line with the aims of the UNESCO instruments on cultural diversity, both the declaration and the convention. Access to their cultural heritage is a possible measure expressly considered by the convention. Repatriation, if understood as a measure to strengthen Indigenous cultures, promotes and protects the diversity of cultural expressions, which is an express objective of the convention.[210] The measures that a state may have to take under international human rights law admittedly go beyond what a state is legally required to do under the UNESCO instruments.

In conclusion, it can be observed that, if national repatriation measures respect the guidelines established under international human rights established in the previous chapter, these measures can mean that a state implements some of its obligations under international cultural heritage law at the same time. This also means that there

[209] See discussions on 1972 World Heritage Convention Sect. 3.2.3.2 above.

[210] Art.1(a) CDCE.

is no need to add additional evaluation principles to examine American and Canadian law.

References

Bandarin F (2012) International trade in indigenous cultural heritage: comments from UNESCO in light of its international standard-setting instruments in the field of culture. In: Graber CB, Kuprecht K, Lai JC (eds) International trade in indigenous cultural heritage - legal and policy issues. Edward Elgar, Cheltenham, UK, pp 306–328

Bengs B (1996) Dead on arrival? A comparison of the Unidroit Convention on stolen or illegally exported cultural objects and U.S. Property Law. Transnatl Law Contemp Probl 6:503–535

Blake J (2006) Commentary on the UNESCO 2003 Convention on the Safeguarding of the Intangible Cultural Heritage. Institue of Art & Law, Leicester, UK

Burri M (2013) The UNESCO Convention on Cultural Diversity: an appraisal five years after its entry into force. Int J Cult Prop 20(4):357–380

Burri M et al (2009) The protection and promotion of cultural diversity in a digital networked environment: mapping possible advances to coherence

Disko S, Tugendhat H (eds) (2014) World heritage sites and indigenous peoples' rights. IWGIA, Copenhagen

Donders Y (2002) Towards a right to cultural identity? Intersentia, Antwerpen; New York

Donders Y (2012) Cultural rights and the convention on the diversity of cultural expressions: included or ignored? In: Kono T, Van Uytsel S (eds) The UNESCO convention on the diversity of cultural expressions - a tale of fragmentation in international law. Intersentia, Cambridge, pp 165–182

Donders Y (2020) Cultural heritage and human rights. In: Francioni F, Vrdoljak AF (eds) Oxford handbook on international cultural heritage law. Oxford University Press, Oxford, UK, pp 379–406

Fechner F (1998) The fundamental aims of cultural property law. Int J Cult Prop 7(2):376–394

Forrest C (2007) Cultural heritage as the common heritage of humankind: a critical re-evaluation. Comp Int Law J South Africa 40:124–151

Forrest C (2010) International law and the protection of cultural heritage. Routledge, Abingdon

Francioni F (2013) Cultural heritage. Max Planck encyclopedia of public international law. Oxford University Press

Graber CB (2012) Stimulating trade and development of indigenous cultural heritage by means of international law: issues of legitimacy and method. In: Graber CB, Kuprecht K, Lai JC (eds) International trade in indigenous cultural heritage - legal and policy issues. Edward Elgar, Cheltenham, UK, pp 3–30

Groenen A (2018) UNIDROIT 1995: tackling the illicit trafficking of cultural property through private law means. Maastricht University, Maastricht

Hausler K (2020) The participation of non-state actors in the implementation of cultural heritage law. In: Francioni F, Vrdoljak AF (eds) The Oxford handbook of international cultural heritage law. Oxford University Press, Oxford, UK, pp 760–786

Kuprecht K (2014) Indigenous peoples' cultural property claims - repatriation and beyond. Springer

McGoldrick D (2002) Culture, cultures, and cultural rights. In: Baderin M, McCorquodale R (eds) Economic, social and cultural rights in action. Oxford University Press, Oxford, pp 447–473

Meijknecht A (2012) The convention on the diversity of cultural expressions - what is its added value for minorities and indigenous peoples? In: Kono T, Van Uytsel S (eds) The UNESCO convention on the diversity of cultural expressions - a tale of fragmentation in international law. Intersentia, Cambridge, pp 201–226

Nafziger J, Paterson RK (2014) Cultural heritage law. Handbook on the law of cultural heritage and international trade. Edward Elgar Publishing, UK

Olivier M (1996) The Unidroit Convention: attempting to regulate the international trade and traffic of cultural property. Golden Gate Univ Law Rev 26:627–674

Prott L (1997) Commentary on the UNIDROIT Convention. Institute of Art and Law

Prott L (2009a) The UNIDROIT Convention on stolen or illegally exported cultural objects - ten years on. Uniform Law Rev 14:215–237

Prott LV (2009b) The history and development of processes for the recovery of cultural heritage. In: Prott LV (ed) Witnesses to history - a compendium of documents and writings on the return of cultural objects. UNESCO Publishing, Paris, pp 2–18

Raschèr AFG (2000) Kulturgüter-Transfer und Globalisierung. Studien zum Kunstrecht. Nomos Verlagsgesellschaft Baden-Baden, Zürich

Scovazzi T (2020) International cultural heritage law: the institutional aspects. In: Francioni F, Vrdoljak AF (eds) The Oxford handbook of international cultural heritage law. Oxford University Press, Oxford, UK, pp 737–759

Scovazzi T, Nafziger J (2007) 2005 - Le patrimoine culturel de l'humanité - The cultural heritage of mankind. Martinus Nijhoff Publishers

Shaheed F (2011) Report of the independent expert in the field of cultural rights on the right of access to and enjoyment of cultural heritage. UN General Assembly, A/HRC/17/38

Srivinas B (2008) The UNESCO Convention for the Safeguarding of the Intangible Cultural Heritage. In: Nafziger J, Scovazzi T (eds) Le patrimonie culturel de l'humanité - The cultural heritage of mankind. Martinus Nijhoff Publishers, Leiden; Boston

Tauli-Corpuz V (2014) Forword. World heritage sites and indigenous peoples' rights. IWGIA, Copenhagen

Vrdoljak AF (2018) Indigenous peoples, world heritage, and human rights. Int J Cult Prop 25 (3):245–281

Part II
Sacred Indigenous Cultural Heritage in U.S. Law

Chapter 4
Repatriation of Sacred Indigenous Heritage in U.S. Law

4.1 Introduction

Part III examines the U.S. example of regulating repatriation of sacred cultural heritage through legal means. In analysing existing intra-national repatriation models NAGPRA, the Native American Graves Protection and Repatriation Act, is the obvious point of departure. It was one of the first laws of its kind to be adopted; it applies to numerous cultural institutions and government agencies within the U.S. (federal or federally funded[1] institutions) and has been in force for roughly three decades. There has been ample discussion of its advantages and disadvantages and case law.[2] The National Park Service, which is the administering agency, has also made a significant amount of material on the act publicly available.[3]

As was highlighted in Chap. 1, this volume seeks to answer how the law can best regulate the repatriation of sacred cultural heritage to Indigenous[4] communities in light of international standards. This comprises three sub-questions: How is the repatriation of sacred cultural heritage regulated in the selected examples? What international standards apply to repatriation? Which method of repatriation is most in line with these standards? The previous two chapters examined international law

[1] See definition of museum 25 U.S.C. Ch. 32 §3001(8) (2019).

[2] Starting with the initial time of adoption of the law, when a special issue was authored by a multitude of authors, see Inouye (1992), also Harjo (2012), Kuprecht (2014), Nafziger (2009) and Tsosie (2012).

[3] Having a look around https://www.nps.gov/subjects/nagpra/index.htm is highly recommended to any institutions or policymakers outside the United States who may lack repatriation/return experience or simply wish to learn more [last accessed 18.08.2021].

[4] Please note that this chapter adopts the capitalization of the terms Indigenous Peoples and Indigenous (except for when used in citations) for reasons explained in Chap. 1. Capital A is used in Aboriginal for similar reasons except for citations, when spelled differently in the original source cited.

V. Tünsmeyer, *Repatriation of Sacred Indigenous Cultural Heritage and the Law*, Studies in Art, Heritage, Law and the Market 3,
https://doi.org/10.1007/978-3-030-89047-6_4

and provided the standard that will be applied in the examination of U.S. law in Chap. 5 and Canadian law (Chaps. 6–8, see Part III). As proposed in Chap. 1, to answer the first sub-question, the applicable repatriation legislation will be analysed paying particular attention to a number of key areas. This allows for a better comparison of the different regulatory frameworks. In particular, the examination will address the scope of the legislation (definition of Indigenous Peoples and sacred objects), whether it mandates a particular outcome, procedure or combination thereof, who takes the final decision on a repatriation request, whether there is a dispute resolution mechanism, and in how far costs associated with repatriation are considered.

To answer both research questions, Part II first needs to map the different applicable laws to examine both the repatriation law and the legal context in which Indigenous communities, museums and governments interact with each other when sacred cultural heritage is concerned. Chapter 1 defined the relevant context as comprising those constitutional law aspects that regulate the legal relationship between the parties, the legal-historical background in which the cultural heritage was taken, Indigenous religious freedom, museum (self-) regulation, and cultural heritage legislation. This chapter begins by summarizing how the relationship between Indigenous Peoples and settler governments involved, which encompasses both the time during which sacred objects were taken and the legal foundations of federal Indian law.[5] This is the primary legal area that regulates the lives of Native Americans.[6] The vast majority of instruments and principles examined in this chapter fall under the umbrella of federal Indian law, including NAGPRA examined in Sect. 4.4. This is further informed by the rules that structure the legal relationship between the different governmental spheres in the U.S. which are laid out in Sect. 4.3. Section 4.5 considers the legal protection of Indigenous religious freedom and the relationship of these rules to repatriation. Finally, Sect. 4.6 considers museum and heritage law and policy. On the basis of these sections, Part II concludes in Chap. 5 by applying the human rights standards distilled in earlier chapters. These findings and the analysis in this chapter will also be used to answer the second research question set out in Chap. 1, namely whether there any additional lessons we can learn from this analysis for national cultural heritage law and policy.

Before proceeding with a summary of the historic evolution of the legal relationship between settler governments and Native Americans, a brief note of caution should be added on the scope of the research. Governmental policies and laws have had (and continue to have) a profound impact on Native Americans, by limiting, transferring or extinguishing ownership rights of vast tracts of land, prescribing membership rules and prohibiting different cultural and religious manifestations.

[5] On Federal Indian Law see also Sect. 4.3.2.7.

[6] The author uses the term Native Americans for the sake of brevity to denote the Indigenous Peoples of the United States, which encompass many different peoples, Native Americans, Native Hawaiians and Native Alaskans. The term Indians is used because of its continued existence in American law.

Moreover, changes in law and policies as well as the fact that hundreds of different peoples and their different cultures are at issue has resulted in a labyrinth of applicable laws. In fact,

> federal Congress, which early in the Nation's history was found to possess extensive power over Indians, has enacted over four thousand treaties and statutes dealing with Native Americans. Regulations and guidelines implementing these laws are even more numerous. The tribes' own laws, and some state statutes dealing with Indians, add to the complexity. There are thousands of reported judicial decisions in Indian law.[7]

As a result, in this volume, I cannot even begin to hope to portray a complete picture of cultural and religious rights or heritage-related laws and policies. Instead, the analysis will focus on NAGPRA as a federal act with a relatively specialized application[8] and it will examine the relationships between the federal level and tribes in the areas of culture and religion more broadly as explained above. Common law[9] or property law[10] avenues for repatriation will not be considered.

Lastly, any provisions from the U.S. Code cited are cited from the latest virtual main edition accessible online at the last moment when it was possible to enter (minor) updates during the editorial process (June 2021) via GovInfo.[11] This is done for the sake of reliability and accuracy, to ensure that the reader can find the precise version discussed here at some indeterminate future date, the version used is therefore the United States Code, 2018 Edition, Supplement 1, Title 25 Indians version, from 2019, that was in effect as of 24th of January 2020.[12] For the Code of Federal Regulations this means that the latest version is the one revised as of October 1, 2020. Currently, a review process of the regulations has been initiated by National Park Services, but because of the timing of the editorial process this could not be considered.

To those readers who may be working in museums and be unfamiliar with the legal landscape, I would also like to highlight that I used the U.S. Code title 25 which is a reorganized structure of relevant pieces of law rather than the actual, positive law. This means that, while the provisions cited are prima facie evidence of the laws

---

[7] Newton et al. (2005), p. xvii.

[8] This also means that NAGPRA does not qualify as a law of general application. Tribes thus maintain tribal sovereignty, see discussion White v University of California, Not Reported in F. Supp.2d (2012), 2012 WL 12335354 [9.10.2012], at 6.

[9] Johnson and Haensly (1992), pp. 155–157 Commenting on People v Van Horn 267 Cal. Rptr. 804 (Ct App.1990) see Riding In (1992), p. 31 Conversely on constraints in using common law Trope and Echo-Hawk (1992), pp. 45–47.

[10] See i.e. Carpenter et al. (2009) and Brown (2010).

[11] Available via: https://www.govinfo.gov/ [last accessed 18.08.2021]. This is done instead of using the version provided by the Office of the Law Revision Counsel, which would have the advantage of being constantly updated to reflect current changes making it harder to use as a source in a publication. The interested reader is referred instead to: https://uscode.house.gov/browse/prelim@title25&edition=prelim [29.06.2021].

[12] 25 U.S.C.—INDIANS—Content Details—USCODE-2019-title25 (govinfo.gov) [last accessed 18.08.2021].

contained therein, it is not legal evidence of the law. This was done with the purpose of this volume in mind: to investigate the legal structure, organization and approach towards repatriation in U.S. law with a view to its compatibility with international human rights standards, and to introduce the subject-matter to readers who may not be familiar with U.S. law (not to bring a case in front of a court).

4.2 Historic Evolution of the Relationship Between Tribes and the Federal Government[13]

> To understand twenty-first century Native American legal issues, one must be familiar with developments often dating back to the sixteenth, seventeenth, and eighteenth centuries. A wealth of seemingly non-legal data affects the legal relationship between Indians and the federal government. Furthermore, Indian law draws on disciplines as varied as anthropology, sociology, psychology, political science, economics, philosophy, and religion. The most significant of these sources is history.[14]

In this statement, the editors of the Cohen Handbook on Federal Indian Law have aptly summarized the need to go beyond contemporary statutes and case law to understand the legal constraints and realities of Indigenous Peoples in today. According to the United States Census Bureau in 2019,[15] the American Population amounted to a total of 328,239,523 with "American Indian and Alaska Native alone" representing an estimated 1.3% of the population and "Native Hawaiian and Other Pacific Islanders alone" representing 0.2% of the population.[16] Collectively, this would amount to an estimated 4,923,593 individuals and does not take into account the 2.8% category of "Two or more races" listed.[17] In 2000, according to Duthu, nearly 2.5 million people identified as American Indian or Alaska Native, with about one-third of that being populations living in "American Indian areas." These areas include "about 310 reservations and the Indian lands in Oklahoma".[18] Moreover, due to international conflicts and transactions, tribes have also been separated by international borders. As a result, members of one Indigenous tribe may live both in

---

[13] This section will put the situation of the Pueblo Indians aside, who, until 1848, lived in a part that was formally Mexico and had special protection under Mexican law. Their different status remained after incorporation into the United States even in the absence of treaties. The next change in status was only in 1912 with New Mexico gaining statehood. See: Newton et al. (2005), pp. 58–60.

[14] Newton et al. (2005), p. 7.

[15] The definite results of the 2020 Census were not yet available at the time of final edits.

[16] https://www.census.gov/quickfacts/fact/table/US/RHI525216#viewtop [last accessed 18.08.2021].

[17] https://www.census.gov/quickfacts/fact/table/US/RHI525216#viewtop [last accessed 18.08.2021].

[18] Duthu (2008), p. 4.

the United States and Canada, the United States and Mexico, or the United States and Russia.[19]

In the contemporary relationship between tribes and federal and state governments, tribes are understood as 'domestic dependent nations' which exercise a certain amount of self-determination over their territories. Nowadays, over 560 federally recognized Indian tribes in the Unites States exercise governmental authority over tribal territories.[20] Neither the question of who is Indigenous for the purposes of U.S. law nor the boundaries of these territories are easy to determine. Moreover, who is recognized as Indigenous for the purposes of federal law does not necessarily coincide with who self-identifies as Indigenous or is accepted by an Indigenous community as a member. On top of this, who qualifies as Indigenous for the purpose of federal law also differs within federal law. To understand this and the complexity of the law applicable to Indigenous cultural heritage and Indigenous cultural and religious rights, it is helpful to go back in history.[21] The historic relationship has been classified according to different stages[22] and has fluctuated between periods of forced assimilation and the relative acceptance of the independent status of Indigenous Peoples (as illustrated in Fig. 4.1).

4.2.1 Treaty Federalism

For present purposes, Brian Duthu's classification of the historic relationship into roughly five general periods is sufficient to gain a general overview.[23] In the initial, formative years of the United States, the relationship between the Indigenous tribes and the incoming government was characterized through treaty-making. Through these treaties, Indian tribes ceded lands in return for various guarantees. In Johnson v McIntosh (1823), Chief Justice Marshall reduced Indian sovereignty over U.S. territory in the form of title to the lands to a right of occupancy, which could be extinguished by the new sovereign.[24] The second case in the (in)famous Marshall trilogy, Cherokee Nation v Georgia (1831) established the trust doctrine and recognized tribes "as 'domestic dependent nations'".[25] This established a trust title for all Indian lands within U.S. borders as being held by the U.S. federal government. As Bradford has aptly summarized, "[a]lthough the trust doctrine generated a host of express obligations in the context of subsequent treaties, statutes, and executive orders creating Indian reservations, political pressure ensured that these judicially

[19] Newton et al. (2005), p. 468.

[20] Duthu (2008), p. xii.

[21] Newton et al. (2005), p. 7.

[22] 5 by Duthu and 6 in the Cohen Handbook, see the illustration of these phases by means of Fig. 4.1.

[23] Duthu (2008), pp. xv–xix.

[24] Newton et al. (2005), p. 75.

[25] Newton et al. (2005), p. 75 Cherokee Nation v Georgia, 30 U.S. 5 Pet. 1 1 (1831).

Fig. 4.1 Overview time periods historic evolution in the U.S.

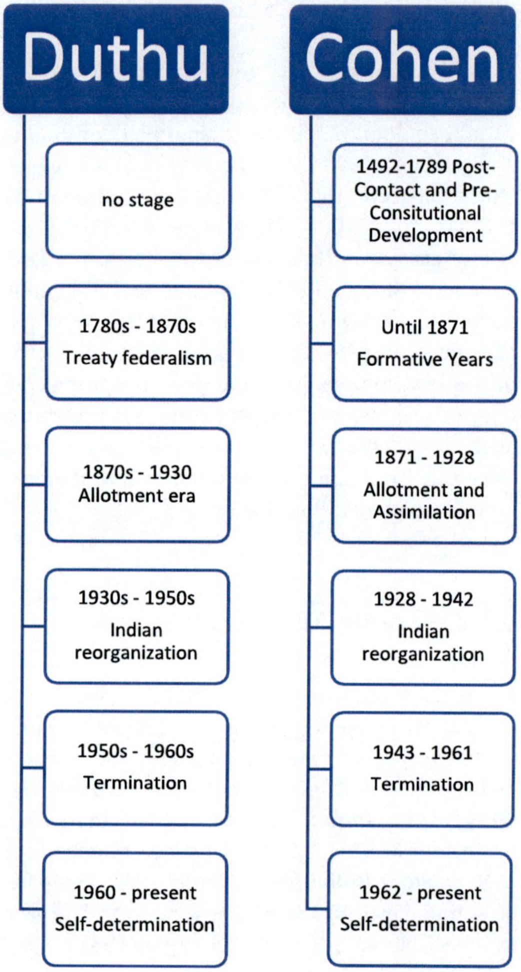

unenforceable obligations were almost never discharged with 'good faith and utter loyalty to the best interests' of the Indian tribes.'"[26] In the last case of the trilogy, Worcester v Georgia (1832), the court established federal plenary power over Indian affairs based on the commerce power which had been allocated to Congress in the Constitution, and it prohibited states "from acting unilaterally to disrupt federal-tribal political and legal arrangements."[27] In the 1830s, with the Indian Removal Act, the government continued its policy of land acquisition and the separation of Native Americans and incoming settlers, this time through forced relocations. The

[26]Bradford (2005), pp. 20–21.

[27]Newton et al. (2005), p. 75.

infamous Trail of Tears[28] is one example of such forced relocations; in this case, those who survived the trails were moved to Oklahoma. The allocated land later became Indian reservations in the 1850s under the Indian 1851 Appropriations Act. The era came to an end with the Appropriations Act of March 1871 when formal treaty-making was officially abandoned. Despite this, however, the federal government continued with agreements, statutes and executive orders "that had legal ramifications similar to treaties."[29]

4.2.2 *Allotment Era (1870s–1930s)*

While the adoption of agreements continued, the attitude of Congress towards Native American uniqueness changed drastically to one of forced assimilation seeking the eradication of the American Indian culture and religion. Laws were adopted which targeted social institutions such as marriage, family and clan relationships and property distributions, which were enforced by Courts of Indian Offences. The Secretary of the Interior argued for prohibitions on tribal dancing and feasting "[i]f it is the purpose of the [U.S.] Government to civilize the Indians, they must be compelled to desist from ... savage rites and heathenish customs."[30] The era received its name from the General Allotment Act (GAA) of 1887, commonly referred to as the Dawes Act. This act sought to assimilate Indigenous communities by converting land held in tribal ownership into land held by individual members.[31] By breaking the connection of a community to its lands and allocating comparatively much smaller land portions to the individual, the policy resulted in reducing Indian lands to roughly one third of their pre-Dawes Act size.[32] This assimilation and 'civilization' policy "was most simply expressed by Richard Henry Pratt: "[k]ill the Indian and Save the Man'."[33] The governmental and social attitudes of the time were also reflected in the relevant case law. For example, in Lone Wolf v Hitchcock (1903) the court held that Congress held the power to abrogate tribal treaty rights unilaterally.[34]

---

[28] For brief historic overview see i.e. https://www.britannica.com/event/Trail-of-Tears.

[29] Newton et al. (2005), p. 75.

[30] As cited in Bradford (2005), pp. 29–30.

[31] Newton et al. (2005), p. 66.

[32] Newton et al. (2005), pp. 78–79 "Of the approximately 156 million acres of Indian land in 1881, less than 105 million remained by 1890, and less than 78 million by 1900. While Indian land holdings were reduced from 138 million in 1887 to 48 million in 1934, an additional 60 million acres that were either ceded outright or sold to non-Indian homesteaders and corporations as "surplus" lands are not included in the 90 million acre loss."

[33] Newton et al. (2005), p. 81.

[34] Lone Wolf v. Hitchcock, 187 U.S. 553 (1903).

4.2.3 Indian Reorganization (1930s–1950s)

The result of centuries of a policy enforcing land confiscation and decades of forced assimilation policies were made visible in the governmental Meriam Report. The report was by no means free of assimilationist mentality,[35] but it emphasized the importance of Indigenous culture and highlighted the horrible living conditions of Indigenous Peoples in the United States. It defined "the goal of Indian policy as the development of all that is good in Indian culture 'rather than to crush out all that is Indian'."[36] The name of the era comes from the 1934 Indian Reorganization Act, which was much edited and ultimately became a piece of compromise legislation.[37] It sought to enable the tribes to organize themselves as governments but it featured, for example, the federal approval of Indian governmental acts which lead to many "standard "boilerplate" documents drafted by the Bureau of Indian Affairs and based on United States constitutional and common law notions rather than historic Native regulations and tribal customs."[38] Reactions were thus divided, with many tribes expressly rejecting the act. However, "a majority of tribes (often after federal pressure) elected to come under the provisions. Attempts to organize under the IRA brought disruption and heightened intra-tribal disputes to some tribes. For others it brought an improved economic structure and a revival or establishment tribal government, courts and policy."[39] Its implementation had to overcome Indian resistance, shortage of funds and resistance in Congress and the BIA. In more recent decades, "many Indian nations initially organized under the IRA have introduced constitutional reform projects aimed at amending IRA constitutions or establishing new constitutions outside the terms of the RIA. These amendments are designed to reshape tribal governments to meet contemporary needs and aspirations while maintaining structures and practices deemed legitimate within the community."[40] Overall, it can be argued that the policy was relatively successful in preventing further land loss but not in re-establishing tribal government and traditional culture.[41]

---

[35] Newton et al. (2005), p. 84.

[36] Newton et al. (2005), p. 84.

[37] Newton et al. (2005), p. 86.

[38] Newton et al. (2005), pp. 87–88.

[39] Newton et al. (2005), pp. 87–88.

[40] Newton et al. (2005), p. 254.

[41] Newton et al. (2005), p. 84.

4.2.4 *Termination (1950s–1960s)*

After a period of comparatively more acceptance of Indigenous distinctiveness, House Concurrent Resolution 108 was adopted. The Resolution is also known as Termination, since Congress exercised its plenary power to assimilate Native Americans into American society by ending their legal status as "wards".[42] As a result of this termination of the Indian status, the trust relationship between the U.S. and a selection of over 100 tribes ended. Termination policy forced tribal governments to dissolve, distributed tribal lands and assets on a per capita basis to reduce overall assets, while the remainder of federal benefits and services were reduced significantly.[43] As a consequence of this legal dissolution, Indigenous nations lost sacred sites and important resources for cultural traditions, economic resources and their political governing structures.[44] Historian Angie Debo has described termination as "the most concerted drive against Indian property and Indian survival since the removals following the act of 1830 and the liquidation of tribes and reservations following 1887".[45] In effect, the resolution did not stand on its own. Other acts, for example, transferred responsibilities away from the Bureau of Indian Affairs (BIA) to other federal agencies and land transfers occurred again.[46] In 1954, another law pushed forced legal assimilation further "by according States extensive jurisdiction over Indian tribes and individuals, granted non-Indian institutions of social control the legal authority to adjudge and condemn Indian domestic relations and employment practices."[47]

This forced legal assimilation can also be witnessed in the case law of the time. Examples are Tee-Hit-Ton v U.S. (1955), which provided that to extinguish Indian title does not give rise to a legal duty to compensate,[48] and Williams v Lee (1959), which created the infringement test. In testing whether state action infringed upon the Indigenous right to self-government on reservation lands, it gave states a

---

[42]This legal status of Native Americans as wards became a powerful narrative. Angie Debo has remarked, that "[t]his legal misconception had crept into the public vocabulary from the court's ruling in Cherokee Nation v Georgia that the relationship of the tribe to the United States "resembles that of a ward to his guardian."" Debo (1970), p. 349 Undoubtedly this understanding fit very well into the assimilatory force of public opinion and U.S. governmental policy that has characterized the relationship between Indigenous and non-Indigenous societies in the U.S. for long periods at a time.

[43]Bradford (2002), pp. 68–69.

[44]Bradford (2002), pp. 68–69.

[45]Debo (1970), p. 349.

[46]Newton et al. (2005), p. 91.

[47]Bradford (2005), p. 48.

[48]It is noteworthy that the rule established in the case was deemed "racially discriminatory" by Erica Daes in the Second Progress Report on Human Rights of Indigenous Peoples, Indigenous People and Their Relationship to Land (UN Doc E/CN.4/Sub.2/1999/18 (1999) (rule in Tee-Hit-Ton Indians v United States, 348 US 272 (1955) is "racially discriminatory").

jurisdictional foothold into Indian Country[49] by enabling it to "protect its interests up to the point where tribal self-government would be affected" where non-Indians were involved.[50]

4.2.5 *Self-determination (1960s–present)*

Since the 1960s, policies have shifted away again from forced assimilation and the relationship can be characterized as one which (seeks to) recognize Indian self-determination. A symbolic shift away from earlier policies of forced assimilation was the adoption of the Menominee Restoration Act in 1973 which repealed the legal termination of the tribe and reinstalled all legal rights which had been lost previously.[51] In the 1970s, Congress stated its aim to turn towards a policy of self-determination by emphasizing "its commitment to the maintenance of the Federal Government's unique and continuing relationship with, and responsibility to, individual tribes and to the Indian people as a whole through the establishment of a meaningful Indian self-determination policy".[52]

Important legislative examples of the self-determination era are the 1975 Indian Self-Determination and Education Assistance Act and the 1994 Tribal Self-Governance Act.[53] The 1975 Act increased Indigenous participation in areas which had previously been under exclusive BIA control such as health, education, economic development, and various social programmes. The 1994 Act in turn has resulted in a growth of self-governing tribes. Bruce Duthu has characterized these acts as "a declaration of independence for tribal governments. They have provided a chance for tribal governments to govern."[54] It may be summarily stated this era is very much characterized by the concept of self-governance, and that tribes are "the primary or basic governmental unit of Indian policy."[55] The laws which will be the focus of the present chapter, notably NAGPRA and the American Indian Religious Freedom Act (hereafter AIRFA), both constitute parts of Federal Indian law which were adopted in this era of self-determination. Relevant cases and principles will

---

[49] 18 U.S. C. § 1151 (2019) defines Indian country as: "(1) All land within the limits of any Indian reservation under the jurisdiction of the United States Government, notwithstanding the issuance of any patent, and, including rights-of-way running through the reservation; (2) All dependent Indian communities within the borders of the United States whether within the original or subsequently acquired territory thereof, and whether within or without the limits of a State; (3) All Indian allotments, the Indian titles to which have not been extinguished, including rights-of-way running through the same."

[50] Williams v Lee 411 US (1959) at 179. See also Duthu (2008), pp. 10–11.

[51] Newton et al. (2005), p. 101.

[52] As cited in Duthu (2008), p. xii.

[53] Newton et al. (2005), p. 103.

[54] Newton et al. (2005), p. 103.

[55] Newton et al. (2005), p. 98.

thus be explored below. Lastly, as will become clear in the context of the self-determination era, the characterization above portrays the historic evolution of governmental policy towards Indigenous Peoples living in the United States as being much neater than it has ever been. Indeed, as the authors of the Cohen handbook caution "there never has been a single, clearly articulated American Indian policy at any given time."[56] This is what makes analysing legislative acts, case law and policy statements in this area so difficult.

4.3 Foundations

4.3.1 Constitution

4.3.1.1 Competences

In setting the stage for an examination of the law governing the cultural rights of American Indians, the first step is to consider the constitutional split of competences and constitutional principles which influence the relationship between tribes, states and the federal level. The constitution mentions "Indians" three times, and the main constitutional competence in terms of American Indians is the commerce clause.[57] The Indian commerce clause is read much more broadly than just referring to its trading component, and it has been described as a plenary power by both Courts and scholars to describe the broad powers held by the Legislature.[58] The necessary and proper clause in Art. I section 8 of the constitution widens Congressional authority to encompass "all Laws which shall be necessary and proper for carrying into Execution the foregoing Powers, and all other Powers vested by this Constitution in the Government of the United States, or in any Department or Officer thereof." Initial constitutional proposals did not feature an Indian affairs provision, yet Madison was

---

[56] Newton et al. (2005), p. 10.

[57] U.S. Constitution. Art I Section 8 Clause 3 "To regulate Commerce with foreign Nations, and among the several States, and with the Indian Tribes;" the other times Indians are mentioned are the apportionment clauses Art.I, clause 3 and in the 14th Amendment. Newton et al. (2005), p. 390: The authors argue that "By excluding 'Indians not taxed' from the population count for apportioning representatives to Congress, the apportionment clauses indicate an understanding of the separate status of tribes as sovereign entities."

[58] Newton et al. (2005), p. 398 "The courts have recognized that Congress has "plenary and exclusive authority" over Indian affairs. The term "plenary" indicates the breadth of congressional power to legislate in the area of Indian affairs, and the term "exclusive" refers to the supremacy of federal over state law. The term "plenary power" is also used as a shorthand for general federal authority to legislate on health, safety, and morals within Indian country, similar to the states' police powers over non-Indians. Courts have upheld broad congressional authority to impose federal policy directly on tribes without their consent." This broad constitutional competence has been characterized as a plenary power by different authors, i.e. Reed (2016), p. 298 Bradford characterizes the allotment policy as an exercise of plenary power, see Bradford (2002), pp. 38–39.

concerned that, irrespective of the right to treat being reserved to Congress, States would encroach upon the power.[59] Since then, the commerce clause has become the foundation of federal Indian law; it is "the most often cited basis for modern legislation regarding Indian tribes, from legislation protecting tribal cultural resources [NAGRPA], to legislation regulating gaming in Indian country."[60]

Historically, the treaty clause[61] was important as a source of federal treaty-making powers. The Supreme Court established that the power to make treaties with Indian tribes was encompassed in the treaty clause.[62] It has also been used to substantiate federal power over Indian affairs.[63] The emphasis on the treaty clause in the early phase was also mirrored in Indian affairs, being very much a matter of military and foreign policy rather than domestic affairs. This approach has changed over time, as highlighted above. In the early twentieth century, in Lone Wolf v Hitchcock (1903), the Supreme Court, comparing treaty making with Indian tribes to the power to make treaties with foreign nations, included the legislative power to abrogate treaty rights unilaterally.[64]

---

[59]Newton et al. (2005), p. 25 According to the authors of the Cohen handbook, "the contrast with the Articles of Confederation, Madison's intent to end state encroachments on federal authority, and contemporary state interference with federal Indian policy, all contribute to the understanding of the Indian commerce clause as a broad grant of power to the federal government and a limit on state power to interfere with federal Indian policy."

[60]Newton et al. (2005), p. 397 Congressional authority vested in it by the commerce clause is also broader than the other commerce clauses, as the Supreme Court highlighted in 1996 in Seminole Tribe of Florida v Florida 517 US 44, 62: "If anything, the commerce clause accomplishes a greater transfer of power from the States to the Federal Government than does the interstate commerce clause. This is clear enough from the fact that the States will exercise some authority over interstate trade but have been divested of virtually all authority over Indian commerce and Indian tribes".

[61]Art.II, Section 2, clause 2 U.S. Constitution "He shall have Power, by and with the Advice and Consent of the Senate, to make Treaties, provided two thirds of the Senators present concur; and he shall nominate, and by and with the Advice and Consent of the Senate, shall appoint Ambassadors, other public Ministers and Consuls, Judges of the supreme Court, and all other Officers of the United States, whose Appointments are not herein otherwise provided for, and which shall be established by Law: but the Congress may by Law vest the Appointment of such inferior Officers, as they think proper, in the President alone, in the Court of Law, or in the Heads of Departments."

[62]First, the Supreme Court established that "The Constitution, by declaring treaties already made, as well as those to be made, to be the supreme law of the land, had adopted and sanctioned the previous treaties with the Indian nations, and consequently admits their rank among those powers who are capable of making treaties. The words 'treaty' and 'nation' are words of our own language, selected in our diplomatic and legislative proceedings, by ourselves, having each a definite and well understood meaning. We have applied them to Indians, as we have applied them to the other nations of the earth. They are applied to all in the same sense."", in Worcester v Georgia, 31 US 515 (1832), at 559. Later it explained that the treaty-making power with Indians corresponded to the treaty-making power with foreign nations, see i.e. United States v Forty-three Gallons of Whiskey 93 U.S. 188.

[63]Newton et al. (2005), pp. 393–394.

[64]Lone Wolf v Hitchcock (1903) 187 US 553, at 566 "Indian tribes by means of treaties, and, of course, a moral obligation rested upon Congress to act in good faith in performing the stipulations entered into on its behalf. But, as with treaties made with foreign nations, Chinese Exclusion Case,

Art. VI of the Constitution, the so-called supremacy clause, provides that the constitution, treaties and federal law are the "supreme law of the land." This translates into federal laws regulating Indian affairs, as well as treaties with tribes, "supersed[ing] conflicting state laws or state constitutional provisions."[65] As was already explained above, the Supreme Court has interpreted the commerce clause in Worcester v Georgia[66] as being exclusive to the Federal Government. Congress also in charge of public lands within states,[67] which is important for present purposes, because the lands either were or still are Indian lands and encompass both sacred sites as well heritage sites. There is no list of enumerated powers; rather the 10th Amendment allocates all powers which have not been reserved for Congress to the states.

4.3.1.2 Constitutional Rights at Issue

The second main way in which the constitution influences the cultural rights and heritage of Indigenous Peoples in general and the repatriation of Indigenous sacred cultural heritage in particular, are constitutional rights, and three in particular. The main rights which have had an impact are the first amendment right, namely the freedom of religion, the 5th Amendment protection of the right to property and the 14th amendment right to equal protection for everyone under the law.

The First Amendment arguments in favour of repatriation have been brought forward mostly in connection with ancient remains. As American Indian scholars Trope and Echo-Hawk summarized: "It is not surprising that Native religious beliefs and practices may be infringed upon when tribal dead are desecrated, disturbed, or withheld from burial by the government."[68] Both in the activist years leading up to the adoption of NAGPRA, and since then, American Indians have (had to) emphasize(d) that grave digging is a serious violation of their religious freedom.[69] Refusal to repatriate older or ancient remains for reasons of scientific research, especially in light of the overwhelming Indigenous ethnicity of the remains, combined with the fact that Indigenous burial grounds remained unprotected by either state or federal legislation until the late twentieth century (in contrast to non-Indigenous burials in cemeteries), is similarly understood as a violation of Indigenous religious beliefs.[70]

---

130 U. S. 581, 130 U. S. 600, the legislative power might pass laws in conflict with treaties made with the Indians. ... The power exists to abrogate the provisions of an Indian treaty, though presumably such power will be exercised only when circumstances arise which will not only justify the government in disregarding the stipulations of the treaty, but may demand, in the interest of the country and the Indians themselves, that it should do so."

[65] Newton et al. (2005), p. 391.

[66] Worcester v Georgia, 31 US 515 (1832), 590–593.

[67] Art. IV, Section 3 Clause 2 U.S. Constitution.

[68] Trope and Echo-Hawk (1992), p. 49.

[69] Riding In (1992), p. 25.

[70] Riding In (1992), p. 25.

Comparable to withholding ancestral remains, withholding sacred objects also impacts the free exercise of religion. The importance of this connection was also recognized during the adoption of AIRFA,[71] and it explains their inclusion in the NAGPRA repatriation scheme. Such congressional action that strengthens Indigenous religious freedom was even more important in light of the Supreme Court cases which restricted Indigenous religious freedom and continue to serve as precedents, such as Employment Division, Department of Human Resources of Oregon v Smith[72] or Lyng v Northwest Indian Cemetery Protective Association.[73] These cases severely limited the protective scope of available constitutional safeguards on the freedom of religion for Native Americans. In Smith, for example, the court did not follow the compelling state interest test developed in earlier case-law.[74]

The importance of the 14th amendment and equality of the law was highlighted especially in the lead-up to the adoption of NAGPRA. A number of authors argued that, while freedom of religion was important, equal burial protection was even more important.[75]

The 5th amendment is relevant for different stakeholders in the repatriation discussion. It is relevant for Indigenous Peoples whose property was excavated irrespective of the legal safeguards aiming to protect against state expropriation and for current holders of ceremonial objects who may hold legal title to the property and are protected from the objects being expropriated. The possibility of repatriation facilitating a 5th amendment takings was also recognized by the Department of Justice[76] and led to the inclusion of provisions both within NAGPRA (§3001(13)) and its accompanying regulations (§10.10(c)(3)). These provisions exempt institutions from the duty to repatriate items if this would result in a 5th amendment taking.

4.3.2 *Relationship Between Different Legal Systems and Actors*

4.3.2.1 American Indigenous Sovereignty

American Indians have a unique status under U.S. law. Their pre-existence as independent, sovereign peoples before the onset of settler colonialism is reflected in U.S. law. This is mainly due to treaties which were adopted before the official end

[71] Johnson and Haensly (1992), p. 158.

[72] Employment Division, Department of Human Resources of Oregon v Smith, 494 U.S. 872 (1990).

[73] Richard E Lyng v Northwest Indian Cemetery Protective Association, 485 U.S. 439 (1988) [hereafter Lyng], see discussion of case below Sect. 4.5.3.

[74] Peregoy (1992), p. 346.

[75] Riding In (1992), p. 26.

[76] Letter of Department of Justice or Secretary of Justice to Senator D.K. Inouye, dated 1.08.1990, reproduced in Inouye (1990), p. 14.

of treaty making in 1871 and they remain valid today. This is not to say that Indigenous sovereignty has always been respected or that it was ever really accepted in U.S. law as full sovereignty comparable to that of a foreign nation under current international law. Given the origins of the U.S. legal system within a history of settler colonialism, this is of course not surprising. That being said, Indigenous sovereignty has survived periods of forced legal assimilation and tribes continue to be characterized as "domestic dependent nations", a term which Chief Justice John Marshall coined in Worcester v Georgia to describe the legal position of American Indians. At the time, he emphasized that tribes had been recognized as "distinct, independent political communities" and that this understanding of their status had been "applied to Indians as we have applied them to the other nations of the earth".[77] He then compared the tribes to a "weaker power" which, under international law, "does not surrender its independence – its right to self-government – by associating and taking protection."[78] While American Indians may thus share some characteristics with other U.S. minorities, they are in a distinct legal position with distinct rights arising out of their position of continuing sovereign existence within the territorial boundaries of the United States.[79]

It is thus not surprising that in contemporary dealings between federal, state and Indigenous governments, as well as individuals, it can be difficult to reconcile the rights and powers of distinct sovereignties. This is also true in the context of cultural heritage which embodies the distinct cultures and worldviews of the parties that are at the heart of concerns for cultural self-governance. The evolution of federal Indian law has led to the problematic construction that Indigenous Peoples are recognized as sovereign entities, which predate the existence of the United States as a sovereign, who have never conceded to said sovereignty but whose rights that arise out treaties made between the tribes and the United States can be unilaterally abridged by the latter. The tensions which are inherent in this peculiar construction, which envelopes tribal sovereignty within US sovereignty, flare up regularly both as a result of administrative actions as well as in court cases. Today, sovereignty struggles are visible especially in the struggle for social and economic activities. As Bruce Duthu has highlighted: "the contours of tribal sovereignty and jurisdiction are often determined as the by-product of cases in which another sovereign – usually state – is asserting authority in Indian Country."[80]

Alison Dussias has traced the different understandings of sovereignty which have been apparent in Supreme Court jurisprudence, varying between a geographically-based and a membership-based understanding of sovereignty.[81] These different constructions show the struggles of the judiciary, even on the highest level, to reconcile the results of past and present federal Indian policies and case law—a

[77] Worcester v Georgia 31 US 515 (1832), at 519.

[78] Worcester v Georgia 31 US 515 (1832), at 520.

[79] Similarly Duthu (2008), p. xxiv.

[80] Duthu (2008), p. 5.

[81] Dussias (1993), pp. 16–17.

truly labyrinthine exercise. This is complicated by the fact that the relevant courts that have to reconcile two cultures with their own claims to sovereignty within the same territory is largely made up of members of the dominant (legal) culture[82] and they are trained purely within that dominant culture.

The different conceptions of a geographically- and membership-based indigeneity can also be found in the types of evidence that can be used to link cultural heritage or human remains and Indigenous communities in NAGPRA, see Sect. 4.4.3.2 below.[83] In tracing Indigenous sovereignty as it evolved within U.S. law, this fundamental inequality between communities and the state, two of the repatriation partners, is brought to the fore-front. This inequality would have always been at the background of any repatriation dialogue between governmental agencies and Native American tribes, as a part of their shared history. However, it continues to be (re-)created within the law. U.S. law defines and shapes the contours of Indigenous identity and Indigenous legal powers within the U.S. legal system, thereby essentially preventing an equal repatriation dialogue. NAGPRA has—unfortunately—stayed true to this heritage as will be seen in Sect. 4.4 below.[84]

4.3.2.2 US: International Law

International legal provisions can become part of U.S. law through treaties being approved by the Senate, in which case they are protected by the above-described supremacy clause, but they may be superseded by a subsequent conflicting federal statute.[85] Moreover, given US Supreme Court jurisprudence, even if treaties have been ratified by the Senate, they are not "self-executing" and so cannot be relied upon directly in a lawsuit. Whether or not a treaty is self-executing will depend on different factors.[86] The authors of the Cohen handbook point to the existence of a three-pronged approach "if each of the following is true: It involves rights and duties

[82] As one example, in a study of state courts, last updated in 2009, on minority judges on the state level, Native Americans judges constitute less than 1% of judges. Native Americans were by far the least represented; the study counted 13 Native American judges out of 1436 judges belonging to minorities. ABA Standing Committee on Judicial Independence ("SCJI"), National database on judicial diversity in state courts (2009). The website data is no longer accessible but the same data has also been used in another publication, see Hemmens et al. (2019), p. 177.

[83] Another federal law recognizing cultural self-governance is the Native American Languages Act, see Reed (2016), p. 279.

[84] Both by excluding non-federally recognized tribes and requiring Indigenous claimants to represent their culture within US legal terms in order to be able to reclaim heritage.

[85] Newton et al. (2005), p. 490.

[86] Cornell Law School, Legal Information Institute entry on self-executing treaty: "A treaty could be identified as either self-executing or non-self-executing by looking at various indicators, including statements that are made by Congress or the Executive regarding the treaty, indeterminate language of the treaty, or if the treaty deals with a matter within the exclusive law-making power of Congress, indicating that Congress must create implementing legislation." Available via: https://www.law.cornell.edu/wex/self_executing_treaty [last accessed 18.08.2021].

of individuals; it does not cover a subject for which legislative action is required by the Constitution; and it does not leave discretion to the parties in the application of the particular provision",[87] which should be sufficient to determine whether the relevant provisions are self-executing.[88] International law can also influence cases before U.S. courts in two other ways, namely "as part of customary international law applied as federal common law, and as an interpretative aid in the construction of United States constitutional or statutory law."[89]

In relation to the relevant international legal treaties, while the United States ratified the ICCPR in 1992, it indicated in its ratification that it did not consider the ICCPR to be self-executing.[90] In connection to the enforceability of the American Declaration of Rights and Duties of Man (hereafter ADRM), the United States has ratified the OAS Charter and the Inter-American Commission on Human Rights has jurisdiction over the compliance of the United States with a number of provisions of the ADRDM.[91] This being said, while the Inter-American Commission has emphasized that signing the Charter makes the ADRDM binding upon the United States, the latter has so far disagreed.[92] As for UNDRIP' while the U.S. changed its initial rejection to a position of support in 2011,[93] this is support for a declaration not a treaty. The statement expressly referred to its declarative status. The statement also—tellingly—emphasizes that the declaration is "not a statement of current international law." On this point, the reader is referred back to the discussion in Chap. 2 and the observation that the UNDRIP rights relevant for present purposes

---

[87] Newton et al. (2005), pp. 490–491 The authors rely on Citizens Living in Nicaragua v Reagan 859 F.2d 929 (DC Cir.1988) US v Green 671 F.2d 46, 50 (1982), US v Noriega 808 F. Supp. 791, 798 (SD Fla. 1992).

[88] This being said, this area seems far from consistent as be seen, for example, in the dissenting opinion Supreme Court case from 2008 José Ernesto Medellín v Texas, 552 US 491 [25.03.2008]. It has been observed that the Supreme Court in Medellín v Texas implied a presumption of non-self-execution, see Dubinsky et al. (2017), p. 10 Another author observed: "The precise nature of this distinction – indeed its very existence – is a matter of some controversy and much confusion. More than one lower federal court has pronounced the distinction 'most confounding'" Vásquez (1995), p. 695.

[89] Newton et al. (2005), p. 489 The presumption is that there was no intention to override the treaty unless it was clearly expressed.

[90] Declarations and Reservations, United States, section 'declarations' (1) "that the United States declares that the provisions of articles 1 through 27 of the Covenant are not self-executing." Via: https://treaties.un.org/Pages/ViewDetails.aspx?src=IND&mtdsg_no=IV-4&chapter=4&clang=_en#EndDec.

[91] Newton et al. (2005), p. 467.

[92] Newton et al. (2005), p. 467 See also discussion of Inter-American human rights system, Sect. 2.4.3, Chap. 2.

[93] See DoJ, press release 12.01.2011 "Announcement of U.S. Support for the United Nations Declaration on the Rights of Indigenous Peoples – Initiatives to Promote the Government-to-Government Relationship & Improve the Lives of Indigenous Peoples" available via: https://2009-2017.state.gov/s/srgia/154553.htm [last accessed 30.07.2021].

are an application of existing international law to the context of Indigenous Peoples (if still limited by the wide margin of state discretion under Art. 27 ICCPR and the permitted limitations under Art. 18 ICCPR). Thus, they *are* very much a statement of current international law. There is, however, no question that it is not self-executing under U.S. law.

4.3.2.3 Federal–Tribal Relationship

The Constitution provides for broad federal powers in Indian affairs. In terms of the relationship between the tribes and the different branches of federal government, the executive has held considerable power in this area both in the past (upheld as a delegation of congressional authority) and it continues to do so even today in an era of relative self-determination.[94] The main executive agency is the BIA, the Bureau of Indian Affairs. Paralleling the historic development outlined above, the Bureau was first under the Department of War until 1849 and it is now under the Department of Interior.[95] In terms of acknowledging the destructive and assimilatory congressional and executive behaviour towards Indigenous Peoples in the past, Congress formally apologized to Native Hawaiians for the overthrow of the Hawaiian kingdom in January 1993.

The apology to Native Americans by contrast is a more controversial issue. It was delivered in 2000 by Kevin Gover, Assistant Secretary of the Interior at the time, on behalf of the BIA for the agency's behaviour. It was seen critically, because Gover, himself Native American,[96] apologized for non-Native behaviour to Native Americans.[97] Furthermore, there was no federal endorsement and the issue remained largely silent until 2009 when the Native American Apology Resolution was signed by President Obama.

However, this apology was a limited one. It had been introduced as a stand-alone bill in the Senate and originally included apologies for governmental behaviour towards Indigenous Peoples of the United States. In the end, a watered-down version was accepted that was attached by the House to a defence appropriations bill and signed in this form. While it recognizes that "there have been years of official depredations, ill-conceived policies, and the breaking of covenants by the Federal Government", the apology by the federal government was not issued by it for its own actions but rather "on behalf of the people of the United States to all Native Peoples for the many instances of violence, maltreatment, and neglect inflicted on Native Peoples by citizens of the United States".[98] In spite of the resolution urging the President "to acknowledge the wrongs of the United States against Indian tribes in

---

[94] Newton et al. (2005), p. 116.

[95] Duthu (2008), p. xxvii.

[96] BIA is nowadays largely staffed with native Americans, Buck (2006), pp. 97–112.

[97] Buck (2006), pp. 97–112.

[98] S.J. Res.14 11th Congress (2009–2010) Section (1)(a)(3) and (4).

the history of the United States", President Obama did not formally apologize (other than signing the defence appropriations bill) and, while a press announcement was sent out on the defence appropriations bill, none was issued for the formal apology.[99] As was mentioned in Chap. 1, one reason to initiate repatriation can be the desire to confront a shared (violent) past, to address past violations and to find a (hopefully fruitful) way forward. Where repatriation seeks to achieve reconciliation, it is easy to see that such an (non-)apology is unlikely to be helpful. This only serves to emphasize that repatriation never occurs in isolation but within a wider socio-legal context which can further obstruct the realization of repatriation goals.

Congressional powers are broad. The three areas of tribal powers which are excluded from this power are: "(1) general statutes that adversely affect rights reserved by treaty, statutes, or a tribe's inherent right of self-government, (2) any instance where tribes are specifically excepted from the applicability of a Congressional statute, including when they are not included but states and local governments are, and (3) any instance where tribes' sovereign immunity would be abrogated, unless Congress makes that abrogation 'express and unequivocal.'"[100] The broad legislative power Congress holds in Indian affairs has also resulted in comparatively broad law-making powers being delegated to administrative agencies, blurring the separation of the legislature and the executive.[101] Congress also has broad powers in relation to certain categories of tribal and individual property, namely the property which it holds in trust and can add to or create new reservations. It "also has the power to take action in derogation of tribal property interests ... without consent of Indian owners."[102] In this context, it is worthwhile noting that the protection offered by the 5th amendment against governmental takings is limited for these kinds of properties; "[b]ecause the government operates both as a trustee and a sovereign with regard to Indian tribes, an action depriving a tribe of property that would be a per se taking under the Court's takings clause jurisprudence may be held to be the action of a trustee and therefore not a taking. In US v Sioux Nation 448 US 371 (1980), the Court stated "Where Congress makes a good faith effort to give the Indians the full value of the land and thus merely transmutes the property from land to money, there is no taking."[103] This obvious conflict of interest, combined with broad legislative and executive powers, presents a continuing danger to tribal self-determination in general and the protection and enforcement of cultural rights, which are so often linked to land in the Indigenous context, in particular.

This trust relationship between the federal level and the tribes can be linked back to Chief Justice Marshall's analogy of the federal-tribal relationship to the relationship of the "ward to his guardian". This comparison has arguably become part of the foundation of federal Indian law and has profound implications, including:

[99] Capriccioso (2010).

[100] Reed (2016), p. 299.

[101] Newton et al. (2005), p. 415.

[102] Newton et al. (2005), pp. 401–402.

[103] Newton et al. (2005), p. 416.

transforming the relationship between the two governments into a trust relationship which obliges the federal government to "protect tribal rights to exist as self-governing entities";[104] requires the interpretations of treaties and agreements to be in line with this obligation to "protect tribal sovereignty and property"[105] and in recent times this duty has also been cited as a reason for initiating new laws which can prove to be beneficial for tribes and have been found to be a useful tool for tribes.[106]

On the other hand, there are obvious problems with a doctrine which allocates so much decision power to the federal level, as it opens up the way for federal decision making without tribal consent, yet with vast consequences for tribes. In the past, it was used to justify significant—unilateral—disposals of tribal property, changes to the relationships between tribes and the federal government—again unilateral—and it has also been used to justify broad congressional powers which would otherwise be difficult to base on the Constitution.[107]

4.3.2.4 Relationship Indigenous Peoples/Tribes: States

The fundamental principle governing the legal relationship between states and tribes derives from the fact that the main power over Indian affairs rests with the federal level. Consequently, if there is no congressional statute to the contrary, "jurisdiction over persons, property, and events in Indian country is retained by tribes."[108] Their geographical proximity yet differing interests in all types of policy sectors, from water purity to protection and access of specific sites to resource development, has made the relationship between individual tribes and the respective states an uneasy one.

Historically, the relationship between tribes and states has by no means been less conflicted than that with the federal level, considering that Indigenous nations stood in the way of state plans for land acquisition and development. In this context, the Supreme Court observed in the 1886 United States v Kagama case: "[The Indian tribes] owe no allegiance to the states, and receive from them no protection. Because of the local ill feeling, the people of the states where they are found are often their deadliest enemies."[109] Since Worcester v Georgia, the rule has been one of tribal independence from states,[110] although this has changed somewhat over time.

---

[104] Newton et al. (2005), pp. 419–420.

[105] Newton et al. (2005), pp. 419–420.

[106] Newton et al. (2005), p. 423.

[107] Newton et al. (2005), p. 422.

[108] Newton et al. (2005), p. 499.

[109] United States v Kagama, 118 US 375, 384 (1886).

[110] Worcester v Georgia 31 US 515, also The Kansas Indians 72 US 737, 757 (1866) "As long as the United States recognizes [a tribe's] national character they are under the protection of treaties and the laws of Congress, and their property is withdrawn from the operation of State laws."

Contemporary clashes seem to centre on resource development, water rights, and conflicts between economic development in the interest of the state versus Indigenous cultural or self-government rights. State powers inside Indian Country differ substantially from its powers within the rest of state territory. Outside of Indian Country, non-discriminatory laws apply unless federal law provides to the contrary.[111] Inside Indian Country, a state may in general regulate neither the property nor the conduct of Native Americans.[112] Another way in which state authority over tribes within Indian Country has been broadened significantly has been by Congressional acts authorizing state jurisdiction.[113] Because of the uncertainties which remain in the relationship between tribal and state jurisdictions, tribal-state cooperative agreements have been concluded in a variety of different areas.[114]

4.3.2.5 Treaties

Another important dimension of the relationship between the United States and individual tribes are the treaties concluded prior to 1871, which continue to be valid treaties with affirming rights and obligations,[115] unless they have been limited since then. At first, treaties concluded between incoming settlers and Indians were not written but rather formal, diplomatic ceremonies.[116] Over time, the US

[111] Newton et al. (2005), p. 513 Example of the latter would be federal laws that protect certain treaty rights such as fishing rights.

[112] State jurisdiction over non-members inside Indian Country is another matter and limited by the pre-emption test originating in William v Lee, which provided that "absent governing Acts of Congress, the question has always been whether the state action infringed on the right of reservation Indians to make their own laws and be ruled by them." Williams v Lee, 358 U.S. 217, 220 (1959). Case law has however been broadening state jurisdiction in this respect, but an in-depth examination of this is beyond the scope of this chapter. See Newton et al. (2005), p. 531, who observe that courts asserted that "strong enough state interests can overcome federal interests reflected in federal law, thereby indicating that the Court's assessment of relative interests can supercede congressional intent."

[113] Newton et al. (2005), p. 537.

[114] Newton et al. (2005), p. 589.

[115] R.S. § 2079 derived from act Mar. 3, 1871, ch. 120, § 1, 16 Stat. 566. Codified as 25 U.S.C. § 71 entitled 'Future treaties with Indian tribes': "No Indian nation or tribe within the territory of the United States shall be acknowledged or recognized as an independent nation, tribe, or power with whom the United States may contract by treaty; but no obligation of any treaty lawfully made and ratified with any such Indian nation or tribe prior to March 3, 1871, shall be hereby invalidated or impaired. Such treaties, and any Executive orders and Acts of Congress under which the rights of any Indian tribe to fish are secured, shall be construed to prohibit (in addition to any other prohibition) the imposition under any law of a State or political subdivision thereof of any tax on any income derived from the exercise of rights to fish secured by such treaty, Executive order, or Act of Congress if section 7873 of title 26 does not permit a like Federal tax to be imposed on such income."

(R.S. § 2079; Pub. L. 100–647, title III, § 3042, Nov. 10, 1988, 102 Stat. 3641.)

[116] Newton et al. (2005), p. 20.

concluded over 370 treaties with Indigenous Peoples in the initial 100 years of its existence.[117] "The contents of the Indigenous treaties varied considerably, but they often included land cession[s], delineation of boundaries, peace guarantees and explicit or implicit mutual recognition of sovereignty."[118] Treaties conducted with Indigenous Peoples, as any treaty to which the US is a party, can be superseded by federal statutes.[119] As Alfredsson points out, an important difference between States and Indigenous Peoples is that the former can seek remedies for the unilateral action of the US under international law, which the latter cannot do.[120] There are different opinions with regard to the status of these treaties under public international law. Special Rapporteur Miguel Alfonso Martínez, in his Study on Treaties Agreements and Other Constructive Arrangements between States and Indigenous Peoples, criticized the dominant viewpoint in legal literature that such treaties are purely a matter of domestic law.[121] This stance is supported by Art. 37 UNDRIP, which affirms the right to the recognition and enforcement of such treaties. This provision was one of those which lead to a delayed passing in UN GA, and it is probably also a reason why treaty states such as Canada and US vetoed UNDRIP initially.[122] Under domestic US law, on the other hand, Indian treaties do not constitute inter-state agreements, but they are covered by the sweeping plenary power[123] on the basis of the Indian commerce clause, introduced in Sect. 4.3.1.1 above.

In terms of interpreting treaties concluded with tribes, the Supreme Court has emphasized that treaties should be liberally constructed in favour of Indigenous parties[124] and that they should be given effect as the tribes themselves would have understood them.[125] However, it has to be remembered that these rules apply only where the meaning of the text is ambiguous. The Supreme Court observed that "the canon of construction . . .[does] not permit reliance on ambiguities that do not exist;

[117] Alfredsson (2011), para 2.

[118] Alfredsson (2011), para 2.

[119] Alfredsson (2011), para 3.

[120] Alfredsson (2011), para 3.

[121] Martinez, A., UN. Special Rapporteur on Treaties, Agreements and Other Constructive Arrangements between States and Indigenous Populations, Study on treaties, agreements and other constructive arrangements between States and Indigenous populations [1999] U.N. Doc. E/CN.4/Sub.2/1999/20, at paras 115–116. At the time, European powers were clearly aware that they were dealing with sovereign powers irrespective of later attempts to portray the situation differently. He highlights that, while the dominant point of view in legal literature views such treaties as domestic issues, this point of view is not shared by Indigenous Peoples (para 117), nor are the subject-matter of such treaties any different from other treaties between sovereign nations under international law (para 123).

[122] Alfredsson (2011), para 9.

[123] Bradford (2002), p. 110.

[124] Bradford (2002), p. 28, footnote 125 text See, e.g., Minnesota v Mille Lacs Band of Chippewa Indians, 526 U.S. 172, 200 (1999); Washington v Wash. State Commercial Passenger Fishing Vessel Ass'n, 443 U.S. 658 (1979), 675–676.

[125] County of Oneida v Oneida Indian Nation, 470 U.S. 226, 246 (1985).

nor does it permit disregard of the clearly expressed intent of Congress."[126] Another important principle of treaty construction is that the treaty is viewed as the granting of rights from Indigenous Peoples to the US. Anything that has not been granted, remains reserved for the respective tribe/nation.[127] Then there is the supremacy clause that applies not only to federal law also applies to Indian treaties. As a result, a State may not enact or enforce a state statute or regulation "that conflicts with treaties between Indian tribes and the United States. The Supremacy Clause further precludes a state from applying its law to Indians located outside the geographical boundaries of an Indian reservation if such application interferes with a tribe's reserved treaty rights."[128] Lastly, plenary power, as conceptualized in the case law, has enabled Congress to terminate federal benefits to American Indians unilaterally as well as restrict or repeal Indian rights which were reserved in treaties.[129]

4.3.2.6 US Law–Tribal Laws

Another important dimension of this legal relationship between the two cultures is the position of tribal law within US law and the relationship of US law to tribal laws. The contours of tribal law naturally depend very much on the content of tribal sovereignty within the US legal system. The possible breadth of legal powers regarding property (including cultural property) is broad and includes (next to the rights in relation to tribally-owned property[130]) governmental powers to allocate and regulate the property of its membership.[131] Tribal laws and traditional rules which govern cultural forms and means of expression can be seen as legitimate subjects of tribal authority either under the tribes broad powers of property or, depending on the cultural expression at issue, as being a matter of internal tribal relations, especially where religious beliefs are at issue.[132] The relationship between tribal law and cultural objects and expressions is of course not unilateral but rather circular given that traditions, customs and objects are existential sources of tribal laws and may even be important in the transmission of tribal laws to future generations. This can also be seen where tribes have adopted constitutions which often emphasize the

[126] South Carolina v Catawba Indian Tribe, Inc., 476 U.S. 498, 506 (1986).

[127] United States v Winans 198 U.S. 371, 381 (1905).

[128] Peregoy (1992), p. 348.

[129] County of Oneida v Oneida Indian Nation, 470 U.S. 226, at 247–248 (1985); United States v Dion, 476 U.S. 734 at 740, Bradford (2002), p. 64.

[130] In relation to tribally-owned lands, and reminiscent of the fluctuating history of US-American Indian relationships, there are different ways in which tribes have acquired interest in lands namely "(1) by action of a prior government; (2) by possession and exercise of sovereignty; (3) by treaty; (4) by act of Congress; (5) by executive action; or (6) by purchase." Newton et al. (2005), p. 969 A more in-depth examination of Indigenous title to land and the mechanisms of federal restraints on tribal land are outside the scope of this study.

[131] Newton et al. (2005), p. 216.

[132] Johnson and Haensly (1992), p. 166.

importance of tribal culture as well as its preservation, protection and promotion.[133] Customs, including traditional responsibilities for certain types of cultural heritage can also be considered by tribal courts as matters of tribal law.[134] US domestic law has also created a space for tribal law and traditions in connection to cultural property, both by virtue of statutory language (i.e. incorporation of traditional religious leader in the definition of sacred objects §3001(3)(c) NAGPRA) and case law, notably Chilkat Indian Village v Johnson. In Chilkat Indian Village v Johnson, the Ninth Circuit not only recognized an Aboriginal right of the Village to four carved wooden posts and a screen which had been removed contrary to its laws, but it found such rights to be potentially enforceable under federal common law, at least against non-Indigenous individuals.[135] The case in question concerned a replevin claim and is outside the scope of this study, but it is worth a brief mention for its inclusion of tribal law (in this case a tribal ordinance regulating heritage within the village property borders) on cultural matters within federal jurisprudence.[136]

On the other hand, difficulties arise with regard to Indigenous oral history which may be crucial evidence before a US court to support an Indigenous claim. Such a testimony can often be blocked by hearsay and best evidence rules.[137] In addition, information that is secret under spiritual rules (not only outside but also inside the tribe) is likewise difficult to evaluate within the US domestic legal system. It can place the judge in a difficult position vis-à-vis the other party and because of its secrecy raise the suspicion that it has been invented only for the purposes of the litigation.[138] When we compare the position of oral traditions within the U.S. and the Canadian legal system, it is notable that both Supreme Courts have allowed hearsay

[133] Newton et al. (2005), p. 278.

[134] As happened in a district court case of the Cheyenne-Arapahoe Tribes where the possession of Sacred Arrows of the Cheyenne was at issue and the determination by the Court was to employ traditional practice and procedure, see Newton et al. (2005), p. 280.

[135] Reed (2016), pp. 286–287.

[136] However, Reed distinguishes cases on title to land from cases on other kinds of property rights by observing: "As in Oneida, the Chilkat court recognized the existence of Tlingit aboriginal title established by the Tribe's laws and customs, and found such rights to be potentially enforceable under federal common law -even against non-indigenous defendants. However, it is interesting to note that in Chilkat, where the property at issue included tribal designs and artifacts rather than land, the enforcement of aboriginal ownership rights within the federal system required an additional step before an equitable remedy could be applied; it required the application of federal common law rules regulating tribal authority over those who are not members of a tribe. It appears that federal courts are comfortable recognizing and enforcing property interests arising under tribal law when the types of property are consistent with those typically addressed by federal common law doctrines, e.g. land or lease rights. However, a federal court may feel less comfortable enforcing property interests arising under tribal law when the type of property at issue lies outside of a court's realm of general expertise. In such situations, these kinds of aboriginal property rights may be curtailed by Due Process considerations." Reed (2016), p. 287.

[137] Babcock (2012), pp. 20–21.

[138] Similarly Babcock (2012), p. 46.

evidence on the basis of necessity and reliability.[139] In the U.S. however, the Court of Claims has required corroboration and limited the admission of oral history to those cases in which "the chain of oral transmission can be traced to Indians who had actual knowledge of the time of pre-contact occupancy[,] a circumstance that even in the recently settled Western states is increasingly impossible[.]"[140] Babcock observes that it is much more common in U.S. cases for oral traditions to be dismissed[141] and that, contrary to Canadian jurisprudence, where he observes a trend of admitting to colonialism and the need to rectify the resulting problems, US courts appear to remain dedicated to the assimilation of Indigenous culture within the dominant culture.[142]

In terms of dispute settlement mechanisms, many American Indian nations operate their own systems which are shaped by the tribes and tribal laws, subject to the requirements of the Indian Civil Rights Act.[143] The provisions of the ICRA mirror some of the constitutional rights of non-Indigenous Americans. This was deemed necessary by Congress, given that Indian nations are not subject to constitutional provisions similar to those that restrict federal and state powers.[144] Tribal law is being used in tribal courts but tribal dispute resolution mechanisms have to be rediscovered or strengthened after legal assimilation and, even when this is the case, they exist 'within U.S. law', meaning both Federal Indian law and the broad, unilateral powers of Congress and the federal executive and its agencies.[145] Their jurisdictional powers can also be used to choose not to operate tribal courts or to cede certain subjects to federal or state courts.[146] Apart from this semi-independent space of tribal law, administered by Indigenous legal experts within U.S. law that is linked to the land they hold as 'domestic dependent nations', tribal law may be applied by federal courts "[i]n the absence of a federal statute or existing federal common law . . . particularly 'when the issue in controversy is one that federal law recognizes as within the purview of tribal governance.'"[147]

4.3.2.7 Federal Indian Law

The above sections have already introduced some of the foundational principles of Federal Indian Law and indicated the relevance of these principles for the present research, given that NAGPRA forms an important element of, and arguably was only

[139] Babcock (2012), p. 58.
[140] Babcock (2012), p. 58.
[141] Babcock (2012), p. 59.
[142] Babcock (2012), p. 60.
[143] Newton et al. (2005), p. 217.
[144] Newton et al. (2005), p. 212.
[145] Bradford (2002), pp. 53–54.
[146] Borrows (2006), p. 129.
[147] Reed (2016), p. 279.

possible in its adopted form because of, Federal Indian Law. Briefly summarized for the purposes of the present discussion, its foundational principles are:

1. Plenary power of Congress, including the right to abrogate treaty rights.
2. Retention of Indigenous self-determination to the extent compatible with the concept of 'domestic dependent nations'.
3. U.S. federal government relationship with Indigenous Peoples akin to a trust relationship.
4. Duty of federal government to protect Indian tribes against intrusions by states and other citizens on their territory and remaining powers arising out of a trust relationship.
   (a) State authority is thus limited.
5. While fundamental tenets of Federal Indian law apply across the board, the tribes often have a unique legal relationship with the United States, both due to treaties and statutes.[148]
   (a) However, these legal, cultural and historic differences are often not reflected in federal policy.[149]
6. Because of the diversity of sources and historic inconsistences, jurisprudence is an important factor in the harmonization of Federal Indian law
7. Canons of interpretation:
   (a) Historically, arising out of a "unique trust relationship between United States and Indians".[150]
      - Field of federal Indian law differs from other fields also in terms of the applicable principles of interpretation. SCOTUS: "[T]he standard principles of statutory interpretation do not have their usual force in cases involving Indian law."[151]

---

[148] Newton et al. (2005), p. 1.

[149] Newton et al. (2005), p. 2.

[150] The authors of the Cohen handbook criticize that this understanding of the relationship between the United States on the one hand and the many different Indigenous Peoples, on the other, has been misused in the past to characterize tribes as wards which facilitates Congressional domination. They suggest a contemporary grounding on the notion of internal sovereignty instead, Newton et al. (2005), p. 123.

[151] Montana v Blackfeet Tribe, 471 U.S. 759 (1985), 766.

- Treaties, agreements, statutes, and executive orders should be construed liberally in favour of American Indians, and ambiguities should be resolved in their favour.[152] However, three Supreme Court judges in Montana v Blackfeet also highlighted that this was not "a license to disregard clear expressions of congressional intent".[153]
- Treaties should be interpreted as the Indigenous Peoples concluding them would have understood them.[154]

(b) Federal pre-emption of state laws.

Federal Indian law encompasses diverse legal areas, including for example hunting, fishing and gathering rights, education and culture and Indigenous sovereignty. NAGPRA is at the heart of federal Indian law on cultural resources.

4.3.3 The American "Indian" Definition in the Law

Before examining NAGPRA in more detail, the difficulties surrounding the definition of who classifies as American Indian within U.S. law needs to be examined briefly, as they also play an important role within NAGPRA. Legal definitions of Indigenous Peoples within the United States differ substantially, even disregarding the distinction between diverse groups such as Inuit, Native Hawaiians and American Indians. An important distinction to be made from the outset is that self-identification, both by the individual and by the community on the one hand is distinct and not necessarily congruent with definitions in federal (Indian) law. Federal legal recognition of both individual and tribal identity has varied significantly over time. As a result, U.S. (Supreme Court) jurisprudence has also had to grapple with Indigenous identity and has, as John Borrows points out, "been too focused on blood quantum and racial categories."[155]

Connected definitions are 'Indian tribes', 'Indian Nations' and 'Indian Country'. For the purpose of federal Indian law, Indian tribes are those Indigenous Peoples who have a legally established relationship with the United States.[156] This legal relationship can fluctuate. The US government has terminated the federal Indian status of tribes (and members) over time only to reinstate it for some tribes later, at times for the purposes of some but not all of the policy areas covered under the umbrella of Indian Affairs. Since 1978, the formal recognition of Indigenous communities operates through an administrative procedure, administered by the

---

[152] Newton et al. (2005), p. 119.

[153] Montana v Blackfeet Tribe, 471 US 759 (1985), 769 dissenting opinion Justices White, Renhquist and Stevens.

[154] Newton et al. (2005), pp. 119–120.

[155] Borrows (2006), p. 131.

[156] Newton et al. (2005), p. 135.

BIA which has been criticized as "overly burdensome, inconsistent and costly".[157] At the same time, Congress retains the power to recognize an Indigenous community as a tribe by means of a formal act.[158] In the period between 1960 to 2009 the BIA recognized 87 new tribes, 49 tribes for the first time and restored recognition for 38 tribes.[159]

In addition, while deferring to tribal membership determinations in defining who classifies as 'Indian', Congress has imposed requirements, including ancestry.[160] Nowadays, the legal definition of 'Indian' under federal law varies depending on the policy area.[161] This contributes to disguising federal—tribal relationships as those between different races rather than acknowledging that "when the federal government deals with Indians, it is addressing members or descendants of members of political entities (Indian tribes), not persons of a particular race."[162] The political power under the Commerce clause of Congress to decide who qualifies as Indian has profound implications for non-federally recognized tribes who "suffer from lack of federal respect for their sovereignty and land bases, lack of protection from state jurisdiction, lack of access to repatriation rights and other forms of cultural protection under federal law, and denial of most benefits available to tribes that enjoy a government-to-government relationship with the United States."[163]

Increasingly, there has been a move to consider as Indian those individuals who are tribal members according to their respective tribal law.[164] This has arguably moved this area of the law to be more in line with international standards which emphasize the right of both the individual and the community to define Indigenous identity rather than the respective non-Indigenous government. It could also mean that—if committed to fully—different tribal law criteria of the over 500 federally tribes would need to be incorporated into federal definitions. This could then mean deference to tribal courts in the case of disputes over membership and Indigenous identity questions as a pre-judicial stage where federal programs are at issue.[165] In terms of the two components of the international right to Indigenous identity (community and self-identification), current U.S. law seems more in line with the communal right to identify its members than the additional criterion of self-identification. This observation is a tentative one, however, as this area is difficult to evaluate given the role of the respective tribal laws in the matter. For now, federal recognition of Indigenous status is complicated, opaque and disharmonious. The

[157] Duthu (2008), p. 18.
[158] Duthu (2008), p. 18.
[159] United States Government Accountability Office (2010), pp. 68–69, Appendix II.
[160] Newton et al. (2005), p. 172.
[161] Dussias (1993), pp. 79–81.
[162] Newton et al. (2005), p. 172.
[163] Newton et al. (2005), p. 139.
[164] Newton et al. (2005), p. 171.
[165] Dussias (1993), p. 84.

understanding of who qualifies as Indian in the NAGPRA has to be understood against the backdrop of these difficulties.

Almost as important as the definition of who qualifies as Indian or an Indian tribe for legal purposes is the determination of 'Indian Country'. This term, albeit not always used congruously, can probably best be defined for present purposes as a geographical area within which tribal laws and customs, as well as federal law that relate to American Indians, generally apply.[166] In 1993, SCOTUS remarked on Indian Country that: "[T]he intent of Congress as elucidated by [court] decisions, was to designate as Indian country all lands set aside by whatever means for the residence of tribal Indians under federal protection, together with trust and restricted Indian allotments."[167]

4.4 Native American Graves Protection and Repatriation Act[168]

4.4.1 Legislative History: Background and Adoption

The two sections above have laid the necessary foundations to understand the complex historic-legal evolution of the relationship between the US (federal and state level) and American Indian tribes. This will explain much of the legislative history of NAGPRA explored in this subsection and render the act's particularities less surprising. Moreover, with this background, it is easier to understand the mechanisms enshrined in the act (see Sect. 4.4.3) as well as some of the reactions and criticisms explored below (see Sect. 4.4.6).

The Native American Graves Protection and Repatriation Act has a twofold purpose of protecting unexcavated Indigenous heritage and to ensure the repatriation of human remains and Indigenous cultural heritage to communities. Native American graves were subjected to systematic grave robbing and ancestral remains were the object of what can only be termed a collecting frenzy. Grave robbing of Indigenous burial sites was incentivized financially by collecting institutions, motivated partially by craniology and facilitated by law and governmental actions. A notorious historic governmental action in this regard was the order of the Army

---

[166] Similarly Newton et al. (2005), p. 182.

[167] Oklahoma Tax Commission v Sac & Fox Nation 508 US 114, 125. SCOTUS in effect cited an earlier version of the Cohen handbook.

[168] Unless stated otherwise, references to NAGPRA will be references to its version as currently in force at the time of writing (2019), not the act as originally adopted. The original sections have been incorporated in 25 USC in Chapter 32 (Native American Graves Protection and Repatriation) with the exception of section 4 NAGPRA on illegal trafficking which was incorporated into Chapter 53 of title 18, United States Code by means of s. 1170. The NAGPRA regulations, however, incorporated in e-C.F.R. Title 43, Subtitle A, Part 10, Subpart C refer to the sections of the original Act.

Surgeon General of the United States who in 1868 ordered "Army medical officers to collect specimens of Indian crania for the Army Medical Museum".[169] This led, *inter alia*, to the decapitation of Indigenous soldiers on battle fields as well as of Indigenous prisoners of war. Grave robbing and the collecting of human remains was facilitated by law until the late twentieth century, because state legislation protecting cemeteries only protected marked cemeteries, which Indigenous burial sites in many cases were not. Professors Carpenter, Katyal and Riley have aptly summarized the resulting need for a repatriation law in observing that the "repatriation statute was necessary not to secure Indians' special rights, but to counteract federal and state laws that facilitated the excavation, examination, and destruction of Indian burial grounds, which were situated predominantly on lands taken from tribes by non-Indians."[170]

Next to the collection and retention of ancestral remains, a vast quantity of sacred objects have been removed from Indigenous communities. The problem of illegitimate property transfers actually came into the public eye as a result of a 1-year study mandated by the American Indian Religious Freedom Act, examined in Sect. 4.5.2 below. In effect, museum records evidenced that, while some objects were sold by their custodians, in many instances the transfer can be traced to military confrontations or as a reaction to the actions of federally sponsored missionaries or Indian agents or they were stolen and then sold, i.e. by 'pothunters'.[171] Both tribes as well as the general public became more and more aware of the dimension of the takings and the losses of Indigenous heritage in Indigenous communities. This led to an Indian burial-rights movement in the 1970s and 1980s.[172] In 1992, it was estimated that "federal agencies and museums possess[ed] between 100,000 and 200,000 Native American human remains, and an estimated ten to fifteen million Native American cultural items."[173] Similarly, it was observed that an estimated 99% of all human remains in federal institutions were of Native American origin.[174] The awareness of the scale of the problem, its historic origins, the inability of either normal laws on property ownership to aid tribes in reclaiming stolen cultural property, or common law protections of cemeteries to protect Indian burial sites effectively from pothunters stimulated Indigenous activism and contributed to ensuring sufficient public and legislative support.

---

[169] Inouye (1992), p. 1.

[170] Carpenter et al. (2009), p. 1062.

[171] Secretary of the Interior Fed. Agencies Task Force, Am. Indian Religious Freedom Act Rep. 77, Aug 1979 (report submitted to Congress), cited by Trope and Echo-Hawk (1992), p. 44.

[172] Nafziger and Dobkins (1999), p. 80. For a first-hand critical account of the activism leading to the adoption of the Act and critical view of its legislative history, see Harjo (2012).

[173] McCain (1992), p. 6.

[174] Marsh (1992), p. 95.

At the same time, individual US museums returned particular Indigenous objects from their collections[175] and discussions were initiated on how to proceed with the extensive collection of ancestral remains held by the Smithsonian, which was resolved in 1989 by means of the National Museum of the American Indian Act (see Sect. 4.6.1.3 below). Several bills which featured the protection of Indigenous burial grounds and/or repatriation were introduced in Congress between 1986 and 1990,[176] until NAGPRA was passed finally. The adoption of the NMAI and NAGPRA are closely linked, one arguably facilitating the other. During his testimony before the Senate Select Committee on Indian Affairs in 1987, Smithsonian Institution Secretary Robert McCormick Adams indicated "that of the 34,000 specimens currently in the Institution's collection, approximately 42.50 or 14,523 are the remains of North American Indians, and another 11.9% or 4061 of the specimens represent Eskimo, Aleut, and Koniag populations", which quickly gave rise to Indigenous calls for repatriation.[177] After several initiatives, in the 101st Congress several bills were introduced that focussed directly on repatriation and the protection of burial sites and called, *inter alia,* for inventories and notices which ultimately led to the adoption of NAGPRA.[178]

In reaction to these initiatives, representatives from the museum community asked for a 1-year period to allow for dialogues to be held between the different communities and museums, the results of which were published in the 'Report of the Panel for a National Dialogue on Museum/Native American Relations'.[179] The Panel gave a number of recommendations, which it expressly saw as policy recommendations not as drafting legislation.[180] It highlighted the need for repatriation claims to be governed by the respect for Indigenous rights ("human rights of Native peoples") and the values of scientific research and public education. On this point the report emphasized that Indigenous rights should be the "paramount principle that should govern resolution of the issue when a claim is made by a Native American group that has a cultural affiliation with remains or other materials. In such cases, the

---

175 Irwin (1997), p. 44 "Prior to this, in the 1980s, the Denver Art Museum returned War Gods to the Zuni; the Heard Museum in Phoenix returned Kiva masks to Hopi elders; the Wheelwright Museum returned eleven medicine bundles to Navajo; the State Museum of New York in Albany returned twelve wampum belts to Six Nation Confederacy and a clan bundle to the Hidatsa; the Boston Peabody Museum returned the sacred pole (plus 270 artifacts) to the Omaha; and many others have made nominal returns as well. But many museums and institutions have ignored requests."

176 See Marsh (1992), p. 94 He reports nine bills in 1989 alone.

177 Inouye (1992), pp. 1–2.

178 Trope and Echo-Hawk (1992), pp. 55–56.

179 Inouye (1992), p. 2.

180 Boyd et al. (1990), p. 489 Part B of Report. In footnote 4, the panel explicitly highlighted the need to define the terms "cultural affiliation", as well as "sacred ceremonial or religious objects" in legislation, observing that "Some members of the panel believe that precise definitions of such terms are essential for interpreting and evaluating the present Report. Their endorsement of the Report is based on the understanding that appropriate definitions will be incorporated in legislation". This foreshadowed some of the issues which have arisen after the adoption of the act for example in the Bonnichsen case, explored in Sect. 4.4.3.2 below.

wishes of the nation or group regarding the disposition of the materials must be followed."[181] It is noteworthy that the panel remained divided on the need to bury all remains, with "a majority of the Panel believe[ing] that all Native human remains are ultimately entitled to a decent burial, even where their cultural affiliation is unknown".[182] All panel members did however condemn past human rights violations and affirm the need to prevent these, thereby emphasizing the human rights nature of the proposed repatriation recommendations.[183] Two members of the panel also rejected the panel position that the wishes of a culturally affiliated tribe for the "reburial, disposition or treatment of the materials must be followed", preferring the ultimate decision-power to remain with the museum.[184]

While preservationist concerns had been uttered to justify rejecting repatriation requests, it is noteworthy that, in adopting NAGPRA, legislators highlighted that repatriation was instead perceived as "[p]reserving Native American and Hawaiian culture . . . in the interest of all Americans, for these unique cultures area part of the history and heritage of our Nation."[185]

4.4.2 *General Characteristics*

4.4.2.1 Structure

Substantively, the act is split in two, one part on native American human remains and objects that are excavated or discovered on Federal or tribal lands after the date of its enactment, and the other providing for a repatriation process. This twofold focus can be explained by the legislative history and the scale of past dislocations that had been uncovered; it sought not only to close gaps in the protection of Indian burial sites to put a stop to pothunting and facilitate Indigenous claims for ancestral remains or objects excavated illegally, but also to address the hundreds of thousands of remains and millions of cultural items that were located in federally funded institutions.[186]

---

[181] Boyd et al. (1990), p. 487 Part A, paras 1–2 of report.

[182] Boyd et al. (1990), p. 496. See footnote 17 in the report.

[183] Boyd et al. (1990), pp. 449–450 Part D, para 1(b) of the report: "In far too many instances, the human rights of Native American nations and people have been violated in the past through collection, display and other use of human remains and cultural materials without Native American consent and in ways inconsistent with Native American traditions and religions. Often, these violations have occurred in the name of science, non-indigenous religion, economic development and entertainment, as well as in pursuance of commercial grave robbing. All Panel members deplore this history and agree that future practices must avoid a repetition of such excesses."

[184] Boyd et al. (1990), p. 499, footnote 418. See also at 487, and footnotes 1 and 2 in the report. One objecting party was an associate professor of anthropology, the other the head of the Division of Physical Anthropology at the Smithsonian at the time.

[185] Rep. Patsy Mink (Hawaii), cited by Newton et al. (2005), p. 106.

[186] Moriwake (1998), p. 273 Moriwake described the Act's scope aptly as "Both sweeping and limited in scope. . . covers everything from inventories and summaries to new excavations . . . On

The increase of protection of Indian burial sites was achieved on federal and tribal lands by providing for Native American ownership or control of cultural objects and human remains, stimulating *in situ* protection.[187] However, the protection could not be extended to state land or private property. At the same time, 32 states had enacted laws that deal with some of the problems that NAGPRA tried to resolve. These primarily focus on reburial and the repatriation of ancestral remains, many disregarding the issue of cultural objects which were acquired by the institution without the consent of the respective community.[188] The repatriation process provides for the obligation to compile an inventory and repatriate on the request of the Indigenous claimant who is entitled to their return under s. 3005 25 U.S.C. 32. NAGPRA features a tiered claimant structure which differs depending on whether ancestral remains or sacred objects or culturally important objects are being reclaimed. The protection of not yet excavated or accidentally excavated remains and objects also works with a tier structure to identify the closest connected party.

4.4.2.2 Parties

In terms of obligations and rights, Indigenous and non-Indigenous parties can be distinguished. Non-Indigenous parties are under obligations either by virtue of holding or controlling specific forms of Indigenous cultural heritage.[189] Indigenous parties are defined broadly by the Act and then narrowed down to parties with standing to make a claim under the implementing regulations.

4.4.2.2.1 Key Definitions of Non-Indigenous Parties

Native American Graves Protection 25 U.S.C. §3001 (2019)
(4) "Federal agency" means any department, agency, or instrumentality of the United States. Such term does not include the Smithsonian Institution. [author note: taken over in regulations, compare 10.2(a)(1)][190]

(8) "museum" means any institution or State or local government agency (including any institution of higher learning) that receives Federal funds and has

the other hand... apply only to federal agencies and federally-funded museums... federal or tribal lands."

[187] McManamon and Nordby (1992), pp. 220–221.

[188] Irwin (1997), p. 44.

[189] There is a second group of non-Indigenous parties, namely those in charge of implementing the framework, which are considered in more detail in Sect. 4.4.5.1. For a definition under regulations see 43 C.F.R. (2020) 10.2(c).

[190] See also 43 C.F.R. (2020) 10.2. (a)(2) Federal agency official means any individual authorized by delegation of authority within a Federal agency to perform the duties relating to these regulations.

possession of, or control over, Native American cultural items. Such term does not include the Smithsonian Institution or any other Federal agency. [author note: taken over in regulations, compare 10.2(a)(3)].[191]

Native American Graves Protection and Repatriation Regulations 43 CFR § 10.2(a)(3) (2020)[192]

i. The term "possession" means having physical custody of human remains, funerary objects, sacred objects, or objects of cultural patrimony with a sufficient legal interest to lawfully treat the objects as part of its collection for purposes of these regulations. Generally, a museum or Federal agency would not be considered to have possession of human remains, funerary objects, sacred objects, or objects of cultural patrimony on loan from another individual, museum, or Federal agency.
ii. The term "control" means having a legal interest in human remains, funerary objects, sacred objects, or objects of cultural patrimony sufficient to lawfully permit the museum or Federal agency to treat the objects as part of its collection for purposes of these regulations whether or not the human remains, funerary objects, sacred objects or objects of cultural patrimony are in the physical custody of the museum or Federal agency. Generally, a museum or Federal agency that has loaned human remains, funerary objects, sacred objects, or objects of cultural patrimony to another individual, museum, or Federal agency is considered to retain control of those human remains, funerary objects, sacred objects, or objects of cultural patrimony for purposes of these regulations.
iii. The phrase "receives Federal funds" means the receipt of funds by a museum after November 16, 1990, from a Federal agency through any grant, loan, contract (other than a procurement contract), or other arrangement by which a Federal agency makes or made available to a museum aid in the form of funds. Federal funds provided for any purpose that are received by a larger entity of which the museum is a part are considered Federal funds for the purposes of these regulations. For example, if a museum is a part of a State or local government or a private university and the State or local government or private university receives Federal funds for any purpose, the museum is considered to receive Federal funds for the purpose of these regulations.

In considering which institutions should be obliged to comply with the NAGPRA, disagreement existed in how far institutions beyond federal agencies should be included, such as university museums.[193] Even after the adoption of NAGPRA,

[191] See also 43 C.F.R. (2020) 10.2. (a)(4) Museum official means the individual within a museum designated as being responsible for matters relating to these regulations.

[192] The regulations then specify a number of key terms, namely 'possession', 'control' and 'federal funds'.

[193] Marsh (1992), p. 99.

uncertainties existed, for example whether museums that receive some support from specific federal agencies were covered or whether tribal repositories would classify as museums under NAGPRA.[194] In this sense, the regulations provided both significant clarification and emphasized the broad scope of the obligations enshrined in NAGPRA and the ambitious scale of this repatriation project. Inventory and repatriation obligations were imposed on state and local government museums, as well as university museums, irrespective of whether the specific institution holding the heritage in question received funding. What mattered was whether the state government, local government or university, as such, received funds (for *any purpose*).[195] The high number of institutions that were placed under this obligation has to be seen in light of the vastness of holdings and their widespread physical distribution and the historic circumstances which led to their dislocation. As was emphasized above, and is highlighted in these definitions as well, while the Smithsonian would otherwise be covered, it is explicitly excluded as it is instead covered by the NMAIA (see Sect. 4.6.1.3).

4.4.2.2.2 Key Definitions of Indigenous Parties

Native American Graves Protection 25 U.S.C. § 3002 (2019)
(6) "Hui Malama I Na Kupuna O Hawai'i Nei" means the nonprofit, Native Hawaiian organization incorporated under the laws of the State of Hawaii by that name on April 17, 1989, for the purpose of providing guidance and expertise in decisions dealing with Native Hawaiian cultural issues, particularly burial issues.

(7) "Indian tribe" means any tribe, band, nation, or other organized group or community of Indians, including any Alaska Native village (as defined in, or established pursuant to, the Alaska Native Claims Settlement Act [43 U.S.C. 1601 et seq.]), which is recognized as eligible for the special programs and services provided by the United States to Indians because of their status as Indians.

(9) "Native American" means of, or relating to, a tribe, people, or culture that is Indigenous to the United States.

(10) "Native Hawaiian" means any individual who is a descendant of the aboriginal people who, prior to 1778, occupied and exercised sovereignty in the area that now constitutes the State of Hawaii.

(11) "Native Hawaiian organization" means any organization which—

[194] McManamon and Nordby (1992), p. 226 "A number of federal agencies supply financial support to museums, and most museums receive at least some federal funds. The committee reports are silent on the question of when and how directly a museum must receive funding in order to qualify as a museum under the NAGPRA definition. We assume that most large museums and many smaller museums within the United States will have to comply with NAGPRA." [NPS employees].

[195] §10(2)(a)(3)(iii) Regulations.

(A) serves and represents the interests of Native Hawaiians,

(B) has as a primary and stated purpose the provision of services to Native Hawaiians,

and

(C) has expertise in Native Hawaiian Affairs, and shall include the Office of Hawaiian Affairs and Hui Malama I Na Kupuna O Hawai'i Nei.

Native American Graves Protection and Repatriation Regulations 43 § 10.2(b) (2020) [standing]

(1) Lineal descendant means an individual tracing his or her ancestry directly and without interruption by means of the traditional kinship system of the appropriate Indian tribe or Native Hawaiian organization or by the common law system of descendance to a known Native American individual whose remains, funerary objects, or sacred objects are being claimed under these regulations.

(2) [Reserved]

(3) (i) Native Hawaiian organization means any organization that:

(A) Serves and represents the interests of Native Hawaiians;

(B) Has as a primary and stated purpose the provision of services to Native Hawaiians; and

(C) Has expertise in Native Hawaiian affairs.

(ii) The term Native Hawaiian means any individual who is a descendant of the aboriginal people who, prior to 1778, occupied and exercised sovereignty in the area that now constitutes the State of Hawaii. Such organizations must include the Office of Hawaiian Affairs and Hui Mālama I NāKūpuna 'O Hawai'i Nei.

(4) Indian tribe official means the principal leader of an Indian tribe or Native Hawaiian organization or the individual officially designated by the governing body of an Indian tribe or Native Hawaiian organization or as otherwise provided by tribal code, policy, or established procedure as responsible for matters relating to these regulations.

The Act uses several concepts of indigeneity, linking past and present individuals by tracing ancestry. On the one hand, it distinguishes clearly between Native American and Native Hawaiian with the latter being clearly defined both in terms of space ("area that now constitutes the State of Hawaii") as well as time ("prior to 1778"). On the other hand, for Native Americans, the definition has led to problems in jurisprudence. In Bonnichsen v US,[196] the judges clearly struggled with accepting a link

[196] Bonnichsen v United States 367 F.3d 864 (2004) United States Court of Appeals, Ninth Circuit.

between contemporary Native American tribes and ancient human remains (the remains of the "Ancient One" or "Kennewick man" were dated at around 9000 years old). In this case, they emphasized the present tense of "is" in "Native American means of, or relating to, a tribe, people, or culture that **is** Indigenous to the United States" and conflated the test for cultural affiliation which should be taking place after the determination of the remains or items as Native American with the initial stage. This was facilitated by the fact that "indigenous to the United States" was not defined further in statute or House/Senate reports.[197] The conflation of the two stages imports a stricter test into the first stage raising the evidentiary hurdles for Indigenous claimants.[198] Judge Gould also clearly adopted a linear (non-Indigenous) construction of cultural identity, observing "[h]uman remains that are 8340 to 9200 years old and that bear only incidental genetic resemblance to modern-day American Indians, along with incidental genetic resemblance to other peoples, cannot be said to be the Indians' "ancestors" within Congress's meaning"[199] Attempts were made to amend the Act to rectify the interpretation resulting from Bonnichsen, in particular the definition of Native American.[200] This resulted in changes to the regulations (rather than amendments in the act). In the regulations the word "is" has been omitted, the definition now reads "[t]he term Native American means of, or relating to, a tribe, people, or culture indigenous to the United States, including Alaska and Hawaii."[201]

Another distinction made in the definitions which has far-reaching consequences for the application of the act is between "Indian tribes" and "Native Americans". While Native American is used to characterize the remains and items that can be reclaimed,[202] Indian tribes or Native Hawaiian organizations are the parties who may have a claim (both under §3002 and §3005). Indian tribes in turn are those tribes which are recognized by the United States for the administration of a program (§3001(7)). This is not in line with the international requirement of Indigenous identity as relying on self-identification and community recognition. The inequality between the two parties that stems from federal Indian law is thus cemented within the repatriation model adopted. An important exception to this observation are lineal descendants, who are recognized throughout the act as having a claim to ancestral remains, items of cultural patrimony or sacred items (§3005(1),(3),(5)(A)). In the regulations, lineal descendants are defined by direct ancestry traced according to common law and irrespective of their membership in a federally recognized tribe or

[197] Dussias (2005), p. 79.

[198] Dussias (2005), p. 134 See also Bonnichsen, 367 F.3d at 875.

[199] Bonnichsen v United States 367 F.3d 864 (2004) United States Court of Appeals, Ninth Circuit at 879.

[200] In particular there were two hearings on S. 536 in 2005, S. Hrg 109-67 and S. Hrg. 109-297. See also https://www.nps.gov/subjects/nagpra/the-law.htm [last accessed 18.08.2021].

[201] Native American Graves Protection and Repatriation Regulations 43 § 10.2(d) (2020).

[202] §3001(3); §3002(c), (d); §3003(a), (b)(2), (d); §3004(a), (b); §3005(a) etc.

"by means of the traditional kinship system of the appropriate Indian tribe".[203] There is an important lesson to be learned here for any other government considering the adoption of repatriation approaches not to rely on ready-made definitions but to use this chance to reconsider any national definitions of Indigenous identity, at least for the purpose of the repatriation. This flexibility in identifying the relative community is also one advantage that international repatriations have over intra-national repatriations. Recognition of a community for the purposes of an international repatriation cannot give rise to the governmental fear of opening the floodgates to other governmental benefits of recognizing Indigenous status, so to speak.

4.4.2.3 Objects covered by NAGPRA and Accompanying Regulations

Native American Graves Protection 25 U.S.C. §3001 (2019)[204]
(3) "cultural items" means human remains and—

(A) "associated funerary objects" [. . .]

(B) "unassociated funerary objects" [. . .],

(C) "sacred objects" which shall mean **specific ceremonial objects** which are **needed by traditional Native American religious leaders** for the practice of traditional Native American religions by their present day adherents, and

(D) "cultural patrimony" which shall mean an object having ongoing historical, traditional, or cultural importance central to the Native American group or culture itself, rather than property owned by an individual Native American, and which, therefore, cannot be alienated, appropriated, or conveyed by any individual regardless of whether or not the individual is a member of the Indian tribe or Native Hawaiian organization and such object shall have been considered inalienable by such Native American group at the time the object was separated from such group.

[203] See §10.14 (b) "*Criteria for determining lineal descent.* A lineal descendant is an individual tracing his or her ancestry directly and without interruption by means of the traditional kinship system of the appropriate Indian tribe or Native Hawaiian organization or by the common law system of descendence to a known Native American individual whose remains, funerary objects, or sacred objects are being requested under these regulations. This standard requires that the earlier person be identified as an individual whose descendants can be traced." There is of course the theoretical exception of claimants who could prove lineal descendancy but who are not members of a recognized tribe.

[204] Emphasis added.

Native American Graves Protection and Repatriation Regulations 43 § 10.2(d) (2020)[205]

What objects are covered by these regulations? The Act covers four types of Native American objects. The term Native American means of, or relating to, a tribe, people, or culture indigenous to the United States, including Alaska and Hawaii.

(1) Human remains [. . .]

(2) Funerary objects [. . .]

(3) Sacred objects means items that are specific ceremonial objects needed by traditional Native American religious leaders for the practice of traditional Native American religions by their present-day adherents. While many items, from ancient pottery sherds to arrowheads, might be imbued with sacredness in the eyes of an individual, **these regulations are specifically limited to objects that were devoted to a traditional Native American religious ceremony or ritual and which have religious significance or function in the continued observance or renewal of such ceremony**. The term traditional religious leader means a person who is recognized by members of an Indian tribe or Native Hawaiian organization as:

(i) **Being responsible for performing cultural duties** relating to the ceremonial or religious traditions of that Indian tribe or Native Hawaiian organization, or

(ii) **Exercising a leadership role** in an Indian tribe or Native Hawaiian organization based on the tribe or organization's cultural, ceremonial, or religious practices.

(4) Objects of cultural patrimony means items having ongoing historical, traditional, or cultural importance central to the Indian tribe or Native Hawaiian organization itself, rather than property owned by an individual tribal or organization member. These objects are of such central importance that they may not be alienated, appropriated, or conveyed by any individual tribal or organization member. Such objects must have been considered inalienable by the culturally affiliated Indian tribe or Native Hawaiian organization at the time the object was separated from the group. Objects of cultural patrimony include items such as Zuni War Gods, the Confederacy Wampum Belts of the Iroquois, and other objects of similar character and significance to the Indian tribe or Native Hawaiian organization as a whole.

As is apparent from the definitions above, sacred Indigenous objects only fall under the repatriation provisions of NAGPRA if they are reclaimed for contemporary religious use. However, current practices do not need to link back to past practices in a continuous chain of practice. It is sufficient that the item was once dedicated to a

[205] Emphasis added.

religious purpose and is needed for this purpose in a religious practice today. The item must thus be used in the ceremony to which it was once dedicated but the practice can be a renewed tradition. Accommodating the revitalization of traditions is an important step to consider in a repatriation, given that the dislocation of the object was motivated by forced assimilation and may have gone hand-in-hand with legal prohibitions of such practices. The legislative history of NAGRPA indicates that Congress was aware of such gaps in time and the reasons therefore.[206] To require either a relatively continuous ceremony or a tradition that is identical to the past is both unrealistic and will be difficult to evidence even if true.

An important element in the definition of sacred objects is the space that it makes for Indigenous traditions and even tribal law. The need for the object is decided upon by the Indigenous individual who (presumably) is responsible for the specific practice or who has an important cultural or religious role. The position of the individual identified as "traditional religious leader" in NAGPRA and the regulations in turn is determined by the Indigenous community itself. The wording of the relevant provisions cited above is broad enough and clearly seeks to emphasize Indigenous responsibility in this area. In this respect, it was important that the act did not seek to define sacredness.[207] To do so would have risked violating Indigenous religious and cultural rights arising out of Art. 18 and 27 ICCPR and contextualized in Art. 12(1) UNDRIP. However, items which are used but incidental to a practice (not "necessary") are not covered. The difficulty here is how to draw the line and who is best qualified to arbitrate necessity in such a case. The act mitigated this difficulty slightly by instating the Review Committee with a mixed composition, representing both the museum community and Indigenous tribes.

Where an item is sacred but no longer used, it may still be an important piece of Indigenous cultural heritage. The incorporation of the category of cultural patrimony in NAGPRA is an important element in strengthening Indigenous cultural rights more broadly, even if the definition is very narrow. The protection of heritage sites against future excavations, examined in Sect. 4.4.4 below, is another important element in protecting Indigenous cultural rights. However, both the Act as well as the regulations highlight that the categories of sacred items and cultural patrimony should be applied narrowly.[208]

4.4.2.4 Types of Land Covered by NAGPRA and Accompanying Regulations

Native American Graves Protection 25 U.S.C. §3001 (2019)

(5) "Federal lands" means any land other than tribal lands which are controlled or owned by the United States, including lands selected by but not yet conveyed to

[206] Dussias (2005), pp. 78–79, 1236.

[207] Trope and Echo-Hawk (1992), p. 66.

[208] Hutt (1992), p. 144.

Alaska Native Corporations and groups organized pursuant to the Alaska Native Claims Settlement Act of 1971 [43 U.S.C. 1601 et seq.]. (…).

(15) "tribal land" means—

(A) all lands within the exterior boundaries of any Indian reservation;

(B) all dependent Indian communities;

(C) any lands administered for the benefit of Native Hawaiians pursuant to the Hawaiian Homes Commission Act, 1920, and section 4 of Public Law 86–3.

Native American Graves Protection and Repatriation Regulations 43 § 10.2(f) (2020)

What types of lands do the excavation and discovery provisions of these regulations apply to? (1) Federal lands means any land other than tribal lands that are controlled or owned by the United States Government, including lands selected by but not yet conveyed to Alaska Native Corporations and groups organized pursuant to the Alaska Native Claims Settlement Act (43 U.S.C. 1601 et seq.). United States "control," as used in this definition, refers to those lands not owned by the United States but in which the United States has a legal interest sufficient to permit it to apply these regulations without abrogating the otherwise existing legal rights of a person.

(2) Tribal lands means all lands which:

(i) Are within the exterior boundaries of any Indian reservation including, but not limited to, allotments held in trust or subject to a restriction on alienation by the United States; or

(ii) Comprise dependent Indian communities as recognized pursuant to 18 U.S.C. 1151; or

(iii) Are administered for the benefit of Native Hawaiians pursuant to the Hawaiian Homes Commission Act of 1920 and section 4 of the Hawaiian Statehood Admission Act (Pub.L. 86-3; 73 Stat. 6).

(iv) Actions authorized or required under these regulations will not apply to tribal lands to the extent that any action would result in a taking of property without compensation within the meaning of the Fifth Amendment of the United States Constitution.

These geographical definitions are relevant not for the repatriation mechanism in NAGPRA but rather for the excavation and discovery provisions, which is why an in-depth analysis will not be carried out here. It suffices to summarize that, given forced migrations as well as legal assimilation programmes, the status of Indigenous lands under the law remains difficult. Non-Indigenous held land within a reservation boundary is covered by NAGPRA, as is current reservation land. Traditional Indigenous lands are not covered—they may be partially covered by the reservation boundaries, or they may located elsewhere.[209] Of course, by understanding tribal land more broadly for the purpose of NAGPRA than is commonly done,[210] Congress arguably attempted to somewhat mitigate the current effects of its past practices on Indigenous cultural rights. Such protection of burial and heritage sites that is more in line with Indigenous traditions decreases the chance of future violations of Indigenous rights. Outside of reservation boundaries, the protection offered does not apply on private, state or local lands.[211]

4.4.2.5 Objectives

In summary, the act sought to achieve several goals, notably the repudiation of past practices and a conscious turn to treating Indigenous remains as human remains rather than objects for collecting.[212] With this emphasis on the respectful treatment of the dead, it built on the NMAI as well as the panel report.[213] It also recognizes the importance of material expressions of culture, notably sacred objects and objects of cultural patrimony as being important to and within Indigenous culture. This was a long overdue movement away from the objectification of Indigenous Peoples towards improving the relationship between all parties concerned. Instead, the focus is placed on Indigenous Peoples as self-determining subjects of the law who claim their human rights. The human rights nature of the act was emphasized repeatedly in the adoption of the Act. Given the interconnection of intangible aspects of culture and material expressions, it is thus not surprising that the act combines different areas of law and is arguably a bit of a patchwork instrument. Its focus on the respectful treatment of Indigenous cultures has been given legal form *inter alia* by the incorporation of tribal law into this federal procedure,[214] the explicit incorporation of oral traditions,[215] and the consultation duty under s. 3002.

It is noteworthy that, in some of its aspects, the NAGPRA foreshadowed provisions in the UNDRIP and important developments in the field of cultural rights which took place in more recent years. For international human rights lawyers, this might be a curious feature given the (almost notorious) disregard the United States government has for important human rights treaties which it refuses to ratify as well as the non-self-executing reservations it has made to the treaties it did ratify. However, NAGPRA, at its core, is not only a human rights instrument but, in domestic law terms, it is a piece of federal Indian legislation adopted in the self-determination era. This is not to say that there are no issues with Indigenous rights

[209] Dussias (2005), p. 81.

[210] Newton et al. (2005), pp. 1237–1238.

[211] For state actions see Seidemann (2010), p. 200.

[212] Dussias (2005), p. 74.

[213] Trope and Echo-Hawk (1992), p. 60.

[214] Definition of sacred objects, see Sect. 4.4.2.3.

[215] S. 3005(4) 25 USC Ch. 32.

protection in the United States (there are plenty). However, the act was adopted against the backdrop of the fundamental principles of federal Indian law, notably Indigenous self-determination in relation to internal affairs and the trust relationship between tribes and the federal government which should also be taken into account in the interpretation of NAGPRA.[216] As such, it arguably provides a minimum standard federal agencies and museums have to adhere to in order to ensure that the federal government fulfils its duties under the trust relationship.

In addition, the act envisions the possibility that federal agencies and museums might wish to go further through a savings clause in §3009(1), which clarifies that chapter 32 should not be construed to "limit the authority of any Federal agency or museum to (A) return or repatriate Native American cultural items to Indian tribes, Native Hawaiian organizations, or individuals, and (B) enter into any other agreement with the consent of the culturally affiliated tribe or organization as to the disposition of, or control over, items covered by this chapter". Given the legalistic approach taken to repatriation in the model enshrined in the NAGPRA, s. 3009 (1) provides important space for flexibility. Given the variety of cultures and tribal laws, as well as museums and other holding institutions, this ensures that holding institutions have to respect their responsibilities, but it acknowledges that they may need to find another route together with the Indigenous claimants to pursue the objectives of the act, namely equal respect for Indigenous cultures, traditions and burial sites.

4.4.3 Repatriation Mechanism

4.4.3.1 Inventory and Summary of Collection

The core provisions on repatriation are s. 3003, providing for a duty to make an inventory of human remains and associated funerary objects, s. 3004 establishing a duty to summarize holdings/collections of unassociated funerary objects, sacred objects, and cultural patrimony and s. 3005 containing the specific repatriation provisions. These are complemented by the federal regulations which supplement NAGPRA.[217]

For any repatriation exercise, a meticulous and detailed inventory of the holdings which have or can be been identified as Indigenous cultural items is a crucial first step. The inventory also has to be (made) accessible to the parties who might have an interest in reclaiming the heritage in question. Both notions arguably reflect a core dimension of Art. 27 ICCPR for Indigenous Peoples, namely access. Without knowing what one may have access to, access to heritage simply cannot be realized.

---

[216] Dussias (2005), pp. 75–76.

[217] Notably Subpart C on Human Remains, Funerary Objects, Sacred Objects, or Objects of Cultural Patrimony in Museums and Federal Collections of title 43 Subtitle A, part 10 C.F.R. (2020).

§3003 reflects and provides for a duty to compile inventories for human remains and associated funerary objects. §3003(a) obliges federal agencies and museums which possess, or control, human remains or associated funerary items in their holdings or collections to compile and make an inventory of these and to identify geographical and cultural affiliation. Under §3003(b)(1), the inventory and any identifications thus made have to be: "(A) completed in consultation with tribal government and Native Hawaiian organization officials and traditional religious leaders; (B) completed by not later than the date that is 5 years after November 16, 1990, and (C) made available both during the time they are being conducted and afterward to a review committee established under section 3006 of this title." However, considerable differences exist(ed) in the size of collections and available information, and therefore a certain degree of flexibility was necessary.[218] §3003(c) thus allowed for an extension of the time period to make an inventory beyond 5 years after if the museum has made a good faith effort to compile the report, which has long since passed.

An important element of this duty to make an inventory is to do so on the basis of information already available at the time (§3003(a) "to the extent possible based on information possessed"). The duty to make an inventory may thus not be read by the holding collection to authorize further testing without the consent of tribes. This is underlined in § 3003(b)(2). This provision obliges holding institutions to provide Indian tribes or Native Hawaiian organizations which have (or should have received) notice under §3003(d) to provide additional documentation upon request. It also emphasizes that the term 'documentation' and anything else in Chapter 32 "shall not be construed to be an authorization for, the initiation of new scientific studies of such remains and associated funerary objects or other means of acquiring or preserving additional scientific information from such remains and objects." The duty to notify any "affected Indian tribes or Native Hawaiian organizations" of determinations of cultural affiliations of particular Native American human remains or associated funerary objects is enshrined in s. 3003(d)(1).[219]

By contrast much less detail had to be compiled and made available in the identification of sacred objects. As pointed out above, the duty to make an inventory does not apply to unassociated funerary items, items of cultural patrimony or sacred objects. § 3004(a) enshrines the duty of the holding or controlling institution to "provide a written summary of such objects based upon available information held

[218] McManamon and Nordby (1992), p. 239.

[219] 25 U.S.C. §3003(d) "(2) The notice required by paragraph (1) shall include information (A) which identifies each Native American human remains or associated funerary objects and the circumstances surrounding its acquisition; (B) which lists the human remains or associated funerary objects that are clearly identifiable as to tribal origin; and (C) which lists the Native American human remains and associated funerary objects that are not clearly identifiable as being culturally affiliated with that Indian tribe or Native Hawaiian organization, but which, given the totality of circumstances surrounding acquisition of the remains or objects, are determined by a reasonable belief to be remains or objects culturally affiliated with the Indian tribe or Native Hawaiian organization."

by such agency or museum. The summary shall describe the scope of the collection, kinds of objects included, reference to geographical location, means and period of acquisition and cultural affiliation, where readily ascertainable." Both the inventory and summary are to be compiled after consulting with Native American governments and traditional leaders.[220] The summary does not constitute an object-by-object inventory, as is the case for human remains and funerary items, and it had to be compiled within three rather than 5 years after adoption of the act.[221] Given the high number of cultural items which fall under this duty, the differentiation between human remains and funerary items, on the one hand, and sacred items, cultural patrimony and unassociated items, on the other, is not surprising. Moreover, NAGPRA was adopted at a time when the collection of human remains and past practices in this regard were in the focus of public attention. However, the duty to provide a summary is absolute in the sense that no time extension was provided either under NAGPRA or its regulations.

Upon reading §3004, one may wonder how tribes and Hawaiian organizations are informed of possible sacred items in the collections that could be connected to them. Unlike the case under section 3003(d), section 3004 does not contain a notification duty. Here the regulations are crucial, 43 C.F.R. §10.8 (2019) supplements §3004 in four ways: first, it features a notification duty as part of a consultation process to both lineal descendants and tribal officials or traditional religious leaders that are, or likely to be, culturally affiliated. It highlights that the purpose of the summaries is to provide "information about the collections to lineal descendants and culturally affiliated Indian tribes or Native Hawaiian organization." Second, it emphasizes that federal agencies retain the responsibility to compile such summaries, irrespective of whether or not they hold the collection. Third, it gives more guidance as to the required content of such summaries:

43 C.F.R. §10.8(b) (2020)

Contents of summaries. For each collection or portion of a collection, the summary must include: an estimate of the number of objects in the collection or portion of the collection; a description of the kinds of objects included; reference to the means, date(s), and location(s) in which the collection or portion of the collection was acquired, where readily ascertainable; and information relevant to identifying lineal descendants, if available, and cultural affiliation.

Fourth, §10.8 also regulates the consultative framework required by 25 U.S.C. § 3004(b)(1)(B). It requires museum and federal agency officials to consult with Indigenous officials and religious leaders who are connected to the items either geographically through their tribal lands, their Aboriginal lands or through cultural

[220] 25 U.S.C. §3003(b)(1)(A), 25 U.S.C. §3004(b)(1)(B).

[221] 25 U.S.C. §3003(b)(1)(B), 25 U.S.C. §3004(b)(1)(A) and (C).

affiliation.[222] Consultation is a crucial element within NAGPRA (and other repatriation schemes). Often identifying the object and determining cultural affiliation will only be possible after consultation among all parties. Consultations can disclose new information, confirm existing knowledge and establish partnerships. However, 'consultation' in and of itself is neither easy nor quick. It will, in all likelihood, cost time, money, and energy. Moreover, as has become clear in the case of NAGPRA, interpretations of what consultation may mean in a given context can differ tremendously.[223] If consultation is understood to mean little more than initiating contact or providing information, potential benefits may not be realized and mutual expectations left unfulfilled. Depending on the desired societal effects of a repatriation framework (i.e. reconciliation), this may risk achieving such goals.

The Act and the regulations link the heritage and the claimant geographically, or alternatively, through a common culture with the original source community. These different options are important given the past forced migrations of communities. In addition to the duty to consult, §10.8 requires the responsible federal and museum officials to provide the information it holds[224] as well as to request both procedural and substantive information from their Indigenous counterpart.[225] While the relevant Indigenous parties have thus hopefully been informed in the consultation process before a repatriation decision is made, §10.8(f) also requires that, prior to any repatriation, a notice of intent to repatriate must be published in the Federal Register.

[222] It appears that the regulations understand Aboriginal lands as areas under Aboriginal occupation that has been recognized by the Indian Claims Commission, a treaty, Act of Congress or Executive Order, see §10.11 (c) (1)(ii).

[223] Nafziger and Dobkins (1999), pp. 90–91.

[224] §10.8(3) "Provision of information. During summary consultation, museum and Federal agency officials must provide copies of the summary to lineal descendants, when known, and to officials and traditional religious leaders representing Indian tribes or Native Hawaiian organizations that are, or are likely to be, culturally affiliated with the cultural items. A copy of the summary must also be provided to the Manager, National NAGPRA Program. Upon request by lineal descendants or Indian tribe officials, museum and Federal agency officials must provide lineal descendants, Indian tribe officials and traditional religious leaders with access to records, catalogues, relevant studies, or other pertinent data for the limited purposes of determining the geographic origin, cultural affiliation, and basic facts surrounding acquisition and accession of objects covered by the summary. Access to this information may be requested at any time and must be provided in a reasonable manner to be agreed upon by all parties. The Review committee also must be provided access to such materials."

[225] §10.8(4) (4) "Requests for information. During the summary consultation, museum and Federal agency officials must request, as appropriate, the following information from Indian tribes and Native Hawaiian organizations that are, or are likely to be, culturally affiliated with their collections: (i) Name and address of the Indian tribe official to act as representative in consultations related to particular objects; (ii) Recommendations on how the consultation process should be conducted, including: (A) Names and appropriate methods to contact any lineal descendants, if known, of individuals whose unassociated funerary objects or sacred objects are included in the summary; (B) Names and appropriate methods to contact any traditional religious leaders that the Indian tribe or Native Hawaiian organization thinks should be consulted regarding the collections; and (iii) Kinds of cultural items that the Indian tribe or Native Hawaiian organization considers to be funerary objects, sacred objects, or objects of cultural patrimony."

As is clear in the substantive requirement,[226] the notice aims to enable a tribe who possibly was not consulted but who may have an interest in the object and wish to be involved.

4.4.3.2 Determining Cultural Affiliation

After the federal agency and/or holding institutions have a better understanding of their holdings, they have to tackle the difficult yet critical task of connecting a sacred object to a possible claimant. This can happen both during as well as after the stocktaking exercise. The determination of cultural affiliation is crucial to repatriation. It is not surprising that both the adopted definitions as well their application by agencies and museums have given risen to case law[227] and a healthy degree of scepticism by academics.[228]

> **Native American Graves Protection 25 U.S.C. §3001 (2019)**
> (2) "cultural affiliation" means that there is a relationship of shared group identity which can be reasonably traced historically or prehistorically between a present day Indian tribe or Native Hawaiian organization and an identifiable earlier group.

> **Native American Graves Protection and Repatriation Regulations 43 C.F.R. §10.8(e)** Using summaries to determine affiliation. Museum and Federal agency officials must document in the summary the following information. They must use this information in determining, as appropriate, the lineal descendants of a deceased Native American individual with whom unassociated funerary objects and sacred objects are affiliated, and the Indian tribes and Native Hawaiian organizations with which unassociated funerary objects, sacred objects, or objects of cultural patrimony are affiliated:
>
> (1) Accession and catalogue entries;

[226] §10.8(f) "...The notice of intent to repatriate must describe the unassociated funerary objects, sacred objects, or objects of cultural patrimony being claimed in sufficient detail so as to enable other individuals, Indian tribes or Native Hawaiian organizations to determine their interest in the claimed objects..."

[227] A number of cases concerned the cultural affiliation of human remains, i.e. White v University of California 765 F.3d 1010 (2014) [dispute on culturally unaffiliated remains], Na Iwi O Na Kupuna O Mokapu v Dalton 894 F. Supp. 1397 (1995) [dispute human remains, finding that NAGPRA did not prohibit further studies for the purpose of accurately identifying cultural identity/ethnicity in an unconvincing analysis of 3003(b)(2)] Fallon Paiute-Shoshone Tribe v United States Bureau of Land Management 455 F.Supp.2d 1207 (2006) [dispute cultural affiliation decision ancient remains, court highlighting difficulty of such decisions for BLM post Bonnichsen].

[228] Brown and Bruchac (2006), pp. 201–208 See also Johnson (2007), pp. 65–89 He traces the history of the term cultural affiliation within the NAGPRA framework.

(2) Information related to the acquisition of unassociated funerary object, sacred object, or object of cultural patrimony, including:

(i) The name of the person or organization from whom the object was obtained, if known;

(ii) The date of acquisition;

(iii) The place each object was acquired, i.e., name or number of site, county, State, and Federal agency administrative unit, if applicable; and

(iv) The means of acquisition, i.e., gift, purchase, or excavation;

(3) A description of each unassociated funerary object, sacred object, or object of cultural patrimony, including dimensions, materials, and photographic documentation, if appropriate, and the antiquity of such objects, if known;

(4) A summary of the evidence used to determine the cultural affiliation of the unassociated funerary objects, sacred objects, or objects of cultural patrimony pursuant to §10.14 of these regulations.

§10.14 Lineal descent and cultural affiliation. (2020)[229]

(c) Criteria for determining cultural affiliation. Cultural affiliation means a relationship of shared group identity that may be reasonably traced historically or prehistorically between a present-day Indian tribe or Native Hawaiian organization and an identifiable earlier group. All of the following requirements must be met to determine cultural affiliation between a present-day Indian tribe or Native Hawaiian organization and the human remains, funerary objects, sacred objects, or objects of cultural patrimony of an earlier group:

(1) Existence of an identifiable present-day Indian tribe or Native Hawaiian organization with standing under these regulations and the Act; and

(2) Evidence of the existence of an identifiable earlier group. [. . .]

(3) Evidence of the existence of a shared group identity that can be reasonably traced between the present-day Indian tribe or Native Hawaiian organization and the earlier group. Evidence to support this requirement **must establish that a present-day Indian tribe or Native Hawaiian organization has been identified from prehistoric or historic times to the present as descending from the earlier group.**

(d) A finding of cultural affiliation should be **based upon an overall evaluation of the totality of the circumstances and evidence pertaining to the connection** between the claimant and the material being claimed and should not be precluded solely because of some gaps in the record.

[229] Emphasis added.

(e) Evidence. Evidence of a kin or cultural affiliation between a present-day individual, Indian tribe, or Native Hawaiian organization and human remains, funerary objects, sacred objects, or objects of cultural patrimony must be established by using the following types of evidence: **Geographical, kinship, biological, archeological, anthropological, linguistic, folklore, oral tradition, historical, or other relevant information or expert opinion.** [. . .]

An important first step in establishing cultural affiliation is the duty to document, which under NAGPRA lies clearly with the respective institution. The framework established requires consultation and mutual learning. However, to achieve a satisfactory consultation can be challenging and museums have (had) to enter consultations with communities often for the first time in a repatriation case.[230]

The key elements to establishing cultural affiliation are a 'shared group identity' between contemporary and past tribes, and a connection that can reasonably be traced historically or prehistorically. By contrast, in Bonnichsen, the court emphasized not only the notion of shared group identity but also the concept of 'identifiable earlier group'.[231] A shared group identity which can be traced back also means that any association of Indigenous Peoples with diverse Indigenous backgrounds cannot apply under NAGPRA.[232] The concept of reasonableness is crucial and should be considered within the specific tribal and museum record context. Otherwise, forced assimilation will make it difficult to meet the standard required to evidence 'cultural affiliation'. The regulations supplement this by clarifying the evidentiary threshold as a 'preponderance of the evidence'.[233] Preponderance of the evidence does not equal scientific certainty.[234] Scientific uncertainty may very well remain even after substantive testing (as was the case in Bonnichsen). The type of evidence to be considered is diverse and reflects the multiculturalism of the task set for the judge. It encompasses Indigenous forms of evidence (such as oral traditions and kinship notions), as well as different scientific fields and expert evidence. Given the vast timelines at issue, the cultural differences and the legal differences between tribal and US law, the broadening of admissible evidence is an important and necessary step. The question that Brown and Bruchac raise is how to evaluate these different forms of evidence when a yardstick is missing.[235] The connected question is then also whether a court and legally trained professionals are really the appropriate forum to determine cultural affiliation and decide on such matters. However, the

[230] Similarly Brown and Bruchac (2006), pp. 207–208.

[231] Newton et al. (2005), p. 1238.

[232] McManamon and Nordby (1992), p. 223.

[233] Marsh (1992), pp. 98–99.

[234] §10.14(f) See also Dussias (2005), p. 82.

[235] Brown and Bruchac (2006), p. 206 "Such dramatic liberalization of evidentiary standards acknowledges the profound differences that exist between cultures. In that sense it is a democratic move. Yet when all kinds of evidence are held to be equally valid, the law risks stumbling into a relativistic quagmire hostile to anything approaching consensual truth."

resolution of such disputes will admittedly be difficult to achieve irrespective of the adjudicative body. One may wonder whether a more representative body could ensure a more equal resolution of such bodies. Something comparable to the Review Committee for example might make for a good adjudicative body, with some necessary changes applied. In NAGPRA the Review Committee is advisory in nature but, if supplemented by additional members who would introduce the necessary legal expertise, both in U.S. law and Indigenous law, and if it would be strengthened to give binding advice with the consent of the parties, it could remedy some of the deficiencies the courts face, as they simply cannot be experts in all relevant matters, and it could address the lack of Indigenous members in the judiciary, at least in the area of repatriation.

For the repatriation of sacred objects, §10.8(e) is key given that information on sacred objects will be compiled via summaries. To establish affiliation with a deceased individual and his descendants or a tribe/Native Hawaiian organization the regulations provide a list of steps to take when researching the provenance of the item. This depends on good recordkeeping in the past by either the museum or the individual who transferred the item, which may not have happened. Establishing the task of tracing the linkage between the claimants and the earlier Indigenous group will be challenging enough, and the wording of the regulations arguably renders this even more difficult (**must establish** that a present-day Indian tribe or Native Hawaiian organization has been **identified from prehistoric or historic times to the present** as descending from the earlier group).[236]

Another challenge in the establishment of cultural affiliation is the exclusion of non-federally recognized tribes. Unrecognized tribes who have evidence to support cultural affiliation have been frustrated by the object being either misidentified or classified as unaffiliated.[237] Individual museums have sought to remedy this by voluntary repatriations,[238] but the flaw in the legal framework persists.

4.4.3.3 Repatriating Sacred Items from Existing Collections

> **Native American Graves Protection 25 U.S.C. §3005. (2019) Repatriation**[239]
> (a) **Repatriation of Native American human remains and objects possessed or controlled by Federal agencies and museums**[. . .]
>
> (2) If, pursuant to section 3004 of this title, the cultural affiliation with a particular Indian tribe or Native Hawaiian organization is shown with respect to unassociated funerary objects, sacred objects or objects of cultural patrimony, then the Federal agency or museum, upon the request of the Indian tribe or Native

[236] 43 C.F.R. § 10.14 (c)(3) (2019).

[237] Brown (2003), pp. 202–204.

[238] Brown and Bruchac (2006), pp. 204–205.

[239] Emphasis added.

Hawaiian organization and pursuant to subsections (b), (c) and (e) of this section, shall expeditiously return such objects.

(3) The return of cultural items covered by this chapter shall be in consultation with the requesting lineal descendant or tribe or organization to determine the place and manner of delivery of such items. [. . .]

(5) Upon request and pursuant to subsections (b), (c) and (e), sacred objects and objects of cultural patrimony shall be expeditiously returned where—

(A) the requesting party is the direct lineal descendant of an individual who owned the sacred object;

(B) the requesting Indian tribe or Native Hawaiian organization can show that the object was owned or controlled by the tribe or organization; or

(C) the requesting Indian tribe or Native Hawaiian organization can show that the sacred object was owned or controlled by a member thereof, provided that in the case where a sacred object was owned by a member thereof, there are no identifiable lineal descendants of said member or the lineal descendants, upon notice, have failed to make a claim for the object under this chapter.

(b) Scientific study

If the lineal descendant, Indian tribe, or Native Hawaiian organization requests the return of culturally affiliated Native American cultural items, the Federal agency or museum shall expeditiously return such items **unless such items are indispensable for completion of a specific scientific study**, the **outcome of which would be of major benefit** to the United States. Such items shall be returned by no later than 90 days after the date on which the scientific study is completed.

(c) Standard of repatriation

If a known lineal descendant or an Indian tribe or Native Hawaiian organization requests the return of Native American unassociated funerary objects, sacred objects or objects of cultural patrimony pursuant to this chapter and **presents evidence which, if standing alone before the introduction of evidence to the contrary, would support a finding that the Federal agency or museum did not have the right of possession**, then such agency or museum shall return such objects **unless it can overcome such inference** and prove that it has a right of possession to the objects.

(d) Sharing of information by Federal agencies and museums

Any Federal agency or museum shall share what information it does possess regarding the object in question with the known lineal descendant, Indian tribe, or Native Hawaiian organization to assist in making a claim under this section.

(e) Competing claims

Where there are multiple requests for repatriation of any cultural item and, after complying with the requirements of this chapter, the Federal agency or museum cannot clearly determine which requesting party is the most appropriate claimant, the agency or museum may retain such item until the requesting parties agree upon its disposition or the dispute is otherwise resolved pursuant to the provisions of this chapter or by a court of competent jurisdiction.

(f) Museum obligation

Any museum which repatriates any item in good faith pursuant to this chapter shall not be liable for claims by an aggrieved party or for claims of breach of fiduciary duty, public trust, or violations of state law that are inconsistent with the provisions of this chapter.

§3005 highlights the legislative intent to address the past, but to accommodate concerns which were expressed loudly by a number of members of the museum community at the time, namely fear for the loss of future knowledge. It is also clear, however, that the focus of the instrument is remedial, intended to address past violations, and preventative in its excavation and discovery provisions.[240] To facilitate repatriation, the provision contains a number of key features. First it contains an obligation for federal agencies and museums to share information with potential claimants; second, the obligation to repatriate once cultural affiliation has been established subject to a limited number of exceptions;[241] third, the obligation to do so in consultation with the respective Indigenous individual or community;[242] fourth, to indemnify museums that have repatriated items in good faith under the Act. Otherwise, museums would be reluctant to repatriate, and negotiations would be impeded. Fifth, it contains an obligation to allow for competing claims to be settled by and among Indigenous claimants rather than by enforcing a specific mechanism; sixth, both NAGPRA[243] and the regulations[244] highlight the reserve

[240]The reasons for this focus have been laid out in Sects. 4.2 and 4.4.1 above.

[241]43 C.F.R. §10.10 (a) (2020) "Upon the request of a lineal descendant, Indian tribe, or Native Hawaiian organization, a museum or Federal agency *must expeditiously repatriate* unassociated funerary objects, sacred objects..." subject to exceptions in §10.10(c) [emphasis added by the author].

[242]43 C.F.R §10.10 (d) (2020) *Place and manner of repatriation.* The repatriation of human remains, funerary objects, sacred objects, or objects of cultural patrimony must be accomplished by the museum or Federal agency in consultation with the requesting lineal descendants, or culturally affiliated Indian tribe or Native Hawaiian organization, as appropriate, to determine the place and manner of the repatriation.

(e) The museum official or Federal agency official must inform the recipients of repatriations of any presently known treatment of the human remains, funerary objects, sacred objects, or objects of cultural patrimony with pesticides, preservatives, or other substances that represent a potential hazard to the objects or to persons handling the objects.

[243]25 U.S.C. §3009 (2019) Nothing in this chapter shall be construed to—(1) limit the authority of any Federal agency or museum to—(A) return or repatriate Native American cultural items to Indian tribes, Native Hawaiian organizations, or individuals, and (B) enter into any other agreement with the consent of the culturally affiliated tribe or organization as to the disposition of, or control over, items covered by this chapter.

[244]43 C.F.R. § 10.15(d) (2020) Savings provisions. Nothing in these regulations can be construed to: "(1) Limit the authority of any museum or Federal agency to: (i) Return or repatriate human

power for federal agencies and museums to repatriate and thus to find repatriation mechanisms together with Indigenous communities that may look different from the NAGPRA model.[245] In this, NAGPRA seems to work as a *de minimis* rule.

For sacred objects, this means that, if a museum has not already established cultural affiliation and consulted with an individual, an Indian tribe or a Native Hawaiian organization, a claimant has to jump five hurdles,[246] namely to show:

1. That the object meets the definitional threshold (essentially that it is necessary in a ceremony today, to which it was dedicated in the past).
2. That the object meets the cultural affiliation standard by a preponderance of the evidence (43 C.F.R. §10.10(a)(ii)(B)), specifically that the conditions of 3005(a)(5) are met [or this step is fulfilled by the agency/museum as result of NAGRPA obligations].
3. That the federal agency or museum does not have a right of possession. Evidentiary standard: evidence that would support a finding, if considered alone before the introduction of evidence to the contrary.[247]
4. Federal agency or museum unable to provide evidence of right of possession.
5. None of exemptions listed in 43 C.F.R.§10.10 (c) apply.

These exceptions to the requirements for repatriation otherwise established by the 25 U.S.C. §§ 3001-3013 and the regulations are summarized in 43 C.F.R. §10.10(c): in paragraph (1) the scientific study exemption of §3005(b); retention in case of competing claims until these are resolved in paragraph (2); where a court of competent jurisdiction has determined that the repatriation … would result in a taking of property without just compensation within the meaning of the Fifth Amendment of the United States Constitution in paragraph (3);[248] and in paragraph (4) where repatriation according to the requirements set out in 43 C.F.R. §10.10 (a) and (b) would not be in accordance with the limitations set out in §10.15. The latter operates as a catch-all provision for various 'other repatriation limitations', such as the failure to make a claim prior to repatriation.

As highlighted above, NAGPRA and the accompanying regulations provide for an exception to the obligation to repatriate where a right to possession exists. The

remains, funerary objects, sacred objects, or objects of cultural patrimony to Indian tribes, Native Hawaiian organizations, or individuals; and (ii) Enter into any other agreement with the consent of the culturally affiliated Indian tribe or Native Hawaiian organization as to the disposition of, or control over, human remains, funerary objects, sacred objects, or objects of cultural patrimony."

[245] Dussias uses this to show how strong congressional support for repatriation was. Dussias (2005), p. 86.

[246] 43 C.F.R. §10.10(a) (2020).

[247] Newton et al. (2005), p. 1240 "Determining right of possession requires both a factual and legal inquiry into whether the original acquisition was with the voluntary consent of an individual or group with the authority to alienate the object, unless the application of this definition would result in an unconstitutional taking."

[248] Newton et al. (2005), p. 1240 Such a finding can only be made by the competent court. A federal agency or museum cannot by itself constitute a takings exception.

legal relationship between NAGPRA and property law raised several 5th amendment concerns in the drafting phase.[249] The next section will highlight the main concerns in drafting NAGPRA but, given the focus of this study on public law mechanisms for return, it will not delve deeper into possible use of property law for repatriation.[250]

4.4.3.4 NAGPRA and Property Law

> **Native American Graves Protection 25 U.S.C. §3001 (2019)**
> (13) "right of possession" means **possession obtained with the voluntary consent** of an individual or group **that had authority of alienation**. The original acquisition of a Native American unassociated funerary object, sacred object or object of cultural patrimony from an Indian tribe or Native Hawaiian organization with the voluntary consent of an individual or group with authority to alienate such object is deemed to give right of possession of that object, **unless the phrase so defined would, as applied in section 3005(c) of this title, result in a Fifth Amendment taking by the United States as determined by the United States Court of Federal Claims** pursuant to 28 U.S.C. 1491 in which event the "right of possession" shall be as provided under otherwise applicable property law. The original acquisition of Native American human remains and associated funerary objects which were excavated, exhumed, or otherwise obtained with full knowledge and consent of the next of kin or the official governing body of the appropriate culturally affiliated Indian tribe or Native Hawaiian organization is deemed to give right of possession to those remains.

In §3001(13) we can see the legal tightrope that legislators will have to walk when they create a legal right to repatriation with a corresponding duty for institutions to deaccession. Where the right to property is protected, a museum owns an object and is not public in a sense that would mitigate a concern for state expropriation, then a law creating a duty repatriate will have to be coupled with compensation and meet national legal standards of justification.

In the case of NAGPRA and the US, §3001(13) provides that, for a right of possession to be valid, not only is a voluntary transfer necessary but also—and this is crucial in the context of sacred objects—the transferor needed to have the authority to alienate such an object. Authority to alienate is not defined further but given the act as a whole and its clear inclusion of tribal/customary law, the authority to alienate must be based in Indigenous tradition, be it tribal law or custom.[251] It is only if such an application would result in a 5th amendment taking—as determined by the Court

[249] In particular by the Department of Justice [statement 17.09.1990], H.R. Rep. No 101-877, 25–28 (1990).

[250] On the usage of property law for repatriation, see i.e. Carpenter et al. (2009) and Brown (2010).

[251] In agreement Trope and Echo-Hawk (1992), pp. 67–68; Strickland (1992), p. 180.

of Federal Claims, not an agency or museum—that this understanding does not apply. In this way, the right to property remains protected by the 5th amendment and the jurisprudence on 5th amendment takings.[252] The purpose of the latter is to limit the exercise of public power. In summary, under the 5th amendment, takings without just compensation are prohibited.[253] Lastly, for those applying NAGPRA, this is a difficult area, as the precedential value of decisions are somewhat limited, given the highly fact-specific nature of finding a right of possession.[254]

Even with this accommodation, institutions which qualify as museums under NAGPRA may find themselves in the difficult position of facing conflicting legal obligations. NAGPRA may require them to repatriate, but state property laws still apply.[255] Museums and scientific organizations have highlighted the tension for culturally unidentifiable remains especially. In these cases no right of possession could be established under NAGPRA, because of the absence of kinship records, while state laws accorded museums legal title to the remains and items removed from private lands with the consent of the owner.[256] This underlines the need for the takings exemption enshrined in §3001(13).[257] On this point, one may highlight again that human remains "are not subject to private ownership" and that, as human remains are not objects to be owned, museums do not loose property rights when they have to repatriate human remains under NAGPRA, as Patty Gerstenblith and others have pointed out.[258] This is of course different from the question of to whom the human remains should be repatriated. A museums' fiduciary duty may create another point of tensions.[259] Thus, even where repatriations can go smoothly, it should be pointed out that museums may have a fiduciary duty to care for their collection and to do so until the very point of repatriation.[260] This being said, repatriation of human remains to which the museum can have no valid title can also not breach its fiduciary duty of care.[261] The provision in NAGPRA of a minimum obligation to repatriate with a modified evidentiary threshold to show that the museum has a right of possession thus certainly mandated the inclusion of

[252]Tracing the historic evolution of takings in context of immovable, see Mangone (2002), SCOTUS affirmed that takings protection also applies to moveable property in Horne et al v Department of Agriculture (Horne II) 135 S. Ct. 2419/576 U.S. (2015).

[253]For a good overview of Supreme Court case law and four types of takings recognized see Meltz (2015), [Report Nr. 97-122]. For more detail at the time of the adoption of NAGPRA, Johnson and Haensly (1992), p. 168.

[254]Hutt (1992), p. 148.

[255]Boyd and Haas (1992), pp. 271–272.

[256]United States Government Accountability Office (2010), pp. 77–78.

[257]United States Government Accountability Office (2010), p. 78.

[258]Gerstenblith (2003), p. 435.

[259]For a more indepth discussion of this common law duty, see Sect. 4.6.2. A comparable common law duty exists in Canada, and is discussed in Sect. 6.3.5.2 in Chap. 6.

[260]Boyd and Haas (1992), p. 258.

[261]Gerstenblith (2003), p. 436.

the takings exception.[262] Nevertheless, where specific items have been donated or willed to an institution with specific conditions, this may be significantly more complicated. After all, even with the adoption of NAGPRA institutional boards will still have duties for their collection and towards the public under common law as well as statutory obligations.[263]

4.4.4 Protection of Unexcavated Sacred Objects After the Entry into Force of NAGPRA

NAGPRA not only provides for the repatriation of sacred objects that were in the collections and holdings at the time of its adoption, but it also increases Indigenous participation in case such items are discovered by accident or within a scheduled excavation. §3002 is the foundation of this mechanism and provides for Indigenous ownership of sacred items discovered on federal or tribal lands[264] after 16.11.1990. Johnson and Haensly have argued that to vest the ownership and corresponding control of the items excavated in Indian Country in the hands Native Americans is a federal interest which can best be understood to arise out of its trust responsibility. They characterize this trust responsibility as forming "a basis for protecting tribal cultures and religions. The Government may also wish to avoid a checkerboard jurisdictional scheme over the control and disposition of cultural items on Indian reservations."[265] §3002(a)(2) lists several potential claimants to sacred objects and objects of cultural patrimony:

> **Native American Graves Protection 25 U.S.C. §3002(a) (2019)**
> The ownership or control of Native American cultural items which are excavated or discovered on Federal or tribal lands after November 16, 1990, shall be (with priority given in the order listed) [. . .]
>
> (2) [. . .] and in the case of unassociated funerary objects, sacred objects, and objects of cultural patrimony—
>
> (A) in the Indian tribe or Native Hawaiian organization on whose tribal land such objects or remains were discovered;

---

[262] One example of clashes between a potential desire to repatriate and duties held by museum can, for example, be in the case of ancient remains and a duty to the public as was the case in White v University of California 765 F.3rd 1010 (2014), at 1023. Group of scientists claimed breach of public trust and sought declaration that remains were not ""Native American" within the meaning of NAGPRA", case dismissed because of tribal immunity.

[263] Boyd and Haas (1992), p. 254.

[264] See §3001(5) and (15) and Sect. 4.4.2.4 above.

[265] Johnson and Haensly (1992), p. 164.

(B) in the Indian tribe or Native Hawaiian organization which has the closest cultural affiliation with such remains or objects and which, upon notice, states a claim for such remains or objects; or

(C) if the cultural affiliation of the objects cannot be reasonably ascertained and if the objects were discovered on Federal land that is recognized by a final judgment of the Indian Claims Commission or the United States Court of Claims as the aboriginal land of some Indian tribe—

(1) in the Indian tribe that is recognized as aboriginally occupying the area in which the objects were discovered, if upon notice, such tribe states a claim for such remains or objects, or

(2) if it can be shown by a preponderance of the evidence that a different tribe has a stronger cultural relationship with the remains or objects than the tribe or organization specified in paragraph (1), in the Indian tribe that has the strongest demonstrated relationship, if upon notice, such tribe states a claim for such remains or objects.

The regulations then specify a hierarchy of claims, with the strongest claim resting in the "Indian tribe on whose tribal land the ... sacred objects, or objects of cultural patrimony were excavated intentionally or discovered inadvertently".[266] On the basis of recognizing Indigenous ownership of Indigenous heritage, NAGPRA then provides both for a mechanism to regulate the intentional excavation of Indigenous remains and heritage as well as their inadvertent discovery. Under

[266] 43 C.F.R. §10.6(a) Priority of custody. This section carries out section 3 (a) of the Act, subject to the limitations of §10.15, regarding the custody of human remains, funerary objects, sacred objects, or objects of cultural patrimony excavated intentionally or discovered inadvertently in Federal or tribal lands after November 16, 1990. For the purposes of this section, custody means ownership or control of human remains, funerary objects, sacred objects, or objects of cultural patrimony excavated intentionally or discovered inadvertently in Federal or tribal lands after November 16, 1990. Custody of these ... sacred objects, or objects of cultural patrimony is, with priority given in the order listed: "(2) ... and with respect to unassociated funerary objects, sacred objects, and objects of cultural patrimony: (i) In the Indian tribe on whose tribal land the human remains, funerary objects, sacred objects, or objects of cultural patrimony were excavated intentionally or discovered inadvertently; (ii) In the Indian tribe or Native Hawaiian organization that has the closest cultural affiliation with the human remains, funerary objects, sacred objects, or objects of cultural patrimony as determined pursuant to §10.14 (c); or (iii) In circumstances in which the cultural affiliation of the human remains, funerary objects, sacred objects, or objects of cultural patrimony cannot be ascertained and the objects were excavated intentionally or discovered inadvertently on Federal land that is recognized by a final judgment of the Indian Claims Commission or the United States Court of Claims as the aboriginal land of an Indian tribe: (A) In the Indian tribe aboriginally occupying the Federal land on which the human remains, funerary objects, sacred objects, or objects of cultural patrimony were excavated intentionally or discovered inadvertently, or (B) If a preponderance of the evidence shows that a different Indian tribe or Native Hawaiian organization has a stronger cultural relationship with the human remains, associated funerary objects, unassociated funerary objects, sacred objects, or objects of cultural patrimony, in the Indian tribe or Native Hawaiian organization that has the strongest demonstrated relationship with the cultural items."

§3002(c), the intentional excavation of sacred objects on tribal lands is only permitted with the consent of the respective community and, in the case of federal lands, the threshold is consultation. In both cases, proof of consultation or consent needs to be given, the excavation needs to be in line with the relevant permit under the Archaeological Resource Protection Act as amended,[267] and the ownership provisions under paragraph (a) need to be respected. The regulations provide considerably more detail on the need to accommodate the Archaeological Resources Protection Act (hereafter ARPA), the steps to take in the planning and consultation process (see §10.3), the custodial hierarchy in an cases of both intentional excavation and inadvertent discovery of sacred objects (see §10.6(a)(2)) as well as requirements for any potential disposition of sacred objects excavated or discovered on federal lands (see §10.6(c)). Sacred heritage and traditions are arguably very much at the heart of a community. As the Supreme Court has recognized the right of a tribe to govern the domestic internal affairs of their members, except for when Congress regulates otherwise,[268] the disposition of excavated or discovered heritage within tribal lands is a matter for the respective tribal law, subject to the custodial hierarchy established in §10.6(a). One part of this structure worth highlighting is the fact that the regulations require that detailed consultations take place before intentional excavations[269] and that, in the case of inadvertent discoveries on federal lands, any activities are halted and consultations begin immediately upon notification.[270] This creates the possibility that the respective form of heritage can be cared for in accordance with Indigenous customs as much as possible.[271] This is one way in which the Indigenous right to maintain and protect past manifestations of heritage under Art. 11(1) UNDRIP can be accommodated where Indigenous communities have been dispossessed of their lands. Administrative burdens on land development processes are a familiar concept within regular heritage law and national heritage law processes can be adjusted to accommodate such rights. Naturally, these may have to be balanced against other rights and interests and problems can arise on how to precisely balance the scale.[272] Within tribal lands, responsibility rests with the respective tribal official in line with Art. 11(1) UNDRIP.[273]

This protection of burial sites put in place in NAGPRA is enforced by means of §4 in the original NAGPRA, a criminal law provision included in the act. It provided

[267] Namely 16 U.S.C. §470cc as per §3002(c)(1).

[268] Highlighting tribal sovereignty in NAGPRA: "one internal domestic matter that falls squarely within this zone of tribal sovereignty is the relationship between the living and the dead." See Trope and Echo-Hawk (1992), p. 50.

[269] 43 C.F.R § 10.5 read in conjunction with § 10.3(b)(2) (2019).

[270] 43 C.F.R § 10.5 read in conjunction with § 10.4(c) (iv) (2019).

[271] Similarly Newton et al. (2005), p. 1242.

[272] This is a common problem that exists not just in the United States. In Canada, for example, a case of developing a religious site into a ski resort involved a difficult/controversial weighing exercise. It was a case which ended up before the Supreme Court (Grizzly Bear Spirit Case). See Chap. 6, Sect. 6.3 for more detail.

[273] 43 C.F.R. §10.4 (e) (2019).

for the insertion of section 1170 establishing illegal trafficking in Native American human remains and cultural items as a crime carrying a fine and/or a prison sentence of up to 1 year for the first and 5 years for a repeat offense.[274] Sherry Hutt has emphasized that, through this mechanism, the standard statutory fines for criminal convictions apply to NAGPRA.[275] They can be quite substantial, as 18 U.S.C. §1170, read in conjunction with section 18 U.S.C. §3559(a), classifies the selling, purchasing, using for profit, or transporting for sale or profit of human remains or cultural items as a class A misdemeanour and the second or subsequent violation as a class E felony. Under 18 USC § 3571, they carry fines of up to $100,000 and $250,000 for each respective offense.

A last element worth mentioning, given the initially critical reception of NAGPRA by some of museum and scientific community[276] is the difference between newly discovered items under §3002, where no accommodation is made for scientific study (it can of course still be consented to by respective Indigenous community or individual that has custody) and heritage that was already in a collection and is covered under §3005(b), which provides for a very narrow exception, permitting scientific study even contrary to the wishes of Indigenous parties for the completion of a specific study which would be "of major benefit to the United States".[277]

4.4.5 NAGPRA in Practice

4.4.5.1 Responsible Organizations

The application of NAGPRA involves a vast number of organizations, institutions, agencies, and individuals. First, there are the different agencies that have relevant holdings even if these may be located elsewhere (for example with a museum). In addition, there are federal agencies responsible for the implementation of NAGPRA, including the need to coordinate NAGPRA with other heritage bodies. This includes the Advisory Council on Historic Preservation (ACHP) and the State Historic Preservation Officers (SHPO). The Department of the Interior [hereafter DOI], which houses the BIA and is thus the key body for the implementation of federal Indian law, was given the key administrative role in this regard.[278] This also complements the DOI's role in federal lands: it has authority over much of the federal land covered by NAGPRA. One of its sub-agencies for the administration of

[274] 18 U.S.C. §1170 (Chapter 53) (2019).

[275] Hutt (1992), p. 146.

[276] Division was already visible in Museum panel report, see Boyd et al. (1990), p. 499, footnote 418. See also at 487 and footnotes 1 and 2 in the report.

[277] Dussias (2005), p. 85.

[278] Dussias (2005), p. 77.

federal lands, the National Park Service, has played a crucial role in the implementation of NAGPRA. At the time of adoption, NPS employees highlighted the complexity of the task ahead for federal agencies who had to: examine records, initiate contacts with museums that retain federal collections, examine records, and identify potential federal responsibilities for collections resulting from multi-agency projects or held by non-federal repositories.[279] Another challenge for agencies who prefer clear regulations and procedures was the inherently necessary vagueness of a number of key concepts enshrined in NAGPRA, *inter alia* sacredness.[280] These concepts had to be kept broad in the law and regulations to create the necessary space for diverse Indigenous Peoples and traditions. As Strumpf rightly predicted at the time of its adoption, the wording of NAGPRA required governmental actors and museums to consult Indigenous communities and individuals on these aspects in order to be able to apply the act.[281] The legal requirement to build clear communication channels is crucial for Indigenous rights which mostly require cross-cultural implementation in a national legal system or even across legal systems. This is an important lesson for any repatriation model, irrespective of the specific goal (be it physical repatriation, or something more amorphous like reconciliation) that the government seeks to achieve.

NAGPRA also established an advisory group, the Review Committee, which does not bind the federal government[282] but monitors and reviews the implementation of the NAGPRA framework,[283] facilitates dispute resolution, and compiles an inventory of culturally unidentifiable remains.[284] Section 3006 provides for a representative committee, three members from nominations by tribes (including two traditional religious leaders), three members from nominations by the museum and scientific community and one member from a list of nominations agreed upon by the other six members. As part of its advisory function, the committee can review and make findings on the cultural affiliation of a cultural item or its return if requested by any affected party.[285] NAGPRA assigns a number of duties to the Secretary of the Interior. These are carried out by the National NAGPRA Program Office (NAGPRA Program Office).[286] National NAGPRA is also responsible for developing the act's implementing regulations.[287] The NAGPRA Program Office also helps in filling vacancies on the Review Committee and provides administrative support to the Committee.[288]

[279] McManamon and Nordby (1992), p. 237.

[280] Stumpf (1992), p. 307.

[281] Stumpf (1992), p. 308.

[282] McManamon and Nordby (1992), pp. 228–229.

[283] Secretary of the Interior (1992), p. 501.

[284] United States Government Accountability Office (2010), p. 11.

[285] 25 USC §3006(c)(3).

[286] United States Government Accountability Office (2010), pp. 2–3, 12.

[287] United States Government Accountability Office (2010), p. 12.

[288] United States Government Accountability Office (2010), p. 12.

Next to the federal agencies, there are numerous institutions which classify as museums receiving federal funds for the purposes of NAGPRA, Indian tribes and Native Hawaiian organizations. While NAGPRA adopts a broad definition of museum, this is counterbalanced with the protection afforded against claims "by an aggrieved party or for claims of breach of fiduciary duty, public trust, or violations of state law that are inconsistent with NAGRPA's provisions."[289]

In terms of enforcing the repatriation obligations imposed on museums, 25 USC §3007(a) and its accompanying regulations provide for civil penalties in the case of non-compliance to be assessed by the Secretary of Interior. §3007(b) lists a number of factors which should influence the amount of the penalty, namely "(1) the archaeological, historical, or commercial value of the item involved; (2) the damages suffered, both economic and noneconomic, by an aggrieved party, and (3) the number of violations that have occurred." Penalties are provided for failing to comply with the requirements of the act by i.e. not completing the required summaries on time (§10.12(b)(1)(ii)); refusing to repatriate human remains, funerary objects, sacred objects, or objects of cultural patrimony to a lineal descendant or culturally affiliated Indian tribe or Native Hawaiian (unless justified under exemptions specified in §10.10(c));[290] not consulting with traditional religious leaders[291] etc. Each failure constitutes a separate violation[292] and—upon determination by the SOI that the institution of a civil penalty action is the appropriate remedy[293]—carries a minimum fine.[294]

In terms of compliance, it should be highlighted that numerous museums have cooperated with tribal organizations and that NAGPRA has indeed led to new partnerships. On the other hand, as Brown and Bruchac highlight, individual museums have responded to the imposed obligations under NAGPRA by restricting access to information and shifting cultural interpretations.[295] Other problems arise due to the toxicity of the objects after a long time of fumigation while in storage, which can hinder the repatriation of sacred objects for revitalization purposes.[296]

The implementation of the act has not only been challenging for museums and federal agencies but also for the tribes themselves. Repatriation has challenged tribes to find new traditions to address reburials hitherto not necessary. Cultural rejuvenation is challenging and some tribes may and have decided against repatriation and

[289] McManamon and Nordby (1992), p. 239.

[290] 43 C.F.R. §10.12(b)(1)(v) (2020).

[291] 43 C.F.R. §10.12(b)(1)(vii) (2020).

[292] 43 C.F.R. §10.12(b)(2) (2020).

[293] 43 C.F.R. §10.12(d)(2)(iii) (2020).

[294] 43 C.F.R. § 10.12(g)(2) (2020) implies a minimum of 25% of the museum's annual budget or $6955 (whichever is less) with the potential for the Secretary to add an additional sum that is decided taking several factors into account. Depending on the circumstances § 10.12(g)(4) creates a possibility for a penalty reduction as well.

[295] Brown and Bruchac (2006), p. 198.

[296] Brown and Bruchac (2006), p. 1987.

reburial in the case of human remains.[297] Challenges have also arisen where tribes have become Christian in the meantime and have had to mitigate the tension between past and present cultural practices.[298] Tensions can also arise between different tribal groups, not only in relation to a specific object but also regarding past traditions and histories, as was the case for example in Hawaii with tensions arising between Hui Mālama I Nā Kūpuna O Hawa'i Nei and other Hawaiian groups.[299]

4.4.5.2 NAGPRA in Numbers

Official annual reports published by the NPS can help to gain an overview of both the scope of the dislocation, the number of repatriations and connected costs. In its aggregate report for the period 1990–2017, the size of the operations under NAGPRA become apparent:

In its aggregate numbers for the period of 1990–2017 on repatriation, the NPS reported 185,475 sets of human remains that were listed in NAGPRA inventories, over 1.5 million associated funerary objects that were listed in notices of inventory completion, 5189 sacred objects and 1668 objects of mixed sacred/cultural patrimony attribution in notices of intent to repatriate.[300] That makes it almost 7000 objects of a (mixed) sacred nature that were covered by notices of intent to repatriate, and the process is still ongoing. This is not surprising given the numbers of objects that are at stake. In the fiscal year 2017, NAGPRA registered 53 sacred objects listed in notices of intent to repatriate and six sacred objects/objects of cultural patrimony were listed.[301] In addition, new summaries were recorded and old summaries were amended. Over the past 27 years, 101.21 million was requested under the NAGRPA grant scheme, with slightly less than 50% being awarded to both tribes and museums (48.45 million).[302] Initial estimations ranged from between $20 million and $50 million for a range of over 5 years, observing "the range is broad because of the uncertainty regarding the cost of compiling an accurate inventory of Native American remains."[303] Overall, the initial fear of museums that NAGPRA would result in an emptying out of museums did not come to pass. By 2017, 34% of human remains inventoried were found to be culturally affiliated with present-day Indian tribes or

297 Brown and Bruchac (2006), p. 209.

298 Brown and Bruchac (2006), p. 209.

299 Traced by Johnson (2004).

300 National Park Service, US Department of the Interior, Fiscal Year 2017 Report National NAGPRA Program [For the period October 1, 2017–September 30, 2017], p. 2.

301 National Park Service, US Department of the Interior, Fiscal Year 2017 Report National NAGPRA Program [For the period October 1, 2017–September 30, 2017], p. 3.

302 Including numbers from 2018, the updated 2019 compilation by National NAGPRA including recipients and awards available via https://www.nps.gov/subjects/nagpra/previously-awarded-grants.htm. In 2017 46.81 National Park Service, US Department of the Interior, Fiscal Year 2017 Report National NAGPRA Program [For the period October 1, 2017–September 30, 2017], p. 2.

303 Marsh (1992), p. 101.

Native Hawaiian organizations. The majority of remains that are unaffiliated (87%) are in museum holdings (rather than Federal agencies).[304] Of course, the numbers given by NPS are only indicative, since the agency has no numbers on final repatriations.[305] Instead, it only received the notices which agencies/museums are obliged to publish in the Federal Register under §10.10(a)(3) read in conjunction with §10.8. This is then another potential addition to repatriation models, namely, to incorporate a duty to gather (and submit) all relevant data to be able to improve implementation throughout the lifetime of the repatriation model.

Under the civil enforcement sections provided for in NAGPRA, as amended and accompanying regulations, in roughly 20 years, 127 letters "alleging one or more failure(s) to comply involving 115 entities" were submitted. 53 entities were investigated, 20 museums were found not to have complied on at least one count. Only eight museums were fined with the evaluation of an additional four still pending at the time of the report.[306]

4.4.5.3 International Returns Under NAGPRA

As was explained above, NAGPRA applies to domestic Indigenous communities only. Canadian First Nations cannot reclaim their cultural heritage or related ancestral remains which have been moved to U.S. holding institutions as they do not classify as tribes under the respective legal provisions. However, there have been instances of noteworthy cooperation between tribes, museums and Canadian First Nations. For example, Native American tribes such as the Nooksack have requested the return of sacred cultural property under NAGPRA from the museum and returned it to Canadian communities, such as the Stó:lō.[307] This took roughly 15 years of cooperation between the tribes and a reframing of the claim from a request to repatriate human remains to reclaiming the statute as object, but ultimately the stone representation of T'xwelatse returned to the Stó:lō.[308] This shows that the line between international and intra-national can be more fluid in practice than one might expect on the basis of the legislation.

[304] National Park Service, US Department of the Interior, Fiscal Year 2017 Report National NAGPRA Program [For the period October 1, 2017–September 30, 2017], p. 4.

[305] National Park Service, US Department of the Interior, Fiscal Year 2017 Report National NAGPRA Program [For the period October 1, 2017–September 30, 2017], p. 6.

[306] National Park Service, US Department of the Interior, Fiscal Year 2017 Report National NAGPRA Program [For the period October 1, 2017–September 30, 2017], pp. 7–8.

[307] Schaepe and T'xwelátse (2018).

[308] Schaepe and T'xwelátse (2018), p. 27.

4.4.6 Evaluation of NAGPRA

4.4.6.1 Initial Hopes

At the time NAGPRA was adopted, several academics[309] and legislators[310] highlighted that NAGPRA represented a national consensus on the protection of Indigenous burial sites and the repatriation of remains and sacred objects. The then chair of the Society for American Archaeology Task Force on Reburial and Repatriation described the compromise achieved as "legislation we can live with".[311] The BLM, one of the agencies discharged with its implementation, hoped for NAGPRA to result both in closer working relationships between agencies and Native Americans as well as new interpretations of archaeological material.[312]

One positive side-effect of the discussions surrounding NAGPRA, already at the time of its adoption, was the realization that more needed to happen on the state level. Once the scope of the past dislocations and continuous grave looting was in the public eye and, given the lack of application of NAGPRA to numerous burial sites located on private and state lands,[313] there was a clear need for legislative action. States reacted in different ways: some states, such as California, copied NAGPRA into state law; others created unmarked burials protection for Native American burials, such as Nevada; some, such as Louisiana, created comprehensive unmarked burials protection schemes and others did not take action.[314] This outcome gives hope for future repatriations in other countries, even in the case of international repatriations. Once investigations into the history of collections begin, repositories are checked and the actual numbers of accumulated items become apparent, chances are that this will trigger more reactions beyond what might have been mandated in the law when the scale of the issue was unknown.

NAGRPA also represented a step forward in terms of bridging U.S. common law and Indigenous customary law and traditions. This includes both its incorporation of Indigenous customary law through the definition of sacred objects in §3001(3)(C) (discussed in Sect. 4.4.2.3 above), and the incorporation of oral history as documentary evidence.[315]

---

[309] Strickland (1992), p. 176.

[310] McCain (1992), p. 5.

[311] Keith W Kintigh as cited by Marsh (1992), p. 103.

[312] Stumpf (1992), pp. 303–304.

[313] Seidemann (2010), p. 199.

[314] Seidemann (2010), p. 200.

[315] Babcock (2012), p. 59 Babcock observes "Interestingly, the Native American Graves Protection and Repatriation Act (NAGPRA) accomplishes statutorily what US courts have been largely unwilling to do; namely putting oral history on an equal footing with documentary evidence. The statue makes storytelling part of the adjudicative process."

4.4.6.2 Congressional and Tribal Evaluation Studies After 20 Years

The Makah Indian Tribe and the National Association of Tribal Historic Preservation Officers published a report in 2008 with a focus on the implementation of NAGPRA by federal agencies [NATHPO report]. The report's main finding focused on insufficient federal agency compliance with NAGPRA. It highlighted a significant backlog in the publication of notices of inventory completion, a lack of standardization and oversight.[316] As factors identified by officials for this result it found: uncertainties and challenges during consultation, insufficient resources, insufficient training of officials, and lack of administrative resources.[317]

The study also recommended[318] a number of steps to be taken which are valuable lessons for other repatriation schemes that look to NAGPRA as a model: many recommendations concerned the need for a clear oversight structure that could monitor compliance and which would be given the information necessary, the need to identify and publish responsible NAGPRA contacts for each agency, the need for more training and funding.[319] Lastly, by means of questionnaires, the report also yielded some (non-representative) views of tribal NAGPRA practitioners. Experiences under NAGPRA appear mixed. Generally, positive reviews were given where individuals experienced governmental officials as open to learn and culturally sensitive. On the level of enforcement, specifically enforcement of unexcavated heritage sites, the evaluation was more negative: 44% believed that the Federal government had not acted responsibly in its duty to protect burials located on federal land, while 31% believed that it had.[320] An interesting result of the study was that both federal officials and tribal respondents were concerned with the looting of unexcavated materials and both reported on positive experiences with the other party: tribal respondents *inter alia* reported favorably on respectful behavior in both treatment and repatriation;[321] federal agency officials reported favorably

---

[316] Makah Indian Tribe and National Association of Tribal Historic Preservation Officers (2008), pp. 30, 31.

[317] Makah Indian Tribe and National Association of Tribal Historic Preservation Officers (2008), p. 24 Interestingly, poor relations between the agency and tribe was only raised once.

[318] Generally speaking, the recommendations were categorized into six general themes: knowledge of process and responsibilities; access to information for Indigenous parties; consultation could be further improved, insufficient resources both for Indigenous claimants and federal agencies; lack of information sharing, reporting standards and evidentiary standards for finding cultural affiliation; insufficient training and technology, Makah Indian Tribe and National Association of Tribal Historic Preservation Officers (2008), pp. 42–45.

[319] Makah Indian Tribe and National Association of Tribal Historic Preservation Officers (2008), pp. 45–49.

[320] Makah Indian Tribe and National Association of Tribal Historic Preservation Officers (2008), p. 20.

[321] Makah Indian Tribe and National Association of Tribal Historic Preservation Officers (2008), p. 24.

on the knowledge of Indigenous partners and positive relationships with Native Americans.[322]

Apparently, in response to the NATHPO and Makah Indian Tribe report,[323] the Chairmen of the Committee on Indian Affairs and the Committee on Natural Resources charged the United States Government Accountability Office [GAO] with the task to determine "the extent to which federal agencies have complied with NAGPRA's requirements for their historical collections; (2) activities taken by the Review Committee to fulfil its role under NAGPRA and what challenges, if any, it faces; (3) actions taken by the NAGPRA Program Office to fulfil its responsibilities under NAGPRA; and (4) extent to which federal agencies reported repatriating Native American human remains and objects."[324] The GAO report, in summary, confirmed that key federal agencies still have not fully complied with the act (after 20 years), criticized the NAGPRA Program Office on several counts and gave a number of recommendations to improve the act's implementation.

As far as agency compliance was concerned, some of the failures in compliance can be explained by the size of the challenge faced. As GAO observed, federal agencies had been assembling collections since the 1800s, "with items numbering in the millions".[325] The workload to distill which parts of the collection fell under the scope of NAGPRA even without the inventory/summary process was considerable. The sources for the materials varied, Forest Services indicated activities that were not initiated by the agency itself but by museums or universities as the main source.[326] By contrast, the Department of Interior "with its land-management agencies – has the largest collection outside of the Smithsonian Institution, with an estimated 146 million objects and documents that cover archaeology as well as disciplines such as art and zoology" which had to be reviewed to distill the cultural items that fell under the scope of the act.[327] To further complicate matters for many agencies, cultural items were held not by the agency but by non-federal institutions spread over multiple locations. In the case of BLM, the collection was spread between "3 BLM facilities and 121 other repositories".[328] A review conducted in 2009 by the Interior Inspector General reported that its "agencies' collections are held in 625 Interior facilities and at least 1,020 non-Interior facilities".[329] To an outsider, the sheer scale of the inventory and summary process (indicated in table below) alone would appear next to impossible.

---

[322] Makah Indian Tribe and National Association of Tribal Historic Preservation Officers (2008), p. 26.

[323] United States Government Accountability Office (2010), p. 2.

[324] United States Government Accountability Office (2010), p. 3.

[325] United States Government Accountability Office (2010), p. 5.

[326] United States Government Accountability Office (2010), p. 5.

[327] United States Government Accountability Office (2010), p. 5.

[328] United States Government Accountability Office (2010), p. 5.

[329] United States Government Accountability Office (2010), p. 8.

Agency personnel also indicated other reasons for the substantial delays in compliance, predominantly lack of financial resources—NAGPRA grants were available to museums and tribes not federal agencies—and other agency priorities due to their mandate.[330] The BIA, for example, indicated that one curator was responsible for an estimated 5.7 million items in its holdings.[331]

In reviewing the work conducted by the NAGPRA Program Office, GAO criticized six points: First, it found inconsistencies between the list of federally recognized tribes maintained by the BIA and by the NAGPRA Program Office.[332] As an aside, as was discussed above, the definition and official federal recognition of an Indigenous community is in itself a problematic process that is far from transparent.[333] GAO found that the publication of notices of items was not satisfactory and consultation was lacking at times.[334] The NAGPRA Program Office also failed in its support of the nomination process of new Review Committee members by insufficiently screening nominations.[335] The Review Committee in turn at times acted outside of its mandate, i.e. by recommending repatriation of culturally unidentifiable human remains to tribes that were not federally recognized. It should be pointed out, however, that, in these cases, the remains were 'culturally unidentifiable', because they were in effect culturally affiliated with non-federally recognized tribes.[336] This reinforces the criticism above, namely that, to make repatriation dependent on federal recognition is questionable, both legally, in light of international legal standards, and historically, in light of the convoluted recognition strategies and programs of the federal government. However, the Department of the Interior indicated that, while it considered the voluntary transfer of unidentifiable human remains to non-recognized tribes permissible, to mandate their return would be not only to violate NAGPRA but also "be contrary to … government-to-government relationship between the United States and federally recognized tribes".[337] On this point, one may wonder in how far this concern of transfers to non-federally recognized tribes is valid when one government in this "government-to-government" relationship has the power to unilaterally award status and to terminate it, and has done both multiple times. It is also somewhat ironic that one of the weaknesses of the Review Committee (its inability to make binding recommendations) actually turned

[330] United States Government Accountability Office (2010), p. 28.

[331] United States Government Accountability Office (2010), p. 28.

[332] United States Government Accountability Office (2010), pp. 14–15. At issue was the (non-) recognition of corporations established pursuant to the Alaska Native Claims Settlement Act.

[333] See Sect. 4.3.3 above.

[334] United States Government Accountability Office (2010), pp. 19–26 Some of the insufficiencies appears to have been caused by a confusion between the differences for inventories and summaries in this regard.

[335] United States Government Accountability Office (2010), pp. 42–44 Changes have been made in the early 2000s in the nomination process, but other problems apparently remained up to the point of the GAO study.

[336] United States Government Accountability Office (2010), p. 34.

[337] United States Government Accountability Office (2010), p. 79.

out to be a strength in this matter. GAO also criticized that the Review Committee had been perceived to favor tribal interest by officials from museums and scientific organizations. Individual Committee members acknowledged a potential bias and "regarded it as understandable because they believe the intent of NAGPRA was to serve Native American interests and overcome years of bias against tribal interests by museums and scientific organizations."[338] Again, the composition of the Committee was set up to represent divergent interests equally and the author concurs with the Committee members that the legislative goal of the act was very clearly restorative, as was supported by the historic background and the legislative history of the act. GAO also highlighted that, as a federal advisory committee, the Review Committee should be balanced and independent.[339]

The insufficiencies detected by GAO were partially due to the framework set in place by NAGPRA and the regulations. There was no indication of a publication deadline for notices[340] of inventories or notices of intent to repatriate in case of summaries. Problems also arose out of case law (notably Bonnichsen as already discussed).[341] The Review Committee recommended amendments to address these concerns (i.e. amending the definition of Native American),[342] which were not incorporated in the act itself. Another criticism was that no centralized data gathering on repatriations had been undertaken by the agencies.[343] Data was thus lacking to facilitate the monitoring processes. The GAO report also highlighted that, while NAGPRA foresaw civil penalties in the case of the non-compliance of museums, no such penalty applied to federal agencies.[344]

4.4.6.3 NAGPRA: Positive Effects and Drawbacks

NAGPRA sought to reconcile very different communities and interests and had to grapple with amorphous and evolving questions on cultural identity. In light of all the difficulties one is confronted with when considering repatriation, NAGPRA should be viewed as a success. It (finally) provided some legislative protection for unexcavated Indigenous remains and heritage backed by criminal sanctions. Given the diverse jurisdictions and competences the protection provided is far from complete.[345] However, it did improve the protection of unexcavated materials significantly, which is crucial given the lack of adequate export controls on cultural

---

[338] United States Government Accountability Office (2010), p. 36.

[339] United States Government Accountability Office (2010), p. 37.

[340] United States Government Accountability Office (2010), p. 24.

[341] Bonnichsen v United States 357 F.3d 962 & 367 F.3d 864 United States Court of Appeals, Ninth Circuit.

[342] United States Government Accountability Office (2010), p. 30.

[343] United States Government Accountability Office (2010), p. 47.

[344] United States Government Accountability Office (2010), p. 53.

[345] Critically, Cryne (2009), pp. 117–118.

heritage elsewhere in U.S. domestic law.[346] It also forced museums to take stock of their collections and confront difficult gaps in their collection history.[347] Senator Daniel K. Inouye, one of the original sponsors of the act, reflected in 2008: "[NAGPRA] is one of the most important statutes enacted to restore honor to Native Americans, Alaska Natives and Native Hawaiians... While there is no question that the Act represents a huge step forward in setting the proper stage for repatriation, there remain areas to be clarified".[348] Skrydstrup has emphasized that the framework "has had direct implications for archaeological and museum practice in the United States".[349] He highlights that, rather than limiting archaeological research (as was feared), publications have increased and a debate has sprung up within the discipline itself as to the methods it employs: "In other words, today it is almost inconceivable to do archaeology and exhibit Native American culture in the United States without the participation of Native American communities. Beyond the direct practical implications at the disciplinary level of archaeology and museum studies, the debate has centred on 'identity politics', cultural survival, revitalization processes and the political sovereignty of descent communities."[350] This has been echoed by anthropologists, who hope that new collaborations which have arisen as a result of NAGPRA "will produce better anthropology than all the thousands of bones and grave goods held by the nations' museums."[351]

Under NAGPRA, museums are obliged to repatriate if the substantive criteria are fulfilled, and this is backed up by civil penalties. From the numbers available, it also does seem as if a significant amount of sacred objects have been repatriated to date[352]—at least by museums.[353] NAGPRA thus was effective in achieving the physical repatriation of a large quantity of Indigenous heritage and human remains. While mandating repatriation, it left actors some legal space to realize that repatriation issues must be solved in context, on a case-by-case basis. These processes can (and as was in the case in the U.S.) sometimes have to be 'jump-started' by a legal process, but the outcome cannot be forced in a uniform manner.[354] An important contribution of NAGPRA was to push institutions into confronting their collections in a more systematic manner and to provide minimum procedural obligations. All the while, the act leaves other avenues open if they are agreed upon by museums and Indian tribes or Native Hawaiian organizations respectively.

---

[346] Nafziger and Dobkins (1999), p. 77.

[347] Nafziger and Dobkins (1999), pp. 84–86.

[348] Makah Indian Tribe and National Association of Tribal Historic Preservation Officers (2008), p. 4 onwards.

[349] Skrydstrup (2010), p. 65.

[350] Skrydstrup (2010), p. 65.

[351] Brown and Bruchac (2006), p. 216.

[352] See Sect. 4.4.5.2 NAGPRA in numbers.

[353] Critically on agency implementation see reports Sect. 4.4.6.2 above and Cryne (2009).

[354] Nafziger and Dobkins (1999), p. 91.

Another important lesson of the act was the realization that consultation and repatriation takes time and significant resources (time, money and people).[355] Financial resources need to be made available to Indigenous claimants, holding institutions and other entities that are obliged to comply with such schemes for a considerable period of time. Identification, consultation and repatriation will take time even with these resources. As NAGPRA highlighted, it is important to realize that such a framework, once set in place, in effect sets an ongoing process into motion. To facilitate repatriation of not just the occasional object but to achieve a systematic inventory system and a consultation and repatriation process requires the provision of sufficient funds over a long period of time. Because of the complexity of establishing a link between heritage and community, questions on access to information also arise. In the case of the NAGPRA Program Office, several databases comprising repatriation data were compiled that are available to the public and searchable by institution as well as tribe/organization.[356] Moreover, to ensure that the programme operates at its best, an obligation to collect data on repatriation processes should be imposed on each agency, and the data needs to be streamlined to facilitate regular programme-wide overviews. It also has to be realized that, even where there is a desire to repatriate within the museum and funds are available, repatriation may be delayed for some time for reasons that are internal to the community in question. Reasons may be a lack of cultural protocols to deal with such a situation,[357] potential spiritual harm that could arise if the object is reintegrated and many more.

NAGPRA has also triggered critical reflection on established legal doctrine. Carpenter, Katyal and Riley emphasize that NAGPRA has allowed for another understanding of the role of property (rights) for group identity. They highlight "certain indigenous cultural property is inextricably bound up with peoplehood, and as such is necessary to a people's identity formation and is nonfungible",[358] which is recognized within the NAGPRA mechanism. Varner, Penneys and Amineddoleh, relying on the reports of the National NAGPRA Program described above, highlight that the impact of the compliance process has been profound, with the process still ongoing.[359] They conclude positively "NAGPRA is not an example of a law whose effect is the opposite of what Congress intended. Rather Congress may proudly claim, in the words of Morris Udall, '[i]n the larger scope of history, this is a very small thing. In the smaller scope of conscience, it may be the biggest thing we have ever done.'"[360] NAGPRA representatives from the Caddo Nation observed "[w]ith

[355] Nafziger and Dobkins (1999), pp. 91–92.

[356] Databases overview available at https://www.nps.gov/subjects/nagpra/databases.htm [last accessed 18.08.2021].

[357] For example, reported by Forest Service NAGPRA staff United States Government Accountability Office (2010), p. 49.

[358] Carpenter et al. (2009), p. 1090.

[359] Varner et al. (2015).

[360] Varner et al. (2015).

the help of the Native American Graves Protection and Repatriation Act . . . we have continued to not only claim and rename our past but also have asserted the identity of the Caddo as being the 'Real Chiefs' governing our history and culture." Museum representatives have emphasized the act's potential for creating new relationships between museums and tribes.[361] These benefits give hope to those considering to adopt their own repatriation model. These benefits may be reaped in repatriation dialogues that are set against a different historical context, as long as procedural and substantive lessons are learned and implemented.

There are, however, a number of deficits to the act as adopted from which important lessons can be drawn. A clear problem within the NAGPRA framework is related to ancient remains and questions of their cultural affiliation in particular.[362] More generally, the question of how to determine cultural affiliation remains difficult. The Bonnichsen case and the 9th circuit interpretation of 'Native American' within the act has been remedied through the regulations, but it showcased some of the difficulties involved. Moreover, case law and surveys into the implementation of NAGPRA have shown how many difficulties courts and agencies can continue to have in accepting oral testimony as evidence on an equal level despite its incorporation into the Act. The bridging between Indigenous and non-Indigenous traditions and beliefs within the law remains difficult. An important lesson is the need to adopt clear guidelines on these matters together with any repatriation scheme (their lack was a reason for the delay in the inventory and summary process[363]). These need to be re-examined regularly, and personnel in institutions and agencies need to be trained specifically for the repatriation process.

Another problem within the act is its exclusion of Indigenous Peoples who have not been federally recognized. Limiting repatriation to federally recognized tribes allocates the power to decide who is Indigenous (and who is not) to the federal government. This is in violation of international standards on the Indigenous right to self-identification elaborated on in Chaps. 1 and 2. Given the importance of sacred objects and human remains for the realization of a number of cultural rights, this element can contribute to the violation of cultural rights, notably Art. 27 ICCPR and Art. 18 ICCPR, of tribes who are not recognized by the federal government. Incorporating governmental recognition as a requirement to repatriation schemes should be avoided in other repatriation schemes.

---

[361] Varner et al. (2015).

[362] See i.e. Tsosie (2012). Also, Nafziger and Dobkins (1999), pp. 93–94; Seidemann (2010); and Echo-Hawk and Zimmerman (2006).

[363] Nafziger and Dobkins (1999), pp. 83–84.

4.5 Legal Protection of Indigenous Religious Freedom and Its Role for Repatriation

4.5.1 Constitutional Rights and Indigenous Sacredness

4.5.1.1 Implications of Constitutional Structure

The focus of the Constitution on protecting individual freedoms from governmental infringement does not align well with the situation of American Indigenous individuals as subjects of multiple sovereign governmental entities (even if the power of those sovereignties differ). First, it protects them from state and federal intrusions not tribal governments.[364] This however does not entail the absence of individual rights, which are enshrined both in individual tribal constitutions and codes as well as in federal statutes, for example the Indian Civil Rights Act.[365] Second, while the federal government is constrained in the exercise of its plenary powers by constitutional provisions, this protection has not always been respected or upheld by the courts. Difficulties have arisen, for instance, with respect to equal protection under the law in the past. As one example, equal protection was used to justify assimilation notably in the termination policy in the 1950s.[366] Existing inequalities therefore require remedial legal acts today that provide preferential benefits to Native Americans[367] and that are distinct from (and additional to) any concerns of differential treatment arising out of the government-to-government relationship. The right to equal protection under the law accommodates such remedial measures, as it merely requires "persons similarly situated be treated alike under the law."[368] Different situations then justify differentiated legal treatment. One constitutional right that has proven difficult, also in more recent times, is the free exercise of religion and concomitant protection from governmental interference.[369] Case law on the first amendment and the establishment clause discussed below demonstrates this fact.

[364] Bill of rights and the 14th Amendment do not apply to tribes out of their own force Nevada v Hicks, 533 U.S. 353 (2001), at 383. See Newton et al. (2005), p. 915 This also had consequences for individual religious freedom, for instance when tribal judges prohibited the performance of sun dances, see Bradford (2002), pp. 44–46.

[365] Newton et al. (2005), p. 916.

[366] Newton et al. (2005), p. 923.

[367] Newton et al. (2005), p. 920.

[368] Newton et al. (2005), p. 921.

[369] Newton et al. (2005), p. 919 Notably, "the special nature of tribal religions, the inseparability of religious and cultural activities, and the distinctive history and relationship between Indian nations and the federal government all contribute to the unusual legal issues."

4.5.1.2 Establishment Clause

The freedom of religion as protected by the first amendment can be a two-edged sword with respect to Indigenous individuals. One fundamental difficulty for Indigenous claimants in establishing a claim under the 1st amendment is the interconnectivity of many activities with their spiritual beliefs. It can therefore be difficult to distinguish the cultural from the religious for Western legal purposes. The repatriation of sacred objects can be linked to treaty provisions, cultural, religious and/or political rights.[370] This clause ("Congress shall make no law respecting an establishment of religion"), however, has caused concerns in connection with Indian rights on more than one occasion. Early Supreme Court cases suggested that the Establishment Clause prohibits any practice that aids one religion, prefers one over the other or aids all religions.[371] It similarly emphasized in Wisconsin v Yoder that "only those interests of the highest order and those not otherwise served can overbalance legitimate claims to the free exercise of religion."[372] This has changed somewhat over the years and "recent decisions have evidenced a greater sympathy for the view that the clause bars "preferential" governmental promotion of some religions but allows governmental promotion of all religion in general."[373] Disagreements on testing a measure under the establishment clause exist, but the *Lemon* tests "remain the primary standard of Establishment Clause validity."[374] According to these tests: (1) neither the purpose of the enactment (2) nor its primary effect of the enactment should advance or inhibit religion. (3) Neither should it lead to an "excessive governmental entanglement with religion".[375] In analysing Supreme Court jurisprudence, the congressional research service differentiated between cases of intentional governmental discrimination which are under strict scrutiny and other cases. In case of the latter, the authors describe the court applying "a standard of formal neutrality".[376]

With regard to the repatriation of sacred objects, it could be observed that this provides the precondition for a free exercise of religion. NAGPRA, if interpreted as governmental support of religion, could, however, have been problematic from the perspective of the establishment clause. Nafziger and Dobkins have rightly observed in this regard that this focus on Native American religion "may be justified . . . as a rectification of past wrongs that resulted in the wrongful takings of such items."[377] In this sense, NAGPRA seeks to remedy previous violations of the establishment clause both in terms of the government sponsoring of looting, the inadequate

---

[370] Newton et al. (2005), p. 937.

[371] Everson v Board of Education 330 US 1 (1947).

[372] Everson v Board of Education 330 US 1, 15 (1947).

[373] Garcia et al. (2017), p. 1074 S.Doc.112-9.

[374] Garcia et al. (2017), p. 1076.

[375] Garcia et al. (2017), p. 1075.

[376] Garcia et al. (2017), p. 1077.

[377] Nafziger and Dobkins (1999), pp. 97–98.

protection of burial sites of Native American religions in comparison to other religions, government-supported missionary programmes etc.

4.5.1.3 Burdening/Infringing on the Free Exercise of Religion

The second element of the 1st amendment at issue is the protection it affords to the free exercise of religion. The Supreme Court understanding of the protection that it offers against governmental interference has been somewhat fluid, and the tests that have been applied have varied over time. Key concerns have been whether the measure specifically targeted religious practices or it was the incidental effect of a generally applicable law, whether the measure enacted a substantial burden on the central observation of religious belief,[378] and whether it served a compelling governmental interest and constituted the least restrictive means of doing so.[379]

Employment v Smith set the standard that "[T]he right of free exercise does not relieve an individual of the obligation to comply with a 'valid and neutral law of general applicability on the ground that the law proscribes (or prescribes) conduct that his religion prescribes (or proscribes)."[380] The court highlighted that, as long as prohibiting the exercise of religion is not the purpose of the measure but "merely the incidental effect of a generally applicable and otherwise valid provision", the First Amendment had not been violated. It is noteworthy that the judges considered that the accommodation of religious practices which were restricted due to generally applicable rules have to be realized within "the political process".[381] Such accommodations can be very difficult to achieve in the case of minority religions such as Native American traditions, where the political processes are, by composition and procedure, majoritarian. Congress reacted by adopting the Religious Freedom Restoration Act (RFRA) to restore the compelling interest test where government substantially burdened the free exercise of religion.[382] Section 2000bb-1 prohibits government from substantially burdening the exercise of religion (even if it is a result of a generally applicable law). Exempted measures have to further a compelling governmental interest (2000bb-1(b)(1)) and be the least restrictive measure available for that purpose (2000bb-1(b)(2)). Initially, Congress enacted RFRA to limit both state and federal governments, which the Supreme Court found to be

378 Garcia et al. (2017), p. 1132.

379 Garcia et al. (2017), pp. 1136–1137.

380 Employment Div v Smith, 494 US 872, 879 (1990) quoting Lee.

381 Employment Div v Smith, 494 US 872, 890 (1990). See also Garcia et al. (2017), pp. 1124–1125.

382 42 USC 2000bb (b) "The purposes of this chapter are- (1) to restore the compelling interest test as set forth in Sherbert v Verner, 374 U.S. 398 (1963) and Wisconsin v Yoder, 406 U.S. 205 (1972) and to guarantee its application in all cases where free exercise of religion is substantially burdened; and (2) to provide a claim or defense to persons whose religious exercise is substantially burdened by government."

unconstitutional.[383] Since then, the applicability of RFRA to federal actions has been confirmed[384] and the compelling interest test applies. Moreover, Congress adopted another mirroring act to apply to state actions in the areas it could base this newer legislation.[385] SCOTUS has accepted the newer legislation.[386]

However, the case law on permissible limitations on the first amendment does not seem to be applied uniformly or in such a manner that one may rely on a test as laid out above to be able to predict the outcome of case. As one author has aptly summarized: "Those hoping for consistent application of a clearly stated principle in cases implicating federal constitutional or statutory law are unlikely to see those hopes realized. Instead, the Court will only make an increasingly chaotic area of law even more chaotic."[387]

At first glance, this may have little to do with questions of how to repatriate cultural heritage. However, the restriction imposed by case law on the free exercise of Native Americans does have an impact on whether, and if so how, they may exercise their religious practices today. NAGPRA required the contemporary use of religious objects as a basis to reclaim religious heritage. Case law has not served adherents to Indigenous religious practices well and if the hope behind NAGPRA was to remedy past assimilatory practices and to facilitate the Indigenous revitalization of practices, then cases such as Smith and Lyng showcase the many difficulties practitioners still face. Repatriation models cannot remedy this. However, expectations of what is necessary to evidence religious practices to substantiate repatriation should be accordingly low. This is especially true for those who are considering implementing a comparable requirement in the case of international repatriations. This is not advisable given the multitude of challenges tribes may face in their practice and the fact that the government enacting the model is not the one that can alter the measure limiting the religious exercise of an affected community.

4.5.2 AIRFA

This chapter examined NAGPRA as well as the difficult relationship between U.S. domestic law and Indigenous cultural and religious distinctiveness. As was highlighted in Sect. 4.2, Indigenous traditional religions have not fared well within

[383] City of Boerne v Flores 521 U.S. 507 (1997).

[384] See i.e. in Gonzales v O Centro Espirita Beneficente Uniao do Vegetal 546 U.S. 418 (2006).

[385] Religious Land Use and Institutionalized Persons Act of 2000, § 2 et seq., 42 U.S.C.A. § 2000cc et seq based on Spending and Commerce Clause.

[386] For example in Holt v. Hobbs 574 U.S. 352 (2015).

[387] Strasser (2016), p. 684 Going on to observe: "Both individuals and the country as a whole deserve more from the court. If history is any guide, however, they are unlikely to get it."

U.S. law. This is true for laws passed by Congress, including the 1883 development of the Indian Religious Crimes Code to prohibit ceremonial activities in the past,[388] as well as before courts today.[389] Examples that received a lot of attention are the Supreme Court case, Employment Division v Smith, where the religious use of peyote was at issue or Lyng, where construction threatened sacred sites. The relationship between tribes, congress and courts remains troublesome. Positive examples of (minority) opinions criticizing the dangers to Indigenous traditions and acts strengthening rights other than NAGPRA exist.

In recent decades, Congress has expressly followed a policy of protecting and preserving the Indigenous right to "believe, express and exercise [their] traditional religious freedom".[390] An early example of this is the 1978 Joint congressional resolution and the linked adoption of the American Indian Religious Freedom Act,[391] adopted after Indigenous activism had been focussing on religious freedom since the early 1970s.[392] Frustration with difficulties with enforcement and in reaction to cases such as Lyng and Smith led to amendments in the 1990s.[393] In addition, in 1996, Executive Order 13-2007 was issued which focused on the protection of sacred sites.[394] Nevertheless, the protection of the Indigenous right to free exercise of their religious beliefs continues to be insufficient, which is at least partially due to case law that remains valid precedence. Examining the case law between 1978 and 2002, Bradford observed that "Indian claimants . . . [had] not won a single case of religious freedom".[395]

4.5.2.1 American Indian Religious Freedom Act (AIRFA) and Repatriation

Lyng brought the lack of sufficient protection of Indigenous religious practices to the forefront, it is discussed further in the next section on access to and use of sacred sites. It showed that the 1st Amendment and the AIRFA resolution by themselves

---

388 Irwin (1997), p. 35.

389 Allison Dussias summarized: "when Native Americans have turned to the federal courts for protection against infringements upon their right to the free exercise of religion, they have faced an uphill battle." See Dussias (1995), p. 636.

390 Newton et al. (2005), p. 108.

391 SJ Res. 102 (11.08.1978), Joint Resolution American Indian Religious Freedom, Public Law 95-341, adopting 42 USC 1996 adopted to remedy limitations that resulted out of Supreme Court decision in Smith.

392 AIRFA Task Force Report (1 year), Appendix A, Legislative History, at 106.

393 Duthu (2008), p. 18 "The act provided no substantive rights enforceable in court but it did lay an important foundation for subsequent legal developments that accorded more meaningful protections for tribal religious rights."

394 Newton et al. (2005), p. 108.

395 Bradford (2002), pp. 44–46.

were insufficient to protect Indigenous religious freedom adequately.[396] AIRFA was an important step on the road to the adoption of NAGPRA in that it—and the activism leading up to it—highlighted the inadequate protection of American Indian religious freedom. Moreover, the 1 year report required by Section 2 of the 1978 AIRFA provided an overview of the distinctiveness of Native American religious, drew attention to inadequate protection of burial sites, and framed AIRFA in reparative terms.[397] Tellingly, in 1979, in response to the concern that AIRFA was akin to the establishment of a religion, the report observed: "It does not constitute the establishment of a religion. The premises of Native tribal religions differ so fundamentally from the religions of the majority in perspective and practice that the traditional dangers against which the establishment clause guards do not exist."[398] Concerns based on the establishment clause were advanced against both AIRFA and NAGRA. The report also listed a summary of consultations. Close to 30 pages detail specific problems Indigenous groups or individuals faced all over the country in the exercise of their religious beliefs, ranging from threats to the resource base for a ceremony, over disturbances of cemeteries, damages or lack of access to sacred sites to problems relating to sacred objects.[399] With regard to the latter, a significant problem was a lack of access to materials needed (feathers, twigs), damage to plant or animal life, a prohibition of certain elements of traditions and problems for individuals crossing borders with sacred objects.[400] As an important prelude to NAGPRA, the consultations also highlighted problems that tribes faced relating to museums. These ranged from complaints about the existence of tribal artifacts in galleries or museums to museum possession of pipes, medicine bags and ceremonial objects, to their inappropriate display and refusals to grant repatriation requests.[401]

Beyond this initial impetus, AIRFA continues to be important to the repatriation of sacred objects for two reasons: it provides a minimum level of protection to Indigenous religious traditions that are dependent on repatriated sacred objects and, without the exercise of such practices, a requirement for their repatriation under NAGPRA would not be fulfilled. Section 1996 provides "[o]n and after August 11, 1978, it shall be the policy of the United States to protect and preserve for American Indians their inherent right of freedom to believe, express, and exercise the traditional religions of the American Indian, Eskimo, Aleut, and Native Hawaiians, including but not limited to access to sites, use and possession of sacred objects, and

[396] Dussias (1995), p. 638.

[397] AIRFA report 1979, at 23 "With the enactment of the American Indian Religious Freedom Act, our Nation is being afforded the opportunity to correct past injustices and to begin anew with regard to treatment of those who adhere to the tenets of traditional Native religions."

[398] Ibid, at 104.

[399] Ibid, at 235–262 [Appendix C].

[400] Ibid, at 252–256.

[401] Ibid, report at 256–257.

the freedom to worship through ceremonials and traditional rites." Section 1996 protects the religious use of peyote.

4.5.3 Access to and Use of Sacred Sites

One of the central cases with respect to Indigenous religious freedom in general and sacred sites, that was already mentioned, is Lyng.[402] The case concerned the paving of a section of road that led through a part of Six Rivers National Forest close to the Hoopa Valley Indian Reservation. A study of American Indian cultural and religious sites found that the entire area "is significant as an integral and indispensable part of Indian Religious conceptualization and practice" and that "successful use of the [area] is dependent upon . . . privacy, silence and an undisturbed natural setting." The study concluded in 1979 that any of the available routes "would cause serious and irreparable damage to the sacred areas which are an integral and necessary part of the belief systems and lifeway of Northwest California Indian peoples".[403] The study recommended that the road not be completed. In 1982 Forest Services declined the recommendation and selected a route that avoided archaeological sites and was removed from practice sites as far as possible.[404] Forest Services also adopted a management plan to allow for harvesting timber in this area of the forest, providing for one-half mile protective zones around the religious sites identified earlier.

Considering the First Amendment implications of the road construction, the Indigenous party argued that the Government's proposed actions would have severe adverse effects on the practice of their religion and that the burden on their religious practice is significant enough to violate the free exercise clause, unless it could be proven that there was a compelling need to complete the road. While the Supreme Court agreed that the beliefs held were sincere and that there would be severely adverse effects on exercising their religious beliefs,[405] it saw no need for a compelling interest test. The Court emphasized that, where the effects of a government program are incidental and where this may "make it more difficult to practice certain religions but which have no tendency to coerce individuals", there was no need for the government to provide a compelling justification for its acts.[406] Instead, the majority opinion saw no reason to distinguish Bowen v Roy and reiterated that "the Free Exercise Clause affords an individual protection from certain forms of governmental compulsion; it does not afford an individual a right to dictate the conduct of

[402] Richard E Lyng et al v Northwest Indian Cemetery Protective Association et al [1988] 485 U.S. 439.

[403] Ibid, at 442.

[404] Ibid, at 443.

[405] Ibid, at 447.

[406] Ibid, at 450.

the Government's internal procedures."[407] The majority added that "even if assume that . . . the G-O road will 'virtually destroy the . . . Indians' ability to practice their religion', the Constitution simply does not provide a principle that could justify upholding respondents' legal claims."[408] The court was critical of the emphasis in the claim on the need for undisturbed naturalness and highlighted that, to decide otherwise could arguably require "de facto beneficial ownership of some rather spacious tracts of public property" and that "[w]hatever rights the Indians may have to the use of the area, however, those rights do not divest the Government of its right to use what is, after all, *its* land."[409] In responding to the dissenting opinion of Justices Brennan Marhsall and Blackmun, the majority also emphasized that the protection offered by the First Amendment was protection from governmental action prohibiting free exercise, not from governmental action that frustrates or inhibits religious practice.[410]

The minority opinion disagreed on several points: first it highlighted the centrality of land-use to Indigenous religions and emphasized that the project could not be justified in compelling interest terms if that was attempted. It also criticized the majority's narrow reading of 'prohibiting' and judged the reading of the claimed violation as non-constitutional as "both unjustified and ultimately unpersuasive."[411] Justice Brennan observed: "I thus cannot accept the Court's premise that the form of the government's restraint on religious practice, rather than its effect, controls our constitutional analysis."[412] Lastly, the court was divided on whether or not Lyng was distinguishable from the precedent. The dissent concluded with a withering evaluation of the majority ruling as "[h]aving thus stripped respondents and all other Native Americans of any constitutional protection against perhaps the most serious threat . . . the Court assures us that nothing in its decision 'should be read to encourage governmental insensitivity to the religious needs of any citizen'. . . . It fails utterly to accord with the dictates of the First Amendment."[413] In Lyng the Court rejected the two-step test developed by lower federal courts (evidence of burden and balance of plaintiff's against government's interest).[414] Critics observed that the Court had both ignored

---

[407] Bowen v Roy 476 U.S. 693 (1986) at 699–700, cited in Richard E Lyng et al v Northwest Indian Cemetery Protective Association et al [1988] 485 U.S. 439, at 668.

[408] Richard E Lyng et al v Northwest Indian Cemetery Protective Association et al [1988] 485 U.S. 439, at 451–452.

[409] Ibid, at 453.

[410] Richard E Lyng et al v Northwest Indian Cemetery Protective Association et al [1988] 485 U.S. 439, at 456.

[411] Ibid, at 465–466. Also, at 468 "Ultimately, the Court's coercion test turns on a distinction between governmental actions that compel affirmative conduct inconsistent with religious belief, and those governmental actions that prevent conduct consistent with religious belief . . . such a distinction is without constitution significance. The crucial word . . . is "prohibit"."

[412] Ibid, at 467.

[413] Ibid, at 476–477.

[414] Marsh (1992), p. 108.

congressional policy as stated in AIRFA and that the case highlighted the difficulties faced by Indigenous religious practitioners in translating the importance of sites for judges "more familiar with religions in which sacred sites do not have comparable importance."[415] Lyng remains valid precedent.

Given that access to sacred sites remains insufficiently protected by jurisprudence, laws and policies protecting Indigenous access are even more important. Executive Order 13007, incorporated as 42 USC section 1996, requires agencies from the executive branch with statutory or administrative responsibility for the management of Federal lands to "(1) accommodate access to and ceremonial use of Indian sacred sites by Indian religious practitioners and (2) avoid adversely affecting the physical integrity of such sacred sites" "to the extent practicable, permitted by law, and not clearly inconsistent with essential agency functions". In addition, the secrecy of sites should be maintained by agencies "where appropriate". This Executive Order is supplemented by others on consultation and coordination[416] and the burial sites protection under NAGPRA. The National Park Service, for example, appears to have accommodated site-specific religious practices on federal lands in specific cases.[417] Dussias similarly highlights that a number of congressional and executive actions have resulted in federal land managements that "are at times based on the heightened sensitivity toward, and respect for, Indian religious needs".[418]

Both the introduction to this research in general and the introduction to this chapter have highlighted the need to consider the legal protection put in place for the exercise of Indigenous religions apart from the repatriation of sacred objects. This has been, predominantly, motivated by the question in how far the repatriation of sacred objects that pursues the revitalization of religious traditions can be successful where Indigenous religious practitioners remain in a position of inequality. In the US federal system, the picture of Indigenous religions is a mixed one. Legislative action has been slow to be developed (and extremely damaging in the past), but some important measures have been taken. Similarly, executive agencies appear to try for better relationships with Indigenous communities, even if the record may remain mixed. In turn some members of the judiciary appear more concerned with the notion of formal equality than substantive equality between religious practitioners.

[415] Dussias (1995), p. 637.

[416] Dussias (2012), p. 358.

[417] Newton et al. (2005), p. 942.

[418] Dussias (2012), p. 357.

4.6 Museum and Heritage Regulation

4.6.1 Federal Heritage Legislation[419]

4.6.1.1 Archaeological Resources Protection Act[420]

In 1979 ARPA replaced the Antiquities Act[421] as the main instrument aimed at the protection of unexcavated material for future generations.[422] It provides protection to an "irreplaceable part of the Nation's heritage"[423] by prohibiting the excavation or removal of 'archaeological resources' from public or Indian lands without a permit. Archaeological resources is broadly defined as "any material remains of past human life or activities" as long as it is over 100 years old and has 'archaeological interest' in line with the accompanying regulations[424] and is located on public or Indian lands.[425] Indian land is defined as "lands of Indian tribes, or Indian individuals" that is owned or controlled by the tribe or the individual and "which are either held in trust by the United States or subject to a restriction against alienation".[426] The

[419] The focus of this chapter rests on the analysis of NAGPRA and its role for the realization for Indigenous cultural and religious rights. There are numerous heritage instruments, some of which have a connection to NAGRPA. This section focusses on two NMAI and ARPA, the former because it has comparable repatriation sections the latter because it has an overlapping focus on the protection of unexcavated materials. The Indian Arts and Craft Act is excluded from consideration since it is focussed on the protection of newly produced crafts the National Historic Preservation Act is excluded because it focusses on the protection of immovable heritage. The NHPA provides for the protection of Indigenous sites ("traditional cultural sites") and for some measure of consultation under the s. 106 procedure in the case a federal undertaking might have an effect on a historic property. Moreover, the act has provided a space for Indigenous administration instead of federal officers for their heritage sites on tribal lands. For more information on the act see Newton et al. (2005), pp. 1252–1260.

[420] 16 U.S.C. §470aa to 470mm (2019) [Chapter 1B Archaeological Resource Protection].

[421] Commentators found ARPA's predecessor ineffective and the Ninth Circuit held that portions of it were unconstitutionally vague which led to the ARPA being adopted by Congress in 1979, see Marsh (1992), p. 128 The Antiquities Act of 1906 had intended to protect heritage from being looted, see Trope and Echo-Hawk (1992), p. 42.

[422] 16 USC 470aa(b) "The purpose of this chapter is to secure, for the present and future benefit of the American people, the protection of archaeological resources and sites which are on public lands and Indian lands, and to foster increased cooperation and exchange of information between governmental authorities, the professional archaeological community, and private individuals having collections of archaeological resources and data which were obtained before October 31, 1979".

[423] 16 U.S.C. 470aa(a)(1) (2019).

[424] 16 U.S.C. 470bb(1) (2019).

[425] In one case, U.S. v Gerber [1993] 999 F.2d 1112, 114 the Seventh Circuit extended the Act to private lands by stating that a criminal conviction under 470ee(c) [editorial: for trafficking archaeological resources interstate or across national borders in violation of State or local law] was not limited to public or Indian lands.

[426] 16 U.S.C. 470bb(4) (2019).

definition is thus narrower than the one adopted in NAGRPA.[427] There is, however, a certain overlap between ARPA, whose definition includes Indigenous heritage as archaeological resources (and prior to the adoption of NAGPRA this included Indigenous human remains) and NAGPRA's protection of Indigenous burial sites and unexcavated cultural resources therein. As NAGPRA is the more recent of the two, it amends ARPA in this respect.[428] ARPA sought to improve the deficiencies in the Antiquities Act, both in concretizing the definition of the protected heritage and increasing the penalties for violating its provision.[429]

With regard to Indigenous cultural heritage, ARPA includes several mechanisms: a permit for excavations or the removal of resources located on Indian lands. Specifically, the "consent of the Indian or Indian tribe owning having such lands" is required and more specific terms may be set.[430] Tribal members can excavate or remove resources on their land without a permit if tribal law regulates the excavation or removal, otherwise a permit including tribal consent has to be requested under ARPA. ARPA also incorporates notification duties [neither consultation nor consent[431] before permits are issued that could prove potentially harmful or destructive to a religious site.[432] In addition, exchange or the ultimate disposal of resources stemming from Indian lands "shall be subject to the consent of the Indian or tribe which owns or has jurisdiction over such lands".[433] The Antiquities Act defined Indigenous remains as resources transforming them into "federal property" (against common law principles on human remains[434]). In fact, prior to NAGPRA, Indigenous remains older than 100 years still qualified as archaeological resources under the ARPA.[435] This feature of ARPA, as well its characterization of Indigenous cultural items as archaeological resources has been criticized by Native Americans.[436] The understanding of Indigenous archaeological resources found on public land[437] (not Indian lands) as property of the United States has been similarly problematic.[438] The concern of ARPA, and its expressly stated purpose, remains the protection of national heritage and the fostering of cooperation and information exchange. There is a clear difference between ARPA and NAGPRA, not only in their purpose but, concomitantly, in their material scope. ARPA defines the

[427] Similarly Newton et al. (2005), p. 1248.

[428] Newton et al. (2005), p. 1248.

[429] Adler (2008), p. 141.

[430] 16 U.S.C. § 470cc (g)(2) (2019).

[431] Dussias (1996), pp. 149–150.

[432] 16 U.S.C. § 470cc (c) (2019).

[433] 16 U.S.C. § 470dd (2019).

[434] Under old common law principles, there can be no property right in human remains. Next of kin hold a limited, 'quasi' property right for some purposes, such as burial.

[435] Irwin (1997), p. 43.

[436] Hutt (1992), p. 137.

[437] 16 U.S.C. §470cc(b)(3) (2019).

[438] Hutt (1992), p. 137.

protected object from a scientific perspective; NAGPRA takes the Native American perspective into account much more strongly.[439]

An important element[440] of enforcing ARPA is the courts' ability to order the forfeiture of objects obtained in violation of federal law (including ARPA).[441] Sherry Hutt has emphasized that one difficulty in ARPA was that the object had to be tied to the nature of the land which could be difficult to establish. She highlights that NAGPRA's focus on the nature of the object instead is an important lesson learned and that it protects items on private land from being trafficked without an interstate transportation requirement.[442] This is an important point to consider within a legal system, albeit within heritage not repatriation law. To ensure adequate protection of a specific object, legal definitions in enforcement provisions must focus on the nature of the object rather than its particular origin, especially where border crossings are easy, and the particular origin is difficult to establish. At the time when NAGPRA was considered, one reason advanced for its adoption was the scale of the looting of burial sites and the inadequate enforcement of the existing protection. Hutt observed that ARPA provides for sufficient criminalization to act as a deterrent but that it was underused prior to 1988 when the jurisdictional limit for a felony was reduced to $500 in damages.[443] This being said, there are a number of important differences between the two instruments, in purpose, scope and procedural mechanisms, which justify NAGPRA's adoption including that of its enforcement provisions.

4.6.1.2 A Patchwork of Export Laws

Another important element in protecting sacred cultural heritage and the cultural rights of Native Americans is to prevent the exportation of their sacred objects. This is especially important given the flourishing tribal art market. The main American export regulation is the Cultural Property Implementation Act (hereafter CPIA) that implements the 1970 Convention on the Means of Prohibiting and Preventing the Illicit Import, Export and Transfer of Ownership of Cultural Property. The United States ratified the Convention in September 1983,[444] however, the US government limited the applicability of the Convention extensively.[445] Apart from emphasizing the instrument's lack of retroactivity and precluding the self-execution of the

[439] In agreement Hutt (1992), p. 142.

[440] Marsh (1992), p. 129.

[441] 16 U.S.C. 470 (2019) gg(b) read in conj. with 470ee(a), (b) or (c).

[442] Hutt (1992), p. 142.

[443] Hutt (1992), p. 141.

[444] List of countries having ratified the 1970 Convention, in alphabetical order available at: http://www.unesco.org/eri/la/convention.asp?KO=13039&language=E&order=alpha [last accessed 21.05.2015].

[445] Forrest (2010), p. 191.

Convention, the U.S. also 'clarified' its understanding of Articles 3, 7(a) and (b), Article 10(a) as well as Article 13(d) in the declaration. These multiple statements in effect amounted to treaty reservations.[446] For present purposes the most important part of the declaration states that the US "*reserves the right to determine whether or not to impose export controls over cultural property*". This is interesting for two reasons: first, it shows that the United States government shared the scholarly opinion that it can be classified as a market country in which art is traded, rather than a source country which produces cultural heritage which should be protected and may not be lost.[447] Second, this self-image as a market nation gives the impression that Indigenous cultural heritage does not seem to be understood as heritage which is important to the state and all of its citizens.

The lack of a discussion about Indigenous heritage is also visible in the reports that the United States submitted to UNESCO. The 1987 Report highlights the implementing instrument, the Cultural Property Implementation Act, a cultural property request submitted by Canada and code of ethics adopted by professionals in the field.[448] The 1995 Report highlighted that the protection afforded by the U.S. under its implementation of the convention is not automatic but on a case-by-case basis and required "a favourable answer from the Director of the United States Information Agency (USIA), in consultation with the State Department and the Treasury Department" before import controls could be established".[449] While the United States facilitates the restitution of illegally exported objects in a number of cases touched upon by the reports, these concerned inter-state returns, not repatriation exercises which took place between a state and an Indigenous community from another state.

However, this initial focus on its character as a market nation, as well as the focus on regulating imports in contravention to the export laws of other countries in the CPIA is slightly misleading. Export controls on Indigenous cultural heritage exists within U.S. law; it is simply included in a variety of instruments that focus on different categories of heritage. This can also be seen in the national report submitted to UNESCO under the periodic reporting mechanism for the 1970 Convention[450] that lists NAGPRA, ARPA and other instruments as responsible for protecting national treasures. Notably, protection occurs indirectly through the prevention of

---

[446] Forrest (2010), p. 191.

[447] The CPIA still does not contain export control limitations, instead it is establishes a framework to regulate the import of ethnographic and archaeological material as defined in 19 U.S.C. §2601(2), which is then supplemented by bilateral or multilateral agreements. See UNESCO Doc. Ref. 24 C/24 at 16, para 18.

[448] UNESCO Doc. Ref. 24 C/24 at 16, para 18.

[449] UNESCO Doc. Ref. 28 C/35 Add at 11–12, para 45.

[450] For example in report 2011–2015: United States of America, Response to UNESCO CL/4102 of March 23, 2015 on implementation of the 1970 Convention on the Means of Prohibiting and Preventing the Illicit Import, Export and Transfer of Ownership of Cultural Property, available via http://www.unesco.org/new/index.php?id=137170, pp. 3–4 [last accessed 18.08.2021].

the unsanctioned trade of Indian, state or federal lands.[451] Protection has been extended through case law in a piecemeal fashion to include cultural heritage which originated on private lands.[452]

Indigenous objects can be classified as archaeological objects which are protected through the Archaeological Resources Protection Act (ARPA) as far as they are located on federal and Indian lands.[453] The ARPA's primary focus rests on protecting and regulating[454] the excavation and removal of 'archaeological resources' as defined in 16 USC 1, §407bb(1).[455] The ARPA was adopted in the 1970s as a response to the weaknesses of the Antiquities Acts its predecessor, especially in terms of enforcement and penalties for violating the protection established.[456] This limited protection, offered predominantly to material located on public or Indian land can be classified as a minimum export control.[457] In addition, the designation remains in governmental, not Indigenous, hands. NAGPRA, as explained in Sect. 4.4.4, changed this by considering Indigenous Peoples as partners in heritage protection, not only through repatriation but also for the protection of unexcavated materials. In addition, section 1170 established trafficking in Native American human remains without right of possession and cultural items contrary to NAGPRA as a crime.

Unfortunately, the protection offered to Indigenous heritage remains limited as it is restricted to those objects located on federal and Indian lands which amount to approximately 30% of the United States.[458] In addition, the general level of protection afforded to sacred Indigenous cultural heritage is limited by the fact that there is no general export control nor does federal law require export permits.[459]

---

[451] Nafziger and Paterson (2014), p. 38.

[452] Nafziger and Paterson (2014), p. 38.

[453] McManamon (2000).

[454] 16 U.S.C. Ch. 1B §407aa(b) (2019)"The purpose of this chapter is to secure, for the present and future benefit of the American people, the protection of archaeological resources and sites which are on public lands and Indian lands."

[455] 16 U.S.C. Ch. 1B §407bb (2019) (1) "The term 'archaeological resource' means any material remains of past human life or activities which are of archaeological interest, as determined under uniform regulations promulgated pursuant to this chapter. Such regulations containing such determination shall include, but not be limited to: pottery, basketry, bottles, weapons, weapon projectiles, tools, structures or portions of structures, pit houses, rock paintings, rock carvings, intaglios, graves, human skeletal materials, or any portion or piece of any of the foregoing items. Nonfossilized and fossilized paleontological specimens, or any portion or piece thereof, shall not be considered archaeological resources, under the regulations under this paragraph, unless found in archaeological context. No item shall be treated as an archaeological resource under regulations under this paragraph unless such item is at least 100 years of age."

[456] McManamon (2000).

[457] Nafziger and Paterson (2014).

[458] Kuprecht (2014).

[459] United States of America, Response to UNESCO CL/4102 of March 23, 2015 on implementation of the 1970 Convention on the Means of Prohibiting and Preventing the Illicit Import, Export

4.6.1.3 National Museum of the American Indian Act

Members of the Smithsonian institutions resisted Indian burial movements for a considerable time.[460] In August 1989, Smithsonian officials then agreed to "return all 'reasonable identifiable' physical remains and burial objects to tribal descendants upon request."[461] This step was significant, as the Smithsonian had been the recipient of over 4000 remains from the Army Medical Museums.[462] These were the remains that had been collected by the army under the order of the Army Surgeon General described above in Sect. 4.4.1. With the creation of the National Museum of the American Indian as a Smithsonian Institution focussed exclusively on the Indigenous Peoples of the Americas, the task to identify and repatriate then passed to the new museum and was incorporated into the NMAI adopted in November 1989 rather than being encompassed into NAGPRA. The provisions in the NMAI have a focus comparable to NAGPRA. Originally, they only covered ancestral remains and associated funeral objects, but with the passing of NMAI Act Amendment of 1996,[463] sacred objects, objects of cultural patrimony, and associated funerary objects were included.[464] Authors have described the construction of the NMAI and the repatriation as "[o]ne of the most significant events symbolizing the new era of support for the presentation, promotion, and extension of Indian arts, culture, and history"[465] and as an "important and symbolic ... capitulation".[466]

As was explained in Sect. 4.4, the NMAI served as inspiration for the drafting of NAGRPA.[467] It is thus unsurprising that the NMAI operates in a similar way to the NAGPRA. It encompasses a duty to make an inventory and repatriate human remains and associated funerary objects.[468] It also provides for a duty to provide a summary of sacred objects, unassociated funerary objects and objects of cultural patrimony and to repatriate these upon the request of the culturally affiliated

and Transfer of Ownership of Cultural Property, available via http://www.unesco.org/new/index.php?id=137170, pp. 4–5 [last accessed 18.08.2021].

460 Members of museum panel report covered in Sect. 4.4.1 above, see FN 182. See also news report covering repatriation efforts by Smithsonian Natural History and the Museum of the American Indian on the change—not only within the Smithsonian but within anthropological and museum community in general: Randall (2018). For changes towards Indigenous Peoples within the Smithsonian over time, see Loring (2009) who traces changes with reference to the Smithsonian's research activities in the Arctic.

461 Riding In (1992), p. 31.

462 National Museum of the American Indian Act 20 USC Chapter 3, Subchapter XIII §80q to §80q-15.

463 Public Law 104-278.

464 20 U.S.C. §80q-9 §80q9a.

465 Newton et al. (2005), p. 106.

466 Riding In (1992), p. 31.

467 Marsh (1992), p. 96.

468 §80q-9 (2019), originally section 11 NMAI.

claimant.[469] Cultural affiliation is either established in the summary process or by the claimant on the basis of a preponderance of the evidence.[470] As is the case for NAGPRA, the NMAI allows for different claimants, both individuals (direct lineal descendants) or entire tribes. Communities can either reclaim a sacred object if they can show that the object was owned or controlled by the tribe or community as a whole, or if control rested in the hands of one of its members on the condition that no lineal descendant exists or has made a claim.[471] Similar to NAGPRA, the NMAI also incorporates a standard which provides for repatriation if evidence is presented "which, if standing alone before the introduction of evidence to the contrary, would support a finding that the Smithsonian Institution did not have the right of possession, then the Smithsonian Institution shall return such objects unless it can overcome such inference and prove that it has a right of possession to the objects."[472] Moreover, the act expressly reserves the right for the Smithsonian institutions to go beyond its provisions both in terms of summaries and repatriations.[473] In this sense, it establishes a minimum rule for repatriation but it allows for more or different agreements with the consent of the tribe. The NMAI also created a review committee to ensure the fair and objective identification and inventory, review any findings upon the request of a party and to facilitate the resolution of disputes.[474] The NMAI operates with terms that are comparable to the NAGPRA, tribes and Native Hawaiian Organization, but it does not define them.

The repatriation policy of the Smithsonian's NMAI[475] adopts terms sacred objects, objects of cultural patrimony and unassociated patrimony that are in line with Section 2(3) of NAGRPA.[476] Sacred objects are thus covered as eligible materials if they are "needed by traditional Native American religious leaders for the practice of Native American religions, including objects needed for the renewal of a religious practice." The repatriation policy uses the same standard of cultural affiliation and method to trace kinship or ancestry. While the NMAI operates with similar definitions as NAGPRA, namely requiring federal recognition of a tribe under the definition of tribe,[477] the policy allows for the consideration of claims by international communities and federally non-recognized tribes on a case-by-case

[469] §80q-9a (2019).

[470] §80q-9a(b) (2019).

[471] §80q-9a(b) (2019).

[472] §80q-9a(c) (2019).

[473] §80q-9a(e) (2019).

[474] §80q-10 (2019), originally section 12 NMAI. As is the case for NAGPRA, the Review Committee under the NMAI must include Indigenous members, including traditional religious leaders.

[475] Smithsonian NMAI (June 2020) available via http://nmai.si.edu/explore/collections/repatriation/ [last accessed 18.08.2021].

[476] NMAI Repatriation Policy, at 1. 25 USC § 3001(c).

[477] NMAI Repatriation Policy, at 4–5 section II C.(2).

basis.[478] The type of admissible evidence is comparatively broad and includes oral traditions. The repatriation policy also provides for the appeal of a decision to the specifically established appeals commission. The latter is however comprised of two members of the board of trustees who made the original decision and the Under Secretary for Museums and Research/Provost.[479]

An important element of the repatriation policy worth highlighting is its protection of culturally sensitive information.[480] In the process of repatriation—especially where the return of sacred objects is at issue—a museum will receive culturally sensitive information. Moreover, the information may be given reluctantly by Indigenous individuals and only because it is required to prove a claim. It is important for an institution to be cognizant of the responsibility it has for the protection of such information and protocols should be put in place together with any repatriation policy that guides staff and institutions in how to balance the need to protect such information with any conflicting access to information obligations.

4.6.2 Nature of Museums and Their General Duties vs Repatriation Legislation

The previous section dealt in detail with the two pieces of federal repatriation legislation in place (NAGPRA and NMAI), their challenges, as well as the more general challenges to religious cultural heritage and practices that Indigenous Peoples face within the United States, in particular under federal Indian law. On the other side of the coin, there are ethical and legal challenges which museum staff and scientists face when confronted with Indigenous religious cultural heritage in the exercise of their regular duties. The challenges range from establishing the religious nature of the object, to establishing its cultural context, to identifying a living community with potential ties, to learning how to consult with Indigenous Peoples (potentially for the first time), to considering their ethical obligations vis-à-vis the general public, to identifying/agreeing on proper care rituals or configuring the appropriate repatriation procedure under NAGPRA, to respecting their legal obligations for their collections. The latter may be significant. Museums in the U.S. are mostly non-profit organizations that are classified either as for public benefit or charitable organizations.[481] They receive significant legal benefits mostly under federal and state tax law for pursuing their educational or scientific purpose in the public benefit.[482] The governing body of such a museum has to comply with a set of

[478] NMAI Repatriation Policy, at 8 Section VI.

[479] NMAI Repatriation Policy, at 6 section IV.A.

[480] NMAI Repatriation Policy, at 7–8 Section V.

[481] Gerstenblith (2003), p. 413.

[482] Gerstenblith (2003), p. 413.

rules which originate in the tax code and in state common law.[483] Their fiduciary obligations are essentially twofold: they owe a duty of loyalty and a duty to care. The former requires that they remain true to the public educational purpose of a museum in their actions and conflicts between self-interest and the public have to be avoided. The latter requires that trustees manage and preserve both a museums' physical assets as well as its financial assets.[484]

These obligations under state (common) law and professional ethics codes remain, even with the adoption of NAGPRA.[485] The question then arises how statutory obligations to deaccession sacred objects can be reconciled with fiduciary obligations to the public. There are, in essence, two answers to this. First, 32 U.S.C. §3005(f) exempts museums acting in good faith from liability under state law or breaches of fiduciary duty or public trust. In this sense, federal law arguably preempts state law in this respect.[486] However, Patty Gerstenblith has argued that NAGPRA, in effect, does not directly mandate the repatriation of sacred objects. Instead, it applies to federally funded institutions, leaving museums with the (admittedly unrealistic) choice of forgoing federal funding (and be subject to the fines imposed by NAGPRA).[487] This tactic, in her view leaves museum directors and trustees with the choice to forego funds or comply with NAGPRA. This would raise the question in how far the choice would comply with the duty of care. As Patty Gerstenblith points out, it seems relatively safe to assume that such decisions would be in line with a museums' duty of care. In the case of repatriation laws that states themselves have enacted, these statutes preempt fiduciary duties under state common law, avoiding the above concern. The foregoing does not apply to the case of voluntary repatriations to non-recognized federal tribes, which are not mandated or fined under NAGPRA. In this case, one may, however, argue that collaboration with non-federally recognized tribes and subsequent repatriations are still compatible with museum fiduciary duties (or even part thereof), given the educational benefits of such cooperation to the respective museum.

As Patty Gerstenblith and others have pointed out, the mission of a museum has changed to include a more educative and even communitarian role.[488] In this sense, the mission of the museum, which it performs for the public, requires the museum to gather knowledge, and considering the contemporary ethics code, also to behave ethically. Repatriation to non-federally recognized tribes avoids wrongful repatriations, can supplement knowledge and enrich the museum's mission to educate the public. To make a choice to deaccession and repatriate the sacred object would then not seem to violate a museum director's fiduciary duty of care. Moreover, when repatriation of sacred objects to non-federally recognized tribes can rest

[483] Gerstenblith (2003), p. 416.
[484] Gerstenblith (2003), pp. 416–420.
[485] Boyd and Haas (1992), p. 254.
[486] Gerstenblith (2003), p. 431.
[487] Gerstenblith (2003), pp. 431–434.
[488] Gerstenblith (2003), p. 414; Fincham (2011).

on the research carried out in line with the mandatory process, the museum does not need to bring additional financial research costs in the equation. However, a museum may have to consider how its duty to care for its financial assets can be reconciled with its duty to fulfil its educative role to the public ethically, depending on the costs of additional man-hours to facilitate the process of repatriation.

Another potential question would be whether the potential choice of a museum not to pursue a superior right of possession to a sacred object may conflict with the museum's fiduciary duty of care. Some have argued that the latter includes a duty only to relinquish the object to a party who has a superior right to possession or control. "If a museum has inferior legal title to all other parties, it is incorrect to conclude that it incurs no duty. Such a position would permit indiscriminate deaccessioning. The museum's duty is, instead, to grant the request only if the party making the request demonstrates a superior interest."[489] There are, of course, a number of remarks to be made in this regard. First, it is somewhat difficult to understand why the museum with the self-confessed problematic legal title should be presumed to be the arbiter when deciding on the validity of Indigenous claims. Even without the difficult history that connects museums, scientists of various disciplines and Indigenous communities, this would imply that a museum that holds the object under at least uncertain circumstances judges the validity of the potentially valid claim by another owner under legal principles which are internal to the system to which the arbiter belongs. NAGPRA and the accompanying regulations arguably establish the standard to decide which community has the closest cultural connection to the heritage or human remains in question. However, given the diversity of communities, there will admittedly always need to be inbuilt flexibility within a repatriation system. This leaves a museum in a comparative position of power that it needs to be mindful of. Second, as members of the museum community have pointed out, repatriation as a human rights question is very well situated within the museum's duty to the public. As the director of the Museum of New Mexico highlighted at the adoption of NAGPRA "the Museum believes that legal issues of fiduciary responsibility rest comfortably below the issues of ethics and civil rights."[490] This being said, NAGPRA, as highlighted in Sect. 4.4.3.4 above, explicitly reserves the application of property and ownership law,[491] as long as its inapplicability would result in an expropriation.

An interesting question, depending on the given context of a repatriation, is in how far professional ethic codes and the otherwise applicable laws give the museum leeway to decide not to pursue a claim to prove a superior property interest under NAGPRA. A strict (or narrow depending on one's point of view) understanding of a conservator's duty in relation to the integrity of an institute's collection would result in such a decision being difficult. The mutual benefits of a repatriation dialogue and

[489] Boyd and Haas (1992), p. 258.

[490] Livesay (1992), p. 296.

[491] Boyd and Haas (1992), pp. 271–272.

consultation (also in terms of enriching the background of the existing collection[492]) that have been evidenced may prove to be a sufficient argument to support an ethical decision not to pursue a claim of a superior property interest, even when it exists. This is provided that state laws give leeway to not to pursue such a claim for those who adopt this very limited understanding of professional museum ethics and in particular the principle of 'service to the public'.

Another attention point for any repatriation legislation follows on from this. In addition to minimum obligations and flexibility for the relevant partners to adopt further-reaching or different solutions if desired, the legislation needs to address existing museum obligations in relation to their collection under the applicable law. In countries where some or many museums are public legal entities, amendments to their legal governing structures may be more easily incorporated into the repatriation legal framework. Even so, difficulties will remain in the case of conditional donations.

The cultural objects which are covered by NAGPRA give museums considerable interpretational leeway. A certain degree of such an interpretational leeway may be inevitable, given the culturally diverse backgrounds of the items in question. This flexibility may be important to ensure the success of a repatriation model. Where such flexibility is incorporated into the law, museum ethics code and repatriation guidelines adopted by a specific institution provide important guidelines and supplement the law. How a repatriation model is applied, and whether it will fulfil its stated or assumed objectives, thus remains influenced, even in cases of federal minimum legislation, by institutional policies and ethical codes. In this sense, it is important to realize that choosing legal stimuli and minimum thresholds in a repatriation framework can indeed act as important trigger points for action (as they have in the U.S. context). However, their incorporation needs to be accompanied by a thorough discussion and potentially an amendment of museum/ institutional ethical codes. For this reason, the next section will analyse selected ethic codes before concluding the analysis of U.S. law.

4.6.3 *Self-regulation of Museums: Code of Ethics of Cultural Institutions*

In the discussion of the NMAI in the section above, some aspects of museum self-regulation were already considered, namely the repatriation policy adopted by the NMAI, which complements and in parts goes beyond the legally mandated repatriation framework. Other important instruments of self-regulation are the code of ethics adopted by different institutions holding sacred objects. There are numerous associations' and institutional codes of ethics, and therefore the following can

[492] This would be in line with those collection duties that focus on the study/explication of the (remainder of the) collection, see principle 12, AAMD 2011 Professional Practices in Art Museums.

provide only a brief glimpse. The examples selected were chosen for their potentially broad applicability given the large constituency of the respective organization.

The following were examined:

1. World Archaeological Congress[493]
   (a) Vermillon Accord on Human Remains 1989
   (b) The Tamaki Makau-rau Accord on Display of Human Remains and Sacred Objects 2006
2. American Alliance of Museums[494]
3. American Anthropological Association[495] 2012 Statement on Ethics
4. The American Association of Museums Curators Committee 2009 Code of Ethics for Curators[496]
5. The Association of Art Museum Directors Report on the Stewardship and Acquisition of Sacred Objects[497]
6. The Association of Art Museum Directors "Professional Practices in Art Museums" (2011)[498]

The common provisions/emphasis in the different examples that were examined were (albeit in varying degrees):

---

[493] Non-profit organization representing archaeologists with globally dispersed electoral colleges, rotating congresses.

[494] Representing a broad spectrum of several hundred US museums, including science centres, zoos etc., as well as umbrella organizations for several professional networks: https://www.aam-us.org/programs/about-aam/ [last accessed 18.08.2021].

[495] "The American Anthropological Association is the world's largest association for professional anthropologists, with more than 10,000 members. Based in Washington, D.C., the Association was founded in 1902, and covers all four main fields of anthropology (cultural anthropology, biological/physical anthropology, archaeology, and linguistic anthropology). While 75% of our members are employed in higher education or are students of anthropology, about 25% of our members work in the public, private, and non-governmental sectors, beyond the academy." http://www.americananthro.org/ConnectWithAAA/Content.aspx?ItemNumber=1665&navItemNumber=586 [last accessed 18.08.2021].

[496] https://www.aam-us.org/wp-content/uploads/2018/01/curcomethics.pdf [last accessed 18.08.2021].

[497] AAMD in August 2021 represents 227 art museum directors in the US, Canada and Mexico, and identifies its mission as "The Association of Art Museum Directors advances the profession by cultivating leadership capabilities of directors, advocating for the field, and fostering excellence in art museums. An agile, issues-driven organization, AAMD has three desired outcomes: engagement, leadership, and shared learning." https://www.aamd.org/about/mission [last accessed 18.08.2021].

[498] By contrast, AAMD 2011 Professional Practices in Art Museums which as appendixes include its documents on deaccessioning and disposal do not mention repatriation or sacred objects. Nor does the 2011 manual list, policies on repatriation requests/cooperation with potential Indigenous/source communities amongst the policies necessary for a museum to adopt (see principle 9, p. 6).

1. Responsibility of museum/profession to the public[499]
2. Mission to collect and preserve, exhibit and educate—importance of the collection[500]
3. Specific recognition of unique nature of sacred objects[501]
4. Responsible treatment of competing ownership conflicts/conflicts of interest[502]

The codes of ethics for museums, curators and anthropologists all highlight the serving role of the institution or profession to the general public. It is clearly the guiding principle on which all others are based. In and of itself, the principle is arguably neutral towards repatriation. Service to the public can be interpreted both to support repatriation or to support the retention of material. 'The public' as a homogenous entity is non-existent but rather it exists as a mass of multiple communities and interests. Their interests may converge or diverge and museums operate at their crossroads and are—as the holder of the material—in a comparative position of power. The benefit of a legal framework which establishes minimum standards or stimuli in favour of repatriation in such a situation is clear. It places the community firmly at the bargaining table and pushes for all stakeholders to enter into a dialogue and at least to open the window for the further realization of Indigenous rights. Ethical frameworks which are adopted and adapted in response to the lessons learned can both further or deter the envisioned success of a legal framework and are thus

[499] "For museums public service is paramount. To affirm that ethic and to elaborate its application to their governance… the American Association of Museums promulgates this Code of Ethics for Museums." American Association of Museums (1993, amended 2000), section I, last paragraph. Curators Committee (2009), p. 3, section I. American Anthropological Association (2012), Principles of Professional Responsibility, paragraph 1 "among our goals are the dissemination of anthropological knowledge and its use to solve human problems", available via: http://ethics.americananthro.org/category/statement [last accessed 18.08.2021]. AAMD definition of museum: "An art museum is a legally organized, not-for-profit institution or component of a not-for-profit institution or government entity with a mission to study, care for, interpret, and exhibit works of art. It is essentially educational in nature, engaging the public and community in regularly scheduled programs and exhibitions" see https://www.aamd.org/about/membership [last accessed 18.08.2021].

[500] American Association of Museums (1993, amended 2000), section III; Curators Committee (2009), p. 3, section I. In the case of AMA accessibility of results and protecting and preserving records, see American Anthropological Association (2012), Principles 5 and 6.

[501] American Association of Museums (1993, amended 2000), Section III, "the unique and special nature of human remains and funerary and sacred objects is recognized as the basis of all decisions concerning such collections." Curators Committee (2009), p. 6, section D; World Archaeological Congress (2006); Association of Art Museum Directors (2006), available via: https://www.aamd.org/standards-and-practices [last accessed 18.08.2021] encourages museums to "use the greatest sensitivity when collecting sacred objects from indigenous societies worldwide", to use "consultation with leaders of indigenous societies … wherever possible to ensure that the object can be collected or removed from its context without damaging the society's central religious beliefs."

[502] American Association of Museums (1993, amended 2000), section III "Competing claims of ownership that may be asserted in connection with objects in its custody should be handled openly, seriously, responsively and with respect for the dignity of all parties involved."; Curators Committee (2009), section V, 7–9.

integral elements of a repatriation model. The danger of justifying decisions which undermine the adopted legal framework in the name of serving the public in such a case are clear. Where repatriation is the outcome of a legal framework that has been adopted in a democratic process, the public, so to speak, has chosen and formulated its interest. For a cultural institution to use the inherent broadness of such a framework unilaterally to supplement its own reading of public interest would arguably be undemocratic. This need not mean that the decision taken might not simultaneously advance cultural rights of other non-Indigenous communities or the interests of future generations. This conflict cannot be eliminated but it should be remembered when a decision is taken. Given that an object needs to be deaccessioned, before it can be repatriated, clearer guidance in deaccessioning policies may be desirable at this point. It is telling that, in their policies on deaccessioning, the AAMD does not consider the sacredness of an object or potentially dubious acquisition conditions. The criterion under which sacred objects in the U.S. may be deaccessioned will most likely have to be that the "museums possession of the object may not be consistent with applicable law."[503]

The Vermillon Accord on Human Remains was clearly adopted in the initial era of NAGPRA. It proposes a 'standard' for repatriation that—similar to NAGPRA—seeks to balance Indigenous interests versus the desire to further education and science.[504] A comparison of the Vermillion Accord with the Tamaki Makau-rau Accord on the Display of Human Remains and Sacred Objects shows that, since then, archaeologists have increased the attention paid to Indigenous rights. The latter, adopted in 2005,[505] still affirms the belief of the respective archaeological community that "the display of human remains or sacred objects may serve to illuminate our common humanity".[506] It does, however, mandate that the permission from the affected community/communities is sought and that, if denied, it should be respected. This applies to both future and existing exhibitions. It also mandates regular consultation "to ensure that the display remains culturally appropriate".[507]

Whatever repatriation model is adopted, it is clear from the U.S. example that it cannot secure the realization of Indigenous cultural rights by itself. However, this does not negate its other (procedural) advantages: dialogue, negotiation and the chance to at least further advance Indigenous cultural rights as articulated in the UNDRIP and other international (legal) instruments. Important spin-off benefits

[503] American Association of Museum Directors, Professional Practices in Art Museums (2011), Appendix B, Policy on Deaccessioning, II (c).

[504] World Archaeological Congress (1989) "Agreement on the disposition of fossil, skeletal, mummified and other remains shall be reached by negotiation on the basis of mutual respect for the legitimate concerns of communities for the proper disposition of their ancestors, as well as the legitimate concerns of science and education."

[505] Adopted at a regional intermediate congress in 2005 in Auckland that focussed on the relationship of Indigenous Peoples and archaeology, see: http://worldarch.org/blog/wac-inter-congress-in-auckland-new-zealand/ [last accessed 18.08.2021].

[506] World Archaeological Congress (2006), preamble.

[507] World Archaeological Congress (2006), principle 6.

from such a dialogue can be the fact that it opens up a space for communities to assert themselves as living rather than vanishing cultures and to shape how their image is translated to 'the public'.[508] Naturally, display and education or heritage in museums are still shaped by the professional judgement and personal interests of the curator.[509]

Another danger in this process of transmitting culture remains even within the repatriation context itself and may be inevitable. As Dussias highlights, the role of Indigenous individuals in presenting their culture to the outside is not as unlimited as might be assumed at first glance. Especially in the legal context, it is not a voluntary release if it is necessary to assert specific legal rights. Moreover, the form is also dictated by legal requirements (both in terms of content and method).[510] Where cultural knowledge is necessitated within a legal framework to support a claim, it has to be surrendered and shaped to fit pre-existing legal moulds. Moreover, making certain knowledge public to support the repatriation of a religious artefact may expose other religious elements to desecration or destruction such as sacred sites.[511] This underlines the need for the process and the parties involved to implement policies which govern the management of any such knowledge, as has been done in the case of the Smithsonian code discussed above in Sect. 4.6.1.3.

References

Adler A (2008) An unintended and absurd expansion: the application of the Archaeological Resources Protection Act to Foreign Lands. New Mexico Law Rev 38:133–158

Alfredsson G (2011) Treaties with indigenous peoples. Max Planck Encyclopedia of Public International Law. Oxford University Press

American Anthropological Association (2012) American Anthropological Association 2012 Ethics code

American Association of Museums (1993, amended 2000) AAM Code of Ethics for Museums. AAM

Association of Art Museum Directors (2006) Report on the Stewardship and Acquisition of Sacred Objects

Babcock HM (2012) "This I know from my Grandfather:" the battle for admissibility of indigenous oral history as proof of tribal land claims. Am Indian Law Rev 37(1):19–61

Borrows J (2006) Indigenous legal traditions in Canada (trans: Canada LCo)

Boyd TH, Haas J (1992) The Native American Graves Protection and Repatriation Act: prospects for new partnerships between museums and Native American groups. Arizona State Law J 24 (1):253–282

Boyd WL, Buffalohead WR, Deloria VJ, Goldstein L, Harjo SS, Echo-Hawk WR, Lyons O, Mayo W, Michael M, Toro H, Snake RAJ, Sullivan M, Ubelaker DH, Welsh PH, Bender P,

[508] Dussias (2009), p. 65.

[509] Dussias (2009), p. 73.

[510] Dussias (2009), pp. 69, 73.

[511] Dussias (2009), p. 85.

Strickland R, Fox M (1990) Report of the Panel for a National Dialogue on Museum/Native American Relations. vol 24. Arizona State Law Journal (1992) Appendix
Bradford W (2002) "With a Very Great Blame on Our Hearts": reparations, reconciliation, and an American Indian plea for peace with justice. Am Indian Law Rev 27(1):1–175
Bradford W (2005) Beyond reparations: an American Indian theory of justice. Ohio State Law J 66 (1):1–103
Brown MF (2003) Who owns native culture? Harvard University Press, Cambridge
Brown MF (2010) Culture, property, and peoplehood: a comment on Carpenter, Katyal, and Riley's "In Defense of Property". Int J Cult Prop 17:569–579
Brown MF, Bruchac MM (2006) NAGPRA from the middle distance: legal puzzles and unintended consequences. In: Merryman (ed) Imperialism, art and restitution. Cambridge University Press, New York, pp 193–217
Buck C (2006) "Never Again": Kevin Gover's apology for the Bureau of Indian Affairs. Wicoza SA Rev 21(1):97–126
Capriccioso R (2010) A sorry saga: Obama signs Native American apology resolution; fails to draw attention to it. Indian Country Today, 13 January 2010
Carpenter KA, Katyal S, Riley AR (2009) In defense of property. Yale Law J 118(6):1022–1125
Cryne J (2009) NAGPRA revisited: a twenty-year review of repatriation efforts. Am Indian Law Rev 34:99–122
Curators Committee (2009) A code of ethics for curators. American Association of Museums
Debo A (1970) A history of the Indians of the United States. University of Oklahoma Press
Dubinsky PR, Fox GH, Roth BR (eds) (2017) Supreme law of the land? Debating the contemporary effects of treaties within the United States Legal System. Cambridge University Press,
Dussias AM (1993) Geographically-based and membership-based views of Indian Tribal Sovereignty: the Supreme Court's changing vision. Univ Pittsburgh Law Rev 55:1–97
Dussias AM (1995) The right to cultural and religious self-determination: lessons from the experience of native Americans. ILSA J Int Comp Law 2:633–641
Dussias AM (1996) Science, sovereignty, and the sacred text: paleontological resources and native American rights. Md Law Rev 55:84–159
Dussias AM (2005) Kennewick Man, Kinship, and the Dying Race: The Ninth Circuit's Assimilationist Assault on the Native American Graves Protection and Repatriation Act. Nebraska Law Rev 84:55–161
Dussias AM (2009) Exhibiting culture in legal settings: courts, agencies, and tribes. Tulsa Law Rev 45:65–87
Dussias AM (2012) Friend, Foe, Frenemy: The United States and American Indian Religious Freedom. Denver Univ Law Rev 90(2):347–431
Duthu NB (2008) American Indians and the Law. The Penguin Library of American Indian History. Penguin Books, New York
Echo-Hawk RC, Zimmerman LJ (2006) Beyond racism: some opinions about racialism and American archaeology. Am Indian Q 30(3):461–485
Fincham D (2011) Deaccession of art from the public trust. Art Antiq Law 16(2):93–129
Forrest C (2010) International law and the protection of cultural heritage. Routledge, Abingdon
Garcia MJ, Devereaux Lewis C, Nolan A, Totten M, Tyson A (2017) The Constitution of the United States: analysis and Interpretation. US Government Printing Office, Washington, DC
Gerstenblith P (2003) Acquisition and deacquisition of museum collections and the fiduciary obligations of museums to the public. Cardozo J Int Comp Law 11:409–465
Harjo SS (2012) Native American Human Rights Acts: a brief account of some ways that native peoples and friends won repatriation and National Indian Museum Laws. Arizona J Int Comp Law 44(2):681–696
Hemmens C, Brody DC, Spohn C (2019) Criminal courts: a contemporary perspective, 4th edn. SAGE Publications
Hutt S (1992) Illegal trafficking in native American human remains and cultural items: a new protection tool. Arizona State Law J 24(1):135–150

Inouye DK (1990) Providing for the protection of native American graves and the repatriation of Native American remains and cultural patrimony – report. U.S. Senate, Washington, DC

Inouye DK (1992) Foreword – repatriation: forging new relationships. Arizona State Law J 24 (1):1–3

Irwin L (1997) Freedom, law and prophecy: a brief history of Native American Religious Resistance. Am Indian Q 21(1):35–55

Johnson G (2004) Naturally there: discourses of permanence in the repatriation context. Hist Relig 44(1):36–55

Johnson G (2007) Sacred claims – repatriation and living tradition. University of Virginia Press, Charlottesville

Johnson RW, Haensly SI (1992) Fifth amendment takings implications of the 1990 Native American Graces Protection and Repatriation Act. Arizona State Law J 24(1):151–173

Kuprecht K (2014) Indigenous peoples' cultural property claims – repatriation and beyond. Springer

Livesay TA (1992) The impact of the Federal Repatriation Act on state-operated museums. Arizona State Law J 24(1):293–301

Loring S (2009) From tent to trading post and back again: Smithsonian anthropology in Nunavut, Nunavik, Nitassinan, and Nunatsiavut – The Changing IPY Agenda, 1882–2007. In: Krupnik I, Lang MA, Miller SE (eds) Smithsonian at the poles: contributions to International Polar Year Science. Smithsonian Institution Scholarly Press, Washington, DC, pp 115–127

Makah Indian Tribe, National Association of Tribal Historic Preservation Officers (2008) Federal Agency Implementation of the Native American Graves Protection and Repatriation Act. NATHPO, Washington, DC

Mangone GJ (2002) Private property rights: the development of takings in the United States. Int J Marit Coastal Law 17(2):195–233

Marsh G (1992) Walking the Spirit Trail: Repatriation and Protection of NAtive American Remains and Sacred Cultural Items. Arizona State Law J 24(1):79–133

McCain J (1992) Foreword: repatriation – balancing interests. Arizona State Law J 24(1):5–6

McManamon FP (2000) The Archaeological Resources Protection Act of 1979 (ARPA). Archaeological method and theory: an encyclopedia. Garland Publishing Co, New York

McManamon FP, Nordby LV (1992) Implementing the Native American Graves Protection and Repatriation Act. Arizona State Law J 24(1):217–252

Meltz R (2015) Takings decisions of the U.S. Supreme Court: a chronology. US Congressional Research Service

Moriwake I (1998) Critical excavations: law, narrative, and the debate on Native American and Hawaiian "Cultural Property" Repatriation. Univ Hawaii Law Rev 20:261–319

Nafziger J (2009) The Protection and Repatriation of Indigenous Cultural Heritage in the United States. In: Bell CE, Paterson RK (eds) Protection of First Nations cultural heritage: laws, policy, and reform. UBC Press, Vancouver, pp 110–152

Nafziger J, Dobkins R (1999) The Native American Graves Protection and Repatriation Act in its first decade. Int J Cult Prop 8(1):77–107

Nafziger J, Paterson RK (2014) International trade in cultural material. Handbook on the law of cultural heritage and international trade. Elgar Online

Newton NJ, Anderson RT, Goldberg CE, LaVelle JP, Royster JV, Singer JW, Strickland R (2005) Cohen's Handbook of Federal Indian Law. 2005 edition with 2007 supplement edn. LexisNexis

Peregoy RM (1992) The legal basis, legislative history, and implementation of Nebraska's Landmark Reburial Legislation. Arizona State Law J 24(1):329–389

Randall K (2018) How the Smithsonian is reuniting thousands of human remains with indigenous communities. Washington City Paper

Reed T (2016) Who owns our ancestors' voices? Tribal claims to pre-1972 recordings. Columbia J Law Arts 40(2):275–310

Riding In J (1992) Without ethics and morality: a historical overview of imperial archaeology and American Indians. Arizona State Law J 24(1):11–34

Schaepe D, T'xwelátse HJ (2018) It's a family affair: Stó:lō experiences in repatriation. BC Stud Autumn (199):27–32

Secretary of the Interior (1992) Charter of the Native American Graves Protection and Repatriation Review Committee. Arizona State Law J 24(1):501–503

Seidemann RM (2010) NAGPRA at 20: what have the states done to expand human remains protections? Mus Anthropol 33(2):199–209

Skrydstrup M (2010) What might an anthropology of cultural property look like? In: Turnbull P, Pickering M (eds) The long way home – the meaning and values of repatriation. Berghahn Books, New York, pp 59–81

Strasser M (2016) Free exercise and substantial burdens under federal law. Nebraska Law Rev 94 (3):633–684

Strickland R (1992) Implementing the national policy of understanding, preserving, and safeguarding the Heritage of Indian Peoples and Native Hawaiians: human rights, sacred objects and cultural patrimony. Arizona State Law J 24(1):175–191

Stumpf GD (1992) A federal land management perspective on repatriation. Arizona State Law J 24 (1):303–320

Trope JF, Echo-Hawk WR (1992) The Native American Graves Protection and Repatriation Act: background and legislative history. Arizona State Law J 24(1):35–77

Tsosie R (2012) NAGPRA and the problem of culturally unidentifiable remains: the argument for a Human Rights Framework. Arizona State Law J 44(2):809–906

United States Government Accountability Office (2010) Native American Graves Protection and Repatriation Act – after almost 20 years key federal agencies still have not fully complied with the act. Washington, DC

Varner EC, Penneys Edelman D, Amineddoleh L (2015) NAGPRA and Congress's Foresight. JURIST – Professional Commentary, 18 January 2015

Vásquez CM (1995) The four doctrines of self-executing treaties. Am J Int Law 89(4):695–723

World Archaeological Congress (1989) The Vermillion Accord on human remains. WAC, South Dakota

World Archaeological Congress (2006) The Tamaki Makau-rau Accord on the display of human remains and sacred objects. WAC, Osaka

Chapter 5
Evaluation of Repatriation in U.S. Law

5.1 Introduction

This research set out to examine how repatriation should be regulated and to better understand the relationship between repatriation, Indigenous[1] cultural rights standards and national law. Two main research questions guide the analysis: First, how should the repatriation of Indigenous sacred cultural heritage be regulated legally in light of international cultural heritage and human rights law standards. In order to establish how repatriation should best be regulated in light of international legal standards, Chap. 4 mapped existing repatriation legislation and a number of connected legal areas. In the examination of NAGPRA, in particular its scope (definition of Indigenous Peoples and sacred objects) was considered, whether they mandate a particular outcome, procedure or combination thereof, who takes the final decision on a repatriation request, whether there is a dispute resolution mechanism, and in how far costs associated with repatriation are considered. This is summarized in Sect. 5.1.

Chapter 4 also considered repatriation of Indigenous cultural heritage within its legal context, defined as the law governing religious freedom, federal Indian law, cultural heritage law and museum (self)-regulation. In terms of the connected legal areas, Indigenous religious freedom, in particular access to sacred sites and AIRFA, and museum self-regulation were examined. This is summarized in Sect. 5.2. On this basis, the international human rights standards were applied in Sect. 5.3. These

---

Please note that this chapter adopts the capitalization of the terms Indigenous Peoples and Indigenous (except for when used in citations) for reasons explained in Chap. 1.

---

[1]Please note that this chapter adopts the capitalization of the terms Indigenous Peoples and Indigenous (except for when used in citations) for reasons explained in Chap. 1. Capital A is used in Aboriginal for similar reasons except for citations, when spelled differently in the original source cited.

V. Tünsmeyer, *Repatriation of Sacred Indigenous Cultural Heritage and the Law*, Studies in Art, Heritage, Law and the Market 3,
https://doi.org/10.1007/978-3-030-89047-6_5

derive from the analysis of international law in part I of this study. The second main research question of this study, asked what—if anything—can we derive from the findings of the country analysis in light of the international standards for the cultural heritage law and policy of the selected countries? Section 5.4 concludes the analysis of U.S. law by summarizing the main research findings, first by extrapolating lessons for any future repatriation model based on the U.S. example to contribute to answer the first research question. Second, it considers whether there are any lessons for U.S. cultural heritage law and policy in general, to answer the second main research question for the example of U.S. cultural heritage law and policy.

5.2 Repatriation of Indigenous Religious Heritage Under NAGPRA

Under NAGPRA, Indigenous religious heritage is protected in two ways. First, NAGPRA facilitates the repatriation of Indigenous religious heritage, albeit with deficits as discussed in Sect. 4.4 in Chap. 4. These are in summary: lack of inclusion of non-federally recognized tribes, reinterpretation of the cultural affiliation criterion with the Bonnichsen case (although this was addressed through the regulations) and lack of uniform control mechanisms of its implementation for a considerable time of its existence. The leeway given to museums in the understanding of cultural affiliation can have both a positive or a negative influence on repatriation and the protection of Indigenous religious heritage according to customary standards, depending on how this gap is filled by self-regulatory instruments, as discussed in Sect. 4.6.3, Chap. 4. The scope of religious heritage under NAGPRA is relatively broad, with the defining criterion being the need of practitioners (as identified by a traditional religious leader) to use the object in contemporary practice. The main characteristics of this repatriation model are summarized in Table 5.1

First, in terms of the legal recognition of Indigenous identity under the repatriation law, NAGPRA incorporates other federal law into NAGPRA. Indian tribes are defined by reference to receiving governmental support under existing programs because of their status as Indian. The analysis has shown that Indigenous self-recognition and communal group recognition is made difficult under existing federal Indian law. The legal recognition of Indigenous identity has fluctuated immensely and the law, as an instrument of assimilatory policies, has left a lasting imprint on the shape of Indigenous identity within the U.S. legal system, as seen in Sects. 4.2 and 4.3.3. Moreover, fluctuations have not stopped but rather continue with the power to recognize federal Indian status (albeit not Indigenous self-identification) resting firmly with Congress as part of its broad plenary power, as detailed in Sect. 4.3. Apart from derailing the efforts of non-recognized communities to realize their human rights more broadly, federal recognition, or the lack thereof, also has very real implications in the context of repatriation and the realization of Indigenous cultural rights. Repatriation is enshrined in federal law, including several hundred

Table 5.1 Summary of NAGPRA repatriation framework

Comparative indicators/Country and repatriation law	US NAGPRA
Objectives of law evidenced in legislative history of law	Ensure equal protection of human remains—remedial—also arguments of equal protection of religious rights
Definition of Indigenous Peoples within act	Follows national definitions of Indigenous Peoples, notion of "federally recognized tribes" by government as eligible to receive governmental support because of Indigenous status
Definition of Indigenous religious heritage	Main criterion for definition is a need by traditional religious leader for contemporary practice. Ultimately definition of sacredness rests with Indigenous religious expert.
Mandated outcome?	Yes. Focus very much on the actual repatriation of human remains (and associated funerary objects), religious objects and cultural patrimony. If conditions are fulfilled obligation to repatriate.
Mandated procedure? What type of procedure?	Partially, there are mandatory elements: (1) First phase inventory/summary with consultation; (2) cultural affiliation standard to link heritage with community; (3) if (1) + (2) fulfilled → duty to repatriate but no specific format, unless scientific exception or competing claims.
Consultation within process and/or FPIC	Yes. Consultation mandated within repatriation process.
Final authority to decide on repatriation request	With museum (decides that cultural affiliation standard not met). But: disputes can be submitted to NAGPRA Review Committee + be brought before courts.
Dispute settlement body and its composition	Review Committee representative, both museum professionals as well Indigenous members including Indigenous religious experts. But no binding authority. Ultimate binding authority rests with courts, judiciary overwhelmingly white, with Native American being among the least newly elected members of the federal judiciary. In the last two decades, 1 elected judges was Native American.[a]
Financial support provided to participants	Yes, federal budget was set aside and available to both museums and tribes (968 awards totaling 48.45 million for the period 1995–2018). Not awarded to federal agencies.

[a]Data from: https://www.fjc.gov/history/exhibits/graphs-and-maps/race-and-ethnicity [last accessed 18.08.2021] New Article III Judges by Race or Ethnicity 1940–2020 in effect lists a total of 3 American Indian judges. For comparison for the same time period there were 2461 white judges

years of assimilatory jurisprudence. It carries within it the historic burdens of this legal area and its pitfalls, which includes an inconsistent and shifting recognition of Indigenous status. For NAGPRA, this translates into an inability to obtain the important religious and cultural heritage necessary for the continued existence of the community as a cultural community for non-recognized peoples and conflicting claims to heritage by multiple communities as a result of past governmental policies.

One argument that has been made against a boundless recognition of Indigenous communities is the concern that to recognize more communities would affect the relationship between the federal government and already recognized tribes as partially sovereign entities within the U.S.. However, one could counter this argument stating that federal recognition under NAGPRA is not a pie that, once split in so many pieces, leaves nothing left to be distributed. This analogy might at most hold true for U.S. grant money to facilitate repatriations. However, in terms of the millions of Indigenous heritage objects, this is more difficult to understand. The lack of facilitating repatriation to non-recognized Indigenous communities has instead led to difficulties in the identification of cultural affiliation of specific objects. Apart from this more practical argument, there is another more foundational objection to such a stance. Indigenous identity and the recognition of that identity is a human right of every Indigenous individual. Political manoeuvring might explain the distribution of benefits, but it does not qualify as a legally valid limitation of the right to self-identification. Such an inconsistent approach, which may severely limit the cultural rights of affected communities in an arbitrary manner, also cannot be justified as a permissible limitation under international cultural rights standards, which is explored in the framework below.

Second, some forms of Indigenous religious cultural heritage are protected under 18 U.S.C. §1170. With the adoption of NAGPRA, this provision extended the protection of criminal law to cover the trafficking of human remains and cultural items. It does not cover religious items as a third category, even though they are covered by the repatriation provisions of NAGPRA. However, a very small number of important religious items are likely to qualify as cultural items, given the interpretation of cultural items under NAGPRA.

NAGPRA has shown both the advantages of legally mandated cross-cultural cooperation as well as its downsides. It can help in creating new partnerships, existing misconceptions on all sides can be adjusted, repatriation on a larger scale with the resulting wealth of knowledge and learning can take place, and existing and historical inequalities can be addressed (if not necessarily corrected). On the other hand, arguably, repatriation requires a cooperative framework and enforced cooperation will not change the mindset of those reluctant to do so, while others would have been willing to cooperate regardless. The advantage of a legal mechanism is then to facilitate the work of those who are willing, by mitigating existing legal obstacles, i.e. in conservation and heritage laws, and by ensuring that Indigenous groups within a country have more of an equal chance of access and use of their heritage than might otherwise be the case. Repatriation on such a scale is also cost-intensive, time-extensive and requires significant manpower. Before adopting such a framework all relevant actors of civil society and government need time for a dialogue about their desired outcomes, to guide reaching the most suitable legal framework. During the process, hopes and aspirations will likely change and therefore inbuilt flexibility is key. The legal framework for repatriation thus needs to allow for the necessary flexibility combined with minimum standards of cataloguing Indigenous objects and repatriating them when requested.

What makes this even more difficult legally is that, while the repatriation model by itself may be created in a flexible way, it is however embedded in a web of more rigid laws which are interwoven with repatriation. Indigenous status, laws protecting the exercise of religion and Indigenous cultural traditions, conservation laws that bind agencies and museums also need to be adapted for repatriation models to function. Given that all of these in turn balance diverse interests, the motivations behind the desired repatriation need to be expressed clearly to allow for the necessary balancing of interests specific to repatriation. If repatriation is aimed at revitalizing Indigenous religions which were stopped because of governmental interference (that violated the free establishment clause), then this desire to undo past interferences should weigh equally in the balancing of interests in how to use public land that was expropriated and is of a sacred nature if the goal is to be achieved. If repatriation is aimed at aiding reconciliation in turn, how successful can it be when treaties concluded between the two parties can be unilaterally abridged by the government? Furthermore, this practice may be permissible within U.S. domestic law, but it violates international human rights standards, and it has also been condemned by CERD.[2] Quite simply (and somewhat obvious), when repatriation seeks to encourage wider societal changes than the return of an object, any repatriation law by itself will be insufficient to achieve this. What is more, notwithstanding all outside non-legal factors that may be necessary, there are multiple legal factors left to consider next to a specific repatriation law to achieve such goals.

5.3 Relevant Legal Context: Summary of Research Findings

5.3.1 Protection of Indigenous Religious Heritage Under Federal U.S. Law

Apart from the protection of Indigenous religious heritage under NAGPRA, Indigenous sacred heritage is also protected to some small degree by federal heritage law,

[2]CERD A/56/18 (paras 380–407 US), 14/08/2001: para 400 "The COM notes with concern that treaties signed by the Government and Indian tribes, described as 'domestic dependent nations' under national law, can be abrogated unilaterally by Congress and that the land they possess or use can be taken without compensation by a decision of the Government. It further expresses concern with regard to information on plans for expanding mining and nuclear waste storage with regard to information on plans for expanding mining and nuclear waste storage on Western Shoshone ancestral land, placing their land up for auction for private sale, and other actions affecting the rights of Indigenous Peoples. The CoM recommends that the State party ensure effective participation by indigenous communities in decisions affecting them, including those on their land rights, as required under articles 5 (c) of the Convention, and draws the attention of the State party to general recommendation 23 on Indigenous Peoples which stresses the importance of securing the 'informed consent' of indigenous communities and calls, inter alia, for recognition and compensation for loss."

namely ARPA. In particular, this applies to potentially unexcavated material which is covered by both ARPA and NAGPRA. Excavations on Indian land require consent. NAGPRA amends ARPA in the relevant sections on the protection of unexcavated heritage and is much more focused on Indigenous rights protection than ARPA (which is focused on resource protection). This legislation addresses unexcavated materials, however, it does not affect the repatriation of material from institutions to communities. Nor is there, to the author's knowledge, any other legislation to this effect apart from what was discussed in Chap. 4.

AIRFA has enshrined U.S. policy to protect Indigenous religious freedom, which is understood to cover, *inter alia*, access to sites and the use and possession of sacred objects. This has led to new policies being implemented in different agencies, both in terms of facilitating access to land as well as how to respect sacred cultural heritage of tribal members who cross the U.S. border, such as traditional bundles. Access to sacred sites is an important component in the adequate protection of Indigenous religious heritage, both in terms of gathering the material components of said heritage and for providing the space to use it. It thus complements NAGPRA both in strengthening practices for which items may be reclaimed and by protecting safe spaces for their use.

In terms of access to and respect of sacred sites, it appears from the literature that the U.S. record is mixed. Despite some laudable Congressional actions, courts have taken steps that have undermined the legal protection offered, most notoriously in Lyng. Similarly, international human rights standards have not been complied with, despite warnings from international treaty bodies. One area in which this has occurred is the failure to obtain free, prior and informed consent, which was considered by CERD in the Western Shoshone case and by the Inter-American Commission of Human Rights in the case of Mary and Carrie Dann.[3] At the core of the case was the decision of the federal government to treat Shoshone treaty lands as ceded as a result of proceedings before the Indian Claims Commission. The lands, thus treated as public lands, were used for military testing and nuclear waste disposal. Both CERD and the IACHR emphasized that the classification was based on proceedings before the Indian Claims Commission which did not conform with international human rights standards on FPIC.[4] Conversely, positive examples of federal agencies which have adopted access and accommodation policies and displayed considerable respect towards the needs of practitioners also exist.[5] While NAGPRA incorporates the findings of the Indian Claims Commission this is less problematic then one might at first assume. Under NAGPRA, the ICC proceedings are used in its decisions to classify land as Aboriginal land, both in NAGPRA to

[3]Case 11.140, 27.12.2002.

[4]Decision 1 (68), CERD/C/USA/DEC/1, 11.04.2006 Early Warning and Urgent Action Procedure Western Shoshone people, para 6. IACHR, Report N° 75/02, Case 11.140 Mary and Carrie Dann United States, December 27, 2002.

[5]This could also be seen even in the critical GAO 20 review report, see Chap. 4, Sect. 4.4.6.2.

protect unexcavated objects under 25 U.S.C. §3002(a)(2)(c)[6] and in the rules on how to proceed with culturally unidentifiable human remains and associated funerary objects.[7] The classification of Aboriginal lands in both cases is broad and includes several alternatives to the Indian Claims Commission process which, problematic as it is, unfortunately also constitutes a legal reality for the tribes in question and thus needs to be incorporated into NAGPRA.

The U.S. legal context on sacred sites teaches us the following lessons: FPIC and comprehensive consultations are important procedural elements to safeguard Indigenous religious rights. The religious background of those in government, executive agencies, legislature and judiciary will likely be fundamentally different from Indigenous religious practitioners. One important difference already highlighted is the place-bound/nature-bound aspect of Indigenous religions. To put it simply, places of worship are not replaceable, nor are the natural materials required for ceremonies nor specific religious objects. It thus appears in the U.S. context that Indigenous religious exercise is not protected in a manner equal to other religions under the applicable civil rights mechanisms. To bridge this gap, consultation and cooperation are crucial. However, consultation is expensive and time-consuming and the resources available to the parties are not distributed equally. Administrative procedures which implement legal consultation requirements need to take this into account. With additional financial support and the support of civil society, i.e. law schools and firms which specialize in Indian law resources and offer voluntary support, the willingness by museums to go the extra mile, and with openness and flexibility among agencies, this inequality may be compensated for.

5.3.2 Museum (Self-) Regulation

This section examined not only NAGPRA but also its sibling, NMAIA that governs the relevant Smithsonian institution. The Smithsonian's own repatriation policy,[8] examined against the legal backdrop of both federal acts, teaches valuable lessons for legal frameworks on repatriation. It orients itself in relation to the federal acts by incorporating its understanding of sacred objects, its standard of cultural affiliation, and its method to trace kinship or ancestry. Yet it is more than a mere copy. With the flexibility of a soft law tool, it also remedies some of NAGPRA's flaws and incorporates valuable lessons. It allows the Museum to consider requests from non-federally recognized tribes and highlights the need to protect sensitive information given to the museum by Indigenous individuals. The repatriation policy can be updated to reflect the continuing learning process that all parties undergo during repatriation procedures. However, museums such as the Smithsonian were reluctant

[6] On the protection of unexcavated heritage see Chap. 4, Sect. 4.4.4.

[7] 43 C.F.R. §10.11 (c) (1)(ii) (2020).

[8] See Chap. 4, Sect. 4.6.1.3.

for a long time to consider repatriation requests and it took public activism and federal acts to trigger a change. It is thus arguably the perfect example for the need to adopt a minimum legal framework requiring cultural institutions to act (once the decision in favour of repatriation has been taken), while allowing institutions some flexibility to go further than the framework. With the act being complemented by the necessary administrative regulations, which are also easier to amend, there is space for all parties to learn from each other and to incorporate relevant experiences into policies and regulations.

Aside from the Smithsonian's repatriation policy, some of the major codes of ethics adopted by cultural institutions were also considered, which showcase how these cultural actors understand their role and duties. As highlighted above, they had a number of commonalities, albeit in varying degrees of emphasis:

1. Responsibility of museum/profession to the public[9]
2. Mission to collect and preserve, exhibit and educate—importance of the collection[10]
3. Specific recognition of unique nature of sacred objects[11]
4. Responsible treatment of competing ownership conflicts/conflicts of interest[12]

The codes shed light on the cultural actors' understanding of themselves as being in a profession in service to the community at large. This service seems to be

---

[9] "For museums public service is paramount. To affirm that ethic and to elaborate its application to their governance... the American Association of Museums promulgates this Code of Ethics for Museums." American Association of Museums (1993, amended 2000), section I, last paragraph. Curators Committee (2009), p. 3, section I. American Anthropological Association (2012), available via: http://ethics.americananthro.org/category/statement [last accessed 18.08.2021] section I Principles of Professional Responsibility "among our goals are the dissemination of anthropological knowledge and its use to solve human problems". AAMD definition of museum: "An art museum is a legally organized, not-for-profit institution or component of a not-for-profit institution or government entity with a mission to study, care for, interpret, and exhibit works of art. It is essentially educational in nature, engaging the public and community in regularly scheduled programs and exhibitions" see https://www.aamd.org/about/membership [last accessed 18.08.2021].

[10] American Association of Museums (1993, amended 2000), section III; Curators Committee (2009), p. 3, section I. In the case of AMA accessibility of results and protecting and preserving records, see American Anthropological Association (2012), Principles 5 and 6.

[11] The AAM observes "the unique and special nature of human remains and funerary and sacred objects is recognized as the basis of all decisions concerning such collections.", see American Association of Museums (1993, amended 2000), section III; Curators Committee (2009), p. 6, section D; World Archaeological Congress (2006); Association of Art Museum Directors, Subcommittee on the Acquisition and Stewardship of Sacred Objects (2006), available via: https://www.aamd.org/standards-and-practices [last accessed 18.08.2021] encourages museums to "use the greatest sensitivity when collecting sacred objects from indigenous societies worldwide", to use "consultation with leaders of indigenous societies . . . wherever possible to ensure that the object can be collected or removed from its context without damaging the society's central religious beliefs."

[12] "Competing claims of ownership that may be asserted in connection with objects in its custody should be handled openly, seriously, responsively and with respect for the dignity of all parties involved.", see American Association of Museums (1993, amended 2000), section III Curators Committee (2009), pp. 7–9, section V.

understood as educative, but it need not necessarily be restricted to this function. Repatriation is compatible with this understanding, both if it is to achieve reconciliation—which is in the interest of the community at large—and if it is to achieve reparations. The actors seem to recognize the unique nature of religious objects. The codes themselves are generally vague, which is arguably necessary to a certain extent given their broad constituency. They do not give much guidance on questions of repatriation but do consider the special nature of sacred objects, albeit to differing degrees. Here it is disappointing that the AAMD report on collecting sacred objects still supports collecting sacred materials, as long as they are not 'central to a society's beliefs'. The report highlights the difficulty for a museum as a 'secular institution' to meet specific demands for the treatment of sacred objects if the category of sacred objects is understood broadly. It advocates a narrow understanding of the term. A parallel to the definition of NAGPRA and the comparable problem of a broad category of sacred objects is drawn. The report also admits to the inability of museums to define sacredness, asking museums to engage in consultation with respective religious leaders where this is possible for acquisitions and to react to requests by Indigenous religious leaders or communities for existing collections.[13]

The report raises several questions. First, if a museum is a secular institution that is admittedly incapable of caring for sacred objects if sacredness were to be understood to reflect the understanding of the source community, why should it acquire new sacred objects? Second, a behavioural standard of 'the greatest sensitivity' to guide new acquisitions does not really require much if anything. Third, one might also have wished that past collecting behaviour, which took place without such consultations were considered together with how to remedy their effects. This is only done indirectly with reference to NAGPRA. In terms of guidance by ethical codes on the deaccessioning of sacred objects, their silence in this regard may be explained by the existence of NAGPRA. This does mean, however, that, in the absence of clearer legal rules on what deaccessioning from the public trust might require,[14] requests for the deaccessioning of sacred objects to tribes who fall outside of NAGPRA (either because they are from outside the US or because they are not federally recognized) do not occur. In summary, while some of the provisions featured are important steps and worth highlighting, overall, these codes underline the need for a law mandating consultation and consent for retention or repatriation if Indigenous religious and cultural rights are to be respected. In how far does the examined legal context comply with relevant international law?

---

[13] Association of Art Museum Directors (2006), Subcommittee on the Acquisition and Stewardship of Sacred Objects (2006), available via: https://www.aamd.org/standards-and-practices at 5 of overall document, (at 2 of report) [last accessed 18.08.2021].

[14] On the need for more legal guidance on deaccessioning (outside of the context of NAGPRA), see Fincham (2011), Donn Zaretsky by contrast, argues that there is no such thing as public trust for museum property which could prevent deaccessioning. See Zaretsky (2015).

5.4 Application of Human Rights Principles to NAGPRA and Related Federal Law

The first part of this research yielded a number of principles deriving from international law that are potential instruments for states to implement their obligations under international law. The research in this chapter focussed on NAGPRA to see what model can be derived from the U.S. practice, which elements should be emulated, and which practices should be avoided or improved. The foundation of the principles in the human rights toolbox developed in the first part of this book is undoubtedly the Indigenous right to cultural self-determination, as enshrined in Art.3 UNDRIP and Art.1 ICESCR/ICCPR.[15] This guiding principle remains fairly vague, however, and it requires further specification, which was achieved on the international level by means of the United Nations Declaration and various soft law instruments. In applying the principles developed to the context of the United States in as far as the latter has been the subject of this research, we can identify a number of measures taken which serve to protect or fulfil the Indigenous right to cultural self-determination. After examining which principles have been incorporated into U.S. law, the next section will look at measures limiting selected rights to examine how rights protection may be negatively affected by state measures. Two rights will be considered that directly involve Indigenous moveable cultural heritage, namely the right to revitalization and the right to the access and use of sacred heritage. As has been explained in the first part of this book, there is no international (human) right to repatriation. However, the repatriation of sacred objects can guarantee their access and use. It will therefore be covered in considering the limitation on access and use of sacred cultural heritage in Sect. 5.3.2.

5.4.1 *Applying Principles from the Human Rights Toolbox to the U.S. Legal Heritage Context*

1. *Respect, protect and fulfil Indigenous religious beliefs also in designing a repatriation framework so long as these are in accordance with international human rights standards.*

Application to the United States: This principle is fulfilled. NAGPRA leaves the definition of sacredness to the respective Indigenous religious leader, who in turn has to be recognized as such by an Indian tribe or Native Hawaiian organization.

2. *The repatriation framework and other examined heritage frameworks have to incorporate consultation of Indigenous rights for measures affecting their*

[15] Compare Daes, E., Principles and Guidelines, principle nr. 2, who terms the right to cultural self-determination the necessary basis for an effective system of Indigenous heritage protection.

cultural rights and FPIC "[w]henever the preservation of their cultural resources, especially those associated with their way of life and cultural expression, are at risk".

Application to U.S.: NAGPRA foresees consultation and participation both within the repatriation process and in the protection of unexcavated heritage. Moreover, the heritage site scheme established by NHPA established not only State Historic Preservation Officers but also Tribal Historic Preservation Officers to provide tribes with assistance in protecting their heritage/cultural resources.

3. *Repatriation of sacred objects guarantees right to control of sacred object. Please note: This principle identifies one possible measure within wide margin of discretion; there is currently no obligation to repatriate sacred objects under international law.*

Application to U.S.: This is fulfilled with the adoption of NAGPRA. However, the exclusion of non-recognized tribes means that not all Indigenous communities within the United States have the opportunity to request the repatriation of their sacred objects.

4. *States may not interfere with Indigenous right to practise and/or revitalize their cultural traditions and customs unless this limitation is in accordance with international human rights law.*

Application to U.S.: The research suggests that the U.S. record in respecting the right to revitalization is mixed. In the context of NAGPRA, one may observe that the statutory text in effect endorses the right to revitalization of religious practices, thereby fulfilling Art.11(1) and Art.34 UNDRIP (and Art.27 ICCPR). 25 U.S.C. §3001(3)(C) (2019) defines the sacredness of an object in relation to its present-day use. While 43 C.F.R.§ 10.2(d)(3) (2020) refers to the object's previous sacredness, it emphasizes present-day usage and expressly envisions the renewal of past traditions. However, problems remain especially in connection with cultural/religious sites that are part of public property. There are attempts to mitigate this, i.e. through the Section 106 consultation Process under National Historic Preservation Act. Problems also exist for Indigenous religious practitioners with materials which are needed for ceremonies, including the religious use of peyote and the use of bald-eagle feathers, partially as a result of case law. Both have been addressed by legislation.[16]

5. *Support Indigenous right to practise and/or revitalize their cultural traditions by creating favourable conditions in which to exercise this right.*

Application to U.S.: The adoption of NAGPRA is one example for a measure that a state can take to create favourable conditions in which Indigenous Peoples may

[16]42 U.S.C. §1996a (2019) on traditional Indian religious use of peyote and 50 C.F.R. §22.22 (2019) establishes a permit system for the use and possession of eagle feathers by Native Americans for Indian religious purposes under certain conditions.

enjoy Art.27 ICCPR and revitalize their cultures. The act leaves the definition of sacred objects to Indigenous religious leaders and requires a current need as a criterion for repatriation rather than continuing practice.

6. *Duty to respect and protect cultural heritage and to mitigate effects of globalization and privatization on culture of marginalized and minority communities, including Indigenous Peoples.*[17]

Application to the United States: This principle is partially realized in U.S. law. NAGPRA criminalizes trade in cultural items obtained in violation of NAGPRA and human remains. Extending coverage to sacred objects would be advisable.

7. *Ensure that Indigenous sacred objects receive special protection under national heritage law but that this does not prevent access to heritage by its Indigenous community. State must actively take steps to eliminate all barriers that prevent Indigenous Peoples for accessing their heritage. Conditions to access are permissible, these have to satisfy the test charted below for limitations on right of access to sacred heritage.*

Application to U.S.: Federal (heritage) law does not include any access prohibitions. NAGPRA mandates the return of many sacred objects. In this case, access is guaranteed unless there is a dispute between different communities. For other objects, the individual holding institutions are responsible for access to and use of their collections. In how far there is a general museum practice that guarantees Indigenous access to their heritage cannot be established based on the present research.

8. *Take measures to prevent conduct aimed desecration of cultural heritage.*[18] *This includes to encourage museums not to display human remains and sacred objects unless with FPIC of affected community.*[19]

Application to U.S.: NAGPRA mandated the repatriation of human remains and sacred objects if a number of conditions are fulfilled. This also stimulated a wider consultation between communities and museums. In this sense, NAGPRA has actually contributed to an atmosphere where museums will consider such matters more ethically even if there is still room for improvement.

9. *The state has a duty to refrain from undue interference with Indigenous right to their heritage and to protect them from undue interference by third parties. It is also under a positive duty to progressively create conditions in which Indigenous Peoples can control etc. their heritage according to their own traditions.*

[17] CESCR, General Comment No.21, para 50(a), (b).

[18] Pineschi (2012), p. 41.

[19] Compare Daes, E., Principles and Guidelines, Guideline 21: "Under no circumstances should human remains or any other sacred elements of an indigenous peoples' heritage be publicly displayed, except in a manner deemed appropriate by the peoples concerned."

Application to U.S.: NHPA established Tribal Historic Preservation Officers (THPOs)[20] responsible for administering and preserving Indigenous heritage within exterior reservation boundaries. There is also a duty to consult THPO for section 106 NHPA process,[21] as the NHPA covers tribal sites of religious importance.[22] The consultation prior to NAGPRA and at regulated points within NAGPRA is also a move towards enabling Indigenous Peoples to have more control over their cultural heritage according to their own traditions.

10. *The state has a duty to refrain from undue interference with right to cultural identity, this includes a prohibition of enforced assimilation. There are three connected duties: First, the obligation not to impose definition of Indigenous identity from the outside. Second, the positive duty to protect the right-holders from undue interference by third parties, including duty to ensure that decision to identify as Indigenous does not result in discrimination. Third, the positive duty to take steps to create favourable conditions for Indigenous Peoples to preserve and develop their cultural identity. This encompasses a wide margin of possible, discretionary measures.*

Application to U.S.: Within NAGPRA the Indigenous right to self-identification has not been respected due to the exclusion of federally non-recognized tribes.

11. *The State has a duty to respect Indigenous right to their own legal traditions*[23] *in accordance with international human rights law.*

---

[20] 42 C.F.R. §137.280 (2019) definition THPO, §137.288 consultation duty "The NHPA requires Federal agencies to take into account the effects of their undertakings, such as construction projects, on properties covered by the NHPA, such as historic properties, properties eligible for listing on the National Register of Historic Places, or properties that an Indian Tribe regards as having religious and/or cultural importance."

[21] 36 C.F.R. §800.1 (2019) "Section 106 of the National Historic Preservation Act requires Federal agencies to take into account the effects of their undertakings on historic properties and afford the Council a reasonable opportunity to comment on such undertakings. The procedures in this part define how Federal agencies meet these statutory responsibilities. The section 106 process seeks to accommodate historic preservation concerns with the needs of Federal undertakings through consultation among the agency officials and other parties with an interest in the effects of the undertaking on historic properties, commencing at the early stages of project planning. The goal of consultation is to identify historic properties potentially affected by the undertaking, assess its effects and seek ways to avoid, minimize or mitigate any adverse effects on historic properties."

[22] 36 C.F.R. § 800.4(b) "*Identify historic properties.* Based on the information gathered under paragraph (a) of this section, and in consultation with the SHPO/THPO and any Indian tribe or Native Hawaiian organization that might attach religious and cultural significance to properties within the area of potential effects, the agency official shall take the steps necessary to identify historic properties within the area of potential effects."

[23] Art.34 UNDRIP describes a number of elements of such legal traditions: Indigenous peoples have the right to promote, develop and maintain their institutional structures and their distinctive customs, spirituality, traditions, procedures, practices and, in the cases where they exist, juridical systems or customs, in accordance with international human rights standards.

Application to U.S.: Tribal courts have broad jurisdiction for anything happening on tribal lands including criminal cases as a result of tribal sovereignty. Jurisdiction shared/mixed with state courts differs depending on state.[24] A study by the national centre for state courts from 2004 found that, for 562 federally recognized tribes, there were 309 tribal justice forums.[25] In terms of representation within the judiciary, Native Americans are severely underrepresented, as pointed out in Table 5.1.[26] Within NAGPRA, the definition of the sacredness of an object appears to be left to Indigenous religious rules which one may consider to be part of Indigenous traditional laws.

5.4.2 Limitations on the Right to Access and Use of Sacred Objects

Chapter 2 introduced the test to evaluate whether a measure that limits the Indigenous right to use and control of sacred objects in effect amounts to a violation of Art.27 ICCPR. It is illustrated through Fig. 5.1. As was pointed out in earlier chapters, only if all answers are answered affirmatively may state take the measure under international human rights law. As the conditions are cumulative, the lack of meeting any of the conditions means that the measure amounts to a violation of Art.27 ICCPR.

As has become apparent in the preceding sections, repatriation is context-dependent. To appreciate in how far NAGPRA is in line with international standards, different factual scenarios will have to be considered:

(1) The state (through its institutions and agencies) holds important religious objects from the Indigenous community, and

(2) (A) a claim is submitted by a state recognized Indigenous community

- (a) with cultural affiliation to a sacred object. This is recognized and the object is returned.
- (b) which is the closest connected community to the object. But the object is not repatriated because it fails the repatriation standard articulated in §3005(c).[27]

---

[24] By virtue of Public Law 280, see also https://www.ncsc.org/Topics/Special-Jurisdiction/Tribal-Courts/Resource-Guide.aspx [last accessed 18.08.2021].

[25] National Centre for State Courts, Tribal Courts Table 33 (2004), available via https://cdm16501.contentdm.oclc.org/digital/collection/spcts/id/159 [last accessed 18.08.2021].

[26] As an additional example, in a study of state courts last updated in 2010 on minority judges on the state level, Native Americans judges constituted less than 1% of judges. Native Americans were by far the least represented. The study counted 13 Native American judges out of 1436 judges belonging to minorities. ABA Standing Committee on Judicial Independence ("SCJI"), National database on judicial diversity in state courts (2009). The website data is no longer accessible but the same data has also been used in another publication, see Hemmens et al. (2019), p. 177.

[27] "If a known lineal descendant or an Indian tribe or Native Hawaiian organization requests the return of Native American unassociated funerary objects, sacred objects or objects of cultural patrimony pursuant to this chapter and presents evidence which, if standing alone before the

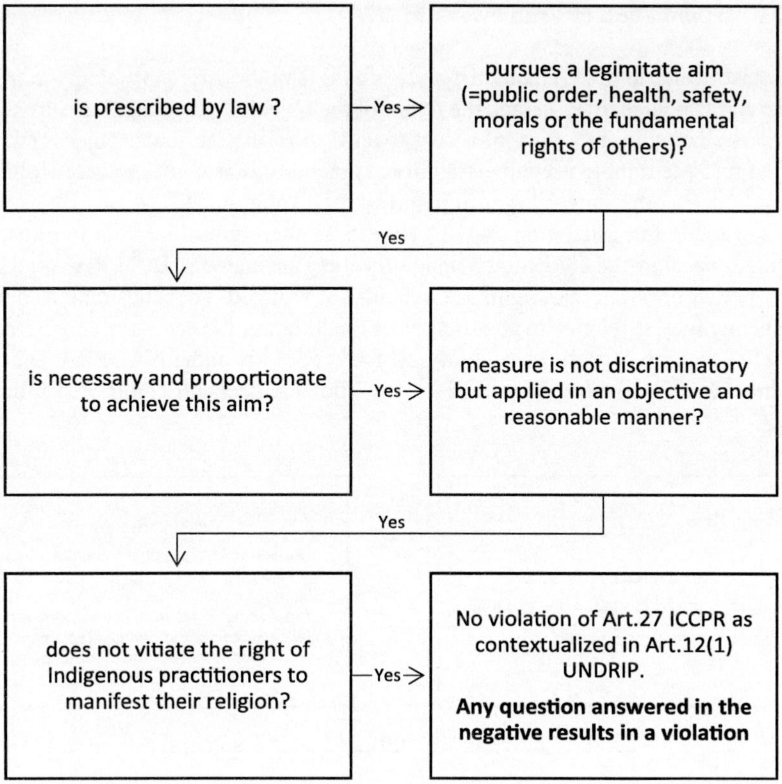

Fig. 5.1 Permissibility of measures that limit access and use of sacred objects (repeated from Chap. 2)

(or)

(2) (B) claim submitted by federally non-recognized Indigenous community inside U.S.

(a) agency/institution refuses to repatriate
(b) agency decides to repatriate

(or)

(2) (C) claim submitted Indigenous community outside U.S.

(a) agency/institution refuses to repatriate
(b) agency/institution decides to repatriate

---

introduction of evidence to the contrary, would support a finding that the Federal agency or museum did not have the right of possession, then such agency or museum shall return such objects unless it can overcome such inference and prove that it has a right of possession to the objects."

5.4.2.1 Application of Framework to 2(A)

In the case scenario of 2(A), the first situation (a) is obviously unproblematic from a human rights perspective. In fact, the return of the object is a laudable measure which ensures the community's right of access to and use of the particular object and even seeks to fulfil its right to revitalize traditional practices. It also goes towards fulfilling that particular community's right to manifest their religion.

In the second constellation 2(A)(b) (Fig. 5.2), the cultural institution refuses to repatriate, because the evidentiary standard set by the state in NAGPRA is not met. Here whether or not human rights are upheld—or violated—depends on the context. The agency may still agree to an arrangement facilitating the access to and use of the object by (members of) the community, which is possible under NAGPRA. Whether it decides to do so would be within its discretion. A decision could then fulfil the

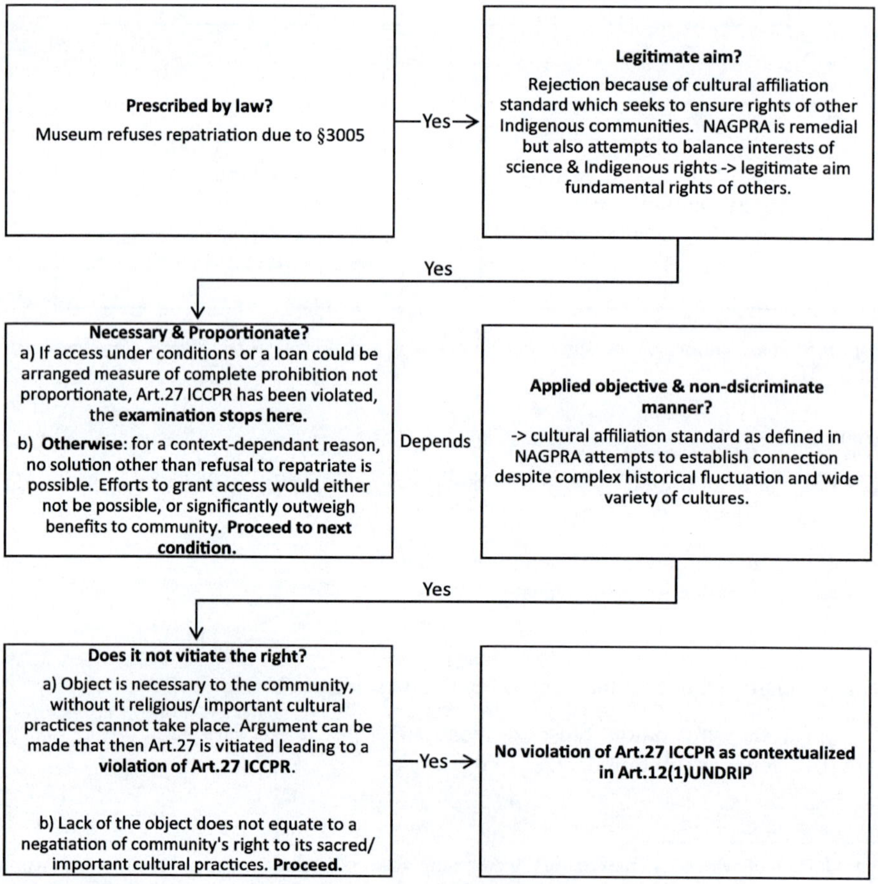

Fig. 5.2 Illustrating scenario 2(A) (b)—refusal to repatriate & no access

community's right of access and the use of the object, reflecting relevant international Indigenous rights standards.

Now let us assume that the decision would be neither to repatriate nor to grant a community which has in fact a close cultural connection to the sacred object access. Or granting access without repatriation could not be possible without a loan because of the geographical distance between institution and community. A loan is refused. Whether the decision is taken by a federal agency or a museum, the limitation in effect arises out of the wording of NAGPRA. It is thus a limitation on the right by the state and has to fulfil the requirements set by such limitations by international law.

As will be seen below, a decision to neither to return a sacred object nor to grant access to and use of the object to an Indigenous community within the U.S. means that NAGPRA can lead to a violation of the Indigenous right to manifest their religion. This will happen when access to and use of the object is denied and there is either (a) a possible compromise regarding access and use that is not realized and/or (b) the object is so crucial to the community that its failure to ensure access to and use of it will vitiate the religious practice of that particular community.

5.4.2.2 Application of Framework to 2(B)

In this scenario (Fig. 5.3), the federal recognition of the Indigenous identity is crucial. As was observed above, the way the federal recognition of tribes operates within the U.S. is a severe limitation of the Indigenous right to self-identification. Depending on the application in an individual case, it may lead to a severe limitation of Art.33 UNDRIP and Art.27 ICCPR. It may even lead to an outright denial of the right of an individual to enjoy his culture, thereby violating Art.27 ICCPR. Connecting this element to NAGPRA, there are two possibilities. First, the institution decides not to repatriate to the closest affiliated tribe, because it is not federally recognized but voluntarily decides to grant access to the object and its use under conditions agreed upon by both parties. In this case, the institution or agency in effect remedies a weakness within NAGPRA and prevents a violation of Art.27 ICCPR. Second, the agency—as a result of NAGRPA—decides neither to repatriate nor to grant access to nor use of the object. As can be seen below, the wording of NAGPRA, when applied to federally non-recognized tribes who have lost much of their cultural heritage, violates both Art.27 ICCPR and Art.18 ICCPR:

Several of the criteria are not met in this factual scenario. The first one would already have sufficed to establish a violation of Art.27 ICCPR as contextualized in Art.12(1) UNDRIP, but if there is disagreement on the application of this element, the test above has shown that several other elements are also not fulfilled. To remedy this insufficiency of NAGPRA, the definition of Indian tribe in §3001(7) should be changed and the definition of Indian tribe as an entity that "is recognized as eligible for the special programs and services provided by the United States to Indians because of their status as Indians" should be dispensed with.

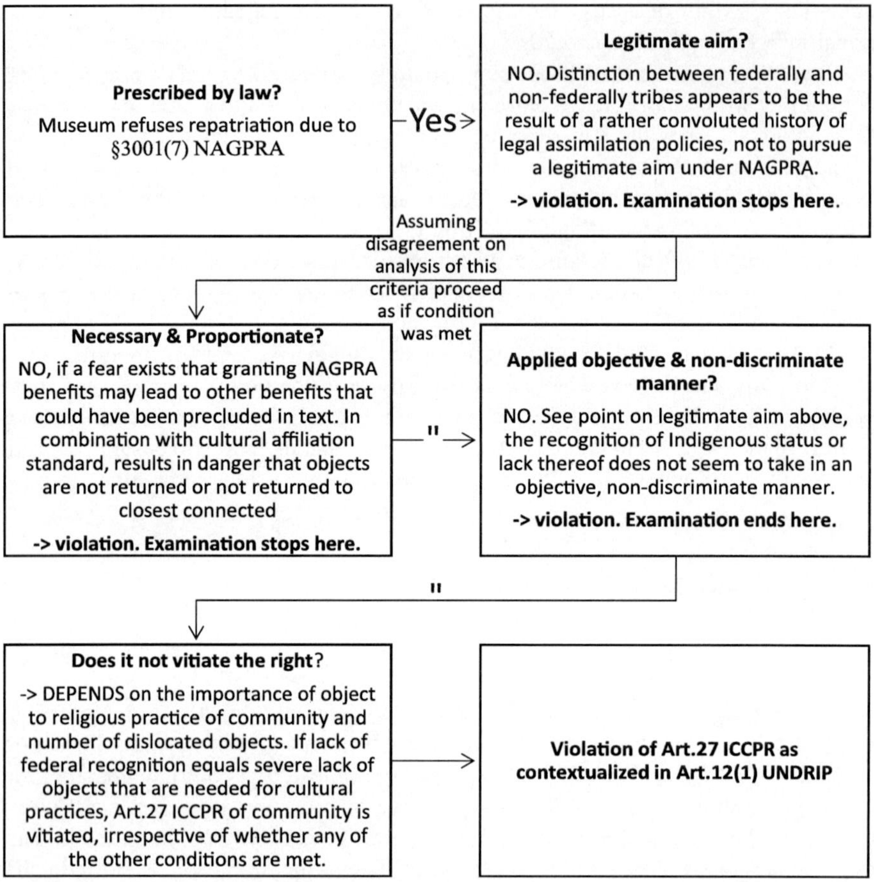

Fig. 5.3 Illustrating scenario 2(B)—analysis the same for both 2(B)(a) and 2(B)(b)

5.4.2.3 Application of Framework to 2(C)

In this constellation, NAGPRA does not apply. The museum is under no legal obligation to repatriate the sacred object. Unlike in the case of NAGPRA, the balancing act between returning the object and deaccessioning it from the public trust and the fiduciary duties of care differs. On the one hand, objects may be in storage and may no longer be displayed as a result of ethical codes and the realization that to do so may desecrate the object and violate the community's religious beliefs. Moreover, repatriation may avoid negative publicity and decrease reputational costs. It may also lead to similar increases of knowledge as has been the case under NAGPRA, thereby furthering the museums educative mission. It may, however, also incur significant financial costs and require time and staff which the museum, in times of financial cutbacks and continuing obligations under NAGPRRA, simply may not have. Moreover, given the very narrow grounds on which museums may deaccession objects under the ethical codes of the AAMD, the museum may risk public censure which can have severe consequences, including asking other members not to loan exhibits.[28] Moreover, in this case, the framework developed cannot be applied, given that a state is under the obligation to protect the relevant rights of individuals *within* its territory. While agency and museum decisions to return sacred objects to Indigenous communities abroad will undoubtedly enhance Indigenous rights and may be pursued for a multitude of reasons identical to those of intra-national repatriations (i.e. reparation, reconciliation), compliance with international human rights obligations is not one of them.[29]

5.5 Concluding Observations to Part II

The above examination yielded a number of interesting results, both as lessons for future repatriation laws as well points for improvement that are more internal to the U.S. system. It has also highlighted the limits of applying a human rights framework to evaluate the strength of Indigenous cultural rights protection within a national system.

For future repatriation models, the lessons may be summarized as follows. First, repatriation models should not incorporate state definitions of Indigenous Peoples within the personal scope of the law. Instead, relying on communal self-identification for the purposes of repatriating sacred objects is recommended. Second, policies should be put in place prior to repatriation and agreed upon in consultations on how to proceed with and protect sensitive information.[30] This is a useful lesson learned from the NMAI repatriation policy. Third, any repatriation model should establish a representative settlement mechanism with the authority to make binding recommendations. Fourth, repatriation is a costly enterprise, both for museums and for Indigenous communities. If it is to be successful, funds need to be set aside from the outside to facilitate repatriation for all parties involved. Fifth, prior to the adoption of a repatriation law, Indigenous parties and museum representatives should meet for consultations to identify respective priorities, identify common grounds and potential pitfalls for the repatriation law before it is adopted. Sixth, depending on the size of the collections open to repatriation and the prospective length of the process, the repatriation law should feature mandatory evaluations of the programme at sensible intervals. Seventh, given the time interval between the

[28] This happened, for instance, for the National Academy in New York which deaccessioned objects to be able to meet expenses and remain open (which is not a permitted use of funds gained from deaccessioning under the AAMD policies). See Fincham (2011), pp. 120–121.

[29] There is one exception, namely where communities have been divided by international borders, in which case, part of the community remains within U.S. borders, and one part abroad (in this case 2 (A) and 2(B) apply).

[30] Brown and Bruchac (2006), p. 216.

original loss of the object and its potential repatriation, the repatriation model should incorporate a variety of sources to provide evidence of a cultural connection between the object and the community. Moreover, care should be taken that Indigenous oral traditions are not prejudiced vis-à-vis other types of evidence.

Recommendations internal to the U.S. can be summarized as follows. First, NAGPRA's scope should be amended so that there is no distinction between federally recognized and non-recognized tribes as claimants. Second, NAGPRA sought to enable a more equal protection of Indigenous religious traditions compared to other religious practices. While NAGPRA did achieve improvements, Indigenous traditional religions continue to be at a disadvantage, mostly because of the connection of the practice to a specific location. If an equal protection of religious practices is to be achieved, neither NAGPRA nor AIRFA have managed to achieve this. Instead, the legal protection of sacred sites and Indigenous access to sacred sites in accordance with Indigenous customs appears to require further consideration. Third, it appears from case law and the literature that Indigenous claimants still face substantial difficulties in translating cultural differences before non-Indigenous courts. While this is a complex problem, and there is no easy solution, one step in the right direction would be to ensure that the judiciary is more representative than it is now. Fourth, U.S. museums could benefit from clearer legal guidance on the content of their fiduciary duties to the public. In addition, the profession's own guidelines should be amended to clarify that deaccessioning Indigenous religious heritage and important cultural objects does not violate the museum's own ethical and fiduciary duties. Fifth, the protection against the trafficking of Indigenous heritage in 18 USC §1170 should be extended to cover all sacred Indigenous heritage not just those objects that are covered because they are also important cultural items.

In terms of evaluating U.S. compliance with international Indigenous rights standards, the record appears more positive than might be expected, given the U.S. refusal to ratify important international human rights treaties and the declaration that UNDRIP is not a statement of current international law. Considering the history of tribal - governmental relations, this is a more recent trend. In fact, much of the relationship between Indigenous and non-Indigenous parties has been characterized by what we would now term a multitude of severe human rights violations. The shift towards a better recognition of Indigenous cultural rights also seems to have very little (if anything) to do with a desire to improve one's governmental human rights records. Instead, it may be explained by a variety of factors. First, the realization that forceful assimilation policies had severe effects and worsened the situation for Indigenous individuals rather than achieve the desired assimilation which led to a governmental shift towards recognizing tribal sovereignty (albeit in limited terms). Second, successful tribal activism which galvanized important legislative and policy changes, notably NAGPRA. Third, the existence of important precedents recognizing tribal sovereignty (again albeit in limited terms). Fourth, Indigenous efforts to maintain sovereign and distinct cultural entities in the face of overwhelming odds to the contrary. These are undoubtedly just some factors, but they suffice to make the point that the outside perception of the human rights record does not appear to be a main or guiding concern for American legislative actions improving (or impairing) Indigenous rights.

The main advances and positive measures which have been examined in this chapter have occurred within the labyrinth known as U.S. federal Indian law and as a result of an increased recognition of tribal sovereignty. However, restrictions on Indigenous rights remain and may even partially be motivated by fears of tribal sovereignty that reaches too far. Examples of this tendency may be a restriction on tribal judicial authority within tribal lands and the extension of state authority in relation to Indigenous individuals, the peculiar shifts in the recognition (and termination) of Indigenous tribal status or the reserve power of Congress to unilaterally alter treaties negotiated between two sovereign powers. In this respect, one may also caution that tribal sovereignty is not a 'one remedy cures all' legal tool.[31] As was evidenced in this chapter, for the area of cultural heritage and cultural rights, tribal sovereignty is undoubtedly important for the protection of Indigenous rights and has served as an important force. However, as a result of history, Indigenous Peoples share their territory with non-Indigenous individuals and governments. In the area of cultural heritage and the protection of cultural rights, much has been achieved as a result of dialogue and consultation between all parties concerned and the apparently genuine desire of individuals to find a middle ground between the different (legal) cultures.

All of this raises the question, what, if anything, can human rights standards add to the debate? At the moment, U.S. legislative measures exceed international minimum standards for the most part, as examined in the section above. The constant and notable exceptions are arguably a number of very important cases. In this respect, one may argue that Congress is under a duty to remedy violations of human rights that occur as a result of judicial action, as it attempted to do with AIRFA to remedy the Supreme Court's decision in Employment v Smith.[32] Apart from this, one may hope that the international standards examined do serve as a barrier should governmental policy shift again to one of assimilation, with the inevitable violations of Indigenous rights this would entail.

References

American Anthropological Association A (2012) American Anthropological Association 2012 Ethics code

American Association of Museums A (1993, amended 2000) AAM Code of Ethics for Museums. AAM

Association of Art Museum Directors A (2006) Report on the Stewardship and Acquisition of Sacred Objects

---

[31] Compare Brown (2010), pp. 570–573.

[32] In agreement Newton et al. (2005), p. 464.

Brown MF (2010) Culture, property, and peoplehood: a comment on Carpenter, Katyal, and Riley's "In Defense of Property". Int J Cult Prop 17:569–579

Brown MF, Bruchac MM (2006) NAGPRA from the middle distance: legal puzzles and unintended consequences. In: Merryman (ed) Imperialism, art and restitution. Cambridge University Press, New York; U.S., pp 193–217

Curators Committee A (2009) A code of ethics for curators. American Association of Museums

Fincham D (2011) Deaccession of art from the public trust. Art Antiq Law 16(2):93–129

Hemmens C, Brody DC, Spohn C (2019) Criminal courts: a contemporary perspective, 4th edn. SAGE Publications

Newton NJ, Anderson RT, Goldberg CE, LaVelle JP, Royster JV, Singer JW, Strickland R (2005) Cohen's handbook of Federal Indian Law. 2005 edition with 2007 supplement edn. LexisNexis

Pineschi L (2012) Cultural diversity as a human right? General Comment No.21 of the Committee on Economic, Social and Cultural Rights. In: Borelli S, Lenzerini F (eds) Cultural heritage, cultural rights, cultural diversity. Studies in intercultural human rights. Nijhoff Publishers, Brill, pp 29–53

World Archaeological Congress W (2006) The Tamaki Makau-rau Accord on the display of human remains and sacred objects. WAC, Osaka, Japan

Zaretsky D (2015) There's no such thing as the public trust, and it's a good thing, too. In: Courtney J (ed) The legal guide for museum professionals. Rowman & Littlefield, Lanham (US), pp 151–155

Part III
Sacred Indigenous Cultural Heritage in Canadian Law

Chapter 6
Indigenous Sacred Heritage on the National Level: Federal Canadian Law and Canadian Museums

6.1 Introduction

> We believe firmly that the time has come to resolve a fundamental contradiction at the heart of Canada: that while we assume the role of defender of human rights in the international community, we retain, in our conception of Canada's origins and make-up, the remnants of colonial attitudes of cultural superiority that do violence to the Aboriginal peoples to whom they are directed. Restoring Aboriginal nations to a place of honour in our shared history, and recognizing their continuing presence as collectives participating in Canadian life, are therefore fundamental to the changes we propose.[1]

The repatriation of Indigenous[2] cultural heritage within Canada takes place within a complicated web of relationships that have been broken in the past and that are being renewed. Difficulties exist at all levels, the federal, the provincial and the local levels. As will be shown below, some cases decided by the Supreme Court in the area of Aboriginal rights have further exacerbated matters. Reconciliation, as a process has been ongoing, and while the observation quoted above was made by the Royal Commission on Aboriginal Peoples 30 years ago, the process remains underway. Positive steps on cultural heritage and repatriation have been taken in different places across the country over the last decades, for example on the provincial level.[3] At the same time, new cases give the opportunity for further improvements. Despite the many remaining hurdles, the positive steps that have been taken give hope that

---

[1] Royal Commission on Aboriginal Peoples (1991), p. 15.

[2] Please note that this chapter adopts the capitalization of the terms Indigenous Peoples and Indigenous (except for when used in citations) for reasons explained in Chap. 1. Capital A is used in Aboriginal for similar reasons except for citations, when spelled differently in the original source cited.

[3] For example, the adoption of the First Nations Sacred Objects Repatriation Act and accompanying regulation in the early 2000s in Alberta and the more recently adopted B.C. Declaration on the Rights of Indigenous Peoples Act which was passed on November 28th 2019.

V. Tünsmeyer, *Repatriation of Sacred Indigenous Cultural Heritage and the Law*, Studies in Art, Heritage, Law and the Market 3,
https://doi.org/10.1007/978-3-030-89047-6_6

Indigenous rights can be advanced further within Canada through legal means. One of the steps taken, for example, has been the change from a veto against the United Nations Declaration on the Rights of Indigenous Peoples in 2007, to a qualified endorsement of the declaration in 2010, to a full endorsement of the Declaration in 2016.[4] This fundamental contradiction at the heart of the country, and indeed, its legal system, observed by the RCAP, remains true today has received renewed attention in recent years. In 2019 the British Columbia Legislature passed an act set to implement the Declaration in the province, both to ensure that provincial laws align with the Declaration and to begin implementing the objectives of the declaration in the province.[5] A similar bill C(C-262) was also introduced on the federal level, but failed in the Senate. Things changed recently, however, when a comparable bill tabled in December of 2020 was passed in June 2021. It contains the express objective to facilitate Canada's implementation of the international standard-setting instrument.[6] With implementing legislation on the United Nations Declaration on the Rights of Indigenous Peoples having been adopted recently, future actions on cultural heritage and legislation are likely.

There are two main research questions that underlie this book: How should the repatriation of Indigenous sacred cultural heritage be regulated legally in light of international cultural heritage and human rights law standards? And second, what—if anything—can we derive from the findings of the country analysis in light of the international standards for the cultural heritage law and policy of the selected countries? To answer the first question, first how the repatriation of sacred cultural heritage is regulated in Canadian law will be addressed. Specifically, federal Aboriginal and heritage law, the repatriation law in Alberta and the modern treaty negotiation process in British Columbia will be analysed. The reasons for the choice of provinces were introduced in the first chapter of this volume. To summarize the reasons briefly, Alberta is the sole Canadian province with specific legislation to enable repatriation, the First Nations Sacred Ceremonial Objects Repatriation Act. British Columbia, in turn, is a province lacking historical treaties between Indigenous Peoples and the Crown. As a result, repatriation and agreements on heritage management responsibilities can be (and have been) embedded in contemporary treaty-making processes. This serves as a valuable contrast to the two other models considered in this volume and will provide an alternative approach to be considered in Part IV, which distils the different repatriation models and considers them in light of international human rights standards. This leads to the second aspect of the analysis of national law, namely, to establish whether these rules and policies are in accordance with Canada's obligations under international human rights law? To answer the first question, the law regulating repatriation in Alberta (see Sect. 7.1,

[4] Millen and Adkins (22.10.2018).

[5] Declaration on the Rights of Indigenous Peoples Act [SBC 2019] Chapter 44 (Assented to 2019-11-28).

[6] United Nations Declaration on the Rights of Indigenous Peoples Act, S.C. 2021, c. 14 (Assented to 2021-06-21).

Chap. 7), the treaty negotiation process and any concluded treaties in British Columbia (see Sect. 7.2, Chap. 7), and federal heritage law, including the institutional code of ethics that govern the federal museum with a large Indigenous heritage collection, the Canadian History Museum (see Sects. 6.3 and 6.4 below), will be examined.

To answer the second question, it is necessary to delve a bit deeper into the context of these different legal areas. As was highlighted in Part I, there is no international human *right* to repatriation *per se*. Instead, repatriation can further or even guarantee a number of cultural rights that are connected to Indigenous cultural rights. This is not surprising as it was already observed that the repatriation of sacred cultural heritage is connected to different legal areas, in particular the legal relationship between the different governmental levels and Indigenous communities (examined in Sect. 6.2), Indigenous religious freedom (examined in Sect. 6.3.3), cultural heritage law (examined in Sect. 6.3.5 for the federal level), and museum (self-) regulation (see Sect. 6.4). Since cultural heritage law is mostly a provincial competence, the federal examination is complemented by an examination of the relevant parts of provincial heritage legislation in Chap. 7. The analysis of U.S. law in the preceding chapter also examined federal Indian law, as it comprised most of the instruments that govern different aspects of the lives of Native Americans. In Canada, the equivalent is the Indian Act, which is a legal remnant of the country's colonial history. It facilitated the removal of Indigenous artefacts in the past and will be examined in Sect. 6.3 below. By contrast, the field of Aboriginal rights law evolved with the constitutional entrenchment of Aboriginal and treaty rights in 1982. All the legal aspects of Indigenous life, including the reclaiming of cultural heritage, are affected by the Aboriginal rights canon. It will be explored in Sect. 6.3.2 below. On the basis of examining federal law in this chapter, and provincial legislation in Chap. 7, this part will conclude by evaluating existing repatriation efforts in light of international human rights standards. Chapter 8 will highlight the lessons that can be derived from this research for the cultural heritage law and policy, in order to answer the second research question.

There is a great diversity in the Indigenous cultures present in Canada. Even within the provinces studied, socio-cultural characteristics vary, as is the case for historic experiences and Indigenous laws.[7] The author made the choice against focussing on one Indigenous People in order to be able to consider the broader legislative interactions which have been put in place on the macro-level. These legal interactions are important for repatriation purposes, since Indigenous material heritage is a much contested 'resource'. Its historic movements exemplifies some of the most important forces which have shaped the contemporary legal position of Indigenous Peoples and which have been reflected in different laws over time: the clash between two sovereign forces, forced assimilation, racism, curtailing or complete

[7] Bell et al. (2008b), p. 203.

negation of civil, political and socio-cultural rights, and mediatory attempts.[8] This can be seen in the different legal areas examined, both in the foundational legal areas examined in the section below and in the more specific fields of cultural heritage and repatriation legislation that are examined later in this chapter.

6.2 Foundations

6.2.1 Constitution

6.2.1.1 Constitutions: An Evolution

Canada came into existence by virtue of the British North America Act 1867, which joined the British colonies of the United Province of Canada, Nova Scotia, and New Brunswick.[9] Prior to this, the region was a self-governing British colony. It took until 1982 for the last legal ties between the countries to be severed by means of the Canada Act 1982[10] This evolution also explains how the country's legal foundation is comprised of a multitude of different instruments.[11] S.52(1) provides for the supremacy of all of these provisions over "any law that is inconsistent with the provisions of the Constitution" which "is, to the extent of the inconsistency, of no force or effect". In addition to these sources, the Supreme Court of Canada found in New Brunswick Broadcasting Co. v Nova Scotia (1993) that the word 'includes' in s.52(2) meant that the definition is non-exhaustive.[12] It has found the Constitution to include, *inter alia*, the non-written rule of parliamentary privilege.[13]

[8]To better appreciate the impact of repatriation on the life of a community and the many legal and bureaucratic hurdles Indigenous Peoples face in specific cases, the interested reader is referred to the cooperative research undertaken in British Columbia, see Bell and Napoleon (2008). For Alberta consult the contributions compiled by Gerald Conaty on the repatriation work undertaken by the Glenbow, see Conaty (2015).

[9]Department of Justice, Government of Canada, About Canada's justice system, available at: http://www.justice.gc.ca/eng/csj-sjc/just/05.html [last accessed 18.08.2021].

[10]Due to this Act, Canada effectively became 'patriated' from the United Kingdom. http://www.justice.gc.ca/eng/csj-sjc/just/05.html [last accessed 18.08.2021].

[11]This includes the Constitution Act 1982 (s.52(2)(a)), several acts and orders which are included in the schedule to the Constitution Act, 1982 (s.52(2)(b)), as well as any future amendments. Most notably, Acts included in the Constitution by virtue of s.52(2)(b) are the Constitution Act 1867 (formerly known as the British North America Act 1867) and the Canadian Charter of Rights and Freedoms. See also Hogg (2007b (loose-leaf updated 2015)), p. 1-7 and 1-8, who counts 30 Acts and orders.

[12]Hogg (2007b (loose-leaf updated 2015)), p. 1-9.

[13]New Brunswick Broadcasting Co. v Nova Scotia [1993] 1 S.C.R. 319.

6.2.1.2 Distribution of Competences and Interpretational Principles

The division of legislative competences is relevant to the protection of cultural property and the rights of First Nations to their cultural heritage on several levels. Firstly, it explains why cultural heritage legislation is marked by a high degree of diversity across Canada. Due to the distribution of legislative competences, different legal regimes govern Indigenous cultural rights and the various forms of Indigenous cultural heritage. Both provinces have a very distinct manner in which they approach the legal protection of 'their' cultural heritage. Secondly, the split also means that each level of government can only implement those (international) treaty provisions for which it has the jurisdiction to act. Thirdly, constitutional principles matter when considering the relationship between the government, Indigenous Peoples and Indigenous cultural heritage. They also affect how Canada can fulfil its obligations under international agreements, notably human rights treaties.

The reception of public international law into Canadian law is governed by two essential, unwritten principles derived from English law. First, foreign affairs (and this includes the ratification of treaties) is a purely executive matter. The second is a principle "established through civil war and revolution" namely "that the Crown is not a source of law. Just as treaty-making is an exclusively executive act, law-making is an exclusively legislative act."[14] Canada can therefore be classified as a dualist legal system. While rules of customary international law directly form part of the common law,[15] any other international law has to be implemented. The 1937 Labour Conventions Reference case established that the level of government that is competent for a subject under Canadian constitutional law is the level with the power to incorporate it into Canadian law through legislation.[16] Canada can thus be described as a predominantly dualist legal system. Implementation powers for international agreements are a result of the general division of legislative powers and are therefore determined by the Canadian constitution.[17] This split of implementation also leads to what has been described as "a variety, a bewildering variety even, of implementation forms".[18] The original distribution of competences in the Constitution Act 1867 favoured a federation with a strong central organ.[19] Thus, the competences of the provincial Legislatures were listed exhaustively, with federal Parliament[20] retaining the remaining power.[21] Due to the subsequent interpretation

[14] van Ert (2010), p. 927.

[15] van Ert (2010), p. 928.

[16] Canada (AG) v Ontario (AG) [1937] UKPC 6, [1937] A.C. 326.

[17] Paterson (2010), p. 234.

[18] van Ert (2010), p. 928.

[19] Hogg (1992), pp. 108–109.

[20] This chapter will adopt the terms used in the Constitution Acts and employ Legislature for a provincial parliament and Parliament for the federal level body.

[21] Hogg (2007b (loose-leaf updated 2015)), p. 5-15.

through case law, the provincial powers, as well their importance, grew significantly.[22]

The areas that are most relevant to repatriation claims are trade, property and civil rights and Indigenous Peoples, as well as land reservations. These areas are split between the two governmental levels. According to s. 92(13) of the Constitution Act 1867, property law is a provincial competence. In Kitkatla Band v British Columbia (2002),[23] the Canadian Supreme Court upheld the BC Heritage Conservation Act as being a valid exercise of the provincial jurisdiction over property rights. Cultural heritage protection has thus been found to be squarely within the jurisdiction of the provincial power under s.92(13). Kitkatla touched upon the difficult interaction between provincial heritage legislation and Indigenous cultural objects and sites which were not located on reserve lands. Most provinces have similar legislation and there is no comprehensive federal legislation in this area. With regard to Indigenous Peoples, it has not yet been settled in the case law whether there is an Aboriginal right (and thus constitutional right) "to [the] protection and control of such resources, or jurisdiction to enact their own laws in relation to these resources."[24] In light of the split of legislative competences between 'property' on the provincial level and 'Indigenous' on the federal level, federal legislation would be difficult to enact. Kitkatla has resulted in considerable powers being given to the province in this regard. Another provincial competence covers the management and sale of public lands that belong to the province under s.92(5). This can be critical depending on where Indigenous Peoples used to reside before dispossession and relocation and the cultural heritage they might have left behind that remains unexcavated. In contrast, Parliament retains power in relation to 'the public debt and property' for federally owned land (s.91(1A)), such as national parks.[25] Legislative authority on trade and commerce rests with the Canadian Parliament according to s. 91 (2) of the Constitution Act 1867.[26] Most important for present purpose is arguably Section 91 (24) of the Constitution Act 1867 which allows Parliament to legislate on matters of "Indians, and lands reserved for the Indians".

If legislative powers such as those addressed above are assigned expressly, this entail an exclusive legislative power, either for the Parliament or for the Legislatures.[27] There are then three important doctrines to consider, the doctrine of interjurisdictional immunity, the paramountcy principle and the pith and substance doctrine. The pith and substance doctrine enables "a provincial law to 'affect' a federal matter" through "read[ing] down [of] the provincial law to exclude the

[22]Hogg (2007b (loose-leaf updated 2015)), p. 5-17, p. 15–18.

[23]Kitkatla Band *v*. British Columbia (Minister of Small Business, Tourism and Culture), [2002] 2 S.C.R. 146, 2002 SCC 31.

[24]Bell (2001), p. 247.

[25]Hogg (2007b (loose-leaf updated 2015)), p. 29-22.

[26]Paterson (2010), p. 234.

[27]Hogg (2007b (loose-leaf updated 2015)), p. 15-38.15.

federal matter."[28] The interjurisdictional immunity might best be classified as an exception to the pith and substance doctrine, as it prohibits provincial laws that reach to the core of a federal subject.[29] The paramountcy principle "applies where there is conflict or inconsistency between provincial and federal law, in the sense of impossibility of dual compliance or frustration of federal purpose. In the case of such conflict or inconsistency, the federal law prevails".[30] Overall, the different levels interact in law-making, in a manner that has also been termed cooperative federalism by the SCC.[31]

6.2.1.3 S.35(1): Judicial Empowerment and Parliamentary Restriction

> **35.** (1) The existing aboriginal and treaty rights of the aboriginal peoples of Canada are hereby recognized and affirmed.
>
> (2) In this Act, *"aboriginal peoples of Canada"* includes the Indian, Inuit and Métis peoples of Canada.
>
> (3) For greater certainty, in subsection (1) *"treaty rights"* includes rights that now exist by way of land claims agreements or may be so acquired.
>
> (4) Notwithstanding any other provision of this Act, the aboriginal and treaty rights referred to in subsection (1) are guaranteed equally to male and female persons.[32]

The addition of s.35 by means of Constitution Act 1982 and the Constitutional Amendment Proclamation in 1983[33] have significantly influenced not only the legal position of Indigenous Peoples in court proceedings but also their relationship with the Canadian authorities. Section 35(1) provides for the constitutional protection of

---

[28] Hogg (2007b (loose-leaf updated 2015)), p. 14-38.13.

[29] Hogg (2007b (loose-leaf updated 2015)), p. 14-38.13.

[30] Tsilhqot'in Nation *v.* British Columbia, 2014 SCC 44, [2014] 2 S.C.R. 256, at para 130.

[31] For example in Reference re Code of Civil Procedure (Que.), art. 35, 2021 SCC 27, paras 304–304 Abella J dissenting.

[32] Subsections 35(3) and (4) were added by the Constitution Amendment Proclamation, 1983 (see SI/84-102).

[33] Section 35.1 was added by the Constitution Amendment Proclamation, 1983 (see SI/84-102). It reads:

35.1 The government of Canada and the provincial governments are committed to the principle that, before any amendment is made to Class 24 of section 91 of the "Constitution Act, 1867", to section 25 of this Act or to this Part,

(a) a constitutional conference that includes in its agenda an item relating to the proposed amendment, composed of the Prime Minister of Canada and the first ministers of the provinces, will be convened by the Prime Minister of Canada; and
(b) the Prime Minister of Canada will invite representatives of the aboriginal peoples of Canada to participate in the discussions on that item.

both Aboriginal and treaty rights. Neither right was defined in the Constitution, nor did the provision clarify whether it was judicially enforceable (unlike the CCRF).[34] The insertion of the word 'existing' has turned out to be similarly problematic. The jurisprudence since 1982 has established that an Aboriginal right is the right to a specific cultural practice that dates to the pre-settler existence of Indigenous Peoples in Canada. An Aboriginal right is specific to a particular community and can be subject to limitations. Since its inclusion, the provision has served the Supreme Court as a basis upon which to develop an entirely new area of law (see Sect. 6.3.2 for a more detailed analysis of Aboriginal rights to cultural heritage) and to redefine the (historic) relationship between Indigenous Peoples and the government (see Sect. 6.2.2.4).

The supremacy of the constitution[35] entails that the constitutional affirmation of Aboriginal rights restricts the powers of both Parliament and the Legislatures.[36,37] Questions that arise from this for the relationship between these different levels include, *inter alia*, the degree of this limitation (i.e. if rights may be limited but not abolished or not limited (at all)), the consequences of such limitations for First Nation/Inuit and Métis sovereignty and questions of cooperation between the different levels of governance.

The courts have been very active in this regard, at times at a great cost to Indigenous Peoples. In Sparrows, the term 'existing' in s.35 has been interpreted to mean existing at the time of the constitutional amendment (17.04.1982).[38] By this time, Indigenous Peoples in Canada had survived targeted assimilation policies and legislation for well over one hundred years. This is perhaps most notable with respect to Aboriginal title and Indigenous self-government. The Canadian judiciary conceptualized Canada's Indigenous Peoples as subjects of the Crown who, in turn, owned unsurrendered Indigenous lands. In St. Catherine's Milling, the Privy Council famously held that Indigenous Peoples held a usufruct over unsurrendered lands and characterized the relationship between Canada's Indigenous inhabitants and the Crown as "one analogous to the feudal relationship of lord and tenant".[39] Only with

[34] Carlson (2005), p. 450.

[35] S.52(1) Constitution Act 1982: The Constitution of Canada is the supreme law of Canada, and any law that is inconsistent with the provisions of the Constitution is, to the extent of the inconsistency, of no force or effect.

[36] Hogg (2007b (loose-leaf updated 2015)), p. 28-29.

[37] Vicaire (2011), p. 18, has aptly described the constitutional process with regard to the Indigenous Peoples of Canada as follows: "Canadian constitutional documents have progressively welded Aboriginal tribes to Canadian society, subordinating their sovereignty at a high price and largely without consultation."

[38] See also Borrows (2016), p. 7 "The assumption in the Sparrow case, that the Crown could unilaterally extinguish rights prior to 1982, is offensive."

[39] St. Catharine's Milling and Lumber Co. v. R [1887] 13 S.C.R. 577, at 604 "The word 'trusts' would not be an appropriate expression to apply to the relation between the crown and the Indians respecting the unceded lands of the latter. As will appear hereafter very clearly, such relationship is not in any sense that of trustee and *cestui que trust*, but rather one analogous to the feudal

Calder[40] would Aboriginal title become anchored in the common law and even then obstacles remain varied and numerous. Peter Vicaire aptly summarized the developments since: "[u]nfortunately, most of the post-Calder judicial decisions suffer from the residual effects of centuries-old colonial mindsets that tenaciously remain today."[41]

6.2.2 Relationship Between Canadian Institutions and Indigenous Peoples

6.2.2.1 Concurrent, Contradicting or Overlapping Jurisdictions: Reconciliatory Principles at the Cost of Indigenous Peoples?

Much of the Aboriginal rights jurisprudence is concerned with the idea of reconciliation. Binnie J. in Mikisew contextualized modern treaty and Aboriginal rights as seeking to realize the fundamental objective of "reconciliation of aboriginal peoples and non-aboriginal peoples and their respective claims, interests and ambitions. The management of these relationships takes place in the shadow of a long history of grievances and misunderstanding."[42] This legal narrative appears time and again in the context of Canada's Indigenous populations. It is central to Aboriginal law and influences contemporary repatriation efforts, either by triggering them or by providing the legal framework in which the requests have to be articulated. This section will briefly consider its meaning and examine how the courts have 'reconciled' different sovereigns, taking the example of the province and Aboriginal peoples.

Reconciliation is used in different ways in the Canadian legal context, and it has different meanings: reconciling the different sovereignties of Indigenous Peoples and the Canadian government, giving effect to treaty rights in light of conflicting non-Indigenous interests, reconciling Indigenous rights with the rights of other Canadians,[43] reconciling Canada with its colonial past,[44] and the ongoing de-colonization process, and the use of treaties to search for "a vibrant and respectful new relationship between peoples".[45] Its frequent use in jurisprudence and policies has ensured that it has a central position in Aboriginal rights. The OED defines it as "[t]he action of restoring estranged people or parties to friendship; the result of this;

relationship of lord and tenant, or, in some aspects, to that one, so familiar in the Roman law, where the right of property is dismembered and divided between the proprietor and a usufructuary."

[40] Calder et al. v Attorney-General of British Columbia [1973] S.C.R. 313.

[41] Vicaire (2011), p. 20.

[42] Mikisew Cree First Nation v. Canada (Minister of Canadian Heritage) [2005] 3 S.C.R. 388, 2005 SCC 69, at para 1.

[43] Tsilhqot'in Nation v. British Columbia [2014], at para 82; Royal Commission on Aboriginal Peoples (1996), p. 16.

[44] Royal Commission on Aboriginal Peoples (1991), p. 17.

[45] Royal Commission on Aboriginal Peoples (1996), p. 35.

the fact of being reconciled"[46] or "the action or an act of bringing a thing or things to agreement, concord, or harmony; the fact of being made consistent or compatible".[47] Reconciliation thus is not congruent with decolonization. However, the existing inequities, including with respect to cultural heritage, have resulted from colonialism. Following this approach, decolonization is necessary in order to restore the 'friendship' between Aboriginal and non-aboriginal people. As will be seen repeatedly, however, big hurdles to these decolonizing efforts remain, despite the frequent use of the term reconciliation.

Without even examining the jurisprudence for how it approaches reconciliation in substance, the composition of the judiciary already leaves room for improvement. On the basis of the available data from 2016, there is an extreme under-representation of Indigenous Peoples among the judiciary. There are no Indigenous judges in the Supreme Court or in the Court of Appeal, or in the Tax Court. Among Federal Courts, Indigenous judges amount to 2.4% of the judiciary. Among federally appointed judges in the Provincial Courts, the numbers are marginally better. Indigenous judges account for 0.7% of the Provincial Supreme Court judges, 1.3% of Provincial Court of Appeals and 0.1% of Superior Court judges.[48] There is clearly a need to work more consciously on the representation of Indigenous Peoples in the judiciary, especially in light of the fact that the field of Aboriginal rights is largely dominated by case law.

An important aspect of the use of reconciliation in the jurisprudence has been to reconcile the different governmental powers that are at play. The courts have used the interpretational doctrines described above to help in this act of 'reconciling' different governmental powers but they have not necessarily progressed as much in decolonizing the relationship. For example, the courts have understood the paramountcy principle to mean that, where a provincial law of general application also covers 'Indians', federal law dealing with the same subject matter will only be paramount in the case of conflict or an inconsistency and does not prohibit the province from legislating on 'Indians' in general.[49] Some of SCC jurisprudence, however, have given raise to questions, especially as it relates to the power of province to also touch upon matters that are at the core of federal jurisdiction in s.91(24), meaning the power to make laws on "the core of Indianness".[50] It also raises questions as to what the core of s.91(24) might be and the corresponding influence of the judiciary in paving the way for or obstructing more recognition of Indigenous rights.

---

[46] http://www.oed.com/view/Entry/159781?redirectedFrom=reconciliation#eid [last accessed 18.08.2021].

[47] http://www.oed.com/view/Entry/159781?redirectedFrom=reconciliation#eid [last accessed 18.08.2021].

[48] Griffith (2016).

[49] Imai (2014), pp. 611–612.

[50] Olthuis Kleer Townshend LLP (2018), p. 16.

In Xeni Gwet'in First Nations v British Columbia, the SCC decided that provincial law could apply to Aboriginal title lands and infringe Aboriginal rights subject to the s.35 infringement and justification test.[51] In Grassy Narrows v Ontario the SCC held that the province acting on behalf of the Crown could take up land thereby limiting treaty rights[52] subject to the Mikisew conditions without breaching those rights.[53] In both cases, limitations arose out of a limitation enshrined in the original treaty. The court distilled four limitations in Mikisew: first, such limitations had to be in line with the purposes of the limitations set out in the treaty. Second, they had to still allow for a meaningful exercise of the treaty right in relation to the territory where it has been and continues to be exercised traditionally. Third, any such measure must be taken only after consultation with the respective Indigenous communities.[54] Fourth, consultation may not exclude accommodation from the outside.[55] Rather, it must seek to *substantially address* the concerns of Indigenous Peoples.[56]

Grassy Narrows, relying on Xeni Gwet'in, also confirmed that the province could infringe treaty rights if the infringement could be justified according to the criteria the court had originally established for infringements of Aboriginal rights in Sparrow examined in Sect. 6.3.2.1 below.[57] As a result, infringements are permitted as long as the legislation causing the infringement pursues a legitimate legislative objective and can be justified.[58] If the aim is legitimate, the analysis progresses to whether the infringement can be justified in light of the fact that the honour of the Crown is always at stake in cases involving Indigenous Peoples.[59] Other questions are whether the infringement is proportionate (only as much as is necessary to effect the desired result), whether fair compensation is available for expropriations and whether consultation requirements have been respected.[60] While both treaty and Aboriginal rights may be infringed upon unilaterally[61] by both provinces and Canada, they may not be extinguished.

---

[51] Tsilhqot'in Nation v. British Columbia [2014].

[52] Imai (2014), p. 626.

[53] Grassy Narrows First Nation v. Ontario (Natural Resources) 2014 SCC 48, [2014] 2 S.C.R. 447, at para 53.

[54] Mikisew Cree First Nation v Canada (Minister of Canadian Heritage) [2005], at para 48, para 49–58, purpose element inferred from para 60.

[55] Mikisew [2005], at para 54.

[56] Ibid, at para 61 relying on Delgamuukw.

[57] Grassy Narrows First Nation v. Ontario (Natural Resources) [2014], at para 53.

[58] Imai (2014), p. 829.

[59] Imai (2014), p. 829.

[60] R v Sparrow [1990] S.C.R. 1075, 1091.

[61] While consultation arguably incorporates an element of multilateralism, courts at all levels have been keen to point out that the duty to consult is a matter of degree and may at times even amount to little more than a duty to inform.

John Borrows rightly criticizes the Supreme Court's decision in of the Xeni Gwet'in First Nations/Tshilqot'in Nations to allow provincial laws of general application to apply to Aboriginal title lands:

> The Court's conclusion cuts against a 250-year-old constitutional principle first outlined in the Royal Proclamation of 1763, and accepted by many First Nations in central Canada in 1764 Treaty of Niagara.... The time tested principles of British and Canadian constitutional law were not followed in the Tsilhqotín Nation decision because of a desire for administrative clarity and efficiency.[62]

In Tsilhqotín Nation v BC the SCC allowed for provincial laws to infringe Aboriginal rights. Since they are protected by virtue of s.35, any such infringement still needs to satisfy the elements of the Sparrow test, meaning that the law must serve a "compelling and substantial objective".[63] It is sadly ironic that the court used a constitutional provision protecting Aboriginal and treaty rights to justify them being subject to limitations by provincial laws, thereby potentially expanding provincial law-making powers. McLachlin C.J. argued that "in this case, applying the doctrine of interjurisdictional immunity to exclude provincial regulation of forests on Aboriginal title lands would produce uneven, undesirable results and may lead to legislative vacuums."[64] So far, interjurisdictional immunity still does apply to provincial laws which affect the remainder of the core of federal power under s.91(24).[65] In her reasoning, McLachlin drew a parallel between s.35 and the Charter and argued that both types of rights act as a limitation on governmental powers. "These limits" she argues "have nothing to do with whether something lies at the core of the federal government's powers" and the doctrine of jurisdictional immunity should not be applied as a result.[66] However, s.35 treaty rights are

---

[62]Borrows (2015), p. 735-737.

[63]Hogg (2007b (loose-leaf updated 2015)), p. 28-16.

[64]Tsilhqot'in Nation v. British Columbia [2014], para 147.

[65]Hogg (2007b (loose-leaf updated 2015)), p. 28-13.

[66]Tsilhqot'in Nation v. British Columbia [2014], paras 139–142: "[139] As discussed, s. 35 of the Constitution Act, 1982 imposes limits on how both the federal and provincial governments can deal with land under Aboriginal title. **Neither level of government is permitted** to legislate in a way that results in a **meaningful diminution of an Aboriginal or treaty right, unless such an infringement is justified** in the broader public interest and is consistent with the Crown's fiduciary duty owed to the Aboriginal group. The result is to protect Aboriginal and treaty rights while also allowing the reconciliation of Aboriginal interests with those of the broader society.

140 **What role** then is left for the application of the **doctrine of interjurisdictional immunity** and the idea that Aboriginal rights are at the core of the federal power over "Indians" under s. 91 (24) of the Constitution Act, 1867? **The answer is none.**

141 The doctrine of interjurisdictional immunity is directed to ensuring that the two levels of government are able to operate without interference in their core areas of exclusive jurisdiction. This goal is not implicated in cases such as this. **Aboriginal rights are a limit on both federal and provincial jurisdiction.**

142 **The guarantee of Aboriginal rights in s. 35 of the Constitution Act, 1982, like the Canadian Charter of Rights and Freedoms, operates as a limit on federal and provincial legislative powers.** The Charter forms Part I of the Constitution Act, 1982, and the guarantee of Aboriginal rights forms Part II. Parts I and II are sister provisions, both operating to limit

different from charter rights in one fundamental point: treaties are agreements between two entities who both possess self-determination rights (albeit to different degrees). This nation to nation element of modern treaty-making has been acknowledged both by British Columbia and the federal government to be a cornerstone in their modern treaty negotiations. A limitation imposed on law-making by virtue of the individual rights of the governed is thus fundamentally different than one which arises out of a level of comity to safeguard government to government treaty-making. To equate the two creates a backdoor through which the province can unilaterally alter the obligations it entered into, and it undermines the legitimacy of the entire process. Any treaty provisions on Indigenous cultural heritage can thus be limited, as can any Aboriginal right to Indigenous cultural heritage, provided the provincial and federal limitation fulfils the Sparrow criteria. One may also wonder in how far this approach to treaty and Aboriginal rights[67] is consistent with the idea of reconciliation, It appears to understand reconciliation as a balancing of Indigenous versus non-Indigenous rights undertaken by non-Indigenous entities and subjugated by Canadian sovereignty.[68]

6.2.2.2 S.91(24) and the Power to Legislate Over 'Indians'

The Parliamentary power to legislate on 'Indians' mentioned above requires further elaboration and can serve as a good entry point into the complex, and frequently adverse, relationship between Canadian governmental authorities and Indigenous Peoples.

According to Hogg, the main motivation behind reserving exclusive Parliamentary competence under Section 91(24) in the nineteenth century seems to have been to protect Indigenous Peoples against incoming settlers. The greater distance between the Parliament and the respective peoples would mean that the former would be more interested in observing the treaties which had been signed than the local settler communities who were seeking less and less regulation. Another possible motivation, according to Hogg, might have been the desire to ensure uniform national policies on Indigenous Peoples.[69]

governmental powers, whether federal or provincial. Part II Aboriginal rights, like Part I Charter rights, are held against government — they operate to prohibit certain types of regulation which governments could otherwise impose. **These limits have nothing to do with whether something lies at the core of the federal government's powers**." Emphasis added.

[67] Ladner (2009), p. 282-283 In evaluating the SCC has observed "The Supreme Court ... has instead viewed Aboriginal and treaty rights as creations of the Canadian constitutional order that is subject to judicial interpretation and parliamentary supremacy. The court has therefore framed reconciliation in a manner that is inconsistent with principles of treaty constitutionalism, and it has done so in a way that disregards Indigenous constitutional orders."

[68] Ladner (2009), p. 283-284.

[69] Hogg (2007b (loose-leaf updated 2015)), p. 28-22.

With regard to the power itself, it is in effect two-fold and covers both a general legislative power over "Indians" and one over "Lands reserved for the Indians".[70] The former is independent of the latter, meaning that Parliament has the exclusive power to legislate over 'Indians' irrespective of their location within a province.[71] This is subject to the exception of laws of general application which the Legislatures may pass and will also govern 'Indians' not on lands reserved for them (and on reserve lands subject to limitations discussed above in i). Furthermore, there remains "an untouchable core" which the Legislatures may not touch upon in line with the notion of interjurisdictional immunity above.[72] According to SCC, only Parliament may legislate on who classifies as Indian,[73] who may possess land on an Indian reserve[74] or on the extinguishment of Aboriginal title.[75]

The scope of s.91(24) rests on three central questions: who qualifies as 'Indian' for the purposes of s.91(24), what laws may be passed in relation to them and which areas classify as "lands reserved for the Indians"? To answer the first question, the federal categorization of Indigenous identity has created three important categories: 'Status' Indians and Non-Status Indians (which both fall under the scope of s.91(24)) and band membership, which remains distinct from these two categories. Indian status in Canada is defined in the Indian Act adopted by Parliament and will be explored further in Sect. 6.2.2.3 below. For now, suffice to say that the Indian Act accords status to descendants of charter members of a band "at the time of the establishment of a reserve or the making of a treaty."[76] This status then entails a number of rights that are granted in the Indian Act, notably the right to live on a reserve. Many changes and reversed classifications have made defining Indian status difficult.

The 2016 governmental census calculated the Aboriginal population to be 1,673,785, around 4.9% of Canada's population.[77] This included those who reported being First Nations (North American Indian), Métis or Inuk (Inuit), Registered or Treaty Indian status that is registered under the *Indian Act* of Canada, and those who reported membership in a First Nation or Indian band. 820,115 had registered or treaty status and classify as Indians for the purposes of s.91(24).[78] 792,140 Canadian

---

[70] Hogg (2007b (loose-leaf updated 2015)), p. 28-22, 28-23.

[71] Hogg (2007b (loose-leaf updated 2015)), p. 28-22, 28-23.

[72] Imai (2014), p. 611-612.

[73] Natural Parents v Superintendent of Child Welfare [1976] 2 S.C.R. 751, at 787.

[74] Derrickson v. Derrickson [1986] 1 S.C.R. 285, at para 57.

[75] Delgamuukw v. British Columbia [1997] 3 S.C.R. 1010, (extinguishment prior to 1982), at paras 172–176. Tsilhqot'in Nation v. British Columbia [2014], at paras 128–152, allows for the impairment not the extinguishment of aboriginal title by the province.

[76] Hogg (2007b (loose-leaf updated 2015)), p. 28-23, 28-24.

[77] See official website of Statistics Canada at: https://www12.statcan.gc.ca/census-recensement/2016/rt-td/ap-pa-eng.cfm [last accessed 19.08.2021].

[78] https://www12.statcan.gc.ca/census-recensement/2016/ref/guides/009/98-500-x2016009-eng.cfm [last accessed 19.08.2021].

citizens had membership in a First Nation or band.[79] The Métis people originate from marriages between French Canadian men and Indigenous woman and classify as Indians under s.91(24). The Inuit who do not fall under the reserve system (and thus not within the Indian Act definition) also qualify as Indian under s.91(24).[80] In summary, four categories of individuals fall under s.91(24): Status-Indian, non-Status Indian as defined above, Métis and Inuit.

To answer the second question, so far Parliament has understood s.91(24) to encompass the power to legislate on matters that would normally be outside its competence as far as non-Indians are concerned.[81] Otherwise, s.91(24) would be an empty provision, as its other powers would provide the necessary powers.[82] In answer to the third question, 'lands reserved' covers not only Indian reserves, both before and after 1867, "it also includes the huge area of land recognized by the Royal Proclamation of 1763 as 'reserved' for the Indians, that is all land within the territory covered by the Proclamation that was in the possession of the Indians and that had not been ceded to the Crown."[83] This area was extended even further by the Supreme Court in Delgamuukw to also cover lands held by Indigenous Peoples under Aboriginal title.[84] It is for this reason that only Parliament may extinguish Aboriginal title.[85]

6.2.2.3 Indian Status Under the Indian Act

The Indian Act is among the most visible legal reminders of Canada's colonial past.[86] Its history is long and predominantly shaped by (forced) assimilation policies enshrined in legal language. Its adoption in 1876 was shaped by a 'civilizing mission', which had started to replace earlier policies of non-interference since about the 1850s. Other acts from this period which preceded the Indian Act had a comparable perspective, such as the 1857 *Act to Encourage the Gradual Civilization*

---

[79] https://www12.statcan.gc.ca/census-recensement/2016/ref/guides/009/98-500-x2016009-eng.cfm [last accessed 19.08.2021].

[80] Reference as to whether "Indians" includes in s. 91 (24) of the B.N.A. Act includes Eskimo in habitants of the Province of Quebec [1939] S.C.R. 104. Hogg (2007b (loose-leaf updated 2015)), p. 28-24.

[81] Hogg (2007b (loose-leaf updated 2015)), p. 28-24.

[82] Hogg (2007b (loose-leaf updated 2015)), p. 28-25.

[83] Hogg (2007b (loose-leaf updated 2015)), p. 28-25, 28-26.

[84] Hogg (2007b (loose-leaf updated 2015)), p. 28-25, 28-26 Delgamuukw v British Columbia, [1997].

[85] Hogg (2007b (loose-leaf updated 2015)), p. 28-25, 28-26.

[86] For governmental recognition of the colonial history of act see for example preamble of Indian Act Amendment and Replacement Act S.C. 2014, c. 38 "Whereas the Indian Act is an outdated colonial statute, the application of which results in the people of Canada's First Nations being subjected to differential treatment; Whereas the Indian Act does not provide an adequate legislative framework for the development of self-sufficient and prosperous First Nations' communities".

of Indian Tribes in this Province, and to Amend the Laws Relating to Indians,[87] adopted by the 5th Parliament of the Province of Canada.[88] Much of this paternalistic 'civilizing' mission can be seen by tracing Indian status under the act. Indian status is the entry point into the Indian Act which continues to determine the relationship between a significant part of the Indigenous population with the Canadian government. Past definitions of Indian status have been employed for assimilatory and/or discriminatory purposes. The effects of these policies are still felt today and are the backdrop to current efforts to restore past traditions which include repatriation requests and cultural revitalization efforts.

The federal approach towards the Act has slowly shifted over the past 50 years. A 1969 federal policy which sought the integration of Indigenous Peoples into Canadian society was widely opposed by Indigenous Peoples and therefore withdrawn.[89] A significant push for reforming Indian status was further provided by the UNHRCee Lovelace decision and resulted in Bill C-31 which reformed Indian status rule and sought to eliminate discrimination. In 1985, Indian bands regained partial control over their membership by means of the power to enact membership codes (which determines access to band resources).[90] Overall, Parliament retained the control to determine Indian status and, with it, eligibility for federal benefits.[91] Indian bands decide on their membership and access to band resources. In light of the focus on eliminating previous discriminatory practices against women, such as Lovelace, membership codes had to be in line with the acquired rights of reinstated women. Failure to respect s.10(4) could (and did in several cases) result in a refusal of the Minister of Indian Affairs to transfer control over the membership list in line with s.10(7).[92] However, reinstated women continued to face discrimination, this time within the bands themselves. This triggered a number of court cases and decisions by the Canadian Human Rights Tribunal.[93] If the Indigenous community has negotiated a modern treaty it will no longer be governed by the Indian Act and the treaties contain their own definitions of indigeneity and membership.[94] Contemporary evaluation of the Indian Act differs. Many point to the colonial origins of the Act and the comparatively few amendments that have been made.[95] Others, such as

---

[87] Robinson (2016).

[88] The united Provinces of Canada was a union of the previous Upper and Lower Canada and was the result of colonial policies to suppress rebellion, the capital moved between Kingston, Montréal, Toronto and Québec City. Stockford Careless (2019).

[89] Grammond (2009), p. 106.

[90] Grammond (2009), p. 108.

[91] Grammond (2009), p. 108.

[92] Grammond (2009), p. 116.

[93] Grammond (2009), p. 117-119.

[94] See for example Maa-nulth First Nations Final Agreement Act, S.B.C. 2007, c. 43, s.29.1.1 "'Maa-nulth First Nation Citizen' means an individual who becomes a citizen of a Maa-nulth First Nation under a Maa-nulth First Nation Law."

[95] Borrows (2016), pp. 5–6 See also account of the effect of the act on women of their family by two members of the Mi'kmaq Nation Simon and Clark (2013), p. Coombe (1993), p. 274 Coombe

Grammond, argue that the act has evolved to one that confers benefits on "members of a disadvantaged ethnic group", notably in the area of reserve lands and tax and seizure exemptions.[96]

6.2.2.4 Honour of the Crown: Fiduciary Duty

The previous sections have sought to sketch out the essential elements in the written sources of Canadian law that shape the relationship between Indigenous Peoples and Canadian institutions. Two further important concepts have been developed by the Courts: the honour of the crown and the Crown's fiduciary duty towards Indigenous Peoples in Canada.

The Honour of the Crown is similar to the notion of fiduciary duty. It was based on s.35(1) as interpreted in Sparrow. In Sparrow the Supreme Court both found that the:

> Government has the responsibility to act in a fiduciary capacity with respect to aboriginal peoples. The relationship between the Government and aboriginals is trust-like, rather than adversarial, and contemporary recognition and affirmation of aboriginal rights must be defined in light of this historic relationship.[97]

and that:

> the guiding interpretative principle derived from Taylor and Williams and Guerin... the honour of the Crown is at stake in dealings with the aboriginal peoples.[98]

Both concepts have been used by SCC in its pursuit of reconciliation, McCabe argues that fiduciary duty was used more heavily post-1982 but that is has been replaced by the Honour of the Crown in this regard "as a more comprehensive principle on which to found conclusions bringing about the necessary and proper reconciliation."[99] In effect, in his words "[t]he reconciliation imperative is central to the law concerning the honour of the Crown that the Court has developed."[100] Reconciliation and the honour of the Crown have aided in the development of a legal duty to consult, accommodate and negotiate.[101]

Fiduciary duties of the Crown to Indigenous Peoples have been developed in connection with s.35(1). Seminal cases in this regard have been Guerin and Wewaykum. The fiduciary relationship between the Crown and Indigenous Peoples

observed that it "curb[ed] constitutional and citizenship rights in the paternalistic guise of Indian protection, while suppressing aboriginal languages, culture, and collective identity... Indian identity has thus been defined and determined by a bureaucracy committed to its disappearance."

[96] Grammond (2009), p. 107.

[97] R v Sparrow [1990], at 1108.

[98] R v Sparrow [1990], at 1114.

[99] McCabe (2008), p. 57.

[100] McCabe (2008), p. 41-42.

[101] McCabe (2008), p. 41-42 Haida Nation v. British Columbia (Minister of Forests) [2004] 3 S.C.R. 511, 2004 SCC 73.

"depends on identification of a *cognizable* Indian interest, and the Crown's undertaking of discretionary control in relation thereto in a way that invokes responsibility 'in the nature of a private law duty'."[102] Interests which have been identified and affirmed to-date have predominantly been concerned with s.35(1) matters, meaning Aboriginal rights and treaty rights.[103] The minimum standard which the Crown must meet are "the basic obligations of loyalty, food faith in the discharge of its mandate, providing full disclosure appropriate to the subject matter, and acting with ordinary prudence with a view to the best interest of the Aboriginal beneficiaries."[104] While the principle binds both the Parliament the Executive,[105] it is not limitless. For example in Wewaykum, the "The Supreme Court (per Binnie J.) . . . went out of its way to make the point that "'fiduciary duty' as a source of plenary crown liability concerning all aspects of the Crown-Indian relationship overshoots the mark"[106] Moreover, the question of suitable remedies if the Crown is held to be liable for a breach of fiduciary duty is not yet settled.[107]

Undoubtedly, the concepts of honour of the Crown and the Crown's fiduciary duty can aid Indigenous litigants before courts and may even do so in repatriation cases. For example, they could be used to argue against future limitations on cultural rights negotiated in modern treaties. However, they remain ambivalent concepts. They leave much room for interpretation by the courts. In addition, both are arguably based on the nineteenth and early twentieth century characterization[108] of Indigenous Peoples as wardens of the guardian Crown. These characterizations were motivated by depictions of Indigenous Peoples as less advanced, incapable of decision making independent of governmental 'guidance'.

Reconciliation is an important element in the relationship between the descendants of settler communities and Canada's Indigenous Peoples, and the court's emphasis on reconciliation in combination with an acknowledgment of historic wrongs is an important step which courts elsewhere still have to take. However, the pure reference to reconciliation alone is not sufficient to achieve it. Its usage as a motivational force in the Supreme Court's jurisprudence can either be a restrictive or enabling force. The concern here is not so much the presence of reconciliation as a *leitmotif* in the legal relationship in the communities and actors in question, which is undoubtedly necessary given past events, but rather its use as a grounding force for the development of rights and entitlements. These are then ascribed to a relationship

[102] Wewaykum Indian Band v. Canada [2002] 4 S.C.R. 245, 2002 SCC 79, para 85, emphasis added.

[103] McCabe (2008), p. 146.

[104] Wewaykum Indian Band v Canada [2002] at para 93.

[105] McNeil (2008), p. 939.

[106] McCabe (2008), p. 190.

[107] McCabe (2008), p. 216.

[108] Giving multiple examples of this characterization, see McCabe (2008), p. 27-28 Cases: Sheldon v Ramsay [1851] O.J. No. 82, 9 U.C.R. 105 at 133. Ontario Mining Co v Seybold [1899] O.J. No. 113, 31 O.R. 386 at 398, Ontario v Canada [1909] S.C.J. No.28, 42 S.C.R.1 at 117–118.

arising out of reconciliation. Reconciliation, however, is a process, with a final aspiration in sight: restoring the relationship between the parties.[109]

This could possibly be achieved by trying to reverse or compensate past harm to the extent that this is possible. The ideal of reconciliation is thus to *re*-gain an equilibrium or rather a balance of some sort. It seems more likely than not that the equilibrium envisioned by the Supreme Court would differ (substantially) if not from the plans of governmental actors then certainly from those of the Indigenous Peoples themselves. It is in effect a question of how to reconcile different entities with varying self-governing powers. If they are to be non-competitive, what kind of power balance should be sought? A very important step would be to anchor Aboriginal and treaty rights more firmly in a notion of shared sovereignty with different holders of self-determination. The alternative would be to retain a process of reconciliation with a yet-to-be-determined future outcome, including through treaty negotiation. This might lead to a similar outcome, but the risk remains that, when the parties do not achieve the envisioned outcome easily, they abandon the process. Even more importantly, it creates a power imbalance rather than the equilibrium ostensibly sought. Treaty rights, themselves already the outcome of a negotiation between Indigenous rights and the overall public interest as represented by the Canadian government, undergo a second limitation.

6.3 Federal Framework

6.3.1 Indian Act

The Indian Act remains the main federal statute that applies to the Indigenous Peoples in Canada on a general level. Its historic roots and long-time assimilatory focus represent a part of Canadian law that targeted Indigenous Peoples specifically, and consistently, with a view to force their assimilation. Because of its role in forced cultural assimilation, the Act played a considerable role in dispossessing Indigenous Peoples off their heritage, as will be discussed below.

6.3.1.1 Historic Background and Evolution of the Act

A consideration of the Indian Act through the repatriation lens focusses on five different aspects: its historic background and past prohibitions, current definitions of Indigenous people, the type of Indigenous property protected under the Act, its effect on Indigenous self-government and its influence on the relationship between province and Indigenous communities. These areas are of interest not because they

[109] http://www.oed.com/view/Entry/159781?redirectedFrom=reconciliation#eid [last accessed 19.08.2021].

provide a legal obligation to repatriate, or prohibit it, but rather because they inform the context in which a return or a refusal thereof operates. The Indian Act can be termed an obstacle to repatriation. Historically it prohibited cultural practices, its past usage suppressed cultural practices and it continues to impede Indigenous cultural self-determination. The Royal Commission remarked in its seminal report: "Conceived under the nineteenth century's assumptions about inferiority and incapacity and an assimilationist approach to the 'Indian question', the *Indian Act* produced gross disparities in legal rights." The Commission characterized its influence on Canadian society at the time: "[t]he Indian Act still holds a symbolic but powerful grip on the thinking of Canadians."[110]

Until 1982, the Indian Act was the most important piece of legislation for Indigenous Peoples living on reserves. It created a comprehensive legal system, applicable to a significant part of the country's Indigenous population.[111] Writing in 1980, Bartlett observed: "The most singular feature of Canadian legislation concerning Indians is that the governmental policy ... that of 'civilizing the Indians' has shown almost no variation since the early 19th century".[112] It continues to regulate membership and governance structures, tax benefits, possession/distribution and management of land and much more. Its assimilatory focus for most of its existence has severely affected Indigenous culture and Indigenous legal orders.[113] Important restrictions enacted in the past included the prohibition of the potlatch and the tamanawas,[114] the prohibition of customary practices[115] and the suppression of Indigenous languages.[116] Restrictions on participation and traditional legal practices have resulted in a contemporary picture of Indigenous law that resembles an incomplete patchwork. Exemplary of this past outlook is an address by Duncan Campbell Scott in 1920, who was Deputy Superintendent General of Indian Affairs: "I want to get rid of the Indian problem. ... That has been the whole purpose of Indian education and advancement since the earliest times....Our object is to continue until there is not a single Indian in Canada that has not been absorbed into the body politic and there is no Indian question."[117]

The inclusion of s.35 has significantly changed the state of affairs, also with regard to the Indian Act. It gave Aboriginal cultural practices and Aboriginal treaties constitutional protection. Soon after 1982, the Supreme Court was confronted with interpreting a section of the Indian Act in Nowegijick *v* The Queen. Dickson

[110] Royal Commission on Aboriginal Peoples (1991), p. 231.

[111] See Sect. 6.2.2 above.

[112] Bartlett (1980), p. 11.

[113] Borrows (2006), p. 10.

[114] Bartlett (1980), p. 13.

[115] There were three additional rounds of prohibitions of customs and dance introduced in 1895, 1914 and 1933. As cited in Bartlett (1980), p. 13.

[116] Coombe (1993), p. 274.

[117] Duncan Campell Scott, Statement, National Archives of Canada, Record Group 10, volume 6810, file 470-2-3, volume 7, pp. 55 (L-3) and 63 (N-3).

J. stated: "It seems to me . . . that treaties and statutes relating to Indians should be liberally construed and doubtful expressions resolved in favour of the Indians." The statement has become a legal benchmark, cited numerous times as a primary authority in subsequent cases.[118] This so-called principle of liberal construction "takes precedence over other canons of statutory interpretation."[119]

The Indian Act is an important factor in current repatriation efforts, given that it expressly prohibited cultural practices for a considerable period of its existence. Examples that are often cited, whose impact is still very much felt in contemporary community life, include the anti-potlatch laws as well as the prohibition of Sundance rituals, which have their origin in the Indian Act.[120] In order to illustrate the impact such historic grievances may have on current repatriation claims, this section will give a brief and widely known example, the potlatch.[121]

For the Kwakwaka'waka community, the potlatch is a ceremony which is essential to community life, as it is used to conduct marriages, transfer the rights and thereby possession of objects, name children etc. It also provides poorer community members with an opportunity to eat, as the chief holds the ceremony and is obliged to provide food for the attendants. It has spiritual, legal, as well as political importance.[122] The banning of the potlatch ceremony was enacted in 1884 when the Indian Act of the federal legislature was amended and through subsequent the revisions in 1895 and 1918, which remained in place until 1951.[123] The amendments in 1918 made the potlatch a summary conviction, eliminating the need to appear before a judge. Thus, Indian agent and magistrate Halliday, who furthered the above amendments significantly, held the power to send First Nations elders and those knowledgeable of the proper conduct for such ceremonies to prison. This power was then used by him to threaten First Nations individuals with prison, forcing them to hand over all the sacred objects that were necessary for a potlatch.[124] Repatriation requests for potlatch items thus not only navigate between vastly different understandings as to the nature of potlatch heritage objects but they are conducted against the backdrop of forced appropriations.

6.3.1.2 Protection of Indigenous Cultural Heritage on Reserve Lands

Past amendments have removed the prohibitions that resulted in the removal of cultural heritage from Indigenous communities. Instead, the current version of the

[118] McCabe (2008), p. 137-138.

[119] McCabe (2008), p. 140.

[120] Bell (2009), p. 19-21 Another negative example which influenced the development of aboriginal community life significantly was the interrelation of the Indian Act with Indian residential schools.

[121] For the role of bah'lats (Potlatch) laws for the Carrier people, see Borrows (2006), p. 63.

[122] Bell et al. (2008a), pp. 46–53.

[123] Bell et al. (2008a), p. 53.

[124] Bell et al. (2008a), p. 53-54.

Act prohibits the trade of a limited category of cultural heritage, guarding against their removal from the community. S.91 of the Indian Act operates as the base-line protection for certain groups of Indigenous cultural heritage on Indian reserve lands:

> 91 (1) No person may, without the written consent of the Minister, acquire title to any of the following property situated on a reserve, namely,
>
> (a) an Indian grave house;
>
> (b) a carved grave pole;
>
> (c) a totem pole;
>
> (d) a carved house post; or
>
> (e) a rock embellished with paintings or carvings.
>
> (2) Subsection (1) does not apply to chattels referred to therein that are manufactured for sale by Indians.
>
> (3) No person shall remove, take away, mutilate, disfigure, deface or destroy any chattel referred to in subsection (1) without the written consent of the Minister.
>
> (4) A person who contravenes this section is guilty of an offence and liable on summary conviction to a fine not exceeding two hundred dollars or to imprisonment for a term not exceeding 3 months.

On the positive side, it may be highlighted that protection from trade is offered for a certain group of Indigenous cultural objects. Also, while Section 91 offers protection to a limited group of objects, it is complemented by the prohibition to trespass (s.30, s.31).[125] On the negative side, there are several peculiarities within this provision, such as, why are these particular objects are protected and not others? The fact that special objects are afforded higher protection is a regular feature in both art and heritage law and, by itself, it is not remarkable. Questions arise in the choice of objects to be protected, who makes the choices that they may be protected and the means of protection. It might have been advisable to include a category under (f) of sensitive/secret/sacred objects or objects which are otherwise deemed to be worthy of special protection by the community in accordance with their traditions. In addition, while it may be justifiable within the (historic) context of the Indian Act, it is obvious that to make the protection of a certain group of objects which are deemed noteworthy of special protection dependent upon whether or not the minister (as defined in s.2(1)) has given his consent, rather than based on the judgement of someone chosen by the community, violates the provisions of the UNDRIP and the right to cultural self-determination. Depending on the object at issue, it also goes against the principles espoused in Art.27 ICCPR, Art.15(1) ICESCR and, in the case

[125] Compare Bell (1992), p. 492.

of religious objects, one may also question whether it does not undermine the protection afforded in Art.18 ICCPR as analysed in Chap. 2.

6.3.1.3 Registration under the Act and Definition

The complexity of Indian status under the Indian Act was briefly raised in Sect. 6.2.2.2 above. The Indian Act defines as "Indian … a person who pursuant to this Act is registered as an Indian or is entitled to be registered as an Indian" (s.2(1)). The register is maintained by the federal Department of Indian Affairs and Northern Development.[126] Significant changes to Indian status were made in 1985,[127] as a response to the Lovelace decision by the UNHRCee. The 17th of April 1985 became a determining factor for Indian status. Being registered or entitled to be registered prior to that date entitles an individual to Indigenous status under s.6(1)(a) and the base line category. It is complemented by band membership, being declared as a band for the purposes of the Act on or after 17.05.1985 (s.6(1)(b)) and by the provisions which seek to remedy the discriminatory exclusions of the children of Indigenous women who had married non-Indigenous men by re-registration. In addition, Indian status is awarded to the children of an Indigenous parent by virtue of s.6(2) in conjunction with s.6(1). There were a number of problems with Bill C-31 and the legislative attempt to remedy previous discriminatory practices, the discussion of which would go far beyond what is necessary for present purposes.[128] For present purposes, it suffices that injustices of past assimilatory and discriminatory definitions have repercussions which persist to this day.

John Borrows proposes an alternative definition to move away from the current focus on race and ancestry. He recalls RCAPs' emphasis that "Aboriginal peoples are not racial groups; they are organic political and cultural entities." Instead, he proposes to focus on the political nature of the community as a reason for Indigenous laws to apply.[129] This proposal would be preferable in the current situation for the following reasons. First, it would better reflect Canada's Indigenous Peoples inherent right to self-governance. This would contribute to remedying the negative impact government assimilationist policies have had on Indigenous membership. Second, it would dispense with the duality under the Indian Act which has resulted in the reality where an individual might have Indian status under the Act but no band membership.[130] Third, this would require the use of Indigenous legal systems, thereby stimulating their growth and strength. Ideally, this would also lead to a reform of the band council system which was introduced through the Indian Act and

[126] S.5(1) read in conjunction with s.2(1).

[127] Imai (2014), p. 91-92.

[128] There is ample literature on this point. Interested readers may consult for example Grammond (2009), p. 110 onwards.

[129] Borrows (2006), p. 130.

[130] Imai (2014), p. 88.

concentrated power in a single government body.[131] The difficulties that arise in relation to achieving this proposal are concerns that Canada is likely to have about its territorial integrity as well as potential resistance within the band governance structure.

6.3.1.4 Aboriginal Self-Government

> The Commission thus concludes that the right of self-determination is the fundamental starting point for Aboriginal initiatives in the area of governance. However, it is not the only possible basis for such initiatives. In addition, Aboriginal peoples possess the inherent right of self-government within Canada as a matter of Canadian constitutional law.[132]

Section 6.2 already elaborated in more detail on the relationship between Indigenous Peoples and the federal and the provincial government. In this sense, this subsection will be brief, bringing together the strands discussed so far. The vast limitations on Aboriginal self-government in the Indian Act not only mirror the Act's historic background explored earlier in this section, but they reflect a conceptualization of Indigenous Peoples under Canadian law as unequal partners in the relationship with less power and rights than the Canadian government. This legal '*lessness*' of Indigenous Peoples is present to some degree in all legal areas addressed in this chapter. They are conceptualized as the less mature wardens who need the Crown's guardianship in the principles of the Crown's fiduciary duty[133] or as an object of federal competence in s.91 CA 1982. Even treaty rights, where arguably Indigenous and non-Indigenous governance structures should meet on an equal basis, are conceptualized as limits on governmental power rather than as a consequence of a tripartite governance structure. This denial of Indigenous Peoples' inherent right to self-government persists in the form of both subversive as well as outright denials.

Despite numerous amendments, the basic tenet of the Act has remained unchanged,[134] arguably for over one hundred years. The amendments in 1951 were motivated by the lack of success of the act and shaped the form of the act for the following decades.[135] Yet, even they did not alter the fundamental assimilatory outlook of the instrument. On the contrary, "the major features of the 1951 Act were the increased imposition of provincial laws and standards on Indians.... It in no

[131] Borrows (2006), p. 137.

[132] Royal Commission on Aboriginal Peoples (1996), p. 183.

[133] This is not to say that both the concept of fiduciary duty and honor of the Crown cannot help an Indigenous claimant in a particular case. Indigenous peoples *are* in a comparatively more vulnerable position because of past and present injustices that continue to persist and are continuing to be perpetuated in the law. But the duality of such concepts (including rights) needs to be acknowledged to be mindful of how they are employed.

[134] Bartlett (1980), p. 13 "The astonishing feature of the amendments up to 1950 is how little, despite their frequency, they have sought to accomplish."

[135] Compare Royal Commission on Aboriginal Peoples (1996), p. 285.

way.... Conferred any power resembling self-determination or self-government upon the Indians."[136] The S.35 jurisprudence has not (yet) changed this power imbalance. There have been attempts to revoke the Indian Act, which were met with resistance in parts of the Indigenous community. Moreover, without a suitable replacement, it would leave regulatory gaps on 'Indian lands' where the Act applies. The treaty negotiations which take place in British Columbia address this for the negotiating parties, as the final agreements replace the Indian Act. They thus represent a significant step forward by the federal and provincial government in recognizing Indigenous self-government in this respect. The problem of unilateral limitations on treaty rights under s.35(1), due to the jurisprudential developments discussed above, mitigates this step somewhat and leaves the door open for future regressions on this point.

6.3.1.5 Section 88: The Provincial Level

Provincial laws apply to Indigenous Peoples in two ways:[137] either *ex proprio vigore*, where they do not interfere with or fall within the sphere of s.91(24) or, second, by their incorporation into federal law. This is the main effect of s.88, it elevates the provincial laws of general application to the level of federal laws capable of being applied to Indians in certain circumstances. S.88 is the result of the 1950/51 amendments which sought to render the Act more effective and resulted in significantly broadening the provincial reach in relation to Indigenous Peoples[138] residing on reserves within the province. It was "[p]assed in 1950 with little political fanfare or opposition".[139] This border has been pushed further at the cost of Indigenous self-governance with Tsilhqotín. Since Tsilhqotín, this power includes the power to pass laws affecting Aboriginal and treaty rights.[140] These are protected by s.35(1), the Constitution Act 1982 and the corresponding case law.[141] Their validity is thus dependent on fulfilling the Sparrow test described in the following section.

The combination of jurisprudence and s.88 complement each other in such a way that the long-standing protection of Indigenous Peoples from provincial power, by allocating legislative power with the federal level has been eroded significantly. There are five narrow[142] exceptions to provincial laws applying to 'Indians': first, singling out 'Indians' for special treatment; second, 'indianness' (laws which "impair 'status or capacity' of Indians, or that affect Indianness'"); third, as a result

[136]Bartlett (1980), p. 14.

[137]Imai (2014), p. 270.

[138]Bartlett (1980), p. 22.

[139]Vicaire (2011), p. 20.

[140]Hogg (2007b (loose-leaf updated 2015)), p. 28-18.

[141]Hogg (2007b (loose-leaf updated 2015)), p. 28-18.

[142]Hogg (2007b (loose-leaf updated 2015)), p. 28-16.

of paramountcy principle; fourth, as a result of the application of Natural Resource agreements;[143] and fifth, as a result of s.35.

6.3.2 *Aboriginal Law in Canada: Rights and Treaties as a* Sui Generis *Domain of the Supreme Court*

By virtue of s.35(1), Aboriginal law is split between rights arising out of historic or modern treaties and unwritten Aboriginal rights originating in the prior existence of Indigenous Peoples in Canada. There is a third pillar of Aboriginal law, namely Indigenous customary law, which is not expressly recognized in s.35(1)[144] and varies in content depending on the people in question. This section focusses first on Aboriginal rights, then discusses the existence of an Aboriginal right to religious cultural objects, before considering Aboriginal treaty rights and their relationship to repatriation. The relationship between the different fields, Aboriginal rights and treaties, Canadian federal and provincial law is fraught with tension. Aboriginal and treaty rights have become firmly embedded in Canadian law, as part of its own field, one which one has largely been developed by the judiciary upon incorporation of s.35(1) in the constitution. In developing the field, the judiciary, especially the SCC adopted court decisions which have been criticized heavily. The following observation by the RCAP aptly summarizes the criticism: "The Supreme Court of Canada, for the most part consistently, has made it clear that Aboriginal and treaty rights are part of the legal regime that defines the rule of law in Canada. These court decisions have come slowly, erratically, and at great cost to Aboriginal people."[145]

6.3.2.1 Aboriginal Rights: Nature and Limitations

6.3.2.1.1 Nature of Aboriginal Rights

> [I]n order to be an aboriginal right an activity must be an element of a practice, custom or tradition integral to the distinctive culture of the aboriginal group asserting the right.[146]

Aboriginal rights under Canadian law are activities which are protected constitutionally by virtue of s.35(1). Constitutional protection undoubtedly opened up the

---

[143] In the three prairie provinces this covers right to game and fish for food.

[144] But it can find entry into the legal arena if we (a) recognize treaties as treaties negotiated between sovereign nations with their own legal systems (b) identify and interpret aboriginal rights in light of the Indigenous law that determines their exercise within the community.

[145] Royal Commission on Aboriginal Peoples (1996), p. 32.

[146] R v Van der Peet [1996] 2 S.C.R. 507, para 45.

possibility for Indigenous Peoples to introduce long-standing concerns in a new form, including the possibility of redress for historical wrongdoing and the recognition of existing Indigenous legal orders.[147] While their constitutional status has been entrenched through the provision, the section does not define the content of the rights in question. As a result, the content of Aboriginal rights has very much been determined by Canadian courts, in particular, the Supreme Court.

The Courts have characterized Aboriginal rights as a *sui generis* legal field. This characterization of Aboriginal rights has been evaluated very differently by scholars. On the positive side, J. Youngblood Henderson has characterized this legal area as "contain[ing] many implicit principles, such as pre-existing systems of Indigenous law or jurisprudences, their distinctive societies or orders, and Aboriginal title or land tenures. These principles sustain and animate knowledge and heritage . . . in an innovative approach to constitutional analysis, which the Court called sui generis legal analysis."[148] Courts have had to develop this area in individual cases in response to governmental assertions which seemed to seek to undermine these rights. As a result, the jurisprudence has created a patchwork in which "judicial insights and principles are juxtaposed on a colonial backdrop that fuses into a new constitutional framework."[149] Youngblood Henderson argues that there has been no opportunity to organize the field and the principles the Court has developed.[150] Gordon Christie, by contrast, has been much more critical. He has characterized the *Van der Peet* test as the result of a "return to hegemony" due to the Court's way of characterizing the Indigenous pre-settler existence as occupancy which is to be reconciled with English-Canadian sovereignty.[151]

The SCC has anchored Aboriginal rights in the long-standing 'use and occupancy' of Canada by Indigenous people before the settler community arrived. There are two important temporal elements to the existence of Aboriginal rights in Canadian law. First, they have been conceptualized as activities that are rooted in a practice prior to European contact. As a result, they do not exist in a uniform manner, but rather they vary from people to people "depending on the customs, practices and traditions that have formed part of their distinctive cultures".[152] Second, the term "existing" in s.35(1) has been interpreted by the Supreme Court to mean existing at the time of the inclusion of s.35 in the Constitution. As a result, any rights that have been extinguished prior to 1982 remain extinguished. Those rights that still existed in 1982 cannot be extinguished easily, but they can be limited. Gordon Christie has argued convincingly that the way in which Aboriginal rights have been given form in

[147] Youngblood Henderson (2006), p. x.

[148] Youngblood Henderson (2006), pp. 66–67.

[149] Youngblood Henderson (2006), p. 51.

[150] Youngblood Henderson (2006), p. 51.

[151] Christie (1998), p. 475-476.

[152] Government of Canada website, Crown-Indigenous Relations and Northern Affairs Canada, https://www.rcaanc-cirnac.gc.ca/eng/1100100028605/1551194878345 [last accessed 19.08.2021].

the jurisprudence has increasingly narrowed their constitutional protection.[153] This, in combination with the jurisprudence on treaty rights and the practical limits of modern treaty negotiation,[154] has left Indigenous people with a choice between "two unsavoury options".[155] In this context, it is worth noting that the Royal Commission on Aboriginal Peoples [RCAP] judged the inclusion of 'existing' "a reflection of both the lack of knowledge of Aboriginal matters among federal and provincial governments and the legal uncertainty in the field at that time."[156] These additional limitations set in addition to the text of s.35(1) seems to be at odds with their purpose, which the Court itself has found to be one of reconciliation.[157] In R v Van der Peet it defined the underlying purpose of s.35(1) as one of "reconciliation of the pre-existing aboriginal societies with the sovereignty of the Crown".[158]

The obvious difficulty with protecting Aboriginal rights is that they are located at the intersection of the Indigenous and the Canadian legal systems.[159] While the Supreme Court recognized that their nature is rooted in the existence of Indigenous cultures, its interpretation of s.35(1), through Guerin and Sparrow,[160] has placed Aboriginal rights firmly within the common law. As will be shown below, the way the concept has been developed by the judiciary also leaves room for repatriation to be considered within the Aboriginal rights. However, the direction in which the test has evolved raises doubts whether a claim for an Aboriginal right to a particular heritage object has a realistic chance of succeeding in court.

---

[153] Christie (1998), p. 470.

[154] See Chap. 7, Sect. 7.2.3.

[155] Christie (1998), p. 470 Parts of argument in FN.

[156] Royal Commission on Aboriginal Peoples (1991), p. 191.

[157] R.V. Van der Peet [1996], at para 50: "It is possible, of course, that the Court could be said to be 'reconciling' the prior occupation of Canada by aboriginal peoples with Crown sovereignty through either a narrow or broad conception of aboriginal rights; the notion of "reconciliation" does not, in the abstract, mandate a particular content for aboriginal rights. However, the only fair and just reconciliation is, as Walters suggest, one which takes into account the aboriginal perspective while at the same time taking into account the perspective of the common law. True reconciliation will, equally, place weight on each."

[158] McCabe (2008), p. 41 Relying on R v Van der Peet at paras 31, 36, 42–43; R v Gladstone (Gladstone No.1) [1996] S.C.J. No.79 at para 72; R v Adams [1996] S.C.J. No.87 and R v Powley [2003] S.C.J. No.43.

[159] Compare Mark Walters referenced in R.V. Van der Peet [1996], para 42: "The challenge of defining aboriginal rights stems from the fact that they are rights peculiar to the meeting of two vastly dissimilar legal cultures; consequently there will always be a question about which legal culture is to provide the vantage point from which rights are to be defined . . . a morally and politically defensible conception of aboriginal rights will incorporate bot legal perspectives."

[160] On these see Hogg (2007b (loose-leaf updated 2015)), p. 28-21.

6.3.2.1.2 Specific Content and Test

The test establishes whether limitations of Aboriginal rights are permissible under Canadian law. It was developed in two Supreme Court decisions, Sparrow and Van der Peet (and R v Powley for Métis rights). Sparrow laid the foundation and essentially requires three questions to be answered, while Van der Peet provides the test for classifying an activity as a right.[161]

There are three essential steps: classifying the activity as an Aboriginal right, proving that there has been an infringement of the Aboriginal right and, finally, considering whether this infringement can be justified. Van der Peet has established that, in order for practice to qualify as a right, it has to originate in a pre-contact custom[162] and be integral to the distinctive[163] culture of an Aboriginal group. Integral should be understood to mean 'central or important' to the culture in question.[164] In R v Sappier, the SCC clarified that it need not be at the core of a culture (previously an element of test), as this would be too restrictive. The aim of the test laid down in Van der Peet was to "provide cultural security and continuity for the particular aboriginal society."[165] R v Sappier also clarified that practices which were crucial to a group's survival were integral under the Van der Peet criteria.[166] With regard to the integral element: "The question to ask is whether the Aboriginal people in question would be who they are without the particular element of their culture in question."[167] There must also be an element of continuity between the pre-contact period custom and the one claimed today. This element of continuity might prove to be a difficult element to fulfil for Indigenous Peoples. By understanding 'existing' as not extinguished until 1982,[168] the SCC has retroactively rubber-stamped over one hundred years of assimilation policies with its approval. The court has, however, placed the threshold to an express elimination before

[161] Panagos (2016), p. 23-25.

[162] Hogg (2007b (loose-leaf updated 2015)), p. 28-23 It need not be identical, but it can for instance be pursued using modern means.

[163] Distinctive is not to be understood as permitting the use of stereotypes for classification or "anthropological curiosities", see R. v. Sappier; R. v. Gray, [2006] 2 S.C.R. 686, 2006 SCC 54, para 42.

[164] R v Van der Peet [1996], para 256.

[165] Imai (2014), p. 713-714.

[166] Imai (2014), p. 716.

[167] Christie (1998), p. 479 R v Van der Peet [1996], para 59.

[168] Hogg (2007b (loose-leaf updated 2015)), p. 28-44.21 in reference to R v Sparrow [1990], at 1091.

1982.[169] Furthermore, if a right was only limited prior to 1982, it is protected by the constitutional provision in its unlimited, pre-contact form.[170]

To evidence that there has been an infringement of the Aboriginal right, the Indigenous claimant has to prove a *prima facie* infringement. This will occur either by showing that the limitation was unreasonable, that it imposes undue hardship upon the claimant or that the action in question denies the right-holders of their preferred means of exercising that right.[171] Once this has been established, the burden shifts to the Crown to show that the infringement may still be justified.[172] The interference causing the infringement must have been based on a valid legislative objective and must be consistent with the honour of the Crown and its duty to Indigenous Peoples.[173] Other questions are whether the "there has been as little infringement as possible in order to effect the desired result; whether, in a situation of expropriation, fair compensation is available; and, whether the aboriginal group in question has been consulted with respected to the conservation measures being implemented"[174] If there has been an infringement, and it cannot be justified, compensation will be considered.

It is noteworthy in this respect that, through its inclusion of the 'practices' element, the Supreme Court has characterized Aboriginal rights as means to protect Indigenous cultures. Specific parts of Indigenous cultures are thus transformed into 'requisite triggers' for the protection of rights under s.35. Aboriginal rights thus carry a communal element within their defining characteristics.[175] More generally, the jurisprudence has drawn a distinction between Aboriginal title and Aboriginal rights as activity-based rights.[176] The latter encompass hunting and fishing rights and, according to RCAP, which used Indigenous representatives' contributions for this overview, "linguistic, cultural and religious rights and rights held under customary systems of Aboriginal law. Also included is the right of self-government."[177]

Apart from this test, there are two additional scenarios to be considered. First, the question arises as to how to proceed in case of an, as of yet, unproved Aboriginal right? Second, how are Aboriginal rights extinguished nowadays in light of their constitutional protection? Concerning the former, courts have developed a "duty to

[169] Sparrow has clarified that the sovereign's intention must have been "clear and plain". J.Y.H remarks critically "The conceptual problems with the clear and plain approach are that if the Sovereign has not explicitly conveyed the intention to Aboriginal peoples, how can it be said that the intention is either honourable or "clear and plain"? Youngblood Henderson (2006), p. 75.

[170] Hogg (2007b (loose-leaf updated 2015)), p. 29-45.

[171] Supreme Court, R v. Sparrow [1990], at 1112-1113. Imai (2014), p. 829.

[172] Hogg (2007b (loose-leaf updated 2015)), p. 28-46.

[173] Mikisew Cree First Nation v Canada (Governor General in Council) [2018], at para 154.

[174] Imai (2014), p. 829.

[175] Compare Panagos (2016), p. 24.

[176] First drawn in R v Adams, affirmed in R v Delgamuukw. See also, Carlson (2005), p. 465.

[177] Royal Commission on Aboriginal Peoples (1996), p. 180.

consult and, if appropriate, to accommodate"[178] Indigenous Peoples in actions which would infringe upon Aboriginal rights or Aboriginal title which are claimed but not proven at the time of the action in question.[179] This has been done on the basis of the honour of the Crown. In Haida Nation, the Court affirmed Delgamuukw and observed that this duty varies depending on the circumstances: "While it is not useful to classify situations into watertight compartments, different situations requiring different responses can be identified. In all cases, the honour of the Crown requires that the Crown act with good faith to provide meaningful consultation appropriate to the circumstances."[180] Also, a duty of consultation does not require the government to obtain consent.[181] With regard to extinguishing existing Aboriginal rights, this can occur in two ways: first, by voluntary surrender by the respective Indigenous community to the Crown or, second, through a constitutional amendment.[182]

Criticism

There are different disconcerting elements of the Aboriginal rights jurisprudence. The most important critique is probably that, despite the constitutional recognition of Aboriginal rights today, previous unilateral actions that clearly sought to extinguish those rights remain valid. Only those rights that were not extinguished prior to 1982 are protected and, while they cannot simply be extinguished unilaterally since 1982, the courts have given the government quite a lot of room to limit these rights. While they have not followed federal and provincial governments in their interpretation of s.35 as an "empty box",[183] the 'box' has been subjected to at least intermittent if not frequent 'thieving' since 1982. From an Indigenous perspective, it would seem as if s.35 is "increasingly used to justify government infringements of Aboriginal rights".[184] This connects to the second strand of criticism, namely the lack of recognition afforded to Indigenous self-government as an inherent right. Instead, Aboriginal self-government has been recognized as an Aboriginal right in a very limited capacity. If we follow the court's reasoning in the R v Pamajewon,[185] it only covers governmental activities which can be classified as traditional activities and if they pass the Van Der Peet test. Furthermore, it is difficult to establish an Aboriginal right, as this requires a large a large amount of historical evidence and a cross-cultural 'translation' of the legal claims. It is not surprising that Aboriginal rights claims have resulted in some of the longest trials in Canada.[186]

---

[178] Haida Nation v British Columbia (Minister of Forests) 2004 SCC 73, 2004 CSC 73, paras 10,15,20.

[179] McCabe (2008), p. 85-87.

[180] Haida Nation v British Columbia (Minister of Forests) [2004], para 41.

[181] Haida Nation v British Columbia (Minister of Forests) [2004], per McLachlin CJ, para 10.

[182] Hogg (2007b (loose-leaf updated 2015)), p. 28–34.21.

[183] See in more detail on empty box theory Youngblood Henderson (2006), p. 45-46.

[184] Borrows (2006), p. 153.

[185] Hogg (2007b (loose-leaf updated 2015)), p. 28-26.

[186] Millen and Adkins (22.10.2018), p. 7 At 7-8 citing Tsilhqot' in which in total took 24 years.

The lack of recognition afforded to Indigenous rights and Indigenous self-determination is especially glaring when contrasted with the way in which Canadian law continues to seek to accommodate the differences between the descendants of the French- and English-speaking societies that settled in Canada. There is evidence that the Canadian legal system is capable of adapting to different legal traditions. John Borrows, using this contrast, argues that although "this [constitutional] framework was not extended to Indigenous peoples, it is not too late to do so."[187]

Another challenge arises in protecting unproven Indigenous rights. Recently, the Supreme Court had the opportunity, for the first time, to decide a case that raised claims both under s.2(a) CCRF and s.35.[188] The Ktunaxa First Nation filed a complaint against British Columbia for developing a year-around ski resort, alleging a violation of s.2(a) CCRF and s.35. The decision to develop the resort had been taken after a decades-long consultation process and a number of changes had been made to the plan as a result. However, it still involved the use of wastewater to create artificial snow and includes a sacred site (Quat'muk), the home of the Grizzly Bear Spirit. After engaging in consultation, the Ktunaxa knowledge keeper disclosed that agreement would not be possible because the development would drive Grizzly Bear Spirit from the sacred area. This would infringe their religious freedom. The provincial minister decided that reasonable consultation and accommodation had occurred and approved the project. The s.35 claim involved an unproven Aboriginal right to a spiritual practice.[189]

In the case of unproven Aboriginal rights that may be affected by a governmental action, consultation obligations arise. The judges did not engage in finding out whether an Aboriginal right under s.35 existed. The Court was clear that a judicial review of an administrative decision was not the place to establish an Aboriginal right.[190] In deciding that the consultation was reasonable, the court observed that the consultation right under s.35 was a procedural right not a substantive right.[191] It does not amount to a right to veto governmental decisions and it operates on a sliding scale.[192] Consent is only required for proven Aboriginal claims and even then only in certain cases.[193] Moreover, it reiterated its previous stance in Haida, namely that "the duty to consult and, if appropriate, accommodate the Aboriginal interest is a two-way street. The obligations on the Crown are to provide notice and information on the project, and to consult with the Aboriginal group.... The obligations on the Aboriginal group include: defining the elements of the claim with clarity (para. 36);

[187] Borrows (2006), p. 102.

[188] Ktunaxa Nation v. British Columbia (Forests, Lands and Natural Resource Operations) 2017 SCC 54, [2017] 2 S.C.R. 386.

[189] For discussion of SCC treatment of s.2(a) CCRF see Sect. 6.3.3.1 below.

[190] Ktunaxa Nation v. British Columbia (Forests, Lands and Natural Resource Operations) [2017], para 84.

[191] Ibid, para 79.

[192] Ibid, paras 79–80.

[193] Ibid, para 80.

not frustrating the Crown's reasonable good faith attempts; and not taking unreasonable positions to thwart the Crown from making decisions or acting where, despite meaningful consultation, agreement is not reached (para. 42)."[194] This is problematic for two reasons: first, Aboriginal rights are often affected by administrative decision-making bodies, including impact assessment boards.[195] This court position will require the investment of significant additional resources next to any impact assessment and consultation process that is already ongoing, in order to be able to establish an Aboriginal claim; second, this increased focus on the procedural dimension inherent in s.35 results in a danger that the substantive protection afforded by this constitutional provision is weakened.

6.3.2.2 A Right to Indigenous Cultural Objects as an Aboriginal Right?

There are different ways in which Aboriginal rights can be related to the question of repatriating Indigenous religious cultural heritage. The first and foremost distinction is between operating within the existing jurisprudence or outside of it. Within the jurisprudence of Aboriginal rights, existing case law can be used as follows:

1. To argue for an Aboriginal right of a specific community to a specific practice or tradition which involves the heritage located outside of the community.
2. To argue for an Aboriginal right of a specific community to the exclusive control or use of a specific heritage object.

Outside or rather apart from adopting an Aboriginal rights discourse to repatriation, Indigenous communities are left with the following options:

1. Approach the holding institution in the hope of engaging in a bilateral/multilateral negotiation in an exercise of cultural self-determination. This happened in Alberta, see Sect. 7.1 in the following chapter.
2. Pursue the return of the object in the broader and on-going societal effort of reconciliation (even if is at a snail's pace with detours and set-backs)
3. Pursue the return of the object as part of modern treaty negotiations if these take place (see Sect. 6.3.2.3 for a critical discussion of treaty rights and Sect. 7.2 for an example and critical discussion of this through the BCTC process)

6.3.2.2.1 The Right to an Indigenous Religious Practice or Tradition

As shown above, there are essentially two ways in which an Aboriginal right can be established which could further repatriation claims. The first is a broader approach, seeking to establish an Aboriginal right to the practice in which an object is used.

---

[194] Ibid, para 80.

[195] Hopkins-Utter (2.11.2017), p.

The object thus needs to be repatriated or the right is limited. The second is a more specific right, focussing on the use of a specific object that is being reclaimed.[196]

In the first case, the first step is the identification of a specific ceremony, practice or tradition. The ceremony or tradition in which the object is used would have to be "integral to the distinctive culture of the Aboriginal group claiming the right". As a next step, it would have to fulfil the continuity element and have to be at least related to the pre-contact era.[197] The specific content of the distinctive or integral element will depend on the specific practice and cannot be 'tested' on a meta-level. There is, however, a good reason for the assumption that the integral element test will be fulfilled in the vast majority of cases. Cultural expressions, such as religious practices and ceremonies, are, by nature, related to the core of a community. With an Indigenous testimony, it should be possible to give evidence of this. Of course, the danger remains that a non-Indigenous judge will apply a non-Indigenous framework to decide this as well as the distinctiveness element[198] and will decide that both are not fulfilled. This is and will be a danger for as long as Indigenous legal orders are insufficiently recognized within Canadian law. Yet it does not take away from the fact that, even with the Courts' narrow construction of Aboriginal rights, Indigenous cultural practices seem to be right at the core of what is afforded protection.

Catherine Bell similarly argues that "the court should look to the history and traditions of the claimant group to determine whether the integral test raised in Sparrow has been met; that is, whether title to an object is essential to the cultural integrity of the group."[199] The author agrees with Bell that "types of objects that are likely to fall within this category are religious objects, ceremonial objects, medicine objects, and objects of particular historical significance."[200] Alternatively, Bell elaborates, if Aboriginal rights were to be understood as rights of a sovereign Indigenous entity, common law would be subordinate to tribal law and Aboriginal claimants would instead have to provide evidence in accordance with Aboriginal customary law to prove an Aboriginal ownership claim.[201] However, such a construction of Aboriginal rights does not sit well with the construction of Aboriginal rights in a manner which would serve the reconciliation of Indigenous pre-existence with Crown sovereignty.

The next step would be to examine whether the relevant ceremony has been extinguished.[202] Given the past prohibitions of Indigenous religious practices due to

[196] For obvious reasons there can be no aboriginal right to repatriation given the need for a pre-contact practice and the fact that objects were removed from their source communities by settlers or government agents.

[197] R. v Van der Peet [1996] , paras 44–46.

[198] This could, for example, occur for shared ceremonial or story-telling aspects.

[199] Bell (1992), p. 509.

[200] Bell (1992), p. 509.

[201] Bell (1992), p. 509.

[202] R. v Sparrow [1990] 1 S.C.R. 1075, at 1093.

the Indian Act, this step could prove difficult to an Indigenous claimant. It will depend on how the court will construct the temporary prohibition of Indigenous practices, including the potlatch. Given that the prohibitions were lifted, and practices resumed (or continued legally in the case of underground practices) before the constitutionally enshrined protection in 1982, it seems plausible to argue that these practices were not 'plainly and clearly' extinguished. If a ceremonial practice has not been extinguished, then it is *prima facie* protected in its original, pre-contact form. In the next step, one would consider whether a practice has been infringed upon and whether the infringement can be justified. It is here that the repatriation of Indigenous cultural objects enters the legal test. There are different ways of reasoning. First, the very existence of an object in federally-funded museums represents a continuous, ongoing limitation of the Aboriginal right to the practice in which the object is used. Second, the act of refusing a repatriation request is an infringement of an Aboriginal right. If the museum is seen as a government agent, as is the case for the Royal British Columbia Museum,[203] one might argue that its actions can be ascribed to the government and any limitations have to be justified in accordance with the test. Otherwise, the most direct way would be to seek the return of the object from the government and then challenge its refusal. In both cases, an infringement of an Aboriginal right will be difficult to prove if an access or use agreement is in place.

The next step for any of these lines of argumentation would be to consider whether the infringement could be justified. The refusal to repatriate would however have to be justified and no less restrictive measure should be available. Possibly, the protection of Canada's cultural heritage would qualify as a legitimate aim. Protection would then embody a very conservative and arguably outdated construction of heritage as including tangible heritage only, disregarding the understanding of living cultural expressions of Indigenous Peoples as a valid part of the country's heritage. However, even with the pursuit of preservation as an objective, the question remains whether no less restrictive measure would be available than an outright refusal to repatriate and keeping the object in the non-Indigenous cultural institution. This seems questionable. Possible measures which are arguably less restrictive and have been adopted voluntarily by a number of museums include: allowing access to and the use of the object at certain intervals for ritual purposes, moving the object to a museum/holding institution on Indigenous lands[204] or employing Indigenous museum personnel to care for Indigenous heritage.[205] In summary, the existence of an Indigenous right to a specific practice which requires the use of a particular heritage object is possible. While this does not entail an Aboriginal right to repatriation, as limitations are permissible, custodial arrangements as well as periodical

[203] S.3(1) Museum Act [S.B.C. 2003], c.12, current as to 10.07.2019. For a further discussion involving the RBCM see Chap. 7, Sect. 7.2.

[204] This can be a costly enterprise for the Indigenous community and could be understood as a repeated colonial expression of outside control over Indigenous heritage if it is made a condition for repatriation.

[205] This can likewise be inadvisable; it might be that the community prefers a non-Indigenous person to handle the object rather than a member from another community.

access to heritage are arguably much less restrictive measures than an outright denial of a request.

6.3.2.2.2 The Right to the Exclusive Control or Use of a Dislocated Object

The second avenue to ensure the right to an object would be to argue for a more specific Aboriginal right, namely the right to exclusively control or use the object (s) in question.[206] The practice would have to be integral and distinctive to the community in question and display an element of continuity with a pre-contact practice.

Depending on the object claimed, it might even be easier to prove the distinctiveness criterion for a specific object than in relation to the complete ceremony. As long as a connection can be proven between the object and the community claiming it, the object-specific claim would make the right distinctive. Whether or not the object is integral to the community's culture would depend on whether a judge will refuse to adopt an Indigenous perspective on the role and position of the heritage within a community or an outside perspective. Given that the test seeks to establish Aboriginal rights and the 'integral' part of the test seeks to establish the position of the right *within* the Aboriginal culture, employing an external framework of evaluation should be rejected as ill-suited for this purpose. The main difficulties would, in all likelihood, arise in proving an element of continuity between the use and control in pre-contact times and currently. Given the focus of governmental policies on the assimilation and expropriation of Indigenous communities enforced through the Indian Act, a great number of traditions were interrupted, which lead to the removal of the object and limited if any control being exercised over it. However, in cases such as the potlatch case, Indigenous communities continued to practice these traditions underground. In addition, in recent decades there have been numerous revitalization efforts and therefore it can be argued that the continuity element is present.[207] Gordon Christies raises another important difficulty under the continuity element: could it possibly be argued that the (perceived) need for exclusive control only exists because of contact with settler communities?[208]

The next step in the application of the test would be to consider whether the right was extinguished. Depending on the object, it could be argued that there was a clear and plain intent to extinguish the exclusive control and/or use of the objects used in ceremonies which were expressly prohibited, such as the potlatch and the tamanawas. However, in the 1951 amendment, the prohibitions were deleted from

---

[206] Christie (1998), p. Christie critically discusses the possible uses of aboriginal rights for the protection of aboriginal culture as well as the dangers thereof. See at 476 onwards for the protection of Aboriginal narratives by means of the aboriginal right to the exclusive control or use of 'culturally significant legends'.

[207] Similarly Christie (1998), p. 476.

[208] Christie (1998), p. 480.

the act and the first legal potlatch was held before the 1982 constitutional amendment. It could thus be argued that there is an existing Aboriginal right to the exclusive use and control of such objects. The argumentation for a legitimate infringement of such rights (refusing control or limiting it by the continuous possession of the object) would follow the argumentation set out above and would have to be viewed with similar scepticism.

In summary, it seems as if the constitutional protection offered to repatriation claims in relation to sacred ceremonial objects is possible but, given the permissible limitations, it might not aid a repatriation claim.[209] In addition, the protection of the Aboriginal right is dependent upon the judge accepting the Indigenous testimony as evidence of the importance and distinctiveness of the object to the community in question. However, a major benefit of the test is the requirement to look for a less restrictive means to pursue a legitimate objective. If a public institution (or a publicly subsidized institution) seeks to ensure the protection of the object, there are compromises which can be sought.[210] More specifically, an Indigenous community could seek to enforce these compromises under an Aboriginal rights claim. Yet, the theoretical existence of this avenue does not alleviate the very real temporal and financial constraints of pursuing a judicial solution in such a case.

6.3.2.3 Treaty Rights: Their Nature, Their Relationship to Repatriation and Their Limitations

6.3.2.3.1 Historic Treaties

Treaties are agreements between Indigenous Peoples and the British Crown in past times and the Canadian governments in modern times. Numerous historic treaties exist which are still valid today and are the continuing source for Indigenous rights and governmental obligations, especially since the constitutional protection of treaties has been enshrined under s.35.[211] At the same time, large stretches of land have not been subject to the treaties in the past, which resulted in modern treaty negotiations starting in the 1970s.[212] There are, however, a number of difficulties to be aware of. First, there have been—and continue to be—vast differences in how the

---

[209] In this respect, the author agrees with Kagan (2005), p. Kagan deplores the weakness of the aboriginal rights approach and takes this as the starting point for developing an alternative approach through the application of common law in order to facilitate repatriation efforts.

[210] One could for example argue for an Aboriginal right to use the sacred object and keep it with its community without changing the property law aspects of the matter.

[211] Simon v The Queen, [1985] 2 S.C.R. 387 affirmed that historical treaties predating Confederation are protected under s.35(1). See also Royal Commission on Aboriginal Peoples (1991), p. 193 S.35(3) clarifies that the protection extends to modern treaties.

[212] Government of Canada website—Crown-Indigenous Relations and Northern Affairs Canada, https://www.rcaanc-cirnac.gc.ca/eng/1100100028574/1529354437231#chp3 [last accessed 19.08.2021].

two sides understand the treaties entered into. As just one example, a number of cases have pointed to the fact that the written version of the historical treaties differs quite substantially from the oral transmissions used at the time. The SCC in Simon v The Queen tried to mitigate this by affirming the principle that, for the interpretation of treaties, the Indigenous understanding at the time should be adopted and that ambiguous terms are to be "construed in their favour".[213] It similarly refused to rely too closely on principles governing international treaties as applied to Aboriginal treaties, which it constructed to be a *sui generis* legal field.[214] The courts have used the concept of the honour of the Crown to mitigate these "deficiencies" in the treaties, for instance in Marshall I.[215] Badger and Marshall put forward a number of principles of treaty interpretation which include that treaties are solemn and sacred, the already mentioned interpretation of ambiguities, the burden of proving extinguishment and the fact that the Courts honour requires "that the promises be given 'meaning and substance'".[216] The scope of these difficulties in the understanding and application of treaties can best be understood if we keep in mind that "there have been over 500 treaties in Canada, many of them drawing on some form of Indigenous legal tradition".[217] It should also be kept in mind that the treaties in the past were negotiated in very different circumstances and that, even a treaty in which both sides agree as to its exact content, will in all likelihood have to be adapted to contemporary challenges.

6.3.2.3.2 Modern Treaties

Modern treaties can serve to resolve unsettled claims and clearly detail existing rights. Contrary to past treaties, modern treaties are no longer viewed as extinguishing Aboriginal rights. However, the agreements concluded have been viewed by the government as settling rights in their definite form as elaborated in the treaty.[218] According to Ash, the governmental position since the 1970s, and still largely prevalent today, has been: "to reach a successful conclusion, an Indigenous party must agree to exchange whatever rights derive from their pre-existence as societies for financial compensation and state recognition of specified rights, on the understanding that governments in Canada ... [have] final legislative authority with respect to the exercise of these rights."[219] The BC treaty negotiations do not follow

---

[213] Simon v The Queen [1985], para 27.

[214] Royal Commission on Aboriginal Peoples (1991), pp. 206–207 Simon v The Queen, [1985] 2 S.C.R. 387, para 33.

[215] McCabe (2008), p. 79-80.

[216] McCabe (2008), p. 77 Relying on R. v Marshall, [1999] 3 S.C.R. 456 at para 52.

[217] Borrows (2006), p. 109.

[218] Compare Bell (1992), p. 510 This can also be seen in the B.C. treaties, for example section 12 in the Tsawwassen Final Agreement, for more discussion see Chap. 7, Sect. 7.2.4.2.

[219] Asch (2014), p. 21.

the extinguishment model, but they do follow what has been termed the 'non-assertion' model. This means that First Nations will not assert rights other than those set out in the treaty.[220] The failure of the BC treaty negotiations to result in a large number of agreements, its length and its costs have raised questions whether the treaty process, as pursued in this province, is sustainable model.[221]

6.3.2.3.3 Limitations of and on Treaty Making

Many of the limitations to using treaty rights in repatriation were already introduced in the preceding sections. The most fundamental limitation remains that the underlying purpose of s.35 is to reconcile Indigenous pre-existence with Canadian sovereignty.[222] It is thus not surprising that the SCC has enabled both the federal as well as the provincial level to limit treaty rights. In Badger (1996), in a bizarre application of analogical reasoning, the Court opined that, since s.35 applies to both Aboriginal as well as treaty rights, the Sparrow doctrine should also be applied to treaty rights.[223] This is especially dubious, given the fact that treaty rights are arrived at by mutual consent.[224] Moreover, it can be presumed that they already include comprises between the initial parties and that the different public interests were considered when the government sought to enforce its position. Why it stands to reason that a legitimate legislative object may again be used to limit treaty rights—unilaterally one might add—is a mystery. Subsequent cases, such as R v Marshall (1999), affirmed this approach and "went a step further, holding that some kinds of laws limiting treaty rights would not need to satisfy any standard of justification. In that case, the treaty right was to fish 'for a moderate livelihood', and the Court held that there was a difference between *defining* the treaty right and *regulating* the treaty right."[225] Since Tsilhqotín Nation v BC, it is clear that, in the eyes of the Court, if the law satisfies the Sparrow standard of justification, s.35 also does not protect treaty

[220] British Columbia Treaty Commission, Annual Report 2003, at 10.

[221] For more see discussion of B.C. treaty process in Chap. 7, Sect. 7.2.3.

[222] Asch (2014), p. 11 Asch has remarked critically that this "prejudices the outcome" as "becomes one based on this singular pre-condition: the agreement on the part of Indigenous peoples that the scope of their political rights, and in particular their right to self-determination, is circumscribed by the fact that, at the end of the day, whatever rights they may have are subordinate to the legislative authority of the Canadian state. Yet, this logically ought not to be the case, if for no other reason than that the political rights of Indigenous peoples already existed at the time that Crown sovereignty was asserted and, therefore it is the question of how the Crown gained sovereignty that requires reconciliation with the pre-existence of Indigenous societies and not the other way around."

[223] P. Hogg rightly observes "We are left with the unsatisfactory position that treaty rights have to yield to any law that can satisfy the Sparrow standard of justification... In my view, the standard of justification for a law impairing a treaty right should be very high indeed." Hogg (2007b (loose-leaf updated 2015)), p. 28-50.

[224] Hogg (2007b (loose-leaf updated 2015)), p. 28-49, 28-50.

[225] Hogg (2007b (loose-leaf updated 2015)), p. 28-50.

rights from provincial infringement.[226] Again, why a provincial legislator should have the power to unilaterally limit a mutual treaty between different self-governing parties remains elusive. McLachlin C.L. constructed s.35 as a limit on both provincial and federal governmental powers,[227] but how this would justify unilateral treaty limitations by either government cannot be explained in any other way than by the position that Indigenous Peoples do not have self-governance rights and ultimately remain subsumed by Canadian sovereignty.

6.3.2.3.4 Treaties and the Repatriation Question

The legal status of treaties is relevant to the repatriation question for two essential reasons: first, the SCC's approach to limiting treaties underlines yet again how Indigenous self-determination has and continues to be denied by different bodies and institutions. It thus informs the broader legal context in which repatriation takes place. Second, and more to the point, a significant number of Indigenous Peoples have never contracted with the Crown. Repatriation questions can thus be dealt with under modern, comprehensive land treaty negotiations if Indigenous Peoples desire to do so and the government is willing. The question which the preceding subsections raises is whether they should. On the positive side, it would be an explicit, written promise of Indigenous control over specific forms of cultural heritage as well as relevant sacred sites which could and have been included in modern treaties (see Sect. 7.2 in the following chapter). However, if these treaties can be limited unilaterally, the question arises which would be the lesser of two evils: the treaty or the right? Both can be limited. The answer will depend on the community and heritage in question, but the fact that the question has to be asked shows how far the legal system still remains from reconciling the Canadian Crown and settler sovereignty with Indigenous self-governance rights.

6.3.3 Indigenous Religious Freedom in the Canadian Charter of Rights and Freedoms

The previous sections have considered whether Aboriginal or treaty rights can protect the Indigenous right to cultural heritage or support repatriation claims. The remaining step is to examine in how far the Charter offers the protection of Indigenous cultural rights. Within Canada, charter rights protect individuals against government actions.[228] It was incorporated in the Constitution in 1982. The Charter

---

[226] Hogg (2007b (loose-leaf updated 2015)), p. 28-51.

[227] Hogg (2007b (loose-leaf updated 2015)), p. 28-50.

[228] Human rights instruments such as the Alberta Human Rights Act, protects individuals against actions committed by other individuals.

is applicable to both the provincial as well as federal governments and now it constitutes the main human rights instrument in the country. Canada has a dualist legal system. Claimants before domestic courts rely on the CCRF rather than the ICCPR. Hogg points to the rule that a "a statute (and presumably a constitution) should be interpreted as far as possible into conformity with international law."[229] Similarities in scope between the two instruments, as well as in language, facilitate this. In addition, Canada has ratified the Optional Protocol to the ICCPR. Decisions of the Committee play a role in the interpretation of the CCRF.[230] Canadians may also petition the IACHR and its jurisprudence may similarly be used as interpretative aid.[231]

Indigenous cultural rights are protected in three ways under the charter. First, religious freedom is protected as a substantive right under s.2(a) CCRF. Second, the charter protects Indigenous individuals from discrimination through s.15 CCRF. Third, s.25 CCRF protects Aboriginal rights from abrogation or derogation under the Charter.

6.3.3.1 S.2(a) CCRF: Freedom of Conscience and Religion

S.2(a) CCRF enshrines the freedom of conscience and religion. One of the leading cases on the freedom of religion, R v Big M Drug Mart (1985), stated that "[t]he essence of the concept of freedom of religion is the right to entertain such religious beliefs as a person chooses, the right to declare religious beliefs openly and without fear of hindrance or reprisal, and the right to manifest religious belief by worship and practice or by teaching and dissemination."[232] It highlighted that "One of the major purposes of the Charter is to protect, within reason, from compulsion or restraint".[233] Hogg highlighted the similarities between the approach of Dickson J. and Art.18 ICCPR.[234] In this sense, the following standards arising from Art.18 ICCPR also fit within the Canadian Charter system:

1. Indigenous Peoples have right to adopt their own (traditional) beliefs. This may not result in *de lege* or *de facto* discrimination.
2. There may be no coercion to adopt/change/reject a religion. Legislative practices such as religious prohibitions which existed in the Indian Act until 1951 have been prohibited under human rights law since the adoption of the ICCPR.

---

[229] Reference as to Powers to Levy Rates on Foreign Legations [1943] S.C.R. 208; Health Services and Support—Facilities Subsector Bargaining Assn. v. British Columbia, [2007] 2 S.C.R. 391, 2007 SCC 27, para 69; Divito v Can [2013] 3 S.C.R.157, 2013 SCC 47, paras 22–27.

[230] Battiste and Henderson (2000), p. 173.

[231] Hogg (2007a (loose-leaf edition updated 2015)), p. 36-41, 36-42.

[232] R. v. Big M Drug Mart Ltd., [1985] 1 S.C.R. 295, para 94.

[233] R. v. Big M Drug Mart Ltd., [1985] 1 S.C.R. 295, para 95.

[234] Hogg (2007a (loose-leaf edition updated 2015)), p. 42-44.

3. Indigenous Peoples have the right to manifest their religion. This includes the right of access to and use of their sacred objects and the right to establish and maintain places to do so.
4. The Canadian state must do its utmost as part of ensuring religious freedom to ensure that relevant sites and other elements of religious practices are protected and "take additional measures in cases where they are vulnerable to desecration or destruction."[235]

While there is a general presumption that Indigenous religious practices are to be protected under the s.2(a) CRF, there are ways in which this protection could be incomplete. For example, if a court (rightly or wrongly) conceptualizes a practice as several distinct activities, some of them may take on religious characteristics, while others do not. The former could still be limited under the Charter, while the latter elements would receive no protection. As a result, a practitioner may find it difficult to practice the complete ceremony. Second, if the entire practice is protected, it might be limited under s.1.[236] The first has occurred when Canadian courts considered Indigenous religious practices in connection with hunting prohibitions under the Wildlife Protection Act. In R v Jack, the defendants hunted meat which was to be burned as a religious ceremony. Testimonial evidence by an Elder and anthropological evidence supported the use of meat in the ceremony. The Indigenous party argued that the hunting prohibition amounted to a violation of religious freedom. The courts rejected the argument and relied heavily on characterizing the hunting practice as not being part of the ceremony. Instead, they characterized the practice as consisting of burning the meat, while hunting was classified as a means of procuring the necessary elements for the practice. The courts consequently argued that the defendants could have relied on meat hunted under conditions permitted by the Act which then could be stored for later use.

A great difficulty in protecting Indigenous religious freedom arises out of a recent Supreme Court case from late 2017. Earlier, the Supreme Court decision in the Grizzly Bear Spirit case was introduced that involved claims both under s.2(a) CCRF and s.35.[237] The Ktunaxa First Nation filed a complaint against British Columbia for developing a year-around ski resort, alleging a violation of s.2(a) CCRF and s.35. The development covered a sacred site (Quat'muk), the home of the Grizzly Bear Spirit. After engaging in consultations, the Ktunaxa knowledge keeper disclosed that agreement was not possible, because the development would drive Grizzly Bear Spirit from the sacred area, thereby significantly impairing if not even destroying the communal dimension of their religious practices. This would infringe their religious freedom. The provincial minister decided that reasonable consultation and accommodation had occurred and approved the project, nevertheless.

---

[235] Art.6(a)(c) 1981 Declaration of General Assembly, Human Rights Council Resolution 6/37 para 9(e). See discussion of Art.18 ICCPR in Chap. 2.

[236] See Sect. 6.3.3.4.

[237] Ktunaxa Nation v British Columbia (Forests, Lands and Natural Resource Operations), 2017 SCC 54. For s.35 claim discussion see Sect. 6.3.2.1.2.

The majority relied on Big Drug Market to observe that s.2(a) comprises two elements, the freedom to hold a religion and the freedom to manifest a religion.[238] The majority then proceeded to test whether the province had infringed the right. To fulfil the infringement test, the claimants had to show that two elements were fulfilled: "(1) that he or she sincerely believes in a practice or belief that has a nexus with religion, and (2) that the impugned state conduct interferes, in a manner that is non-trivial or not insubstantial, with his or her ability to act in accordance with that practice or belief."[239] Both the majority and minority agreed on the elements of the test and on the fact that the first element of test, a sincere belief, was fulfilled.[240] They did, however, disagree substantively on the application of the second element. The majority opinion mistakenly decided that the decision neither affected the community's right to their religious beliefs *nor* their right to manifest their religion.[241] It characterized the claim not as seeking the protection of the religious activity (holding the belief or manifesting it), but rather as seeking the protection of the content of the religion, namely Grizzly Bear Spirit, which it found to be outside the scope of s.2(a) CCRF.[242] To do otherwise, the majority claimed, "would put deeply held personal beliefs under judicial scrutiny".[243] It is striking that despite the 30 year time gap the decision taken by the Canadian Supreme Court in Ktunaxa closely resembles the one taken by the by the US Supreme Court in Lyng. While the SCC makes no reference to Lyng, both the split in majority vs minority as well as the resulting lack of protection of Indigenous religious sacred grounds from both cases closely resemble each other. This is more than unfortunate, given the problems which Lyng created for the protection of Indigenous religious traditions and the criticisms that were brought against the Lyng decision. It is not surprising that the consequences of Ktunaxa are similarly worrisome for the Indigenous freedom of religion as pointed out below.

The minority in Ktunaxa aptly pointed out that state actions that render a religious belief meaningless interfere with an individual's ability to act in accordance with their beliefs.[244] Because the development would cause Grizzly Bear Spirit to leave "[a]ll songs, rituals, and ceremonies associated with Grizzly Bear Spirit would become meaningless".[245] More importantly, "[t]his kind of state interference is a reality where individuals find spiritual fulfillment through their connection to the

[238] Ktunaxa Nation v British Columbia (Forests, Lands and Natural Resource Operations) [2017], para 63.

[239] Ibid, para 68 relying on Multani v. Commission scolaire Marguerite-Bourgeoys [2006] 1 S.C.R. 256, 2006 SCC 6, para 34.

[240] Ktunaxa Nation v British Columbia (Forests, Lands and Natural Resource Operations) [2017], paras 68–69 and 123.

[241] Ibid, para 70.

[242] Ibid, paras 70–71.

[243] Ibid, para 72.

[244] Ibid, para 126.

[245] Ibid, para 117.

physical world. The connection to the physical world, specifically to land, is a central feature of Indigenous religions".[246] To dismiss such claims as seeking to protect the 'object' of a religious practice rather than the practice leaves large elements of Indigenous religious practices without any protection against governmental action under the Charter.[247] Moldaver J. continued, however, that, while the ministerial decision breached the Ktunaxa Nations' religious freedom, this breach was justified. He opined that the minister balanced the right proportionately with the relevant legal objectives, namely to administer Crown land and to dispose of it in the public interest and sought to limit it as little as reasonably possible.[248] As a result of this decision, the protection of Indigenous religious freedom is severely limited. One may thus wonder whether repatriation requests for specific objects that are based on a fear of the desecration of grounds would similarly remain without Charter protection.

One could still argue that Indigenous practitioners need their sacred heritage in order to practice their religion, thereby emphasizing the practice element of the claim. Moreover, even if one could claim that a governmental decision not to return an object would infringe the right, this decision could still be reasonable, even if the practice was no longer possible as a result—adopting the minority's reasoning. This framework is comparatively broad, and definitely broader than the limitations permissible under Art.18(3) ICCPR explored in Chap. 2. It is difficult to see how the decision to permit a ski resort is necessary to protect public safety, order, health, morals, or the fundamental rights and freedoms of others. This is a crucial element to protect Indigenous religious freedom under the ICCPR. This Supreme Court decision therefore results in a dual risk of future violations of Indigenous religious rights. Overall, there are a number of court decisions that have been phrased in a way that emphasizes reconciliation at the cost of Indigenous Peoples. However, as this analysis has only looked at case law incidentally, it is insufficient evidence to prove an overall trend.

6.3.3.2 S.15 CCRF Equality and Aboriginal Rights Protection

S.15(1) enshrines equal treatment, prohibiting discrimination on the basis of race, national or ethnic origin, colour, religion, sex, age or mental or physical disability. Paragraph 2 clarifies that the right to equal treatment does not prohibit affirmative action (action that seeks the "amelioration of conditions of disadvantaged individuals or groups"). The Supreme Court has affirmed that equal treatment need not mean identical treatment.[249] John Borrows has argued that to apply the principle to

[246] Ibid, para 127.

[247] Compare Ibid, para 131.

[248] Ibid, para 119, using Doré framework para 136.

[249] Law v Canada (Minister of Employment and Immigration) [1999] 1 S.C.R. 497.

Indigenous legal traditions "it can be argued that the fact of their difference does not necessarily raise concerns about equality, fairness, certainty, and so on."[250]

S.15 has different dimensions in the repatriation context. As discussed in Chap. 2, in its General Recommendation No.23, CERD called upon states to "[e]nsure that indigenous communities can exercise their rights to practise and revitalize their cultural traditions and customs and to preserve and to practise their languages".[251] Especially in the Canadian context, the contemporary scarcity of some forms of Indigenous heritage is the result of past assimilationist policies. As a result, state measures that support Indigenous cultural rights, including repatriation programmes, qualify as measures to protect Indigenous rights equally. In effect, Indigenous Peoples are both in a disadvantaged position in terms of contemporary rights protection because of past violations and they may require the state to take different measures in order to ensure that they can effectively enjoy rights equal to other citizens. It must be underlined that these are *two distinct categories*. Canada's Indigenous Peoples, for historical and cultural reasons, are members of *both categories*. Both require the government to take distinct measures which arise *independently of* any requirements under Aboriginal and treaty rights. Even when past effects have been remedied, Indigenous distinctiveness will still require different measures to be taken to ensure that their substantive rights are protected equally.

6.3.3.3 S.25 CCRF: Aboriginal Rights, Treaty Rights, and the Charter

The relationship between Charter and Aboriginal and treaty rights in the broader sense is governed by s.25 CCRF. While s.35 CA 1982 has become the foundation for *sui generis* Aboriginal law developed by the Supreme Court, s.25 CCRF details the relationship between Aboriginal rights, treaty rights and the Royal Proclamation, on the one hand, and the Charter on the other.[252] In R v Kapp, the Supreme Court drew a parallel between the modern treaty process and s.25, observing that it "reflects the notions of reconciliation and negotiation present in the treaty process".[253] In line with the Supreme Court's understanding of reconciliation in other cases, s.25 has been read to operate as a shield. It only protects Aboriginal and treaty rights in the case of an irreconcilable conflict between Charter rights and rights listed in s.25.[254] As was emphasized in R v Kapp, the primacy of s.25 "was clearly intended" and it serves to protect Indigenous rights "from erosion based on the

[250] Borrows (2006), p. 125.

[251] CERD General Recommendation No.23 (1997), para 4.

[252] The wording of s.25 suggests that the category of protected rights is to be understood broadly: "The guarantee in this Charter of certain rights and freedoms shall not be construed so as to abrogate or derogate from any aboriginal, **treaty or other rights or freedoms that pertain to the aboriginal peoples of Canada** . . ." [emphasis added].

[253] R. v. Kapp, [2008] 2 S.C.R. 483, 2008 SCC 41, para 120.

[254] Ibid para 79.

Charter".[255] However, this shielding function of s.25 is not an absolute one. The majority in R v Kapp has narrowed the shielding function by drawing a distinction between the impairment of an Aboriginal right and it being incidentally affected. Relying on Van der Peet, it argued that "only laws that actually impair native rights will be considered, not those that simply have incidental effects on natives." [256] Moreover, s.28, which ensures gender equality, applies regardless.[257]

6.3.3.4 Procedural Aspects

The rights in the Charter can be limited in accordance with S.1 CCRF. It provides that the protection offered by the Charter is "subject only to such reasonable limits prescribed by law as can be demonstrably justified in a free and democratic society." The reasonable and demonstrably justified test was developed in R v Oakes and must satisfy four criteria:

1. sufficiently important objective: The law must pursue an objective that is sufficiently important to justify limiting a Charter right.
2. Rational connection: The law must be rationally connected to the objective.
3. Least drastic means: The law must impair the right no more than is necessary to accomplish the objective
4. Proportionate effect: The law must not have a disproportionately sever effect on the persons to whom it applies.[258]

Concerning the standard of judicial review, in 1982 there was significant discussion whether a charter and the ensuing judicial review of charter rights was desirable given the non-elected position of judges. The final result is less judicial supremacy than in the U.S., but not complete parliamentary supremacy. It was given form in s.33 ("the notwithstanding clause"). It enables Parliament or the Legislatures to overrule the Supreme Court, but it has seldom been used.[259] Concerning the standard of review, laws that aim at curtailing a Charter right are unconstitutional, if the objective is constitutional but the effect of law is to reduce Charter rights, it will be unconstitutional unless it falls under s.1.[260]

In terms of interpretation, Canada's constitution has been characterized as a 'living tree' to allow for it to be a flexible rather than static instrument. As early as 1930, Edwards v A-G highlighted the need for a generous interpretation, not to give Parliament more power but rather to ensure "full effect to civil liberties".[261] This

[255] Ibid, paras 81, 80.

[256] Ibid, para 79.

[257] Ibid.

[258] Hogg (2007a (loose-leaf edition updated 2015)), p. 38-18.

[259] Hogg (2007a (loose-leaf edition updated 2015)), p. 36-37, 36-38.

[260] Hogg (2007a (loose-leaf edition updated 2015)), p. 36-22.

[261] Hogg (2007a (loose-leaf edition updated 2015)), p. 36-28.

approach allows a flexible interpretation which allows Charter provisions to be given full effect, while keeping up with changing times both for the Charter and other constitutional provisions.[262]

6.3.4 *Canada's Implementation of UNDRIP*

As observed in the introduction, in June 2021 Bill C-15 'The United Nations Declaration on the Rights of Indigenous Peoples Act' became law in Canada.[263] Because the Act was passed just prior to finalizing edits, not much can be said here as to its effects. It is nonetheless noteworthy as it contains within it the potential for real advancement of Indigenous Rights within the Canadian legal system. The Act has two purposes, affirm the applicability of the Declaration in Canadian law and provide a framework for its implementation (s.4). However, much about the Act remains unclear, as can be seen in the discussions in the legislature and the general public debate. This starts with the stated purpose of the act. The Minister of Justice of Canada has emphasized, for example, that "affirm the Declaration as a universal international human rights instrument with application in Canadian law;" in s.4(a) is not to mean that the Declaration has direct legal effect within the Canadian legal system, contrary to what one may have expected based on the wording. Rather "the objective of these acknowledgements is to recognize existing legal principles".[264] It appears that, instead, the main focus is to use the declaration "to inform the process of developing or amending laws and as part of interpreting and applying them".[265] This to be done together with Indigenous Peoples.

One of the open questions in the discussions leading up to the Act's adoption and for the future is how the approach to free, prior and informed consent will influence the legal consultation duties under Canadian law. The question is in how far there really will be a strengthening of Indigenous rights in Canada as a result of increasing existing rights so that there are closer to the international standards. Or, alternatively, if UNDRIP will instead be used as window dressing, with Canadian law being read as being consistent with international standards. The Minister of Justice was quick to point out that FPIC in UNDRIP is not a veto power, adding that the governmental obligations provided for in the declaration "are not absolute".[266] And that this should

[262] 'Living tree' concept i.e. in Canada (Attorney General) v. Hislop [2007] 1 S.C.R. 429, 2007 SCC 10, paras 94,144 (interpretation of Charter generally).

[263] United Nations Declaration on the Rights of Indigenous Peoples Act (S.C. 2021, c. 14).

[264] House of Commons Debates, 43-2, No. 60 (17 February 2021) 1810 (Hon David Lametti) "the objective of these acknowledgements is to recognize existing legal principles and not give the declaration itself direct legal effect in Canada."

[265] House of Commons Debates, 43-2, No. 60 (17 February 2021) 1810 (Hon David Lametti) "the objective of these acknowledgements is to recognize existing legal principles and not give the declaration itself direct legal effect in Canada."

[266] House of Commons Debates, 43-2, No. 60 (17 February 2021) 1815 (Hon David Lametti).

have a result, or in the words of the Expert Mechanism on the Rights of Indigenous Peoples "Withholding consent is expected to convince the other party not to take the risk of proceeding with the proposal."[267] The Expert Mechanism even cautioned "Arguments of whether Indigenous Peoples have a "veto" in this regard appear to largely detract from and undermine the legitimacy of the free, prior and informed consent concept".[268] The problem here is of course that under UNDRIP "consent" does mean that Indigenous Peoples have the right not to consent.[269] Of course, FPIC depends on context but the right to give (or withhold) consent is more than a right to be consulted. The discussion on whether FPIC under UNDRIP implies a veto or not does showcase some of the problems of the consultative process under Canadian law. If FPIC is understood to be a purely procedural right, it undermines the goal of the provision, for how free and informed can consent be if the party giving it knows that ultimately government and businesses can overturn it and even a lengthy and very costly court process may not secure it?

The most noteworthy elements of the Act (from an Indigenous rights perspective) are arguably in the preamble. These include the rejection of the doctrine of terra nullius and colonialism,[270] the understanding of the Declaration rights as minimum standards which "must be implemented in Canada"[271] and much more. The question remains, of course, what courts and the government will make out of the Act. The preamble is part of the Act and must be taken into account in its implementation and application.[272] However, it is also true that the preamble text goes much further than the text in sections 1-7, and it remains to be seen which direction will be followed.

6.3.5 *Heritage Legislation and Museum Framework*

The position of Indigenous cultural heritage within the federal legislative framework is multifaceted. To understand in how far these forms of heritage are protected and what this protection means at the federal level, possible export prohibitions as well as potential protections in federal (read national) museum(s) should be given attention.

---

[267] Human Rights Council, Study of the Expert Mechanism on the Rights of Indigenous Peoples, Free, prior and informed consent: A human-rights based approach, U.N. Doc.A/HRC/39/62 [10.08.2018], para 26(a).

[268] Ibid.

[269] For a discussion of the B.C. legislation implementing UNDRIP and the challenges of FPIC, see Sayers (2020), p. 14.

[270] United Nations Declaration on the Rights of Indigenous Peoples Act (S.C. 2021, c. 14), recitals 9 and 10.

[271] United Nations Declaration on the Rights of Indigenous Peoples Act (S.C. 2021, c. 14), recital 2.

[272] Joffe (2021), p. 1.

6.3.5.1 Export Regulation

Canada adopted a system that sought to protect specific forms of cultural heritage through export controls in 1975. By then, a considerable portion of Indigenous cultural heritage created until this point had already been removed from the country.[273] It also accepted the 1970 UNESCO Convention at roughly the same time, on the 28th of March 1978.[274] The Cultural Property Export and Import Act (CPEIA) aims "to keep in Canada, in the public domain, that which is deemed to be of **national** importance."[275] The act will only prevent the permanent export of a limited number of objects, namely those that are of "outstanding significance" and of "national importance".[276]

Generally, Indigenous cultural heritage is protected either because of its archaeological or artistic value. In the first group of listed objects, "ceremonial and religious articles" are protected by virtue of being archaeological objects.[277] This is under the condition that the object was excavated or recovered within Canada no less than 75 years after its burial, regardless of its value.[278] In the second category, s.4(2)(b) CPEIA includes "objects that were made by, or ... that relate to, the aboriginal peoples of Canada and that have a fair market value in Canada of more than five hundred dollars." The Canadian Cultural Property Control List classified these objects as ethnographic material culture and they are included subject to their financial value, unless they are younger than 50 years or were made by a person still alive.[279] The objects featured in the Export Control List are subject to export control that considers whether they are of outstanding significance and of national importance.

These criteria are cumulative[280] and only if an object qualifies either as an ethnographic or archaeological object on the list, as well as satisfying both elements

---

[273] Prott and O'Keefe (1989), p. 458.

[274] List of countries having ratified the 1970 Convention, in alphabetical order available via http://portal.unesco.org/en/ev.php-URL_ID=13039&URL_DO=DO_TOPIC&URL_SECTION=201.html#STATE_PARTIES [last accessed 19.08.2021].

[275] UNESCO, Reports of Member States on the action taken by them to implement the Recommendation on the Means of Prohibiting and Preventing the Illicit Export, Import and Transfer of Ownership of Cultural Property (1964) and the Convention on the Means of Prohibiting and Preventing the Illicit Import, Export and Transfer of Ownership of Cultural Property (1970), [1978] UNESCO Doc. Ref. 20 C/84, p.15. Emphasis added.

[276] S.11(1) CPEIA. CPEIA current to 2019-06-06-06-28 at time of editing.

[277] Canadian Cultural Property Export Control List [C.R.C. c.448] current to 2019-06-06 at time of editing, Group I s.4(2)(a)(vi).

[278] Canadian Cultural Property Export Control List [C.R.C. c.448], Group I s.4(1) read in conjunction with s.4(2)(a)(vi).

[279] S.4(3)CPEIA and Canadian Cultural Property Export Control List, Group II s.2.

[280] This is expressed by the use of the connector 'and' between subparagraphs (a) and (b) as well as the wording of s11(3) CPEIA "Where an expert examiner determines that an object that is the subject of an application for an export permit that has been referred to him is of outstanding significance under paragraph (1)(a) **and** meets the degree of national importance referred to in

of section 11(1), it may it not be exported. If an object meets the protective criteria, the export permit is delayed, and the object may be bought by an institution or a government under s.29(5). It therefore seems as if Indigenous cultural heritage will be prohibited from leaving the country in exceptional cases. Moreover, the reason for this protection does not lie in the cultural link the Indigenous community has with the object, but rather in its economic or historic or archaeological value. However, if a private seller wishes to sell an important religious artefact, agency practice has established that an Aboriginal community can apply to be accepted as a designated organization for the particular object and purchase the object to keep it in Canada.[281] As was shown above, and most importantly for present purposes, the focus of CPEIA rests on keeping objects in Canada. If a sacred object is found on private lands and smuggled into the United States, for example, this would amount to a violation of the CPEIA. However, if an important object is found and offered for sale in the United States, the act also does not provide for information to be sent to First Nations. In effect, the act in the way it was adopted does not consider First Nations interests to their heritage at all.[282] The singular focus has the unfortunate side effect that contemporary Indigenous rights standards which exist on the international level are not considered within the Act.[283]

6.3.5.2 Fiduciary Duties and the Deaccessioning of Indigenous Heritage

Chapter 4 introduced the concept of fiduciary duties, albeit in the U.S. legal context. These fiduciary duties require the trustees and directors of a museum not to place themselves in a position of conflict between the interests of the institution and their own.[284] The duty of care requires the exercise of reasonable care and skill in the management and preservation of the museum assets.[285] In Canada, privately funded museums are far less common. Instead, many museums are controlled by the government and set up as (government) corporations.[286] As a result, they still incur fiduciary duties, but the standard of behaviour that can be expected should arguably not be as high as for museum directors whose museum is established as a

---

paragraph (1)(b), the expert examiner shall forthwith in writing advise the permit officer who referred the application not to issue an export permit in respect of the object and shall provide the permit officer with the reasons therefor." (emphasis added by the author).

[281] Institutions or public authorities may make a purchase offer under s.29, the Department of Canadian Heritage has give guidance that aboriginal governing bodies can classify as public authorities, see: https://www.canada.ca/en/canadian-heritage/services/designation-institutions-cultural-property.html [last accessed 19.08.2021]. Funds may be made available.

[282] This was experienced by the Saanich people in the case of the SDDLNEWHALA ("Stel-nuh-quay-la") medicine bowl. For a Saanich account of this experience, read Henry (1995), p.

[283] Kuprecht (2014), pp. 105–106.

[284] Nafziger et al. (2010), p. 711.

[285] Nafziger et al. (2010), p. 726.

[286] Nafziger et al. (2010), p. 713.

trust.[287] Nevertheless, the duties in operating a Crown corporate museum may create tension between the duty to further the public interest and more economically-driven behaviour.[288]

Concerning repatriation requests, it has to be shown that a decision to repatriate is in line with the museum's mission. If the museum's ultimate purpose is to serve the public either through education or identity formation, repatriation can be reconciled with this purpose based on several arguments. First, if repatriation is motivated by ethical reasons, transparency about the history of the object and the reasons for the repatriation can serve an important educative function. Cooperation with Indigenous communities can also yield important new knowledge to educate. Second, if the museum mission supports identity formation through the conservation and transmission of heritage, repatriation can support this mission, first, in revitalizing local or regional Indigenous communities and strengthening the multicultural identity of the community the museum serves and, second, if the repatriation is accompanied by educative material it can also strengthen identity formation. Repatriation would not violate the museum director's fiduciary duties in any of these cases.

Regarding the deaccessioning of Indigenous sacred heritage in Canada, guidance on deaccessioning comes mostly from non-binding codes of ethics. Case law guidance comes from U.S. jurisprudence, there is a lack of Canadian cases on deaccessioning decisions. In the context of the United States, the discussion on deaccessioning was limited by the fact that NAGPRA established a statutory obligation to deaccession if certain conditions are fulfilled. Outside of the NAGPRA framework, the jurisprudence seems to suggest that a decision to deaccession is given a certain deference by the court.[289] In the absence of federal legal criteria for deaccessioning, a museum will be guided first by its governing act, second by any self-regulatory code it adopted and third by industry standards.[290] In the following section, it will be examined how the first two influence repatriation decisions. Non-binding industry guidelines are discussed further below.[291]

---

[287] Paterson (2007), p. 428.

[288] Nafziger et al. (2010), p. 713.

[289] Nafziger et al. (2010), p. 715 See also Rockwell et al v Trustees of the Berkshire Museums et al (7.11. 2017) WL 6940932.

[290] Additional restrictions may also arise in the case of conditional donations.

[291] See Sect. 6.4.2.

6.3.5.3 National Canadian Heritage and the Repatriation Question

There are currently nine national museums in Canada[292] governed by federal law, namely the Museums Act.[293] Given the focus of this research on the repatriation of Indigenous cultural heritage removed in the past, the Canadian Museum of History [hereafter CMH] is the museum which will be considered in more detail in this section.[294] It is also adopted its own repatriation policy. The Museum Act emphasizes the need to preserve the heritage of Canada for present and future generations. The museum's role is conceptualized as "preserving and promoting the heritage of Canada . . . and in contributing to the collective memory and sense of identity of all Canadians".[295] Its purpose is to "enhance knowledge, understanding and appreciation" of the past.[296] In order to further this purpose, the CMH may collect objects,[297] but also it may "sell, exchange, give away, destroy or otherwise dispose of museum material in its collection".[298] This is on the condition that any revenue thereby obtained is reinvested in the collection. The main limitation of the museum's power to deaccession Indigenous cultural heritage then arises from two sources. First, if the museum decides to repatriate Indigenous objects this must still further its overall mission.[299] Repatriation can definitely be argued to contribute to the collective identity of all Canadians, both in terms of addressing difficult stretches of shared history and in furthering reconciliation. Second, the CMH "may deal with property only in accordance with the terms on which it was acquired or is held".[300] Depending on the origin of a particular item, for example a donation, there may be conditions attached that will prevent the museum from repatriating the item, even if it may wish to do so.

The CMH has repatriated objects and human remains and continues to respond to community requests for repatriation. According to its website, the museum has

---

[292] https://www.canada.ca/en/services/culture/cultural-attractions/museums-galleries/national-museums.html [last accessed 19.08.2021].

[293] Museums Act S.C. 1990, c.3 governs the seven museum corporations National Gallery of Canada, the Canadian Museum of History, the Canadian Museum of Nature, the National Museum of Science and Technology, the Canadian Museum for Human Rights and the Canadian Museum of Immigration at Pier 21. The Canadian Museum of History Corporation also oversees the operation of and includes the Canadian War Museum and any other affiliated museums under s.7(2) Museums Act S.C. 1990, c.3. Museums Act current as to 2021-06-28 at time of editing.

[294] Apart from the museums, there is also Parks Canada. It is a federal government agency that is responsible for national historic sites, national parks and national marine conservation areas. It has also established a repatriation policy and repatriated a number of items. For more information see: Myles (2010).

[295] S.3(a) Museums Act S.C. 1990, c.3.

[296] S.8 Museums Act S.C. 1990, c.3.

[297] S.9(1)(a) Museums Act S.C. 1990, c.3.

[298] S.9(1)(c) Museums Act S.C. 1990, c.3.

[299] S.9(1) Museums Act S.C. 1990, c.3.

[300] S.9(2) Museums Act S.C. 1990, c.3.

engaged in repatriation in three different ways since the 1990s. First, it has acted in response to requests received from First Nations, second, it developed a programme focusing specifically on giving Indigenous individuals access to the collection to identify and potentially request sacred objects,[301] and third through the treaty process.[302] The Museum also engaged in the Nunavut Repatriation Project.[303] As another example, in the early 2000s, the museum corporation detailed that it was actively engaged "in the negotiation of repatriation in the context of comprehensive claims and/or self-government with approximately 34 First Nations."[304]

The Repatriation policy adopted by the CMH (then the Canadian Museum of Civilization)[305] covers human remains and associated burial objects as well as ethnographic and archaeological objects as of June 30th 2001. It does not cover "those parts of the CMCC collection … bound by treaties" (S.1). The policy sets a number of requirements for repatriation requests:

1. They must be made in writing (S.5(1))
2. They must originate from Aboriginal individuals, Aboriginal governments, comprehensive claims negotiations or self-government negotiations' (S.5(2))
3. The subject of the repatriation request may not be claimed by another competing request (S.5(4))

The request will then evaluated on the basis of four criteria, namely "the *historical relationship* of the requestor(s) to the human remains or objects concerned; the *conditions* under which the materials requested *were acquired* by the museum; the possibility of competing claims to the material; and, *the character of the objects*, i.e. whether they meet the criteria set out in Section 6."[306] It is noteworthy that, in its criteria for repatriation, the museum displays a clear preference for repatriation requests which originate from Indigenous governments. S.6(2) prescribes that human remains and associated burial objects "will be repatriated only to an Aboriginal Government or an organization designated in writing for this purpose by an

[301] Sacred Materials project which "provides First Nations with an opportunity to review collections held by the Corporation, identify objects requiring special care, and discuss repatriation, as required." Information provided by Canadian Museum of History, Website, available at: http://www.historymuseum.ca/learn/research/repatriation/#tabs [last accessed 19.08.2021]. Project established in 1993, Summary Report Corporate Plan 2011–2012 to 2015–2016, at 15 available at: http://www.historymuseum.ca/wp-content/uploads/2015/09/corp2011e.pdf [last accessed 19.08.2021].

[302] http://www.historymuseum.ca/learn/research/repatriation/#tabs [last accessed 19.08.2021].

[303] Summary Report Corporate Plan 2014–2015 to 2018–2019, p. 42, available via: https://www.historymuseum.ca/about/the-corporation/#tabs [last accessed 19.08.2021].

[304] Summary of the Corporate Plan 2003–2005 to 2007–2008 and Summary of the Operating and Capital Budgets 2003–2004, p. 9, available at: http://www.historymuseum.ca/wp-content/uploads/2015/09/corp03e.pdf, [last accessed 19.08.2021].

[305] Repatriation Policy [2001] adopted by the Canadian Museum of Civilization Corporation, available at: http://www.historymuseum.ca/wp-content/uploads/2015/09/REPATRIATION-POLICY.pdf [last accessed 19.08.2021].

[306] Art.5(3) Repatriation Policy 2001.

Aboriginal Government." Indigenous religious heritage, by contrast, can be repatriated both to an Aboriginal Government or an individual according to s.6(3). S.6(3) (i) requires an individual or groups of individuals to have "an undisputed historical relationship to the objects and the objects are demonstrated to have been acquired under conditions which were illegal at that time" for the repatriation to be successful. As an alternative to repatriation, the repatriation policy allows the museum to conclude custodial arrangements with Indigenous Peoples. As one example of such a Custodial Arrangement, the museum refers to an agreement reached with the Nisga'a in the Nisga'a treaty. It arranges shared possession on a rotational basis for Nisga'a objects that are part of the museum's collection.[307] The repatriation policy reserves the right of the museum to reproduce records of repatriated objects (s.6(5)) and clarifies that the repatriation policy does not preclude any research on its collections being carried out by its staff (s.9(1)).

There may also be further conditions included in repatriation agreements. For example in the early 1980s confiscated potlatch material was returned by a Canadian museum with the condition that these objects remain in Canada as part of its national heritage.[308] Similar conditions can be envisioned under the CMH 2001 policy, given that the policy recalls the institution's mandate in s.2 which is to be achieved "by establishing, maintaining and developing for research and posterity a collection of objects of historical or cultural interest". Moreover, the CMH operates within the constraints of the Museum Act and the purpose it allocates to the institution remains one of "preserving and promoting the heritage of Canada . . . and in contributing to the collective memory and sense of identity of all Canadians" (s.3(a)).

6.4 Canadian Museum Documents

6.4.1 1992 Museum Task Force Report

The Canadian museum sector experienced an upheaval in the late 1980s and early 1990s. Several museum controversies surrounding museum exhibitions arose. One such exhibition, "The Spirit Sings", was organized by the Glenbow Museum in 1988 during the Calgary Winter Olympics. The museum granted Shell Canada exclusive corporate sponsorship for the exhibition. The company was commercially exploiting land which, at the same time, was claimed by the Lubicon Nation."[309] The exhibition also contained a number of masks the display of which was rejected by the First Nations. It sparked a boycott by the Lubicon Lake First Nation and a national discourse on the relationship between museums and Indigenous communities in

[307] CMH Website, http://www.historymuseum.ca/learn/research/repatriation/#tabs [last accessed 19.08.2021].

[308] Glass (2004), p. 132.

[309] Bolton (2009), p. 145.

Canada.[310] This collaboration between museums and First Nations has led to the creation and adoption of the Museum Task Force Report.[311]

The Task Force Report was drafted by experts in the cultural field, including both Indigenous and non-Indigenous experts, after nation-wide consultations. The final principles and recommendations set out to create the framework for an equal partnership between Indigenous Peoples and museums in all areas of Indigenous cultural heritage.[312] Equality in the sense of the principles requires both parties to appreciate the other's knowledge of and interest in Indigenous cultural heritage. It also entails addressing misrepresentations of Indigenous Peoples in the past,[313] the involvement of Indigenous individuals in relevant policies and funding programmes, the planning of exhibitions and all other activities carried out by a museum.[314] Recommendations address interpretation, access, repatriation, training and implementation.

The removal of Indigenous culture and cultural heritage is addressed by repatriation and loan provisions, the creation of Indigenous cultural community centers and recommendations of special access to items in museum storage. Notably, "museums are identified as having the potential to engage with living cultures, not just objects."[315] *Intra-national* repatriation recommendations cover the obligation to return human remains[316] and a broad category comprising 'objects of cultural patrimony'. For the latter, the recommendations require that any decision be taken jointly with Indigenous Peoples as equal partners. Five different options are recommended: restitution or reversion, transfer of title, loan of materials, replication of materials and shared authority to manage cultural property. With regard to international repatriations, the report emphasizes the need for governmental involvement and asks both representative organizations, the Canadian Museum Association and the Assembly of First Nations to lobby for repatriation with international actors.[317] The recommendations on repatriation options take special note of the need to return sacred ceremonial objects. Restitution is defined as the transfer or return of the legal title over any objects which "are judged by current legal standards to have been acquired illegally".[318] This is to be based on the applicable legal

---

[310] "The Spirit Sings" exhibition was a watershed in Canadian museology." Task Force Report, 1994, at 7.

[311] Ibid, 1994, at 1.

[312] Ibid, at 4. The report speaks of Indigenous interpretation which "includes all facets of museum administration, research, public program and exhibition planning, and the presentations that result from such planning". One example is s.3(b)(v) "museums are urged to share management of their collections", at 9.

[313] Ibid, at 4.

[314] Ibid, at 7 (principles).

[315] Ibid, at 4.

[316] Ibid, at 8, recommendation 3(a).

[317] Ibid, at 9, recommendation 3 (c).

[318] While restitution thus covers a broad category of objects, this is however softened by the fact that is one of the recommended options, ibid, at 9., 3(b)(i).

framework for the de-accessioning of objects. Transfer of title is also considered for legally-obtained cultural heritage. Here, the report recommends that museums support requests for the transfer of title in relation to sacred and ceremonial objects, as well as objects "that have an ongoing historical, traditional or cultural importance". In addition, the report asks museums to negotiate mutual loan agreements for sacred and ceremonial objects to be used by Indigenous communities in ceremonies and festivals. The agreement should address the foreseen use, length of time and possible risks to the physical integrity of the object.[319]

The recommendations try to balance Indigenous and conservationist interests. With respect to the heritage at issue here, this means that museums are required to "recognize the legitimate right of access by Aboriginal peoples to sacred materials, cultural objects and relevant documentation." Access includes not only physical access to but also ceremonial use of the heritage in question.[320] Indigenous Peoples are, in return, required to "also recognize the legitimate concerns of museums with respect to the care, maintenance and preservation of their holdings." In general, the Task force report regulates the repatriation of heritage as a means to support revitalization and engage with living Indigenous cultures on an equal level. In general, the recommendations clearly advocate moving beyond legal considerations in favour of creating long-lasting cultural/heritage partnerships between Indigenous communities and cultural institutions.[321] Its preference for the creation of partnerships explains its preference for negotiations between the involved parties based on moral and ethical considerations. The focus on individual local agreements also has to be understood as an acknowledgement of the vast regional differences which exist (ed) in Canada at the time in terms of cooperation levels and the differences among Indigenous cultures and their ensuing preferences.

Today, the majority of museums with Indigenous collections hire Indigenous individuals, but as Bolton suggests, too often on a contractual, limited basis.[322] Similarly, while the report triggered budgetary promises for an increase in Indigenous museum staff, "funding priorities are still a source of frustration for Aboriginal cultural workers trying to break into the perpetually cash-trapped museum world."[323] In an interview with Bolton, Lee-Ann Martin, the first coordinator of the task force, highlighted the report's development of a framework of cooperation between non-indigenous museums and Indigenous communities as its "most significant effect".[324] The Task Force Report certainly brought the differences in Indigenous and traditional museum approaches to access, preservation and heritage to

[319] Ibid, 3(b)(iii) at 9.

[320] Ibid, at 4.

[321] In general: "There is a strong consensus that Partnerships should be guided by moral, ethical and professional principles and not limited to areas of rights and interests specified by law", ibid, at 4. A specific example is recommendation 3(b)(ii), at 9.

[322] Bolton (2009), p. 151-152.

[323] Bolton (2009), p. 151.

[324] Bolton (2009), p. 152.

light. Traditionally, museums would have viewed access and preservation as opposite goals to be remedied, as certain types of access may damage the physical integrity of an object.[325] This can be at odds with perspectives which emphasize heritage as a procedural,[326] cultural element which interacts with community members and with which Indigenous individuals interact. However, different Canadian repatriation policies were based on the Task Force Report, which shows how important it was in influencing this museum policy area.[327]

One observation both captures the drive behind the original report and could arguably still be used today in connection to the debate on the role of museums for the reconciliatory process: "There is a strong consensus that partnerships should be guided by moral, ethical and professional principles and not limited to areas of rights and interests specified by law."[328] After all, the importance of such partnerships was again highlighted by a more recent report, and the role of museums and archives in reconciliation received renewed attention. This was triggered by the findings of the Truth and Reconciliation Commission of Canada that was set up to implement parts of the Indian Residential Schools Settlement Agreement. The process sought to facilitate reconciliation and gather testimonies from residential school survivors and communities. In 2015, the Commission published the information gathered and its findings in a number of reports.[329] This culminated in a Call to Action, which comprises over 90 specific calls to action, designed to advance reconciliation and address the long-lasting effects of residential schools among Indigenous communities.[330] The Commission called upon the Canadian Association of Museums and the Canadian Association of Museums in collaboration with Indigenous Peoples to investigate in how far national museum policies were in line with the UNDRIP, distil best practices and make recommendations for a better alignment of institutional policies and practices with Indigenous human rights statements. The federal government was to provide funding for these activities. In spring 2019, it committed to providing the CMA with 1 million CAD to implement action call 67 and align museum policies with UNDRIP.[331]

[325] Clavir (2002), p. 33, 40-41.

[326] Clavir (2002), p. 35.

[327] Myles (2010), p. 50.

[328] Task Force Report on Museums and First Peoples [1992, reprinted 1994], A Report jointly sponsored by the Assembly of First Nations and the Canadian Museums Association, available at: http://museums.in1touch.org/uploaded/web/docs/Task_Force_Report_1994.pdf, p. 4. [last accessed 19.08.2021].

[329] Available via the website of the National Centre for Truth and Reconciliation at: http://nctr.ca/reports.php [last accessed 19.08.2021].

[330] Truth and Reconciliation Commission of Canada (2015) Calls to Action. Truth and Reconciliation Commission of Canada, Winnipeg, Manitoba.

[331] Katz (22.04.2019).

6.4.2 *Canadian Museum Association Guidelines*

6.4.2.1 Ethical Guidelines

Similar to the Code of Ethics issued by ICOM examined in Chap. 3, the Canadian Museum Association has issued ethical guidelines. They are designed to provide both institutions and individuals active for museums with guidelines on expected standards of behavior, both in the general exercise of their functions and in specific cases.[332] They are of a general nature and they exist next to individual museum codes of conduct. The main roles of museums as perceived/identified by the CMA are the stewardship of cultural heritage for future generations and public service in advancing knowledge and understanding.[333]

Similar to the Task Force Report, which influenced the drafting of the guidelines,[334] the guidelines seek to establish a standard of behavior that goes beyond legal requirements.[335] Indigenous religious heritage and traditions are taken into consideration both in terms of general museum practice and specifically in relation to requests for repatriation. Procedurally, museum actors are required to "actively seek out" information on culturally sensitive objects "before using the material in any way".[336] Museums are also asked to adopt clear loan policies, including on "loans of regalia and other objects for ceremonial purpose."[337] In terms of accessibility, museums are to ensure that the presentation of its collection generally occurs in a culturally respectful manner by involving different groups in the planning process.[338] More specifically with regard to Indigenous religious heritage, the guidelines acknowledge that it "may be appropriate to restrict access to certain objects, to honor the protocols and ceremonies of that community regarding storage, treatment, handling and display, or to facilitate special access as appropriate."[339] The guidelines give no indication of what the CMA would consider as appropriate circumstances to restrict access other than that any decision taken under the guidelines is to be taken ethically. B.1 describes ethics as "based upon the underlying values of honesty, fairness, respect, excellence and accountability". In addition, "museum ethics must reflect an ongoing dialogue between the museum community and the society it serves". Arguably, to act in accordance with the Task Force Report

---

[332] Canadian Museums Association [CMA], Ethics Guidelines (2006) Ottawa, guidelines A.1 and A.2.

[333] CMA, Ethics Guidelines, C.1.

[334] Bolton (2009), p. 150.

[335] CMA, Ethics Guidelines, B.1 "Museum ethics represent more than the avoidance of contractual or legal liability".

[336] CMA, Ethics Guidelines, C.3, emphasis added. Also, G "it is the responsibility of museums to actively seek it out from knowledgeable members of the appropriate cultural groups before using the object in any way."

[337] CMA, Ethics Guidelines, E.3.

[338] CMA, Ethics Guidelines, F.

[339] CMA, Ethics Guidelines, G.

Recommendations of 1994 would constitute ethical behaviour under the definition of the CMA guidelines, even if the latter are comparatively less strong in their support of Indigenous cultural rights. The CMA guidelines lack the Task Force's emphasis on equality.

In terms of repatriation agreements, both documents clearly favour case-by-case negotiations. This is understandable given by the vastly different cultural and legal requirements applicable across Canada, which renders a countrywide detailed solution undesirable. The guidelines mitigate this necessarily broad statement. Institutions are required to have clear policies in place which describe the procedure following a repatriation request.[340] In the case of international repatriation requests that originate from states (not Indigenous communities), the museum is tasked with facilitating negotiations "rather than await action at a government or political level." The guidelines offer the strongest support for requests for the return of human remains, directly associated funerary objects and culturally sensitive objects if the community can show a historical relationship.[341] In addition, museums are asked to "facilitate the return of material which may have been acquired under circumstances that invalidate the museum's claim to title."[342]

6.4.2.2 Deaccessioning Guidelines

The CMA published a specific set of deaccessioning guidelines in 2015. The guidelines marked a slight turn from the very strong emphasis of the ethics guidelines on the retention of collections that was previously the sole guidance on deaccessioning.[343] The deaccessioning guidelines frame deaccessioning as "a necessary and appropriate tool in the collections management for any museum or gallery".[344] However, the guidelines expressly exclude the disposal of material through return or repatriation. As no CMA repatriation guidelines or policies exist, the ethics guidelines examined above establish the only CMA guidance. This constitutes a missed opportunity to reflect on the elements that are necessary in museum repatriation practices or to establish best practices within Canada. On the one hand, the deaccessioning of cultural material for curatorial reasons, as considered in the guidelines, will usually differ substantially from returns motivated by historic dislocations, reconciliatory efforts or the cultural cooperation. On the other hand, it might have been useful to acknowledge the possibility that a museum may

[340] CMA, Ethics Guidelines, G.

[341] CMA Ethics Guidelines, G "Museums should be committed to the return of . . .".

[342] CMA Ethics Guidelines, G "Museums should be committed to the return of . . .".

[343] CMA Ethics Guidelines, E.4 "generally there is a strong presumption against the disposal of accessioned collections to which the museum has acquired legal title".

[344] CMA Deaccessioning Guidelines, 2015 (reviewed and updated for HTML in 2020), B. introduction, available via: https://www.museums.ca/site/deaccessioning_guidelines [last accessed 19.08.2021].

wish to deaccession an Indigenous object for one of the reasons listed in the guidelines[345] that are not linked to a repatriation request. In such cases, the procedure to be followed may differ from other deaccessioning cases, for example by creating a different method of divestment.[346]

The CMA is also engaged in a process on reconciliation, in response to the calls for action by the TRCC. Part of this process was to survey its non-Indigenous member institutions on their engagement with Indigenous Peoples.[347] 1548 were sent the survey of which 1499 were non-Indigenous (291 responded), 49 self-identified as Indigenous (13 responded). Interestingly, in answer to the question "for which activities does your institution engage with Indigenous communities or entities?" only 19 respondents selected accession/deaccession as an activity, 37 repatriation and 57 museum loans. On exhibits 229 of the 304 respondents engaged with Indigenous communities. 187 institutions had no specific policies in place for working together with Indigenous communities. Overall, the response to these and other questions shows the need for further action within the institutions and by the CMA as the overarching body.

References

Asch M (2014) On being here to stay. Toronto University Press, Toronto

Bartlett RH (1980) Indian Act of Canada: an unyielding barrier. Am Indian J 6:11–26

Battiste M, Henderson JY (2000) Protecting indigenous knowledge and heritage: a global challenge. Purich, Saskatoon

Bell C (2001) Protecting Indigenous heritage resources in Canada: a comment on Kitkatle v British Columbia. Int J Cult Prop 10(2):246–263

Bell C, Napoleon V (2008) First Nations Cultural Heritage and Law - Case Studies, Voices, and Perspectives. UBC Press, Vancouver

Bell CE (1992) Aboriginal claims to cultural property in Canada: a comparative legal analysis of the repatriation debate. Am Indian Law Rev 17(2):457–522

Bell CE (2009) Restructuring the relationship: domestic repatriation and Canadian law reform. In: Bell CE, Paterson RK (eds) Protection of first nations cultural heritage: laws, policy, and reform. UBC Press, Vancouver, pp 15–77

Bell CE, Raven H, McCuaig H (2008a) Recovering from colonization: perspectives of community members on protection and repatriation of Kwakwaka'wakw cultural heritage. In: Bell CE, Napoleon V (eds) First nations cultural heritage and law: case studies, voices and perspectives. UBC Press, Vancouver, BC, pp 33–91

---

[345] CMA Deaccessioning Guidelines, 2014, D.1: "improved care for the object(s), improved access to the object(s), retention of an object(s) within the community or removal of a potentially hazardous item".

[346] CMA Deaccessioning Guidelines, 2014, G. For example, by preferring communities, or community cultural institutions over bigger museums.

[347] All numbers and questions in this paragraph were taken from CMA's Reconciliation Program National Survey Results (accessed 30.07.2021) available at: https://www.museums.ca/site/muse_article_reconciliationsurvey_2020.

Bell CE, Statt G, Mookakin Cultural Society (2008b) Repatriation and heritage protection: reflections on the Kainai experience. In: Bell CE, Napoleon V (eds) First nations cultural heritage and law: case studies, voices, and perspectives. UBC Press, Vancouver, pp 203–257

Bolton S (2009) Museums taken to task: representing first peoples at the McCord museum of Canadian history. In: Timpson AM (ed) First nations, first thoughts: the impact of indigenous thought in Canada. UBC Press, Vancouver, pp 145–169

Borrows J (2006) Indigenous Legal Traditions in Canada (trans: Canada LCo)

Borrows J (2015) The durability of terra nullius: Tsilhqotín Nation v British Columbia. UBC Law Rev 48(3):701–742

Borrows J (2016) Unextinguished: rights and the Indian Act. Univ New Brunswick Law J 67:3–35

Carlson KM (2005) Does constitutional change matter – Canada's recognition of aboriginal title. Arizona J Int Comp Law 22:449

Christie G (1998) Aboriginal rights, aboriginal culture, and protection. Osgoode Hall Law J 36 (3):447–484

Clavir M (2002) Heritage preservation: museum conservation and first nations perspectives. Ethnologies 24(2):33–45. https://doi.org/10.7202/006638ar

Conaty GT (ed) (2015) We are coming home - Repatriation and the restoration of Blackfoot cultural confidence. AU Press

Coombe RJ (1993) The properties of culture and the politics of possessing identity: native claims in the cultural appropriation controversy. Can J Law Jurisprud 6(2):249–285

Glass A (2004) Return to sender. J Mater Cult 9(2):115–139. https://doi.org/10.1177/1359183504044368

Grammond S (2009) Identity captured by law. McGill-Queen's University Press

Griffith A (2016) Diversity among federal and provincial judges. Policy Options, 4.05

Henry D (1995) Back from the Brink: Canada's first nations' right to preserve Canadian heritage. University of British Columbia Law Review Special Issue:5–12

Hogg PW (1992) Constitutional law of Canada, 3rd edn. Carswell, Scarborough; Ont

Hogg PW (2007a (loose-leaf edition updated 2015)) Constitutional law of Canada, vol II. Thomson Reuters Carswell, Toronto

Hogg PW (2007b (loose-leaf updated 2015)) Constitutional Law of Canada, vol I. Thomson Reuters Canada, Toronto

Hopkins-Utter SR (2.11.2017) Case Comment: Ktunaxa Nation v. British Columbia (Forests, Lands and Natural Resource Operations). Shane R. Hopkins Law Corporation, https://canliiconnects.org/en/commentaries/46976

Imai S (2014) The 2015 annotated Indian Act and aboriginal constitutional provisions. Carswell, Thomson Reuters Limited, Toronto, Canada

Joffe P (2021) Bill C-15 Legal Significance of the Preamble, Assembly of First Nations, available via: https://www.afn.ca/wp-content/uploads/2021/01/C-15_Preamble_ENG-1.pdf. Accessed 19 August 2021

Kagan T (2005) Recovering aboriginal cultural property at common law: a contextual approach. Univ Toronto Faculty Law Rev 63:1–41

Katz B (22.04.2019) Canadian Museum Association Receives $1 Million to Foster Reconciliation With Indigenous Peoples. Smithsonian Magazine

Kuprecht K (2014) Indigenous peoples' cultural property claims - repatriation and beyond. Springer

Ladner KL (2009) Take 35: reconciling constitutional orders. In: Timpson AM (ed) First nations, first thoughts: the impact of Indigneous thought in Canada. UBC Press, Vancouver, p 279

McCabe JTS (2008) The honour of the crown and its fiduciary duties to aboriginal peoples. LexisNexis Canada, Markham

McNeil K (2008) Fiduciary obligations and aboriginal peoples. In: Gillen MR, Woodman F (eds) The law of trusts: a contextual approach. Emond Montgomery, Toronto

Millen R, Adkins S (22.10.2018) BC treaty process and the realization of free, prior and informed consent. Blake, Cassels & Graydon LLP, pp 1–14

Myles V (2010) Parks Canada's policies that guide the repatriation of human remains and objects. In: Turnbull P, Pickering M (eds) The long way home - the meanings and values of repatriation. Berghahn Books, New York, pp 48–56

Nafziger JAR, Renteln AD, Paterson RK (2010) Cultural law: international, comparative and Indigenous. Cambridge University Press, Cambridge

Olthuis Kleer Townshend LLP (2018) Aboriginal law handbook, 5th edn. Thomson Ruiters, Canada

Panagos D (2016) Uncertain accommodation: aboriginal identity and group rights in the Supreme Court of Canada. UBC Press, Vancouver

Paterson RK (2007) Totems and teapots: the Royal British Columbia Museum Corporation. Univ Br Columbia Law Rev 40(1):421–437

Paterson RK (2010) Canada. In: Kono T (ed) The impact of uniform laws on the protection of cultural heritage and the preservation of cultural heritage in the 21st century // The impact of uniform laws on the protection of cultural heritage and the preservation of cultural heritage in the 21st century. Martinus Nijhoff Publishers, Leiden; Boston, pp 233–246

Prott LV, O'Keefe PJ (1989) Law and the cultural heritage, vol. 3. Movement. Butterworths, London [etc.]

Robinson A (2016) Gradual Civilization Act. The Canadian Encyclopedia. https://www.thecanadianencyclopedia.ca/en/article/gradual-civilization-act

Royal Commission on Aboriginal Peoples (1991) Looking forward, looking back, vol 1. RCAP, Ottowa, p 17

Royal Commission on Aboriginal Peoples (1996) Restructuring the relationship, vol 2. RCAP, Ottowa, p 16

Sayers J (2020) Opportunities and barriers for the B.C. Declaration of Rights Act in Hayden King (Ed) The UN Declaration on the Rights of Indigenous Peoples in Canada: Lessons from B.C., Yellowhead Institute (Special Report December 2020), pp 13–15

Simon C, Clark J (2013) Exploring inequities under the Indian act. Univ New Brunswick Law J 64:103–122

Stockford Careless JM (2019) Province of Canada (1841-67). The Canadian Encyclopedia. https://www.thecanadianencyclopedia.ca/en/article/province-of-canada-1841-67

van Ert G (2010) Dubious Dualism: the reception of international law in Canada. Valparaiso Univ Law Rev 44(3):927–934

Vicaire PS (2011) Two roads diverged in a wood - a comparative analysis of indigneous rights in a North American constitutional context. Judges J 50(3):18–25

Youngblood Henderson J (2006) First nations jurisprudence and aboriginal rights. Native Law Center, University of Saskatchewan, Saskatoon, Canada

Chapter 7
Repatriation of Sacred Indigenous Cultural Heritage in Provincial Law: Alberta and British Columbia

7.1 Alberta

Repatriation efforts in Alberta arose against the backdrop of a controversial museum exhibition "The Spirit Sings". The controversy led to the creation and adoption of the Museum Task Force Report in 1992.[1] The Glenbow Museum, in turn, engaged in both repatriations and resulted in an increased involvement of Indigenous individuals in museum activities since then. These efforts ultimately culminated in the adoption of a piece of rather specific repatriation legislation. When the repatriation legislation was discussed in the legislature, Pearl Calahasen, in one of her contributions summarized both the underlying conflict between two cultures and also introduced one of the reasons for the return of objects today, contemporary spiritual practices: "The sacred ceremonial objects in these institutions have for some time been part of two worlds, Madam Speaker, one of museums and collections and one still reflecting First Nations' traditions.... By returning the sacred ceremonial objects, which are vital to the practice of traditional ceremonial life today, I believe Bill 2 sets us on a new and even more promising course in the year 2000, this millennium . . . ."[2] These themes will reappear in the course of the following sections within the Alberta context, but are also mirrored in some of the American discussions in the US context, covered in earlier chapters.

Please note that this chapter adopts the capitalization of the terms Indigenous Peoples and Indigenous (except for when used in citations) for reasons explained in Chap. 1. Similarly Aboriginal is capitalized unless the lower case was used in a citation.

[1] Task Force Report, 1994, at 1.

[2] Pearl Calahasen, Métis, Alberta Minister for Aboriginal Affairs and Northern Development at second reading of Bill which became the First Nations Sacred Objects Repatriation Act, the first legislation of its kind in Canada. 6.03.2000, 24th Legislature, 4th session, Alberta Hansard (8) 2000, at 262–263.

V. Tünsmeyer, *Repatriation of Sacred Indigenous Cultural Heritage and the Law*, Studies in Art, Heritage, Law and the Market 3,
https://doi.org/10.1007/978-3-030-89047-6_7

7.1.1 *Heritage Legislation*

7.1.1.1 Historical Resources Act[3]

The Historical Resources Acts affords provincial protection to different forms of heritage through the creation of different heritage categories and strong ministerial powers. The central broad category being protected is historical resources,[4] which comprise both movable heritage (defined as historic objects[5]) as well as immoveable heritage (defined as historic sites[6]) and can be further divided into archaeological resources and paleontological resources.[7] Without ministerial permission,[8] no person may destroy, disturb, alter, restore, or repair a historic resource or remove a historic object from a historic resource.[9]

The Act does not address the Indigenous communities' role or Indigenous interests in the protection of Indigenous heritage under the provincial heritage framework.[10] Moveable Indigenous heritage[11] can be subsumed under the Act both as archeological resources,[12] if it was or is buried, or alternatively as a historic object or resource.[13] The Act vests all ownership of archaeological resources in the Crown in Right of Alberta.[14] The date of acquisition of an archaeological resource is of importance. Unless resources have been acquired prior to the 5th of July 1978, ownership is vested in the Crown.[15] Archaeological resources may not be

---

[3] This section considers the Historical Resources Act, RSA 2000, c H-9, retrieved on 200-01-20.

[4] Defined in s. 1(e) HRA as "(e) "historic resource" means any work of nature or of humans that is primarily of value for its palaeontological, archaeological, prehistoric, historic, cultural, natural, scientific or aesthetic interest including, but not limited to, a palaeontological, archaeological, prehistoric, historic or natural site, structure or object."

[5] Defined in s. 1(d) HRA as "(d) "historic object" means any historic resource of a movable nature including any specimen, artifact, document or work of art."

[6] Defined in s. 1(f) HRA.

[7] Archaeological resources are 'works of man' (s. 1(a) HRA) versus paleontological resources as 'works of nature' s. 1(h) HRA.

[8] It has to be granted expressly, i.e. in the case of provincial historic resources s. 20(9) and/or implicitly by lack of objection within a certain period of time after notice of the intended action is published for registered historical resources. See i.e. s. 19(5) H.R.A.

[9] S. 19(5) HRA for registered historic resources.

[10] Of note is that the Regulations to the HRA do however make one exception to safeguard Indigenous ceremonial practices, namely the general prohibition of gathering ammonite shell, Dispositions (Ministerial) Regulation, Alta Reg 101/1998, retrieved on 2020-01-22, see s. 9(d).

[11] Bell (1992), p. 484.

[12] Both as works of humans that are primarily of value for their cultural or their historic significance and which are or have been buried in Alberta s. 1(a) HRA.

[13] Either on the basis of its cultural, archaeological or historic value under s. 1(e) read in conjunction with s. 1(d) HRA.

[14] S. 32(1) HRA.

[15] S. 2(1) Alberta Regulation 101/98. For archaeological resources acquired after 5.07.1978, the option of custodial agreements remains under s. 4 Alberta Regulation 101/98.

transported outside of Alberta subject to ministerial permission,[16] or be altered, marked or damaged without an excavation permit or ministerial permission.[17] With regard to the prohibition of transport outside of Alberta one can question whether this is ultimately unconstitutional, given the constitutional division of competences discussed in the previous chapter which reserves international and inter-province trade for the federal level. In any event, one possible advantage of the HRA, as argued by Catherine Bell, could be for Indigenous communities to use the vast ministerial powers to effect provincial protection for heritage objects for which they would otherwise lack the funding or training.[18] Such agreements might be able to satisfy both provincial heritage and Indigenous cultural needs. This is, however, very much dependant on the negotiated agreement.

7.1.1.2 The First Nation Sacred Ceremonial Objects Repatriation Act[19] and the Blackfoot First Nations Sacred Ceremonial Objects Repatriation Regulation

The First Nation Repatriation Act is the only legislation of its kind in Canada. Ms. Calahasen, the Associate Minister of Aboriginal Affairs, and Métis herself, spoke in support of the Bill in legislative session: "This bill is giving back what is rightfully ours, but we need to ensure we have processes in place, for this is truly significant for our own survival."[20] She summarized the bill as pursuing three goals: the creation of basic principles for repatriation, starting a consultative process, and amending the Glenbow–Alberta Institute Act to give effect to the Blackfoot Agreement.[21] The latter is the subject of the sole operating regulation under the Act.

The specific focus of the Alberta legislation on ensuring the repatriation or at least partial return of sacred objects can be explained by the fact that it was originally intended to aid a very specific repatriation between the Blackfoot First Nation and the Glenbow Museum.[22] In addition, it could be argued that sacred ceremonial

[16] S. 33(1) HRA or if the resource was disposed of by Minister under s. 32(3) HRA by operation of s. 33(2).

[17] S. 34(1) HRA or if the resource was disposed of by Minister under s. 32(3) HRA by operation of s. 34(2).

[18] Bell (1992), pp. 485–486.

[19] First Nations Sacred Ceremonial Objects Repatriation Act; in Revised Statutes of Alberta, 2000; c. F-14 [hereafter First Nations Repatriation Act or FNSCORA].

[20] Alberta, 24th Legislature, 4th session, House records of discussions on 1.03.2000, Alberta Hansard Issue 7, at 187.

[21] Alberta, 24th Legislature, 4th session, House records of discussions on 1.03.2000, Alberta Hansard Issue 7, at 187.

[22] Bell (2009b), p. 41.

objects are often essential to the survival of First Nations communities,[23] hence otherwise resistant actors might be more open to acknowledging their moral obligation to return them than is the case in repatriation claims for other objects. For other heritage objects, arguments brought forward by museums, such as sharing First Nations culture with the public or preserving artefacts for the future, may resonate much more strongly with the legislature.[24] In effect, the act seeks to harmonize the preservationist role of museums with First Nations cultural revitalization efforts by locating ownership and responsibility for ceremonial/religious objects with Indigenous communities, as can be seen in the preamble.[25]

Repatriation is defined as the transfer of title to a sacred ceremonial object by the Crown to a First Nation and the latter's acceptance thereof.[26] Section 1(d) of the Act defines a sacred ceremonial object as an object which:

1. was used by a First Nation in the practice of sacred ceremonial traditions,
2. is in the possession and care of the Royal Alberta Museum or the Glenbow–Alberta Institute or on loan from one of those institutions to a First Nation, or is otherwise in the possession and care of the Crown, and
3. is vital to the practice of the First Nation's sacred ceremonial traditions.

This section introduces a number of criteria that narrow the scope of potential sacred ceremonial objects which may be reclaimed. Repatriation applications are only covered if they concern objects which are held by the two public institutions or are in Crown possession and a use criterion (both past and future) and the use of which is '*vital*'.[27] This threshold is arguably higher than the necessity element in NAGPRA. There is no definition of 'sacred' contained in the Act. The legislative discussions emphasize the importance of the objects for contemporary spiritual

---

[23] Also acknowledged in FNSCORA, preamble, recital 2: "WHEREAS First Nations desire the return of sacred ceremonial objects that are vital to the practice of their sacred ceremonial traditions".

[24] Some statements made during the reading of the Bill would support such a reading, i.e. Alberta, 24th Legislature, 4th session, House records of discussions on 6.03.2000, Alberta Hansard Issue 8, at 263: Ms Olsen "I think it's important to note that in the preamble, under what I would state as the set of principles, the items desired for return are those "that are vital to the practice of . . . sacred ceremonial traditions." "That's important, because there are a number of artefacts in museums across this country and certainly in this province. . . . I think that's an important delineation, because some of those artefacts will in fact remain with the current museums and those places. So it's not an attempt to take all of those items which have been in the possession of different museums and galleries and give them all back to the community." Alberta, 24th Legislature, 4th session, House records of discussions on 6.03.2000, Alberta Hansard Issue 8, at 263.

[25] FNSCORA Preamble, recital 3: "WHEREAS the Crown desires to harmonize the role museums play in the preservation of human heritage with the aspirations of First Nations to support traditional values in strong, confident First Nations communities". Similarly Bell (2009b), p. 41.

[26] S. 1(d) FNSCORA.

[27] Also underlined as an important criterion to narrow scope, see legislative discussion Alberta, 24th Legislature, 4th session, House records of discussions on March 6th, at 263.

practice and use.[28] This would suggest that sacredness is to be defined from the perspective of the practicing Indigenous individual.

S. 2(1) FNSCORA establishes a general right for First Nations to apply for the repatriation of a specific object if the responsible Minister,[29] defined by s. 1(c), agrees [s. 2(2)]. After a sacred ceremonial object is repatriated, it is held by the community on behalf of all its members.[30] The Act itself is relatively vague and leaves much, such as the process of repatriating, questions of representation and consultation, to be defined in further regulations. This includes the definition of who may apply for repatriation.[31] The only regulation in force at the time of writing is the Blackfoot Regulation.[32] The Act creates a strong presumption in favour of repatriation,[33] but this may depend on ministerial practice, given that the Minister[34] is given the right to refuse repatriation if "in the Minister's opinion, repatriation would not be appropriate."[35] "Appropriate" is not defined further. A reading of the (at times rather lively) discussions in the Alberta legislature shows that, while the bill was passed unanimously, there was considerable disagreement on the possible scope of ministerial discretion under s. 2(2) FNSCORA.[36] Proponents of the Act explained its broadness as being a product of consultation with the Indigenous Peoples of the province. Moreover, it would allow the use of different procedures initiated and necessitated by different Indigenous communities.[37] It is worth highlighting that political support was strong at the time and that individual submission favoured the

---

[28] Alberta, 24th Legislature, 4th session, House records of discussions on March 6th, at 263. Olsen, at 265 Krzycka, at 267 Nicol. Other comments also highlighted the educative function, see at 264, at 265.

[29] The designated minister for FNSCORA (and the Glenbow-Institute Act) is the Minister of Culture and Tourism, s. 6(1) (f), (h) Designation and Transfer of Responsibility Regulation, Alta Reg 44/2019, <https://canlii.ca/t/554j0> retrieved on 2021-08-19.

[30] S. 3 FNSCORA.

[31] S. 1(b) FNSCORA.

[32] See for instance s. 2(3), s. 5 FNSCORA.

[33] S. 2(2) FNSCORA "The minister **must** agree to the repatriation..." emphasis added.

[34] The minister is determined under s. 16 Government Organization Act, see S. 1(c) FNSCORA.

[35] S. 2(2) FNSCORA.

[36] Alberta, 24th Legislature, 4th session: House records of discussions on 6.03.2000, Alberta Hansard Issue 8 at 262–267, House records of discussions on 3.04.2000, Alberta Hansard Issue 22, at 687–685. House records of discussions on 18.04.2000, Alberta Hansard Issue 37, at 1106–1107.

[37] The minister of community development expressly identified this as an objective at the legislative reading "we hope to keep regulations minimal, and they will be created in consultation with the First Nations people to whom they apply". Alberta, 24th Legislature, 4th session, House records of discussions on 6.03.2000, Alberta Hansard Issue 8 at 266–267.

introduction of the Act as "long overdue"[38] and as a means to "promote the living traditions of First Nations".[39]

Catherine Bell explains the general vagueness of the Act, since it was originally intended to only aid the negotiations between the Blackfoot First Nations and the Glenbow- Alberta Institute.[40] Without the Act and the accompanying regulation examined below, repatriation objects held by the institution were held on behalf of the citizens of Alberta,[41] rendering repatriation decisions difficult. In effect, the act was a political solution sought by the Glenbow to overcome significant bureaucratic hurdles and resistance among provincial officials.[42] The advantage of the current lack of regulations is that it leaves room to negotiate repatriation to realize Indigenous cultural traditions, while creating a strong presumption in favour of repatriation. However, it should be acknowledged that the Act could have provided Indigenous Peoples, who are not covered by the Blackfoot agreement, with much more certainty, by explicitly requiring a cooperative mechanism rather than broad ministerial discretion and specifying a review and/or dispute resolution mechanism in case of disagreement. Moreover, by leaving much of the specific procedural elements to the negotiation of future regulations, it further increases both the length of time and costs which have to be invested in repatriation efforts.[43] The Royal Alberta Museum emphasizes that the Act is an enabling legislation which came into effect with the Blackfoot Regulation which was specific to them. It details "Additionally, RAM is working collaboratively with Indigenous communities and their elders to uphold the Calls to Action put forward by the Truth and Reconciliation Commission of Canada", emphasizing the possibility to facilitate access to sacred objects upon request on a case-by-case basis.[44] The desire to facilitate access to sacred heritage is also clearly motivated by Articles 11 and 12 of UNDRIP, which are cited together with Canada's desire to support UNDRIP. The focus of the Act on sacred objects has clearly been influencing the museum's repatriation practice. The phrasing used in the Act is certainly at odds with the principles of cultural self-determination. It takes some steps towards, but ultimately falls short of, guaranteeing Indigenous control over Indigenous ceremonial objects for nations other than the Blackfoot Nations. A positive effect has undoubtedly been the repatriation of several

[38] Alberta, 24th Legislature, 4th session, House records of discussions on 3.04.2000, Alberta Hansard Issue 22, at 678.

[39] Alberta, 24th Legislature, 4th session, House records of discussions on 6.03.2000, Alberta Hansard Issue 8, at 264.

[40] Bell (2009b), p. 41.

[41] Glenbow–Alberta Institute Act, RSA 2000, c G-6, s. 20(2). See discussion in Sect. 7.1.1.3 below.

[42] Conaty (2015b), p. 12 See account from museum perspective Janes (2015), and for the perspective of a government official Ives (2015).

[43] Bell (2009b), p. 42.

[44] Royal Alberta Museum, archived website from 3.05.2019, archived at: https://web.archive.org/web/20190503104739/https://royalalbertamuseum.ca/collections/cultural-studies/repatriation/ [last accessed 19.08.2021].

hundred objects through the original Blackfoot Agreement and over forty subsequent agreements with the Blackfoot Nations.[45]

The main function of the Blackfoot First Nation Sacred Ceremonial Objects Repatriation Regulation[46] [hereafter Blackfoot regulation] was to give effect to the Blackfoot agreements which had already been negotiated at the time. It is therefore comparably short, comprising ten sections and an appendix listing the agreements to be given effect. Most notably is the procedure of repatriation which operates through a legal society who acts on behalf of the Indigenous community reclaiming the object.[47] Thus, repatriation does not hinge on a return to band councils which have been the result of legislative interventions, examined in Sect. 3.1.3 in Chap. 6, and may not reflect ceremonial realities.[48] The community must have used the object in the past and provide assurances that it will be returned to ceremonial use upon its repatriation.[49] The Regulation is clearly motivated by efforts to support cultural revitalization efforts, an element which also surfaced in the legislative discussions in the adoption of the Act. The Act also provides for the publication of intended repatriation decisions to give other communities the opportunities to file a competing application.[50] According to Catherine Bell, First Nations can choose to work under the act to request a transfer of title. In this case, negotiations on a community basis are then implemented by means of a regulation.[51] But this is not necessary, and it seems as if communities are negotiating with the Royal Alberta museum without such a framework. It seems as if the act and its accompanying regulation have strengthened repatriation negotiations even for communities other than the Blackfoot First Nations.[52]

7.1.1.3 Glenbow–Alberta Institute Act

Complementing the Act and the Blackfoot Agreement, changes to the Glenbow–Alberta Institute Act were introduced to facilitate the Museum's long-time repatriation efforts. Under the Act, the institute's collection assets were transferred to Crown ownership in 1996[53] and under the act they are to be held "on behalf of the

[45] Otiena Ellwand, Interview with C. Robertson from Royal Albert Museum, 27.05.2016, archived website available at: https://web.archive.org/web/20160527225310/http://edmontonjournal.com/news/local-news/alberta-government-to-expand-policy-around-return-of-sacred-items-to-indigenous-communities [last accessed 19.08.2021].

[46] Alberta Regulation 98/2004, with amendments up to and including Alberta Regulation 59/2014.

[47] S. 3 Alberta Regulation 98/2004.

[48] Bell (2009b), p. 42.

[49] S. 4(d) and (e)(i) Alberta Regulation 98/2004.

[50] Sections 6–7 Alberta Regulation 98/2004.

[51] Bell (2009a), p. 83.

[52] Compare Bell (2009a), p. 83.

[53] S. 20(1) Glenbow–Alberta Institute Act.

people of Alberta".[54] However, s. 20(3) now permits the repatriation of collection assets in accordance with s. 20(3). This also means that possibilities for the Glenbow to repatriate legally are clearly restricted to vital sacred ceremonial objects whose repatriation is deemed appropriate by the minister. To get a better understanding of the wealth of material that is covered by the term 'collection assets', an appendix reveals that Indigenous museum holdings "exceed 20,000 pieces, including 13,0000 North American Indian and Eskimo artefacts. Other significant collections include South American Indian, West African, Indonesian and Australian including nearly 50 bark paintings."[55]

S. 21(1) imposes full responsibility on the Institute to ensure "reasonable public access to the collection assets" and provide curatorial care for its assets with the exception of repatriated objects. "Reasonable" public access arguably gives the museum another way of entering partnerships with Indigenous communities. It enables the museum to weigh Indigenous religious concerns against the public interest in heritage display and to accommodate Indigenous concerns about the display of and access to Indigenous heritage that has not been repatriated but may be of significance. In addition, long-term loans could be negotiated between Indigenous Peoples, the museum and the minister under s. 22(2). It allows for the possibility to negotiate future agreements between the Minister and the Institute on the institute's care and access responsibility, without the need of another legislative amendment. Both repatriation and other agreements designed to increase the museum's inclusive character are fully in line with its legally mandated objectives "to promote and encourage the acquisition and diffusion of knowledge .... In the manner that best serves the educational and cultural needs of the peoples of Alberta".[56] "Cultural needs" leaves the museum space to navigate between different cultural aspirations and historic experiences. Notably, this includes support for cultural revitalization efforts, which are an Indigenous right under s. 11(1) UNDRIP as an objective for the museum under its governing act.

7.1.2 Evaluation of Legal Repatriation Opportunities Within Alberta

A closer look at Alberta reveals a distinct approach to repatriation, different from the U.S. model in the preceding chapter and the treaty process followed in parts of British Columbia, examined below. These differences have legal, historic and cultural origins. The constitutional split of competences examined above entails varying provincial responses. Museums have to act within the differing legislative

[54] S. 20(2) Glenbow–Alberta Institute Act.

[55] Glenbow–Alberta Institute Act, Schedule, Descriptive Summary of Collections and Public Displays, at 18.

[56] S. 3 Glenbow–Alberta Institute Act.

frameworks set upon them. Nationwide policies, as they are set by the CMA, can give important guidance, but they cannot prescribe specific repatriation mechanisms. More importantly, given the vast cultural differences among the Indigenous Peoples of Canada, one national framework is as likely (if not even more likely) to hinder fruitful, mutually respectful relationships between cultural institutions and communities as it is to aid such efforts.

Repatriations between the Glenbow Institute, the Royal Alberta Museum and the Indigenous Peoples of the province have spurred a comparatively tailored legislative framework from the bottom up. The advantage of this model is that the regulations have the capacity to take different cultural protocols into account in the repatriation process. At the same time, the overarching legislative act remains in place and does not require further amendments. The danger in this model is that the framework for such regulatory freedom is broad in scope, with the possible danger of abuse. In the case of the FNSCORA, the danger was a resulting ministerial abuse of power. However, if the framework legislation requires regulations governing repatriation requests to be agreed upon in a consultative process, such dangers could be mitigated. One could argue that such legislation can empower Indigenous Peoples. In its absence, Conaty argues that museums remain in positions of power that can reinforce colonial patterns of the community as the supplicant and the museum acting as the benevolent irrespective of its intentions.[57] In fact, the colonial past is an indelible part of all contemporary relocation and revitalization efforts. It will always be part of repatriation efforts, be they the result of voluntary negotiations or mandated by law. The question that should guide the adoption of specific repatriation legislation may be compared to the question that should frame modern treaty negotiations: which steps can be taken to remedy colonial efforts to ensure that contemporary cultural agreements and efforts take place on a level of substantive equality? Case-specific legislation can help to balance power inequalities, if it is carefully drafted through a consultative process. In many cases, legislative action in the form of amendments to enable deaccessioning for the purpose of repatriation is necessary for public institutions.

In the meantime, localized repatriation negotiations between the museum and the community can take significant steps towards addressing power imbalances inherited through colonialism and support cultural revitalization.[58] At both levels, actors need to consider not only museum policies and the applicable law but also Indigenous cultural and legal requirements. This is an inevitable consequence of a policy that is aligned with the Indigenous right to cultural self-determination. The repatriation process thus has to navigate two very different cultural and legal traditions.

[57] Conaty (2015a), p. 37.

[58] For a First Nation perspective on repatriation, read for example: Yellow Old Woman (2015), pp. 183–204.

7.2 British Columbia

The repatriation of Indigenous sacred cultural heritage in British Columbia is set against a patchwork of actors and legal frameworks. The Royal British Columbia Museum is the central public museum that houses Indigenous heritage in British Colombia. It is structured as a provincial Crown Corporation.[59] It acts as a government agent[60] and has an educative and conservative purpose. It can also be called upon by the province to manage specific cultural heritage.[61] It has the legal power to decide on the disposal of items out of its collection,[62] for example in repatriation cases. The First Nations participate in what is called modern treaty negotiations with the provincial government and the federal government. In addition to the provincial heritage legislation and the RBCM's founding statute, the law setting up the facilitating organ for the treaty negotiations as well as any treaties that have been negotiated within said framework also influence repatriation.

7.2.1 Legal and Historical Background to Current Repatriation Requests

7.2.1.1 Lack of Treaty Making

A number of different factors have caused this patchwork approach. The first important factor is the lack of historic treaties between First Nations and the incoming settler government, which has left much of the province subject to unsettled claims.[63] As a result, the province pursues a modern treaty-making strategy, which it has characterized as necessary for three main reasons: first, "to meet legal obligations to clearly define the rights and responsibilities of both the Province and First Nations. They provide a cooperative way to resolve issues and help avoid future conflict in the courts;" second, to "address these economic and social injustices by providing First Nations with the authority to manage their own affairs and become less dependent on government support;" and, third, "to bring certainty to land and resource rights, treaties will maximize opportunities for economic development and job creation for all British Columbians."[64] Comprehensive treaty

[59] S. 2 Museum Act [S.B.C. 2003], c. 12.

[60] S. 3(1) Museum Act [S.B.C. 2003], c. 12, current as to 10.07.2019.

[61] S. 4(d)(f)(g) Museum Act [S.B.C. 2003], c. 12, current as to 10.07.2019.

[62] S. 5(2)(b) Museum Act [S.B.C.2003], c.1 2 current as to 10.07.2019.

[63] Hogg (2007 (loose-leaf updated 2015)), pp. 28–35.

[64] British Columbia, Provincial Government, Website from July 2017 archived via: http://web.archive.org/web/20170707010350/http://www2.gov.bc.ca/gov/content/environment/natural-resource-stewardship/consulting-with-first-nations/first-nations-negotiations/about-first-nations-treaty-process [last accessed 19.08.2021].

negotiations cover a vast array of different rights. They also involve cultural matters including the control or management of cultural heritage and they may even include repatriation agreements.

This governmental policy to adopt treaties stands in marked contrast to the initial policy of considering the province's territory *terra nullius*, held by provincial authorities since the 1880s.[65] However, the Supreme Court's ruling in Calder v Attorney General of British Columbia recognized Aboriginal title on the basis of historic occupation as a legal right in Canadian law in 1973. The court thus forced both the federal as well as the provincial government into developing a policy to deal with unextinguished Aboriginal title claims.[66] This federal comprehensive lands claims policy, released in August 1973,[67] continues to this day. In British Columbia, however, the province held a considerable part of Crown land and remained uncompromising.[68] Indigenous activism, starting from the 1970s and increasing through the 1980s, increased pressure upon the province and forced the province to recognize the legal presence of Indigenous title claims in its territory.[69] This led to the adoption of a tripartite process which involved the province, the federal government and the First Nations Summit, which was created to represent Indigenous interests in these negotiations.[70] Section 7.2.3 explores this process in more detail.

As John Borrows points out, the great advantage of treaties is that they are "one way to recognize Indigenous peoples' right to make decisions in accordance with their laws to share or give land to others."[71] An important element of treaties which Borrows highlights is their mutuality. Treaties guarantee rights both to Indigenous Peoples and the rest of the population.[72] This also means that treaties are vehicles of communicating between two different legal cultures. It is important to recognize that both historic and modern treaties are bridges between these different traditions and that, in their interpretation, both traditions will have to be used. The interpretation of such treaties thus always requires the interpreter to engage in a "translation process".[73] This is a challenge for which non-Indigenous judges trained purely in Canadian law are ill-equipped and which needs to be mitigated by the incorporation of treaty interpretation by Indigenous legal experts, including relevant elders.

65 de Costa (2004), p. 135.

66 de Costa (2004), p. 135.

67 Cruickshank (2006).

68 de Costa (2004), p. 135.

69 de Costa (2004), p. 135.

70 de Costa (2004), p. 136. See website of FNS: http://www.fns.bc.ca/about/about.htm [last accessed 19.08.2021].

71 Borrows (2006), p. 93.

72 Borrows (2006), p. 93.

73 Borrows (2006), p. 97.

7.2.1.2 The Royal British Columbia Museum and Repatriation

Modern treaties are important for repatriation within the province, because they cover outstanding rights, including cultural rights in general and the right to specific cultural heritage objects in particular. These rights, once the treaty has been ratified, will lead to direct repatriations from the RBCM. As a governmental agent, the RBCM has been obliged in the Museums Act to return an artefact in its collection to an Indigenous community. This obligation arises when the repatriation has been laid down in a treaty or other type of agreement with the province and any conditions set therein have been met.[74]

By contrast, if an Indigenous community approaches the museum outside of any treaty or agreement, the museum may decide to return an object in accordance with its disposal power, but only after its cultural significance and the public interest in its retention have been considered, and this is in accordance with any (ethical) standards the museum may have adopted.[75] These standards include the museum's 'Indigenous cultural collections and repatriation' policy. The museum clarifies that it seeks a collaborative approach towards the care and management of its Indigenous collection, and expressly recognizes UNDRIP as one of foundational documents for its policy. It also administers repatriation grants which are supported financially by the province to help Indigenous communities with repatriation. Moreover, the museum works together with an Indigenous Advisory and Advocacy Committee, composed of Indigenous community members.[76] It advises the museum on "respectful and effective engagement with Indigenous communities on matters relating to the Museum's governance, corporate planning, operations and repatriation."[77] Cooperation between the museum and Indigenous communities is established through Custodial Agreements or Memoranda of Understanding that set out the agreement on care, preservation, interpretation, and exhibition of the heritage,[78] including specific requirements for sacred materials. The policy also foresees loan agreement with an Indigenous community for the use of their Indigenous heritage, subject to mutual agreement.[79] It pursues an active repatriation policy, including not only ancestral remains and burial materials, but also for cultural materials. Outside of the treaty process, requests for cultural materials are negotiated on a case-by-case basis and cover materials which have entered the collection between 1884 and 1951 and are requested by communities, not individuals.[80] This timeframe is motivated by

[74] S. 5(7) Museum Act.

[75] S. 5(2)(b) Museum Act.

[76] Collison et al. (2019), p. 40.

[77] Collison et al. (2019), p. 40.

[78] Royal British Columbia Museum, Indigenous Collection and Repatriation Policy [Revised August 2018], available via: https://royalbcmuseum.bc.ca/documents/105663/Indigenous-Collections-and-Repatriation-Policy, at 3 [last accessed 19.08.2021].

[79] Ibid, at 4.

[80] Ibid, at 5–6.

the cultural prohibitions enforced during this time period on Canadian Indigenous communities through the Indian Act, mentioned in Chap. 6, Sect. 6.3.1. As evidenced in the policy, these prohibitions constitute another important historic factor that influences contemporary repatriation efforts in the province.

7.2.1.3 Provincial Adoption of UNDRIP and the Hope for a New Relationship

In recent years, the provincial government has signalled that, like the federal government, it seeks to strengthen its relationship with the First Nations in its territory. This included the desire to work together on UNDRIP implementation legislation passed in 2019,[81] and now work on its implementation, including through the preparation off the legally mandated Action Plan.[82] Another important step could be the sharing of provincial gaming revenue, which will provide First Nations with some of the resources necessary to invest in their communities.[83] Both have been explicitly linked to the province's commitment to reconciliation.[84]

The jurisprudence of the Canadian Supreme Court has undoubtedly been important in spurring the province into action. The Delgamuukw case brought about an important rethinking of the relationship between the provincial government and Indigenous Peoples. This was articulated in a 2005 'vision document' in which the ministry articulated its desire for the new relationship with the provinces' first nations: "We are all here to stay. We agree to a new government-to-government relationship based on respect, recognition and accommodation of Aboriginal title and rights. Our shared vision includes respect for our respective laws and responsibilities."[85] Among the express goals in this document were notably "[t]o achieve First Nations self-determination through the exercise of their aboriginal title"[86] and "[t]o revitalize and preserve First Nations cultures and languages".[87] The 2015 SCC Tsilhqot'in decision, for all its flaws explored in the previous chapter, gave hope to a

[81] Declaration on the Rights of Indigenous Peoples Act [SBC 2019] Chapter 44 (Assented to 2019-11-28).

[82] Horgan, J (26.11.2020) Mandate Letter to the Honourable Murray Rankin, Minister of Indigenous Relations and Reconciliation, available via https://www2.gov.bc.ca/assets/gov/government/ministries-organizations/premier-cabinet-mlas/minister-letter/rankin_mandate_2020.pdf [last accessed 19.08.2021].

[83] https://www2.gov.bc.ca/gov/content/governments/indigenous-people/first-nation-gaming-revenue-sharing [last accessed 19.08.2021].

[84] Holmwood and Plank (2018).

[85] BC Ministry of Aboriginal Relations and Reconciliation. The New Relationship – Vision Document (2005), available at: http://www2.gov.bc.ca/assets/gov/environment/natural-resource-stewardship/consulting-with-first-nations/agreements/other-docs/new_relationship_accord.pdf, at 1 [last accessed 19.08.2021].

[86] Ibid, at 2.

[87] Ibid.

renewal of the reconciliation process and spurred some governmental action.[88] It was the first case to declare Aboriginal title over land and required the province to undergo several years of negotiations with the Tsilhqot'in Nation government to operationalize the court decision.[89] In 2018, all parties concerned updated their previous vision to reflect both changes in case law and the new federal support of the UNDRIP and improved government-to-government relationships with First Nations. This included an express commitment to implement the UNDRIP which is characterized as containing "minimum standards for the survival, dignity and well-being of the Indigenous Peoples of the world, including in British Columbia" by the provincial and Indigenous governments.[90] An important step in this direction has been the adoption of the Declaration on the Rights of Indigenous Peoples Act in November 2019. Its statutory purpose is threefold: affirm the application of UNDRIP to the laws of British Columbia, contribute to its implementation and contribute to the building of intergovernmental relationships.[91] The act foresees the creation of an action plan in cooperation and consultation with Indigenous Peoples to implement the declaration. This is crucial, as UNDRIP needs implementation on the national and regional level, and how this implementation looks like can only be decided together with Indigenous Peoples. In is therefore important that both pieces of legislation (provincial and the federal UNDRIP implementation discussed in the previous chapter) provide the room for an implementation framework to be developed together, hopefully on a nation-to-nation level. In how far this potential is realized will depend on the action plan and its implementation. At the moment, it is too early to give evaluate the outcome,[92] but criticism has been levied against the implementing process so far not being inclusive enough, and draft legislation being tabled without cooperating with Indigenous Peoples.[93] Moreover, some of the difficulties that exist with the provincial legislation mirror the federal Act. Specifically, questions remain on FPIC, and Aboriginal rights. The concerns for FPIC in B.C. are similar to the ones on the federal level, briefly put, FPIC on the international level goes further than Canadian legal practice. The question that arises here is then whether existing practice will be changed or maintained.

Another open question pertains to the relationship between UNDRIP and the Aboriginal rights canon as developed by the Supreme Court on the basis of section 35. UNDRIP, as developed on the international level, arguably goes further than the Canadian Aboriginal rights canon, at least in part. It is arguably for this very reason that UNDRIP implementing legislation is even necessary within the

[88] Rustad et al. (2015).

[89] Millen and Adkins (2018), pp. 8, 10.

[90] First Nations Summit et al. (2018), p. 2.

[91] Declaration on the Rights of Indigenous Peoples Act, s. 2.

[92] At the time of final edits the consultations on the draft action plan have not yet been completed. As it is currently unclear what final shape the Action Plan will take, the draft version was not taken into account in the final edits.

[93] Sayers (2020), pp. 13–15.

Canadian federal and provincial context to begin with. The question is then whether s. 35 rights will be approached with the understanding that they are the minimum standard and should be strengthened and increased, or whether international standards will be read through the lense of s. 35 and the corresponding jurisprudence.[94]

Lastly, the new policy approach adopted in 2018 also foresees support for First Nations efforts to revitalize, strengthen and continue their distinct cultures to enable their cultural survival.[95] This makes the research objective to evaluate Canadian law on the repatriation of cultural heritage in light of UNDRIP even more appropriate.

7.2.2 British Columbia Heritage Conservation Act

7.2.2.1 Relevant Provisions

In British Columbia, tangible cultural heritage is subject to the protection of the Heritage Conservation Act.[96] For the purpose of encouraging and facilitating the protection and conservation of provincial heritage material, the ministry is obliged to create a "Provincial heritage register".[97] For present purposes, section 4 is relevant, which allows the province "to enter into a formal agreement with a first nation with respect to the conservation and protection of [. . .] heritage objects that represent the cultural heritage of the aboriginal people". Such an agreement may feature specific schedules that designate which objects or sites are of cultural and/or ceremonial value and, according to s. 5, must specify what actions would be viewed as a desecration by the respective First Nation. Section 4 is hardly, if ever, used in practice.[98] This means that the theoretical potential for the Heritage Act to make room for and, depending on the agreement, further the implementation of existing international Indigenous rights is not used. One may question why s. 4 is disregarded. Is it because these issues can and are being subsumed under the broader treaty-making process with the BCTC? Given the duration of these negotiations might explain why s. 4 is not used.

There is, however, an important provision which is not dependent upon the adoption of such an agreement: S. 8 affirms that the Heritage Conservation Act does not "abrogate or derogate from the aboriginal and treaty rights of a first nation". This is important for two reasons: first, because it may be possible to establish an

---

94 Pasternak (2020), p. 18 raises the fear that "domestic legal precedents will be paramount over international legal principles".

95 First Nations Summit et al. (2018), pp. 4, 5.

96 Heritage Conservation Act [R.S.B.C. 1996], c. 18, https://canlii.ca/t/53mj9 [last accessed 19.08.2021].

97 Ibid, s. 2, 3.

98 Union of British Columbia Indian Chiefs, First Nations Heritage Planning Toolkit (April 2013) [hereafter UBCIC Toolkit], available via: https://www.ubcic.bc.ca/ubcic_publications, at 48 [last accessed 19.08.2021].

Aboriginal right to practice a specific cultural tradition (depending on the practice) and possibly even a right to exclusively control an object as explained earlier in this volume;[99] second, because ownership, protection, management and/or ownership of cultural heritage may be (partially) protected by means of treaties which are protected under s. 35 Constitution Act. Section 8.1 complements s. 8 by recognizing the heritage management powers of First Nations on their treaty land and exempting this area from the application of parts of the Act, including the otherwise strong ministerial powers.[100] It thus paves the way for Indigenous control over their cultural heritage on treaty lands, from designation to protection, subject to the community successfully negotiating a treaty (which is a considerable enterprise, see Sect. 7.2.3).

If neither treaties nor s. 4 agreements apply, there is the option to designate an object (irrespective of its ownership, be it a museum, a gallery or a private person) as provincial heritage under the designation procedure in s. 10. First, the person who has possession of the object [s. 10 (b)(i)], as well as "any person or party who, in the opinion of the minister, is or may be the owner of the object or has or may have a proprietary interest in the object" [s. 10 (b)(ii)] and "any other prescribed person" [s. 10 (c)] must be given notice. A First Nation could fall under either of the last two categories and thus has the right to file an objection notice according to s. 10(2), which will have to be considered in accordance with s. 10 (3)–(5).

In terms of protected objects, Indigenous cultural heritage is classified under several categories: burial places; Aboriginal rock paintings or carvings; objects that are located in "a site that contains artifacts, features, materials or other physical evidence of human habitation or use before 1846;" and Indigenous objects covered by an s. 4 agreement.[101]

7.2.2.2 The Heritage Conservation Act and Its Relationship to Indigenous Control over Their Cultural Heritage

7.2.2.2.1 Provincial Control over Indigenous Heritage

The Act impacts Indigenous control over their heritage in different ways, from the general to the specific. First, there is *prima facie* provincial control over Indigenous heritage. Indigenous and provincial interpretations of protection may vary significantly for a particular category of heritage. The Act arguably seeks to consider Indigenous interests through s. 4 and s. 8.1. However, overall, the Act does not seem to balance between Indigenous and provincial interests, and it does not respect Aboriginal cultural rights sufficiently. Rather, the balancing in the Act appears to

[99] See Chap. 6, Sect. 6.3.2.2.

[100] "If a treaty first nation, in accordance with its final agreement, makes laws for the conservation and protection of, and access to, heritage sites and heritage objects on its treaty lands, sections 9, 12.1 to 12.8, 16.1, 18 and 20 (1) (a) do not apply in relation to those treaty lands."

[101] S. 12.1(2)(b),(c),(d),(h).

be between two *provincial* interests: "preserving heritage objects and sites" (where preservation is understood as the physical preservation of the object) vis-à-vis "the proper utilization of provincial lands and resources".[102] When the Supreme Court had the opportunity to review the act for compliance with Aboriginal rights, it seemed to read Indigenous rights in their heritage as sufficiently protected within the provincial desire to protect heritage. "The Act considers First Nations' culture as part of the heritage of all residents of British Columbia. It must be protected, not only as an essential part of the collective material memory which belongs to the history and identity of First Nations, but also as part of the shared heritage of all British Columbians... At the same time, heritage conservation schemes such as the Act here must strike a balance between conservation and other societal interests, which may require the destruction of heritage ... after a careful review by the minister."[103] However, an Aboriginal right to their heritage and their interests in their heritage are not congruent with those of the province. They may be in individual cases, but the community is more likely to view the heritage as part of its living culture and identity, whereas the province may view it as an important part of its (shared) history.

While it may seem as if s. 4 and s. 8 seek to balance Indigenous interests with provincial interests, s. 4 leaves it up to the province whether or not it seeks to enter into such an agreement (the province "may"). Sec. 4(4)(a) allows the province and first nation to enter into an agreement which includes a "schedule of heritage sites and heritage objects that are of particular spiritual, ceremonial or other cultural value to the aboriginal people for the purpose of protection under section 12.1 (2) (h)". However, it has not really been used in practice. In a toolkit explaining the heritage management process in BC to Indigenous communities, a representative Indigenous body explained that the province was not negotiating s. 4 agreements with individual First Nations;[104] a pilot project was finally established in 2016[105] (after initial negotiations failed)[106] with the implementation and negotiation of the first agreement apparently still underway.[107] The fact that this section has not been used

[102]These are the interests distilled by Hall, J.A. in his reading of the BCHCA in Kitkatla v BC [2000] BCCA 42 (see below for further discussion), para 101. I would agree with his reading of the main interests of the Act, the problem arises in equating the lack of the legislator's concern for Indigenous interests in its balancing exercise with a corresponding lack of effect of the act on aboriginal status, aboriginal rights and indigeneity in how the act *operates* [contrast Hall, J.A para 109].

[103]Kitkatla Band v British Columbia (Minister of Small Business, Tourism & Culture) [2002] SCC 31 para 45.

[104]See UBCIC Toolkit, at 48.

[105]Union of British Columbia Indian Chiefs, pilot project announcement, website available via: https://www.ubcic.bc.ca/jwgfnhc.

[106]The Midden (2012), Province Disappoints, First Nations Disengage: No Section 4 Agreement in Sight, Volume 44, number 3/4, p. 5. Available at: https://journals.uvic.ca/index.php/midden/issue/view/917 [last accessed 19.08.2021].

[107]https://thestsa.ca/resources-relations/agreements/heritage-conservation-act-s4-pilot-project/ [last accessed 19.08.2021].

before, despite the apparent desire of First Nations is telling. The treaty negotiations referred to in s. 8.1, because of their complexity, take decades, are costly and involve many other important issues. Moreover, even if an agreement has been concluded, the minister still retains the power to issue a permit that allows for the desecration of burial sites as well as items covered by section 4 agreements.[108] Sacred objects identified under an s. 4 agreement, as well as burial sites, continue to be protected from desecration by provincial legislation unless the permit has been issued.[109] The power to issue permits covering Indigenous heritage—including potential desecration—thus is in the hands of the provincial government (except for heritage located on treaty lands negotiated under the BC Treaty process). While the minister may decide to make the permit conditional on either consultation with or the consent of Indigenous Peoples,[110] this power appears to be discretionary. As was the case previously, the minister *may* require the permit holder to consult an Indigenous community without obtaining their consent, and he *may* require the permit holder to require their consent. He *may* also decide to do *neither*.

Recent amendments to the Act pave the way for greater consideration of Indigenous interests by incorporating one additional consultation requirement, namely with regard to existing heritage sites that are not covered by an s. 4 agreement. If the minister decides to define the extent of a protected site or exempt it from this protection that is not covered by a s. 4 agreement, this may only be done after the First Nations have been afforded consultation.[111] This is an important safeguard, given the apparent provincial refusal to enter into s. 4 agreements. Overall, despite improvements in the Act, there are still changes which can be made to the framework in order to align it better with the rights articulated in the United Nations Declaration. It is also important for the legal framework to incorporate the Indigenous right to their cultural heritage adequately, because provincial and Indigenous conceptualizations of heritage may differ considerably, and they have in the past.[112] It remains to be seen in how far future amendments to the act, also in light of the recent UNDRIP implementation act will improve the situation.

One example of provincial and Indigenous heritage conceptualizations going wrong was in Kitkatla Band v British Columbia (Small Business, Tourism and Culture) 2000 B.C.C.A. 42, which concerned culturally modified trees (CMTs). The case comprised both a constitutional as well as an administrative law

[108] S. 12.1(2)(b) BCHCA (formerly 13(2)(b)), and S. 12.1(2)(h) (formerly 13.(2)(h)) BCHA.

[109] S. 12.1 (2)(b), (h) BCHCA.

[110] S. 12.5(1)(b) BCHA.

[111] S. 12.1(4), (5) BCHCA.

[112] See for example UBCIC Toolkit, at 14–16 on the differences in valuing sites and the obstacles Indigenous communities face in achieving protection for their sacred sites. The provincial Archaeological Branch seems to interpret the Act to only cover sites with a physical or archaeological expression or human alteration. By contrast, the Indigenous toolkit observes on at 16 "[T]his viewpoint stands in opposition to the fact that sites may be significant to First Nations because they *do not* have alterations."

challenge.[113] The Kitkatla Band found itself going against the Act in an attempt to save trees which were modified artificially.[114] A logging permit had granted the logging of CMTs in a specified area. Of a total of 116 standing CMTs and 61 fallen CMTs, 76 of the standing CMTs and all of the fallen CMTs were (largely) to be preserved "for study by those interested in the history and provenance of these objects".[115] The Kitkatla argued that the removal or modification of the CMTs would go to the heart of their identity. Both Kitkatla and the province agreed that the majority of items at issue, under the contested category, would be considered to be Aboriginal.[116] Their modification or destruction would thus go to the core of s. 91 (2). The province, however, relied heavily on the fact that the ambit of the provision was general and that "non-aboriginal heritage objects or other evidence of human habitation will also be caught."[117] The majority of the Court of Appeal, as well as LeBel J. of the Supreme Court,[118] agreed with the province on this reading. The Court of Appeal held that heritage protection is within provincial power and the BCHCA to pursue heritage conservation as its valid legislative aim. In the Supreme Court judgment, LeBel J. agreed with this finding. He highlighted that an act having a disproportionate effect on a (group of) individuals would not disqualify it from being a law of general application.[119]

The Supreme Court agreed with the Court of Appeal and found the pith and substance of the contested provisions, as well as the overall Act, to be heritage protection and conservation.[120] This included s. 13(2) (now s. 12.1(2)) as heritage

[113] The administrative law challenge concerning the relevant issues which the minister had to address before issuing the permit succeeded. The second element concerned a constitutional challenge alleging that the province had acted *ultra vires* in allowing the minister to enable the destruction or modification of the CMTs as these objects 'stand at or near the core of aboriginal identity'. See Kitkatla Band v British Columbia (Minister of Small Business, Tourism & Culture) [2002] SCC 31, para 32, and thus fell within the federal power s. 91(24).

[114] The case did not consider the repatriation of Indigenous heritage. It is however relevant since (a) the Kitkatla argued for the existence of an Aboriginal right to heritage conservation, (b) it evidences the constraints which Indigenous peoples face under Canadian law because of the split of competences in combination with the jurisprudence on the applicability of provincial law as well as Aboriginal and treaty rights.

[115] Hall, J.A. para 99 in Kitkatla Band v. British Columbia (Minister of Small Business, Tourism and Culture) [2000] BCCA 42.

[116] Category (d) "damage, excavate, dig in or alter, or remove any heritage object from, a site that contains artefacts, features, materials or other physical evidence of human habitation or use before 1846." Kitkatla v BC [2000] BCCA 42, para 56.

[117] Kitkatla v BC [2000] BCCA 42, para 57.

[118] Kitkatla Band v British Columbia (Minister of Small Business, Tourism & Culture) [2002] SCC 31 para 40 only speaks of "different impacts on the persons to whom it applies" but in paras 68–69 LeBel J. makes clear that "while provincial legislation that singles out aboriginal peoples would be ultra vires, 'singling out' should not be confused with disproportionate effect."

[119] Kitkatla Band v British Columbia (Minister of Small Business, Tourism & Culture) [2002] SCC 31.

[120] Kitkatla Band v British Columbia (Minister of Small Business, Tourism & Culture) [2002] SCC 31 paras 52–63.

conservation.[121] The statement by LeBel J. was less convincing that the "Act clearly considers them ['Native cultural interests'] as an essential part of the interests to be preserved and of the cultural heritage of British Columbia as well as of all First Nations" and that it strikes an "appropriate balance between native and non-native interests".[122] The provisions in the Act which do take Indigenous interests into account are not used enough (see above). Aboriginal interests in their heritage, as defined by themselves, are not an "essential part", rather the conservation of Aboriginal heritage as the cultural heritage of British Columbia is the essential interest intended to be preserved. This is not the same as preserving Aboriginal heritage as identified by Aboriginal interests.

Similarly, the consideration of the effect of Act and ministerial permits under s. 13 on Aboriginal rights was disconcerting, given that the band argued for the existence of an Aboriginal right to heritage conservation and protection. Hall, J.A. from the Court of Appeal observed: "One's lineage and heritage in the general sense is an important circumstance for us all but objects and sites, the primary subjects of the HCA, do not appear to me to rise to the level of importance of territorial rights or 'way of life' rights — such latter subjects in the aboriginal field as hunting and fishing rights and practices for instance."[123] Catherine Bell has criticized that "[i]t is hard to imagine what defines the identity of a people and is worthy of section 91(24) protective jurisdiction if objects and sites integral to the contemporary spiritual life and historical memory of a people do not."[124] LeBel, J. declined to comment on the general existence of such a right. Instead, he concentrated on the importance of the heritage for the Aboriginal group as going to the core of the s. 91 (24) power. He considered evidence on the relative importance of CMTs to the Kitkatla Band as "sparse".[125] He did, however, leave the path open for a category of heritage objects to fall under s. 91(24), albeit a very narrow path: "in some future case, it might very well happen that some component of the cultural heritage of a First Nation would go to the core of its identity ... that it would affect the federal power over native affairs and the applicability of provincial legislation."[126]

The last problematic aspect of the case is its treatment of unestablished Aboriginal rights. The Court of Appeal denied the need for the minister to consider the potential impact of the permit on Aboriginal rights which had not yet been proven by court claims, requiring the First Nation to seek separate remedies instead, namely a court declaration stating that they had existing Aboriginal title or an Aboriginal right. Braidwood, J.A. argued that, since s. 8 declares "that the application of any provision in the HCA is not to impact on the determination of aboriginal rights. This being so,

[121] Ibid, para 60.

[122] Ibid, para 62.

[123] Hall, J.A. para 102 in Kitkatla v BC [2000] BCCA 42.

[124] Bell (2001), p. 252.

[125] Kitkatla Band v British Columbia (Minister of Small Business, Tourism & Culture) [2002] SCC 31, para 50.

[126] Ibid, para 78.

those claiming an aboriginal right can be assured that any action taken under the HCA will have no impact on the determination of such rights. To destroy a piece of evidence while preserving the fact of the evidence cannot affect the existence of any underlying aboriginal right."[127] One may wonder how this will affect an Indigenous group that claims the existence of an Aboriginal right to a practice which requires a specific form of heritage threatened under the permit system. One may also wonder in how far this right could still be practiced if all that is left at the time of a trial is "evidence" of the "underlying aboriginal right", because the minister is not required to consider the potential impact of his decision on such rights.[128] This case leaves Indigenous heritage interests vulnerable to provincial development interests, rather than allowing federal intervention in cultural heritage matters (which admittedly, as Catherine Bell points out, would be unpopular).[129] In this sense, the original argument for making s. 91(24) a federal competence, rather than a provincial competence, considering the province has an economic interest in Indigenous lands, arises again.

This and other, similar, actions show that, while the Act may be aimed at protecting a specific heritage source, this mostly does not correspond to the affected First Nation's understanding of protection and conservation. It also does not take s. 35 rights sufficiently into account.

7.2.2.2.2 The B.C. Heritage Conservation Act and Repatriation: Obstacle, Neutral Party or Facilitator?

The Act's impact on repatriation is neutral, as it is neither an obstacle nor support. This is due to the fact that it refrains from regulating or interfering with the ownership aspects of protected objects or sites. Instead, it allows for the registration and protection of the object, despite it possibly remaining in the possession of a private person, or a First Nation. Moreover, it could be argued that the explicit prohibition of desecrating a burial place,[130] a heritage object or a site,[131] except with ministerial permission, reflects a level of recognition by the province for the spiritual, religious or cultural importance of Indigenous heritage to Indigenous Peoples. In terms of Aboriginal rights to their heritage, the result is mixed. The Heritage Act requires the minister to afford a First Nation whose heritage site or object would be affected by a permit to be consulted (absent a s. 4 agreement). There is also the

[127] Braidwood, J.A. Kitkatla v BC [2000] BCCA 42, para 86.

[128] Similarly Bell (2001), p. 252 "The proper question is not whether protection of Aboriginal heritage objects and sites is a 'core' Aboriginal right and therefore a matter of exclusive federal jurisdiction, but whether the particular CMTs at issue are integral or a 'central and significant part' of the 'distinctive' culture of the Kitkatla."

[129] Bell (2001), p. 257.

[130] S. 13(2)(b).

[131] S. 13(2)(a).

possibility to negotiate cooperative heritage agreements under s. 4 and any agreements made in modern treaties are protected under s. 8.1.

These modern treaties provide a legal path for the province to enter into agreements with Indigenous communities for Indigenous heritage on province lands. Increasing cooperation with Indigenous Peoples for the protection of their heritage and recognizing their interests was recommended in the RCAP report ‘Gathering Strength’.[132] Reconciliation is a proclaimed objective of the province of British Columbia. The province pursues an express policy on reconciliation which is led by the Ministry of Aboriginal Relations and Reconciliation. Treaties have been identified as an important way to achieve this, but the province has also negotiated other agreements. While treaty negotiations have a number of advantages in terms of addressing Indigenous rights and self-governance claims more holistically, there is a danger in seeking to regulate Indigenous participation, management or the control of Indigenous heritage predominantly through the BC treaty process, as seems to be the unofficial policy. These negotiations take a considerable amount of time and until a final agreement is reached no cooperation exists. An alternative would be to try to seek more s. 4 agreements to bridge the gap until a First Nation is in the final stage of the process. S. 4 agreements should also be pursued more actively with regard to First Nations not engaged in the treaty process.

However, absent s. 4 or s. 8.1 agreements (which are scarce), the Act does not enable Indigenous Peoples to take an active role with regard to Indigenous heritage not located on reserve lands.

7.2.3 British Columbia Treaty Process

7.2.3.1 The Process of Negotiating Comprehensive Treaties When Parties Share a Territory

In British Columbia, the federal government and the provincial government have been involved in treaty negotiations with First Nation communities. Indigenous governments need to negotiate with both non-Indigenous governmental levels for a number of reasons, one which being the split of competences mentioned in the previous chapter. After all, each level can only implement those parts that lie within their jurisdiction. The negotiations are undertaken with the help of an independent facilitator, set up to facilitate the negotiations, the British Columbia Treaty Commission, in short BCTC.[133] Private parties such as companies or private museums

[132] Royal Commission on Aboriginal Peoples (1996), p. 560.

[133] For a brief provincial summary and justification of current negotiation efforts to the wider public, see: https://www2.gov.bc.ca/gov/content/environment/natural-resource-stewardship/consulting-with-first-nations/first-nations-negotiations/about-first-nations-treaty-process [last accessed 19.08.2021].

cannot be part of such domestic treaty negotiations, as a result the discussions on repatriation provisions in the treaties are limited to public museum holdings.

The treaty process was launched in 1992 as a cooperative effort by the provincial and federal legislator. It focussed primarily on settling unresolved Aboriginal title claims to land. The underlying focus points to the governmental desire for further economic growth (rather than, or at least less than reconciliation). In recent years, there appears to have been a slight shift and the federal government announced a desire to renew the relationship with Canada's Indigenous first peoples "based on the recognition of rights, respect, cooperation and partnership".[134] The start of this process was problematic, with disparate views among the parties on how to proceed with the drafting,[135] and the process remains heavily debated. At this point in time, it is unclear in how far a new approach will evolve[136] and how it will affect the overall relationship of the federal level with Indigenous Peoples in general and the treaty negotiations in British Columbia in particular.

In line with the original aim of settling outstanding land claims, the definition of Indigenous Peoples is very broad and inclusive. The main component of a First Nation is that it is an Aboriginal body with traditional territories within the province, which is authorized by its constituency to enter into treaty negotiations.[137] At the time of writing, the BCTC is involved in (in some cases already completed) negotiations with 76 bands,[138] subsumed under 65 negotiations.[139] Consequently, a significant proportion of Indigenous BC is negotiating with the federal and provincial governments.

The negotiation process is divided into six stages, separated as follows. In the first stage, a First Nation is given the opportunity to initiate the negotiation by filing a "statement of intent" with the respective authority. Ensuring the administration necessary to enable a negotiation is the central aim of the second stage, involving

[134] Crown-Indigenous Relations and Northern Affairs Canada (2018b), p. 3.

[135] Lamirande (2019), Aboriginal Peoples Television Network (APTN).

[136] Brake (2018).

[137] Treaty Commission Act, [R.S.B.C. 1996], c. 461, s. 1(1) ""**first nation**" means an aboriginal governing body, however organized and established by aboriginal people within their traditional territory in British Columbia, that has been mandated by its constituents to enter into treaty negotiations on their behalf with Her Majesty in right of Canada and Her Majesty in right of British Columbia."

[138] The band is a federal governmental definition of a group of Indigenous peoples in the Indian Act. See s. 2(1) Indian Act. The process covers slightly more than a third of Indigenous peoples in the province through either active or completed negotiations. https://www.bctreaty.ca/negotiation-update as consulted on 19.08.2021.

[139] On 23.01.2020, three negotiations had reached the final stage of treaty implementation, 16 are in the fifth stage, 34 in stage four, 2 in stage three and 6 in stage two. On 19.08.2021 7 nations had reached the final stage (but these include a separate listing of the different Maa-nulth First Nations), 17 stage five, 31 stage four, 2 stage three, 5 stage two and four First Nations were in the so-called Tripartite Reconciliation stage. See http://www.bctreaty.ca/negotiation-update (numbers regularly updated, last accessed 19.08.2021).

the setting up of negotiation teams and consultation mechanisms.[140] In the third stage the parties conclude a first agreement, the framework agreement. It sets the agenda for the rest of the negotiation. An important element of this agreement is the need for ratification at the community level via processes established in stage two.[141] In the fourth stage, the parties negotiate AIPs (agreements-in-principle) upon the various legal points. These AIPs then form the basis for the next step of the treaty process, the negotiation of the final treaty. The last stage consists of cooperative efforts to implement the final treaty. An important element of these negotiations, indicated by the term 'comprehensive', is the understanding that they should address all points the parties want to settle and that there should be no unilateral refusal of individual points. DeCosta characterizes this as "an acknowledgment of the 'nation-to-nation' character" emphasized in Indigenous activism in 1980s prior to the Commission's creation.[142]

In the past, a number of advantages have been identified for First Nations, as well as for the provinces, to participate in the treaty-making process, most notably legal certainty, which is a key component of the process. It is a means of ensuring that all parties can be sure of the content of their rights for the future. For the province, this certainty is important for its economic development and in its representation of the non-Indigenous citizens of the province.[143] For First Nations, the treaty negotiation process is one way to negotiate directly with the government,[144] with the intention to clarify Indigenous rights and self-governance possibilities. As was addressed above, the legal provisions guarantee protection for Aboriginal rights but leave the content up to the courts to define. In these cases the outcome is not guaranteed, and the decision is ultimately made by someone not trained in Indigenous cultures or laws. In addition, court proceedings are costly and lengthy, and the courts have emphasized the need for negotiations to resolve Aboriginal rights and title claims.[145]

7.2.3.2 Challenges Within and for the BCTC and the Treaty Process

However, the BCTC process has been challenged both from within and from the outside. The duration and the costs for all parties involved, but especially for First Nations, have led to it being called troubled and a failure.[146] Another notable

[140] de Costa (2004), p. 136.

[141] de Costa (2004), p. 136.

[142] de Costa (2004), p. 137.

[143] British Columbia Ministry of Indigenous Relations and Reconciliation, https://www2.gov.bc.ca/gov/content/environment/natural-resource-stewardship/consulting-with-first-nations/first-nations-negotiations/about-first-nations-treaty-process [last accessed 19.08.2021].

[144] See for example First Nation Summit's emphasis on direct negotiations and the right of each First Nation to choose how to negotiate with Canadian government: http://fns.bc.ca/about [last accessed 19.08.2021].

[145] B.C. Teachers' Federation and Committee (1998), p. 5.

[146] Borrows (2015) and O'Neil and Shaw (2016).

challenge includes the role of historic wrongdoing and possible compensation. According to De Costa, disagreements on the role and reason for financial compensation offered in agreements (i.e. as compensation for past violations or as basis for future development) have constituted a noteworthy obstacle.[147] The provincial government apologized in 2003 to First Nations for the actions of past governments.[148] This apology has explicitly been linked to governmental efforts on reconciliation.[149] It is, however, worth noting that, in the four final agreements mentioned so far, there is no explicit apology by either the provincial or the federal government for historic wrongdoing. The closest to an apology is the following statement in two of the final agreements:

> Canada and British Columbia acknowledge **the perspective of** [Maa-nulth First Nations/ Tsawwassen First Nation] that harm and losses in relation to their aboriginal rights have occurred in the past and express regret **if any actions or omissions of the Crown** have contributed to that perspective, and the Parties rely on this Agreement to move them beyond the difficult circumstances of the past;[150]

This is neither an admission of past wrongdoing nor an apology. In effect, it eschews both.

When cultural heritage matters are negotiated via processes such as the BC treaty process, it has to be remembered that the parties engaging in the negotiating face different administrative, budgetary and mandate restraints. First Nations have significantly less financial resources and capacity at their disposal leading to unequal negotiating positions.[151] To provide First Nations with financial resources, a combination of government contributions coupled with lending agreements have been concluded in the past.[152] The borrowing component required Indigenous communities to go into debt to ensure the recognition for existing rights.[153] The costs incurred represent(ed) a significant burden to the Indigenous communities involved. The Hul' qumi' num, for example, argued before the Inter-American Commission of Human Rights that the $13 million debt incurred due to the BC treaty process was one reason

[147] de Costa (2004), pp. 140–141.

[148] CBC News (2003), available at: https://www.cbc.ca/news/canada/b-c-offers-apology-to-first-nations-for-inequity-intolerance-isolation-and-indifference-1.398592 [last accessed 19.08.2021]. Incidentally, the same government was responsible for the referendum on the BC treaty process that was heavily criticized by First Nations.

[149] B.C. Ministry of Aboriginal Relations and Reconciliation (2017).

[150] Emphasis added by the author, all statements can be found in the preambles of the respective final agreements which are available online at: http://www.bctreaty.ca/treaties-and-agreements [last accessed 19.08.2021].

[151] de Costa (2004), p. 138.

[152] Allocations used to be made up of a maximum of 80% loans and a minimum of 20% non-repayable contributions split between the federal government and the province. See BCTC, Reconciling Prosperity, Annual Report 2017, available via http://www.bctreaty.ca/annual-reports p. 56 [last accessed 19.08.2021].

[153] de Costa (2004), p. 138. He also highlights the debts' negative impact on first nations' access to commercial credit.

why they could not continue availing themselves of all administrative challenges against individuals taking action that affects their lands, sacred spaces and other interests.[154] There is, however, a chance that the treaty process will be given new life and that the potential advantages of treaty negotiations, including a fuller realization of UNDRIP rights, can be achieved. In April 2018, the federal government commenced with a 100% non-repayable contribution budget for participating treaty nations.[155] This means that First Nations will no longer have to incur new debt in securing their rights. In 2019, the federal government went the necessary step further and announced loan forgiveness for outstanding treaty negotiation loans.[156] This is an important and visible effect of the government's desire to renew its relationship with Indigenous Peoples mentioned earlier in this section.

The BC treaty process is a lengthy one, which should not be surprising given its scope. Negotiation times vary immensely. Of the three agreements which reached the final stage at the time of writing,[157] the negotiation periods to reach stage six ranged from between 15 to 20 years.[158] In 2017, a sample of eight negotiations out of the 42 negotiations showed that the negotiations had been in stage four for over 16 years on average.[159] The length of proceedings has also been criticized internationally. The Inter-American Commission on Human Rights considered the length of the proceedings as an "unwarranted delay on the part of the State to find a solution" to the land claims of the Hul' qumi' num Treaty Group.[160] In fact, it went even further and characterized the proceedings as an ineffective mechanism to protect the rights that were being claimed by the Hul' qumi' num.[161] Given the length of the process, interim measures are not only advisable but necessary, given that resources affected by resource developments are also part of negotiations.[162] When Indigenous

[154]IACHR, Report Nr. 105/09 Admissibility Hul'qumi'num Treaty Group Canada [30.10.2009], para 16.

[155]BCTC, Annual Report 2018, available via http://www.bctreaty.ca/annual-reports, p. 12 [last accessed 19.08.2021].

[156]BCTC, News Release 19.03.2019, available via http://www.bctreaty.ca/news-releases [last accessed 19.08.2021].

[157]On 19.08.2021 seven nations are listed as having reached stage six, the three treaties for these negotiations were considered for the analysis. The Lheidli T'enneh Treaty was not considered as it has not been signed at this date, any other treaties remain for future analysis.

[158]British Columbia, Provincial Government, information on Maa-nulth First Nations, available via: http://www.bctreaty.ca/negotiation-update and http://www2.gov.bc.ca/gov/content/environment/natural-resource-stewardship/consulting-with-first-nations/first-nations-negotiations/first-nations-a-z-listing/maa-nulth-first-nations [last accessed 19.08.2021].

[159]Time of negotiations considered from: 'Namgis Nation, Da'naxda'xw Awaetlala Nation, Haisla First Nation, Katzie Indian Band, Musqueam Nation, Sechelt Indian Band, Tlatlasikwala Nation and Wet'suwet'en Hereditary Chiefs available at: http://www.bctreaty.ca/negotiation-update [last accessed 19.08.2021].

[160]IACHR, Report Nr. 105/09, para 37.

[161]Ibid, para 38.

[162]The BCTC recommends the government to increase the adoption of land agreements for this very reason which serve to temporarily protect important areas that are part of the process, https://

Peoples negotiate in good faith only to witness their lands and territories being developed in a manner that negatively affects the traditional use of their land, this does not reflect positively on the overall process. Moreover, private lands are not part of the negotiations, which can be problematic for First Nations whose traditional territories are overwhelmingly in private hands. The need for stepping-stone agreements and the possibilities of sector agreements was also raised in 2015 in order to improve the process.[163] All parties were clearly unsatisfied with the process for many reasons, including those addressed here. Negotiations are complicated further by the fact that two of the parties involved, the federal and provincial governments, are political bodies with changing composition. This became very much apparent in the process of the 2002 referendum that rose in response to allegations of a lack of transparency and the undemocratic nature of the BCTC in the 1990s. The referendum questions have been characterized as vague as well as "transparently malicious" and it resulted in an Indigenous protests and public ballot burning by Indigenous protesters.[164] Similarly, Indigenous communities may also not speak in a unified voice, as community rejections of stage four agreements suggest.[165]

Evaluations of the process seem to vary between extremely critical and moderately critical. John Borrows observed in 2015: "Furthermore, the 20-year-old treaty process in British Columbia has been a dismal failure up to this point. First Nations are deeply indebted to Canadian governments from decades-long negotiations with very little to show for their efforts. Very few agreements have been signed."[166] A Tripartite Working Group, composed of government and Indigenous representatives, identified a number of reasons for the difficulties they were encountering. These included the length of the process, the higher than expected number of negotiation tables (communities negotiating individually rather than as a nation) lack of coordination between governmental negotiators and the departments responsible for implementing agreements and much more.[167] The report supported a proposal to negotiate incrementally with intermediate agreements that could serve as important motivations for the final agreements and more certainty on the ground.[168]

The case of negotiations of the Yale First Nation highlights some of the problems. The negotiations had in fact advanced to the adoption of a final agreement and passed from stage five to stage six with the implementation deadline scheduled for

---

www.bctreaty.ca/land-and-resources, or see archived link: http://web.archive.org/web/20181023091837/http://www.bctreaty.ca/land-and-resources [last accessed 19.08.2021]. See also de Costa (2004), p. 141.

[163] Crown-Indigenous Relations and Northern Affairs Canada, Government of Canada, Multilateral Engagement Process to Improve and Expedite Treaty Negotiations in British Columbia (2015), see https://www.rcaanc-cirnac.gc.ca/eng/1465231252132/1539697344543 [last accessed 19.08.2021].

[164] de Costa (2004), pp. 143–144.

[165] de Costa (2004), p. 145.

[166] Borrows (2015), p. 731.

[167] Tripartite Working Group (2002), see especially at 2, 10–11.

[168] Ibid.

2016 when the First Nation announced it would not be able to proceed with the implementation phase. It appears that one of the reasons is overlapping fishery rights with another First Nation.[169] This means that, at this point, the First Nation had incurred a significant amount of debt (prior to the changes in the policy). Certainty in relation to the promised rights and benefits remains doubtful. Overlapping territorial claims is indeed a larger problem which challenges the negotiations. As Turner and Fondahl observe on the process: "An underlying assumption is that such a map of mutually exclusive Indigenous territories can indeed be drawn. Yet Indigenous peoples cognize territoriality in a wide variety of ways some of them substantially different from those common to State governments."[170] By their own words, the policy of the Commission (and the Government) is not to assign any land until the dispute is resolved amongst the respective Indigenous nations.[171] This would respect Indigenous rights to self-determination, aligning with Art. 3 UNDRIP, Art. 18 UNDRIP and Art. 26 UNDRIP. However, Turner and Fondahl point out that in BC these policies of not assigning land until the dispute has been resolved amongst and by Indigenous Nations has "been ignored repeatedly."[172] The combination of the fact that the BCTC cannot compel settlement of disputes prior adoption as it is a facilitatory body, combined with the fact that participation in the negotiation processes is voluntary means that First Nations that have raised overlapping claims, but who are not part of the negotiations face the impairment of their rights. This has also led to court cases,[173] however, the problem of overlapping claims remains.[174] This means that the process through settling exclusive rights risks discriminating against non-participating First Nations in the case of overlapping claims.

7.2.4 Culture and Heritage in Final Agreements

At the time of writing, seven first nations have reached stage six: Maa-nulth First Nations [Huu-ay-aht, Ka:'yu:'k't'h/Che:k'tles7et'h', Toquaht, Uchucklesaht,

[169] O'Neil and Shaw (2016).

[170] Turner and Fondahl (2015), p. 475.

[171] British Columbia Treaty Commission (2014); Turner and Fondahl (2015), p. 476.

[172] Turner and Fondahl (2015), p. 476.

[173] Cook v. British Columbia (Minister of Aboriginal Relations & Reconciliation), 2007 BCSC 1722, 2007 CarswellBC 2858.

[174] Turner and Fondahl (2015) proposed the creation of an Indigenous Territories Tribunal whose inquires into overlapping claims could be used by the Commission. The authors were inspired by the Waitangi Tribunal of New Zealand.

Ucluelet],[175] Tla'amin Nation (Sliammon),[176] Tsawwassen First Nation.[177] The Yale First Nation[178] also reached stage six but currently remains stalled. To be able to evaluate the advantages and disadvantages of such a comprehensive treaty negotiation process for repatriation and the related cultural rights, this section will examine the three final agreements that had been ratified at the time of writing.[179]

7.2.4.1 Maa-nulth First Nations Final Agreement[180]

An example of how repatriation can be embedded in modern treaty negotiations are the Maa-nulth First Nations Treaties. As part of the final agreement, Indigenous heritage objects have been returned to a Maa-nulth First Nation by the RBCM. In total, the museum and the Huu-ay-ath identified 51 heritage objects; 17 were transferred in 2016 and the remaining 34 are to stay with the museum until requested otherwise by the community.[181] Some of the objects had been taken from the community over 100 years ago.[182]

The MFNFA is a comprehensive modern treaty covering governance, financial, territorial, resource and cultural matters. It replaces the Indian Act after a transitional period,[183] constituting a "full and final settlement" of Aboriginal rights (including

[175] Maa-nulth Final Agreement, available at: http://www2.gov.bc.ca/assets/gov/environment/natural-resource-stewardship/consulting-with-first-nations/agreements/maa-nulth_final_agreement_signed_june_2008__april_2009.pdf [last accessed 19.08.2021]. British Columbia, Provincial Government, information on Maa-nulth First Nations, available at: http://www2.gov.bc.ca/gov/content/environment/natural-resource-stewardship/consulting-with-first-nations/first-nations-negotiations/first-nations-a-z-listing/maa-nulth-first-nations [last accessed 19.08.2021].

[176] Available at: http://www.bctreaty.ca/sites/default/files/Tlaamin-Final-Agreement_Initialled_1.pdf [last accessed 19.08.2021].

[177] Available at: http://www.bctreaty.ca/sites/default/files/Tsawwassen_final_initial_1.pdf [last accessed 19.08.2021].

[178] Available at: http://www.bctreaty.ca/sites/default/files/Yale-Final-Agreement_Feb10_0.pdf [last accessed 19.08.2021].

[179] On 19.08.2021 7 nations had reached the final stage (but these include a separate listing of the different Maa-nulth First Nations), 17 stage five, 31 stage four, 2 stage three, 5 stage two and four First Nations were in the so-called Tripartite Reconciliation stage. See http://www.bctreaty.ca/negotiation-update (numbers regularly updated, last accessed 19.08.2021) As observed, the Yale Treaty negotiations are currently halted. The Lheidli T'enneh First Nation had negotiated and initialled a Final Agreement, but this was not ratified by the community. All final agreements and Agreements in Principle are available by the BCTC at: http://www.bctreaty.ca/treaties-and-agreements-in-principle [last accessed 19.08.2021].

[180] Ratified by all parties 2012–2013, effective as of 5.4.2016.

[181] https://royalbcmuseum.bc.ca/first-nations/first-nations-repatriation/return-cultural-treasures-huu-ay-aht-first-nations [last accessed 19.08.2021].

[182] Ibid.

[183] Maa-Nulth Final Agreement, s. 1.6.1 (except for determination of Indian status), in more detail ch. 16 of Final Agreement.

title)[184] and seeks to set out s. 35 rights exhaustively for the Maa-nulth First Nation.[185] It also includes a release of past claims.[186] With regard to cultural rights, the agreement provides the Maa-nulth-aht, *inter alia*, with the right to practice their culture and use their language[187] and rights to harvest, barter and trade a number of different resources.[188] The agreement also provides each Maa-nulth First Nation with the right to harvest wildlife and migratory birds and gather plants for ceremonial purposes, subject to measures necessary for conservation, public health or public safety.[189]

Chapter 20 of the agreement is the most important chapter for present purposes, it comprises a number of different repatriation or access modalities. In substance, it can be split into three main parts, rules on artefacts (moveable Indigenous heritage), heritage sites and places (immoveable Indigenous heritage) and human remains. The first subsection focusses on artefacts and is based on the importance of Maa-nulth First Nation artefacts for the continuation of the Nation's culture, values and traditions, **irrespective** of whether an artifact is in the possession of the Nation or one of the acknowledged public institutions which (still) hold (dislocated) Maa-nulth heritage.[190] This influences how the treaty regulates the two categories (those to be held by the respective First Nation and those (to be) held by the cultural institution). The agreement establishes the presumption that each Maa-nulth First Nation owns any artifact discovered within a Heritage Site on its lands discovered after the agreement becomes effective.[191] As for dislocated objects, the return of artefact is regulated differently depending on the holding institution, the treaty covers three public bodies: the Canadian Museum of Civilization (now the Canadian Museum of History), Parks Canada Agency, and the Royal British Columbia Museum.[192]

The provisions covering the two museum holdings are relatively similar. In both cases, the treaty operates via the incorporation of a split list, which covers objects which will be returned to the respective First Nation and those which remain in museum ownership. The artefacts will be returned after the treaty has entered into effect, within 5 years of it entering into effect or upon a date agreed upon by the two

[184]Maa-Nulth Final Agreement, s. 1.11.1.

[185]Maa-Nulth Final Agreement, s. 1.11.2.

[186]For Canada, BC and all other persons in s. 1.11.6 Maa-Nulth Final Agreement, similarly also Tsawwassen agreement, see below. Reflects declared governmental objective of certainty for negotiations.

[187]Maa-Nulth Final Agreement 6.4.1 in conj. with 21.1.1.

[188]Maa-Nulth Final Agreement, section 6.4. pp. 70–72.

[189]Maa-Nulth Final Agreement, s. 11.1.1–2, s. 12.1.1–2, s. 24.6.1–2 in conj. with the definition of domestic purposes in s. 29.1.0.

[190]The agreement encompasses Parks Canada Agency, the Canadian Museum of Civilisation and the Royal British Columbia Museum.

[191]Maa-Nulth Final Agreement, s. 20.1.2.

[192]This is combined with an obligation incumbent on the federal level, to "make reasonable efforts to facilitate Maa-nulth First Nation's access to their Artefacts and Human Remains in other public collections in Canada at their request", see s. 20.3.1.

parts; transfer includes all legal interests and possession of the artifact.[193] This is combined with limiting museum liability in the case of loss or damage until transfer.[194] Objects acquired by the public institution after the treaty entered into effect or whose origin was undetermined until after that point will be part of the museum holdings unless both the museum and the First Nation agree that the object will be transferred.[195] The treaty obliges both parties to negotiate and to *attempt* to reach an agreement. Custodial arrangements have to be in accordance with First Nation law and practices as well as federal or provincial laws and policies, depending on the identity of the holding institution.[196]

The treaty gives an indicative list of matters which can be regulated via a custodial arrangement, including conditions of maintenance, storage and handling and conditions of access to and use of Maa-nulth First Nation artefacts, which includes their study, reproduction or display.[197] The possession of objects which will remain with the federal museum is shared between the First Nation and the museum, depending on the museum's resources and any custodial arrangement made.[198] In the case of the Royal Museum of British Columbia (hereafter referred to as RBCM), possession remains with the museum, but the treaty highlights that the parties have the option to negotiate lending, replication as well as professional and technical training. This is, however, worded in soft language and is optional, depending on the willingness of both parties.[199] The provisions on the collections held by Parks Canada Agency are brief by comparison. Both parties are obliged to make reasonable efforts to determine whether an object in the permanent collection is of Maa-nulth origin. The treaties leave it up to the parties to negotiate a transfer or loan agreement if the Maa-nulth origin of an object has been established after the treaty has entered into effect, or if such an object enters the permanent possession or is under the control of Parks Canada Agency after that date.[200] In case of competing claims related to an artifact, either the province (for objects held by the RBCM) or the federal level may request the Maa-nulth First Nation to resolve the dispute with the contesting Nation or community.[201]

Lastly, Chapter 20 emphasizes the right of the Maa-nulth First Nation Governments to develop heritage management processes for sites on their lands and obliges both the province and the First Nation to seek to agree on a list of key sites of cultural

---

[193] Maa-Nulth Final Agreement, s. 20.2.2, s. 20.2.24.

[194] Maa-Nulth Final Agreement, s. 20.2.6, 20.2.28(b). Limited to loss or damage resulting from dishonesty, gross negligence, or malicious or wilful misconduct of the museum employees or agents.

[195] Maa-Nulth Final Agreement, s. 20.2.10, s. 20.2.33.

[196] Maa-Nulth Final Agreement, s. 20.2.16, s. 20.2.37 respectively.

[197] Maa-Nulth Final Agreement, s. 20.2.38.

[198] Maa-Nulth Final Agreement, s. 20.2.13 for Canadian Museum of Civilization.

[199] Maa-Nulth Final Agreement, s. 20.2.39.

[200] Maa-Nulth Final Agreement s. 20.2.22.

[201] Maa-Nulth Final Agreement, s. 20.2.9, s. 20.2.32.

and historic significance to the respective First Nation, which are outside of their lands and are to be protected via provincial heritage designation (see Sect. 7.2.2 above).[202]

7.2.4.2 Tsawwassen First Nation Final Agreement [TFNFA]

There are a number of important provisions in the Tsawwasen Final Agreement which relate to Indigenous heritage: cultural self-determination; management, protection and control of cultural resources and repatriation of cultural heritage in government possession.[203] Chapter 1 defines key terms: "'Cultural Heritage Site' means an area within a National Park or National Marine Conservation Area **that has heritage value to a group**, including aboriginal people, a community and other Canadians, and may include a traditional use, archaeological, funereal or sacred site;" "Cultural Property" refers either to "**ceremonial regalia and similar personal property** associated with a chief, clan or family;" or "other personal property that **has cultural significance** to Tsawwassen First Nation".[204] Lastly, "Tsawwassen Artifact" means any object created by, traded to, commissioned by, or given as a gift to a Tsawwassen individual or that originated from the Tsawwassen community, past or present, and that **has past and ongoing importance to the culture or spiritual practices** of Tsawwassen First Nation, but does not include any object that has been traded to, commissioned by, or given as a gift to another aboriginal individual or community.

Cultural Heritage Sites[205] are defined in broad terms. The defining term is "heritage value", which is capable of encompassing all cultural elements a group may wish to claim. The non-exhaustive list of examples could indicate a focus in the negotiations to ensure the traditional use of Indigenous lands as well the protection of funeral sites. Cultural Property and Tsawwassen Artefacts by contrast are defined in slightly narrower terms. In essence, the personal connection of the property combined with a requirement of cultural or ceremonial/religious significance makes up this category.

Furthermore, the agreement recognizes a ceremonial right to fish and to harvest wildlife and migratory birds otherwise subject conservation, publish health or public safety requirements.[206] The Agreement similarly provides for a right to harvest renewable resources in National Parks or National Marine Conservation Ares that

[202]Maa-Nulth Final Agreement, s. 20.6.0. The treaty also foresees the option of giving or changing place names in the Nuu-chah-nulth language, see s. 20.7.0.

[203]Most relevant is Chapter 14 on cultural heritage.

[204]Tsawwassen Final Agreement, p. 6.

[205]The Agreement also defines "Heritage Resources" as "include[ing] archaeological sites, traditional use sites, culturally modified trees, trails and routes, burial or other funereal sites, structural features, and cultural landscapes."

[206]Tsawwassen Final Agreement, ch. 9, s. 1 and 2, p. 75, read in conj. with definition of 'domestic purposes' p. 6, in ch. 1. Ch. 10 s. 1 and 2, p. 95 read in conj. with definition of 'domestic purposes',

are "wholly or partly within Tsawwassen Territory" for ceremonial purposes. In addition, the agreement recognizes the right to exchange regalia, traditional or artistic objects for ceremonial purposes.[207] Similarly, Chapter 13 TFFNA recognizes the right to gather plants for ceremonial purposes and to exchange regalia, traditional or artistic objects made from such plants for ceremonial purposes.[208]

The Chapter 14 on culture and heritage provides broad rights (the right of First Nation to practise their culture and use their language, law-making powers relating to the right to culture and heritage resources) as well as specific rights (right to make laws for devolution of Cultural property of a Tsawwassen Member who dies without a valid will). The Tsawwassen First Nation realized its law-making capabilities with its 2009 Culture and Heritage Act. The Act follows the terminology adopted in the TFNNA explored above. The Act establishes a number of cultural rights and obligations. S. 3 provides Tsawwassen members with the right to individually and collectively: "(a) enjoy, advance and promote the Hun'qum'i'num language, Tsawwassen art, literature, lifestyle, value systems and ways of living together, (b) engage in the spiritual, material, intellectual and emotional features of Tsawwassen society, (c) preserve and protect Tsawwassen First Nation history, traditions, traditional beliefs and symbols, (d) advance, promote and participate in Tsawwassen First Nation ceremonies, songs, dance, storytelling, and naming practices, and (e) engage in other practices of Tsawwassen culture." It obliges the Executive Council to "negotiate an agreement about the ownership, return of, care, custody, control or exhibition of, and respect to be accorded to, Tsawwassen Artifacts held" by non-Tsawwassen individuals or organizations inside or outside Canada.

In terms of cultural heritage, the agreement considers the future discovery of artefacts in three ways. If an object enters into museum holdings in the future, a custodial agreement can be negotiated. For buried heritage, its location is determinative. The Tsawwassen agreement establishes Indigenous ownership over Tsawwassen artefacts discovered on Tsawwassen lands after the effective date.[209] Artefacts discovered outside of the nation's lands may be subject to a lending or transfer agreement with Canada. The Royal British Columbia Museum agrees to share any information on Tsawwassen artefacts or human remains in other public collections. To obtain the necessary information is crucial to any repatriation effort.[210] Comparably, Chapter 14 does not prescribe the participation of the Tsawwassen people in the management and protection of their heritage resources

p. 6 ch. 1. Ch. 11 s. 1 and 2, p. 105, read in conjunction with definition of 'domestic purposes', p. 6, ch. 1.

[207]Tsawwassen Final Agreement, Ch. 12, s. 6, p. 111.

[208]Tsawwassen Final Agreement, Ch. 13, s. 1 & 2 (read in conj. with p. 6 ch. 1 definition of 'domestic purposes'), s. 6, p. 119.

[209]Tsawwassen Final Agreement, Ch. 14 s. 14.

[210]Tsawwassen Final Agreement, Ch. 14 s. 16.

which are located outside of Tsawwassen lands and within Tsawwassen Territory.[211] Rather it opens up the opportunity for further negotiations or agreements.

In light of the jurisprudence on Aboriginal and treaty rights under s. 35, it is important to note that section 12 of the TFNFA provides for the final agreement to be the final and exhaustive record of the Tsawwassen First Nation's Aboriginal and other s. 35 rights. The agreement notably deviates from Supreme Court jurisprudence which has stated that, in case of doubt, agreements with first nations have to be interpreted in favour of the First Nations to safeguard the honour of the Crown.[212] Moreover, treaty rights negotiated today do not entail the extinguishment of Aboriginal rights (unlike in the past). They seek to provide certainty by clearly stating the content of rights, but this does not equal extinguishment.[213] Moreover, it has always been clear that treaties need to have an inbuilt flexibility in order to allow the parties to adapt to changing circumstances. For all of these reasons, section 12 may be in line with the provincial and federal governmental perspective, but it needs to be rejected from a viewpoint that supports Aboriginal rights.

7.2.4.3 Tla'amin First Nation Final Agreement

In the preamble, the treaty is identified as a means to seek reconciliation. Moreover, the Tla'amin emphasize their cultural, historic and religious links to their lands and waters as well as the need to "preserve, protect and enhance Tla'amin heritage language and culture".[214]

Similar to the Tsawwassen treaty, the Tla'amin First Nation Final Agreement [hereafter Tla'amin treaty] includes a number of provisions which affect Indigenous rights to their cultural heritage. These are cultural (including ceremonial and language) rights and the right to (cultural) self-determination. The treaty recognizes, *inter alia*, a right to harvest fish and aquatic plants,[215] wildlife[216] and migratory birds,[217] and to gather plants[218] for ceremonial purposes within a specified area

[211] Tsawwassen Final Agreement, Ch. 14 ss. 18–25, pp. 127–128. Tsawwassen Territory refers to those lands the First Nation initially indicated in its statement of intent, Tsawwassen lands are those lands which are recognized as Tsawwassen lands in the appendix to the final agreement.

[212] Tsawwassen Final Agreement, ch. 2 s. 60, p. 31. "There will be no presumption that doubtful expressions... are to be resolved in favour of any particular Party."

[213] See Report of the British Columbia Claims Task Force (28.06.1991), p. 11.

[214] Tla'amin Final Agreement, preamble, recital l and m.

[215] Tla'amin Final Agreement, ch. 9 s. 1 & 2 read in conj. with definition of domestic purpose in ch. 1.

[216] Tla'amin Final Agreement, ch. 10 s. 1 & 2 read in conj. with definition of domestic purpose in ch. 1.

[217] Tla'amin Final Agreement, ch. 11 s. 1 & 2 read in conj. with definition of domestic purpose in ch. 1.

[218] Tla'amin Final Agreement, ch. 12 s. 16 & 17 read in conj. with definition of domestic purpose in ch. 1.

which may be limited by measures necessary for conservation, public health or public safety.

Also similar to the Tsawwassen treaty, Chapter 14 on culture and heritage recognizes the First Nation's right to practise the Tla'amin culture and language in accordance with the treaty provisions.[219] Importantly, Tla'amin citizens may exercise these rights "*except* as otherwise provided under *Tla'amin law*."[220] This recognition of Indigenous laws is an important element of respecting the First Nation's right to self-determination and to strengthen revitalization efforts. As is the case for the Maa-nulth First Nations, the Tla'amin treaty includes a list of already identified artefacts which will be returned to the First Nation. The broad right to culture and language is given more substance by providing not only for concrete rights applicable in the future relationship between the Indigenous community and the different government actors,[221] but by also addressing the effects of past assimilation policies and laws. This is done in relation to artefacts, heritage sites, place names, and human remains. The provisions on artefacts are based on the recognition of the importance of Tla'amin artefacts for the continuation of Tla'amin culture irrespective of the current holding institution.[222] The removal of the artefacts is partially remedied by a number of rules addressing public holding institutions. The RBCM is required to return specific items to the Tla'amin Nation via rules comparable to those applicable in the Maa-nulth treaty.[223] For those that will remain with the museum in Victoria, there is an obligation to seek to reach custodial arrangements.[224] In the case of the former Canadian Museum of Civilization, the treaty briefly touches upon the option for the museum and the Tla'amin First Nation to negotiate an agreement. Once it has been agreed that an artefact is of Tla'amin origin by both the museum and the First Nation, it can either be covered by a repatriation or a custodial agreement. The repatriation provisions are complimented by provisions which go some steps towards ensuring better access to dislocated objects. Canada is obliged to "make reasonable efforts to facilitate access" to Tla'amin heritage and human remains which are held in other public collections.[225] The RBCM in turn is obliged to share any information it has on Tla'amin heritage and ancestral remains in other public collections located in Canada upon request.[226] The combination of information sharing about the location of heritage with an (albeit limited) obligation on the

[219] Tla'amin Final Agreement, ch. 14, s. 1.

[220] Tla'amin Final Agreement, ch. 14, s. 2, emphasis added.

[221] For example, Tla'amin Final Agreement, and notably sections 31–33 which oblige the province and the Tla'amin Nation to enter into a harvesting agreement for Monumental Cedar and Cypress for Cultural Purposes. Cultural Purpose means the use for a purpose that "was integral to Tla'amin culture before contact, is primarily for totem poles, dugout canoes . . .; is not carried out for profit." See definition in Ch. 1, p. 7.

[222] Tla'amin Final Agreement, ch. 14, s. 10, p. 160.

[223] Tla'amin Final Agreement, ch. 14, s. 15–19 including comparable limited liability, pp. 161–162.

[224] Tla'amin Final Agreement, ch. 14, s. 20, s. 21, p. 162.

[225] Tla'amin Final Agreement, ch. 14, s. 22, p. 162.

[226] This is similar to the Tsawwassen Agreement, ch. 14, s. 16.

side of the federal Government to enable access to that heritage has the capacity to improve the cultural rights of the Tla'amin continuously. Through this, it can aid the creation of a partnership between First Nations and cultural and governmental actors that has the capacity to foster mutual respect and is sustainable in the long-term.

Similar to the provisions in the Maa-nulth treaty, for ancestral remains, the obligations on the side of the federal government are stronger than for artefacts. Any human remains held by Canada when the treaty comes into effect will have to be returned.[227] Similarly, any ancestral remains or burial objects that enter into its permanent possession after the treaty has entered into force will have to be returned at the request of the First Nation.[228] This provision is incredibly important, given that many Indigenous ancestral remains are still located outside of Canada. The Tla'amin and Maa-nulth treaties ensure that, also in these cases, the ancestral remains will be returned to the respective First Nation. British Columbia, in turn, is obliged to enter into negotiations and *attempt* to reach an agreement with the Tla'amin if ancestral remains "that are reasonably considered to be of Tla'amin ancestry" are found off Tla'amin lands and enter the province's permanent possession after the treaty has entered into force. This obligation should have been worded more strongly in order to guarantee Art. 12(1) UNDRIP.

As regards immovable heritage, the treaty recognizes the right of Tla'amin to legislate on the protection, conservation and access to heritage sites on Tla'amin lands.[229] Moreover, similar to the Maa-nulth treaties, the Tla'amin treaty also has provisions with regard to naming or changing the names of geographic features within Tla'amin lands. It includes a list of already agreed upon geographic features and a provision enabling the province and the nation to cooperate on the naming of other features in the future.[230]

The treaty replaces the Indian Act for the participating parties after a transitional period.[231] Similar to other modern treaties, it acknowledges the need to resolve potential conflicts between the treaty and obligations Canada may have entered or will enter into under international law. The treaty provides both for a consultation obligation before Canada enters into agreements which could affect a treaty right adversely,[232] as well as a dispute resolution mechanism via arbitration in case of conflict between an international obligation and Tla'amin law. The Tla'amin Nation in turn has committed to remedy the law or exercise thereof "to the extent necessary to enable Canada to perform its obligations". Given the much broader legislative and territorial powers of Canada, this provision is certainly understandable. Canadian courts have interpreted the duty to consult not to require consent, depending on the foreseeable effect of a measure. As a result, the effects of this arrangement on

[227] Tla'amin Final Agreement, ch. 14, s. 24, p. 163.

[228] Tla'amin Final Agreement, ch. 14, s. 25, p. 163.

[229] Tla'amin Final Agreement, ch. 5, s. 17(b) p. 79, ch. 14 s. 4(b), s. 5–7, pp. 159–160.

[230] Tla'amin Final Agreement, ch. 14, s. 28, s. 29, p. 163.

[231] Tla'amin Final Agreement, ch. 2, s. 30–32.

[232] Tla'amin Final Agreement, ch. 2, s. 24, p. 26.

Tla'amin treaty rights will very much depend on the good faith of the Canadian government in its approach to consultation and whether it will respect its treaty obligations not to enter international treaties which might otherwise allow it to circumvent such obligations.

In this and other agreements, the obligation to meet periodically to review existing practices to realize respective treaty obligations as start of a new relationship which requires continuous efforts and interactions is a positive development.[233]

7.2.5 *Evaluation of Repatriation Chances in BC*

Several factors influence the right of Indigenous communities to their heritage within British Columbia. First, not all Indigenous communities in British Columbia engage in the treaty process. If the Canadian government and the province rely exclusively on the final treaties as a means to fulfil their obligations to respect Aboriginal rights under s. 35 (as the little use of s. 4 would suggest)[234] and to enact its promise to realize the UNDRIP, this is inadequate to protect Indigenous heritage rights. Second, as has been pointed out by international bodies,[235] the duration of the negotiations means that they are insufficient to protect particular individual human rights. Third, the agreements reached so far have, for the most part, given Indigenous Peoples law-making and enforcement rights for heritage located on the lands the province recognized as Indigenous lands. These rules do not apply to any heritage located elsewhere in the province for which the BCHA still applies in full force. In the absence of any legal mechanisms for such cases, it is to be hoped that the successful negotiations will create a basis of voluntary cooperation. For the many negotiations which have not yet reached this stage, the danger of Indigenous cultural heritage being used as a bargaining chip to gain concessions in land, resource of governance matters remains. Fourth, the author would argue that—contrary to the argument made by the SCC in Kitkatla—the way the Heritage Conservation Act leaves licensing power to desecrate sites and remove heritage objects up to the Minister for any Indigenous heritage object or site if no s. 4 agreement has been taken threatens to leave Aboriginal ceremonial rights unprotected. These rights should be protected as Aboriginal rights under s. 35(1).

The primary purpose of the BC treaty process is not the repatriation of Indigenous heritage or the protection of Indigenous cultural rights. Rather its express aim is reconciling the different rights and interests in the province, reconciling Indigenous and non-Indigenous citizens and providing for legal certainty. As was emphasized

[233] Tla'amin Final Agreement, ch. 2, s. 58–65, pp. 33–34.

[234] For a discussion of obligations under international law, taking into account Chaps. 2–3, and see evaluation in Chap. 8.

[235] HRCee, George Howard v. Canada, Communication No. 879/1999, U.N. Doc CCPR/C/84/D/879/1999, para 8.4.

above, there are thus a multitude of rights and interests that require negotiation. Focussing on everything within one all-encompassing treaty negotiation has a number of advantages. Negotiations take place between different cultures and people of different backgrounds and with divergent interests. To find common ground takes time and, once it has been found, it can be used to negotiate on a multitude of interests. Moreover, given that cultural heritage stands not in isolation but is connected to a multitude of other factors (including environmental protection, land rights, language and educational policy), it can arguably be advantageous to negotiate all of these issues among the same parties within the same negotiation process. The disadvantages are the length of the process, the imbalance of resources, lack of satisfactory approach towards overlapping claims, and that the final treaty will regain only a fraction of their original lands for Indigenous Peoples. In relation to the repatriation of cultural heritage, in particular, it can result in repatriation agreements. However, it can also result in mere provisions that state the option to negotiate in the future. If the negotiations only reach this result, but they have required no negotiation on cultural resources with museums in the meantime, this severely curtails Indigenous cultural rights. In either case, if the repatriation of religious heritage is motivated by the desire to revitalize religious practices, waiting 20 years significantly impairs the practitioners' right to manifest their religion. There is therefore a need to consider repatriating specific categories of Indigenous cultural heritage as soon as an agreement on the particular issue of repatriation has been reached or to agree on interim measures.

The need for interim measures is also pressing to guarantee the Indigenous right to protect, control and manage their cultural heritage (Art. 31(1) UNDRIP). It will not be served by a treaty agreement that comes after crucial sites and areas have been desecrated and repurposed for, for example, ski resorts or logging sites. One element of a sincere, good faith effort to negotiate on the side of the government would be to refrain from developing those parts of public lands which are being claimed as part of the treaty-making process. Moreover, while treaties can give Indigenous Peoples greater security than they would have before the courts, this picture is also incomplete. Given that the Canadian judiciary has interpreted treaty rights to be subject to unilateral limitations by the Crown, it is still doubtful in how far treaties will really be more advantageous in the long run. This might be remedied by the fact that the negotiating parties agree that the core of the treaty may stand but that future challenges can arise which require addendums by the parties to the treaty.[236] This could mean that the parties can adapt the provisions of the treaty should the Canadian judiciary undermine features of the treaty through its interpretation and endangers reconciliation.

With regard to evaluating the general level of protection afforded to Indigenous heritage within the modern treaties that have been negotiated so far, the following may be observed. The treaties do include provisions on law-making and management powers for the protection of Indigenous heritage on Indigenous lands which are

[236] Crown-Indigenous Relations and Northern Affairs Canada (2018a).

protected at the constitutional level by virtue of s. 35(1). The constitution thus protects Indigenous Peoples within Canada as distinct socio-cultural entities who have rights independent of provincial or federal action or their status as Canadian citizens. This is a remarkable step away from a very long history of forced assimilation. In addition, there are a number of provisions in the treaties which seem to give credence to the governmental emphasis on reconciliation and may open up a path for Indigenous communities towards long-term partnerships.

The difficulty which may arise in this area arguably lies in the apparent inability or unwillingness of some governmental actors and parts of the judiciary to fully accept that these rights originate in the self-determining status of Indigenous communities. In addition, given that modern treaties seek to set out the s. 35 rights of Indigenous communities concerned[237] exhaustively, in order to promote (legal) certainty for the government, Indigenous and business actors, any future limitations imposed on s. 35(1) by judicial interpretations risk depriving the rights of their meaning. Where governmental limitations on treaties imposed unilaterally can easily be justified as a balancing exercise of Indigenous interests against the general public interest, as long as some consultation has taken place, this misses the fact that the original treaty (both historic and modern) already contained a balancing exercise of Indigenous and public interests. Instead, when there is a potential measure, the government should have to balance modern interests on both sides and consider the balancing act which already took place when the treaty was negotiated.

The need to respect existing Indigenous rights is reiterated in provincial heritage legislation. S. 8 BCHCA provides that neither the Act nor any s. 4 agreements abrogates or derogates from existing Aboriginal and treaty rights. Moreover, the Act's prohibition on the damage or desecration of Indigenous cultural heritage signals that the province knows of the need to protect Indigenous cultural and religious heritage according to Indigenous standards. Unfortunately, the space within the BCHCA to take the different characteristics and cultural rights of the province's many Indigenous Peoples into account has not been realized.

The treaties that have been negotiated through the BCTC not only address the management and protection of heritage sites and the ownership of Indigenous heritage objects excavated after the treaties' entry into effect, they also provide for explicit repatriation obligations and feature provisions stimulating future cooperation between cultural institutions and the Indigenous community, including more negotiations. This provides the potential for museum and Indigenous community to meet as equals, to address past grievances and to establish new cultural relationships. This can help Indigenous Peoples in revitalizing past traditions and restoring the cultural health of their communities. Museums may discover a new way in which to act as mediators between different cultures. A willingness to consider the removal of Indigenous objects from an Indigenous rather than a traditional museologist's perspective has already helped in addressing some of the negative consequences of forced assimilation policies which are still very present in contemporary community

[237] See for example, Tla'amin Final Agreement, ch. 2 s. 41, p. 29.

life. First Nations view the refusal to return such items as a sign that colonial power relations have not ceased to exist but are still present, if only in undercurrents.[238] Apart from creating new relationships on the local cultural level, such efforts also contribute towards achieving the reconciliatory objectives which underlie the constitutional protection of Aboriginal and treaty rights.

References

B.C. Ministry of Aboriginal Relations and Reconciliation (2017) FACTSHEET: reconciliation at the heart of relationship with aboriginal peoples

B.C. Teachers' Federation and Committee TPE (1998) Understanding the B.C. Treaty Process – an opportunity for dialogue. First Nations Summit

Bell CE (1992) Aboriginal claims to cultural property in Canada: a comparative legal analysis of the repatriation debate. Am Indian Law Rev 17(2):457–522

Bell C (2001) Protecting indigenous heritage resources in Canada: a comment on Kitkatle v British Columbia. Int J Cult Prop 10(2):246–263

Bell C (2009a) Repatriation of cultural material to First Nations in Canada: legal and ethical justifications. Cultural heritage issues: the legacy of conquest, colonization, and commerce. Brill Nijhoff, Leiden

Bell CE (2009b) Restructuring the relationship: domestic repatriation and Canadian law reform. In: Bell CE, Paterson RK (eds) Protection of First Nations cultural heritage: laws, policy, and reform. UBC Press, Vancouver, pp 15–77

Bell CE, Raven H, McCuaig H (2008) Recovering from colonization: perspectives of community members on protection and repatriation of Kwakwaka'wakw Cultural Heritage. In: Bell CE, Napoleon V (eds) First Nations cultural heritage and law: case studies, voices and perspectives. UBC Press, Vancouver, pp 33–91

Borrows J (2006) Indigenous legal traditions in Canada (trans: Canada LCo)

Borrows J (2015) The durability of terra nullius: Tsilhqot'in Nation v British Columbia. UBC Law Rev 48(3):701–742

Brake J (2018) Trudeau to address First Nation chiefs amid growing opposition to Indigenous rights framework. APTN News, 4.12

British Columbia Treaty Commission (2014) Annual Report 2014. https://www.bctreaty.ca/sites/default/files/BCTC-Annual-Report-2014.pdf. Last accessed 19 Aug 2021

CBC News (2003) B.C. offers apology to First Nations for 'inequity, intolerance, isolation and indifference'. CBC News, 12 March 2003

Collison JN, Bell SK̲L, Neel L-A (2019) Indigenous repatriation handbook. Royal BC Museum and Haida Gwaii Museum at K̲ay Llngaay

Conaty GT (2015a) The development of museums and their effects on First Nations. In: Conaty GT (ed) We are coming home. AU Press, Edmonton, pp 37–69

Conaty GT (ed) (2015b) We are coming home – repatriation and the restoration of Blackfoot cultural confidence. AU Press

Crown-Indigenous Relations and Northern Affairs Canada (1.12.2018a) Treaty Principals sign Accord to transform treaty negotiations in B.C. https://news.gov.bc.ca/releases

Crown-Indigenous Relations and Northern Affairs Canada (2018b) Engagement document: working together to create the foundation for the Federal Recognition and Implementation of the Inherent and Treaty Rights of Indigenous Peoples in Canada

[238] Bell (2009b), p. 20 See also, Bell et al. (2008).

Cruickshank DA (2006) Calder Case. The Canadian Encyclopedia. https://www.thecanadianencyclopedia.ca/en/article/calder-case. Last accessed 19 Aug 2021

de Costa R (2004) Treaties in British Columbia: comprehensive agreement making in a democratic context. In: Langton M, Palmer L, Tehan M, Shain K (eds) Honour among nations? Treaties and agreements with indigenous people. Melbourne University Press, Melbourne, pp 133–146

First Nations Summit, Assembly of First Nations, Union of British Columbia Indian Chiefs, Government of British Columbia (2018) Joint agenda: implementing the commitment document – shared vision, guiding principles, goals and objectives. https://www2.gov.bc.ca/gov/content/environment/natural-resource-stewardship/consulting-with-first-nations/first-nations-negotiations/reconciliation-other-agreements. Last accessed 19 Aug 2021

Hogg PW (2007 (loose-leaf updated 2015)) Constitutional law of Canada, vol I. Thomson Reuters Canada, Toronto

Holmwood J, Plank S (2018) B.C. government, First Nations will share gaming revenue, co-develop legislation to implement UN declaration. B.C. Office of the Premier, 29 November 2018

Ives JW (2015) Moving toward repatriation. We are coming home: repatriation and the restoration of Blackfoot cultural confidence. Athabasca University Press, Edmonton

Janes RR (2015) The Blackfoot Repatriation: a personal epilogue. We are coming home: repatriation and the restoration of Blackfoot cultural confidence

Lamirande T (2019) Indigenous rights framework far from dead as Trudeau government rolls it out in pieces. Nation to Nation

Millen R, Adkins S (2018) BC treaty process and the realization of free, prior and informed consent. Blake, Cassels & Graydon LLP, pp 1–14

O'Neil P, Shaw R (2016) Yale First Nation puts hold on treaty implementation. Vancouver Sun, 2 November 2016

Pasternak S (2020) B.C. might want to align with UNDRIP, but does UNDRIP align with B.C.? In King H (ed) The UN Declaration on the rights of indigenous peoples in Canada: lessons from B.C. Yellowhead Institute (Special Report December 2020), pp 17–19

Royal Commission on Aboriginal Peoples (1996) Gathering strength, Vol 3. RCAP, Ottawa, Canada

Rustad J, Phillip S, Chamberlin B, Wilson J, John E, Casimer C, Phillips R, Gottfriedson BC S (2015) Proposed commitment document.

Sayers J (2020) Opportunities and barriers for the B.C. declaration of rights act. Yellowhead Institute, pp 13–15. December 2020, Special Report. https://yellowheadinstitute.org/wp-content/uploads/2020/12/yellowhead-institute-bc-undrip-report-12.20-compressed.pdf

Tripartite Working Group (2002) Improving the treaty process. Report of the Tripartite Working Group, 25 February 2002

Turner C, Fondahl G (2015) "Overlapping Claims" to territory confronting treaty-making in British Columbia: causes and implications. The Canadian Geographer/Le Géographe canadien 59 (4):474–488

Yellow Old Woman H (2015) Bringing back Iitskinaiksi at Siksika. In: Conaty GT (ed) We are coming home: repatriation and the restoration of Blackfoot cultural confidence. Athabasca University Press, Edmonton, pp 183–204

Chapter 8
Evaluating the Position of Indigenous Sacred Cultural Heritage in Canadian Law

8.1 Introduction[1]

Part III analyses how Canadian law regulates the relationship between Indigenous Peoples and their sacred cultural heritage, in particular, in how far it allows for the repatriation of sacred cultural heritage to Indigenous communities. Both federal and provincial law were considered and the special position of Indigenous Peoples under the Canadian constitution was taken into account. Next to these legal aspects, repatriation in Canada has been supported by museum action, which is reflected in the analysis of museum statutes and codes in Chaps. 6 and 7. All of the above helps to answer the research questions that underlie this country analysis. First, how is the repatriation of sacred cultural heritage regulated in Canadian law: is there a distinct approach or model? Second, are these rules and policies in accordance with Canada's obligations under international human rights law? Third, are there any lessons that can be learned from this analysis for the cultural heritage law and policy that we examined? Here, first the results of the previous two chapters will be summarized to show how Canadian law regulates repatriation. Afterwards, the analysis conducted in Chaps. 6 and 7 will be used to evaluate in how far Canadian law is in line with the human rights law principles that were set out in Chap. 2.

Please note that this chapter adopts the capitalization of the terms Indigenous Peoples and Indigenous (except for when spelled differently in citations) for reasons explained in Chap. 1. Similarly Aboriginal is capitalized unless the lower case was used in a citation.

---

[1] Please be aware that this chapter functions as the final synthesizing analysis and conclusion to Part III. The analysis and bulk of the sources are located in Chaps. 6 and 7.

V. Tünsmeyer, *Repatriation of Sacred Indigenous Cultural Heritage and the Law*,
Studies in Art, Heritage, Law and the Market 3,
https://doi.org/10.1007/978-3-030-89047-6_8

8.2 Existing Repatriation Efforts Through Process-Oriented Models

To answer the first question, repatriation within Canada largely occurs on an individual level between a museum and a community. Legally, the federal level may have the competence to legislate on matters that relate to Aboriginal peoples, but it lacks the constitutional competence to legislate on property and provincial civil rights matters. The Supreme Court has affirmed that the protection of cultural heritage within the province is firmly within the provinces' legal competences. As this is unlikely to change, federal legislation comparable to NAGPRA is therefore quite simply not a realistic legal solution to repatriation demands within the country. Even if this option was legally possible; the cultural and legal differences between different first nations and the different provincial heritage legislation cast doubt on whether a federal heritage repatriation act would be advisable. It was shown how, for British Columbia, the absence of historic treaties affect contemporary heritage rights and repatriation negotiations today. The final treaties that have been negotiated cover an array of cultural rights and even feature repatriation provisions. Federal repatriation legislation would end up as an additional factor in an already complex web of legal relationships that differ from nation to nation; it would not simplify repatriation requests for First Nations. This is not to say that the absence of federal action does not have consequences. NAGPRA provides for a clear right to repatriation. This strengthens the position of the Indigenous community. Moreover, because of the existence of the federal legal framework, federal funds were set aside to support repatriation endeavours. This is noticeably lacking in the Canadian context. Of course, the absence of a federal law does not mean that the governments could not establish a repatriation fund. Along the same lines, a clear federal policy that acknowledges the existence of an Aboriginal right to the use and control of a sacred object would go a long way to strengthen the position of Indigenous claimants in the provinces. This initiative could guide communities through the steps and the evidence they need to bring to have such a right recognized by the government. Given the fact that the judiciary has reigned almost supreme over the legal rules that govern the field of Aboriginal rights, clear federal support for the existence of such a right would be an important measure to protect s.35 rights.

In the absence of such measures, the main power to regulate repatriation legally will remain with the provinces and without any provincial framework with the individual museum. Since the adoption of the Museum Task Force Report in the early 1990s, Canadian museums have taken important steps to collaborate with First Nations on heritage matters, in general, and to agree on custodial measures for sacred objects and repatriation measures in particular. One of the laws examined was even adopted in response to museum negotiations and efforts, namely the repatriation legislation in Alberta. The First Nations Sacred Ceremonial Objects Repatriation Act provides the legal possibility for museums and Indigenous communities to negotiate repatriation, including a more specific legal arrangement that can be adopted by means of a regulation. The wording of the repatriation law still leaves a lot of power

Table 8.1 Summary of Alberta repatriation framework

Comparative indicators/Country and Repatriation law	Canada–Alberta [Alberta Regulation 96/2004, Blackfoot First Nations Sacred Ceremonial Objects Repatriation Regulation]
Objectives of law evidenced in legislative history of law	Gives effect to an agreement already negotiated, namely between the Blackfoot First Nation and Glenbow Museum. Also, harmonize museum goals with First Nation revitalization desire;[a] adopt basic repatriation principles, amend act of museum with large ethnographic collection (Glenbow Institute).
Definition of Indigenous Peoples within act	[FNSCORA] As defined in regulations. [96/2004] very specific, only 3 Blackfoot First Nations listed
Definition of Indigenous religious heritage	[FNSCORA] Very specific: past usage + only if in possession of 2 museums or Crown + *vital* to practice of Indigenous religious practice.
Mandated outcome?	Yes, giving effect to a negotiated agreement, repatriation of very specific items. Outcome negotiated before the law was passed, law only passed to ensure that agreement could be realized.
Mandated procedure? What type of procedure?	No. Incorporates governmental approval for previous negotiations.
Consultation within process and/or FPIC	Incorporated after the fact. Negotiations with a small number of Indigenous communities took place before passing the act.
Final authority to decide on repatriation request	Designated Minister or person so authorized by minister
Dispute settlement body and its composition	No. [But normal court avenues open]
Financial support provided to participants	No, regulation specifically excludes governmental liability for costs incurred in the repatriation process.

[a]First Nations Sacred Ceremonial Objects Repatriation Act, RSA 2000, c F-14, <https://canlii.ca/t/52vmw> retrieved on 2021-08-20, preamble

with the minister, as was already criticized during its legislative process. Overall, however, it signals legal support for individual repatriations which can again strengthen the position of Indigenous communities.

The goal of the analysis of these different repatriation laws was to distil different repatriation models, which may provide useful lessons for future repatriation efforts. The two provinces regulate repatriation very differently. In Alberta, summarized in the first Table 8.1, repatriation was bottom-up, between the museum and the Indigenous community. The agreement was thus specific to the actors involved and the contested parts of the collections and could be tailor-made to fit their needs. Moreover, the (relatively) close proximity between Indigenous community and museum in these bottom-up negotiations decreased the risk of miscommunication. Face to face meetings are easier to arrange, and can happen more frequently, if the distance between community and museum is manageable. The establishment of trust paved the way for a better collaboration in the future. Moreover, because the negotiations take place 'on the ground', they were less politicized than in the case of the BC treaty negotiation process. Their explicit focus on specific objects meant that they were also quicker. The success of this model very much depends on the willingness of the cultural institution, however. Moreover, additional legal hurdles that are likely to exist for public museums that wish to deaccession parts of their collection still need to be eliminated after an agreement has been reached. The resulting ex post legislative approval bears the risk of changing the agreements made. In Alberta, this delayed legal approval of the agreement entailed the desire to create a broader repatriation law. However, the danger is that the negotiations are simply made applicable to a wide group of applicants. This means that the necessary consultation and dialogue phase to draft an appropriate legal framework is skipped. This also occurred in Alberta.

In British Columbia, summarized in Table 8.2, modern treaty negotiations can succeed in securing the repatriation of Indigenous cultural heritage and protecting a

Table 8.2 Summary of British Columbia repatriation framework

Comparative indicators/Country and Repatriation law	Canada, British Columbia [British Columbia Treaty Negotiation Process]
Objectives of law evidenced in legislative history of law	Reconciliation of three governmental entities: First Nations, Canada and British Columbia. Explicit aim to forge a new relationship, to settle rights and provide for legal and economic certainty and to improve the situation of First Nations.
Definition of Indigenous Peoples within act/process	Very broad/ inclusive, Aboriginal governing body established by Indigenous community within their traditional territories within British Columbia.
Definition of Indigenous religious heritage	Not applicable, to be decided at negotiation tables where applicable.
Mandated outcome?	Not specifically. Process designed to end in the adoption of a treaty but what to be included in the treaty is decided in negotiations.
Mandated procedure? What type of procedure?	Yes. Treaty negotiations of a very broad scope, encompassing land claims, cultural rights etc.
Consultation within process and/or FPIC	Yes. Consultation is a mandatory part of the process; the process also enables the realization of FPIC. Problems exist however with regard to overlapping claims.
Final authority to decide on repatriation request	Not possible to determine. Organic treaty negotiation process among three governments that enter government to government negotiations.
Dispute settlement body and its composition	For different types of disputes on the treaties after they have been negotiated, the treaties include provisions on dispute resolution.[a]
Financial support provided to participants	Important changes after decades of process. System used to be up to 80% loan advancement with a minimum of 20% non-repayable contribution funding split between the province and the federal level. Since April 2018, shift to 100% non-repayable contribution funding, in 2019 loan forgiveness for outstanding loans was announced.

[a]Maa-Nulth Final Agreement ch.25, Tsawwassen Final Agreement ch.27, Tla'amin Final Agreement, ch.26

number of important cultural rights at the same time upon the treaty's entry into force. Yet, these are lengthy, cost-intensive and cultural rights still need to be protected in the interim. To be fair, however, their wide scope does offer the chance to reconsider the relationship between the different (legal) cultures in its entirety. This cannot be achieved without the investment of necessary resources and good faith in the negotiations. Both negotiations are also likely to occur behind closed doors. While this may be crucial to the success of the negotiations, it also means that there is no societal confrontation with the historical reasons that make these negotiations necessary. In Canada the latter arguably occurred regardless, namely because of the work of important commissions that documented, analysed and confronted the country's colonial past, notably the Truth and Reconciliation Commission.

8.3 Comparative Evaluation in Light of International Human Rights Law

8.3.1 Applying Standards and Obligations from the Human Rights Toolbox to the Canadian Legal Heritage Context

To answer the second question, the findings of the country analysis will be combined with the results of the human rights analysis conducted in the first part of this volume. This toolbox contains a number of principles that can guide the implementation of Indigenous human rights within national laws on cultural heritage and the tests that can be applied to evaluate whether a measure that limits a particular cultural right amounts to a violation of the international standard. As was the case for the United States, first the principles will be addressed. To help the reader, each principle is stated briefly, together with its legal basis, before it is applied to the Canadian legal context.

1. *Respect, protect and fulfil Indigenous religious beliefs also in designing a repatriation framework so long as these are in accordance with international human rights standards.*

Application to the Canada: In Alberta, sacredness is defined by the elders, knowledgeable religious Indigenous practitioners. This is both for the application of FNSCORA and by the RAM to decide on access requests for religious objects. Within the BC treaty process, sacred objects that are included in repatriation agreements appear to be identified in collaboration with Indigenous communities. The RBCM also actively collaborates with Indigenous communities in the repatriation process, as well as agreeing on specific care protocols for religious cultural heritage. While the conditions for a successful repatriation request with the CMH appear very restrictive, there appears no definition of sacredness from the 'outside' and the possibility to decide on custodial agreements with Indigenous Peoples is expressly mentioned.

2. *The repatriation framework and other examined heritage frameworks have to incorporate consultation of Indigenous rights for measures affecting their cultural rights and FPIC "[w]henever the preservation of their cultural resources, especially those associated with their way of life and cultural expression, are at risk".*

Application to Canada: The federal export legislation does not consider Indigenous interests in the protection of cultural heritage. Under the legislation, important Indigenous cultural heritage can thus be exported contrary to the wishes of its source community, which violates the community's right of FPIC. However, this is slightly mitigated as the case law has established the duty to consult Indigenous Peoples in decisions that affect their Aboriginal and treaty rights. If a treaty right to a heritage resource exists, for example, there is an obligation to consult prior to issuing export permission. This is also the case where an Aboriginal right to the heritage can be established. This process is however uncertain and may require litigation to realize the right. Moreover, in so far as this can be observed from the analysis, the jurisprudence on permissible infringements of Aboriginal and treaty rights does not align fully with UNDRIP. In looking at the Aboriginal rights canon and discussion as part of the context of heritage legislation and repatriation, some tentative remarks can be made: From the analysis it appears that the areas of FPIC and permissible infringements on treaty rights in the case law are especially problematic. For example, one may ask whether a unilateral right to infringe upon a treaty (even subject to conditions that include consultation) in effect respect Art.37 (1) UNDRIP. This has been amply discussed by First Nations scholars themselves and in the Aboriginal rights literature. For present purposes it did however require repetition as the problems that exist in the heritage legislation are both mirrored elsewhere and appear to be part of wider, systemic problem. To bring this back to the duty to consult, it therefore does not relieve Canada of its obligation to amend its export regulation accordingly as case-law has created a situation in which the duty to consult based on precedence is insufficient protection of the aboriginal right to heritage without changes to the legislation. In British Columbia, the provincial heritage legislation provides the opportunity for Indigenous Peoples to enter agreements on heritage matters, thereby participating in the decision-making process. It is under-utilized, however. Next to this, the treaty negotiations in British Columbia do seek to operationalize Indigenous participation in decision-making, including with respect to cultural resources.

3. *Repatriation of sacred objects guarantees Indigenous right to control of sacred object. Please note: This principle identifies one possible measure within a wide margin of discretion; there is currently no obligation to repatriate sacred objects under international law.*

Application to Canada: This principle appears to have been partially realized within Canada. There are a number of repatriation programmes available within

Canada, depending on the identity of the holding institution, the identity of the Indigenous community requesting the object and the location of both object and community. For example, repatriation possibilities differ substantially between Alberta and Canada. All of this also means that the chances of regaining a religious cultural object are not the same for each Indigenous community within Canada.

4. *States may not interfere with Indigenous right to practise and/ or revitalize their cultural traditions and customs unless this limitation is in accordance with international human rights law.*

Application to Canada: As far as can be established from the research undertaken, the federal and provincial governments do not appear to be unduly interfering with the Indigenous efforts to revitalize their cultural traditions. On the federal level, forced assimilation laws that targeted cultural practices and heritage have been repealed since 1951. In terms of federal support for cultural revitalization efforts, the Museum Task Force Report of the 1990s demanded a number of changes which would have supported the revitalization of Indigenous cultures. However, while museums took action on a number of points, federal support in this area was somewhat lacking. Recently, the federal level has signalled its intent to implement UNDRIP. This has already led to some financial changes, so there is hope that further measures will be taken to fulfil this right. Amendments to the CPEIA that consider Indigenous interests in their heritage as separate interests would be another step to support revitalization. A legal area that has a significant negative impact on revitalization efforts is the SCC's understanding of s.35 protecting rights that existed at the time of the constitutional amendment. The effects of this have been mitigated somewhat by requiring an express extinguishment and by protecting the right in its pre-contact form absent extinguishment. However, given the long period of forced assimilation with legal and policy measures which very clearly sought to extinguish rights, this approach remains a barrier to revitalization.

In Alberta, there is no consideration of Indigenous interests in their heritage under the provincial heritage legislation. Apart from this legislation, there is possible room for negotiations that protect Indigenous heritage that is important for revitalization efforts. However, the act vests all power quite clearly in the non-Indigenous government, which impairs the fulfilment of the right. In British Columbia, by contrast, there is an express governmental desire to support revitalization—including the desire to implement UNDRIP. At this point, it is still unclear how this will translate into clear legislative and policy measures with respect to cultural heritage. It is clear that the provincial heritage framework requires some changes to support revitalization efforts, most notably a clear policy that prioritizes cooperative agreements with Indigenous communities under section 4 BCHCA and the incorporation of Indigenous heritage values within the legislative framework. Without these changes, the act will continue to grant all decision power to the provincial government and Indigenous sacred cultural heritage will be not be protected sufficiently against desecration, i.e. in the course of development. This inability to protect their heritage undermines revitalization efforts. Within the BC treaty process, cultural rights are negotiated and protected in the final treaties in a way that supports revitalization efforts. However, it takes a long time to reach this stage of the process and interim measures protecting the contested resources—including cultural heritage—are crucial.

Moreover, the sincerity of the provincial declaration in supporting cultural revitalization efforts may be doubted in light of the provincial decision to develop a ski resort, including the use of waste water which leads to the desecration of Indigenous sacred sites making it impossible for Ktunaxa practitioners to continue manifesting their religion, casts a shadow on this approach.[2] One may also argue that the Supreme Court's application of section 2(a) CCRF deprives nature-based religious traditions of effective protection for their right to manifest under the Charter. This represents a substantial interference with the right to religion and the right to revitalize cultural traditions. Therefore, while the governmental record with respect to respecting Indigenous revitalization efforts currently appears to be good rather than bad, the record is mixed and can change quickly.

5. *Support Indigenous right to practise and/ or revitalize their cultural traditions by creating favourable conditions in which to exercise this right.*

Application to Canada: On the federal level, it appears as if the federal government is currently undertaking some projects that actively support Indigenous revitalization efforts (which does of course not mean that Indigenous rights are not violated or limited). Similarly, in Alberta there is still room to make the existing repatriation legislation widely applicable to all Indigenous communities, but the continued existence of the repatriation act remains a positive sign. In British Columbia, in recent years there has been an increase in agreements also made outside the treaty process which support Indigenous efforts at self-governance and control over cultural heritage. Moreover, the efforts to find a way to implement UNDRIP within the province allows us to hope that the province will not unduly interfere with revitalization efforts. Yet, the provincial decision to develop a ski resort in the Grizzly Bear Spirit case raises some doubt as to the sustainability and sincerity of these efforts. Also, it has to be remembered that actions have to be taken because of the substantial gap in the rights protection afforded to Indigenous individuals compared to other citizens. The BCHA is still underutilized and past efforts have not always led to actual improvements for Indigenous individuals. Therefore, while the governmental record with respect to respecting Indigenous revitalization efforts currently appears to be good rather than bad, this can change quickly.

6. *Duty to respect and protect cultural heritage and to mitigate effects of globalization and privatization on culture of marginalized and minority communities, including Indigenous Peoples.*[3]

[2] Ktunaxa Nation v British Columbia (Forests, Lands and Natural Resource Operations), 2017 SCC 54 (CanLII), see Chap. 6 Sect. 6.3.3 for further discussion.

[3] CESCR, General Comment No.21, para 50(a), (b).

Application to Canada: Federal export legislation protects sacred ceremonial objects insufficiently. While an Aboriginal object is protected by virtue of being sacred, regardless of its potential market value, the law does not really recognize Indigenous communities as independent actors under the framework (other than the agency practice of accepting Aboriginal governing bodies as public institutions that can apply to hold a particular piece of movable heritage). Moreover, sacred Indigenous heritage is only explicitly protected as archaeological material. This means that it has to have been buried for at least 75 years and excavated to be considered. The framework also does not protect relatively new sacred objects. Section 4 (3) CPEIA excludes objects younger than 50 years old or whose maker is still alive. Given the continuing demand for Indigenous/Aboriginal cultural heritage on the art market, both flaws need to be remedied in order to protect the Indigenous right to manifest their religion better.

7. *Ensure that Indigenous sacred objects receive special protection under national heritage law but that this does not prevent access to heritage by its Indigenous community. State must actively take steps to eliminate all barriers that prevent Indigenous Peoples for accessing their heritage.*[4] *Conditions to access are permissible, these have to satisfy the test charted below for limitations on right of access to sacred heritage.*

Application to Canada: There is no specific access prohibition that arises out of federal law. As a result, it is the responsibility of individual museums and government agencies to provide for access and/or repatriation policies. The national Canadian Museum of History has done this and also expressly mentions deciding on other caretaking arrangements for sacred materials if desired.

8. *Take measures to prevent conduct aimed desecration of cultural heritage.*[5] *This includes to encourage museums not to display human remains and sacred objects unless with FPIC of affected community.*[6]

Application to Canada: The ethical considerations of museum storage and display so far seem to have mostly arisen from within the Canadian museum community rather than national legal or policy measures. An important step was taken by the Canadian Museums Association and the Assembly of First Nations with the creation of the joint Task Force in the 1990s. However, the renewed governmental commitment to reconciliation may serve as an important factor in further improving the relationship between Indigenous peoples, museums and the museum public. As a result of this commitment, for example, the CMA has received governmental funding to work cooperatively with Indigenous Peoples. This undoubtedly

[4] CESCR, General Comment No 21, para 55(d). Shaheed (2011), p. 18, para 68.

[5] Pineschi (2012), p. 41.

[6] Compare Daes Principles and Guidelines, Guideline 21: "Under no circumstances should human remains or any other sacred elements of an indigenous peoples' heritage be publicly displayed, except in a manner deemed appropriate by the peoples concerned."

can help in further improving museum practice. It thus appears as if the federal government is implementing this principle.

9. *The state has a duty to refrain from undue interference with the Indigenous right to their heritage and to protect them from undue interference by third parties. It is also under a positive duty to progressively create conditions in which Indigenous Peoples can control etc. their heritage according to their own traditions.*

Application to Canada: On the federal level, s.91 of the Indian Act protects a select number of cultural heritage objects located on reserve lands from trade. Sacred cultural objects are not included as a category. Moreover, permission for title transfer rests with a federal minister, namely the Minister of Indian Affairs and Northern Development. Therefore, while there is some protection from outside interference, there is no protection from governmental interference in this respect, breaching this principle. It opens up a space for a violation of Art.27 ICCPR by the Canadian government, depending on the circumstances of the individual case. In Alberta, the provincial heritage legislation neither respects nor protect the Indigenous right to their heritage. In fact, it does not consider Indigenous cultural heritage as being of interest to a specific subgroup of people at all. Title to all archaeological resources discovered after 1978 rests in the Crown and Indigenous communities are not considered (they might try to apply as custodians for their cultural heritage). Moreover, all decision powers rest with the provincial minister under the Act. In British Columbia, the treaty process and negotiation with Indigenous partners addresses a wide range of substantive issues, including culture and cultural rights. The concluded treaties include the right of Indigenous communities to their heritage and address artefacts, heritage sites, language and culturally relevant rights such as harvesting materials necessary for sacred ceremonies. Outside of the treaty process, the provincial heritage legislation allows for some consideration of Indigenous interests but it does not guarantee an Indigenous right to their heritage.

10. *The state has a duty to refrain from undue interference with right to cultural identity, this includes a prohibition of enforced assimilation. There are three connected duties: First, the obligation not to impose definition of Indigenous identity from the outside. Second, the positive duty to protect the right-holders from undue interference by third parties, including duty to ensure that decision to identify as Indigenous does not result in discrimination. Third, the positive duty to take steps to create favourable conditions for Indigenous Peoples to preserve and develop their cultural identity. This encompasses a wide margin of possible, discretionary measures.*

Application to Canada: As was described in the beginning of this section, the Indigenous Peoples of Canada have survived a long history of forced assimilation due to the country's colonial history. Reminders of this are everywhere, including in the law. The Indian Act is a clear example of this. Even though it was redrafted completely in 1951 and amended several times, it has shaped Indigenous (self-) identification significantly by incorporating a federal definition of who classifies as Indian for the purposes of federal law, which continues to violate international human rights standards. It has also included discriminatory provisions in the recognition of federal Indian status between Indigenous men and women and, despite changes to the provision, the effects continue to be felt. The Canadian state has also not protected Indigenous peoples from outside interference with their cultural identity.[7] These actions continue to negatively affect the way in which Indigenous peoples can enjoy their cultural rights within Canada, including the right to cultural identity. However, the federal government has confronted some of the colonial past and steps are being taken to create favourable conditions for Indigenous peoples to preserve and develop their cultural identity. This has included changes to the Indian Act and also the option for the Indigenous community to opt out of parts of the Indian Act in favour of increased self-governance of their lands. Moreover, steps are being taken in response to the Residential School Settlement Agreement and the reports of the national Truth and Reconciliation Commission.

11. *The State has a duty to respect Indigenous right to their own legal traditions*[8] *in accordance with international human rights law.*

Application to Canada: It is impossible to evaluate on a general level given the vast difference between provinces and different treaties covering different First Nations. There are two areas of concern that were examined in federal law. With respect to the Aboriginal rights doctrine, the jurisprudence requirements call for Aboriginal claimants to translate their cultural-legal claims into common law legal concepts. Given that Indigenous legal traditions are thus made subordinate to the common law system and a right once proven can be unilaterally changed by the federal or provincial government (albeit subject to limitations), this does not seem to qualify as respect for Indigenous legal traditions. However, whether the doctrine will in fact lead to a violation of Art.27 ICCPR will depend on its individual application by the respective Canadian authority. Second, under the Indian Act, the band council has the power to make bylaws under s.81 of the Indian Act. However, the band council was initially created by the Indian Act and the legislative powers are very restricted and decided upon by the non-Indigenous federal Parliament. This hardly qualifies as respect for the Indigenous right to their own legal traditions. The repatriation law in Alberta is phrased in a comparatively broad way, which would allow for different repatriation methods depending on the specific legal and cultural traditions of the community concerned. However, the overall power to reject an application rests with the responsible provincial minister. Moreover, there is only

[7] As one prominent example, outside interference by churches was sponsored by the government in the case of residential schools which forcefully tried to assimilate Indigenous children. These operated for more than 150 years; the last residential school closed in 1986. In residential schools, Indigenous children were subjected to widespread emotional, psychological, sexual, and physical abuse. For more information see: http://nctr.ca [last accessed 19.08.2021].

[8] Art.34 UNDRIP describes a number of elements of such legal traditions: Indigenous Peoples have the right to promote, develop and maintain their institutional structures and their distinctive customs, spirituality, traditions, procedures, practices and, in the cases where they exist, juridical systems or customs, in accordance with international human rights standards.

one operationalizing regulation in force to date. For Indigenous communities other than the Blackfoot First Nations, it is therefore of no use. There are thus further steps to take for the provincial government in fulfilling this dimension of Art.27 ICCPR. In British Columbia, the negotiated treaties that were examined have incorporated law-making powers, *inter-alia* for cultural heritage on Indigenous lands. There thus appears to be at least some respect for Indigenous legal traditions, including their revitalization. Overall, there seems to be a renewed emphasis on Indigenous self-governance within Canadian law and policy at the moment, which includes Indigenous peoples using their own legal traditions. There seems to be at least partial respect for Indigenous legal traditions in some Canadian legal instruments.[9]

8.3.2 Measures Limiting the Right to Use and Control of Sacred Objects

8.3.2.1 Right of Access to and Use of Sacred Objects

A violation of a specific human right can only be established within a given context. For this reason, here, different constellations will be considered that can illustrate the differences and obstacles that Indigenous communities may face when they seek to access and use their sacred objects.

Three scenarios will be considered: first, a First Nation other than the Blackfeet applies for access to and use of a sacred object held in the Royal Alberta Museum; second, a First Nation from British Columbia that is engaged in the treaty process seeks access to and use of objects located in the RBCM (B); third, a First Nation from British Columbia that is not engaged in the treaty process seeks access to and use of objects located in the RBCM (C). To evaluate their compliance with human rights standards the test and figure developed in Chap. 2 will be used.

8.3.2.2 Application of the Framework to Alberta

Both provincial museums in Alberta are covered by the provincial repatriation legislation. The Blackfoot First Nations negotiated the return of specific heritage objects. This was legalized by means of a regulation. Their access to and use of these objects is therefore guaranteed. Sacred objects are covered only if they are *vital* to the ceremony. As for other Indigenous communities within Alberta, many appear to be engaged in repatriation negotiations. The legislative history of the act suggests that, should they desire to structure repatriation by means of an act that operationalizes

[9]There are also specific Indigenous courts which incorporate elders and Indigenous traditions in criminal law cases, the Gladue courts, that operate on restorative justice principles. These are, however, outside the focus of the present research.

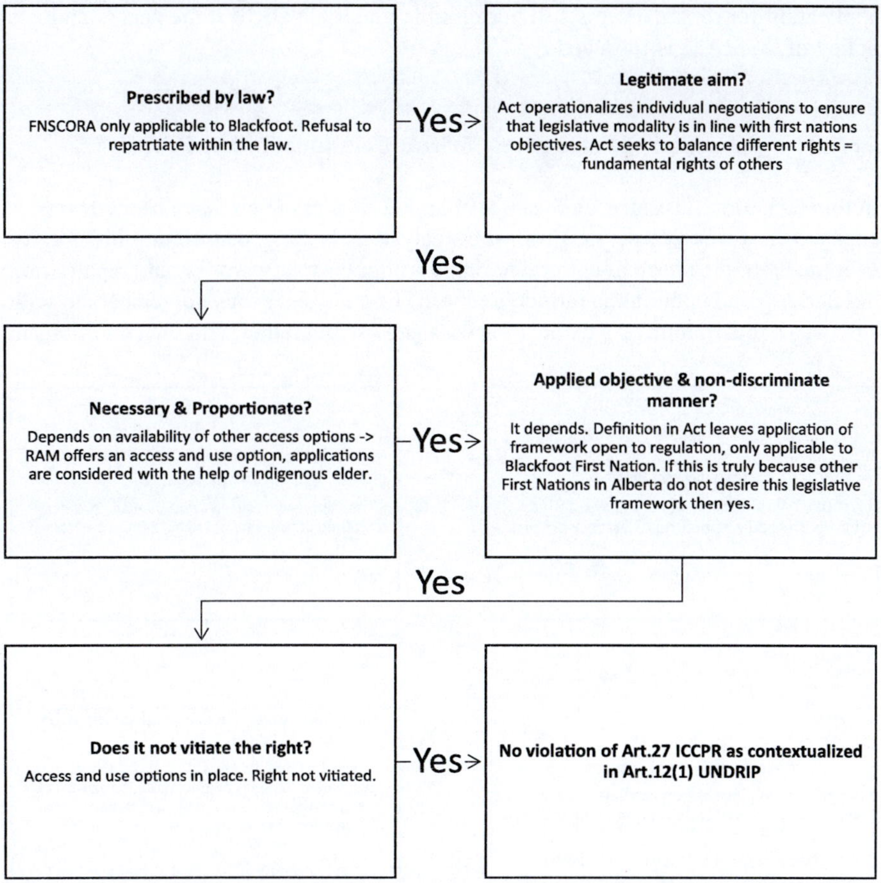

Fig. 8.1 Does a decision by RAM not to repatriate an item to a First Nation other than the Blackfoot violate Art.27 UNDRIP?

FNSCORA for their particular community, this option may be available. However, no second operationalizing regulation exists, which means that other Indigenous individuals cannot make use of the repatriation act. Nevertheless, there is the possibility of access to and use of sacred ceremonial items that are located with RAM if individuals are accompanied by an elder. The museum decides on applications for access on an individual basis. This makes it impossible to assess in how far the right to access and use of objects is guaranteed. The information made available by the RAM does suggest that the museum actively supports the implementation of Art.11 and Art.12 UNDRIP. This indicates that, at least for the collection of sacred objects that is located with the RAM, the right to access and use of sacred objects is being realized. Considering a hypothetical situation in which an application for repatriation by an Indigenous individual who is not Blackfoot is denied, as Fig. 8.1 illustrates, even if no repatriation is negotiated, a decision to reject an application for repatriation is still permissible under UNDRIP if the access and use policy of the RAM is followed.

8.3.2.3 Application of Framework British Columbia Treaty Process

In this scenario, illustrated by means of Fig. 8.2, it is assumed that a treaty nation is engaged in a treaty process. From the analysis it is clear that communities have negotiated for the return of cultural heritage within the treaty process and repatriation has been agreed upon in the ratified treaties. The analysis is thus not concerned with a denial of repatriation or a denial of access and use but rather with the conditions in

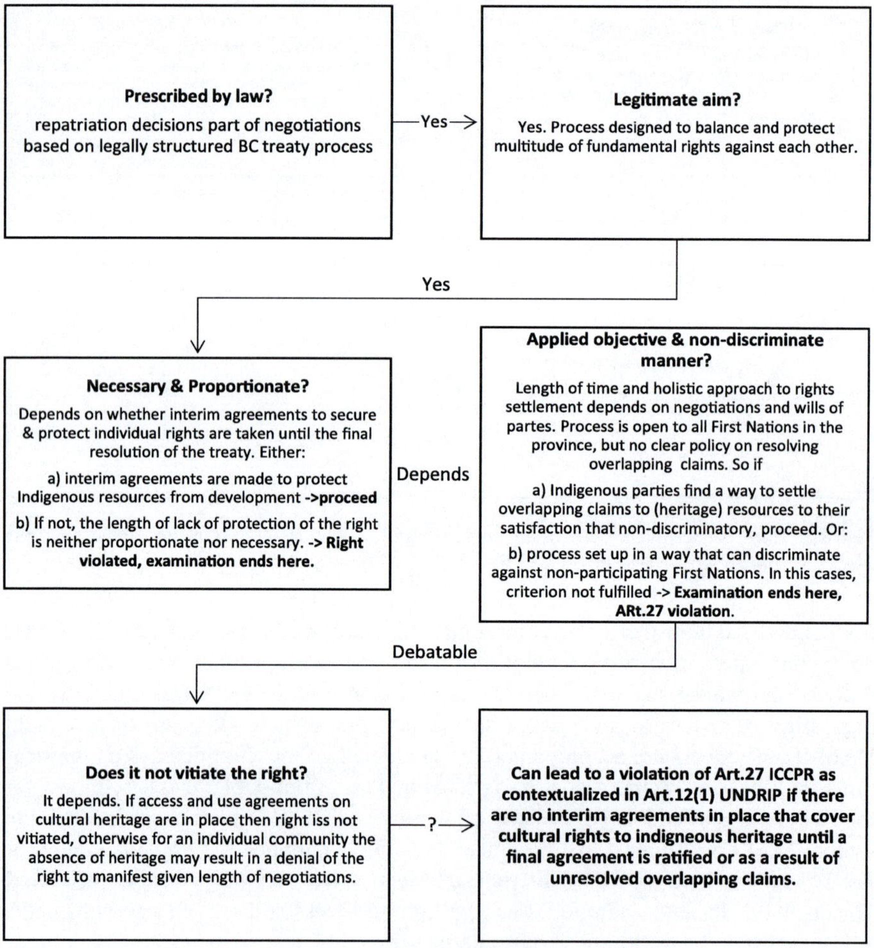

Fig. 8.2 Does the B.C. treaty process violate Art.27 UNDRIP in so far as it relates to sacred cultural heritage?

which the negotiations take place. This refers to the considerable time until the right is guaranteed, and the costs of the negotiation that communities had to incur until recently. Having to wait several years to over two decades before an item may be repatriated severely limits the right of access to and use of the item. The limitation is prescribed by law and the RBCM may not take steps to undermine the treaty process. It is clearly instructed to return an item within the process only if it is subject to an agreement and the conditions within an agreement have been fulfilled. The limitation also pursues a legitimate aim to protect the treaty process which seeks to settle outstanding Indigenous rights and reconcile Indigenous rights with non-Indigenous rights. The limitation can also be argued to be necessary, given that to allow outside repatriation agreements while cultural rights negotiations are ongoing at the same time can lead to distrust among the actors and risk the achievement of the final treaty. However, if there is no access and use agreement in place to bridge the time until the treaty has been negotiated, then the measure is not proportionate simply because of the duration of the negotiations. As the Human Rights Committee observed, negotiations are not analogous to legal remedies and their duration can mean that they are unreasonably prolonged to be effective remedies for a specific individual's rights breach.[10] In the present context, a less restrictive measure would be available, namely interim agreements that cover access and use of objects during the negotiation period. If these are not concluded, the right of access to and use of the heritage has been violated.[11]

Assuming such an agreement is in place the next step of the test becomes relevant. The measure is based on objective reasons—the time period arises because of the difficulty of the individual negotiation tables. It can also be argued that it is applied in a non-discriminatory manner, as all First Nations who enter into treaty negotiations face this risk. However, in the case of overlapping claims, the question arises how these are settled. The BCTC has expressed its preference for First Nations negotiating overlapping claims with each other.[12] While it may make the process less predictable, this is an important element of respecting Indigenous self-determination. This presumes however, that no exclusive claims are awarded until claims are resolved by the involved Indigenous nations. Some authors have pointed out that this is not the case. The process thus potentially disadvantages Indigenous peoples who do not participate in the process (or may only decide to do so in the future), given that Indigenous understandings of territoriality may not/do not overlap with Canadian governmental understandings of exclusive territory. Moreover, assimilation policies in the past have led to frequent relocations and shifting within

---

[10] HRCee Communication No. 879/1999, para 8.4.

[11] This is supported by a decision on admissibility of the IACHR. It judged the treaty process as being insufficient to guarantee an Indigenous community's land claims, partially because of its length. It, *inter alia*, commented on the necessity of interim measures. See IACHR, Report Nr. 105/09 Hul'qumi'num Treaty Group v Canada. Admissibility [30.10.2009]. See Chap. 7, Sect. 7.2.3.

[12] British Columbia Treaty Commission (2014).

groups, also leading to overlapping claims.[13] If there is no clear policy on how to deal with overlapping claims, as the decision of the Yale First Nation to withdraw from the process suggests, this is a fundamental weakness of the process. It also means that it is not applied in an objective manner in a way that would satisfy the Art.27 ICCPR test. The last element of the test would be whether it possibly vitiates the right. Given the assumption that an access and use agreement has been reached for the duration of the negotiation, the limitation is reasonable and the right has not been violated.

8.3.2.4 Application of Framework to British Columbia Beyond Treaty Process to a Sample Case

In this case, illustrated by Fig. 8.3 an Indigenous community seeks the return of a sacred object from the RBCM. The RBCM is legally classified as a governmental agent and its actions can thus be attributed to the government, including any potential human rights limitations. Assuming that the object stems from the period during which cultural objects are most likely to have been taken by force/under duress or other questionable means, namely 1884–1951, in this case the material falls under the repatriation policy and a community can request the heritage from the museum. The museum will decide on a case-by-case basis, but it is "committed to the originating community acquired under circumstances that render the Museum's claim invalid".[14] It is important that the museum does not require illegality at the time of acquisition. Instead the policy seems to consider the unethical acquisition to invalidate its claim to a particular piece. If the museum agrees to the repatriation request, which seems likely for a substantiated and documented request, then the right of access and use will be fulfilled in any event.

How does this change if the museum denies the request and only allows an access and use agreement? In this case, the limitation on access and use is set out in the custodial agreement. It is prescribed by law, namely by the power of the museum to decide on whether or not to dispose of a piece of heritage,[15] and it pursues a legitimate aim, namely the conservation of cultural heritage to protect the cultural rights of other residents of the province. Whether or not the decision is necessary cannot be invalidated without knowing the reasons behind the refusal. Assuming that it was necessary, then it would still have to be proportionate. If the museum offers the possibility for an access and use agreement, then the decision to grant limited access will fulfil the proportionality requirement. If the limitations arise because of the condition of the object, for example, the limitation would also be based on objective reasons and applied in a non-discriminatory manner. Lastly, as

[13] Turner and Fondahl (2015), p. 475.

[14] Royal British Columbia Museum (2018), p. 5.

[15] S.5(2)(b) Museum Act [S.B.C. 2003], c.12, current as to 10.07.2019.

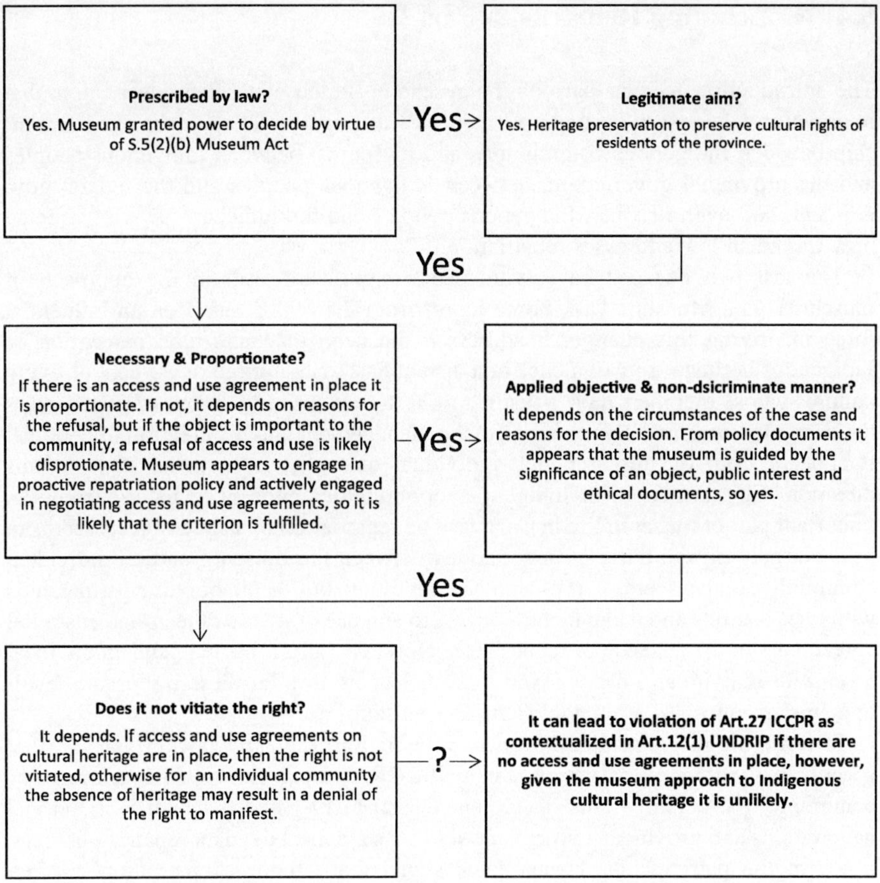

Fig. 8.3 Would a decision by the RBCM to refuse repatriation violate Art.27 UNDRIP?

access and use are still protected, the exercise of the right is not denied. The limitation is permissible.

If there is no access or use agreement, the evaluation of the necessity and proportionate criterion would depend on the specific circumstances. If it is motivated by concerns for the physical integrity of the object, then it will fulfil the necessity criterion. However, depending on the importance of the object for the community, it might not be proportionate to deny it access to its heritage in order to allow other visitors the possibility to view the object that are much less connected to it. Moreover, if the object is crucial to the exercise of a specific practice or if it is an important piece of the community's heritage, one might argue that the denial of access and use will result in a denial of the community's right to enjoy their cultural life, or to manifest their religion. If this is the case, the decision amounts to a human rights violation.

8.4 Concluding Remarks to Part III

The introduction to this part of the research started with the observation that repatriation takes place in a complicated web of (legal) relationships. The relationship between Indigenous communities and museums, between Indigenous peoples and the provincial government, between Indigenous peoples and the federal government, and even between Indigenous peoples and the judiciary have all affected how Canadian law addresses repatriation.

The last two decades have witnessed a significant shift in the approach of museums. The Museum Task Force report from the 1990s has been an influential force in driving this change. It addressed the need to change the perception of Indigenous heritage from evidence of a distant past to an important element of living cultures whose members have a distinct right to it. It spoke in favour of partnerships between museums and communities in the management and the creation of heritage. It appears from the research that individual museums have taken steps in this direction. Engagement with Indigenous communities appears to have become an important part of museum life in Canada. The repatriation of sacred objects seems to occur largely on the basis of negotiations between the museum and an individual community. It also seems part of a greater attempt to build collaborative partnerships with First Nations and it can include access to and use of sacred objects and custodial agreements in the absence of repatriation. However, all of this happens on the local level with individual museums and it is unclear in how far these important developments are mirrored among all Canadian museums.

In terms of the legal dimension to repatriation, the only law in Canada that specifically requires repatriation, the FNSCORA, arose out of such a museum-community partnership. This development also highlighted that, while individual negotiations and provincial tailor-made solutions are ideal to adapt repatriation to the needs of the participants, a clear legal signal that supports repatriation is often necessary. In British Columbia, the absence of historical treaty-making has given both the government and Indigenous peoples the space to engage in more respectful partnerships to further reconciliation and Indigenous (cultural) self-determination. Such treaties have resulted in repatriation agreements. However, the negotiations are lengthy, and the results depend on the individual negotiation tables. Moreover, because of the wide scope of the negotiations, there is a danger that the negotiations link the repatriation of sacred objects to other interests. The individual repatriations may get lost in the process as a result. In order to ensure that Indigenous rights are protected during the negotiation process, interim measures need to be taken. Overall, repatriation efforts seem to succeed due to museum and Indigenous efforts. This seems to happen more in spite of the applicable law than because of any specific legal protection of Indigenous heritage interests (this even holds true for Alberta, where FNSCORA was enacted after negotiations had been concluded).

The comparison between Alberta and British Columbia yielded two different repatriation avenues that both emphasize procedural elements overreaching a specific outcome. This procedural focus can be explained both by the goals that were pursued and the context in which these models operate. In Alberta, repatriation negotiations had already occurred between the Blackfoot First Nations whose sacred objects represented the largest chunk of provincial collections. This was a bottom-up negotiation that was approved 'after the fact' by law. In British Columbia, the treaty negotiations are set up to further the reconciliation of the different governments, peoples and rights. This, combined with the large array of unsettled claims, resulted in a choice for negotiations with a wide scope. In terms of the human rights dimension of these two models, the treaty negotiations require interim measures to protect individual rights until a treaty is negotiated. Before the changes introduced in 2018, an important point of critique would have been the significant debts that Indigenous peoples have had to incur to secure their existing rights. This seems to have changed, however. The individual negotiations in Alberta seem to further Indigenous heritage rights compliance and museums appear to be important driving forces that act together with Indigenous communities to support the rights of Indigenous communities to their heritage, such as the access to ceremonial objects.

Looking at the realization of Indigenous heritage rights outside the repatriation framework, some positive developments can be noted. On the federal level, there has been an important shift towards the full support of the United Nations declaration. This may impact future repatriation applications as well as access and use arrangements. A positive sign of this support has been federal funding to support research into how museum policies and actions are in line with UNDRIP. This also provides the chance to see how museums have been faring in implementing the Museum Task Force Report more generally, on which information is still missing. If the future results of this research into museum compliance with UNDRIP are heeded, there may be important legislative and policy measures in the (near) future. However, there are also areas in which the provincial and federal governments need to take legislative steps to implement UNDRIP. The federal export legislation does not recognize Indigenous rights to their heritage. This needs to change. Hopefully the recent adoption of the UNDRIP Act will provide impetus to do so. Provincial heritage legislation likewise requires further amendments to incorporate Indigenous rights to their heritage. This includes a change away from conceptualizing Indigenous heritage predominantly as evidence of Canada's past and to recognize it as an important resource for the cultural life of contemporary Indigenous communities and the enjoyment of human rights.

There is also the concern that the stringent test required by international law to justify a limitation of the freedom of religion protected under Art.18(1) ICCPR may no longer be respected for certain Indigenous religions under Canadian law. In the Grizzly Bear Spirit Case, the majority disregarded nature as an important element of Indigenous religious freedom altogether as not falling under the constitutional protection of religious freedom. The minority did take the important step to consider the specific characteristics of Indigenous nature-based religions but (relying on precedent) applied a framework testing the limitation which is considerably more permissive than the one developed under Art.18(3) ICCPR. Overall, there is room for the further incorporation of Indigenous legal customs within the Canadian legal order. Canadian jurisprudence does seem to operate against Indigenous interests in many cases. This tendency is not helped by the fact that Indigenous peoples are underrepresented, especially among the judiciary. Quite apart from the necessary steps that need to be taken to mitigate this understanding of freedom of religion, taking steps to have a more representative judiciary would also be advisable. In terms of the Grizzly Bear Spirit case specifically, this was decided recently. It is still uncertain how it will affect Indigenous practitioners in the enjoyment of their ceremonial practices. Hopefully, it will not undermine the strengthening effect that repatriation and museum cooperation has had on the revitalization of Indigenous culture and rights.

References

British Columbia Treaty Commission (2014) Annual Report 2014 available at: https://www.bctreaty.ca/sites/default/files/BCTC-Annual-Report-2014.pdf. Accessed 19 August 2021

Pineschi L (2012) Cultural diversity as a human right? General comment no.21 of the committee on economic, social and cultural rights. In: Borelli S, Lenzerini F (eds) Cultural heritage, cultural rights, cultural diversity. Studies in intercultural human rights. Nijhoff Publishers, Brill, pp 29–53

Royal British Columbia Museum (2018) Indigenous Collections and Repatriation Policy. https://royalbcmuseum.bc.ca/documents/105663/Indigenous-Collections-and-Repatriation-Policy

Shaheed F (2011) Report of the independent expert in the field of cultural rights on the right of access to and enjoyment of cultural heritage. UN General Assembly, A/HRC/17/38

Turner C, Fondahl G (2015) "Overlapping claims" to territory confronting treaty-making in British Columbia: causes and implications. Can Geogr/Le Géographe canadien 59(4):474–488

Part IV
Repatriation of Sacred Indigenous Cultural Heritage Through the Law

Chapter 9
Repatriation Models

9.1 Introduction

This research began with the question how the repatriation of sacred Indigenous[1] cultural heritage should be regulated legally in light of international cultural heritage and human rights standards. Part I considered both international cultural heritage law and international human rights law. The analysis of international human rights law provided a framework which can be used in evaluating national cultural heritage law, in general, and repatriation laws, in particular, to check their compliance with human rights. Repatriation that is regulated in accordance with these standards is also sufficient under international cultural heritage, since the relevant treaties do not require the repatriation of Indigenous cultural heritage, but such actions can qualify as measures that endorse cultural heritage and measures that support specific forms of intangible cultural heritage, notably religious rites. Overall, international cultural heritage law still needs to be adapted (further) to reflect contemporary human rights standards, notably Indigenous rights. It is thus not surprising that international cultural heritage law does not contain more specific standards.

In order to make recommendations for a specific legal form to structure repatriation, this book examined the existing repatriation legislation. This served as the basis for the exploration of different avenues to regulate repatriation and to analyse the relationship with the standards advanced in part I. As examples of different regulatory choices, the author examined the repatriation of sacred objects in the United States and Canada, in particular in British Columbia and Alberta. Part II analysed the legal context in the US, including federal Indian law and its historic evolution, before delving deeper into the particulars of the federal repatriation framework NAGPRA. Furthermore, part III examined Canadian law, with a special

[1] Please note that this chapter adopts the capitalization of the terms Indigenous Peoples and Indigenous (except for when used in citations) for reasons explained in Chap. 1.

V. Tünsmeyer, *Repatriation of Sacred Indigenous Cultural Heritage and the Law*,
Studies in Art, Heritage, Law and the Market 3,
https://doi.org/10.1007/978-3-030-89047-6_9

focus on aboriginal rights law, the First Nations Sacred Ceremonial Objects Repatriation Act in Alberta and the treaty negotiation process in British Columbia. Both examinations of the national law examined in how far the states acted in accordance with their obligations under international rights law in the context of sacred cultural heritage. In both sections, the application of the human rights framework showed not only a mixed (albeit largely positive) compliance record, but it also yielded important insights into the strengths and weaknesses of the particular repatriation systems. Combining these insights, it is possible to examine whether there are different regulatory models to repatriate sacred objects, their relationship to human rights, if they have distinct advantages and disadvantages, and which model should be chosen under which circumstances. These questions are the focus of this chapter. Afterwards, all findings are summarized in the conclusions in the following chapter.

Over the course of this volume three different legal mechanisms to structure repatriation were addressed: first, the US federal law covering entire an country and a large number of museums mandating the repatriation of specific categories of heritage (and human remains); and second, a law focussing on only two public museums, where the law was the result of negotiations which required legal changes to allow the museum to realize the negotiated expectations. This was the case for Alberta and the Glenbow Institute. In this case, the repatriation framework focused on a very specific goal, namely, to enable a specific institution to repatriate already identified objects to already identified Indigenous communities. Third, repatriation that was embedded in wider treaty negotiations in Canada was examined (British Columbia). In this case, there was no mandated repatriation. Instead repatriation depended on the priorities of the individual negotiation tables. All of the examples display very different ways of using the law, despite some close legal parallels between the selected examples in terms of their dominant legal system (common law) as well as their history. The reasons for the adoption of the particular legislation in each jurisdiction can be found in their respective legal contexts. While the (legal) reasons behind adopting repatriation legislation will inevitably differ for future repatriation laws, the US and Canadian examples teach valuable lessons for future repatriation models.

The analysis of the different examples has shown that the models have their own distinctive advantages and disadvantages and experience has showcased lessons which should be heeded in any future repatriation law. Moreover, examining the legal context in light of the human rights principles and tests developed in the first section of this book has also brought to light which elements of a repatriation framework can serve to protect or even fulfil human rights obligations and which may create a risk for practitioners to unwillingly limit or even violate Indigenous rights. In the following sections, the different mechanisms (Sect. 9.2) to distill the existing models (Sect. 9.3) will be compared. Afterwards it will be considered which lessons should be heeded for all repatriation frameworks and in how far the specific models distilled in Sect. 9.3 are transferrable to the context of international repatriations (Sect. 9.4).

9.2 Comparative Analysis

9.2.1 Comparison of the Different Repatriation Laws

If the three different repatriation mechanisms are compared, it seems that, while they share certain commonalities, there are distinct features which make classification possible. In fact, legal repatriation models which are more goal-oriented can be distinguished from those that are more process-oriented.

The cases examined showcase three distinct legal approaches to the repatriation of religious heritage to Indigenous communities. Overall, there are differences between those emphasizing a specific goal (US & Alberta) and the treaty negotiation process in British Columbia emphasizing the procedural element. This is not to say that the other component of process/outcome has been neglected, but rather that these repatriation schemes differ in terms of their emphasis and how they approach repatriation.

In the United States, the repatriation of religious objects came to the forefront of public awareness during the debate on the unequal protection of Indigenous religious practices and the repatriation of human remains. Indigenous activism and the public knowledge of the sheer mass of Indigenous human remains which had been stored in cultural institutions and by governmental agencies, combined with the continuing inequality of burial site protection between Indigenous and non-Indigenous citizens, ultimately led to the adoption of NAGPRA. As a result, NAGPRA pursues two goals: the repatriation of Indigenous remains associated funerary objects and religious objects and the protection of burial sites. The repatriation part of this legal scheme is focussed on realizing this desired outcome: actual, physical repatriation if a number of conditions are fulfilled. These conditions both serve to alleviate museum concerns which existed at the time (i.e. loss of knowledge to science) and to facilitate a relatively smooth repatriation, despite the long period between the original loss of the human remains/religious object/cultural patrimony and its return to the community. Once the conditions were fulfilled, museums had to repatriate, regardless of whether they were supportive of the obligation or reluctant to do so (both attitudes were present at the time).NAGPRA also provides for the opportunity for museums and Indigenous Peoples to reach different agreements, but the obligation to repatriate if no other agreement has been reached constitutes the core of the framework. The law thus provides for a minimum standard of repatriation by which museums have to abide, while opening the way for further cooperation. NAGPRA has already resulted in large-scale repatriations of human remains and religious objects, and it continues to result in repatriations to this date. It has, undoubtedly, led to more equality for Indigenous religious practitioners (at least those that belong to federally recognized tribes). For the equal protection of Indigenous religious practices, however, much more remains to be done. Included here are, *inter alia*, the protection of sacred sites from desecration and private access to such sites for ceremonial practices. Both are outside the scope of a repatriation-specific law, yet they continue to present problems for practitioners, despite the presence of AIRFA and the RFRA.

Next to the repatriation of cultural heritage and human remains, NAGPRA has also resulted in increased cooperation and better understanding between individual museums and Indigenous communities. The shape of the legal framework likely played an important role in this, by remedying some of the inequalities between Indigenous Peoples and museums that had existed prior to NAGPRA. It incorporated mandatory consultations and placed Indigenous interests at the center of the mechanism by creating an obligation for museums to repatriate. This addressed the previous power imbalances, which too often placed Indigenous communities in the position of pleading for the return of their heritage while the museum was both in possession of the heritage and in the position to decide on the claim. NAGPRA also created a representative advisory body that brought both parties together to advise in the case of disputes. NAGPRA has shown that the law can play an important role in achieving physical repatriation, while also furthering other objectives, such as better cooperation between Indigenous Peoples and non-Indigenous actors. The necessary historical research to establish the origins of an object or of human remains before its arrival in the museum, if done in partnership with Indigenous communities, can also become an important element of ongoing decolonization processes.

The repatriation legislation in Alberta (FNSCORA), by comparison, operated on a much smaller scale and was more specific than NAGPRA. Namely, the focus here was to ensure that the law did not remain an obstacle to repatriation agreements that had already been concluded between First Nations and the Glenbow museum. In the case of Alberta, the law can play very different roles in relation to the repatriation of religious objects. In this case, given that the Glenbow museum held the objects in trust for the people of the province, legal obligations prevented the parties from coming to a cooperative agreement. Only after the intervention of the legislature, which gave ex post legal approval, were the agreements ready for implementation. The legislation continues to apply to two museums only: the Glenbow and the Royal Alberta Museum. This shows what is possible if support is present in the legislature. However, it arguably also highlights the benefits of adopting legislation that would allow museums to come to similar agreements with Indigenous Peoples both inside and outside the province, if certain conditions are met. This would eliminate the need for continuous parliamentary action, indicate societal support for the repatriation of Indigenous cultural heritage and strengthen the position of other First Nations seeking agreements similar to the Blackfoot agreements.

FNSCORA would actually allow for other First Nations to also have agreements. It is only in combination with the regulations that the legislative framework adopted is restricted to the Blackfoot Agreements. FNSCORA would actually allow for the return of a sacred ceremonial object to another First Nation subject to governmental agreement,[2] were it not for the fact that the statute defines 'First Nation' by reference to the regulations. The accompanying regulation to the act restricts First Nation to

[2]S 2 First Nations Sacred Ceremonial Objects Repatriation Act, RSA 2000, c F-14.

three specific First Nations.[3] However, according to practitioners other communities do not desire a similar framework, suggesting that the adoption of such regulations would be possible.[4] In addition, it should be pointed out that, even if this element of the mechanism were to be changed or additional regulations adopted, the framework still leaves Indigenous parties comparatively weaker than other repatriation laws. While section 2 creates a "general right to apply for repatriation" it is limited to a "right to apply". The ultimate decision power within FNSCORA rests with the designated governmental official who is under an obligation to agree with the application, unless in her opinion "repatriation would not be appropriate". Clearly, appropriate is a rather vague term that could have benefitted from clarification if the desire had been to enable the repatriation of sacred objects to all contemporary Indigenous communities who had a need of them.

In the British Columbia Treaty negotiation process, repatriation occurs as part of a larger conversation between the respective Indigenous communities, the provincial and the federal government. The focus of these very resource-intensive processes (with respect to time, money and people) is different from the other examples. Here the emphasis rests very much on reconciling the different sovereignties at play. Such a new partnership gives all parties concerned more legal certainty as to their rights and duties and is hoped to improve the socio-economic situation of the Indigenous nations involved. This was and continues to be an extremely ambitious undertaking and it thus not surprising that many of the negotiations are still ongoing and that it took decades to reach agreement in those that have been completed.

As was pointed out previously, the process has been viewed rather critically. With the changes introduced in the financing structure and further potential debt-release changes for completed treaties in late 2018, however, an important deficit has been remedied. Participating communities no longer have to incur debt in order to negotiate for their existing rights. As for the duration of the negotiations, it should be remembered that the treaties seek to establish new relationships between parties after hundreds of years of inequality and they cover a wide range of both legal rights and resources. Their duration thus does not seem too surprising given the goals underlying the process. Yet, considering the focus here on the repatriation of religious heritage, the duration of negotiations can have negative consequences, since religious heritage is needed for religious practices today, not in 20 years. While treaty negotiations can be an important tool for securing and implementing Indigenous rights, their duration can also risk (further) limitations or even violations of specific rights, including the right to religion. This can occur, for example, when religious objects are only repatriated after the final completion of the treaty. Access to heritage is barred in the meantime and no safeguards against the desecration of religious heritage or sacred sites are in place. The final agreements examined

---

[3] S1(b) First Nations Sacred Ceremonial Objects Repatriation Act, RSA 2000, c F-14 read in conjunction with 1(b) Blackfoot First Nations Sacred Ceremonial Objects Repatriation Regulation, Alta Reg 96/2004.

[4] Personal communication with Alberta museum staff.

displayed a mix between comparatively specific repatriation provisions[5] and much softer provisions which provide for the possibility of future agreements,[6] either on returning the artifact or agreeing on custodial arrangements. The scope of the negotiations and their resulting duration can negatively impact the negotiations of repatriation-specific agreements, both because of the simple passage of time and because in such wide-scale negotiations every single point to be negotiated becomes a potential bargaining chip.

This comparison is illustrated in the comparative Table 9.1.

Apart from this comparison of repatriation legislation, the national country chapters also considered whether there were other avenues for repatriation in the legal areas that were analysed. The examination of Canadian law also considered in how far existing constitutional provisions could be used to pursue repatriation, namely s.35. As was described in detail in Sect. 6.2 of the Chap. 6, section 35 incorporates treaty rights and aboriginal rights into the Canadian constitution. Aboriginal rights are activities which are (an element of) "a practice, custom or tradition integral to the distinctive culture of the aboriginal group asserting the right."[7] There are a number of guidelines on what may be classified as an aboriginal right that arises out of the jurisprudence which are of less relevance for the purposes of this chapter. It is of importance here that the Canadian Supreme Court has defined aboriginal rights in such a way that they can be broadly classified as cultural rights. Practices are protected because of their importance to the distinctive culture of the individual Indigenous community. However, by restricting the constitutional protection to those activities that are integral to the respective group, the Supreme Court narrowed the protection of s.35(1). Moreover, the importance of a practice relative to the overall cultural distinctiveness of the group claiming the right has become a matter for judicial evaluation. The difficulty of judging such a matter in a court of law, which is shaped and presided over by representatives of another (legal) culture aside, is not a challenge unique to the Canadian legal context. It is also the case in international law that cultural rights are, by their nature, more difficult to grasp legally because of the vague matter they protect. In international law, this difficulty led to cultural rights being underdeveloped for several decades before they were given a more robust theoretical underpinning. The effort to give them concrete form continues to this day.

Similarly, the debate of how to shape aboriginal (cultural) rights is taken up anew with each case that is brought before a Canadian court. At the moment, neither an

[5]Maa-nulth, Final Agreement, lists of objects to be repatriated. Tla'amin Final Agreement, Ch.14 s.5-19, Yale First Nation repatriation agreement list with RBCM.

[6]Tsawwassen Final Agreement, option to come to an agreement on Tsawwassen cultural objects enter RBCM holdings after effective date of treaty and to negotiate outside of final agreement for objects in possession of either Tsawwassen First Nation or museum, see Chapter 14, paras 11, 12. Yale First Nation repatriation provisions covering CMoC 6.2.1 to 6.2.5.

[7]R v Van der Peet [1996] 2 S.C.R. 407, para 45.

Table 9.1 Comparative table repatriation legislation

Country/ comparative indicators	Canada – Alberta[a]	Canada, British Columbia[b]	United States[c]
Objectives of law evidenced in legislative history of law	Gives effect to agreement already negotiated, namely between Blackfoot First Nation and Glenbow Museum. Also, harmonize museum goals with first nation revitalization desire[d]; adopt basic repatriation principles, amend act of museum with large ethnographic collection (Glenbow Institute).	Reconciliation of three governmental entities: First Nations, Canada and British Columbia. Explicit aim to forge new relationship, to settle rights and provide for legal and economic certainty and to improve the situation of First Nations.	Ensure equal protection of human remains—remedial—also arguments of equal protection of religious rights.
Definition of indigenous peoples within act	[FNSCORA] As defined in regulations. [96/2004] very specific, only three Blackfoot First Nations listed.	Very broad/inclusive, aboriginal governing body established by indigenous community within their traditional territories within British Columbia.	Follows national definitions of indigenous peoples, notion of "federally recognized tribes" by government as eligible to receive governmental support because of indigenous status.
Definition of indigenous religious heritage	[FNSCORA] Very specific: past usage + only if in possession of two museums or Crown + *vital* to practice of indigenous religious practice.	Not applicable, to be decided at negotiation tables where applicable.	Main criterion for definition is need by traditional religious leader for contemporary practice. Ultimately definition of sacredness rests with indigenous religious expert.
Mandated outcome?	Yes, giving effect to negotiated agreement, repatriation of very specific items. Outcome negotiated before the law was passed; law only passed to ensure that agreement could be realized.	Not specifically. Process designed to end in adoption of treaty but what is to be included in treaty is decided in negotiations.	Yes. Focus very much on the actual repatriation of human remains (and associated funerary objects), religious objects and cultural patrimony. If conditions are fulfilled obligation to repatriate.
Mandated procedure? What type of procedure?	No. Incorporates governmental approval for previous negotiations.	Yes. Treaty negotiations of very broad scope, encompassing land claims, cultural rights etc.	Partially, there are mandatory elements: (1) First phase inventory/summary with consultation; (2) cultural affiliation standard to link heritage with community; (3) if

(continued)

Table 9.1 (continued)

Country/ comparative indicators	Canada – Alberta[a]	Canada, British Columbia[b]	United States[c]
			(1) + (2) fulfilled → duty to repatriate but no specific format, unless scientific exception or competing claims.
Consultation within process and/or FPIC	Incorporated after the fact. Negotiations with a small number of communities took place before passing the act.	Yes. Consultation is a mandatory part of the process. Process also enables realization of FPIC.	Yes. Consultation mandated within repatriation process.
Final authority to decide on repatriation request	Designated Minister or person so authorized by minister.	Not possible to determine. Organic treaty negotiation process among three governments that enter government to government negotiations.	With museum (decides that cultural affiliation standard not met). But: disputes can be submitted to NAGPRA Review Committee and can be brought before courts.

[a] First Nations Sacred Ceremonial Objects Repatriation Act, RSA 2000, c F-14, Alberta Regulation 96/2004, Blackfoot First Nations Sacred Ceremonial Objects Repatriation Regulation
[b] British Columbia Treaty Negotiation Process
[c] Native American Graves Protection and Repatriation Act
[d] First Nations Sacred Ceremonial Objects Repatriation Act, RSA 2000, c F-14, preamble

aboriginal right to a specific ceremony which requires the repatriation of a religious object nor an aboriginal right to its use has been established before a court. However, as was shown in Chap. 6, depending on the specifics of the case, the existence of such a right can be argued. Cultural objects, and especially religious objects, seem to fit squarely within the definition of "integral to the distinctive culture" that is used by the Supreme Court. Once such an aboriginal right has been judicially established, the precedent will strengthen the bargaining positions of other communities. However, establishing such a right before a court is costly. Moreover, because of the integrity and distinctiveness criteria, a successful case may not necessarily help other communities in regaining their objects or even help the same claimant community to regain other items. A legal framework (i.e. at the provincial level) establishing a duty to repatriate subject to conditions, or even merely a duty to negotiate, is more likely to ensure an equal chance at repatriation. The latter may also forge new partnerships between museums or even governmental agencies and communities, which are unlikely to arise in the adversarial setting of a court room.

9.2.2 *Relationship Between the Goal Behind a Repatriation Law and the Adopted Legal Structure*

All legal repatriation avenues cost the participants significant amounts of resources, albeit it in differing degrees. It is important therefore that a legal repatriation framework is successful. What would make it successful? A framework that achieves its legislative goal could be termed successful. Alternatively, if the aim is too far-reaching to be attained by implementing the framework, it should at least contribute to its achievement. The next requirement for a framework builds on a basic principle of international law, namely that human rights treaties give rise to rights and obligations that the state has to respect at the national level. If they are not implemented, this does not negate their existence. Therefore, if human rights are accepted as the underlying framework governing the interaction between a state and its citizens, they also need to be respected in any legal interaction between the two. A successful repatriation framework would thus contribute towards strengthening human rights and at a minimum not violate them. There are arguably many potential legislative goals which can underlie repatriation models, but what do the examples here reveal about legislative goals? Have the frameworks been successful in achieving them? And how do they interact with underlying human rights?

The mechanisms examined above pursued four categories of legislative goals: first, the physical repatriation of sacred cultural heritage and/or human remains;[8] second, ensuring the equal protection of human remains for Indigenous Peoples;[9] third, remedying some of the inequalities in the protection of Indigenous religious and cultural rights;[10] fourth, facilitating reconciliation.[11] Generally, the repatriation frameworks appear to have been successful at achieving their legislative goals. In the case of British Columbia, it is arguably too early to tell in how far the treaty negotiation process will be successful at achieving reconciliation. It does not seem to be the best mechanism to ensure the repatriation of cultural objects specifically, but to be fair that was not the goal the overarching mechanism sought to realize.

[8]US NAGPRA; Alberta First Nations Sacred Ceremonial Repatriation Act, RSA 2000, c F-14. Alberta, Glenbow Institute Act, s.20(3) exempting cultural objects repatriated under FNSCRA from the main collection being held by the Crown on behalf of the people of Alberta. By amending the statute governing public collections physical repatriation was facilitated.

[9]US, NAGPRA, provisions repatriating human remains to ensure equal protection of human remains in order to remedy past grave-robbing practices. Coupled with protections of unexcavated remains/burial sites. This goal will not be considered further, given the exclusion of human remains from the scope of this research. For justification of research scope, see Chap. 1.

[10]In the United States, linked to arguments on repatriation remains was the desire to remedy inequalities in the protection of religious rights for Indigenous Americans. In Alberta it was to harmonize museum goals with first nation revitalization desire, see First Nations Sacred Ceremonial Objects Repatriation Act, RSA 2000, c F-14, preamble.

[11]In British Columbia the reconciliation of three governmental entities: First Nations, Canada and British Columbia. The explicit aim was to forge new relationships, to settle rights and provide for legal and economic certainty and to improve situation of First Nations.

Have the repatriation mechanisms been successful in achieving the legislative goal that was set for them? In terms of achieving the actual repatriation of sacred objects, NAGPRA was the most successful simply in terms of scale. The mandatory repatriation provision was the appropriate choice to handle a large number of institutions, with a large number of objects and remains, and with mixed feelings on whether or not to repatriate. By comparison FNSCORA is a good example of how the legal process can react flexibly to eliminate legal barriers, provided there is sufficient political will. While it was successful in providing for the repatriation of the negotiated heritage to the Blackfoot nations, it also showed the capriciousness of the legislative process. While FNSCORA theoretically enables repatriation claims by other First Nations, the regulation does not apply them. RAM emphasizes that while the regulation only applies to the Blackfoot First Nations, negotiations are under way about what the process might look like as desired by the Cree, Nakota, and Saulteaux.[12] Yet, even if the regulations are adjusted, the ultimate power to decide on a repatriation request is given to the Minister of Culture and the process remains unequal in terms of the distribution of powers between the parties. However, we can also see that successful repatriations and the Canadian truth and reconciliation commission's call to action that included museums have significantly influenced museum policy. The online information on repatriation provided by RAM is linked to the notion of community engagement and cooperation, and express mention is made of articles 11 and 12 of UNDRIP, and the opportunity of access to ceremonial objects is also expressly mentioned.

The last repatriation mechanism that was part of this comparison are the treaty negotiations in British Columbia, Canada. It is too early to say in how far the treaty negotiations in British Columbia are successful in achieving the reconciliation of Indigenous and non-Indigenous sovereignties, clarifying outstanding claims and rights. They have been successful at achieving the first wave of modern treaties which cover a wide array of rights and respective obligations. This, in itself, is a significant achievement. They also represent an attempt to find a new place for Indigenous distinctiveness in modern society against the backdrop of settler colonialism and the realization that all inhabitants of the country "are here to stay".[13] In terms of facilitating repatriation and/or access to cultural heritage, the result is mixed. The negotiations have succeeded with a number of repatriation agreements and the physical repatriation of objects. Where this is not the case, they include an agreement for further negotiations. Moreover, future discoveries of heritage objects are also considered. Apart from the provisions listing specific objects, the provisions on future negotiations do not resolve existing repatriation claims. Where the origin of an object is not known or where the provision simply seeks to cover the potential

[12]Royal Alberta Museum, currently https://royalalbertamuseum.ca/collections/cultural-studies/indigenous-studies/community-engagement [last accessed 19.08.2021], compare website from 3.05.2019, archived at: https://web.archive.org/web/20190503104739/https://royalalbertamuseum.ca/collections/cultural-studies/repatriation/.

[13]Delgamuukw v. British Columbia, [1997] 3 S.C.R. 1010, para 186.

future entry of an Indigenous object into a museum collection, this may be understandable. However, where the existence of linked cultural heritage is known, one may have wished for stronger repatriation provisions. This being said, provided that Canada enables Indigenous access to ceremonial objects in public collections, it complies with Art.12(2) UNDRIP and upholds the commitment it made in 2016. To give one example of this, in the Tla'amin agreement, Canada is obliged to "make reasonable efforts to facilitate access" to Tla'amin heritage and human remains which are held in other public collections not covered by the agreement.[14] As long as the final mechanisms regulating access are "fair, transparent and effective" and developed "in conjunction with the indigenous peoples concerned", Art.12(2) is respected.

9.2.3 Comparing the Relationship Between Indigenous Cultural Rights and Different Repatriation Laws

This research project also focused on the relationship between human rights, in particular cultural rights and repatriation laws. The initial hope was to distil one or more repatriation model(s) that can strengthen Indigenous cultural rights. In the course of examining both the individual repatriation legislation, as well as their legal context, a number of important lessons were learned about the relationship between Indigenous cultural rights and repatriation. They are concerned in particular with the right to manifest one's religion, the right to revitalize cultural traditions, the right to Indigenous cultural heritage, and the right to cultural identity. To allow for a better comparison, Table 9.2 summarizes the key features of the different repatriation legislation with respect to each of the enumerated rights.

In this comparison, illustrated by means of Table 9.2, it can be seen that the different repatriation mechanisms can all lend themselves to strengthening Indigenous cultural rights. In how far this happens depends on the specifics incorporated into the mechanism. In treaty negotiations, everything depends on the participants. They can lend themselves to strengthening Indigenous cultural rights or result in substantively weakening them. A well-designed mandatory repatriation framework, which also considers the protection of still buried Indigenous heritage from an Indigenous perspective, is stronger than a mere repatriation framework. In this case, it is crucial that this framework is developed respecting international legal standards given its mandatory nature. Misidentification of objects, no or wrongful repatriations, can all risk Indigenous access to sacred objects (Art.11(1) UNDRIP). Access, however, is guaranteed as part of Art.18(1) read in conjunction with Art.27 ICCPR. When these rights are denied as a result of a mandatory framework established by the state, it risks violating its international human rights obligations.

[14] Tla'amin Final Agreement, ch.14, s.22, at 162.

Table 9.2 Comparative table relationship repatriation legislation and human rights

	Canada, Alberta	Canada, B.C.	U.S.A., NAGPRA
Right to manifest religion	FNSCORA and Blackfoot Regulation ensure the return of sacred objects that were used in the past and are vital to contemporary practices → protects right. Arguable whether the requirement that an object is 'vital' is not too high a threshold. 'Necessary' would have encompassed more heritage for potential claims.	Process is flexible, possibility to address rights and claims of parties. Examined treaties included repatriation agreements of sacred materials as well as provisions on future negotiations.	Return of necessary objects for ceremonial practices. Violation: non-federally recognized tribes who do not have access to objects in private. But, problem outside of NAGPRA (protection and access to sacred sites) can limit or even violate individual practitioners' right to religion
Right to revitalize cultural traditions	Facilitates revitalization, no continuing practice element needed.	Treaties provide right to gather materials for ceremonial purposes.	Seeks to facilitate revitalization → no continuing practice required, only contemporary need. Other laws address need for specific materials for ceremonies (i.e. eagle feathers)
Right to protect/control/manage Indigenous heritage	Provincial heritage legislation does not address Indigenous control/management of Indigenous heritage. Strong ministerial power may be used to negotiate agreements that provide provincial protection to Indigenous heritage but not specifically provided for in act.	Treaties address heritage management to be placed in Indigenous control within agreed-upon territorial boundaries. Provincial heritage legislation in turn provides agreements to protect heritage from desecration but insufficiently used. Any management/controlling right arising out of existing treaties remains unaffected by heritage legislation. Makes treaty negotiations more crucial for the protection of Indigenous cultural rights.	Consultation prior and within NAGPRA in several places, also addresses Indigenous control over buried heritage (only on Indian land). Other Heritage legislation establishes tribal heritage management program
Right to cultural identity, in particular the right to self-identification.	FNSCORA defines First Nations by reference to regulations—only enabling regulation Blackfoot regulation. As a result, limits right	Respected, Indigenous communities can enter negotiations as long as the aboriginal governing body is established by an	Exclusion of non-federally recognized tribes violates right to distinct cultural identity for respective

(continued)

Table 9.2 (continued)

	Canada, Alberta	Canada, B.C.	U.S.A., NAGPRA
	to cultural identity for other communities. Blackfoot regulation does not define Blackfoot identity from the outside, respects Blackfoot self-identification.	Indigenous community within their traditional territories within British Columbia.	Indigenous communities.

Apart from this, a mandatory framework may not necessarily align with either the legal context or the societal goals pursued by the legislator, or both. There are also other goals, such as reconciliation and limiting the amount of heritage which may potentially be removed from public collections (while considering Indigenous rights at the same time). However, any model can be made to respect Indigenous rights. In the examination of the different legislative approaches to repatriation, elements that were critical in light of international standards did not go to the heart of the mechanism. They can thus be changed while keeping the regulatory model as a choice in the legislative toolbox. Part I yielded 12 broader human rights standards which concerned both repatriation legislation, in particular, and cultural heritage legislation, in general. The standards were broadly based on the rights under examination, i.e. the duty to respect, protect and fulfil, the right to manifest one's religion within the repatriation framework, subject to the limitations permissible under international law. In the preceding chapters, 11 standards were applied to the national legal framework. Through this, the relationship between the standards and the repatriation frameworks was elucidated as summarized above. This relationship can be operationalized via a set of guidelines, to facilitate of government and heritage actors. In particular, a set of guidelines can help in guiding the adoption of repatriation frameworks, to align them closer to international human rights law.

Moreover, to answer the second research question, a number of guidelines can be formulated are applicable to cultural heritage law and policy more generally can be formulated. These give more concrete guidance to states and derive from the analysis of the national legal context in light of the selected broader international legal standards.

In both cases the guidelines, are of varying legal nature, this is reflected in how they are worded. The term guideline was chosen as an umbrella term to reflect the intention that it should guide states and other willing heritage actors in aligning their behaviour closer with international human rights law.

9.2.3.1 Human Rights Guidelines for Repatriation Frameworks

In order to ensure that any repatriation framework (irrespective of modality) aligns with international human rights standards, a repatriation framework has to be designed to respect human rights from the ground up, starting with drafting the instrument. Nine guidelines have to be respected within the instrument and in its implementation:

Drafting phase

1. The repatriation framework itself should be developed in cooperation with the Indigenous Peoples concerned. It is important to collaborate with Indigenous Peoples to ensure respect for different Indigenous cultural rights that can be affected by the framework. This operationalizes different elements of a number of rights, in particular Art.11(2) UNDRIP and Art.38 UNDRIP.

Repatriation legislation: Scope

2. Respect Indigenous beliefs in the definition of religious object by respecting Indigenous authority and practices to identify sacredness. Interference with Indigenous religious practices only permissible under the (very narrow) conditions of Art.18(3) ICCPR and the additional limitation imposed by Art.27 IRCCPR.
3. Respect Indigenous right to self-identification; do not impose governmental definition of Indigenous identity that is contrary to Indigenous self-identification. The definition of Indigenous Peoples used may not exclude Indigenous Peoples within the territory who identify as Indigenous in line with Art.33(1) UNDRIP.

Repatriation legislation: Regulating repatriation procedure

4. In connecting a sacred object to a community, Indigenous customary legal traditions should be respected. If scientific methods are used to connect a sacred object with a community, the framework should require museums to obtain FPIC for measures that affect Indigenous cultural rights.
5. The repatriation framework should not require a continuing practice between the initial practice and the time of reclaiming if the object is reclaimed for contemporary use. This is an important safeguard to ensure that a state respects the Indigenous right to revitalization. It is also part of the fulfil dimension of the freedom of religion. A decision not to repatriate must be permissible under the relevant limitation clauses of Art.27 ICCPR and Art.18(3) ICCPR.
6. Respect the Indigenous right to their own legal traditions by incorporating Indigenous customary practices within repatriation framework if they are in accordance with international human rights law. Examples of measures that can be taken in accordance with Indigenous legal traditions are

    a. identify link between object and community,
    b. identify custodian of heritage,
    c. Incorporate oral testimony where relevant.

Implementing repatriation legislation

7. Identifying Indigenous cultural heritage should be done in consultation with Indigenous Peoples to guarantee Art.31 UNDRIP.
8. Do not dictate conditions for Indigenous Peoples to fulfil upon repatriation of sacred object in order to respect Indigenous right to their own heritage under Art.31 UNDRIP
9. Sacred heritage in public collections that is not repatriated must be made accessible to Indigenous religious practitioners in private, in accordance with Art.12(1) UNDRIP and Art.18(1) ICCPR.

Lastly, a good practice to fulfil the relevant rights discussed is the provision of the resources necessary for Indigenous Peoples to take advantage of these opportunities. This encompasses financial resources and training for both Indigenous Peoples and museums that are engaged in repatriation.

9.2.3.2 Human Rights Guidelines Applicable to National Cultural Heritage Law and Policy

This dissertation has considered repatriation in its legal context, both in terms of its connection to human rights and in the interaction of different national legal areas and their interaction with repatriation. In the individual country chapters, recommendations were made to adjust national cultural heritage law where applicable. Compiling these insights, the research has also yielded a number of guidelines and good practices applicable to legislation that affects Indigenous cultural heritage in general. These are:

1. States should encourage museums to ensure that, where custodial agreements are made for sacred cultural heritage and it is not repatriated, the Indigenous right to maintain and protect their heritage in accordance with their traditional practices under Art.11(1) UNDRIP is still protected.
2. Heritage legislation and policy has to require FPIC for governmental measures that affect Indigenous cultural rights, for example:

    a. State archaeological branches that issue excavation permits for potential Indigenous sites qualify as governmental actors who have to obtain FPIC.
    b. Public museums that exhibit sacred cultural heritage in a way that could lead to its desecration.
    c. Any action that interferes with a sacred site that is sanctioned or conducted by a governmental actor can affect Indigenous rights. Consultation is a minimum requirement, depending on the impact, FPIC will be necessary. Any legislation or policy measure that affects sacred sites should not unduly interfere with Indigenous Peoples right of access to sites. This is an important measure to respect Indigenous right to manifest their religion.

3. States should take measures to protect and fulfil Indigenous access to sacred sites. A wide margin of discretionary measures is possible.
4. States should take measures to prevent third-person conduct that desecrates Indigenous cultural heritage. This includes encouraging private museums not to display sacred objects unless with the FPIC of the affected community.
5. States have to incorporate Indigenous rights to their heritage in export legislation. This includes a duty to attempt to prevent culturally important and sacred objects from leaving state territory without the consent of the tribe by adapting the legislation and implementation accordingly.
6. States should protect and fulfil Indigenous rights to their cultural heritage. The state is under the positive duty to progressively create conditions in which Indigenous Peoples can control their heritage according to their own traditions. There are many different measures states can take, for example:

   a. Include Indigenous staff in national/regional/local heritage administration to care for Indigenous heritage.
   b. Encourage museums to employ Indigenous staff, support heritage management/museology studies for Indigenous individuals.
   c. Accommodate Indigenous heritage laws covering Indigenous lands within the national heritage law scheme.

7. States can fulfil Indigenous rights to their cultural identity by supporting programs that address the results of past discriminatory practices which may continue to affect Indigenous rights to preserve and develop their own cultural identity, for example residential schools.

Lastly, this research leads to an obvious observation, which bears stating nonetheless, because of its importance. The presence of religious cultural heritage within an Indigenous community is vital to the protection of their cultural rights. For Indigenous Peoples to enjoy their cultural rights, however, much more is needed than control of their (religious) cultural heritage. Instead, their enjoyment of cultural rights requires adequate legal conditions in such diverse areas as constitutional law, environmental law, federal Indian law/aboriginal rights law, cultural heritage law, export laws and many more (depending on the legal system in question). The discussion, adoption and implementation of repatriation laws can thus help to disclose unequal or insufficient protection in other, related legal areas. Depending on the goal that the legislature wishes to pursue with the repatriation of Indigenous cultural heritage, for example, to ensure the equal protection of Indigenous religious practices, more work may need to be done.

9.3 Repatriation 'Models'

The comparison between the three mechanisms has highlighted how different mechanisms can be successful at repatriation while still considering the particularities of the given legal (and historical) context. This has been complemented by an analysis of the relevant international legal instruments. This resulted in a framework of rights and permissible limitations which then could be applied to the selected repatriation laws.[15] Through this a number of guidelines were developed (see preceding paragraphs) which need to be respected in any intra-national repatriation model to ensure that the state respects its human rights obligations towards its Indigenous citizens. With the help of this comparison, and bearing the principles in mind, the different repatriation models will be addressed.

First, two cautionary remarks are warranted. As explained in the introductory chapter, this study only looked at three different mechanisms to regulate the repatriation of sacred objects. Other repatriation avenues are possible that have not been researched in this contribution but elsewhere.[16] Next to this, as was mentioned in the beginning, available private law avenues have not been considered. Second, the mechanisms selected could also be tweaked slightly. For example, a legislator could decide to simply amend the act governing public collections to enable any museum with public collections to decide unilaterally on the repatriation of Indigenous cultural heritage. In this case, the museum would be the ultimate body deciding upon repatriation and the deaccessioning of objects which it holds on behalf of the public.[17]

Keeping this in mind, the frameworks will be examined for the purposes of distilling different repatriation models. All mechanisms have been (partially) successful at achieving varying legislative goals and have even gone beyond achieving physical repatriation. This has happened both in the cases that emphasized the specific goal of repatriation and even seems to have started in the case of British Columbia. Here the process was structured around a particular procedure to achieve more intangible goals, notably reconciliation. The cases have shown that the question as to which legal avenue is most suitable then depends not only the legal context in the given country but also on the primary goal that underlies the efforts made for repatriation. This highlights that there is no one set path to follow with repatriation that will guarantee the best possible outcome.

The mechanism that is selected needs to match the goals of the parties involved, the legal context that surrounds it and the historic and societal background that

[15] It also yielded a number of helpful guidelines for national heritage law and policy as a by-product which can be found in Chap. 10, Sect. 10.3.1.

[16] Kuprecht (2014), advocating for cultural diplomacy as a repatriation tool in international repatriations. Van Beurden (2017) advocates the development of a set of principles for the return of colonial cultural objects comparable to the Washington Principles for the Return of Nazi-looted art.

[17] This would be a slightly adapted version of the mechanism employed in Alberta, Canada.

underlies it. The examples given below can provide actors with a helpful starting point in how to approach the legal side of repatriation. Advantages and disadvantages can be considered carefully, and, in light of their respective context, it may be possible to merge different elements. In this case, it should be pointed out that some repatriation features do not lend themselves well to achieving certain (legislative) goals. Notably, a framework will have to prioritize either procedural elements or substantive goals. Opting for procedural elements will mean there is an emphasis on the consultation and participation of Indigenous Peoples from the outset. The final outcome of the repatriation framework may then not necessarily reflect the initial hopes of the participants. Setting substantive goals from the outset, by contrast, can easily re-introduce discriminatory practices rooted in colonialism. Even in situations where the decolonization process has advanced considerably, setting substantive goals without some amount of flexibility for actors can strengthen power asymmetries between Indigenous and non-Indigenous actors considerably.

The different cases that were examined highlighted that repatriation frameworks can achieve different outcomes and that legal frameworks that are not specifically addressed at repatriation (such as the treaty negotiations in British Columbia) can comprise repatriation agreements. Table 9.3 provides an overview of the correlation between models and their suitability to achieve different legislative goals, as examined in the previous sections. Using this approach to evaluate the relationship between the legislative goal and each model, it is clear that the models may either mandate a particular goal, encourage its realization, not endorse or hinder its achievement (neutral), or potentially hinder its achievement. These relationships are summarized in the following table:

Considering which models can help in achieving which goals, it is clear that all models can achieve repatriation. Model 4 is the weakest guarantor to achieve physical repatriation. This is simply because of the scope of the negotiations and the necessary priorities which may have to be set. The large scope and the

Table 9.3 Relationship model and legislative goal

	Goals		
Models	Repatriation	Remedy unequal protection of religious and/or cultural rights	Reconcile different sovereign claims
Model 1: Mandatory repatriation provision	Mandates goal	Partially encourages	Depends: Neutral or hinders
Model 2: Voluntary negotiation between community and museum	Encourages goal	Partially encourages	Neutral
Model 3: Hybrid of repatriation and Indigenous heritage law	Depends: Encourages or mandates	Encourages goal	Partially encourages
Model 4: Large scale treaty negotiations	Depends: Encourages but can also hinder	Yes. But duration of negotiation can also increase inequalities	Encourages goal

government to government negotiations preclude direct repatriation agreements between museums and communities and can thus hinder repatriation efforts.

Similarly, all repatriation models can help to address the comparatively weaker protection of Indigenous cultural rights albeit to varying degrees. This is because their full realization rests on many factors other than Indigenous control over important (religious) cultural heritage. The examination of Canada and the United States was restricted in scope. However, even with this restriction, to the need to adjust laws and policies to ensure private access to sacred sites on public lands, access to necessary ritual resources, and a more inclusive heritage management policies that fully incorporates Indigenous stewardship for Indigenous cultural heritage became apparent. Moreover, there are difficulties in protecting Indigenous rights from restrictions that have resulted from the judiciary which—maybe not so coincidentally—is clearly represented by Indigenous members.

The last legislative goal that was found in the analysis, to reconcile the different sovereignties' (Indigenous and settler) claims to land, resources and governance, is unsurprisingly the most difficult to achieve. Reconciliation in this respect is a difficult and broad term. In the dictionary, to reconcile is defined as "to restore to peace or unity" and "to settle or to resolve".[18] If we take the Canadian example, we can see that the negotiations in British Columbia in effect attempt to achieve all of this. The goal goes beyond the settling or resolving of different claims to encompass restoring the relationship between the different parts of society. Many Canadian authors have written extensively on this topic[19] and the Canadian Supreme Court has dealt with the notion of reconciliation repeatedly.[20] For present purposes, it is sufficient to highlight the ambitious scope of the Canadian project of reconciliation considering the words of the Truth and Reconciliation Commission: *"Reconciliation must create a more equitable and inclusive society by closing the gaps in social, health, and economic outcomes that exist between Aboriginal and non-Aboriginal Canadians"*.[21] In as far as the relationship of reconciliation and repatriation is concerned, the cases examined suggest that repatriation can contribute to but not secure reconciliation.[22] While negotiations between museums and Indigenous

---

[18] The Oxford English Dictionary Online, available at www.oed.com, entry "reconcile" [last accessed 9.12.2019].

[19] For example, Murphy (2009), p. Ladner (2009), p; Nagy (2014), p; Asch (2014), p.

[20] For example, in Tsilhqot'in: "What is at stake is nothing less than justice for the Aboriginal group and its descendants, and the reconciliation between the group and broader society." Tsilhqot'in Nation v. British Columbia [2014] 2 SCR 257, para. 23.

[21] For an indicative list of the various definitions of reconciliation see BC Minister of Aboriginal Relations and Reconciliation and First Nation Leadership Council (2015), p. 5.

[22] Compare Morton (2010), pp. 104–105 John Morton has considered the relationship between the two in the Australian context and observed: "I view repatriation in precisely these terms – as the simultaneous retrojection of the national spirit into the deep past and projection of that spirit into an indefinite future. A such it as an aspect of so called 'symbolic reconciliation'; though what the symbolism elides is the altogether more messy and turbulent business of 'practical reconciliation' as an aspect of national governance - not simply as a matter of dealing with health issues and the like, but also in terms of the difficulties involved in all matters where Indigenous Australians are in

Peoples are unlikely to affect government to government relationships, mandatory repatriation laws may even hinder reconciling claims. This can occur when the mandatory provision is adopted unilaterally without the consultation and participation of Indigenous Peoples which can ultimately exacerbate existing tensions. Modern treaty negotiations have had weaknesses, but they have resulted in building the foundations for this enterprise for some Indigenous communities. Concerning model 3, a well-designed hybrid legislation that addresses both repatriation and access to and the management of Indigenous heritage and is designed cooperatively, can help to balance the different claims in the sphere of cultural rights but not for the other areas of concern.

Having established this overview of the role of the different repatriation laws in achieving not only repatriation, but other related goals, it is important to consider the mechanisms in more detail. One of the central research questions posed in the beginning was whether the three cases examined have distinct approaches towards achieving repatriation, which was termed '(legal) models'. In the following section, the different models are considered with respect to the goal they can help to achieve and their advantages and disadvantages. Each description also lists a number of elements which would have to be included in their adoption, in addition to the human rights concerns already outlined.

9.3.1 Goal 1: Repatriation of Sacred Objects

9.3.1.1 Model: Mandatory Repatriation Provision Enshrined in Law

Advantages:

- Can be used in cases where many different institutions hold objects.
- Addresses the power imbalance between an Indigenous claimant and a museum. In situations where Indigenous Peoples hold no legal claim to an object, a museum remains in more powerful position in negotiations. A mandatory repatriation, obliging holding institutions to repatriate under certain conditions, remedies this. The resulting consultations can be more equal as a result and can result in long-lasting partnerships.
- Provides for a duty to engage in repatriation. This necessitates an inventory and identification process that can lead to a better understanding of the collection (history).
- Process becomes a chance for re-examination of the past, both inside and outside of the museum community, because of: (a) the potential scale of repatriation

apposition to negotiate with Australian institutions, including museums. Hence repatriation is embedded in the relationship between myth and history – between the myth of an essential national unity and the ongoing histories of conflict and accommodation in the Australian people's myriad relationships with each other."

exercise (b) it occurs after legislative action, meaning after political debate. It is more in the public eye than closed one-on-one negotiations.

- Obligatory nature of mechanisms can improve the cultural rights of numerous Indigenous communities provided that the law is formulated respecting international legal standards.
- Provided that the scope is formulated inclusively, this model provides an equal chance for different Indigenous communities within negotiations. This is not the case for individual negotiations with museums where personal rapport, distance between the museum and the community and financial resources will be more likely to influence negotiation outcomes.
- Can be used both for international repatriations and intra-national repatriations by the same institution.
- Museums will likely be obliged to engage in multiple repatriations. Lessons from individual negotiations can be directly applied to ongoing and future repatriation efforts because the knowledge and experience is already "in-house".

Disadvantages:

- If the law does not include a clause to allow for other agreements to be made, then the mandatory mechanism can prevent other mutually beneficial arrangements from occurring.
- Mandatory nature of process means that definitions of participants, objects etc. become even more crucial to avoid excluding Indigenous communities and violating their cultural rights.
- Depending on the scope of the model and the number of institutions/Indigenous communities, this process will be very costly. It requires financial resources to be set aside in advance and potentially adjusted after the inventory-process is completed and the numbers of potential repatriations more reliable.

Elements to include:

- Before a mandatory repatriation law is designed and adopted, Indigenous Peoples should be consulted and potentially involved in the drafting process to ensure that their cultural and religious rights are respected. This can also ensure that the repatriation framework does not result in the desecration of an object because of scientific efforts to establish a cultural link between the claimant community and the sacred objects.
- The definition of Indigenous Peoples used may not exclude Indigenous Peoples within the territory who identify as Indigenous in line with Art.33(1) UNDRIP.
- The repatriation framework should not require continuing practice between initial practice and time of reclaiming. Contemporary needs and past use prior to removal should be sufficient. This protects Arts.11(1), Art.12(1) UNDRIP.
- Identifying prospective objects should be done in consultation with Indigenous Peoples.

- The repatriation framework should include an escape clause allowing holding institutions and Indigenous people to decide together to opt for different custodial arrangements.
- The repatriation framework should also include a clause to ensure that sacred heritage in public collections that is not repatriated must be made accessible to Indigenous religious practitioners in private, in accordance with Art.12 (1) UNDRIP and Art.18(1) ICCPR.

9.3.1.2 Model: Voluntary Negotiations Between a Museum and the Indigenous Community; Afterwards the Agreement Is Incorporated into the Law if Necessary

Advantages:

- Very flexible mechanism. Negotiations can be adapted in multiple ways depending on the needs of the participants.
- The potential outcome of negotiations (= repatriation agreement) is very flexible. It can be adapted to the individual needs of a museum/holding institution and community.
- Can be initiated by one or both parties whenever they are ready for negotiations, be it museum or community. Note that it would be advisable for the museum to initiate contact and then leave it to community to decide when/whether to take the next step. Communities might not know that the museum potentially holds their sacred objects. Informing communities and then leaving the initiation of negotiations to them enables Indigenous communities to realize their rights. At the same time, this approach does not re-enforce power imbalances that the decolonization process (and maybe even the actual repatriation negotiation) seeks to remedy.
- Neither the start nor the duration of negotiations are dependent on a mandatory timeframe.
- Negotiations are between the actual actors involved, not part of a political process that may overcomplicate matters or politicize the result.

Disadvantages:

- Negotiations cover public collections, but they are behind closed doors. Merely receiving legislative/political approval after the fact circumvents the democratic process. This can be a missed chance for a much-needed public and societal debate on the extent of past removals, colonial assimilation policies and existing inequalities in the exercise of cultural rights.
- Because the entire process is flexible and up to the parties, there is no obligation to ensure that Indigenous rights are respected.
- When the entire process is initiated by non-governmental actors, this decreases the chance of governmental funds being set aside to support repatriation efforts specifically. These can be costly for parties who are likely to operate with already limited resources.

- When heritage laws and/or the law governing the public collection do not clearly permit repatriation, whatever agreement is negotiated will still require legislative approval.
- The additional legislative approval ex post will extend time limits and a positive outcome is not guaranteed. As a result, the negotiation parties may have invested significant time and resources without receiving the intended results. An alternative could be to amend the law governing public collections to allow the museums negotiation and deaccessioning powers in relation to certain categories of items. This would have many of the same disadvantages as the ex post legislative approval (negotiations behind closed doors, no obligation to ensure actor respects Indigenous rights, no repatriation funds). It would, however, allow for speedier processes and can share some of the advantages of this model (flexibility, only involving actors directly involved, if museum adopts carefully designed repatriation policy can put Indigenous Peoples on almost equal footing).

Elements to include:

- Institutional website should have a clear repatriation policy online that is easily (!)[23] accessible and can be found via a simple search function. Any necessary documents to initiate a repatriation claim should also be available online, easy to understand and accompanied by a guideline explaining the steps of a repatriation procedure.
- An institution should adopt a broad understanding of Indigenous Peoples when trying to identify potential claimants. Once the communities are broadly identified and notified, the museum can leave it to respective community to identify itself as Indigenous upon initiating a repatriation claim.
- An institution should adopt a repatriation policy and initiate an inventory process to establish the identity of its holdings on the basis of already existing documents and research. Before initiating any new research into the objects, they should consult the potential claimant communities to ensure that the actions do not result in the desecration of an object because of scientific efforts to establish a cultural link between the claimant community and the sacred objects.
- If there is no enabling law in the beginning but rather an ex-post legal permission of previous negotiations, the law still may not exclude Indigenous Peoples within the territory who identify as Indigenous in line with Art.33(1) UNDRIP.
- If the legislation goes beyond incorporating the negotiated agreement, the repatriation framework should not require continuing practice between initial practice and time of reclaiming. A contemporary need and past use prior to removal should be sufficient. This protects Arts.11(1), Art.12(1) UNDRIP. Moreover, sacred heritage in public collections that is not repatriated must be made accessible to Indigenous religious practitioners in private, in accordance with Art.12 (1) UNDRIP and Art.18(1) ICCPR.

[23] In this author's experience, this is often not the case.

9.3.2 *Goal 2: Remedy Unequal Protection of Indigenous Religious/Cultural Rights*

9.3.2.1 Model: Address Effects of Past Inequalities Through Repatriation and Strengthen Indigenous Cultural Rights Through Heritage Management Provisions

Advantages

- This approach recognizes that past assimilatory practices have led to the relocation of human remains, sacred objects and important Indigenous heritage. This has an effect, *inter alia*, on the enjoyment of the right to religion and the right of Indigenous Peoples to enjoy their own culture. By inserting both repatriation provisions and covering until now buried materials and human remains, this repatriation framework has a better chance of realizing Indigenous cultural rights. Repatriation remedies some of the current effects of past assimilatory laws and policies. Addressing rights and responsibilities in relation to buried heritage in return can reduce future removals and strengthen cultural revitalization efforts.
- As has been the case of the United States, repatriation can serve to strengthen Indigenous rights. Control over Indigenous heritage is an important prerequisite to the enjoyment of different Indigenous rights and a right in itself (Art.31 UNDRIP).
- This approach recognizes that the repatriation of cultural heritage alone is unlikely to improve the living situation of Indigenous Peoples. It can help in realizing cultural rights, and it can be an important step in addressing past injustices, but there are limitations to its benefits. In recognizing this and coupling repatriation with other changes in the legal protection of Indigenous cultural rights, more can be achieved than with purely repatriation-focused mechanisms, such as one-on-one negotiations.

Disadvantages:

- However, a model covering repatriation and Indigenous control over heritage cannot address the many inequalities that continue to exist for Indigenous individuals today by itself. For example, the control over religious objects is of limited benefit when sacred sites cannot be accessed in private. The repatriation of important cultural objects to museums that are located closer to Indigenous communities is of little value when those museums lack important resources such as funding and training.
- This model may create expectations among civil society that inequalities in the protection of Indigenous cultural rights are remedied once the legal framework has been implemented. Yet, they can only *help* in the realization of Indigenous rights. Further actions will be necessary and they also require societal support and political will.

Elements to include:

- Include a provision providing repatriation or private access and use of, or control over, sacred objects. In cooperation with Indigenous communities, repatriate human remains in so far as they have not been repatriated yet.
- Include a provision establishing Indigenous rights to manage, control and use Indigenous heritage, not only on Indigenous lands but also on public lands.
- Include a provision regulating Indigenous control over unexcavated Indigenous heritage. Establish permit procedures jointly with Indigenous communities to regulate future discoveries.

9.3.3 Goal 3: Reconciling Different Sovereignties

9.3.3.1 Model: Modern Treaty Negotiations That Address Land Claims, Resource Rights, Cultural Rights, Governing Rights and More of the Different Sovereign Entities

Advantages:

- Indigenous Peoples and the descendants of former settler communities reside in the same territory. Due to colonization, generally, their co-existence has not been mediated by fair and equal negotiations but rather by right of might. The consequent losses, combined with long-term assimilatory laws and policies have resulted in disenfranchised, disadvantaged and poorer living situations for Indigenous communities. Treaty negotiations that address the full range of claims and rights can address many of the (presumed) root causes of the problem.
- In negotiating modern treaties, there is also a better chance of improving the inequalities in the protection of cultural rights, since the full spectrum of necessary activities and resources that are specific to an Indigenous people can be addressed.
- The long negotiation period that results from such a wide range of topics can also be an advantage in building sustainable relationships between the parties. Better relationships between the different governing bodies will increase the chances of reconciling their different demands and needs.
- The scope of such negotiations necessitates a framework to structure them. Such a framework represents a chance to equip parties with the necessary resources to increase the chances of success. It also provides regulatory space to ensure that Indigenous procedural rights are protected. Both of these factors are not necessarily present in private negotiations between museums and Indigenous communities.

Disadvantages:

- Reconciliation cannot occur when the mechanism itself exacerbates existing inequalities. Parties coming to the table are unlikely to have the same resources available. To give only one example, to have a chance at reconciliation, financial resources must be made available to Indigenous nations to support negotiation endeavors (note: *not* as a loan).
- By necessity, the wide range of issues to be negotiated will require a long negotiation period (years, possibly even decades, see B.C. example). In the meantime, Indigenous rights are vulnerable to additional limitations, violations or even extinction before a new treaty can fully protect them.
- This is not the most efficient mechanism to ensure the repatriation of sacred heritage, because it addresses many other needs as well. As a result, resources (time/money/people) are focused on many different issues other than repatriation. As a result, the mechanism is not advisable where the aim is the actual physical repatriation of Indigenous heritage within a given timeframe for different reasons, i.e. closure of an ethnographic museum.
- Because of the duration and costs, this model needs sufficient support from civil society and the political will of changing governments, which may be difficult to sustain the longer the process lasts.

Elements to include:

- Before the negotiations can commence, ample funds need to be set aside to enable Indigenous communities to meet negotiating costs.
- An act providing the framework the negotiations should follow must be adopted. Such a framework will need to address who is authorized to negotiate (note: *remember* Indigenous right of self-identification), how negotiation funds may be accessed, possible legal areas to be covered, an outline of the different steps of the negotiations, how and at which stage the different parties acquire the consent of their constituencies, establish a body to provide secretarial support during the negotiations and consider establishing a representative mediating or dispute settlement body to cover disputes arising during or even after the treaties. While, strictly speaking, the last element could be provided by existing dispute settlement mechanisms, notably the courts, these exist by and large within one of the different legal cultures. It will thus be difficult for them to settle disputes that in effect arise at the border of their legal sphere and Indigenous laws and traditions. Moreover, a representative body would increase the chances among the participants of accepting the settlement of a dispute.
- The final treaties should also include a provision which allows for all parties to introduce modifications to the treaty jointly in the future.

9.4 Conclusion to Chapter 9

The analysis concludes that repatriation can be a crucial piece in improving the human rights of Indigenous communities but it requires the corresponding national legal context. Nationally, different models can be used which can all achieve the physical repatriation of sacred objects, albeit at varying speeds and with different side-benefits. The different models lend themselves to pursue very different objectives next to repatriation. The crucial first step in adopting any legal framework for repatriation is therefore an open dialogue between the actors involved to establish a common goal, if possible. This way, the cooperation can yield mutually beneficial results next to repatriation which may otherwise be lost. With this knowledge, a suitable repatriation framework can be chosen.

As a next step, designing the repatriation framework should be in accordance with human rights and strengthen them as much as possible. The guidelines established can provide helpful in this respect. In the national context, a state has the full spectrum of human rights obligations to respect, protect and fulfil vis-à-vis its citizens. There is, in effect, no one repatriation model that should be followed in light of international standards. Instead, all models have their difficulties, but they can be adjusted to respect the human rights guidelines listed in Sect. 9.2.3.1. Instead, the author recommends that the repatriation model should be chosen and structured to reflect the aim that motivated the actors to engage in repatriation in the first place. Is the desire purely to repatriate as many objects as possible? Then a mandatory repatriation framework is advisable. But if repatriation is motivated by the desire to address a country's problematic history and treatment of the respective Indigenous communities then the author's recommendation would differ. All of this may not be immediately clear to the parties at the outset. This is why it is so important to start with a consultative dialogue that engages all parties before a framework is drafted, let alone adopted.

In the meantime, the debate on the benefits and limits of repatriation remains heated. It was seen repeatedly that repatriation is a complex matter and the question of whether to return or not can in effect not be answered on a purely theoretical level. Instead, its answer depends on the specific context of the cultural heritage that is being reclaimed. Important questions in this regard are not only whether the cultural and historical context of an object can be established but whether potential recipients actually wish to receive the object. Moreover, as was highlighted throughout this research, the mere desire to return is insufficient if it is not coupled with providing the necessary resources to transform repatriation from a political gesture into an act that can have actual benefits to the claimant community.

References[24]

Asch M (2014) On being here to stay. Toronto University Press, Toronto, Canada
BC Minister of Aboriginal Relations and Reconciliation, First Nation Leadership Council (2015) British Columbia - First Nations Proposed Commitment Document. online draft document
Kuprecht K (2014) Indigenous peoples' cultural property claims - repatriation and beyond. Springer
Ladner KL (2009) Take 35: reconciling constitutional orders. In: Timpson AM (ed) First nations, first thoughts: the impact of indigneous thought in Canada. UBC Press, Vancouver, Canada, p 279
Morton J (2010) Consigned to oblivion: people and things forgotten in the creation of Australia. In: Turnbull P, Pickering M (eds) The long way home - the meanings and values of repatriation. Berghahn Books, New York, pp 96–113
Murphy M (2009) Civilization, self-determination, and reconciliation. In: Timpson AM (ed) First nations, first thoughts: the impact of indigenous thought in Canada. UBC Press, Vancouver, Canada, pp 251–278
Nagy R (2014) The Truth and Reconciliation Commission of Canada: genesis and design. Can J Law Soc/La Revue Canadienne Droit et Société 29(Special Issue 02):199–217. https://doi.org/10.1017/cls.2014.8
van Beurden J (2017) Treasures in trusted hands - negotiating the future of colonial cultural objects. Interdisciplinary studies in culture, history and heritage. Sidestone Press, Leiden

[24]Please be aware that Part IV (Chaps. 9 and 10) construct repatriation models and analyse their relationship on the basis of the research conducted in the previous chapters, including the sources referenced there.

Chapter 10
Summary, Conclusion and Recommendations

10.1 Introduction

This study aimed to consolidate the lessons that exist from almost 30 years of regulating repatriation through the law, to facilitate the work of actors who are now about to engage in repatriation. This is reflected in the research questions posed at the outset, namely *how should the repatriation of Indigenous sacred cultural heritage be regulated in light of international human rights and cultural heritage law standards? And second, is there anything else we can derive from these findings for the national cultural heritage law and policy of Canada and the United States?* Since the adoption of the first legal instruments that regulated the repatriation of Indigenous cultural heritage a lot has changed, in particular in the Indigenous rights movement. To reflect these changes and provide recommendations that are based not only on experience but also are up to date in light of legal advances that were made, the author analysed the repatriation laws in light of international human rights law. This is crucial, as there is continued reticence of state actors to align international cultural heritage law with human rights standards, and this has impacted Indigenous Peoples in particular. The first section will answer the first central research and summarize the relevant analysis that was necessary to reach this answer. The second section will then consider whether there are any other lessons that derive from the analysis for national cultural heritage law and policy of Canada and the United States. The third section compiles the important lessons learned into recommendations for future repatriation mechanisms as well as research. This book will conclude with a short outlook discussing the possible future of repatriation and avenues for further research.

Please note that this chapter adopts the capitalization of the terms Indigenous Peoples and Indigenous (except for when used in citations) for reasons explained in Chap. 1.

V. Tünsmeyer, *Repatriation of Sacred Indigenous Cultural Heritage and the Law*, Studies in Art, Heritage, Law and the Market 3,
https://doi.org/10.1007/978-3-030-89047-6_10

10.2 How Should the Repatriation of Indigenous Sacred Cultural Heritage Be Regulated Legally in Light of International Cultural Heritage and Human Rights Law Standards?

This research proposed to derive standards from international cultural heritage and international human rights to evaluate which mechanism should be used to structure repatriation legally. This section will elaborate on the human rights guidelines which should be respected and the reasons for this (see Sects. 10.2.1 and 10.2.2). Then the findings of Chap. 3 will be summarized, which showed that there is no need for additional guidelines based on international cultural heritage law (see Sect. 10.2.3). Finally, Sect. 10.2.4 will answer the first research question.

Cultural heritage is an important resource for a wide range of human rights. This connection has been highlighted on the international level, *inter alia* through the works of the Special Rapporteur in the field of cultural rights. Unsurprisingly, repatriation of cultural heritage affects a number of Indigenous rights, and the research that was undertaken has clarified this connection. In particular, we have seen how repatriation of sacred heritage can be a measure that a state can take to strengthen a number of different rights, including the Indigenous right to cultural heritage and the Indigenous right to their religious practices. Furthermore, the research emphasized that human rights law also demands certain elements to be included in a repatriation framework to respect and protect different rights. In international human rights law, there is no state obligation to repatriate sacred heritage. However, repatriation is a means to realize a number of obligations that a state has towards the Indigenous Peoples within its territory. First, it complies with duty to fulfil the freedom to manifest religion; an alternative measure to fulfil this right would be to guarantee Indigenous access and use of sacred objects that are under governmental control. Second, it fulfils the Indigenous right to minority culture, including the right to control cultural heritage. Third, it is a measure to protect and fulfils the Indigenous right to their cultural identity, including the right to revitalize their cultural traditions.

In the course of the analysis, more general human rights standards were drafted, which were derived by considering the relevant treaty articles and their relationship to repatriation.[1] This analysis was informed by the general comments of the respective treaty bodies, the reports of different special rapporteurs and expert committees. Because of the broadness of the relevant cultural rights articles and the specific nature of repatriation and Indigenous cultural practices, the observations in part I were still rather broad in nature. The standards derived in Part I were therefore applied to the outcomes of the national legal analysis. This yielded a nine more specific guidelines. These principles operationalize Indigenous cultural rights for the actors who engage in repatriation and may be unfamiliar with the specifics of the human rights canon.

---

[1] See Chap. 2 for standards and the human rights provisions on which they are based, in particular Sect. 2.6.1.

10.2.1 Repatriation-Specific Guidelines

These guidelines can be structured in accordance with the procedure of adopting a repatriation law. This means that there are human rights standards and obligations which have to be respected in the drafting phase of the law, those that have to be incorporated into the repatriation legislation itself, and those which need to be respected in the implementation of the repatriation legislation. These are indicated below.

Drafting phase

1. The repatriation framework itself should be developed in cooperation with the Indigenous Peoples concerned. It is important to collaborate with Indigenous Peoples to ensure respect for different Indigenous cultural rights that can be affected by the framework. This operationalizes different elements of a number of rights, in particular Art.11(2) UNDRIP and Art.38 UNDRIP.

Repatriation legislation: Scope

2. Respect Indigenous beliefs in the definition of religious object by respecting Indigenous authority and practices to identify sacredness. Interference with Indigenous religious practices only permissible under the (very narrow) conditions of Art.18(3) ICCPR and the additional limitation imposed by Art.27 IRCCPR.
3. Respect the Indigenous right to self-identification; do not impose a governmental definition of Indigenous identity that is contrary to Indigenous self-identification. The definition of Indigenous Peoples used may not exclude Indigenous Peoples within the territory who identify as Indigenous in line with Art.33(1) UNDRIP.

Repatriation legislation: Regulating repatriation procedure

4. In connecting a sacred object to a community, Indigenous customary legal traditions should be respected. If scientific methods are used to connect objects to communities' actors should obtain FPIC for measures that affect Indigenous cultural rights.
5. The repatriation framework should not require a continuing practice between initial practice and the time of reclaiming if the object is reclaimed for contemporary use. This is an important safeguard to ensure that a state respects the Indigenous right to revitalization. This is also part of the fulfil dimension of freedom of religion. A decision not to repatriate must therefore be permissible under the relevant limitation clauses of Art.27 ICCPR and Art.18(3) ICCPR.
6. Respect Indigenous rights to their own legal traditions by incorporating Indigenous customary practices within a repatriation framework if these are in accordance with international human rights law. Examples of measures that can be taken in accordance with Indigenous legal traditions are

a. identify linkage between object and community,
b. identification of custodian of heritage,
c. incorporation of oral testimony where relevant.

Implementing repatriation legislation

7. Identifying Indigenous cultural heritage should be done in consultation with Indigenous Peoples to guarantee Art.31 UNDRIP.
8. Do not dictate conditions for Indigenous Peoples to fulfil upon the repatriation of sacred objects in order to respect Indigenous right to their own heritage under Art.31 UNDRIP.
9. Sacred heritage in public collections that is not repatriated must be made accessible to Indigenous religious practitioners in private, in accordance with Art.12(1) UNDRIP and Art.18(1) ICCPR.

10.2.2 Evaluating Whether State Measures on Sacred Indigenous Cultural Heritage Amount to a Human Rights Violation

There is another dimension to the research question of how repatriation of sacred cultural heritage should best be regulated in light of international human rights standards. On top of asking which actions a state should take under a repatriation legislation to respect international standards we should also ask which steps it may *not* take under these standards. To be in line with international standards, not only must the drafted repatriation law respect international standards, but the actual practice of a state in engaging with Indigenous Peoples and their sacred cultural heritage must also be in line with human rights standards. A difficulty that has appeared at different stages of this research is that human rights are quite broad on the international level, especially in the area of cultural rights. However, human rights only gain their actual value for Indigenous individuals and communities in their specific application to the challenges they face. The research repeatedly emphasized the margin of discretion that states have in deciding how they implement an existing obligation. Moreover, a state can also take measures that limit Indigenous rights if these measures are in line with the limitation clauses under the relevant treaties. Limitation clauses are a necessary part of human rights to allow for balancing the different rights that inevitably clash with each other. All of this means that the actions a state may not take with regards to a repatriation legislation cannot be elaborated in the abstract.

To reflect this and give repatriation actors more guidance to evaluate state actions, I thus also elaborated on the steps that are necessary to evaluate whether state actions that limit human rights amount to violations. There is no obligation to repatriate sacred heritage and no specific right to the repatriation of Indigenous sacred cultural heritage. But there is a right that is very closely connected to repatriation. The repatriation of sacred objects is not mandated under UNDRIP but states are asked to enable repatriation or access agreements in order to protect the Indigenous right to manifest, practise, develop and teach their spiritual and religious traditions, customs and ceremonies. State practice that limits the Indigenous right to their spiritual and religious traditions is thus likely to affect repatriation; the actions may even be caused by repatriation legislation. In particular, the author focussed on whether a state measure still permits access and use of sacred objects (Art.12(1) UNDRIP) which has been interpreted to be a contextualization of Art.27 ICCPR and—depending on the context—a pre-condition for Indigenous individuals to manifest their religion under Art.18(1) ICCPR. Both articles impose binding human rights obligations upon states (Fig. 10.1).

Whether or not a state violated its obligations under international law and went beyond what is permitted under the existing limitation clauses can only be judged in a given case. Testing how this takes shape for all communities that fall under a given repatriation law is beyond the scope of this thesis. The analysis can however identify which conditions a state measure has to fulfil that limits Indigenous access to and control of sacred objects and apply these to the selected repatriation cases to give

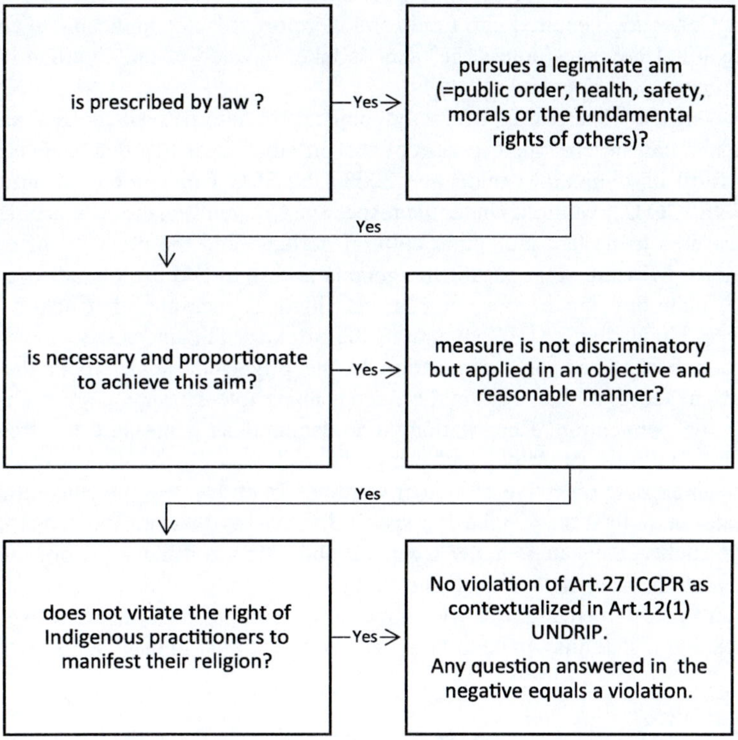

Fig. 10.1 Test to evaluate limitations imposed on the Indigenous right to access and use of their sacred objects (repeat of Chap. 2)

practitioners further guidance, as was done in the US and Canadian context. Mock scenarios were considered to highlight the instances where a state measure might prove problematic. Together, the human rights guidelines and the test can be used to evaluate repatriation frameworks for their compatibility with international standards.

10.2.3 Standards Arising Out of International Cultural Heritage Law

The first research question employs international human rights law and international cultural heritage as a measuring standard by which to evaluate repatriation legislation. The guidelines elaborated above, however, are based on human rights law alone. As was seen in Chap. 3, international cultural heritage law does not oblige states to return cultural heritage taken during colonialism to Indigenous communities, either abroad or within their own territory. However, existing ICHL instruments incorporate provisions that do affect *intra-national* repatriation. The most concrete example of a return obligation for sacred Indigenous heritage exists in the 1995 UNIDROIT Convention. However, it applies to sacred objects that leave the country after the Convention entered into force, and therefore it is not applicable to colonial sacred cultural heritage (unless the latter is taken outside of the community for a second time).

However, the repatriation of sacred objects, or alternatively access and use agreements, can be classified as one of the possible measures that a state has to take to fulfil its obligations under the 2003 UNESCO Convention and under the 2005 UNESCO Convention. Under the respective Convention, the state is obliged to take measures to protect intangible cultural heritage and the diversity of cultural expressions. Measures that ensure Indigenous access to and use of sacred cultural heritage, including repatriation, can be classified as measures that achieve both objectives. Under the 2003 Convention, the artefacts fall under the scope of the convention because of their connection to the protected ritual. Under the 2005 Convention, access to their cultural heritage is a possible measure expressly considered by the convention. Repatriation, if understood as a measure to strengthen Indigenous cultures, promotes and protects the diversity of cultural expressions, which is an express objective of the convention.[2] In both cases, the conventions do not create an obligation to take the specific measures that are the focus of this research. Rather, the state is under a general obligation to achieve the objectives of the conventions and, in line with the particular treaty provisions, repatriation or access and use agreements qualify as measures to achieve these objectives. The measures that a state may have to take under international human rights law go far

[2] Art.1(a) CDCE.

beyond what a state is legally required to do under the UNESCO instruments. For this reason, it was sufficient to apply the principles developed in Chap. 2 to evaluate the three repatriation examples in Chaps. 4–8.

10.2.4 Different Mechanisms to Regulate Repatriation in Light of International Standards

As Chap. 9 and the comparative analysis of the different repatriation laws showed, there are different ways (models) in which repatriation can be structured. Chapter 9 distinguishes between four different models: a mandatory repatriation legislation, bottom-up negotiations between Indigenous communities and the holding institution that facilitated through the law, a combination of heritage management and repatriation provisions and modern-day treaty negotiations. These models have distinct advantages and disadvantages that were elaborated upon in the previous chapter.

What they have in common is that all of them can be constructed to respect relevant human rights guidelines provided that all actors are aware of them and guide their behaviour accordingly. In this aspect the state as body that incurs obligations under international law needs to be proactive. Advance guidance is important in this respect, especially to museums who may not be aware of considering the human rights dimension of their actions given that they do not incur obligations under the relevant treaties. In this respect it should be noted that bottom-up negotiations (model two) should best be combined with ex ante legislative approval in which the state elaborates upon the need to respect human rights standards. To answer the first research question, there are thus different ways to regulate repatriation of sacred cultural heritage in light of international human rights and cultural heritage law standards. The important element in evaluating the standard is then not so much which model was chosen, but whether the model was drafted and implemented in a way that respects these guidelines.

Does this mean that repatriation legislation can be structured any which way provided these guidelines are respected? The analysis suggests that this is not the case. It appears as if different repatriation mechanisms lend themselves to pursue different goals. Each model has distinct advantages and disadvantages. Instead of recommending one way to regulate repatriation, the author would thus recommend to first take stock of the factors that interact with and shape the repatriation framework: What is the legal-historical context and the legal system in place? What are the legal rules that are in place that a repatriation framework has to adhere to that cannot be changed by adopting a particular model? What is the scale of relocation (number of objects and institutions), the diversity of Indigenous communities and their hopes and needs for the process (this will become apparent in the initial collaborative consultation process, see human rights principles above), the willingness (or lack thereof) of museums to repatriate, and the general Indigenous rights record within the country? And perhaps most important, in light of all of this information, what is the underlying aim that the actors hope to achieve through the repatriation framework?

The analysis has highlighted how important it is to clarify the aims that the framework seeks to achieve. This then leads us to answering the research question of how repatriation should be regulated with the following proposition: How a repatriation framework is structured should be guided by the consideration which repatriation model has the best chance of realizing the goal that the actors want to achieve and factor in the legal, historical and cultural factors at play. Goals differ and there are different ways in which repatriation can be achieved. Repatriation is a resource-intense endeavour, and therefore every care should be taken to facilitate the achievement of the goals sought. This includes taking care in the consultation, drafting and implementing process to adopt the legal framework to the legal preconditions that cannot be changed as well as to the needs and resources of the actors at play. The discussion of the different models, their advantages and disadvantages and elements to be included can prove to be a useful starting point for this. Not all models lend themselves equally well to achieving all aims. An important first step for all cases is thus to consult and agree upon common objectives that the repatriation framework should (help to) achieve.

This then leads us to the next step. Once consultations have taken place expectations have been spelled out, the chosen framework needs to be drafted and implemented in a way that respects the human rights guidelines elaborated upon in this research. This can be done for all models. The guidelines are, in effect, not dependent on a specific approach. Instead, what is necessary is governmental awareness and willingness to adopt a rights-based approach to their heritage legislation and management, including through—but not limited to—repatriation legislation. For the case of intra-national repatriations, this has the added benefit of aligning repatriations with steps that the government should take to further its compliance with international human rights treaties in any event. The preceding chapters have shown that repatriation and Indigenous cultural rights are closely connected. Repatriation legislation cannot only respect but also advance Indigenous human rights and achieve very different legislative goals at the same time. At a minimum, any repatriation legislation should thus be rights-based and respect the guidelines derived in Chap. 9.

10.3 What—If Anything—Can We Derive from the Findings of the Country Analysis in Light of the International Standards for the Cultural Heritage Law and Policy of the Selected Countries?

The second research question gave room to consider the contextual analysis of national law in light of the international legal standards that were the outcome of the analysis of international law in Part I. Chapters 4 to 8 looked beyond the repatriation-specific legislation at the national level to the legal relationship of Indigenous Peoples and the respective government actors at the national and regional level, the historic roots of contemporary cultural rights struggles of Indigenous Peoples, the rules that guide museum actors and the values enshrined in national cultural heritage law. All of this has shown that national cultural heritage and policy still has some ways to go to fully align with contemporary human rights standards. This goes for the specific cultural heritage law that is drafted by the legislatures, the way it is implemented by the relevant cultural agencies and even for museum and the way they guide their own actions through industry-specific codes of ethics.

10.3.1 Guidelines to Incorporate into National Cultural Heritage Law and Policy

The application of human rights standards to the legal context in which repatriation is situated, in particular national cultural heritage law, yielded a number of additional lessons on the national cultural heritage law and policy that affects Indigenous rights to their sacred cultural heritage. This answers the second research question posed in this study, which left room for any insights that may be gained by looking so closely at the legal relationship between cultural rights on the one hand and Indigenous cultural heritage that rests in museum and/or state control on the other. Chapters 5 and 8 recommended some changes for the United States and Canada respectively. Generalizing these recommendations, they can be summarized in the guidelines below to answer the second research question:

1. States should encourage museums to ensure that, where custodial agreements are made for sacred cultural heritage and it is not repatriated, the Indigenous right to maintain and protect their heritage in accordance with their traditional practices under Art.11(1) UNDRIP is still protected.
2. Heritage legislation and policy has to require FPIC for governmental measures that affect Indigenous cultural rights, for example:

    a. State archaeological branches that issue excavation permits for potential Indigenous sites qualify as governmental actors who have to obtain FPIC.

b. Public museums that exhibit sacred cultural heritage in a way that could lead to its desecration.
c. Any action that interferes with a sacred site that is sanctioned or carried out by a governmental actor can affect Indigenous rights. Consultation is a minimum requirement, depending on the impact, FPIC will be necessary. Any legislation or policy measure that affects sacred sites should not unduly interfere with Indigenous Peoples' rights of access to sites. This is an important measure to respect Indigenous rights to manifest their religion.

3. States should take measures to protect and fulfil Indigenous access to sacred sites—a wide margin of discretionary measures is possible.

    a. States should take measures to prevent third-person conduct that desecrates Indigenous cultural heritage. This includes encouraging private museums not to display sacred objects unless with the FPIC of affected community.

4. States should (better) incorporate Indigenous rights into their heritage in export legislation. This includes taking steps to prevent cultural and sacred objects from leaving state territory without the consent of the tribe.
5. States should protect and fulfil Indigenous rights to their cultural heritage. The state is under the positive duty to progressively create conditions in which Indigenous Peoples can control their heritage according to their own traditions. There are many different measures states can take, for example:

    a. Include Indigenous staff in national/regional/local heritage administration to care for Indigenous heritage.
    b. Encourage museums to employ Indigenous staff, support heritage management/museology studies for Indigenous individuals.
    c. Accommodate Indigenous heritage laws covering Indigenous lands within national heritage law schemes.

6. States can fulfil Indigenous rights to their cultural identity by supporting programs that address the results of past discriminatory practices which may continue to affect Indigenous rights to preserve and develop their own cultural identity, for example residential schools.

Mostly, these guidelines constitute steps that states should take in their cultural heritage legislation. This is not surprising, given that human rights law imposes obligations upon states. However, they are also measures that museums can decide to take by themselves (without state intervention) if they wish to align their behaviour with human rights standards. For example, museums can make sure to collaborate and consult with Indigenous Peoples on exhibitions that deal with Indigenous cultures and history, including the effects of colonialism. This strengthens the Indigenous right to their cultural identity. To respect the Indigenous right to their heritage, they can acquire their free, prior and informed consent and guidance on dealing with sacred cultural heritage. Similarly, museum boards can try to staff their institution in a more representative manner and encourage the training and employment of Indigenous curators, while keeping an open mind to alternative traditions of what conservation and care-taking might mean. Various museums in both countries have already taken these steps. Some of these measures could also be taken by European museums who might not have the same experience of collaborating with Indigenous communities and can take inspiration from their (North-American) colleagues.

10.4 Recommendations: Lessons for Future Repatriation Laws

This research took a detailed look at the ways in which the law can structure repatriation. Furthermore, repatriation legislation was examined in light of Indigenous rights standards, to link the strengthening of Indigenous human rights at the international level to the national legal level. Human rights implementation occurs at the national level. Sacred cultural heritage is connected to a variety of different human rights. To connect the two is crucial. It operationalizes international standards for Indigenous Peoples in their everyday life, concretizes the human rights dimension for cultural heritage actors who may not be familiar with it and reminds the states of the obligations it incurred when ratifying the major human rights instruments in the field.

Calls for the return of Indigenous colonial cultural heritage from European museums to communities or state governments abroad are not new. What is new is the wide-spread debate and willingness among European museums to consider repatriation. We might be witnessing an evolution that is comparable to the shift that occurred decades earlier in the museum sector in North America. It has had a profound impact on the conservation of Indigenous cultural heritage, museum collaborations with Indigenous Peoples and exhibits of Indigenous culture and history. If there will be renewed repatriations from Europe, this will happen internationally, but it may also give rise to further inter-national repatriations from former colonies. Given that there is a wealth of materials from which to learn, the research thus asked how should repatriation be structured legally in light of international cultural heritage and human rights law standards? The recommendation was to be based on the analysis of US and Canadian legal experience, to be measured against a standard based on the relevant international law. The research has yielded a number of important insights for both international and intra-national repatriations, in general, and intra-national repatriations, in particular. It has shown that there is a possibility to structure repatriation in a way that implements contemporary human rights standards. To aid in this process, nine guidelines were presented.

Next to this, the wealth of experience in Canada and the United States that was analysed has also yielded some additional insight into aspects which should be considered in repatriation that are not necessarily connected to the question of human rights. An important question in this regard is in how far these lessons that were learned in the context of intra-national repatriations are transferable to international repatriations. This is considered in Sect. 10.4.2 below.

10.4.1 General Lessons Applicable to Repatriations

The comparison between the different mechanisms, their advantages and disadvantages and the analysis of their relationship to human rights have highlighted a number of important lessons for future repatriations. First, before any repatriation law is drafted, a government should schedule time for a dialogue among all parties: museums, Indigenous Peoples, scientists, government officials (including heritage agencies) and civil society. Through this, the different positions and wishes will become clearer. Questions to consider are, for example: Is there a basic desire to repatriate on the side of (some of the) museums? What are the reasons identified in favor and against repatriation? What is the scope of the relevant public collections? Is there any provenance information available? What do actors hope that the repatriation process should achieve? Is there common ground among them, for example, the desire to gain knowledge on the history of collections or to address past injustices? All of this can help in choosing the best repatriation model and to draft it accordingly as highlighted above. In considering the experiences analysed in Chaps. 4–8, a number of elements that should be avoided can be distinguished from those that should be incorporated.

10.4.1.1 Elements to Be Avoided

From the examined cases, the following particularities should be avoided: First, one may be tempted to draft a definite end date by which a repatriation should be completed. This should be avoided, irrespective of whether repatriation features mandatory repatriation provisions or focusses predominantly on procedural elements (negotiation, consultation, FPIC), since experience has shown that these processes take time. Second, a rigid and detailed description of religious heritage should be avoided. Different Indigenous cultures will have different religious practices and different forms of cultural heritage. It is best to leave identifying religious cultural heritage to knowledgeable Indigenous practitioners. Aside from all human rights concerns in this matter (which are a reason in and of themselves to avoid this), rigid definitions risk misidentification of objects and the exclusion of objects which should fall under the scope of the mechanism from an Indigenous perspective. Third, in the wording of the actual repatriation process, the law should not be too rigid. In particular, it should leave some flexibility for Indigenous Peoples and museums to find different resolutions jointly. Depending on the goal behind the repatriation process, it may be better to set minimum repatriation requirements while leaving the opportunity for other arrangements to be made if both parties agree.

Correspondingly, there are also a number of elements that should be included that are examined below.

10.4.1.2 Elements to Be Included

Inventory and Consultation

In drafting the scope of the repatriation law, both Indigenous individuals and communities have to be included, to respect their human rights and to avoid imposing outside standards and norms in a renewed assimilatory attempt. Members of the museum communities should of course also be included in the consultations to account for different custodial practices. If museums are not sure as to the content of their collection, the legislator may consider incorporating timelines for the completion of the inventory process, depending on the extent of consultation possibilities. Given that identification should occur jointly with Indigenous Peoples, and especially for larger collections, a longer time period will be necessary. This is especially the case where the museum is not allocated additional funding for this stage of the process and it has to undertake considerable research work next to its regular operations. Overall, it is important to schedule a longer period of time to account for consultation.

Given the need to incorporate a consultation requirement both in the identification process of religious heritage and as part of repatriation process, realistic timelines are crucial. Moreover, this is a process that takes time, money and resources. This includes considering alternative means of access and consultation, most notably online, if the community is located a long distance away from the museum. As was evidenced in the case of NAGPRA, the duration of the consultations is dependent on a multitude of factors, including the number of objects, the records available, the number of Indigenous parties etc. Apart from this, if the ensuing repatriation process itself is open-ended and left to Indigenous communities and museums, this should be balanced by incorporating deadlines for museums to react to repatriation requests by Indigenous Peoples. Conversely, timelines should be set for Indigenous Peoples to lodge complaints appealing repatriation decisions.

Identifying Sacredness and the Connecting Community

As was highlighted in the proposed guidelines, it is important to define the sacredness of an object from the perspective of the Indigenous practitioners. This can be done, for example, by incorporating Indigenous laws on sacred practices and by leaving the identification of sacredness to religious leaders. The law thereby creates a space for incorporating Indigenous understandings of sacredness and linked personal responsibility that are difficult for non-Indigenous policy makers to understand and define.[3] Aside from the human rights concerns that endorse this approach, there is also the simple fact that relying purely on Western record-keeping and identification

[3] Bell (1992), pp. 462–463.

methods misidentifies the object. The assumption that because a written record is necessarily more reliable than an oral histories has proven false in practice. This way, written records can be complemented by oral histories. Procedural rules should allow for different types of evidence to be presented and to be weighed equally.[4] This is an important lesson from both Canada and the United States which highlights the need to ensure that Indigenous evidence is evaluated on an equal footing with non-Indigenous evidence, as prejudice against oral evidence continues to exist. If this results in fears that the potential number of religious objects will be unlimited (the familiar opening the floodgates argument), one may consider incorporating a limiting criterion of contemporary usage, as was done in NAGPRA. Moreover, the mechanism should allow for the possibility to update rules at predetermined intervals, to allow for changes depending on the lessons learned. This goes for rules on identifying objects, linking objects to communities etc.

Allow for Flexible Solutions

As was highlighted above, there is a need to combine the rigidity of a repatriation law with at least some degree of flexibility to allow Indigenous Peoples and museums to find other mutually satisfying solutions. This way, the advantages of a mandatory legal framework are maintained, while the disadvantages of using Western law to consider Indigenous legal and cultural claims is mitigated in part.[5]

Preparing Resources in Advance

The repatriation mechanism should also prepare repatriation sufficiently in terms of resources. This means that individuals who will be responsible for implementing the repatriation law should be provided with additional training. Moreover, additional training should be scheduled further along the implementation process to account for additional lessons learned. Next to this, a state should set aside *sufficient* funds to provide for the needs of *all* implementing parties. These will be needed in all stages of the process.

Establish a Clear Oversight Structure for the Implementation Phase

The legal requirement to build clear channels of communication is crucial for Indigenous rights, which mostly require cross-cultural implementation in a national legal system or even across legal systems. This is an important lesson for any repatriation model, irrespective of the specific goal (be it physical repatriation or a broader goal of reconciliation) that the government seeks to achieve. This requires, for example, a clear oversight structure for the implementation of a repatriation law, first indicating who is given the power to monitor compliance and second obliging all implementing parties to submit the necessary information at regular intervals.

[4] On admissibility of Indigenous oral testimony see Babcock (2012).

[5] Compare Coombe (1993), pp. 263–264 Coombe observes "Even more debilitating for Native claims, perhaps, is the law's rigid demarcation between ideas and expressions, oral traditions and written forms, intangible works and cultural objects, personal property and real property. The law rips asunder what First Nations people view as integrally related, freezing into categories what Native peoples find flowing in relationships."

This includes information on the number of religious items, repatriation requests submitted, repatriation requests granted and the number of items finally repatriated (a lesson from the US). It also requires the identification and publication of contacts for individuals within museums and governmental agencies who are responsible for the implementation of a repatriation model. Correspondingly, Indigenous communities who have submitted repatriation claims should be required to indicate a contact person within their submission.

Establish a Dispute Settlement Mechanism
Lastly, the repatriation mechanism should also provide for a representative settlement mechanism in the case of disagreement between the parties from the outset, i.e. in the case of disagreements on the cultural link between a community and heritage objects. In both countries, there were difficulties that Indigenous claimants faced in translating their claims to a largely non-Indigenous judiciary that practices fully within the common law system. The repatriation mechanism should thus establish a representative dispute settlement mechanism with the authority to make binding decisions in the case of disagreement. It is necessary that this body includes Indigenous individuals, including those that are experienced in Indigenous religious expressions. Otherwise, judges who are trained exclusively in the language and law of one culture will end up having to try to mediate between the two perspectives.

10.4.1.3 Lessons for Museums

The preceding analysis also highlighted four important lessons for museums. First, in most cases, the repatriation law will need to cover different Indigenous cultures, thereby leaving (ample) space for a museum to act in a way suitable to its own collection and the distinctive cultural needs of Indigenous claimants. It is crucial that the museum formulate clear deaccessioning policies that incorporate the particularities of repatriating Indigenous cultural heritage. Second, as was learned in the United States, the repatriation of sacred materials will likely disclose very sensitive cultural information. A museum should plan for this well in advance and adopt institutional guidelines on how to deal with such information acquired in the course of repatriation. Third, irrespective of any repatriation claims that are being negotiated, museums with Indigenous cultural heritage should consult with Indigenous Peoples, in particular elders, priests and other cultural experts about Indigenous curatorial traditions.[6] This not only can prevent the desecration of important religious heritage before it is repatriated but it can also allow for mutual learning covering the entirety of the Indigenous collection. Lastly, as was seen in the Canadian example, the composition of museum personnel does not necessarily

[6] In agreement Kreps (2009), p. 195. She observed: "The word curator is derived from the Latin word curare, which means 'to take care of'. If we think of curators as caretakers and guardians of culture, we can see how certain individuals in many societies, such as priests, ritual specialists, shamans, and elders, are curators."

reflect the museum's cultural collections. Museums with significant Indigenous collections, especially in countries with resident Indigenous communities, should consider hiring Indigenous curators and museum personnel. It would be helpful if the museum followed some of the Canadian examples considered, in considering (the impact of) their work within the framework of human rights, in particular UNDRIP.

10.4.2 Transferability of Models to International Returns

The previous section provided a number of lessons that are generally applicable both to intra-national as well as international repatriations. Some of these will be more difficult to achieve in the international context, most notably consultation. However, this should not be taken to excuse a state (or museum) from disregarding consultation (altogether). Indeed, this has been one important lesson to take away from all intra-national repatriations. Irrespective of its human rights context, consultation and cooperation with Indigenous Peoples is crucial to successful repatriations for three reasons. First, it balances the scales and moves away from colonial power asymmetries. It is thus an important part of the decolonizing process and a means to hopefully avoid assimilation. Second, knowledge is pooled that would otherwise not be accessible. Third, because of the complex history behind objects coupled with poor record keeping, identifying sacred objects and their connected Indigenous community may otherwise not be possible. Another lesson that will be more difficult to realize in the context of international repatriations is to establish a clear oversight structure and to establish a representative dispute settlement mechanism. The arguments that speak to their necessity in the national context still hold true in the international scenario, but the sheer physical distance will render their operation more difficult. Another point to consider is that line between intra- and international repatriation may be more fluid depending on the collaboration between the parties involved. There have been incidents, for example, where Native American tribes have reclaimed heritage on behalf of Canadian First Nations, and then returned it to them.[7] Where there is a willingness for collaboration amongst museums and collaboration amongst Indigenous communities much can be achieved. In fact, to the individuals involved it may appear as if the only barrier is a too restrictively formulated law.

It was thus shown that there are important lessons to be learned from the cases examined, not only for intra-national repatriations but also for European countries that are considering confronting their colonial collections, as has been happening in the Netherlands, France and Germany. European states do not entertain comparable obligations under human rights treaties for Indigenous communities located abroad, as they do for those within their territory. However, if they do decide to engage in

[7] For further discussion see Chap. 4.

repatriation efforts, the effects this will have on Indigenous cultural rights (positive or negative) do not disappear with the increased geographical distance between communities and the state (even if the legal obligation may). This becomes even more important, because the contemporary wave of repatriation calls seems motivated by the desire to address historic/colonial wrongs. The desire to address historical violations of human rights should thus not lead to a contemporary rights limitation. To approach repatriation legislation through a rights-based method by incorporating the listed principles can help with this. In light of the origin of the dislocated object and the reasons to consider repatriation in the absence of legal obligations, respecting human rights standards in these cases may thus not be a legal obligation but an ethical imperative.

The next question may be in how far the models that have been developed in Sect. 10.3 are transferable to the context of international repatriations. Considering the different models, the first two are also suitable to an international context, namely a mandatory repatriation law and negotiations that take place between museums with public collections and the individual communities that are given legislative approval. Both cases would result in establishing the necessary legal basis to enable the international repatriation of sacred heritage. In the international context, and especially for museums that have amassed a very diverse collection of Indigenous cultural heritage, a legal framework establishing repatriation powers for individual negotiations would probably be easier. This is for the simple reason that provenance research, consultation and cooperation must cover different geographical areas and cultures. This could render drafting and implementing a mandatory framework more difficult in terms of the material and personal scope, in establishing a representative dispute settlement authority and in establishing timelines that are realistic. As for museums tasked with its implementation, they might be confronted with a multitude of claims covering vastly different parts of their collection.

Nevertheless, the advantages of a mandatory framework that is combined with flexible provisions allowing for different arrangements to be made remain true in the international context. It can balance the scales of power slightly when repatriation is not at the discretion of museums but obligatory upon request by Indigenous Peoples. If drafted accordingly, it can involve claimant communities. This could be a benefit given that international repatriation efforts often continue to operate at the interstate level or between a museum and the government of a former colonial power. Moreover, it would help in providing equal chances for a diversity of Indigenous communities to regain their sacred objects. This is not necessarily the case for repatriations which take place in numerous, individual negotiations. As a result, it might be advisable to merge the two and design a repatriation framework that gives museums the legal power to repatriate; the duty to do so if a set of circumstances are fulfilled; sets aside a budget for provenance research, training, repatriation negotiations and the final process of repatriation; and establishes a dispute settlement mechanism that is of mixed composition. It could comprise both museum personnel as well as a register of Indigenous experts and religious practitioners from the different former colonies. The Indigenous representatives would then shift depending on the colonial background of the claim and overall composition would have to be balanced between museum officials and Indigenous representatives. So far, however, discussions in Europe appear to be a mix of museum soft law approaches and proposals that lean more towards returns and the focus on intergovernmental relationships than on the mandatory involvement of communities. Examples for this are the National Museum of World Cultures in the Netherlands[8] and the German Museums Association's Guidelines on Dealing with Collections from Colonial Contexts.[9] The Dutch proposal, for example, is clear in its emphasis on intergovernmental relationships to avoid a "neocolonial repetition of the past", which means that views of the governments of former colonies are sought, respected and accommodated.[10] As was highlighted in Chap. 1, this also reflects the structure of contemporary international law (with both its advantages and disadvantages). From the perspective of Indigenous rights this can lead to international returns that exclude the community of origin. In theory those Indigenous communities and nations do have rights vis-à-vis their governments, including rights to the heritage in question. From a legal perspective the observation made in chapter one is worth repeating: every international, intergovernmental return bears the potential for repatriation within it. In how far this is realistic in practice, in light of both the precarious position of many Indigenous communities within their countries of origin, and the insufficient funds of governments and museums across the globe, is of course another matter.

The other two models are not suited to international repatriation. Modern-day treaty negotiations are aimed at reconciling different sovereign powers existing within the same territory and are unsuitable for international repatriations. The third model, remedying the unequal protection of cultural rights will only be partially possible in the international context. Remedying the effects of past removals is an important step and, for many Indigenous communities, this may actually only work if international repatriations take place. In the case of international repatriations, there is likely no possibility to guarantee alternative access options for heritage which forms part of public collections. This is all the more reason to take repatriation requests seriously that claim religious cultural heritage that is needed for contemporary practices. However, as the examination of intra-national repatriations showed, repatriation alone will not balance the scales of cultural rights. More needs to be done, and these actions will predominantly be in the hands of the national government of the territory in which the Indigenous community resides.

[8]The Dutch National Museum of World Cultures is in fact an amalgam of the Museum Volkenkunde, the Tropenmuseum and the Afrika Museum.

[9]Deutscher Museumsbund (2021).

[10]Gonçalves-Ho Kang You et al. (2021), recommendation 3. The advice was followed by the minister in her proposal, see I. van Engelshoven, Beleidsvisie Collecties uit een koloniale context (29.01.2021) [Letter of government, Appendix], p. 4.

10.5 Outlook

This study started by situating contemporary repatriation requests in a colonial history of taking and re-contextualizing cultural artefacts, legitimized by international law. This past practice continues to legitimize the contemporary ownership of sacred cultural heritage that was taken and is reclaimed by either his or her descendants or the descendant community. Indigenous communities who request repatriation thus frequently find themselves facing different legal obstacles and diverse arguments made against repatriation, including the need for the conservation of the object and the general public's right of access to it. I acknowledged this debate but decided to build upon it by asking how repatriation should be regulated rather than whether or not it should. This research thus started with the assumption that there are reasons that motivate parties to engage in repatriation. The motivation to repatriate, however, does not simply dissolve the legal obstacles that arise, for example out of cultural heritage protection and museum (self-)regulation.

Parts II and III have shown that there are different ways of navigating the different obstacles to repatriation, and that this can be done while observing the applicable human rights standards (even if this is not done in all of the cases that were examined). These are various, for example open communication between all parties, the respect for and incorporation of Indigenous legal and cultural practices, the provision of adequate resources to all parties. Important steps were taken in both the United States and Canada. However, there is room for improvement both with regards to the different repatriation laws as well as in heritage law and policy in general to increase respect for international standards endorsed in UNDRIP and by both governments. The research also indicated some problems that are of a more systemic nature and could not be examined in detail in this research. To give one example that goes beyond repatriation and cultural rights, there are clear problems in how Indigenous claimants have to navigate the common-law system in front of the judiciary. Clearly, there is need for Indigenous judges trained in Indigenous law on Canadian and United States benches—at least if there is a desire to respect Indigenous rights and move further in the decolonization of the relationship between all parties involved. Otherwise, the burden of translating between different legal traditions (and cultural practices) will remain solely on Indigenous practitioners. This is unlikely to bring a real reconciliation between the different interests involved. Instead, it resembles past assimilation practices albeit in a modern disguise.

The research into the applicable standards in international cultural heritage and human rights law in Part I also highlighted the need for further research into Indigenous cultural rights, in particular the status of individual UNDRIP articles. The author followed international legal opinion in considering UNDRIP to be more than a mere declaration and approached the articles that were considered as interpretations of binding cultural rights. This has helped to concretize Art.27 ICCPR and Art.15(1)(a) ICESCR which remain too broad in the context of Indigenous cultural rights to give concrete guidance to practitioners on the ground. A particular frustration in this regard is the vagueness of the limitation clause of Art.27 ICCPR ("shall not be denied"). This can definitely benefit from further concretization and guidance through the treaty committee in its individual opinions, which so far has been sparse. Admittedly, only a handful of cases that considered Indigenous cultural rights under Art.27 ICCPR reached the merits stage. Because the scope of the right can only be determined in its context, it remains unclear where exactly the denial of the right starts and the limitation ends. Further research on the limitation clause of Art.27 ICCPR could help in concretizing the right.

Part IV has showcased the lessons that can be learned from intra-national repatriation and the analysis suggests that many could be implemented in international repatriation, albeit at a different cost or with slight alterations. Admittedly, in international repatriations, there is no international obligation to repatriate in the relevant cultural heritage treaties nor is the relationship between a state and the recipient community the same under human rights law. Instead there is a growing trend towards the repatriation of important cultural heritage, both religious and other cultural objects, as well as human remains. When states decide for their own reasons to engage in repatriation, human rights do give guidance on elements to be included in the repatriation framework. As was established above, a number of principles work in both the intra-national and the international context. Apart from this, two of the models, the one centred on museum to community negotiations and the mandatory legal framework one, can be used in international repatriations. In the international context there is a bigger risk that the human rights benefits of a specific framework are neglected for the sake of expediency or for political reasons. This raises another problematic point. The present research has considered the return of sacred objects for the benefit of a living community which can live with that heritage in accordance with its own traditional practices. Contemporary efforts on international repatriations focus predominantly on returning cultural heritage to the governments of former colonies.[11] This can be because of political calculation on both ends. Former colonial powers may wish to strengthen their ties with governments abroad. Or they may simply wish to refrain from interfering in the national affairs of the former colony for obvious historical reasons. Former colonies, by contrast, may still struggle with cultural tensions between various Indigenous Peoples and be hesitant to invite a national debate on the closest connected community next to other more pressing matters. For now, in the absence of clear legal obligations to the contrary and the lack of a clear legal relationship between the recipient community and the state abroad, governments remain free to do as they wish in international repatriations and they lack legal accountability. However, the experiences in Canada and the United States suggest that structuring repatriation legally, in a manner that is respectful of Indigenous rights standards can bring very real benefits to the relationship between museums and communities.

The good news is that, as long as the need to respect human rights and the specific principles elaborated upon in this research are remembered, parties are free in

[11] One exception are the NMVW guidelines in the Netherlands, which expressly include communities and governments and were released in 2019.

designing the framework that best suits their needs. The important part would seem to be to orientate the repatriation framework in relation to the reasons that motivated the decision to repatriate on the one hand and human rights on the other. Here the research took a first step in laying out which legislative objects were pursued by the frameworks examined and how they fared in achieving them on the basis of the material available. However, to ensure that the framework adopted is most effective in achieving the desired result, more research is needed. To measure the effectiveness of the models in light of their legislative aim went beyond the scope of this research. It would require more collaborative empirical research of individual repatriation negotiations as those introduced in Chap. 1. Because of the diversity of communities and repatriation scenarios, this is cannot be achieved in a single systematic manner across all models. The most that can be done through future research is to pick sample repatriation cases and investigate the effectiveness of different models, albeit the results will still be limited to their respective context. This would hold true for mapping the results of such research that already exists. For policy actors, it is recommended that, once parties within a legal system have decided upon the goals they wish to achieve and considered the legal obstacles they face within their system, they decide on a model that—based on its structure—is most likely to help them to achieve these objects. A research project could then be designed to investigate which elements could further the effectiveness of the model and the research could be tailored to the needs of the respective legal system, for example France or Germany, where there seems to be a growing desire to repatriate colonial heritage.

The research has shown that to structure repatriation legally can bring real benefits. If repatriation actions follow up on the renewed calls for repatriation, they should be undertaken after consultation with the respective Indigenous communities and the adoption of a suitable repatriation legislation. Repatriation will interact with the national applicable legislation in any event, be it the national legislation that structures museums or national heritage legislation. It thus seems prudent to consider these interactions in advance and draft a framework that will be as advantageous for all parties involved as possible, rather than leaving repatriation to ad hoc negotiations and cultural diplomacy efforts. The recent wave of calls for repatriation in Europe, in any event, does give rise to the hope that we will see some changes in how Indigenous collections and communities are approached by museums in Europe. If we heed the lessons from our colleagues abroad, there is also the very real chance that we can further Indigenous rights at the same time as confronting our own, difficult, past.

References[12]

Babcock HM (2012) "This I know from my Grandfather:" The battle for admissibility of indigenous oral history as proof of tribal land claims. Am Indian Law Rev 37(1):19–61

Bell CE (1992) Aboriginal claims to cultural property in Canada: a comparative legal analysis of the repatriation debate. Am Indian Law Rev 17(2):457–522

Coombe RJ (1993) The properties of culture and the politics of possessing identity: native claims in the cultural appropriation controversy. Can J Law Jurisprud 6(2):249–285

Deutscher Museumsbund (2021) Leitfaden Umgang mit Sammlungsgut aus kolonialen Kontexten, 3. Fassung 2021

Gonçalves-Ho Kang You L, Balai L, Bloksma B, Gosselink M, Lidchi H, Smeulders V, Tarekat Dipowijoyo H, Visser J, Bersee S, Keizer E (2021) Colonial collections and a recognition of injustice. Raad voor Cultuur, The Hague

Kreps C (2009) Indigenous curation, museums, and intangible cultural heritage. In: Smith L, Akagawa N (eds) Intangible heritage. Routledge, New York, pp 193–206

Nationaal Museum van Wereldculturen, Return of Cultural Objects: Principles and Process Nationaal Museum van Wereldculturen (7 March 2019)

[12]Please be aware that Part IV (Chaps. 9 and 10) construct repatriation models and analyse their relationship on the basis of the research conducted in the previous chapters, including the sources referenced there.

Bibliography

Primary Sources: International Law

Treaties

Council of Europe, Protocol 1 to the European Convention on Human Rights and Fundamental Freedoms, 20 March 1952, ETS 9

International Institute for the Unification of Private Law (UNIDROIT), UNIDROIT Convention on Stolen or Illegally Exported Cultural Objects (24 June 1995)

International Labour Organization (ILO), Indigenous and Tribal Populations Convention, C107, 26 June 1957

International Labour Organization (ILO), Indigenous and Tribal Peoples Convention, C169, 27 June 1989

League of Nations, Covenant of the League of Nations, 28 April 1919

Organization of African Unity (OAU), African Charter on Human and Peoples' Rights ("Banjul Charter"), 27 June 1981, CAB/LEG/67/3 rev.5, 21 I.L.M. 58 (1982)

Organization of American States (OAS), American Convention of Human Rights, "Pact of San Jose", Costa Rica, 22 November 1969

Organization of American States (OAS), Charter of the Organization of American States, 30 April 1948

United Nations, Charter of the United Nations, 24 October 1945, 1 UNTS XVI

UN Educational, Scientific and Cultural Organization (UNESCO), Constitution of the United Nations Educational, Scientific and Cultural Organization (UNESCO), 16 November 1954

UN Educational, Scientific and Cultural Organization (UNESCO), Convention Concerning the Protection of the World Cultural and Natural Heritage, 16 November 1972

V. Tünsmeyer, *Repatriation of Sacred Indigenous Cultural Heritage and the Law*, Studies in Art, Heritage, Law and the Market 3,
https://doi.org/10.1007/978-3-030-89047-6

UN Educational, Scientific and Cultural Organization (UNESCO), Convention for the Protection of Cultural Property in the Event of Armed Conflict, 14 May 1954

UN Educational, Scientific and Cultural Organization (UNESCO), Convention for the Safeguarding of the Intangible Cultural Heritage, 17 October 2003

UN Educational, Scientific and Cultural Organization (UNESCO), Convention on the Means of Prohibiting and Preventing the Illicit Import, Export and Transfer of Ownership of Cultural Property 1970, 14 November 1970

UN Educational, Scientific and Cultural Organization (UNESCO), Convention on the Protection and Promotion of the Diversity of Cultural Expressions, 20 October 2005

UN General Assembly, International Covenant on Civil and Political Rights, 16 December 1966, United Nations, Treaty Series, vol. 999, p. 171

UN General Assembly, International Covenant on Economic, Social and Cultural Rights, 16 December 1966, United Nations, Treaty Series, vol. 993, p. 3

UN General Assembly, International Convention on the Elimination of All Forms of Racial Discrimination, 21 December 1965, United Nations, Treaty Series, vol. 660, p. 195

Case-Law

Committee on the Elimination of Racial Discrimination Decision 1 (68), CERD/C/USA/DEC/1, 11.04.2006 Early Warning and Urgent Action Procedure - Western Shoshone people

Human Rights Committee, Sandra Lovelace v. Canada, Communication No. R.6/24, U.N. Doc. Supp. No. 40 (A/36/40) (1981)

Human Rights Committee, Ivan Kitok v Sweden, Communication No. 197/1985, U.N. Doc. CCPR/C/33/D/197/1985 (1988)

Human Rights Committee, Lubicon Lake Band v. Canada, Communication No. 167/1984 (26 March 1990), U.N. Doc. Supp. No. 40 (A/45/40) (1990)

Human Rights Committee, Ilmari Länsman v Finland, Communication No. 511/1992 U.N. Doc. CCPR/C/52/D/511/1992 (1994)

Human Rights Committee, Jouni E. Länsman v Finland, Communication No. 671/1995, U.N. Doc. CCPR/C/58/D/671/1995 (1996)

Human Rights Committee, Concluding Remarks France [8.04.1997] UN Doc CCPR/C/79/Add.8

Human Rights Committee, George Howard v. Canada, Communication No. 879/1999, U.N. Doc CCPR/C/84/D/879/1999

Human Rights Committee, Views adopted by the Committee under article 5 (4) ofthe Optional Protocol, concerning communication No. 2668/2015 (Tiina Sanila-Aikio), U.N. Doc CCPR/C/124/D/2668/2015 [20.03.2019]

International Court of Justice (ICJ), Case Concerning East Timor (Portugal v. Australia), 30 June 1995

Inter-American Commission on Human Rights (IACHR), Report Nr. 75/02, 11.140 Mary and Carrie Dann v. United States [27.12.2002]

Inter-American Commission on Human Rights (IACHR), Report Nr. 40/04 Case 12.053 Maya Indigenous Communities of the Toledo District Belize [2004]

Inter-American Commission on Human Rights (IACHR), Report Nr. 61/08 Case 12.435 Grand Chief Michael Mitchell Canada [2008]

Inter-American Commission on Human Rights (IACHR), Report 6/14 Case 12.788, Residents of the Village of Chichupac and Neighbouring Communities, Municipality of Rabinal Guatemala [2016]

Inter-American Commission on Human Rights (IACHR), Report Nr. 105/09 Admissibility Hul' qumi' num Treaty Group Canada [30.10.2009]

Inter-American Court of Human Rights, Mayagna (Sumo) Awas Tingni Community v Nicaragua, Inter Am. Ct. H.R. (ser. C) No. 79 (31.08.2001)

Inter-American Court of Human Rights, Moiwana Community v. Suriname, Inter-Am. Ct. H.R. (series C) No. 124 (15.06.2005)

Inter-American Court of Human Rights, Sawhoyamaxa Indigneous Cmty. v. Paraguay, Inter-Am. Ct. H.R. (ser. C) No. 146 (29.03.2006)

Inter-American Court of Human Rights, Xákmok Kásek Indigenous Community v Paraguay, Inter-Am. Ct. H.R. (ser. C) No. 214 (24.08.2010)

Permanent Court of International Justice (PCIJ) Rights of Minorities in Upper Silesia Minority Schools 1928 Series A, No 15,29

Permanent Court of International Justice (PCIJ) Customs Régime between Germany and Austria (Protocol of March 19th, 1931), Advisory opinion, PCIJ Series A/B No 41, ICGJ 287 (PCIJ 1931)

Other

Bielefeldt, H. Special Rapporteur on freedom of religion or belief, Report, [24.12.2012] U.N. Doc. A/HRC/22/51

Committee on Economic, Social and Cultural Rights, General Comment No. 3 The Nature of States Parties' Obligations (Art. 2, Para. 1, of the Covenant) [1990] U.N. Doc. E/1991/23

Committee on Economic, Social and Cultural Rights, General Comment No.12: The right to Adequate Food [1999] U.N. Doc. E/C.12/1999/5

Committee on Economic, Social and Cultural Rights, General Comment No.20 Non-discrimination in economic, social and cultural rights (art. 2, para. 2, of the International Covenant on Economic, Social and Cultural Rights) [2009] U.N. Doc. E/C.12/GC/20

Committee on Economic, Social and Cultural Rights, General Comment No.21, Right of everyone to take part in cultural life (Art.15(1)(a) ICESCR) [2009] U.N. Doc. E/C.12/GC/21

Committee on the Elimination of Racial Discrimination, General Recommendation XXI [1996] U.N. Doc. A/51/18

Committee on the Elimination of Racial Discrimination, General Recommendation XXIII [1997] U.N. Doc. A/52/18

Committee on the Elimination of Racial Discrimination, Report of the Committee at Fifty-eighth and Fifty-ninth session [1996–1997] U.N Doc. A/56/18

Committee on the Elimination of Racial Discrimination, Decision Kyrghystan [2010] U.N. Doc. CERD/C/KGZ/DEC/1

Committee on the Elimination of Racial Discrimination, Decision Nigeria [2010] U.N. Doc. CERD/C/NGA/DEC/1

Committee on the Elimination of Racial Discrimination, Decision Côte d'Ivoire [2011] U.N. Doc. CERD/C/CIV/DEC/2

Committee on the Elimination of Racial Discrimination, Decision 1/85 Iraq [2014]

Committee on the Elimination of Racial Discrimination, Statement on Libyan Arab Jamahiriya [2011]

Committee on the Elimination of Racial Discrimination, Statement on Syrian Arab Republic [2011]

Committee on the Elimination of Racial Discrimination, Statement on Recent Migrant Crisis [2015]

Daes, E. UN Special Rapporteur on Protection of the Heritage of the Indigenous People, Final report of the Special Rapporteur [1995] UN Doc E/CN.4/Sub.2/1995/26

Daes, E., Standard-setting Activities: Evolution of standards concerning the rights of indigenous peoples [1996] U.N. Doc. E/CN.4/Sub.2/AC.4/1996/2

Daes, E., Second Progress Report on Human Rights of Indigenous Peoples, Indigenous People and Their Relationship to Land (UN Doc E/CN.4/Sub.2/1999/18 (1999)

Daes, E, Report of the seminar on the draft principles and guidelines for the protection of the heritage of indigenous people [28.01-1.03.2000] U.N. Doc: E/CN.4/Sub.2/2000/26

Declaration on the Value and Importance of Universal Museums (10.12.2002), signed by different museum directors, published by British Museum.

Deschênes, J., United Nations Sub-Commission on the Prevention of Discrimination and Protection of Minorities Proposal Concerning a Definition of the Term 'Minority' U.N. Doc. E/CN.4/Sub.2/1985/31 & Corr. 1

First Session of the Intergovernmental Meeting of Experts on the Preliminary Draft Convention for the Safeguarding of Intangible Cultural Heritage, CLT-2002/CONF.203/5 [December 2002]

Glossary Intangible Cultural Heritage, prepared by an international meeting of experts at UNESCO 10.06-12.06.2002, available at: http://www.unesco.org/culture/ich/doc/src/00265.pdf [last accessed 19.08.2021]

Historical Background to the preparation of the preliminary Draft Convention for the Safeguarding of the Intangible Cultural Heritage [Doc. Ref.: CLT-2003/CONF.205/INF.6] available at: http://www.unesco.org/culture/ich/doc/src/04557-EN.pdf [last accessed 19.08.2021]

Human Rights Committee, Concluding Remarks France [8.04.1997] UN Doc CCPR/C/79/Add.80

Human Rights Committee, General Comment No.18 Non-Discrimination [1989] U.N. Doc. HRI/GEN/1/Rev.9 (Vol. I)

Human Rights Committee, General Comment No. 22 Freedom of Religion (Art.18) [1993] U.N. Doc. CCPR/C/21/Rev.1/Add.4

Human Rights Committee, General Comment No. 23 Rights of Minorities (Art.27) [1994] U.N. Doc. CCPR/C/21/Rev.1/Add.5

Human Rights Committee, General Comment No. 29 States of Emergency (Art.4) [2001] UN Doc CCPR/C/21/Rev.1/Add.11

Human Rights Committee, General Comment No. 31 Nature of the General Legal Obligation on States Parties to the Covenant [2004] U.N. Doc. CCPR/C/21/Rev.1/Add.13

ICOM Code of Ethics (2004), available at: https://icom.museum/wp-content/uploads/2018/07/ICOM-code-En-web.pdf [last accessed 19.08.2021]

Human Rights Council, Resolution 6/36 Expert Mechanism on the Rights of Indigenous Peoples [14.12. 2007] UN Doc A/HRC/RES/6/36

Human Rights Council, Resolution 6/37 Elimination of all forms of intolerance and of discrimination based on religion or belief [14.12.2007] A/HRC/RES/6/37

Human Rights Council, Report of the Special Rapporteur on the situation of human rights and fundamental freedoms of indigenous peoples, S. James Anaya [11.08.2008] U.N. Doc. A/HRC/9/9

Human Rights Council, Promotion and protection of the rights of indigenous peoples with respect to their cultural heritage, Study by the Expert Mechanism on the Rights of Indigenous Peoples, U.N. Doc. A/HRC/30/53 [19.08.2015]

Human Rights Council, Resolution 33/20 Cultural rights and the protection of cultural heritage [30.09.2016] UN Doc A/HRC/RES/33/20

Human Rights Council, Study of the Expert Mechanism on the Rights of Indigenous Peoples, Free, prior and informed consent: A human-rights based approach, U.N. Doc.A/HRC/39/62 [10.08.2018]

Human Rights Council, Report of the Expert Mechanism on the Rights of Indigenous Peoples, Repatriation of ceremonial objects, human remains and intangible cultural heritage under the United Nations Declaration on the Rights of Indigenous Peoples, U.N. Doc. A/HRC/45/35 [21.07.2020].

ILA Constitution, available via: https://www.ila-hq.org/index.php/about-us/aboutus2 [last accessed 19.08.2021]

ILA Resolution No 4/2006 adopted at the 72nd Conference of the International Law Association, held in Toronto, Canada, 4-8 June 2006, available via the website of the cultural heritage committee of the ILA at: http://www.ila-hq.org/en/committees/index.cfm/cid/13 [last accessed 19.08.2021]

ILA, The Hague Conference Report—Committee on the Rights of Indigenous Peoples (2010), Available via the committee publications at www.ila-hq.org [last accessed 19.08.2021]

ILA Toronto Conference (2006) Cultural Heritage Law Committee Report, available via: http://www.ila-hq.org/en/committees/index.cfm/cid/13 [last accessed 19.08.2021]

Inter-American Commission on Human Rights (2000), 'Report on the Situation of Human Rights of Asylum Seekers Within the Canadian Refugee Determination System'

International Commission of Jurists (2008), 'Background paper for the Day of General Discussion—Right to take part in cultural life (article 15(1)(a) of the Covenant)', (E/C.12/40/7: CESCR), 1–14

International Labour Office (2009) Indigenous and tribal peoples' rights in practice: a guide to ILO Convention No. 169 Geneva, ILO

International Labour Office (2013) Understanding the Indigenous and Tribal Peoples Convention, 1989 (No. 169) Handbook for ILO Tripartite Constituents, Geneva

International Labour Organization, ILO (2008), 'Comments submitted for the Day of General Discussion—The right to take part in cultural life', (E/C.12/40/12: CESCR), 1–4.

Intergovernmental Committee for the Safeguarding of the Intangible Cultural Heritage, Ethical Principles for Safeguarding Intangible Cultural Heritage (Windhoek, Namibia, 30 November to 4 December 2015), part of Basic Texts of the 2003 Convention for the Safeguarding of Intangible Cultural Heritage (2018 Edition)

Intergovernmental Committee for the Safeguarding of the Intangible Cultural Heritage, Ethical Principles for Safeguarding Intangible Cultural Heritage, tenth session (Windhoek, Namibia, 30 November to 4 December 2015), part of Basic Texts of the 2003 Convention for the Safeguarding of Intangible Cultural Heritage Compilation (2018 Edition) available via: https://ich.unesco.org/en/convention. [last accessed 19.08.2021]

International Institute for the Unification of Private Law (UNIDROIT), Draft UNIDROIT Convention on the International Return of Stolen or Illegally Exported Objects and Explanatory Report prepared by UNIDROIT Secretariat [December 1994] Document reference Conf. 8/3

International Institute for the Unification of Private Law (UNIDROIT), Special Committee to review the practical operation of the 1995 UNIDROIT on Stolen or Illegally Exported Cultural Objects—first meeting [June 20120] Document reference DC8/CS/1/ Doc. 3

Inter-Agency Support Group on Indigenous Issues and UNESCO, Indigenous peoples: development with culture and identity in the light of the UNDRIP [18.02.1010] U.N. Doc. E/C.19/2010/17 UNPFII

IUCN World Conservation Congress, Jeju, Korea, 6–15 September 2012, Resolution 5.055, Implementation of the United Nations Declaration on the Rights of Indigenous Peoples in the context of the UNESCO World Heritage Convention.

Maastricht Guidelines on Violations of Economic, Social and Cultural Rights, (Maastricht, 22-26.01.1997) Sec. II.6, available at: http://www1.umn.edu/humanrts/instree/Maastrichtguidelines_.html [last accessed 19.08.2021]

Martinez, A., UN. Special Rapporteur on Treaties, Agreements and Other Constructive Arrangements between States and Indigenous Populations, Study on treaties, agreements and other constructive arrangements between States and indigenous populations [1999] U.N. Doc. E/CN.4/Sub.2/1999/20

Martínez Cobo, J. Special Rapporteur, Study of the Problem of Discrimination Against Indigenous Populations Final report (last Part) [30.09.1983] U.N. Doc. E./CN.4//Sub.2/1983/21/Add.8,

Organization of American States (OAS), American Declaration on the Rights of Indigenous Peoples, 15 June 2016

Organization of American States (OAS), American Declaration of the Rights and Duties of Man, 2 May 1948

Operational Guidelines of the Convention on the Diversity of Cultural Expressions last approved by the Conference of Parties at its fifth session (Paris, 10–12 June 2015)

Operational Directives for the Implementation of the Convention for the Safeguarding of the Intangible Cultural Heritage (as amended June 2018)

Rodriguez, L., independent Expert, The right of everyone to own property alone as well as in association of others [1993] U.N. Doc. E/CN. 4/ 1994/19

Second Session of the Intergovernmental Meeting of Experts on the Preliminary Draft Convention for the Safeguarding of the Intangible Cultural Heritage—General Comments received from Member States, Doc Ref Doc.CLT-2003/CONF.205/5

Shaheed, Farida (2010), 'Report of the independent expert in the field of cultural rights on the conceptual and legal framework of her mandate', (A/HRC/14/36: UN General Assembly), 1–20.

Shaheed, Farida (2011), 'Report of the independent expert in the field of cultural rights on the right of access to and enjoyment of cultural heritage', (A/HRC/17/38: UN General Assembly), 1–20.

Shaheed, Farida (2012), 'Report of the Special Rapporteur in the field of cultural rights on the enjoyment of cultural rights by women', (A/67/287: UN General Assembly), 1–24.

The Australia ICOMOS Charter for Places of Cultural Significance ("Burra Charter"), 1979 version

United States Comment to Declaration, AG/RES. 2888 (XLVI-O/16) American Declaration on the Rights of Indigenous Peoples (Adopted at the third plenary session, held on June 15, 2016)

UNIDROIT Convention on the International Return of Stolen or Illegally Exported Cultural Objects—Acts and Proceedings, available at. http://www.unidroit.org/english/conventions/1995culturalproperty/1995culturalproperty-acts-e.pdf [last accessed 19.08.2021]

UN Commission on Human Rights, Resolution 2005/40 on Elimination of All Forms of Intolerance and of Discrimination Based on Religion or Belief, U.N. Doc E/CN.4/RES/2005/40 (19.04.2005)

UN Commission on Human Rights, Resolution 2003/26 'Promotion of the Enjoyment of the Cultural Rights of Everyone and Respect for Different Cultural Identities' U.N. Doc E/CN.4/RES/2003/26 (22.04.2003)

UN Commission on Human Rights, Resolution 2005/20 'Promotion of the Enjoyment of the Cultural Rights of Everyone and Respect for Different Cultural Identities', U.N. Doc E/CN.4/RES/2005/20 (14.04.2005)

UN Educational, Scientific and Cultural Organization (UNESCO), Declaration of Principles of International Cultural Co-operation (4.11.1966)

UN Educational, Scientific and Cultural Organization (UNESCO), Reports of Member States on the action taken by them to implement the Recommendation on the Means of Prohibiting and Preventing the Illicit Export, Import and Transfer of Ownership of Cultural Property (1964) and the Convention on the Means of Prohibiting and Preventing the Illicit Import, Export and Transfer of Ownership of Cultural Property (1970), [1978] UNESCO Doc. Ref. 20 C/84

UN Educational, Scientific and Cultural Organization (UNESCO), 18th General Conference, 18 C/ Resolution 3.428 Contributions of UNESCO to the return of cultural property to countries that have been victims of de facto expropriation (1974)

UN Educational, Scientific and Cultural Organization (UNESCO), 20th General Conference Document Reference: Resolution 20 C/ Resolution 4/7.6/5 (1978)

UN Educational, Scientific and Cultural Organization (UNESCO), Recommendation on the Safeguarding of Traditional Culture and Folklore (15.11.1989)

UN Educational, Scientific and Cultural Organization (UNESCO), Universal Declaration on Cultural Diversity (2.11.2001)

UN Educational, Scientific and Cultural Organization (UNESCO), Recommendation concerning the Protection and Promotion of Museums and Collections, their Diversity and their Role in Society (Paris, 17 November 2015)

UN Educational, Scientific and Cultural Organization (UNESCO), UNESCO Policy on Engaging with Indigenous Peoples, 201 Ex/6 (Paris 2018)

UN Educational, Scientific and Cultural Organization (UNESCO), World Heritage Committee, Decision 31 COM 31 B (2007)

UN Educational, Scientific and Cultural Organization (UNESCO), World Heritage Committee, Operational Guidelines 2008

UN Educational, Scientific and Cultural Organization (UNESCO), World Heritage Committee, Operational Guidelines 2015

UN Educational, Scientific and Cultural Organization (UNESCO), World Heritage Committee, Operational Guidelines 2017

UN General Assembly, Declaration on the Elimination of All Forms of Intolerance and of Discrimination Based on Religion or Belief, U.N. Doc A/RES/36/55 (25.11.1981)

UN General Assembly, Resolution 60/147, Basic Principles and Guidelines on the Right to a Remedy and Reparation for Victims of Gross Violations of International Human Rights Law and Serious Violations of International Humanitarian Law (2005)

UN General Assembly Resolution 63/174, Effective promotion of the Declaration on the Rights of Persons Belonging to National or Ethnic, Religious and Linguistic Minorities, U.N. Doc A/RES/63/174 (2009)

UN General Assembly, Resolution 55/91 Human rights and cultural diversity, U.N. Doc A/RES/55/91 (2000)

UN General Assembly, Resolution 3187 Restitution of works of arts to countries victims of expropriation (1973)

UN General Assembly, Universal Declaration of Human Rights, 10 December 1948, 217 A (III)

UN General Assembly, United Nations Declaration on the Rights of Indigenous Peoples, U.N. Doc A/RES/61/295 (2007)

UN High Commissioner for Human Rights, Annual Report of the United Nations High Commissioner for Human Rights—The rights of indigenous peoples, U.N. Doc A/HRC/10/51 [14.01.2009]

UN Human Rights Council Resolution 14/9, Promotion of the enjoyment of the cultural rights of everyone and respect for cultural diversity, U.N. Doc A/HRC/RES/14/9 (2010)

UN Human Rights Council Resolution 6/1, Protection of cultural rights and property in situations of armed conflict, U.N. Doc A/HRC/RES/6/1 (2007)

UN Office of the High Commissioner for Human Rights (2010), 'Minority Rights: International Standards and Guidance for Implementation', (New York and Geneva).

UN Permanent Forum on Indigenous Issues, Background paper prepared by the Secretariat of UNPFII on the concept of indigenous people [2004] UN Doc PFII/2004/WS.1/3

UN Secretary General, Compilation of Guidelines on the form and content of reports to be submitted by States Parties to the International Human Rights Treaties [3.06.2009] U.N. Doc. HRI/GEN/2/Rev.6

UN Special Rapporteur on Freedom of Religion or Belief, Framework for Communications—International Standards on freedom of religion or belief, available at: http://www.ohchr.org/EN/Issues/FreedomReligion/Pages/Standards.aspx [last accessed 19.08.2021]

UN Special Rapporteur on Freedom of Religion or Belief, Report of the Special Rapporteur on freedom of religion or belief [24.12.2012] U.N. Doc. A/HRC/22/51

Washington Conference Principles on Nazi-Confiscated Art [3.12.2008], principle II. Vilnius Forum Declaration [5.10.2000]

World Archaeological Congress, WAC (1989), 'The Vermillion Accord on Human Remains', (South Dakota USA: WAC).

World Archaeological Congress, (2006), 'The Tamaki Makau-rau Accord on the Display of Human Remains and Sacred Objects', (Osaka, Japan: WAC).

Primary Sources: National Law

National Law: Canada

Blackfoot First Nations Sacred Ceremonial Objects Repatriation Regulation, Alta Reg 96/2004, retrieved 2020-01-23

Canadian Charter of Rights and Freedoms, s 7, Part 1 of the Constitution Act, 1982, being Schedule B to the Canada Act 1982 (UK), 1982, c. 11

Constitution Amendment Proclamation, 1983 (SI/84-102)
Canadian Cultural Property Export Control List, C.R.C. c.448, retrieved on 2020-01-22
Designation and Transfer of Responsibility Regulation, Alta Reg 80/2012
Dispositions (Ministerial) Regulation, Alta Reg 101/1998, retrieved on 2020-01-22
Cultural Property Export and Import Act, RSC 1985, C-51, retrieved on 2019-07-16
Declaration on the Rights of Indigenous Peoples Act, S.B.C. 2019, Chapter 44 (B.C.), retrieved on 2020-01-20
First Nations Sacred Objects Repatriation Act (Alberta), retrieved on 2020-01-22
Glenbow-Alberta Institute Act, RSA 2000, c G-6, retrieved on 2020-01-22
Historical Resources Act, RSA 2000, c H-9, retrieved on 2020-01-22
Heritage Conservation Act, RSBC 1996, c 187, retrieved on 2020-01-22
Indian Act Amendment and Replacement Act, S.C. 2014, c. 38
Museum Act, S.B.C. 2003, c 12, retrieved on 2020-01-23
Museums Act, S.C. 1990, c 3, retrieved on 2020-01-22
The Constitution Act, 1867 (UK), 30 & 31 Victoria, c. 3
The Constitution Act, 1982, being Schedule B to the Canada Act 1982 (UK), 1982, c. 11
Treaty Commission Act, [R.S.B.C. 1996], c. 461, retrieved on 2020-01-20
United Nations Declaration on the Rights of Indigenous Peoples Act, S.C. 2021, c. 14

National Law: United States

Constitution of the United States, Art I, Art. II, Art. IV, Art. VI, Amend. I, Amend. V
American Indian Religious Freedom Act (AIRFA), Pub. L. 95-341, 42 U.S.C. §1996
Archaeological Resources Protection Act (ARPA), Pub. L. 96–95 as amended, 16 U.S.C. §§ 470aa–470mm (2019)
Native American Graves Protection and Repatriation Act (NAGPRA), Pub. L. 101-601, 25 U.S.C. 3001 et seq. (and 18 U.S.C. §1170)
Native American Graves Protection and Repatriation Regulations, Code of Federal Regulations (2020), Title 43, Subtitle A, Part 10
National Museum of the American Indian Act (NMAI), Pub. L. 101-185, 20 U.S.C, Chapter 3, Subchapter XIII §80q to §80q-15
An Act to amend the National Museum of the American Indian Act to make improvements in the Act, and for other purposes, Pub. L. 104-278, 110 Stat. 3355
Senate Joint Resolution, SJ Res. 102, Joint Resolution American Indian Religious Freedom, Pub. L. 95-341 (11.08.1978),
Senate Joint Resolution, SJ Res. 14, A joint resolution to acknowledge a long history of official depredations and ill-conceived policies by the Federal Government regarding Indian tribes and offer an apology to all Native Peoples on behalf of the United States.111th Congress (2009–2010) 11th Congress (2009–2010)
United States Code (2019), Title 18 § 1151

United States Code (2019), Title 25, Chapter 32
United States Code, Title 42 §1996a
Code of Federal Regulations (2019), Title 36, §800.1
Code of Federal Regulations (2019), Title 42, §137.280, §137.288
Code of Federal Regulations (2019), Title 50, §22.22

Case-Law: Canada

Calder et al. v. Attorney-General of British Columbia [1973] S.C.R. 313
Canada (Attorney General) v. Ontario (AG) [1937] UKPC 6, [1937] A.C. 326
Canada (Attorney General) v. Hislop [2007] 1 S.C.R. 429, 2007 SCC 10
Cook v. British Columbia (Minister of Aboriginal Relations & Reconciliation), 2007 BCSC 1722, 2007 CarswellBC 2858
Delgamuukw v. British Columbia [1997] 3 S.C.R. 1010
Derrickson v. Derrickson [1986] 1 S.C.R. 285
Divito v. Canada (Public Safety and Emergency Preparedness) [2013] 3 S.C.R. 157, 2013 SCC 47
Grassy Narrows First Nation v. Ontario (Natural Resources) [2014] 2 S.C.R. 447, 2014 SCC 48
Haida Nation v. British Columbia (Minister of Forests) [2004] 3 S.C.R. 511, 2004 SCC 73
Health Services and Support – Facilities Subsector Bargaining Assn. v. British Columbia [2007] 2 S.C.R. 391, 2007 SCC 27
Kitkatla Band v. British Columbia (Minister of Small Business, Tourism and Culture) [2000] BCCA 42
Kitkatla Band v. British Columbia (Minister of Small Business, Tourism and Culture) [2002] 2 S.C.R. 146, 2002 SCC 31
Ktunaxa Nation v. British Columbia (Forests, Lands and Natural Resource Operations) 2017 SCC 54, [2017] 2 S.C.R. 386
Law v Canada (Minister of Employment and Immigration) [1999] 1 S.C.R. 497
Mikisew Cree First Nation v. Canada (Minister of Canadian Heritage) [2005] 3 S.C.R. 388, 2005 SCC 69
Multani *v.* Commission scolaire Marguerite-Bourgeoys [2006] 1 S.C.R. 256, 2006 SCC 6
Natural Parents v. Superintendent of Child Welfare [1976] 2 S.C.R. 751
New Brunswick Broadcasting Co. v. Nova Scotia [1993] 1 S.C.R. 319
Ontario Mining Co v. Seybold [1899] O.J. No. 113, 31 O.R. 386
Ontario v. Canada [1909] S.C.J. No.28, 42 S.C.R.1
R v. Adams [1996] S.C.J. No.87
R v. Gladstone (Gladstone No.1) [1996] S.C.J. No.79
R. v. Kapp, [2008] 2 S.C.R. 483, 2008 SCC 41
R. v Marshall [1999] 3 S.C.R. 456
R v. Powley [2003] S.C.J. No.43

R. v. Sappier; R. *v*. Gray [2006] 2 S.C.R. 686, 2006 SCC 54
R v. Sparrow [1990] S.C.R. 1075
R. v. Big M Drug Mart Ltd., [1985] 1 S.C.R. 295
R v. Van der Peet [1996] 2 S.C.R. 507
Reference as to whether "Indians" includes in s. 91 (24) of the B.N.A. Act includes Eskimo in habitants of the Province of Quebec [1939] S.C.R. 104
Reference as to Powers to Levy Rates on Foreign Legations [1943] S.C.R. 208
Reference re Code of Civil Procedure (Que.), art. 35, [2021] 2021 SCC 27
Simon v. The Queen, [1985] 2 S.C.R. 387
Sheldon v. Ramsay [1851] O.J. No. 82, 9 U.C.R. 105
St. Catharines Milling and Lumber Co. v. R [1887] 13 S.C.R. 577
Tsilhqot'in Nation v. British Columbia, 2014 SCC 44 [2014] 2 S.C.R. 256
Wewaykum Indian Band *v*. Canada, [2002] 4 S.C.R. 245, 2002 SCC 79

Case-Law: United States

Bonnichsen v United States 367 F.3d 864 (2004) United States Court of Appeals, Ninth Circuit
Bowen v Roy 476 U.S. 693 (1986)
Cherokee Nation v Georgia, 30 U.S. 5 Pet. 11 (1831)
City of Boerne v Flores 521 U.S. 507 (1997)
County of Oneida v Oneida Indian Nation, 470 U.S. 226 (1985)
Employment Division v Smith, 494 U.S. 872 (1990)
Everson v Board of Education 330 U.S. 1 (1947)
Fallon Paiute-Shoshone Tribe v United States Bureau of Land Management 455 F. Supp.2d 1207 (2006)
Gonzales v O Centro Espirita Beneficente Uniao do Vegetal 546 U.S. 418 (2006)
Holt v. Hobbs 574 U.S. 352 (2015)
Horne et al v Department of Agriculture (Horne II) 135 S. Ct. 2419 / 576 U.S._ (2015)
José Ernesto Medellín v Texas, 552 U.S. 491 [25.03.2008]
Minnesota v Mille Lacs Band of Chippewa Indians, 526 U.S. 172 (1999)
Montana v Blackfeet Tribe, 471 U.S. 759 (1985)
Na Iwi O Na Kupuna O Mokapu v Dalton 894 F. Supp. 1397 (1995)
Nevada v Hicks, 533 U.S. 353 (2001)
Lone Wolf v. Hitchcock, 187 U.S. 553 (1903)
Oklahoma Tax Commission v Sac & Fox Nation 508 U.S. 114 (1993)
People v Van Horn 267 Cal. Rptr. 804 Ct App. (1990)
Richard E Lyng et al v Northwest Indian Cemetery Protective Association et al 485 U.S. 439 (1988)
Seminole Tribe of Florida v Florida 517 U.S. 44
South Carolina v. Catawba Indian Tribe, Inc., 476 U.S. 498 (1986)
Tee-Hit-Ton Indians v United States, 348 U.S. 272 (1955)

The Kansas Indians 72 U.S. 737 (1866)
United States v Dion, 476 U.S. 73 (1986)
United States v Forty-three Gallons of Whiskey 93 U.S. 188 (1876)
United States v Kagama, 118 U.S. 375, 485 (1886)
United States v Gerber, 999 F.2d 1112 (1993) United States Court of Appeal, 7th Circuit
Washington v Wash. State Commercial Passenger Fishing Vessel Ass'n, 443 U.S. 658 (1999)
White v University of California, Not Reported in F.Supp.2d (2012), 2012 WL 12335354 (9.10.2012)
Williams v Lee, 358 U.S. 217 (1959)
Worcester v Georgia, 31 U.S. 515 (1832)

Other: Canada

Alberta, 24th Legislature, 4th session, House records of discussions on 1.03.2000, Alberta Hansard Issue 7
Alberta, 24th Legislature, 4th session, House records of discussions on 6.03.2000, Alberta Hansard Issue 8
British Columbia Claims Task Force, Report (28.06.1991).
B.C. Ministry of Aboriginal Relations and Reconciliation (2017), 'FACTSHEET: Reconciliation at the heart of relationship with Aboriginal peoples', (https://news.gov.bc.ca/).
Campell Scott, Duncan, Statement, National Archives of Canada, Record Group 10, volume 6810, file 470-2-3, volume 7, pp. 55 (L-3) and 63 (N-3)
Government of British Columbia, Government of Canada, Maa-nulth First Nations, Maa-nulth First Nations Final Agreement (2009)
Government of British Columbia, Government of Canada, Tla'amin Nation, Tla'amin Final Agreement (2014)
Government of British Columbia, Government of Canada, Tsawwassen First Nation, Tsawwassen First Nation Final Agreement (2007)
Government of British Columbia, Government of Canada, Yale First Nation, Yale First Nation Final Agreement (initialled 2010)
House of Commons Debates, 43-2, No. 60 (17 February 2021)
Royal British Columbia Museum (2018), 'Indigenous Collections and Repatriation Policy', (https://royalbcmuseum.bc.ca/documents/105663/Indigenous-Collections-and-Repatriation-Policy).
Royal Commission on Aboriginal Peoples (1991), 'Looking Forward, Looking Back', (1; Ottowa: RCAP).
Royal Commission on Aboriginal Peoples (1996a), 'Restructuring the Relationship', (Volume 2; Ottowa: RCAP).
Royal Commission on Aboriginal Peoples (1996b), 'Gathering Strength', (Volume 3; Ottowa, Canada: RCAP).

Truth and Reconciliation Commission of Canada (2015), 'Calls to Action', (Winnipeg, Manitoba: Truth and Reconciliation Commission of Canada).

Other: United States

ABA Standing Committee on Judicial Independence ("SCJI"), Study commissioned on available at: https://apps.americanbar.org/abanet/jd/display/national.cfm

AIRFA Task Force Report PL 95-341, Department of the Interior [August 1979, Washington DC] RC 012180, ED190329 available via US – ERIC database

American Anthropological Association, AMA (2012), 'American Anthropological Association 2012 Ethics code'.

American Association of Museums, AAM (1993, amended 2000), 'AAM Code of Ethics for Museums', (AAM).

Association of Art Museum Directors, AAMD (2006), 'Report on the Stewardship and Acquisition of Sacred Objects'.

Curators Committee, American Association of Museums (2009), 'A Code of Ethics for Curators', (American Association of Museums).

Department of Justice [statement 17.09.1990], H.R. Rep. No 101-877 (1990)

National Park Service, US Department of the Interior, Fiscal Year 2017 Report National NAGPRA Program [For the period October 1, 2017–September 30, 2017]

House of Representatives, Providing for the Protection of Native American Graves, And For Other Purposes, H.R. Rep. No 101-877 (1990).

United States Government Accountability Office, GAO (2010), 'Native American Graves Protection and Repatriation Act - After Almost 20 Years Key Federal Agencies Still Have Not Fully Complied with the Act', in GAO (ed.), (Washington, DC).

United States of America, Response to UNESCO CL/4102 of March 23, 2015 on implementation of the 1970 Convention on the Means of Prohibiting and Preventing the Illicit Import, Export and Transfer of Ownership of Cultural Property, available via www.unesco.org

Secondary Sources

Books, Book Chapters and Articles

Abungu, George (2009), 'The Declaration: A Contested Issue', in Lyndel Prott (ed.), *Witnesses to History - A Compendium of Documents and Writings on the Return of Cultural Property* (Paris: UNESCO Publishers), 121–122.

Adler, Andrew (2008), 'An unintended and absurd expansion: The application of the Archaeological Resources Protection Act to Foreign Lands', *New Mexico Law Review,* 38, 133–158.

Ahdar, Rex and Leigh, Ian (2005), 'Legal Protection of Religious Freedom', *Religious Freedom in the Liberal State* (Oxford: Oxford University Press), 98–126.

Ahmed, Mohsen Al Attar, Aylwin, Nicole, and Coombe, Rosemary (2008), 'Indigenous Cultural Heritage Rights in International Human Rights Law', in Catherine Bell and Robert Patterson (eds.), *Protection of First Nations' Cultural Heritage: Laws, Policy and Reform* (Vancouver: UBC Press), 311–342.

Åhrén, Matthias (2008), 'Protecting Peoples' Cultural Rights: A Question of Properly Understanding the Notion of States and Nations?', in Francesco Francioni and Martin Scheinin (eds.), *Cultural human rights* (Leiden, Boston: Martinus Nijhoff Publishers), 91–118.

Alfredsson, Gudmundur (2011), 'Treaties with Indigenous Peoples', in Rüdiger Wolfrum (ed.), *Max Planck Encyclopedia of Public International Law* (March 2011: Oxford University Press).

Antkowiak, Thomas M. (2013), 'Rights, Resources, and Rhetoric: Indigenous Peoples and the Inter-American Court', *University of Pennsylvania Journal of International LAw,* 35 (1), 113–188.

Asch, Michael (2009), 'Concluding Thoughts and Fundamental Questions', in Catherine E. Bell and Robert K. Paterson (eds.), *Protection of First Nations cultural heritage* (Vancouver: UBC Press), 394–411.

Asch, Michael (2014), *On Being Here To Stay* (Toronto, Canada: Toronto University Press).

Asmuss, Kerstin (2011), *Ansprüche indigener Völker auf Rückführung rechtswidrig ausgeführten Kulturgutes: Eine Untersuchung für Ansprüche aus Art. 5 UNIDROIT-Konvention 1995 und aus allgemeinem Völkerrecht* (1. edn., Veröffentlichungen aus dem Institut für Internationale Angelegenheiten der Universität Hamburg; Baden-Baden: Nomos) 260 S.

Babcock, Hope M (2012), '"This I know from my Grandfather:" The Battle for Admissibility of Indigenous Oral History as Proof of Tribal Land Claims', *American Indian Law Review,* 37 (1), 19–61.

Bandarin, Francesco (2012), 'International trade in indigenous cultural heritage: comments from UNESCO in light of its international standard-setting instruments in the field of culture', in Christoph B. Graber, Karolina Kuprecht, and Jessica Christine Lai (eds.), *International Trade in Indigenous Cultural Heritage - Legal and Policy Issues* (Cheltenham, UK: Edward Elgar), 306–328.

Barkan, E (2009), 'Making Amends: A New International Morality?', in Lyndel Prott (ed.), *Witnesses to History - A Compendium of Documents and Writings on the Return of Cultural Objects* (Paris: UNESCO Publishing), 78–94.

Bartlett, Richard H. (1980), 'Indian Act of Canada: An Unyielding Barrier', *American Indian Journal,* 6, 11–26.

Battiste, Marie and Henderson, James Youngblood (2000), *Protecting indigenous knowledge and heritage: A global challenge* (Saskatoon: Purich).

Bell, Catherine (2001), 'Protecting Indigenous Heritage Resources in Canada: A Comment on Kitkatle v British Columbia', *International Journal of Cultural Property,* 10 (2), 246–263.

Bell, Catherine (2009a), 'Repatriation of Cultural Material to First Nations in Canada: Legal and Ethical Justifications', in Ann M. Nicgorski and James Nafziger (eds.), *Cultural Heritage Issues: The Legacy of Conquest, Colonization, and Commerce* (Leiden: Brill Nijhoff), 81–106.

Bell, Catherine and Napoleon, Val (2008), *First Nations Cultural Heritage and Law - Case Studies, Voices, and Perspectives* (Vancouver: UBC Press).

Bell, Catherine E. (1992), 'Aboriginal Claims to Cultural Property in Canada: A Comparative Legal Analysis of the Repatriation Debate', *American Indian law review,* 17 (2), 457–522.

Bell, Catherine E. (2009b), 'Restructuring the Relationship: Domestic Repatriation and Canadian Law Reform', in Catherine E. Bell and Robert K. Paterson (eds.), *Protection of First Nations cultural heritage: Laws, Policy, and Reform* (Vancouver: UBC Press), 15–77.

Bell, Catherine E. and McCuaig, Heather (2008), 'Protection and Repatriation of Ktunaxa/ Kinbasket Cultural Resources: Perspectives of Community Members', in Catherine E. Bell and Val Napoleon (eds.), *First Nations cultural heritage and law: Case Studies, Voices, and Perspectives* (Vancouver, BC: UBC Press), 312–364.

Bell, Catherine E., Statt, Graham, and Mookakin Cultural Society (2008a), 'Repatriation and Heritage Protection: Reflections on the Kainai Experience', in Catherine E. Bell and Val Napoleon (eds.), *First Nations Cultural Heritage and Law: Case Studies, Voices, and Perspectives* (Vancouver: UBC Press), 203–257.

Bell, Catherine E., Raven, Heather, and McCuaig, Heather (2008b), 'Recovering from Colonization: Perspectives of Community Members on Protection and Repatriation of Kwakwaka'wakw Cultural Heritage', in Catherine E. Bell and Val Napoleon (eds.), *First Nations cultural heritage and law: Case Studies, Voices and Perspectives* (Vancouver, BC: UBC Press), 33–91.

Bengs, Brian (1996), 'Dead on Arrival? A Comparison of the Unidroit Convention on Stolen or Illegally Exported Cultural Objects and U.S. Property Law', *Transnational Law and Contemporary Problems,* 6, 503–535.

Besson, Samantha (2011), 'Sovereignty', in Rüdiger Wolfrum (ed.), *Max Planck Encyclopedia of Public International Law* (April 2011: Oxford University Press).

Bettinger-Lopez, Caroline (2009), 'The Inter-American Human Rights System: A Primer', *Clearinghouse Review,* 42 (6), 581–595.

Beurden, Jos (2014), 'How to Break the Deadlock in the Debate about Colonial Acquisition?', in Valentina Vadi and Hildegard Schneider (eds.), *Art, Cultural Heritage and the Market*, 165–182.

Blake, Janet (2006), *Commentary on the UNESCO 2003 Convention on the Safeguarding of the Intangible Cultural Heritage* (Leicester, UK: Institue of Art & Law).

Blake, Janet (2014), *Exploring Cultural Rights and Cultural Diversity* (Builth Wells, UK: Institute of Art & Law).

Bolton, Stephanie (2009), 'Museums Taken to Task: Representing First peoples at the McCord Museum of Canadian History', in Annis May Timpson (ed.), *First Nations, First THoughts: The Impact of Indigenous Thought in Canada* (Vancouver, Canada: UBC Press), 145–169.

Borrows, John (2006), 'Indigenous Legal Traditions in Canada'.

Borrows, John (2015), 'The durability of terra nullius: Tsilhqot'in Nation v British Columbia', *UBC Law Review,* 48 (3), 701–742.

Borrows, John (2016), 'Unextinguished: Rights and the Indian Act', *University of New Brunswick Law Journal,* 67, 3–35.

Boyd, Thomas H. and Haas, Jonathan (1992), 'The Native American Graves Protection and Repatriation Act: Prospects for New Partnerships Between Museums and Native American Groups', *Arizona State Law Journal,* 24 (1), 253–282.

Boyd, Willard L, et al. (28.02.1990), 'Report of the Panel for a National Dialogue on Museum/Native American Relations', (24; Arizona State Law Journal (1992) Appendix), 487–500.

Bradford, William (2002), '"With a Very Great Blame on Our Hearts": Reparations, Reconciliation, and an American Indian Plea for Peace with Justice', *American Indian Law Review,* 27 (1), 1–175.

Bradford, William (2005), 'Beyond Reparations: An American Indian Theory of Justice', *Ohio State Law Journal,* 66 (1), 1–103.

Brown, Michael A. (2010), 'Culture, Property, and Peoplehood: A Comment on Carpenter, Katyal, and Riley's "In Defense of Property"', *International Journal of Cultural Property,* 17, 569–579.

Brown, Michael F. (2003), *Who owns native culture?* (Cambridge, Mass.: Harvard University Press).

Brown, Michael F. and Bruchac, Margaret M. (2006), 'NAGPRA from the Middle Distance: Legal puzzles and unintended consequences', in Merryman (ed.), *Imperialism, Art and Restitution* (New York; U.S.: Cambridge University Press), 193–217.

Buck, Christopher (2006), '"Never Again": Kevin Gover's Apology for the Bureau of Indian Affairs', *Wicoza SA Review,* 21 (1), 97–126.

Burri, Mira (2013), 'The UNESCO Convention on Cultural Diversity: An Appraisal Five Years after Its Entry into Force', *International Journal of Cultural Property,* 20 (4), 357–380.

Burri, Mira, Graber, Christoph B., and Steiner, Thomas (2009), *The Protection and Promotion of Cultural Diversity in a Digital Networked Environment: Mapping Possible Advances to Coherence.* in CrossRef online database].

Capriccioso, Rob (13.01.2010), 'A sorry saga: Obama signs Native American apology resolution; fails to draw attention to it', *Indian Country Today.*

Carlson, Kirsten Matoy (2005), 'Does Constitutional Change Matter - Canada's Recognition of Aboriginal Title', *Arizona Journal of International and Comparative Law,* 22, 449.

Carpenter, Kristen A., Katyal, Sonia, and Riley, Angela R (2009), 'In defense of Property', *The Yale Law Journal,* 118 (6), 1022–1125.

Cassese, Antonio (1995), *Self-determination of peoples: A legal reappraisal* (Cambridge: Grotius Publ.) XVIII, 375 S.

Chamberlain, Kevin and Vrdoljak, Ana Filipa (2014) *Controls on the export of cultural objects and human rights* [online text], Edward Elgar Publishing

Champagne, Duane (2012), 'Indigenous self-government, cultural heritage and itnernational trade: a sociological perspective', in Christoph B. Graber, Karolina Kuprecht, and Jessica Christine Lai (eds.), *International Trade in Indigenous Cultural Heritage - Legal and Policy Issues* (Cheltenham, UK: Edward Elgar), 31–58.

Charlesworth, Hilary (2008), 'Universal Declaration of Human Rights (1948)', in Rüdiger Wolfrum (ed.), *Max Planck Encyclopedia of Public International Law* (Max Planck Institute, Heidelberg: Oxford Public International Law).

Charters, Claire (2012), 'Reparations for Indigenous Peoples: Global International Instruments and Institutions', in Federico Lenzerini (ed.), *Reparations for Indigenous Peoples: International and Comparative Perspectives* (Oxford Online Scholarship), 163-96.

Christie, Gordon (1998), 'Aboriginal Rights, Aboriginal Culture, and Protection', *Osgoode Hall Law Journal,* 36 (3), 447–484.

Clavir, Miriam (2002), 'Heritage Preservation: Museum Conservation and First Nations Perspectives', *Ethnologies,* 24 (2), 33–45.

Collison, Jisgang Nika, Bell, Lucy Sdaahl K̲'waas, and Neel, Lou-Ann (2019) *Indigenous Repatriation Handbook* [online text], Royal British Columbia Museum

Conaty, Gerald T. (2015a), 'The development of museums and their effects on First Nations', in Gerald T. Conaty (ed.), *We are coming home* (Edmonton, Canada: AU Press), 37–69.

Conaty, Gerald T. (ed.), (2015b), *We are coming home - Repatriation and the restoration of Blackfoot cultural confidence* (AU Press).

Coombe, Rosemary J and Turcotte, Joseph F (2012), 'Indigenous cultural heritage in development and trade: perspectives from the dynamics of cultural heritage law and policy', in Christoph B. Graber, Karolina Kuprecht, and Jessica Christine Lai (eds.), *International Trade in Indigenous Cultural Heritage - Legal and Policy Issues* (Cheltenham, UK: Edward Elgar), 272–305.

Coombe, Rosemary J. (1993), 'The Properties of Culture and the Politics of Possessing Identity: Native Claims in the Cultural Appropriation Controversy', *Canadian Journal of Law and Jurisprudence,* 6 (2), 249–285.

Coombe, Rosemary J. (2004), 'The Properties of Culture and the Politics of Possessing Identity: Native Claims in the Cultural Appropriation Controversy', in Patty Gerstenblith (ed.), *Art, Cultural Heritage, and the Law* (Durham, North Carolina: Carolina Academic Press), 541–547.

Cruickshank, David A. (2006), 'Calder Case', *The Canadian Encyclopedia* (https://www.thecanadianencyclopedia.ca/en/article/calder-case).

Cryne, Julia (2009), 'NAGPRA Revisited: A Twenty-Year Review of Repatriation Efforts', *American Indian Law Reviev,* 34, 99–122.

de Costa, Ravi (2004), 'Treaties in British Columbia: Comprehensive Agreement Making in a Democratic Context', in Marcia Langton, et al. (eds.), *Honour Among Nations?: treaties and agreements with indigenous people* (Melbourne, Australia: Melbourne University Press), 133–146.

de Jong, Cornelis (2000), *The freedom of thought, conscience and religion or belief in the United Nations: (1946 – 1992)* (Antwerpen [u.a.]: Intersentia [u.a.]).

Debo, Angie (1970), *A History of the Indians of the United States* (University of Oklahoma Press).

Desmet, Ellen (2008), 'The UN Basic Principles and Guidelines on the Right to a Remedy and Reparation: A Landmark or Windowdressing? An Analysis with Special Attention to the Situation of Indigenous Peoples', *South African Journal on Human Rights,* 24 (1), 71–103.

Desmet, Ellen (2011), *Indigenous rights entwined with nature conservation* (Cambridge; Portland: Intersentia International Specialized Book Services).

Disko, Stefan and Tugendhat, Helen (eds.) (2014), *World Heritage Sites and Indigenous Peoples' Rights* (Copenhagen: IWGIA).

Donders, Yvonne (2002), *Towards a right to cultural identity?* (Antwerpen; New York: Intersentia).

Donders, Yvonne (2007), 'The legal framework of the right to take part in cultural life', in Yvonne Donders and Vladimir Volodin (eds.), *Human Rights in Education, Science and Culture: Legal Developments and Challenges* (Aldershot, Hampshire: Ashgate Publishers), 231–272.

Donders, Yvonne (2008a), 'Background Paper for the General Day of Discussion - Right to take part in cultural life (article 15(1)(a) of the Covenant)', (E/C.12/40/13: CESCR), 1–7.

Donders, Yvonne (2008b), 'The History of the UNESCO Convention on the Protection and Promotion of the Diversity of Cultural Expressions', in Hildegard Schneider and Peter van den Bossche (eds.), *Protection of Cultural Diversity from a European and International Perspective* (Antwerp: Intersentia), 1–29.

Donders, Yvonne (2012), 'Cultural Rights and the Convention on the Diversity of Cultural Expressions: Included or Ignored?', in Toshiyuki Kono and Steven Van Uytsel (eds.), *The UNESCO Convention on the Diversity of Cultural Expressions - A Tale of Fragmentation in International Law* (Cambridge: Intersentia), 165–182.

Donders, Yvonne (2020). Cultural Heritage and Human Rights, in *Oxford Handbook on International Cultural Heritage Law*. F. Francioni and A. F. Vrdoljak (Eds). Oxford, UK, Oxford University Press: 379–406.

Dorough, D. S. and S. Wiessner (2020). Indigenous Peoples and Cultural Heritage, in *The Oxford Handbook of International Cultural Heritage Law*, F. Francioni and A. F. Vrdoljak (Eds). Oxford, UK, Oxford University Press: 407–430.

Dubinsky, Paul R. , Fox, Gregory H. , and Roth, Brad R. (eds.) (2017), *Supreme Law of the Land? Debating the Contemporary Effects of Treaties within the United States Legal System* (Cambridge University Press).

Dussias, Allison M (1993), 'Geographically-Based and Membership-Based Views of Indian Tribal Sovereignty: The Supreme Court's Changing Vision', *University of Pittsburgh Law Review,* 55, 1–97.

Dussias, Allison M (1996), 'Science, Sovereignty, and the Sacred Text: Paleontological Resources and Native American Rights', *Md. L. Rev.,* 55, 84–159.

Dussias, Allison M (2005), 'Kennewick Man, Kinship, and the Dying Race: The Ninth Circuit's Assimilationist Assault on the Native American Graves Protection and Repatriation Act', *Nebraska Law Review,* 84, 55–161.

Dussias, Allison M (2009), 'Exhibiting Culture in Legal Settings: Courts, Agencies, and Tribes', *Tulsa Law Review,* 45, 65–87.

Dussias, Allison M (2012), 'Friend, Foe, Frenemy: The United States and American Indian Religious Freedom', *Denver University Law Review,* 90 (2), 347–431.

Dussias, Allison M. (1995), 'The Right to Cultural and Religious Self-determination: Lessons from the Experience of Native Americans', *ILSA Journal of International and Comparative Law,* 2, 633–41.

Duthu, N. Bruce (2008), *American Indians and the Law*, ed. Colin G Calloway (The Penguin Library of American Indian History; New York: Penguin Books).

Echo-Hawk, Roger C and Zimmerman, Larry J (2006), 'Beyond racism: some opinions about racialism and American archaeology', *The American Indian Quarterly,* 30 (3), 461–485.

Evans, Malcolm D (2001), 'Human Rights, Religious Liberty and the Universality Debate', in Richard O'Dair and Andrew Lewis (eds.), *Law and Religion* (Oxford: Oxford University Press), 205–226.

Fechner, Frank (1998), 'The Fundamental Aims of Cultural Property Law', *International Journal of Cultural Property,* 7 (2), 376–394.

Fincham, Derek (2011), 'Deaccession of Art from the Public Trust', *Art Antiquity and Law,* 16 (2), 93–129.

Fink, Caroline (2000), 'Minority Rights as an International Question', *Contemporary European History,* 9 (3), 385–400.

Forrest, Craig (2007), 'Cultural heritage as the common heritage of humankind: a critical re-evaluation', *Comparative and International Law Journal of Southern Africa,* 40, 124–151.

Forrest, Craig (2010), *International law and the protection of cultural heritage* (Abingdon: Routledge).

Francioni, Francesco (2008), 'Culture, Heritage and Human Rights: An Introduction', in Francesco Francioni and Martin Scheinin (eds.), *Cultural human rights* (Leiden; Boston: Martinus Nijhoff Publishers), 1–15.

Francioni, Francesco (2013), 'Cultural Heritage', *Max Planck Encyclopedia of Public International Law* (Oxford University Press).

Garcia, Michael J., et al. (2017), 'The Constitution of the United States: Analysis and Interpretation', (Washington, DC: US Government Printing Office).

Gerstenblith, Patty (2001), 'The Public Interest in the Restitution of Cultural Objects', *Connecticut Journal of International Law,* 16 (2), 197–246.

Gerstenblith, Patty (2003), 'Acquisition and Deacquisition of Museum Collections and the Fiduciary Obligations of Museums to the Public', *Cardozo Journal of International and Comparative Law,* 11, 409–465.

Glass, Aaron (2004), 'Return to Sender', *Journal of Material Culture,* 9 (2), 115–139.

Golay, Christopher and Cismas, Iona (2010), 'Legal Opinion: The right to property from a human rights perspective', 1–31. <http://www.geneva-academy.ch/docs/publications/ESCR/humanright-en.pdf>.

Graber, Christoph B. (2012), 'Stimulating trade and development of indigenous cultural heritage by means of international law: issues of legitimacy and method', in C. B. Graber, Karolina Kuprecht, and Jessica Christine Lai (eds.), *International Trade in Indigenous Cultural Heritage - Legal and Policy Issues* (Cheltenham, UK: Edward Elgar), 3–30.

Graber, Christoph B. and Lai, Jessica Christine (2011), 'Indigenous Cultural Heritage and Fair Trade: Voluntary Certification Standards in the Light of WIPO and WTO Law and Policymaking', *SSRN Electronic Journal.*

Grammond, Sébastien (2009), *Identity Captured by Law* (McGill-Queen's University Press).

Groenen, Amoury (2018), 'UNIDROIT 1995: Tackling the Illicit Trafficking of Cultural Property Through Private Law Means', (Maastricht University).

Groni, Christian (2008), 'Background Paper for the General Day of Discussion - Right to take part in cultural life (article 15(1)(a) of the Covenant)', (E/C.12/40/3: UN CESCR), 1–24.

Hadjioannou, Marina (2005), 'The International Human Right to Culture: Reclamation of the Cultural Identities of Indigenous Peoples under International Law', *Chapman Law Review,* 9, 201–228.

Harding, Sarah (1997), 'Justifying repatriation of Native American cultural property', *Indiana law journal,* 72 (3), 723–774.

Harding, Sarah (1999), 'Value, Obligation and Cultural Heritage', *Arizona State Law Journal,* 31, 291–354.

Harding, Sarah (2009), 'Perpetual Property', *Florida Law Review,* 61, 285–327.

Harjo, Suzan Shown (2012), 'Native American Human Rights Acts: A Brief Account of Some Ways That Native Peoples and Friends Won Repatriation and National Indian Museum Laws', *Arizona Journal of International and Comparative Law,* 44 (2), 681–696.

Hausler, K. (2020). The Participation of Non-State Actors in the Implementation of Cultural Heritage Law in *The Oxford Handbook of International Cultural Heritage Law*, F. Francioni and A. F. Vrdoljak (Eds.). Oxford, UK, Oxford University Press: 760–786.

Hemmens, Craig, Brody, David C., and Spohn, Cassia (2019), *Criminal Courts: A Contemporary Perspective* (4th edition edn.: SAGE Publications).

Henry, Diana (1995), 'Back from the Brink: Canada's First Nations' Right to Preserve Canadian Heritage', *University of British Columbia Law Review,* Special Issue, 5–12.

Hogg, Peter W (2007 (loose-leaf edition updated 2015)), *Constitutional law of Canada (Volume II)* (II; Toronto, Canada: Thomson Reuters Carswell).

Hogg, Peter W (2007 (loose-leaf updated 2015)), *Constitutional Law of Canada (Volume I)* (I; Toronto: Thomson Reuters Canada).

Hogg, Peter W. (1992), *Constitutional law of Canada* (3rd edn.; Scarborough; Ont: Carswell) lxxii, 1478.

Holmwood, Jen and Plank, Sarah (29.11.2018), 'B.C. government, First Nations will share gaming revenue, co-develop legislation to implement UN declaration', (B.C. Office of the Premier).

Hutt, Sherry (1992), 'Illegal Trafficking in Native American Human Remains and Cultural Items: A new Protection Tool', *Arizona State Law Journal,* 24 (1), 135–150.

Imai, Shin (2014), *The 2015 Annotated Indian Act and Aboriginal Constitutional Provisions* (Toronto, Canada: Carswell, Thomson Reuters Limited).

Inouye, Daniel K (1990), 'Providing for the Protection of Native American Graves and the Repatriation of Native American Remains and Cultural Patrimony – Report', in Select Committee on Indian Affairs (ed.), (Washington, D.C.: U.S. Senate).

Inouye, Daniel K (1992), 'Foreword - Repatriation: Forging New Relationships', *Arizona State Law Journal,* 24 (1), 1–3.

Irwin, Lee (1997), 'Freedom, Law and Prophecy: A brief history of Native American Religious Resistance', *American Indian Quarterly,* 21 (1), 35–55.

Ives, John W. (2015), 'Moving Toward Repatriation', in Gerald T. Conaty (ed.), *We are coming home: repatriation and the restoration of Blackfoot cultural confidence* (Edmonton: Athabasca University Press), 223–240.

Janes, Robert R. (2015), 'The Blackfoot Repatriation: A Personal Epilogue', in Gerald T. Conaty (ed.), *We are coming home: repatriation and the restoration of Blackfoot cultural confidence*, 241–262.

Johnson, Greg (2004), 'Naturally There: Discourses of Permanence in the Repatriation Context', *History of Religions,* 44 (1), 36–55.

Johnson, Greg (2007), *Sacred Claims - Repatriation and Living Tradition* (Charlottesville: University of Virginia Press).

Johnson, Ralph W. and Haensly, Sharon I. (1992), 'Fifth Amendment Takings Implications of the 1990 Native American Graces Protection and Repatriation Act', *Arizona State Law Journal,* 24 (1), 151–173.

Kagan, Tamara (2005), 'Recovering Aboriginal Cultural Property at Common Law: A Contextual Approach', *University of Toronto Faculty of Law Review,* 63, 1–41.

Katz, Brigit (22.04.2019), 'Canadian Museum Association Receives $1 Million to Foster Reconciliation With Indigenous Peoples', *Smithsonian Magazine.*

Kenney, Cortelou C (2011), 'Reframing Indigenous Cultural Artifacts Disputes: An Intellectual Property-based Approach', *Cardozo Arts & Entertainment Law Journal,* 28 (3), 502–552.

Kowalski, Wojciech (2005), 'Types of Claims for Recovery of Lost Cultural Property', *Museum International,* 57 (4), 85–102.

Kreps, Christina (2009), 'Indigenous curation, museums, and intangible cultural heritage', in Laurajane Smith and Natsuko Akagawa (eds.), *Intangible Heritage* (New York: Routledge), 193–206.

Kuprecht, Karolina (2014), *Indigenous Peoples' Cultural Property Claims - Repatriation and Beyond* (Springer).

Kuprecht, Karolina and Siehr, Kurt (2012), 'International trade in moveable tangible cultural heritage of indigenous peoples: a European perspective', in Christoph B. Graber, Karolina Kuprecht, and Jessica Christine Lai (eds.), *International Trade in Indigenous Cultural Heritage - Legal and Policy Issues* (Cheltenham, UK: Edward Elgar), 246–271.

Kymlicka, Will (1995), *Multicultural Citizenship - A liberal Theory of Minority Rights* (Oxford (UK): Oxford University Press).

Ladner, Kiera L (2009), 'Take 35: Reconciling Constitutional Orders', in Annis May Timpson (ed.), *First Nations, First Thoughts: The Impact of Indigneous Thought in Canada* (Vancouver, Canada: UBC Press), 279.

Lavrysen, Laurens (2014), 'Positive Obligations in the Jursprudence of the Inter-American Court of Human Rights', *Inter-American & European Human Rights Journal,* 7, 94–115.

Lenzerini, Federico and Scott, John (2012), 'International indigenous and human rights law in the context of trade in indigenous cultural heritage', in Christoph B. Graber, Karolina Kuprecht, and Jessica Christine Lai (eds.), *International Trade in Indigenous Cultural Heritage* (Cheltenham, UK: Edward Elgar), 61–87.

Lerner, Natan (1991), *Group rights and discrimination in international law* (The Hague: Martinus Nijhoff) xiv, 181.

Livesay, Thomas A (1992), 'The Impact of the Federal Repatriation Act on State-Operated Museums', *Arizona State Law Journal,* 24 (1), 293–301.

Lixinski, Lucas (2014), 'Heritage for Whom? Individuals' and Communities' Roles in International Cultural Heritage Law', in Federico Lenzerini and Anna Filipa Vrdoljak (eds.), *International Law for Common Goods - Normative Perspectives on Human Rights, Culture and Nature* (Oxford: Hart Publishing), 193–213.

Loring, Stephen (2009), 'From Tent to Trading Post and Back Again:Smithsonian Anthropology in Nunavut, Nunavik, Nitassinan, and Nunatsiavut - The Changing IPY Agenda, 1882-2007', in Igor Krupnik, Michael A Lang, and Scott E Miller (eds.), *Smithsonian at the Poles: Contributions to International Polar Year Science* (Washington, DC: Smithsonian Institution Scholarly Press), 115–127.

Lubina, Katja (2009), 'Contested Cultural Property - The Return of Nazi Spoliated Art and Human Remains From Public Collections', (Maastricht University).

Makah Indian Tribe and National Association of Tribal Historic Preservation Officers, NATHPO (2008), 'Federal Agency Implementation of the Native American Graves Protection and Repatriation Act', (Washington, DC: NATHPO), 1–50.

Mangone, Gerard J. (2002), 'Private Property Rights: The Development of Takings in the United States', *The International Journal of Maritime and Coastal Law,* 17 (2), 195–233.

Marleau, Robert and Montpetit, Camille (2000), 'House of Commons Procedure and Practice', in House of Commons (ed.), (Canada, Parliament, House of Commons).

Marsh, Gene (1992), 'Walking the Spirit Trail: Repatriation and Protection fo NAtive American Remains and Sacred Cultural Items', *Arizona State Law Journal,* 24 (1), 79–133.

Mazzuoli, Valerio de and Ribeiro, Dilton (2015), 'Indigenous Rights before the Inter-American Court of Human Rights', *Indonesian Journal of International & Comparative Law,* 2, 522–553.

McCabe, J. Timothy S. (2008), *The Honour of the Crown and its Fiduciary Duties to Aboriginal Peoples* (Markham, Canada: LexisNexis Canada).

McCain, John (1992), 'Foreword: Repatriation - Balancing Interests', *Arizona State Law Journal,* 24 (1), 5–6.

McGoldrick, Dominic (2002), 'Culture, Cultures, and Cultural Rights', in Mashood Baderin and Robert McCorquodale (eds.), *Economic, Social and Cultural Rights in Action* (Oxford: Oxford University Press), 447–473.

McManamon, Francis P (2000), 'The Archaeological Resources Protection Act of 1979 (ARPA)', in Linda Ellis (ed.), *Archaeological Method and Theory: An Encyclopedia* (New York, London: Garland Publishing Co).

McManamon, Francis P. and Nordby, Larry V. (1992), 'Implementing the Native American Graves Protection and Repatriation Act', *Arizona State Law Journal,* 24 (1), 217–252.

McNeil, Kent (2008), 'Fiduciary Obligations and Aboriginal Peoples', in Mark R. Gillen and Faye Woodman (eds.), *The Law of Trusts: A Contextual Approach* (Toronto, ON: Emond Montgomery).

Meijknecht, Anna (2001), *Towards international personality: The position of minorities and indigenous peoples in international law* (Antwerp: Intersentia) xiv, 271.

Meijknecht, Anna (2012), 'The Convention on the Diversity of Cultural Expressions - What is Its Added Value for Minorities and Indigenous Peoples?', in Toshiyuki Kono and Steven Van Uytsel (eds.), *The UNESCO Convention on the Diversity of Cultural Expressions - A Tale of Fragmentation in International Law* (Cambridge: Intersentia), 201–226.

Meltz, Robert (2015), 'Takings Decisions of the U.S. Supreme Court: A Chronology', (US Congressional Research Service).

Merryman, John (1986), 'Two Ways of Thinking About Cultural Property', *The American Journal of International Law,* 80 (4), 831–853.

Metcalfe, Eric (1996), 'Illiberal Citizenship? A Critique of Will Kymlicka's Liberal Theory of Minority Rights', *Queen's Law Journal,* 22 (1), 167–207.

Millen, Roy and Adkins, Sam (22.10.2018), 'BC Treaty Process and the Realization of Free, Prior and Informed Consent', *Blake, Cassels & Graydon LLP,* p. 1–14.

Moriwake, Isaac (1998), 'Critical Excavations: Law, Narrative, and the Debate on Native American and Hawaiian "Cultural Property" Repatriation', *University of Hawaii Law Review,* 20, 261–319.

Morton, John (2010), 'Consigned to Oblivion: People and THings Forgotten in the Creation of Australia', in Paul Turnbull and Michael Pickering (eds.), *The Long*

Way Home - The Meanings and Values of Repatriation (New York: Berghahn Books), 96–113.

Moustakas, John (1989), 'Group Rights in Cultural Property: Justifying Strict Inalienability', *Cornell Law Review,* 74 (6), 1179–1227.

Murphy, Michael (2009), 'Civilization, Self-Determination, and Reconciliation', in Annis May Timpson (ed.), *First Nations, First Thoughts: The Impact of Idnigenous Thought in Canada* (Vancouver, Canada: UBC Press), 251–278.

Museums and Galleries Commission, United Kingdom (2009), 'Restitution and Repatriation: Guidelines for Good Practice 2000', in Lyndel Prott (ed.), *Witnesses to History - A Compendium of Documents and Writings on the Return of Cultural Objects* (Paris: UNESCO Publishers), 130–149.

Myles, Virginia (2010), 'Parks Canada's Policies that Guide the Repatriation of Human Remains and Objects', in Paul Turnbull and Michael Pickering (eds.), *The Long Way Home - The Meanings and Values of Repatriation* (New York: Berghahn Books), 48–56.

Nafziger, James (2009), 'The Protection and Repatriation of Indigenous Cultural Heritage in the United States', in Catherine E. Bell and Robert K. Paterson (eds.), *Protection of First Nations cultural heritage: Laws, Policy, and Reform* (Vancouver: UBC Press), 110–152.

Nafziger, James and Dobkins, Rebecca (1999), 'The Native American Graves Protection and Repatriation Act in Its First Decade', *International Journal of Cultural Property,* 8 (1), 77–107.

Nafziger, James and Paterson, Robert K. (2014a), 'International Trade in cultural material', in James Nafziger and Robert K. Paterson (eds.), *Handbook on the law of cultural heritage and international trade* (Elgar Online), 19–43.

Nafziger, James and Paterson, Robert K. (2014b), 'Cultural Heritage Law', in James Nafziger and Robert K. Paterson (eds.), *Handbook on the Law of Cultural Heritage and International Trade* (UK: Edward Elgar Publishing), 1–18.

Nafziger, James A. R., Renteln, Alison Dundes, and Paterson, Robert K. (2010), *Cultural Law: International, Comparative and Indigenous* (Cambridge: Cambridge University Press).

Nagy, Rosemary (2014), 'The Truth and Reconciliation Commission of Canada: Genesis and Design', *Canadian Journal of Law and Society / La Revue Canadienne Droit et Société,* 29 (Special Issue 02), 199–217.

Nationaal Museum van Wereldculturen (7 March 2019), 'Return of Cultural Objects: Principles and Process'.

Newton, Nell Jessup, et al. (2005), *Cohen's Handbook of Federal Indian Law* (2005 edition with 2007 supplement edn.: LexisNexis).

Niezen, Ronald (2009), *The rediscovered self: Indigenous identity and cultural justice* (Montréal [Que.]: McGill-Queen's University Press).

Niezen, Ronald (2010), *Public justice and the anthropology of law* (Cambridge, UK; New York: Cambridge University Press) xiv, 254.

Nimni, Ephraim (2008), 'Background Paper for the Day of General Discussion - Right to take part in cultural life (article 15(1)(a) of the Covenant)', (E/C.12/40/17: CESCR), 1–16.

Nowak, Manfred (2005), *U.N. Covenant on Civil and Political Rights - CCPR Commentary* (Kehl: N.P. Engel).

O'Keefe, Patrick (2009), 'Repatriation of Sacred Objects', in Lyndel Prott (ed.), *Witnesses to History - Documents and writings on the return of cultural objects* (Paris: UNESCO), 225–238.

O'Keefe, Roger (2011), 'Cultural Life, Right to Participate in, International Protection', in Rüdiger Wolfrum (ed.), *Max Planck Encyclopedia of Public International Law* (Max Planck Institute of International Law, Heidelberg: Oxford Public International Law).

O'Keefe, Roger (2013), 'Tangible Cultural Heritage and International Human Rights Law', in Lyndel Prott, Ruth Redmond-Cooper, and Stephen Urice (eds.), *Realising Cultural Heritage law - Festschrift for Patrick O'Keefe* (IAL Institute of Art and Law), 87–95.

Olivier, Monique (1996), 'The Unidroit Convention: Attempting to Regulate the International Trade and Traffic of Cultural Property', *Golden Gate University Law Review,* 26, 627–674.

Olthuis Kleer Townshend LLP (2018), Aboriginal Law Handbook 5th Edition, Thomson Ruiters, Canada

Panagos, Dimitrios (2016), *Uncertain Accommodation: Aboriginal Identity and Group Rights in the Supreme Court of Canada* (Vancouver, Canada: UBC Press).

Pasqualucci, Jo M. (2006), 'The Evolution of International Indigneous Rights in the Inter-American Human Rights System', *Human Rights Law Review,* 6 (2), 281–322.

Pasternak, S (2020) B.C. might want to align with UNDRIP, but does UNDRIP align with B.C.? in King, H. (Ed) pp. 17–19 The UN Declaration on the Rights of Indigenous Peoples in Canada: Lessons from B.C., Yellowhead Institute (Special Report December 2020)

Paterson, Robert K. (2007), 'Totems and Teapots: The Royal British Columbia Museum Corporation', *University of British Columbia Law Review,* 40 (1), 421–437.

Paterson, Robert K. (2010), 'Canada', in Toshiyuki Kono (ed.), *The Impact of Uniform Laws on the Protection of Cultural Heritage and the Preservation of Cultural Heritage in the 21st Century // The impact of uniform laws on the protection of cultural heritage and the preservation of cultural heritage in the 21st century* (Leiden; Boston: Martinus Nijhoff Publishers), 233–246.

Paterson, Robert K. (2014), 'Collecting "Tribal Art"- Sacred or Secular?', *International Journal of Cultural Property,* 21, 305–318.

Pentassuglia, Gaetano (2013), 'Protecting Minority Groups through Human Rights Courts - The Interpretative Role of European and Inter-American Jurisprudence', in Ana Filipa Vrdoljak (ed.), *The Cultural Dimension of Human Rights* (Oxford University Press), 73–116.

Peregoy, Robert M. (1992), 'The Legal Basis, Legislative History, and Implementation of Nebraska's Landmark Reburial Legislation', *Arizona State Law Journal,* 24 (1), 329–389.

Pineschi, Laura (2012), 'Cultural Diversity as a Human Right? General Comment No.21 of the Committee on Economic, Social and Cultural Rights', in Silvia Borelli and Federico Lenzerini (eds.), *Cultural Heritage, Cultural Rights, Cultural Diversity* (Studies in Intercultural Human Rights: Nijhoff Publishers, Brill), 29–53.

Prott, Lyndel (1986), 'Cultural Rights as People's Rights in International law', *Bulletin of the Australian Society of Legal Philosophy,* 10 (1), 4–19.

Prott, Lyndel (1997), *Commentary on the UNIDROIT Convention* (Institute of Art and Law).

Prott, Lyndel (2009a), 'The UNIDROIT Convention on Stolen or Illegally Exported Cultural Objects - Ten Years On', *Uniform Law Review,* 14, 215–237.

Prott, Lyndel and O'Keefe, Patrick (1992), 'Cultural Heritage or Cultural Property', *International Journal of Cultural Property,* 1 (2), 307–320.

Prott, Lyndel V. (2009b), 'The History and Development of Processes for the Recovery of Cultural Heritage', in Lyndel V. Prott (ed.), *Witnesses to History - A Compendium of Documents and Writings on the Return of Cultural Objects* (Paris: UNESCO Publishing), 2–18.

Prott, Lyndel V. and O'Keefe, Patrick J. (1989), *Law and the cultural heritage / Vol. 3, Movement* (London [etc.]: Butterworths).

Prott, Lyndel V. (ed.), (2009c), *Witnesses to History - Documents and writings on the return of cultural objects* (Paris, France: UNESCO Publishing).

Randall, Kayla (2018), 'How the Smithsonian is Reuniting Thousands of Human Remains with Indigenous Communities', *Washington City Paper.*

Raschèr, Andrea F.G. (2000), *Kulturgüter-Transfer und Globalisierung* (Studien zum Kunstrecht; Zürich: Nomos Verlagsgesellschaft Baden-Baden).

Reed, Trevor (2016), 'Who Owns Our Ancestors' Voirces? Tribal Claims to Pre-1972 Recordings', *Columbia Journal of Law & The Arts,* 40 (2), 275–310.

Riding In, James (1992), 'Without Ethics and Morality: A Historical Overview of Imperial Archaeology and American Indians', *Arizona State Law Journal,* 24 (1), 11–34.

Rivière, Françoise, et al. (2007), 'UNESCO Forum on Memory and Universality, UNESCO Headquarters Paris, 5 February 2007', in Lyndel Prott (ed.), *Witnesses to History* (Paris: UNESCO), 45–77.

Robinson, Amanda (2016), 'Gradual Civilization Act', *The Canadian Encyclopedia* (https://www.thecanadianencyclopedia.ca/en/article/gradual-civilization-act).

Rustad, John, et al. (2015), 'Proposed Commitment Document', in BC Ministry of Aboriginal Relations and Reconciliation and First Nations Leadership Council (eds.), 1–11.

Sarr, Felwine and Savoy, Bénédicte (2018), 'The Resitution of African Cultural Heritage. Toward a New Relational Ethics', (N 2018-26).

Savoy, Bénédicte (2021), Afrikas Kampf um Seine Kunst. C.H.Beck, Ulm

Sayers, Judith (2020), Opportunities and Barriers for the B.C. Declaration of Rights Act in Hayden King (Ed.) The UN Declaration on the Rights of Indigenous Peoples in Canada: Lessons from B.C., Yellowhead Institute (Special Report December 2020), pp. 13–15

Scheinin, Martin (2005), 'Indigenous Peoples' Rights Under The International Covenant On Civil And Political Rights', in Joshua Castellino and Niamh Walsh (eds.), *International Law and Indigenous Peoples* (Leiden: Martinus Nijhoff Publishers), 3–15.

Scovazzi, Tullio and Nafziger, James (2007a), *2005 - Le patrimoine culturel de l'humanité - The cultural heritage of mankind* eds Hague Academy of International Law. Center for Studies and Research (Martinus Nijhoff Publishers).

Scovazzi, Tullio and Nafziger, James (2007b), *2005 - Le patrimoine culturel de l'humanité - The cultural heritage of mankind*, eds Hague Academy of International Law Center for Studies and Research (Martinus Nijhoff Publishers).

Scovazzi, T. (2020). International Cultural Heritage Law: The Institutional Aspects, in *The Oxford Handbook of International Cultural Heritage Law*, F. Francioni and A. F. Vrdoljak (Eds.). Oxford, UK, Oxford University Press: 737–759.

Secretary of the Interior, US (1992), 'Charter of the Native American Graves Protection and Repatriation Review Committee', *Arizona State Law Journal,* 24 (1), 501–503.

Seidemann, Ryan M (2010), 'NAGPRA at 20: What Have the States Done to Expand Human Remains Protections?', *Museum Anthropology,* 33 (2), 199–209.

Shelton, Dinah (2013), 'The Inter-American Human Rights Law of Indigenous Peoples', *University of Hawaii Law Review,* 35 (2), 937–982.

Simon, Cheryl and Clark, Judy (2013), 'Exploring Inequities under the Indian Act', *University of New Brunswick Law Journal,* 64, 103–122.

Singh, Kavita (2009), 'Universal Museums: The View from Below', in Lyndel Prott (ed.), *Witnesses to History - A Compendium of Documents and Writings on the Return of Cultural Property* (Paris: UNESCO Publishers), 123–129.

Skrydstrup, Martin (2010), 'What Might an Anthropology of Cultural Property Look Like?', in Paul Turnbull and Michael Pickering (eds.), *The Long Way Home - The Meaning and Values of Repatriation* (New York: Berghahn Books), 59–81.

Srivinas, Burra (2008), 'The UNESCO Convention for the Safeguarding of the Intangible Cultural Heritage', in James Nafziger and Tullio Scovazzi (eds.), *Le patrimonie culturel de l'humanité - The cultural heritage of mankind* (Leiden; Boston: Martinus Nijhoff Publishers).

Stamatopoulou, Elissavet (2008), 'Background Paper for the Day of General Discussion - Right to take part in cultural life (article 15(1)(a) of the Covenant)', (E/C.12/40/9: CESCR).

Stamatopoulou, Elsa (2007), *Cultural rights in international law: Article 27 of the Universal Declaration of Human Rights and beyond* (Boston: Martinus Nijhoff).

Stockford Careless, James Maurice (2019), 'Province of Canada (1841-67)', in Richard Foot and Andrew McIntosh (eds.), *The Canadian Encyclopedia* (https://www.thecanadianencyclopedia.ca/en/article/province-of-canada-1841-67).

Strasser, Mark (2016), 'Free Exercise and Substantial Burdens under Federal Law', *Nebraska Law Review,* 94 (3), 633–684.

Strickland, Rennard (1992), 'Implementing the National Policy of Understanding, Preserving, and Safegaurding the Heritage of Indian Peoples and Native

Hawaiians: Human Rights, Sacred Objects and Cultural Patrimony', *Arizona State Law Journal,* 24 (1), 175–191.

Stumpf, Gary D. (1992), 'A Federal Land Management Perspective on Repatriation', *Arizona State Law Journal,* 24 (1), 303–320.

Swepston, Lee (2005), 'Indigenous Peoples in International Law and Organizations', in Joshua Castellino and Niamh Walsh (eds.), *International Law and Indigenous Peoples* (Leiden: Martinus Nijhoff Publishers), 53–66.

Tauli-Corpuz, Victoria (2014), 'Forword', in Stefan Disko and Helen Tugendhat (eds.), *World Heritage Sites and Indigenous Peoples' Rights* (Copenhagen: IWGIA), xii–xv.

Tennant, Chris (1994), 'Indigenous Peoples, International Institutions, and the International Legal Literature from 1945-1993', *Human Rights Quarterly,* 16 (1), 1–57.

Thomas, Nicholas (2018), 'Should colonial art be returned home?', *Financial Times,* 6.12.

Thornberry, Patrick (2002a), *Indigenous peoples and human rights* (Manchester: Manchester University Press) 1 online resource (1 v.).

Thornberry, Patrick (2002b), *Indigenous peoples and human rights* (Manchester: Manchester University Press).

Thornberry, Patrick (2008), 'Background Paper for the Day of General Discussion - Right to take part in cultural life (article 15(1)(a) of the Covenant)', (E/C.12/40/15: CESCR).

Tomuschat, Christian (2010), *Human Rights - Between Idealism and Realism* (Oxford University Press).

Trope, Jack F. and Echo-Hawk, Walter R. (1992), 'The Native American Graves Protection and Repatriation Act: Background and Legislative History', *Arizona State Law Journal,* 24 (1), 35–77.

Tsosie, Rebecca (2012a), 'International trade in indigenous cultural heritage: an argument for indigenous governance of cultural property', in Christoph B. Graber, Karolina Kuprecht, and Jessica Christine Lai (eds.), *International Trade in Indigenous Cultural Heritage - Legal and Policy Issues* (Cheltenham, UK: Edward Elgar), 221–245.

Tsosie, Rebecca (2012b), 'NAGPRA and the Problem of Culturally Unidentifiable Remains: The Argument for a Human Rights Framework,' *Arizona State Law Journal,* 44 (2), 809–906.

Turner C, Fondahl G (2015), "Overlapping Claims" to territory confronting treaty-maing in British Columbia: causes and implications. The Canadian Geographer / Le Géographe canadien 59(4), pp. 474–488

van Beurden, Jos (2017), *Treasures in Trusted Hands - Negotiating the Future of Colonial Cultural Objects* (Interdisciplinary Studies in Culture, History and Heritage; Leiden: Sidestone Press).

van der Schyff, Gerhard (2004), 'The historical development of the right to freedom of religion', *South African Law Journal,* 2, 259–272.

van Ert, Gib (2010), 'Dubious Dualism: The Reception of International law in Canada', *Valparaiso University Law Review,* 44 (3), 927–934.

Vásquez, Carlos Manuel (1995), 'The four doctrines of self-executing treaties', *American Journal of International Law,* 89 (4), 695–723.

Vicaire, Peter Scott (2011), 'Two Roads Diverged in a Wood - A comparative analysis of indigneous rights in a North American constitutional context', *The Judges Journal,* 50 (3), 18–25.

Virgil (1792), *The Works of Virgil - Volume II,* trans. Dryden (J. Rivington and Sons).

Vrdoljak, Ana Filipa (2008a), *International law, museums and the return of cultural objects* (Cambridge [u.a.]: Cambridge University Press).

Vrdoljak, Ana Filipa (2008b), 'Self-Determination and Cultural Rights', in Francesco Francioni and Martin Scheinin (eds.), *Cultural human rights* (Leiden; Boston: Martinus Nijhoff Publishers), 41–78.

Vrdoljak, Ana Filipa (2014), 'Human Rights and Cultural Heritage in International Law', in Federico Lenzerini and Ana Filipa Vrdoljak (eds.), *International Law for Common Goods* (Oxford: Hart Publishing), 139–173.

Vrdoljak, Ana Filipa (2018), 'Indigenous Peoples, World Heritage, and Human Rights', *International Journal of Cultural Property,* 25 (3), 245–281.

Watson, Irene (2015), *Aboriginal Peoples, Colonialism and International Law*, eds Mark A. Harris and Claire Charters (Raw Law; Abingdon: Routledge).

Welsh, Peter H. (1992), 'Repatriation and Cultural Preservation: Potent Objects, Potent Pasts', *University of Michigan Journal of Law Reform,* 25 (3&4), 837–866.

Whitby-Last, Kathryin (2010), 'Legal Impediments to the Repatriation of Cultural Objects to Indigenous Peoples', in Paul Turnbull and Michael Pickering (eds.), *The Long Way Home - The Meanings and Values of Repatriation* (New York: Berghahn Books), 35–47.

Wiener, Michael (2015), 'Interpretation of the 1981 Declaration through the Mandate Practice of the United Nations Special Rapporteur on Freedom of Religion or Belief', in Malcolm D Evans, Peter Petkoff, and Julian Rivers (eds.), *Changing Nature of Religious Rights under International LAw* (Oxford: Oxford University Press), 51–80.

Xanthaki, Alexandra (2018), 'Articles 11(1), 12, 13(1), 15 and 34', in Jessie Hohmann and Marc Weller (eds.), *The UN Declaration on the Rights of Indigenous Peoples* (Oxford: Oxford University Press), 273–298.

Yellow Old Woman, Herman (2015), 'Bringing Back Iitskinaiksi at Siksika', in Gerald T. Conaty (ed.), *We are coming home: repatriation and the restoration of Blackfoot cultural confidence* (Edmonton: Athabasca University Press), 183–204.

Young, James O. and Brunk, Conrad G. (eds.) (2009), *The ethics of cultural appropriation* (Chichester, U.K; Malden, MA: Wiley-Blackwell).

Youngblood Henderson, James (2006), *First Nations Jurisprudence and Aboriginal Rights* (Saskatoon, Canada: Native Law Center, University of Saskatchewan).

Yupsanis, Athanasios (2010), 'ILO Convention NO. 169 Concerning Indigenous and Tribal Peoples in Independent Countries 1989–2009: An Overview', *Nordic Journal of International Law,* 79, 433–456.

Zaretsky, Donn (2015), 'There's No Such Thing as the Public Trust, and It's a Good Thing, Too', in Julia Courtney (ed.), *The Legal Guide for Museum Professionals* (Lanham (US): Rowman & Littlefield), 151–155.

Newspaper Articles

(12.03.2003), 'B.C. offers apology to First Nations for 'inequity, intolerance, isolation and indifference'', *CBC News*.
Brake, Justin (2018), 'Trudeau to address First Nation chiefs amid growing opposition to Indigenous rights framework', *APTN News,* 4.12.
Braun, Stuart (2019), 'Looted colonial art: Is there the political will to return pilfered artifacts?', *Deutsche Welle,* 5.01.
Griffith, Andrew (2016), 'Diversity among federal and provincial judges', *Policy Options,* 4.05., available at: https://policyoptions.irpp.org/2016/05/04/diversity-among-federal-provincial-judges/ [last accessed 19.08.2021]
Harris, Gareth (2017), 'What restitution experts have to say about President Macron's pledge to return African artefacts', *The Art Newspaper,* 29.11.
Hickley, Catherine (2018), 'Berlin Museums chief calls for rules on restitution of colonial artefacts', *The Art Newspaper,* 16.02.
Hickley, Catherine (2019), 'Dutch museums take initiative to repatriate colonial-era artefacts', *The Art Newspaper,* 14.03.
Lamirande, Todd (2019), Indigenous rights framework far from dead as Trudeau government rolls it out in pieces, *Nation to Nation*, Aboriginal Peoples Television Network, 15.07.
O'Neil, Peter and Shaw, Rob (2.11.2016), 'Yale First Nation puts hold on treaty implementation', *Vancouver Sun*.

Online Sources

All Links Were Last Accessed 30.07.2021

American Alliance of Museums, available at: https://www.aam-us.org/programs/about-aam/
American Anthropological Association, available at: https://www.americananthro.org/ConnectWithAAA/Content.aspx?ItemNumber=1665&navItemNumber=586
British Columbia, Ministry of Aboriginal Relations and Reconciliation. The New Relationship – Vision Document (2005), available at: http://www2.gov.bc.ca/assets/gov/environment/natural-resource-stewardship/consulting-with-first-nations/agreements/other-docs/new_relationship_accord.pdf

British Columbia, Ministry of Indigenous Relations and Reconciliation, website, available at: http://www.gov.bc.ca/arrtreaty/negotiating/why.html

British Columbia Ministry of Indigenous Relations and Reconciliation (2019), 'About First Nations Treaty Process', available at: https://www2.gov.bc.ca/gov/content/environment/natural-resource-stewardship/consulting-with-first-nations/first-nations-negotiations/about-first-nations-treaty-process

British Columbia, Provincial Government, Website from July 2017 archived via: http://web.archive.org/web/20170707010350/http://www2.gov.bc.ca/gov/content/environment/natural-resource-stewardship/consulting-with-first-nations/first-nations-negotiations/about-first-nations-treaty-process

British Columbia, Provincial Government, information on Maa-nulth First Nations, available at: https://www2.gov.bc.ca/gov/content/environment/natural-resource-stewardship/consulting-with-first-nations/first-nations-negotiations/first-nations-a-z-listing/maa-nulth-first-nations

B.C. Teachers' Federation and Committee, Tripartite Public Education 'Understanding the B.C. Treaty Process—An Opportunity for Dialogue', available via: http://www.fnesc.ca/publications/Copyrighted_Publications/Understanding%20the%20BC%20Treaty%20Process%201998_Cpyrt.pdf

British Columbia Treaty Commission, Website archived version: http://web.archive.org/web/20181023091837/http://www.bctreaty.ca/land-and-resources

British Columbia Treaty Commission, Where are We, Annual Report 2003, available via: http://www.bctreaty.ca/annual-reports

British Columbia Treaty Commission, Reconciling Prosperity, Annual Report 2017, available via http://www.bctreaty.ca/annual-reports

British Columbia Treaty Commission, Annual Report 2018, available via http://www.bctreaty.ca/annual-reports

British Columbia Treaty Commission, Negotiation Update, archived version from 12.07.2019 available at: http://web.archive.org/web/20190712083820/http://www.bctreaty.ca/negotiation-update , updated version available at: http://www.bctreaty.ca/negotiation-update

British Columbia Treaty Commission, News Release 19.03.2019, available via http://www.bctreaty.ca/news-releases

British Columbia Treaty Commission, overview of treaties and agreements in principle, available at: http://www.bctreaty.ca/treaties-and-agreements

Canadian census data, available via official governmental website of Statistics Canada at: http://www.statcan.gc.ca/daily-quotidien/171025/dq171025a-eng.htm

Canadian Museum Association, Ethics Guidelines [2006], available at: http://www.museums.ca/uploaded/web/docs/ethicsguidelines.pdf

Canadian Museum Association, Deaccessioning Guidelines [2020] available https://www.museums.ca/site/deaccessioning_guidelines

Canadian Museum of Civilization Corporation, Summary Report Corporate Plan 2003-2005, 2007-2008 2014-2015, 2018-2019, available via https://www.historymuseum.ca

Canadian Museum of Civilization Corporation, Repatriation Policy [2001] available via: http://www.historymuseum.ca/wp-content/uploads/2015/09/REPATRIATION-POLICY.pdf

Canadian Museum of History, Website, available at: http://www.historymuseum.ca/learn/research/repatriation/#tabs

Cornell Law School, Legal Information Institute entry on self-executing treaty, available at: https://www.law.cornell.edu/wex/self_executing_treaty

Crown-Indigenous Relations and Northern Affairs Canada, Government of Canada, Multilateral Engagement Process to Improve and Expedite Treaty Negotiations in British Columbia (2015), available at: https://www.rcaanc-cirnac.gc.ca/eng/1465231252132/1539697344543

Crown-Indigenous Relations and Northern Affairs Canada (1.12.2018), 'Treaty Principals sign Accord to transform treaty negotiations in B.C.', available via: https://news.gov.bc.ca/releases

Crown-Indigenous Relations and Northern Affairs Canada, Government of Canada (2018), 'Engagement document: Working together to create the foundation for the Federal Recognition and Implementation of the Inherent and Treaty Rights of Indigenous Peoples in Canada', available via: https://www.rcaanc-cirnac.gc.ca/eng/1531511313025/1539960167883

Culturally Affiliated Native American Inventories Database, available via https://www.nps.gov/subjects/nagpra/databases.htm

Department of Justice, Government of Canada, About Canada's justice system, available at: http://www.justice.gc.ca/eng/csj-sjc/just/05.html

Deutscher Museumsbund (2021) Leitfaden Umgang mit Sammlungsgut aus kolonialen Kontexten, 3. Fassung 2021. Available via: https://www.museumsbund.de/wp-content/uploads/2021/03/mb-leitfanden-web-210228-02.pdf

Ellwand, O., Interview with C. Robertson from Royal Albert Museum, 27.05.2016, archived website available at: https://web.archive.org/web/20160527225310/http://edmontonjournal.com/news/local-news/alberta-government-to-expand-policy-around-return-of-sacred-items-to-indigenous-communities

Federal Judicial Centre, demography of Art. III judges, available at: https://www.fjc.gov/history/exhibits/graphs-and-maps/race-and-ethnicity

First Nations Summit website, available at: http://fns.bc.ca/about

First Nations Summit, et al. (2018), 'Joint Agenda: Implementing the Commitment Document - Shared Vision, Guiding Principles, Goals and Objectives', available at: https://www2.gov.bc.ca/gov/content/environment/natural-resource-stewardship/consulting-with-first-nations/first-nations-negotiations/reconciliation-other-agreements , 1-6.

Federal Foreign Office of Germany (30.04.2021) Press release: Statement on the handling of the Benin Bronzes in German museums and institutions. Available via: Statement on the handling of the Benin Bronzes in German museums and institutions - Federal Foreign Office (auswaertiges-amt.de)

Government of Canada website – Indigenous and Northern Affairs, https://www.canada.ca/en/indigenous-northern-affairs.html

Hopkins-Utter, Shane R. (2.11.2017), 'Case Comment: Ktunaxa Nation v. British Columbia (Forests, Lands and Natural Resource Operations)', available via: http://shulaw.ca/case-comment-ktunaxa-nation-v-british-columbia-forests-lands-and-natural-resource-operations-2017-scc-54-canlii/

Horgan, J (18.07.2017) Mandate Letter to the Honourable Scott Fraser, Minister of Indigenous Relations and Reconciliation, available via https://www2.gov.bc.ca/gov/content/governments/organizational-structure/ministries-organizations/ministries/indigenous-relations-reconciliation

International Law Association (ILA), website available at: https://www.ila-hq.org/index.php/about-us/aboutus2

International Law Association (ILA), overview of committees available at: https://www.ila-hq.org/index.php/committees?committeeID=9

International Labour Office (2009) website, www.ilo.org International Labour Office (2009) Indigenous and tribal peoples' rights in practice: a guide to ILO Convention No. 169, Geneva, ILO, ebook available at: http://www.ilo.org/wcmsp5/groups/public/%2D%2D-ed_norm/%2D%2D-normes/documents/publication/wcms_106474.pdf

Merriam Webster Online Dictionary, entry 'preserve' available at: http://www.merriam-webster.com/dictionary/preservation

National NAGPRA grant overview: https://www.nps.gov/subjects/nagpra/previously-awarded-grants.htm.

National Centre for State Courts, Tribal Courts Table 33 (2004), available via https://cdm16501.contentdm.oclc.org/digital/collection/spcts/id/159

National Centre for Truth and Reconciliation, website available via: http://nctr.ca

National Museum of the American Indian Repatriation Policy (2020), available via: https://americanindian.si.edu/explore/repatriation

Parzinger, Hermann and Polenz, Ruprecht (2016), 'Wir müssen den Mut zu schwierigen Themen haben', available at: https://www.preussischer-kulturbesitz.de/newsroom/dossiers-und-nachrichten/dossiers/dossier-sammlungswelten/wir-muessen-den-mut-zu-schwierigen-themen-haben.html

Royal Alberta Museum, archived website: archived website from 3.05.2019, archived at: https://web.archive.org/web/20190503104739/https://royalalbertamuseum.ca/collections/cultural-studies/repatriation/

Royal British Columbia Museum, Indigenous Collection and Repatriation Policy [Revised August 2018], available via: https://royalbcmuseum.bc.ca/documents/105663/Indigenous-Collections-and-Repatriation-Policy

Royal British Columbia Museum, Return of Cultural Treasures to Huu-ay-aht First Nations, information available at: https://royalbcmuseum.bc.ca/first-nations/first-nations-repatriation/return-cultural-treasures-huu-ay-aht-first-nations

Task Force Report on Museums and First Peoples [1992, reprinted 1994], A Report jointly sponsored by the Assembly of First Nations and the Canadian Museums Association, available at: http://museums.in1touch.org/uploaded/web/docs/Task_Force_Report_1994.pdf

Te Papa Tongerewa (Museum of New Zealand), Return of Toi Moko from overseas to New Zealand with governmental support, information available at: https://www.tepapa.govt.nz/about/repatriation/repatriation-maori-and-moriori-remains

The Oxford English Dictionary Online, available at www.oed.com , entries "dilemma", "indigenous", "preserve", "recovery", "reconcile"

Tripartite Working Group '"Improving the Treaty Process" - Report of the Tripartite Working group', available via: http://www.fns.bc.ca/

Union of British Columbia Indian Chiefs, First Nations Heritage Planning Toolkit (April 2013) [UBCIC Toolkit], available via: https://www.ubcic.bc.ca/ubcic_publications

Union of British Columbia Indian Chiefs, pilot project announcement, website available via: https://www.ubcic.bc.ca/jwgfnhc

UN DESA website, indigenous peoples > UNDRIP [last accessed 27.08.2019] https://www.un.org/development/desa/indigenouspeoples/declaration-on-the-rights-of-indigenous-peoples.html

US census data available at: https://www.census.gov/quickfacts/fact/table/US/RHI525216#viewtop

US Department of Justice, press release 12.01.2011 "Announcement of U.S. Support for the United Nations Declaration on the Rights of Indigenous Peoples - Initiatives to Promote the Government-to-Government Relationship & Improve the Lives of Indigenous Peoples" available via: https://2009-2017.state.gov/s/srgia/154553.htm

UN Voting Record for A/RES/61/295, via https://digitallibrary.un.org/?ln=en

UNESCO Website on intangible cultural heritage, available at: http://www.unesco.org/culture/ich/index.php?lg=en&pg=00310

UNIDROIT, Website, available at: http://www.unidroit.org/about-unidroit/overview

Varner, Elizabeth C., Penneys Edelman, Diane, and Amineddoleh, Leila (2018), 'NAGPRA and Congress's Foresight', available at: https://www.jurist.org/commentary/2015/01/varner-edelman-amineddoleh-nagpra/

Weblink Washington City Paper article, archived for reference: https://web.archive.org/web/20181103225306/https://www.washingtoncitypaper.com/news/article/21027853/how-the-smithsonian-is-reuniting-thousands-of-human-remains-with-indigenous-communities